Winston Churchill's Illnesses 1886–1965

Courage, Resilience and Determination

Allister Vale and John Scadding

FRONTLINE BOOKS

First published in Great Britain in 2020 by
Frontline Books
An imprint of
Pen & Sword Books Ltd
Yorkshire – Philadelphia

ISBN 978 1 52678 949 5

Typeset by Mac Style
Printed and bound in the UK by TJ International Ltd,
Padstow, Cornwall.

Pen & Sword Books Limited incorporates the imprints of Atlas,
Archaeology, Aviation, Discovery, Family History, Fiction, History,
Maritime, Military, Military Classics, Politics, Select, Transport,
True Crime, Air World, Frontline Publishing, Leo Cooper, Remember
When, Seaforth Publishing, The Praetorian Press, Wharncliffe
Local History, Wharncliffe Transport, Wharncliffe True Crime
and White Owl.

For a complete list of Pen & Sword titles please contact

PEN & SWORD BOOKS LIMITED
47 Church Street, Barnsley, South Yorkshire, S70 2AS, England
E-mail: enquiries@pen-and-sword.co.uk
Website: www.pen-and-sword.co.uk

Or

PEN AND SWORD BOOKS
1950 Lawrence Rd, Havertown, PA 19083, USA
E-mail: Uspen-and-sword@casematepublishers.com
Website: www.penandswordbooks.com

Winston Churchill's Illnesses 1886–1965

Contents

Foreword   viii
Acknowledgements   x
List of Plates   xv
Introduction   xvii

Chapter 1   Pneumonia in March 1886 in Brighton   1

Chapter 2   Fall and Concussion in January 1893 in Branksome
                 Dene   6

Chapter 3   A Shoulder Injury in October 1896 in Bombay
                 (Mumbai)   11

Chapter 4   Donation of a Skin Graft in 1898 after the Battle of
                 Omdurman   16

Chapter 5   Appendicitis in October 1922 in London   20

Chapter 6   A Serious Accident in December 1931 in New York   31

Chapter 7   An Attack of Enteric Fever in September 1932 in
                 Austria   47

Chapter 8   Chest Pain During Christmas 1941 at the White
                 House   57

Chapter 9   Pneumonia in February 1943 in London   73

Chapter 10   Pneumonia and Atrial Fibrillation in December 1943
                 in Carthage   88

Chapter 11   Recuperation in January 1944 in Marrakech   119

Chapter 12   Pneumonia in August–September 1944 in London   127

Chapter 13	A High Temperature in January 1945 on the Way to Yalta	143
Chapter 14	Diagnosis of Inguinal Hernia in September 1945 at Lake Como	150
Chapter 15	Repair of Inguinal Hernia in June 1947 in London	168
Chapter 16	First Stroke in August 1949 in Monaco	182
Chapter 17	Cerebrovascular Disease January 1950–March 1952 in London	194
Chapter 18	Churchill Unveils a Portrait of Lord Moran in July 1951	206
Chapter 19	Acute Stroke in June 1953 in London	210
Chapter 20	Churchill's Triumph at the Conservative Party Conference in October 1953 in Margate	229
Chapter 21	Acute Ataxic Stroke in June 1955 in London	246
Chapter 22	A Further Stroke in October 1956 in the South of France	262
Chapter 23	Pneumonia, Jaundice, Rigor and Atrial Fibrillation February–April 1958 on the Riviera and at Chartwell	273
Chapter 24	Two Strokes: April 1959 at Chartwell and October 1959 in London	288
Chapter 25	Right Finger Gangrene in May 1959 in Washington	303
Chapter 26	Fracture of Fifth Thoracic Vertebra and Stroke in November 1960 in London	309
Chapter 27	Hip Fracture in June 1962 in Monte Carlo, Femoral Vein Thrombosis and Jaundice in London	333
Chapter 28	Vascular Episode in the Left Leg in August 1963 at Chartwell	351
Chapter 29	Churchill's Skin Diseases	359

Chapter 30   Did Churchill Suffer from the 'Black Dog'?   372

Chapter 31   Was Churchill an Alcoholic?   398

Chapter 32   Churchill's Terminal Illness in January 1965 in
   London   410

Chapter 33   Churchill's Doctors   429

Notes   454
Select Bibliography   494
Index   498

Foreword

My great-grandfather suffered bouts of poor health. After obtaining access to several closed medical archives, as well as unearthing some that were unknown previously, Allister Vale and John Scadding have written the definitive account of Churchill's illnesses. Their expertise as physicians has been brought to bear on the interpretation of the evidence, much of it available for the first time. I would like to pay tribute to them for their dedication and determination to spend thousands of hours setting the history of Churchill's medical challenges into modern day context.

They have already published some of their meticulous research on his illnesses in the medical press. That these papers have met with acclaim in the medical community does not surprise me; I have read them all with great interest too. As a result of their research the authors have corrected many repeatedly perpetuated errors. For example, we now know that Churchill did not suffer a heart attack in Washington over Christmas and New Year in 1941. The ECG taken shortly after the event confirms this and is published for the first time in the book with the detailed notes of Sir John Parkinson, Churchill's cardiologist.

Similarly, there has always been much talk about Churchill's 'black dog' (although Churchill only ever mentioned it in one letter, in 1911). In our family we always felt that he was referring to his personal low moments – unsurprising, perhaps, given the great stress and pressure he often worked under. He was fortunate to be supported by his wife, Clementine, to whom he was devoted. Their correspondence shows the extraordinary support that she gave him. At times Churchill would cry, and he could be emotional in both happiness and sorrow. But it was never felt in the family that he suffered from clinical depression and this volume confirms that view.

Helpfully the authors have placed each illness in its historical setting and have cited multiple non-medical sources to support their conclusions regarding the impact of each illness on Churchill, his family and colleagues and on his work output.

What picture emerges of Churchill during these illnesses? That he was seriously ill from pneumonia on several occasions and had repeated strokes is now not in doubt. It is remarkable that he was able to continue to function as Prime Minister for two terms after suffering repeated illness at a time when investigation and treatment options were limited. The care Churchill received from more than thirty eminent physicians and surgeons (their short biographies are included) and from carefully chosen nursing staff was exemplary.

Allister Vale and John Scadding provide a rich picture of the Man – his fears, his frustration at being ill, his insights, his requests for detailed medical information, his penetrating intelligence and his enduring wit. But above all, his reaction to serious illness demonstrated his personal courage, resilience, his sense of duty and his determination to continue to serve in high office. This is perhaps best manifested by his ability to continue during many stroke episodes, which was truly remarkable. For even when those around him predicted that he was finished, he bounced back again to fight another day. As Lord Moran, his personal physician from 1940, concluded: 'Winston has nine lives!'

Vale and Scadding have produced a well-researched and highly readable book that will be essential reading for Churchillians and other historians of the period, as it provides so much new material and many new insights. Clinicians and general readers alike who wish to understand the impact of illness on arguably the greatest leader of the twentieth century will also find the book of great interest.

Randolph Churchill
Crockham Hill
July 2020

Acknowledgements

We could not have written this book without access to the medical and nursing notes written by colleagues.

By courtesy of Jamie Wilson, the present Lord Moran, we have had access to his grandfather's original papers (PP/CMW/F/6/1-5) in the Library at the Wellcome Collection and permission to cite unpublished parts of Lord Moran's medical records. We are also grateful to Lord Moran and Little, Brown Book Group for allowing us to cite substantial parts of his grandfather's book, *Winston Churchill: The Struggle for Survival*.

We are most grateful to Toni Hardy, Collections Information Analyst, at the Library at the Wellcome Collection, for granting permission for us to access Dr Thomas Hunt's previously closed medical records (GC/46/D.5) relating to Sir Winston Churchill.

The Royal College of Physicians holds the medical records of Dr Davis Evan Bedford CBE, Lord Brain and Sir John Parkinson. Pamela Forde, Archive Manager at the College, facilitated access to these records with the permission of Professor Dame Jane Dacre PRCP. Elva Carey (daughter) and John Phillips (grandson) kindly granted permission for us to cite Sir John Parkinson's medical reports on Sir Winston Churchill, and generously provided a family photograph of Sir John. Michael Brain DM FRCP, Lord Brain's son, allowed us to quote verbatim from his father's clinical records, which make up a substantial part of several chapters; we are in his debt.

Lord Richardson's daughters, Anne Stafford and Clare Wales, generously not only gave us access to their father's unpublished autobiography but also allowed us to use the portrait of Lord Richardson drawn by their mother, Sybil, in 1980. We are most grateful to Professor AWF Edwards FRS for permission to publish the notes and correspondence (WCHL 6/59; CHUR 1/134) of his father, Harold Edwards CBE FRCS, and himself, which are archived at the Churchill Archives Centre, Churchill College Cambridge. Charles Barne kindly allowed us to publish information from his grandfather's (Lieutenant Colonel Anthony Barne) diary and records. Jeremy and Mark Cunningham and Lavinia Winch generously provided a typed version of their parents' (Colonel and Mrs Cunningham) diaries. All relate to Churchill's holiday on Lake Como in 1945.

The Pulvertaft family, particularly Robert and Robyn Pulvertaft, have generously allowed us to quote from the unpublished autobiography of Professor RJV Pulvertaft, which contains much medical information on Churchill's illness in Carthage in December 1943. We are most grateful to Ms Louise King, Archives Manager at the Royal College of Surgeons of England, for granting access to the previously closed clinical records (MS0279) of Professor Sir Herbert Seddon relating to his care of Sir Winston Churchill during three illnesses.

We are very grateful to Valerie Herbert for granting us permission to cite the clinical notes of Sir Crisp English regarding Winston Churchill's appendicectomy (WCHL 6/64), which were donated by her late husband, Veryan Herbert, to the Churchill Archives Centre, Churchill College, Cambridge. She also generously provided the photograph of Sir Crisp English.

The unpublished diary of Nurse Dorothy Pugh yielded important information regarding Churchill's pneumonias in February 1943 and August 1944. Access to the diary and to Nurse Pugh's photograph was kindly provided by Stephen Rubin OBE; Mr Rubin, Dr Robert Pugh and Mrs Sara LeFleur (respectively son and daughter of Mrs Pugh) granted us permission to publish the entries. The letters from Nurse Doris Miles to her husband while she nursed Churchill through the February 1943 illness, as well as additional clinical information and the photograph of Nurse Miles, were kindly made available by her daughter, Jill Rose, in advance of the publication of her book: *Nursing Churchill.* We are grateful to Dr Pugh and Jill Rose for providing biographical details of their mothers. Gill Morton generously allowed us to cite her recollections of nursing Churchill in the Middlesex Hospital in 1962. We have drawn considerably on Roy Howells book *Simply Churchill,* though we have been unable to identify the current copyright holder.

The nursing records (WCHL 6/66) covering the period November–December 1960 when Sir Winston Churchill suffered a fracture of a thoracic vertebra and stroke are held by the Churchill Archives Centre, Churchill College, Cambridge.

Churchill historians owe a huge debt to Sir Martin Gilbert, his official biographer, not only for his biography but also for compiling the related *Churchill Documents,* a monumental task completed by Larry Arnn and published by Hillsdale College Press. These works have been cited frequently. Celia Lee (*Winston and Jack: The Churchill brothers* and *The Churchills.*

A family portrait) generously provided advice on Churchill's early life and illnesses. We are very grateful to Dr Richard Griffiths who provided much additional biographical material on Dr Roose, and to Peter Roose, great-great-grandson of Dr Roose, who added additional biographical details on the family. The following archivists/librarians generously provided much information regarding Dr Roose's early training and qualifications: David Allen, Royal Society of Chemistry; Jessica Borge, King's College London Archives; Alexandra Browne, Trinity Hall, Cambridge; Deirdre Bryden, Queen's University, Kingston, Canada; Estela Dukan, Royal College of Physicians of Edinburgh; Steven Kerr, Royal College of Surgeons of Edinburgh; Janet Payne, Apothecaries' Hall.

We are delighted to acknowledge the assistance of colleagues who have provided expert advice on areas outwith our expertise. We are most grateful to Professor David Baldwin who kindly advised on the psychiatric aspects, Dr Brian Cooper for advice on the gastroenterological aspects, Ian A Donovan on Churchill's appendicectomy, Professor Jason B Harris on paratyphoid infections, Philip Nicholl on Churchill's vascular episodes and Andrew L. Wallace on Churchill's shoulder injury. We are most grateful to Dr Anthony Daniels and Dr Ian White who co-authored the chapters *Did Churchill Suffer from the Black Dog?* and *Churchill's Skin Diseases*, respectively. Professor David Werring kindly refereed multiple published papers in the *Journal of the Royal Society of Medicine* and provided much useful advice on Churchill's cerebrovascular disease.

We are very grateful to Wyn Beasley, Past Vice-President of the Royal Australasian College of Surgeons and Churchill's medical biographer (*Churchill: The Supreme Survivor*), who kindly provided copies of the papers published by Julian Ormond Smith PPRACS on Thomas Dunhill and for his comments on Smith and the likely operation on Churchill alluded to by Smith as well as his general advice. We are very grateful to William Attenborough for allowing us to cite information from his detailed studies on Churchill (*Churchill and the 'Black dog' of Depression*) and to him and McFarland & Co. Inc. for permission to cite from *Diagnosing Churchill: Bipolar or 'Prey to Nerves'*). We acknowledge the help of Lord Owen and Dr Alex Proudfoot on specific aspects and we thank Dr John Mather for our discussions in recent years on Churchill's health. Richard Langworth CBE of the Hillsdale Churchill Project generously answered questions by return and arranged for our published papers on Churchill's illnesses to be reviewed for the Project by Professor Antoine Capet, which elicited further important information.

We are grateful also for his permission to cite from *Winston Churchill, Myth and Reality* and his response to the accusation that Churchill was a drunk (https://richardlangworth.com/noonan-churchill-alcohol).

We thank the Editors of the *Journal of the Royal College of Physicians of Edinburgh*, the *Journal of the Royal Society of Medicine* and the *Journal of Medical Biography*, who allowed us to use material we published in these journals. Professor Warren Kimball kindly allowed us to quote from his article on Churchill's alcohol consumption in *Finest Hour*. Professor David Freeman, Editor of *Finest Hour*, gave us permission to cite material from several other articles published in the *Journal*.

Our colleagues Rachael Brookes, Damian Ballam and Michael Owen kindly added the multitude of citations to a citation manager to ensure accuracy.

Rather than paraphrasing Sir Winston Churchill's words, we have cited them extensively. These are reproduced with the kind permission of Curtis Brown, London on behalf of The Estate of Winston S. Churchill. Copyright ©The Estate of Winston S. Churchill. The Correspondence of Lady Clementine Churchill is reproduced with the permission of Curtis Brown, London on behalf of the Master, Fellows and Scholars of Churchill College, Cambridge. Copyright ©The Master, Fellows and Scholars of Churchill College, Cambridge. Extracts from *A Thread in the Tapestry* and *Keep on Dancing* by Sarah Churchill are reproduced with the permission of Curtis Brown, London on behalf of the Master, Fellows and Scholars of Churchill College, Cambridge. Copyright ©The Master, Fellows and Scholars of Churchill College, Cambridge. We are grateful to Niall Harman of Curtis Brown for his assistance in arranging these permissions. With the assistance of Hannah Binymin extracts from *Clementine Churchill* by Mary Soames have been reproduced by permission of The Random House Group Ltd © 2001. Random House Group Ltd also gave permission for extracts to be published from Martin Gilbert's *Never Despair: Winston S Churchill 1945-1965* © 1998 and *In Search of Churchill* © 1994; Nassir Ghaemi's *A First-Rate Madness* © 2011 and General Lord Ismay's *The Memoirs of Lord Ismay* © 1960. We are also grateful to Faber for permission to cite extracts from Dilks D, ed. *The Diaries of Sir Alex Cadogan OM 1938-1945.* © 2010. Citations from Violet Bonham Carter *Winston Churchill as I Knew Him* and Pottle M ed. *Daring to Hope: The Diaries and Letters of Violet Bonham Carter 1946-1969* were reproduced by kind permission of Aitken Alexander Associates Ltd.

Her Majesty the Queen generously allowed us to cite from her correspondence and that of her father, King George VI, to Sir Winston

Churchill. Quotations from the Sir John Colville's *Fringes of Power* are reproduced by permission of Hodder and Stoughton Limited. John Mulligan of the Podkin Press has generously allowed us to cite Sir Anthony Montague Browne's recollections on Churchill's illnesses from the *Long Sunset*. We thank Debbie Schlosser for her permission to cite extracts from her mother's (Elizabeth Nel née Layton) book (*Winston Churchill by His Personal Secretary*) and recollections. David Higham Associates granted permission to cite the *War Diaries 1939–1957* of Field Marshall Lord Alanbrooke and HarperCollins Publishers Ltd gave permission for us to cite from *Churchill's Black Dog and Other Phenomena of the Human Mind* © Anthony Storr, 1989.

In a number of cases, despite extensive efforts, it proved impossible to identify the current copyright holder of some cited publications either via the publisher or by other means. We will willingly include a credit to these works in subsequent printings or editions.

Andrew Roberts (*Churchill: Walking with Destiny*) and Allen Packwood OBE (*How Churchill Waged War*) generously encouraged us throughout the time we published the medical papers and wrote this book. We thank them both for their advice and their willingness to endorse our book. In his role as Director of the Churchill Archives Centre, Churchill College, Cambridge, Allen Packwood kindly ensured that if we could not find documents in the Archive digitally, we could call upon one of the archivists, most frequently Tom Davies.

We are grateful for the support of all at Frontline Books: Tara Moran (Commissioning Editor), Alison Flowers (Editor), Lisa Hoosan (Production Manager) and Jon Wilkinson (jacket design). Our thanks also to Christopher Phipps, who has produced a comprehensive and meticulous index which greatly enhances ease of reference to the text.

Randolph Churchill, on behalf of the Churchill family, could not have been more supportive and encouraging throughout. Moreover, he trusted us to write accurately about his great-grandfather's illnesses. On several occasions Randolph was responsible for closed Archives being opened to us. We are very much in his debt not only for this support but also for his Foreword.

Note on Drug Names

The current recommended International Nonproprietary Name (rINN) for each drug prescribed for Churchill has been used for consistency throughout.

List of Plates

1. Brighton School, 29 and 30 Brunswick Road, Hove, on the celebration of Queen Victoria's Golden Jubilee on 20 June 1887.
2. Winston (right), brother Jack (middle) and Bertie Roose (the son of the Churchill family doctor on the left) in 1887.
3. Winston Churchill campaigning in Dundee and speaking seated; Mrs Churchill is sitting next to him.
4. Rose room (Queens' room), White House
5. Winston Churchill MP addresses a joint session of the US Congress on 26 December 1941 in Washington DC.
6. Winston Churchill at the controls of the Boeing 314 flying boat, RMA *Berwick*.
7. ECG performed on Winston Churchill 6 February 1942.
8. Nurse Pugh who nursed Churchill in February 1943 and August/September 1944.
9. Churchill's temperature chart when he developed pneumonia in London in February 1943.
10. Nurse Doris Miles who nursed Churchill in February 1943 receiving the Gold Medal for Excellence in Nursing.
11. Churchill, dressed in his siren suit and dressing gown, stands beside General Eisenhower on Christmas Day 1943.
12. Churchill's temperature chart when he developed pneumonia in Carthage in December 1943.
13. Churchill sits in the sunshine in Marrakech, Morocco, in January 1944 during a period of convalescence after falling ill with pneumonia.
14. Churchill speaking at the Council of Europe on 17 August 1949.
15. Portrait of Lord Moran painted by Professor Pietro Annigoni and unveiled by Churchill on 10 July 1951 at the Royal College of Physicians.
16. Sir Winston Churchill's triumphant speech at the Conservative Party Conference 10 October 1953 after recovering from a stroke.
17. Sir Winston Churchill disembarking after flying back from Nice on 3 April 1958.

18. Sir Winston Churchill, Anthony Montague Browne and President Eisenhower on a Marine helicopter on 6 May 1959 while visiting Washington DC.
19. Lord Moran arrives with a present at 28 Hyde Park Gate to celebrate Sir Winston Churchill's 86th birthday on 30 November 1960.
20. Sir Winston Churchill being admitted to the Middlesex Hospital on 29 June 1962.
21. Lord Moran reads a medical bulletin to the press outside Sir Winston Churchill's home in January 1965.
22. Dr Davis Evan Bedford CBE (1898–1978).
23. Lord Brain Bt FRS (1895–1966).
24. Viscount Dawson GCVO KCB KCMG (1864–1945).
25. Lieutenant General Sir Robert Drew KCB CBE (1907–91).
26. Sir Thomas Dunhill GCVO CMG (1876–1957).
27. Harold Edwards CBE (1899–1989).
28. Sir Crisp English KCMG (1878–1949).
29. Dr Thomas Hunt CBE (1901–80).
30. Sir Geoffrey Marshall KCVO CBE.
31. Lord Moran MC (1882–1977).
32. Sir John Parkinson (1885–1976).
33. Professor Robert Pulvertaft OBE (1897–1990).
34. Lord Richardson Bt LVO (1910–2004).
35. Dr EC Robson Roose (1848–1905).
36. Sir James Paterson Ross Bt KCVO (1895–1980).
37. Professor John Guyett Scadding in 1943 (1907–99).
38. Professor Sir Herbert Seddon CMG (1903–77).
39. Professor Sir Lionel Whitby CVO MC (1895–1956).

Introduction

Sir Winston Churchill was arguably the greatest statesman of the twentieth century. His political life spanned more than sixty years and he held high office for much of this time. He is generally regarded as the man through whose military and political skill, diplomacy, inspiration and powers of persuasion the Second World War was won.

Much has already been written about Churchill's health, though we consider that little that has been published is evidenced based, for example the suggestion that he suffered from a bipolar disorder. Churchill became ill at critical moments in British and world history, so it is legitimate both to understand the effects of his many illnesses on him and to consider his ability to continue in high office during them. Perhaps the most relevant illnesses in this respect relate to his gradually increasing cerebrovascular disease, manifested by a series of strokes, the first occurring in 1949, some fifteen years before his death at the age of 90.

A great deal has been written about the ethical aspects of reporting, in the public domain, about the health of any individual. This is not the place to rehearse all the arguments. We each guard information about our own personal health with care. However, when it comes to famous individuals, there are matters of great public interest. It is reasonable to speculate about the effect, for example, that Robert Schumann's deteriorating mental health had on his music compositions, or Beethoven's profound deafness on his later works. But in relation to our national political leaders, there is a genuine public interest in the potential effect of illness on the ability to govern.

The difficulties of balancing confidentiality and the public good were exemplified by suppression, during their lifetimes, of the degree of President Roosevelt's disability resulting from polio and the fact of President Kennedy's adrenal insufficiency (Addison's disease). The doctors of world leaders, and indeed of others holding public office, frequently release selective information to the public, with the expectation that the public believes that the whole truth is being revealed.

When an individual has made public comment about a personal health problem, it may seem not unreasonable to provide an objective medical view, but only with the individual's permission. Lord Moran claimed[1,2] to have received Sir Winston's permission to write his book,[3] and this claim has been supported by Sir Herbert Seddon, one of Churchill's surgeons,[4] though not by other close colleagues.[5] As Lord Moran's biographer has stated: 'By giving medical details about his recently dead patient, by quoting private conversations without consent from those involved, and by publishing in the face of Lady Churchill's objection, Moran affronted a large body of public opinion and raised questions about medical professional behaviour.'[6]

The opprobrium expressed at the time by members of Churchill's family,[7-10] his closest colleagues[5,11,12] as well as medical colleagues[13,14] is balanced by the view that a man as great as Churchill could not have any privacy, but that 'he belongs to the world, alive or dead, and anything related to him, especially his health problems, are of universal interest (cited by Robitscher[15])'. On this view medical disclosures made after the death of an individual, in order to set the historical record straight, are justifiable. In his defence, Moran wrote:

> A writer [*The Times* Medical Correspondent] complains that I have violated the convention governing the relations between patient and doctor. I believe the obligation is absolute in the life-time of a patient. I would, however, submit that it is not applicable to a great historical figure, such as Sir Winston Churchill, after his death, since it is inevitable that his illnesses will be described in detail by the laity.[1]

Lord Moran sought the advice of the historian, Professor GM Trevelyan, who advised: 'It is inevitable that everything about this man will be known in time. Let us have the truth.'[1]

Lord Brain, another of Churchill's physicians, clearly pondered this dilemma in regard to his own medical case notes:

> I doubt if there are any absolute ethical rules and sometimes there is a conflict of obligations. The main thing is to see that no avoidable harm is done, and that there may well come a time after Churchill himself is dead, when publication of this account of his health may do no harm to anyone and actually be of some historical importance.[16]

Fifty-five years have now passed since Sir Winston Churchill's death and we believe the time is apposite to review his illnesses again and in detail. Our approach to this account of Churchill's health has been primarily to set the record straight. We have sought the blessing of the Churchill family in our documentation of Sir Winston's health and we owe a particular debt to Randolph Churchill who has supported our endeavours throughout the book's gestation. We believe that our account of a supremely accomplished and gifted world leader not only amplifies what has been published previously but also sets the record straight.

We document all Churchill's major illnesses, from an episode of childhood pneumonia in 1886 until his death in 1965. We have adopted what we hope is a thorough approach in gaining access to numerous sources of information. We have depended heavily on the writings of Churchill's personal physician, Sir Charles Wilson, later Lord Moran, and the clinical notes of the neurologist Russell (later Lord) Brain. But we have also cited extensively from the clinical records of the numerous distinguished physicians and surgeons invited to consult on Churchill during his many episodes of illness. These include not only objective clinical data, but also personal reflections. In addition to these contemporaneous medical and nursing notes, we have sought the comments and reflections of Churchill's family, friends and political colleagues.

We believe this compendium presents a uniquely comprehensive medical, personal and rounded picture of this remarkable man, who remained active in public and political life until his late 80s. His ability to continue despite his illnesses is, we believe, well demonstrated in our book, the subtitle of which was chosen to reflect his core personal attributes of courage, resilience and determination. For example, could any other world leader, we wonder, have chaired a meeting of his Cabinet in Downing Street on the day following a stroke, without his colleagues noticing that anything was wrong?

We cite Churchill's own spoken and written words extensively; he was exquisitely talented in the economical and expressive use of the English language, very often with great wit, pithy and sometimes waspish, but always relevant to the situation, and highly memorable.

We have already published accounts of some of the illnesses described here in peer reviewed medical journals and, given the responses we have received, we believe our post hoc clinical reflections and conclusions to be sound, based as they are on our extensive clinical experience. Of course, our interpretations are made with the benefit of knowledge derived from medical advances since the time of Churchill's death in 1965, which in some areas have been huge. For example, throughout all his stroke episodes, Churchill never had the diagnostic benefit of a computerized X-ray (CT) head scan, let alone a magnetic resonance (MRI) scan, which we now take for granted in routine clinical practice.

With hindsight, it would be easy to be critical of those looking after Churchill at the time, but we have nothing but admiration for the skill of the physicians and surgeons involved in his care. On so many occasions, they kept the great man going and ready to fight another day.

Chapter 1

Pneumonia in March 1886 in Brighton

Nourishment, stimulants and close watching will save your boy.[1]

Winston Churchill explained later why he went to school in Brighton.[2] 'Our family doctor, the celebrated Robson Roose, then practised at Brighton; and as I was now supposed to be very delicate, it was thought desirable that I should be under his constant care. I was accordingly, in 1883 [Churchill is mistaken, it was 1884[3,4]], transferred to a school at Brighton kept by two ladies [Charlotte (headmistress) and Kate Thomson].'[2] The Brighton School was based at 29 and 30 Brunswick Road, Hove (Plate 1), which Bertie, the son of Robson Roose, also attended (Plate 2). Churchill remained at the school for three years.

Churchill did not mention directly the physical abuse he received previously at the hands of the Reverend Herbert William Sneyd-Kynnersley, Headmaster at St George's School, Ascot, which was also undoubtedly a factor in his transfer to Brighton. He does state, however, that he was in a low state of health at St George's (Churchill camouflaged the school by calling it St James's[2]) and after a serious illness he was transferred to the Brighton School where he benefited from the gentle surroundings and bracing air.[2]

In addition, Winston's 'weak chest' may also have been a factor in his move to Brighton, as it was in the choice of school later (see below). There is some evidence that Winston was prone to severe bouts of asthma during his three-year residence in Ireland (1877–1880).[5] This statement is based on the recollections of Peregrine Spencer-Churchill (son of John 'Jack' Spencer-Churchill, Winston's brother) and family correspondence, which suggested that the family believed the months of heavy rain was the precipitant (personal communication from Celia Lee).[5] At the time, Winston's grandfather, the Duke of Marlborough, was Viceroy of Ireland and his father was Private Secretary to the Viceroy.

2 Winston Churchill's Illnesses 1886–1965

13 March–17 April 1886: Severe Pneumonia and Recovery

It is not known when Winston first became ill or when Dr EC Robson Roose, a fashionable physician who treated the Churchill family (see p. 448), was summoned to assess him, though his mother, Lady Randolph Churchill, was informed of Winston's illness on 13 March. She hurried to Brighton and stayed at the Bedford Hotel.[4,5] Lord Randolph Churchill sent a telegram to her from London which stated that he would arrive in Brighton at 9.10 (presumably in the evening) on 13 March. Initially, Roose would not let the Churchills see Winston,[5] presumably because he was so ill.

Roose wrote to Lord Randolph on 14 March at 10.15 pm stating that Winston's temperature was 104.3°F (40.2°C) and that the right lung was 'generally involved – left lung of course feeling its extra work but, as yet, free from disease!'[6] Winston's respiratory rate and pulse were increased.[6]

Recognising the impact these observations might have on the Churchills, Roose wrote: 'This report may appear grave yet it merely indicates the approach of the crisis.'[6] The 'crisis' was the turning point of the disease in pre-antibiotic days, after which the patient either improved or deteriorated. Roose informed Lord Randolph that he was in the room next to Winston to watch his patient during the night 'for I am anxious'.[6]

At 6 am on 15 March, Roose wrote to Lord Randolph stating that as Winston's high temperature indicated 'exhaustion' he had used stimulants, by the mouth and rectum, with the result that at 2.15 am the temperature had fallen to 100°F (37.8°C) and at 6 am was 100.3°F.[7] It is probable the stimulant was alcohol (see below). Roose confirmed that he would not see patients in London that day but care for Winston.[7]

Lord Randolph wrote to his wife on 15 March: 'The return of the fever is most distressing: I think you do much good by remaining with him. I send the sandwiches & sherry. Tell Roose he will find me here and not at the Orleans [Club, a residential club at 64 King's Road, Brighton, frequented by Lord Randolph and friends] … Give dear Winny my love when he is himself.'[8]

Roose wrote again to Lord Randolph at 1 pm on 15 March stating that Winston's temperature was now 103°F [39.4°C] but that he was taking nourishment better.[1] Roose indicated that his strategy was to keep Winston's temperature under 105°F (40.6°C), and he predicted that by Wednesday, 17 March Winston's fever would have subsided, and the crisis past.[1] 'Nourishment, stimulants and close watching will save your boy.'[1] Roose informed Lord Randolph that he would remain at Winston's bedside until 3.30 pm when he would walk to the Orleans Club and leave a report but not be absent from Winston's bedside for more than an hour. He concluded: 'Pardon this shaky writing. I am a little tired.'[1]

Roose wrote his third letter to Lord Randolph at 11 pm on 15 March which stated that Winston was holding his own, and his temperature was 103.5°F (39.7°C).[9] On the morning of 16 March Roose informed Lord Randolph that after an anxious night during which Winston was delirious, his temperature was now 101°F (38.3°C) and the left lung was still uninvolved.[10] Roose again remained in Brighton rather than attend his London practice.[10]

There was better news on 17 March. Roose wrote to Lord Randolph at 7 am before he made his way to his London practice stating there was good news.[11] Winston had had 6 hours sleep and was no longer delirious. His temperature had fallen to 99°F (37.2°C), his pulse was 92 beats per minute and his respiratory rate was 28 per minute. 'He sends you and her ladyship his love.'[11] Roose left Dr Joseph Rutter, Physician to Sussex County Hospital, Brighton (see p. 450), 'in whom I have every confidence',[11] in charge of Winston's care after a joint consultation at 8.45 am. Rutter's fee was £2 2 shillings (approximately £268 in 2019) each visit.[4] The fee Roose charged is not known but is likely to have been far greater.

Roose indicated to Lord Randolph that he would not return that night to Brighton as he hoped that Winston would not relapse with 'nourishment the *avoidance* of *chill, rest* and quiet'.[11] To reinforce this message, Roose also wrote to Lady Randolph Churchill from the station to impress upon her the absolute necessity of quiet and sleep for Winston and that Mrs Everest (Winston's nanny and chief confidante) should not be allowed in the sick room today. 'I am so fearful of relapse knowing that we are not quite out of the wood yet.'[12]

Roose promised, however, that he would return to Brighton on 18 March or Friday, 19 March 'as the lung will I hope begin to be clearing up and must be carefully examined'.[11] Lord Randolph informed his wife from the Carlton Club, London, that he would return to Brighton on 19 March when Roose would examine Winston again.[13] No correspondence of this further professional encounter has survived.

On 17 April, Lord Randolph informed his wife that Winston was getting on well 'and is attended by Dr Gordon [this practitioner cannot be identified[14]]. He cannot go out yet as the weather is raw'.[4] Winston was delighted, however, by a locomotive steam engine his father had given him.[4]

Medical Aspects

Churchill developed pneumonia aged 11 years. He later wrote that: 'I very nearly died from an attack of double pneumonia.'[2] In fact, it was only right-sided. He was treated in the school in Brighton he was attending with close watching, nourishment and stimulants (probably alcohol orally and rectally) by the family physician, Dr Robson Roose, with the assistance of another physician, Dr Joseph Rutter. Roose was exemplary in his professional commitment to his young patient and assiduous in informing Lord Randolph of his son's clinical progress.

Pneumonia was a common illness in children at the time and a major cause of mortality. Between the ages of 5 and 14 years, pneumonia accounted for almost 10 per cent of all childhood deaths in the late nineteenth century.[15]

What of the treatment ('I used stimulants, by the mouth and rectum') administered by Roose? It is probable that Roose refers to alcohol (ethanol) when he uses the term 'stimulants'. In a paper published in 1861 on the *Use of stimulants in pneumonia*, Russell[16] sets out to demonstrate 'the great value of stimulants in the treatment of pneumonia, and to advocate their fearless administration … extending my advocacy to the freest employment of brandy even in hourly doses'.

Furthermore, Yeo[17] confirms that in 1884 alcohol was widely used in the treatment of pneumonia. The author was of the opinion that if 'cardiac exhaustion, with sleeplessness and delirium' were observed, the 'free use of alcoholic stimulants' was essential. Waters[18] reported on his experience of treating pneumonia as a physician between 1861 and 1881. 'In a large majority of cases … some alcoholic stimulant – wine or brandy, more frequently the latter – was given early in the disease, usually from the beginning of treatment, and continued throughout the attack … In the most severe cases, brandy was given every hour, or hour and a half.'

In his Croonian Lecture at the Royal College of Physicians in 1872, Bristowe[19] reviewed the treatment of pneumonia. He reported that Professor RB Todd, first Dean of the Medical Department, King's College Hospital, London, and his followers treated pneumonia mainly by the administration of alcohol in large quantities. In contrast, Bristowe[19] claimed that he had refrained altogether from the use of alcohol, excepting during the period of convalescence, 'without any diminution of success'. It was accepted at the time, even by those clinicians who did not routinely prescribe alcohol in the treatment of pneumonia, that if the patient was a heavy drinker alcohol must be prescribed to prevent the onset of the alcohol withdrawal syndrome.[19]

The decision to send Churchill to Harrow rather than Eton after his attendance at the Brighton School was because of this attack of pneumonia. It was considered that Harrow-on-the-Hill would be more bracing and less injurious to his lungs than Eton (a low-lying area) surrounded by the 'fogs and mists of the Thames Valley'.[3] Churchill subsequently enjoyed good health as a young man, with a distinguished military and then political career, up until the onset of medical problems in his seventh decade. We believe that this episode of childhood pneumonia did not have any bearing on his later episodes of pneumonia in the 1940s and 1950s,[20-2] though his tobacco smoking habit may have been important. As his son wrote: 'Winston never suffered from lack of lung power, either on the political platform or in the House of Commons.'[3]

Chapter 2

Fall and Concussion in January 1893
in Branksome Dene

*The eldest son of Lord and Lady Randolph Churchill ... met with an
accident yesterday afternoon*[1]

Winston Churchill, while still at Harrow, failed his first attempt to pass the entrance examination for Sandhurst in July 1892, finishing 390th in a list of 693 candidates with 5,100 marks. He returned to Harrow in September 1892 to make a second attempt at the examination in December 1892.[2] On 20 January 1893 Churchill heard that he had once again failed the examination. On this occasion, he was placed 203rd out of 664 candidates with 6,106 marks.[2] He had done well enough, however, for his Headmaster, the Reverend JEC Welldon, to recommend that he transfer to the crammer in South Kensington, London, run by Captain Walter James which specialized in preparing its pupils for the entrance examination to Sandhurst.[2]

Before Churchill took up his place at the crammer, arrangements had been made for the family to spend their 1892–3 Winter holiday at Canford, Branksome Dene, near Bournemouth.[3] Lord Randolph Churchill's sister, Cornelia Spencer-Churchill, had married Sir Ivor Guest Bt (later Baron Wimborne) in 1868 and owned an estate at Canford, which consisted of 40 or 50 acres of pine forest descended by sandy undulations terminating in cliffs to the smooth beach of the English Channel.[3] It was described by Churchill as a small, wild place and through the middle there fell to the sea level a deep cleft called a 'chine'. Across this chine a rustic bridge nearly 50yd long had been thrown.[3]

10 January 1893: The Accident

Churchill suffered a serious accident at Branksome Dene on 10 January. *The Times* reported on 11 January 1893: 'The eldest son of Lord and Lady

Randolph Churchill, who is staying with his mother and the Dowager Duchess of Marlborough at Branksome Dene, Bournemouth, met with an accident yesterday afternoon. He was climbing a tree, when a branch on which he was standing broke, and he fell some distance to the ground. No bones were broken, but he was very much shaken and bruised.'[1]

The Times underestimated the injuries suffered which were explained more fully by Churchill himself in his autobiography, *My Early Life.* Churchill was 18, his younger brother, Jack, was aged 12 and a cousin aged 14. The two younger children proposed to chase Winston.[3] After he had been hunted for 20 minutes and was rather short of breath, Winston decided to cross the bridge.[3] Arriving at the centre of the bridge, Winston saw to his consternation that the pursuers had divided their forces. One stood at each end of the bridge; capture seemed certain. The chine which the bridge spanned was full of young fir trees. Their slender tops reached to the level of the footway. 'Would it not be possible to leap on to one of them and slip down the pole-like stem, breaking off each tier of branches as one descended, until the fall was broken,' Winston asked himself.[3]

> I looked at it. I computed it. I meditated. Meanwhile I climbed over the balustrade. My young pursuers stood wonder struck at either end of the bridge. To plunge or not to plunge, that was the question! In a second I had plunged, throwing up my arms to embrace the summit of the fir tree. The argument was correct; the data were absolutely wrong.[3]

The measured fall was 29 ft on to hard ground, though the branches may have slowed the fall. Lady Randolph, summoned by the concern of the other children that 'Winston won't speak to us', hurried down with 'energetic aid and inopportune brandy'.[3] Lord Randolph travelled over at 'full express from Dublin where he been spending his Christmas at one of old Lord Fitzgibbon's once celebrated parties'.[3]

Churchill later recalled that members of the Carlton Club (The Club associated with the Conservative Party in St James's, London) made a joke about his accident: 'I hear Randolph's son met with a serious accident. Yes? Playing a game of Follow my Leader – well, Randolph is not likely to come to grief in that way!'[3]

Churchill's Injuries

Churchill claimed it was an axiom with his parents that in a serious accident or illness the highest medical aid should be invoked, regardless of cost. 'Eminent specialists stood about my bed ... I was shocked and also flattered to hear of the enormous fees they had been paid.'[3] At least three doctors were involved in Winston's care. Firstly, Dr Robson Roose (see p. 448), the Churchill family general practitioner, who had looked after Winston when he suffered from severe pneumonia in 1886.[4] Secondly, in all probability, Professor William Rose (see p. 449), who held the chair in Surgery at King's College Hospital, London. The *Companion Volume*[5] identified the surgeon as Dr John Rose of 17 Harley Street, but this cannot be correct as the only doctor with this surname and practising at this Harley Street address was Professor William Rose. Thirdly, Lily, Dowager Duchess of Marlborough, identified Dr (Henry) Couling (see p. 432) as being in attendance when Winston was staying with her in Brighton.

No medical notes of the accident have been found, though three letters published in *Companion Volume 1*[5] are relevant. Despite extensive searches, in several archives, the original letters in the *Blenheim Papers* have not been found. However, based on autobiographical evidence, and that from Churchill's aunt (see below), Churchill suffered concussion (mild traumatic brain injury), a right shoulder injury and a ruptured kidney. Churchill later claimed it was three days before he regained consciousness.

In all probability Churchill also suffered damage to his cervical spine in this accident. When he was investigated by Professor Sir Herbert Seddon (see p. 451) for a fracture of his fifth thoracic vertebrae following a fall in November 1960, Seddon recorded: 'Golding [Dr Campbell Golding, Radiologist (see p. 437)] took superb pictures and they showed an old lesion of the 4th and 7th cervical vertebrae which were all fused ... I then recalled a serious accident the young Churchill had suffered on 10 January 1893 when he jumped from a bridge at Bournemouth.'[6] Lord Moran recorded that: 'Seddon tells me that without this protective block it is probable that one of the cervical vertebrae would have been fractured in his fall [in 1960], and then we should have been in real trouble. Winston, as I have said before, seems to have nine lives.'[7]

Convalescence

Churchill states that after the accident he was 'carried to London'[3] to his grandmother's house at 50 Grosvenor Square where the Churchill family was living to save money. Despite his injuries, Churchill later recalled following with keen interest from his bed the political events of 1893.[3]

A handwritten letter to his brother, Jack, on 3 February from 50 Grosvenor Square, London stated: 'I am going to try and go to Brighton tomorrow, but I feel far from well enough. The doctors say I shall not be cured for 2 months. I pass the greater part of my time in bed.'[8] Churchill clearly managed the journey as he was staying with Lily, Dowager Duchess of Marlborough, at 26 Brunswick Terrace, Brighton on 9 February 1893 when she wrote to Lord Randolph:

The Dr (Couling) came again this morning and reported Winston is doing very well: not quite 'fit' yet but going on nicely. Do you want him to go up Sunday or Monday? If you do not I will be so pleased to keep another week – after wh[ich] I 'believe' he will have nothing left of that nasty fall but its memory. You know he fell on his right side, and I discovered the right shoulder wasn't quite right, so I've had my masseuse rub it for him – and it is already better.

Rose had written to Roose on 8 February: 'I certainly agree with you that young Mr Churchill should not at present return to hard study any more than he should vigorous exercise. It would be better to wait and see if the albumin will entirely disappear from the brain [presumably urine].'[5] On 9 February Roose wrote to Lord Randolph: 'Winston has still a little albumin so I sent on to Rose and now forward his reply.'[5]

Churchill later claimed it was more than three months before 'I crawled from my bed.' As Randolph Churchill explained in his biography of his father, Winston had somewhat exaggerated the length of his convalescence. In fact, Churchill was able to go back to the crammer by the end of February 1893 to study for entrance to Sandhurst.

While preparing for his third attempt, Churchill lived at 'home' at Grosvenor Square, but spent Easter at his Aunt Lily's home in Brighton. The results of the third attempt were announced at the start of August 1893 and Churchill came 95th out of 389 with a mark of 6,309; 104 candidates were successful.[2] His mark was too low to achieve an infantry cadetship, but enough for a cavalry cadetship. Churchill's highest mark was in English History (1278) and his lowest in Latin (362).[2] On 30 August 1893 Churchill discovered that other aspirants had failed to take up their cadetships that year and that he had been given the opportunity of going into the Infantry (60th Rifles).[2] Churchill joined the 4th Hussars and not the 60th Rifles.

Medical Aspects

With the exception of a cervical fracture, the injuries Churchill suffered are common after a fall from this height. There is evidence from some studies, but not others, that the distance fallen is a dominant factor influencing vertical deceleration patterns.[9] The fact that in all probability Churchill hit several tree branches during his fall may have also affected the type of injuries he suffered. Some studies have shown that there exists a significant correlation between the height of fall (if greater than or equal to 25 ft) and the Glasgow Coma Scale (a numerical score used to estimate a patient's level of consciousness after head injury), Injury Severity Score (which standardizes severity of traumatic injury based on the worst injury of six body systems), blood transfusion requirements and the risk of death.[9]

Orthopaedic injuries are heavily influenced by the site and position of impact, as well as the height of the fall. 'Jumpers' (intentional) more often land on their feet than 'fallers'.[10] Spinal injuries are very common in high falls (as here), but are more usually lumbar rather than cervical.[10]

In a study of 64 children (mean age 7.4 years) of whom 14 had fallen more than 20 ft, the head was injured in 25 (39 per cent) patients (concussion occurred in 8), fractures of the extremities occurred in 22 (34 per cent), abdominal injuries in eight (12 per cent) and spinal injuries in four (6 per cent).[11] Splenic injuries (n=5) were more common than kidney injury (n=3).[11] In another study intra-abdominal injuries occurred in 13.8 per cent of 116 patients (mean fall height 19 ± 10 ft), with splenic injury being three times more common than kidney injury.[9] In 39 deer hunters falling a mean of 12.5 ± 5.9 ft from a tree stand, 5 suffered concussion, 11 incurred a lower extremity fracture, 1 a shoulder dislocation and 1 a renal laceration.[12]

As the mortality in one study was some 30 per cent in those falling more than 25 ft (mean 37.9 ± 13.1),[9] Churchill was very fortunate to survive this prank.

Chapter 3

A Shoulder Injury in October 1896 in Bombay (Mumbai)

I had sustained an injury which was to last me my life … and to be a grave embarrassment in moments of peril, violence and effort.[1]

The 4th Hussars embarked on the P&O steamship *Britannia* at 10 am on 11 September 1896 to sail to Bombay (now Mumbai).[2] The Regimental diary recorded the 4th Hussars strength as 22 officers, 2 warrant officers, 448 NCOs and other ranks.[2] Among the officers was Lieutenant Winston Churchill, 1 of 10 lieutenants; there were 5 lieutenants junior to him.[2]

Britannia reached Port Said on 20 September 1896 where it was re-supplied with coal.[2] The subsequent passage through the Suez Canal took three days.[2] The *Britannia* dropped anchor off the Sassoon Dock on the east side of Bombay Island on 2 October 1896 at 3 pm.[2] Manchester has written that the identity of the designer of the Dock 'has not survived, luckily for his reputation. It is a triumph of incompetence, so ill-suited to disembarkation that impatient immigrants often choose to come ashore in skiffs, a risky procedure which could cripple a man before he set foot on Indian soil.'[3]

The plan was that the 4th Hussars were to disembark en masse at 8 pm when it would be cool, but Churchill and two other officers were allowed to disembark early in a tiny boat.[1] It took the party 15 minutes to reach the quays of the Sassoon Dock when disaster struck.[1]

2 October 1896: The Accident

Churchill wrote later:

We came alongside of a great stone wall with dripping steps and iron rings for hand-holds. The boat rose and fell four or five feet with the surges. I put out my hand and grasped at a ring; but before I could get my feet on the steps the boat swung away, giving my right shoulder a sharp and peculiar wrench. I scrambled up all right, made a few remarks of a general character, mostly beginning with the earlier letters of the alphabet, hugged my shoulder and soon thought no more about it.[1]

Banta, an orthopaedic surgeon, has concluded that it would appear that Churchill 'had sustained injury to the capsular attachments, rendering the shoulder prone to recurrent instability. Obviously, a cavalry officer with chronic instability of his dominant shoulder joint was precluded from effectively wielding his sword in combat.'[4]

Despite this injury, Churchill continued to play polo, though this required the wearing of a leather belt so that his right arm could not swing too freely. Churchill continued to play until 1927 when at the age of 52 he played his last game in Malta with Sir Roger Keyes, Commander-in-Chief Mediterranean.[5]

Recurrent Dislocations

In a letter to his mother, Lady Randolph, dated 5 January 1898 Churchill wrote: 'You must excuse my handwriting as I have dislocated my shoulder at polo and am all strapped up. So painful it was – and I fear it may ultimately end my polo career for it may slip out again.'[6]

On 9 February 1899 Churchill wrote both to his mother and his brother, Jack, regarding a fall on the previous evening while he was serving in the Army in Jodhpore: 'Last night I fell downstairs and sprained both my ankles & dislocated my right shoulder. I am going to struggle down to polo this afternoon strapped up etc, but I am a shocking cripple and doubt very much whether I shall be able to play in the tournament.'[7] To his brother, he added: 'my arm is weak and stiff & may come out again at any moment'.[7]

This fall took place when Churchill was coming down to dinner the night before departure for Meerut where the polo tournament was to be held four days hence. He described the incident in *My Early Life*: 'I got it put back in fairly easily, but the whole of the muscles were strained. By the next morning I had lost the use of my right arm. I knew from bitter experience it would take three weeks or even more before I could hit a polo ball hard again, and even then it would only be under the precaution of having my elbow strapped to within a few inches of my side.'[8] Although Churchill told his three team mates to 'take me out of the team', after further discussion it was decided Churchill should still play.[8] 'Accordingly with my elbow strapped tight to my side, holding a stick with many an ache and twinge, I played in the first two matches of the tournament. We were successful in both'[8] The 4th Hussars then met the 4th Dragoon Guards in the Final and won the Inter-Regional Tournament of 1899.[8]

Following the accident, Churchill wrote that:

> Since then at irregular intervals my shoulder has dislocated on the most unexpected pretexts; sleeping with my arm under the pillow, taking a book from the library shelves, slipping on a staircase, swimming, etc. Once it very nearly went out through too expansive a gesture in the House of Commons, and I thought how astonished the members would have been to see the speaker to whom they were listening, suddenly for no reason throw himself upon the floor in an instinctive effort to take the strain and leverage off the displaced arm bone.[1]

Wallace, an orthopaedic surgeon with a major clinical interest in shoulder surgery, has written that it is rare to find images of Churchill:

> with his shoulder elevated in full flexion and external rotation: the so-called 'apprehension' position might have put him at risk of subluxation, so it seems he was careful to avoid it.[9] In countless photographs throughout his career, he is seen with his arm elevated purely in flexion, anterior to the coronal plane and in the 'safe zone'.[9] However, there is at least one image where he was able to achieve a position of nearly full abduction and external rotation, but only when the arm was supported on the railing of an open-topped car.[9] Nonetheless, it is also clear from other photographs of him holding his left (non-injured) arm aloft, that he was able to achieve the normal range of at least 90 degrees of abduction and 90 degrees external rotation.[9]

Wallace concludes that there was no anatomical restriction of motion in the injured shoulder and 'it was indeed a cautionary posture that he adopted to avoid the risk of recurrent instability'.[9]

Writing more than thirty years later, Churchill counselled younger readers of *My Early Life*:

> to beware of dislocated shoulders. In this, as in so many other things, it is the first step that counts. Quite an exceptional strain is required to tear the capsule which holds the shoulder joint together; but once the deed is done, a terrible liability remains. Although my shoulder did not actually go out, I had sustained an injury which was to last me my life, which was to cripple me at polo, to prevent me from ever playing tennis, and to be a grave embarrassment in moments of peril, violence and effort.[1]

Medical Aspects

Churchill sought non-surgical treatment. Wallace has explained: 'The concept of this brace was to prevent the arm being rotated and elevated to the position of subluxation, whilst still allowing enough movement to effectively swing the stick and connect with the ball.'[9] Although Churchill continued to wear the brace when playing polo until his last match in 1925, there are images of him swimming, shooting, playing golf and fishing without the brace, so it seems he had some measure of dynamic control over the instability episodes.[9] Churchill wrote to his mother on 6 April 1905 to inform her that in addition to the brace: 'I have begun electrical treatment to tighten up my dislocated shoulder. It is rather pleasant.'[10] This use of electrotherapy was unlikely to be therapeutic but was harmless except for the costs involved.

Beasley, an orthopaedic surgeon and medical historian, has discussed whether Churchill should have opted for surgical intervention. Would it have changed the course of his life, or indeed the war?

> If his original injury had been managed by a period of adequate immobilization, he might well have been spared the recurrences he wrote about. So far as operation for these recurrences is concerned, he might in 1923 (when he was out of parliament and 'available') have become one of Blundell Bankart's [Consultant Orthopaedic Surgeon, Middlesex Hospital, London and Royal National Orthopaedic Hospital] early cases ... however, after a lapse of more than a quarter-century he

had probably come to terms with the disability and the precautions needed to minimize it.[11]

Churchill's decision to manage his shoulder problem non-operatively was clearly the safest and simplest method. Modern operative management, based on Bankart's pioneering work, yields dependable and reliable outcomes.[12] While not without complications, the curse of multiple recurrences can largely be prevented.

Churchill considered this accident:

was a serious piece of bad luck. However, you never can tell whether bad luck may not after all turn out to be good luck. Perhaps if in the charge of Omdurman [see p. 16] I had been able to use a sword, instead of having to adopt a modern weapon like a Mauser pistol, my story might not have got as far as the telling. One must never forget when misfortunes come that it is quite possible they are saving one from something much worse; or that when you make some great mistake, it may very easily serve you better than the best-advised decision. Life is a whole, and luck is a whole, and no part of them can be separated from the rest.[1]

Chapter 4

Donation of a Skin Graft in 1898 after the Battle of Omdurman

He will take my skin with him, a kind of advance guard, into the next world[1]

In summer 1898 the 23-year-old Lieutenant Winston Churchill of the 4th Hussars, while on leave from his Regiment in Bangalore, India, was serving with the 21st Lancers in Sudan. This supernumerary posting had been arranged using many of Churchill's political and military connections, even though it had been opposed by Major General Sir Herbert Kitchener, Sirdar (Commander-in-Chief) of the Egyptian Army.[2] In part, this may have been because Churchill had sought and obtained a commission to act also as a special correspondent 'as opportunity served'[2] for the *Morning Post* for which he was well compensated at a rate of £15 (£1,900 in 2019) a column.[2,3]

Churchill's reports in the *Morning Post* formed the basis of *The River War: An Historical Account of the Reconquest of the Soudan*, first published in 1899. Churchill had to pay his travel expenses to the Sudan and was informed that 'in the event of your being killed or wounded in the impending operations, or for any other reason, no charge of any kind will fall on British Army funds'.[2]

Churchill participated in the last British cavalry charge in history at the Battle of Omdurman in September 1898:

I fired 10 shots with my pistol – all necessary … I am sorry to say I shot 5 men for certain and two doubtful. The pistol was the best thing in the world … The Dervishes showed no fear of cavalry … they tried to hamstring the horses, to cut the bridles – reins – slashed and stabbed in all directions and fired rifles at a few feet range.[4]

Churchill witnessed the bravery of Private Thomas Byrne in rescuing Lieutenant Richard Molyneux. Reporting from Atbara Fort, Sudan on 16 September 1898, he wrote an anonymous article, the fourteenth in the series of dispatches, which was published in the *Morning Post* on 11 October 1898:

> As the charging squadron of the 21st Lancers closed with the enemy in the action of the 2nd September, Private Byrne was struck by a bullet, which passed through his right arm and inflicted a severe wound. His lance fell from his hand, but he succeeded in drawing his sword. This delayed him, and he was one of the last men to get clear of the stabbing and hacking mass of Dervishes alive. Safety was then in sight.[5]

But Molyneux had been wounded.

> Dismounted, disarmed and streaming with blood, this officer was still endeavouring to make his way through the enemy and to follow the line of charge. He was beset on all sides. He perceived Private Byrne, and called on him for help. Whereupon, without a moment's hesitation, Byrne replied, 'All right, sir,' and turning, rode at the four Dervishes who were about to kill his officer. His wound, which had partly paralysed his arm, prevented him from grasping his sword, and at the first ineffectual blow it fell from his hand, and he received another wound from a spear in the chest. But his solitary charge had checked the pursuing Dervishes. Lieutenant Molyneux regained his squadron alive, and the trooper, seeing that his object was attained, galloped away, reeling in his saddle. Arrived at his troop, his desperate condition was noticed and he was told to fall out. But this he refused for some time to do, urging that he was entitled to remain on duty and have 'another go at them.' At some length he was assisted from the field fainting from loss of blood.[5]

Byrne was awarded the Victoria Cross for the action at Omdurman.

Skin Graft

Three days after the battle, the 21st Lancers started northwards on their march home. Churchill was allowed to sail down the Nile in the big sailing boats which contained the Grenadier Guards. In Cairo, he found Molyneux, who was now proceeding to England, in the charge of a hospital nurse.

Churchill decided to keep him company. While Churchill was talking to Molyneux, the doctor came in to dress his wound.[6]

It was a horrible gash, and the doctor was anxious that it should be skinned over as soon as possible. He said something in a low tone to the nurse, who bared her arm. They retired into a corner, where he began to cut a piece of skin off her to transfer to Molyneux's wound. The poor nurse blanched, and the doctor turned upon me. He was a great raw-boned Irishman. 'Oi'll have to take it off you,' he said. There was no escape, and as I rolled up my sleeve he added genially 'Ye've heeard of a man being flayed aloive? Well, this is what it feels loike'. He then proceeded to cut a piece of skin and some flesh about the size of a shilling from the inside of my forearm. My sensations as he sawed the razor slowly to and fro fully justified his description of the ordeal. However, I managed to hold out until he had cut a beautiful piece of skin with a thin layer of flesh attached to it: This precious fragment was then grafted on to my friend's wound. It remains there to this day and did him lasting good in many ways. I for my part keep the scar as a souvenir.[6]

Molyneux was the third son of the 4th Earl of Sefton. After recovery from his injuries at Omdurman, he continued to serve in the Army. After the First World War, he retired and was appointed groom in ordinary to King George V and began his long connexion with the Royal Family.[7] After the death of King George V in 1936 he became, until her death in 1954, extra equerry to Queen Mary.[7]

On 22 January 1945 Molyneux wrote to Churchill who was then Prime Minister:

Like everyone else I have followed your amazing performances; and become ever prouder of having a bit of your pelt. I never mention and always conceal it, for fear people might think I was bucking [talking boastfully]. Routing out old papers yesterday I found an amusing letter from you dated 1897, so even then must have thought it worth keeping, which has incited me to write these lines.[8]

Churchill replied: 'Thank you so much dear Dick. I often think of those old days, and I should like to feel that you showed that bit of pelt. I have frequently shown the gap from which it was taken.'[9]

On 21 January 1954 Lord Moran (see p. 443), Churchill's personal physician from 1940, recorded that Churchill showed him a scar on his right arm. "'That's where I gave some skin for grafting to Dick Molyneux after the battle of Omdurman – it hurt like the devil. His death is in today's paper." The P.M. grinned. "He will take my skin with him, a kind of advance guard, into the next world".'[1]

Medical Aspects

The success of this homograft taken without anaesthetic is remarkable given the circumstances and is a testimony to the skill of the Irish doctor and the appropriateness of follow-up dressings. It suggests too that Molyneux's wound had not become infected prior to the graft. In the 1900s, even if the skin graft took, the resulting scar was often thin, weak and prone to ulcerate.[10] Douglas et al.[10] reviewed their results in 29 patients, all of whom received local anaesthetic; 7 were homografts. In 18 out of these 29 cases, 80 to 100 per cent of the grafts adhered; in 7 cases 48 to 80 per cent adhered; in three cases 5 to 15 per cent of the grafts adhered and 1 was a complete failure. Churchill was proud to show 'the gap from which it was taken'.[9]

Quite apart from Churchill's unreserved willingness and selflessness in donating a small piece of his own skin, entailing a risk of serious infection to himself in the pre-antibiotic era, this account demonstrates his resolve to be personally involved in a conflict he judged to be both justifiable and important. Furthermore, it is evidence of his personal bravery in the front line of military conflict. By all accounts, he was fortunate to have survived unscathed.

We suggest that this and other early experiences of hand-to-hand fighting gave Churchill an unrivalled insight into the physical and psychological demands of battle, and shaped his approach to strategy and his responsibilities to individual soldiers as Prime Minister and Commander-in-Chief during the Second World War.

Chapter 5

Appendicitis in October 1922 in London

I had lost not only my appendix but my office as Secretary of State[1]

The Conservative Party had increasingly regretted its four-year political impotence within a Coalition led by David Lloyd George, Liberal and Prime Minister, and decided to try to bring the Coalition to an end.[1] On the morning of 19 October 1922, an independent Conservative had beaten the Coalition candidate at a by-election in Newport.[1] That same morning 273 of the 335 Conservative MPs met at the Carlton Club in London to discuss whether or not to remain in the Coalition.[2] Austen Chamberlain (Conservative, Lord Privy Seal and Leader of the House of Commons) urged them to remain, but another Conservative member of Lloyd George's Cabinet, Stanley Baldwin, the President of the Board of Trade, pressed for an end to the association with Lloyd George. He was supported by Bonar Law, the former Conservative leader; only 88 MPs wished to remain in the Coalition.[2]

Churchill, a Liberal MP at that time and Secretary of State for the Dominions and Colonies in the Coalition government, had tried a week earlier to persuade Baldwin not to turn against the Coalition.[1] He had also planned to speak at Bristol on 17 October to put the case for a Coalition election, and to defend its policies,[1] but on the morning of 16 October 1922 he felt unwell and was not able to speak at the meeting.[3]

16–18 October 1922: History of the Illness

Churchill complained on 16 October to Edward Marsh, his Private Secretary, about pains in his side.[1] That evening it was announced from the Colonial Office that Churchill was suffering from acute gastroenteritis and was strictly confined to bed.[3] In fact, he had developed acute appendicitis. Sir Crisp English (see p. 436) also recorded a history of indigestion for 'some time'.

Gilbert states that it was on 17 October that Churchill's doctors decided it was necessary to operate for appendicitis;[1] we consider this unlikely, as a surgical opinion was not sought on that day. In addition, Beasley, a medical historian, has stated that Lord Dawson, English and Dr Hartigan had a consultation on 16 October.[4] Although these clinical records have not survived, it is far more probable that Churchill was first assessed by Hartigan, his long-standing London general practitioner, on 16 October, who kept a 'watching brief' and did not seek a surgical opinion until late on 18 October, and the operation did not take place until 9.45 pm on that day.

This opinion is based on the practice adopted by English of operating urgently for appendicitis. Specifically, he wrote that operation should be undertaken 'at the very earliest moment' in the first 24 hours of diagnosis.[5] 'Immediate operation' should be undertaken if the diagnosis had been made 24–48 hours before.[5] On the third and fourth day after the diagnosis was made, English stated the outlook was critical and that it was 'usually safest to operate at once; but each case calls for most careful consideration'.[5]

This opinion is also supported by the contents of a letter Churchill dictated on 18 October to James Allison, the acting Chairman of the Dundee Liberal Association. He explained that: 'I cannot tell whether I shall have to be operated on or not. If I am I shall be out of the fight altogether, but will send an election address as soon as I have sufficiently recovered ... I will send a fuller message when I know what the verdict of the doctors is.'[1] This letter strongly implies that no decision over operation had been taken even during the day on 18 October.

Furthermore, in all probability, Dawson did not review Churchill until 2 November. If Dawson had been involved from 16 October, he would have been aware of the clinical details and would not have required these to be set out in an extensive letter. Most probably this was a new referral by English who requested a second opinion from a very senior and ennobled physician because of his concern that Churchill, a well-established political figure, might not be fit enough to travel to Scotland and campaign.

At some point between 16 October and 18 October Churchill was moved from his sick bed in Sussex Square, London W2 to a nursing home in Dorset Square, London NW1, a mile away.

18 October 1922: Operation

The operation took place at the nursing home at 4 Dorset Square, Marylebone, London on 18 October at 9.45 pm.[6] English was the surgeon, and he was assisted by Dr Thomas Hartigan (see p. 438). A Dr Chaldecot (probably Dr JH Chaldecott) was stated by English to be the anaesthetist, and he used ether administered by the open drop method.[6]

A 5in-long oblique incision was made in the skin and the muscles were split. A black gangrenous perforated appendix was identified;[6] the appendix was necrotic from its tip to the caecum. The mesentery was oedematous.[6] 'The appendix was removed with difficulty.'[6] The wound was sewn up using ten-day Van Horn chromic catgut No. 2 with through and through sutures, and a 'fairly large drainage tube was sown in'.[6]

The Times announced on 19 October that Churchill had been operated on successfully for appendicitis the previous evening and was doing very well.[7]

On 21 October Sir Maurice Hankey, Secretary of the Cabinet, recorded in his diary: Masterton Smith [Sir James Masterton Smith, Permanent Under-Secretary of State for the Colonies], told us a characteristic story of Winston Churchill, who had been stricken down quite suddenly with appendicitis and had been operated on two days ago. On coming to from his anaesthetic he immediately cried 'Who has got in for Newport? Give me a newspaper'. The doctor told him he could not have it and must keep quiet. Shortly after, the doctor returned and found Winston unconscious again with four or five newspapers lying on the bed. Masterson Smith was to see Winston that afternoon, and the patient insisted on seeing Lord Birkenhead [Lord High Chancellor] and others, though less than two days have elapsed since the operation.[8]

Post-operative Course

Two samples were sent for bacteriology on 22 October and were examined by Dr William Broughton-Alcock, who practised from 20 Grosvenor Street, London and was Director, Central Laboratory, Ministry of Pensions. The first sample was a serous exudate coming through the wound. A moderate number of leucocytes (white cells) were present on direct microscopic examination, and only a few gram-negative cocco-bacilli and a gram-positive diplococcus (probably staphylococcus) were present. The second sample was obtained by English from the deep part of the wound using a pipette. Direct microscopic examination showed equal numbers of leucocytes and red cells. A few gram-negative cocco-bacilli and short bacilli were seen after a careful search of the film.[6] These samples confirmed that no clinically significant infection was present at the wound site.

Lord Stamfordham, Private Secretary to King George V, wrote to Churchill on 25 October:

> The King desires me to say, firstly that he trusts you are making steady progress and that you must not impede it by your natural eagerness to join the Political Fray! – and further to express his great regret that you were unable to be present here this morning to hand over your seal of office and take leave of His Majesty. The King will look forward to seeing you when you are convalescent – he will be back in London on the 2nd November.[9]

Parliament was dissolved by Royal Proclamation on 26 October and elections were fixed for 15 November.[10] Churchill announced he would stand again to retain his seat in Dundee.

On 1 November 1922 Lloyd George, Prime Minister, wrote to Churchill: 'I have the honour to inform you that the King has been pleased to approve that you be appointed a member of the order of the Companions of Honour.'[11]

Churchill, although physically weak, was not mentally inactive during his forced absence from the political fray.[12] From the West End of London, he bombarded Dundee with a stream of manifestos and political essays. One was a long document of 2,000 words addressed to his new chairman, Mr Robinson, which *The Times* published in full.[12,13] The other four, of almost equal length, were entitled *Winston S. Churchill: Notes for his constituents.*[11]

2 November 1922: Review by Lord Dawson

English invited Lord Dawson (see p. 433) to review Churchill on the morning of 2 November.[6] In preparation for this consultation, English wrote to Dawson on 1 December as follows:[6]

1. Tomorrow will be the sixteenth day from the date of operation.
2. The stitches are all out; the wound is soundly healed except where the drainage tube was inserted. This too looks as if it would heal quickly but of course it may be some days before it finally closes.
3. He was moved to Sussex Square yesterday on a stretcher by ambulance and gets into a chair for the first time today.
4. Temperature has been subnormal for more than a week and he has had daily massage to keep his muscles fit.
5. He is very anxious if possible to go to Dundee on Friday the 10th and from a carrying chair to address a meeting on the 11th. He does not propose to do walking of any kind and I think fully realises the importance of being careful. As soon as the election is over he would come south and by December 6 would be ready to take a long holiday.
6. The main point of the consultation is whether or not this is practicable.
7. I have told him that we have let him go 50% faster than the average case, mainly because he has really made a very good and quick recovery. I said that the two things we want to guard him against are, a weak scar and from getting over-tired after a serious illness, in other words, the consultation is to decide how much we may let him do without running any risks or putting too much strain on him. As a matter of fact, he has shown surprising powers of recuperation.[6]

On 2 November a press statement was issued which stated that:

Mr Churchill's medical advisers, Lord Dawson, Sir Crisp English and Dr Hartigan, have consented to his fixing provisionally Saturday, November 11th, as the date when he can address a public meeting in Dundee. Whether in fact Mr Churchill will be able to fulfil this engagement must depend upon the progress made in the next four or five days, when a further consultation will be held.[11]

HAL Fisher, President of the Board of Education until 19 October 1922, wrote in his diary on 2 November: 'Thence to Sussex Square where I see Winston in bed. He is recovering from his operation for appendicitis, but seems quite vigorous.'[11]

Mrs Churchill had gone to Dundee on 6 November to represent her husband and had taken 7-week-old daughter, Mary, with her. As Mary (Soames) later pointed out, it was hardly a cheering omen that the house where she and her mother stayed was in Dudhope Terrace.[14]

Churchill also wrote to his wife on 6 November from the nursing home. Hartigan had examined their daughter, Sarah, that morning and said she had:

a little cold behind the nose which would naturally cause a certain irritation of the ear, and that there was no connection whatever between this and the glands [Sarah suffered from tubercular glands in her neck about this time]. Her temperature is normal and she is quite all right. We are, however, keeping her indoors for a day or two as a precautionary measure ... I do hope you were not too tired by your long journey. I thought it was a great effort for you to cart yourself and your kitten [daughter, Mary] all that way last night. Jack Wodehouse [Lord Wodehouse, one of Churchill's personal private secretaries] telephoned this morning that you are all right and were addressing a meeting this evening. Do take it easy. The mere fact of your presence will I am sure be highly beneficial ... The doctors were quite content this morning with my progress and seem to think there is no doubt that I shall be able to keep my engagement at Dundee.[14]

11–16 November 1922: Dundee

Churchill arrived in Dundee on 11 November. He was still very weak. Churchill has described the events in Dundee:

On the 21st day after my operation I addressed two great assemblies. The first, a ticket meeting, was orderly and I was able to deliver my whole argument. The evening meeting in the Drill Hall was a seething mass of eight or nine thousand people, among whom opponents greatly predominated. I was unable to stand, my wound was still open. I had to be carried in an invalid chair onto the platform and from place to place (Plate 3). There is no doubt a major operation is a shock to the system. I felt desperately weak and ill. As I was carried through the yelling crowd of Socialists at the Drill Hall to the platform, I was struck by looks of passionate hatred on the faces of some of the younger men and women. Indeed but for my helpless condition I am sure they would have attacked me.[15]

The result was announced on 16 November, and Churchill's majority of 15,000 was swept away; he was beaten by over 10,000 votes. Churchill was present at the counting of the votes, and he soon became aware that his fate was sealed. 'He was a somewhat miserable picture of feverish restlessness, and he was completely dejected when Sheriff Malcolm was declaring the result.'[16]

Churchill was out of Parliament for the first time in twenty-two years. As Churchill left Dundee by the night train, he was seen off by a crowd of friendly students. Asked to say a few words from his sleeping compartment window, he told the students that 'he had always been a Democrat, and had always believed in the right of the people to make their own institutions. He bowed to that now, even though he thought that it was misguided.' Churchill quit Dundee and was 'carried back to a long convalescence in London and the south of France'.[10]

18–30 November 1922: Recovery from Loss of Seat and Office

On 18 November, TE Lawrence (Lawrence of Arabia) wrote to Churchill:

Dear Mr Churchill

This is a difficult letter to write – because it follows on many unwritten ones. First I wanted to say how sorry I was when you fell ill, and again when you had to have an operation. Then I should have written to say I was sorry when the Government resigned. I meant to write & congratulate you on getting better: but before I could do that you were in Dundee and making speeches. Lastly I should write to say that I'm sorry the poll went against you – but I want to wash out all these lost opportunities, & give you instead my hope that you will rest a little: six months perhaps. There is that book of memoirs to be made not merely worth £30,000 [approximately £1,690,000 in 2019] but of permanent value. Your life of Lord Randolph shows what you could do with memoirs. Then there is the painting to work at, but I feel you are sure to do that anyhow: but the first essential seems to me a holiday for you.[11]

Bishop Welldon, Churchill's Headmaster at Harrow, wrote to him on 24 November 1922, 'It is sometimes an advantage to a statesman that he should be temporarily excluded from the House of Commons: He is missed then, as I suppose Mr Bonar Law has been missed, and I do not doubt your star will rise again and will shine even more brightly than before.'[11]

Two weeks after Churchill's electoral defeat, on 30 November, he was 48 years old. On 21 November Churchill informed Stamfordham that: 'I sail for the Mediterranean on Friday, 1st December, and shall not return, except momentarily, till the Spring is far advanced.'[11] Churchill kept his postponed appointment with the King on 28 November.[11] Churchill, his wife and their children stayed for a six-month holiday in the South of France at the Villa Rêve d'Or near Cannes. He spent most of his time writing his memoirs and painting. Churchill returned alone to England on two occasions to supervise the rebuilding of Chartwell and to discuss his forthcoming war memoirs with naval experts.[17]

Correspondence Between Churchill and Crisp

Churchill wrote from Cannes to English on 9 March 1923:

My dear Sir Crisp English,
You will be glad to hear that I am getting on very well and have experienced so far no ill effects from the wound. The indigestion has been very tiresome, but has been getting steadily better out here through strict attention to eating dry at lunch – a horrible infliction. I have been playing polo since the middle of February and derive great benefit from it. But on Thursday of last week I was forced to exert myself unduly in a match, with the result that I have had a very unpleasant recurrence of indigestion and was a good deal exhausted. It is difficult in a match to avoid sometimes being forced to make exceptional exertions. However, I am much better now and hope to be able to compete satisfactorily. Enclosed please find a cheque for your skilful services and my very best thanks are once again repeated for all the trouble and care you took in my case. Everyone seems very much astonished that I should be playing so soon after a serious operation.[6]

English wrote a handwritten note to Churchill on 18 October 1942:

It is exactly 20 years this evening since I had the honour of doing the operation upon you for acute appendicitis. The notes of your case remind me of the great severity of the attack which you had and the splendid way which you defeated it. I still operate on a great many of these cases, but honestly do not meet any with the great determination which you showed. With all gratitude and good wishes.[18]

English wrote to congratulate Churchill on 9 May 1945:[19]

May we, as millions of others would like to, thank you with the utmost gratitude for the glorious way in which you have brought victory for our country. My wife, daughter and I were within five yards of you, when you left the American Embassy this afternoon, and it was the greatest pleasure to see you looking so wonderfully well and young; and I thought of October 1922, when as a most excellent patient, you gave us a considerable help; and again when your daughter was ill in 1925.
Yours ever faithfully
Crisp English[19]

Churchill sent Crisp a telegram on 11 June 1945: 'Thank you so much for your Victory letter. Winston Churchill.[20]

Twenty-five years after the operation, English wrote again to Churchill (24 November 1947):

It is now just 25 years ago since I operated upon you for appendicitis at 4 Dorset Square and since then I have followed up all your splendid activities with much pleasure, and send you all the best of good wishes and good luck for many more years to come. Personally, I am still 'carrying on' at this same address. Yours very sincerely, Crisp English
PS Yesterday was 22 years since I operated upon Miss Churchill: All good wishes to her.[22]

Churchill replied the following day:

My dear Crisp English
How nice of you to write to me. I have never had the slightest trouble all these twenty-five years. Of course we went over the old ground again

the other day [11 June 1947] when I had my operation for hernia. The cuts are pretty well merged into one, so it looks much bigger. Thank you so much for all you say in your letter and for your kind thoughts. I do not know whether you can find the time to look through this little book of Secret Session Speeches, which I send you. They differ from ordinary speeches as they give the vitals of the story.

Yours very sincerely

WSC[23]

After receiving the book English wrote to Churchill on 2 December 1947:

Thank you very much for your very nice letter and for the most attractive book which will give me <u>very great pleasure</u>. I am very glad to hear that all has gone so very well with you, and again wish you many years of good health and happiness.

Yours very sincerely,

Crisp English[24]

Medical Aspects

Churchill presented with pain in his side (presumably the right side) and 'gastroenteritis', which suggests vomiting and possibly diarrhoea. It is not surprising that Hartigan was uncertain of the diagnosis when Churchill first presented and this probably explains the delay in English being invited to operate. Once English had examined Churchill, the operation was scheduled for that night. English used a McBurney incision, which involves splitting of the three muscle layers of the abdomen rather than cutting through them vertically. The operation report has right rectus sheath crossed out, suggesting that English did consider a vertical incision until the last moment. English was frank enough to state the appendix was removed with difficulty. Ether anaesthesia does not provide good muscle relaxation, and the greater the dose administered, the greater the post-operative nausea and vomiting, though this was not a severe problem in Churchill's case.

It was customary in 1922 to keep patients in bed for several weeks after an appendicectomy, though English advocated getting patients out of bed as soon as possible.[25] Specifically, in cases without drainage, he recommended the patient be got out of bed the day after operation.[25]

The wound infection rate after an open operation for a perforated appendix was very high in the pre-antibiotic era. It is a tribute to the operative technique of English that Churchill did not develop a wound infection, despite late operation and the presence of necrosis. English placed a fairly large drainage tube into the peritoneal cavity and when the wound started to 'weep' he did not hesitate to use a pipette to extract fluid which might have been the early stages of an abscess. However, the microbiological examination of fluid samples showed only a few organisms of a species which rarely caused infection after an appendicectomy. Moreover, the absence of a wound infection is confirmed by the letter English wrote to Dawson, which stated that the wound had healed by the fifteenth day, except where the drainage tube was inserted.

Churchill himself later wrote of this experience:

At the crucial moment I was prostrated by a severe operation for appendicitis, and in the morning when I recovered consciousness I learned that the Lloyd George Government had resigned, that I had lost not only my appendix but my office as Secretary of State for the Dominions and Colonies, in which I conceived myself to have had some Parliamentary and administrative success.[1]

Chapter 6

A Serious Accident in December 1931 in New York

My New York misadventure ... I was conscious through it all[1]

Winston Churchill was 57 years old, he no longer held high political office and was isolated from the leadership of the British Conservative Party over his opposition to greater Indian self-government.[2] His aim in going to the United States in December 1931 was to recoup some of the money he had lost (more than $75,000;[3] equivalent to $1,260,245 in 2019) on the New York stock market.[3,4] He had contracted with Louis Alber, President of the Affiliated Lecture and Concert Association Incorporated, to give forty lectures during his visit, for a guaranteed minimum fee of $50,000.

Churchill was unable to obtain passage for himself, his wife Clementine, his daughter Diana and detective, Inspector Walter Thompson, on a British liner.[5] Of necessity, therefore, for Churchill to meet his contractual commitments, he had to travel on the *Europa*, a German liner. Thompson, who had been Churchill's bodyguard up to 1929 when he lost office as Chancellor of the Exchequer, was provided on this occasion because there had been threats to Churchill's life from Indian Nationalists; Churchill paid all Thompson's personal expenses.[5] Thompson described subsequently that the *Europa* provided the party with 'gorgeous accommodations, superb food, fine companions, and service of a kind I'd never experienced before, afloat or ashore'.[5]

Thompson later recalled that soon after 4 am on 11 December, when he was cleaning his weapons, he was disturbed in his cabin on the *Europa* by forty reporters, who had joined the ship that day from a 'far from seaworthy launch' in order to obtain an interview with Churchill.[5] After Churchill had breakfasted, he met the press and gave interviews in the ship's lounge.[5]

After the ship had docked at about 11 am, Churchill was welcomed to New York by a number of celebrities and several hundred policemen.[5] Churchill was staying in a 39th floor suite at the Waldorf Astoria. On 12 December 1931, he gave his first lecture at Worcester, Massachusetts on 'Pathway of the English-speaking People',[4] which 'went extremely well. The people were almost reverential in their attitude.'[6] After dinner on 13 December, Churchill was telephoned at half-past nine by his longstanding friend Bernard Baruch, Head of the War Industries Board during the two years Churchill was Minister of Munitions, asking him to meet a few mutual friends who were gathered at Baruch's house on Fifth Avenue.

13 December 1931: The Accident

Churchill explained what happened in two articles published in the London *Daily Mail* (see below), but which are now more readily accessible in *Finest Hour*.[1] Churchill descended the thirty-nine storeys which separated his suite from street level by lift. It occurred to him that he did not know the exact number in Fifth Avenue of Baruch's house. The telephone book listed only Baruch's business address. Churchill knew it was somewhere near 1100. He thought it probable he would pick it out from the windows of his taxicab. When the taxicab got near the eleven-hundreds, Churchill peered out of the cab window and scanned the houses as he sped past but could not see any like the one he remembered. Churchill reached the twelve-hundreds, and he was certain he had overshot the house. He told the cabman to turn around and go back slowly so that he could scan every building in turn. Churchill was concerned that as it was now nearly half-past ten, his friends would be concerned as they knew he had started an hour before. Churchill told the cabman to stop where he was on the Central Park side of the avenue so that he could walk across the road and inquire at the most likely house.[1]

I no sooner got out of the cab somewhere about the middle of the road and told the driver to wait than I instinctively turned my eyes to the left. About 200 yards away were the yellow headlights of an approaching car. I thought I had just time to cross the road before it arrived; and I started to do so in the prepossession – wholly unwarranted – that my only dangers were from the left. The yellow-lighted car drew near and I increased my pace towards the pavement, perhaps twenty feet away. Suddenly upon my right I was aware of something utterly unexpected and boding mortal peril. I turned my head sharply. Right upon me, scarcely its own length away, was what seemed a long dark car rushing forward at full speed ... Then came the blow.[1]

The car was driven by an unemployed mechanic from Yonkers, New York, Edward F Cantasano, whose name was misreported by journalists at the time as Mario Contasino. He had not been involved in an accident in the previous eight years. Churchill admitted to the Police that he was 'entirely to blame; it is all my own fault'.[1] After Churchill had recovered, he arranged to meet Cantasano at the Waldorf Astoria for tea and gave him an autographed copy of his book, *The Unknown War*, Volume V of *The World Crisis*.
Churchill later described the trauma:

I felt it on my forehead and across the thighs. But besides the blow there was an impact, a shock, a concussion indescribably violent ... it blotted out everything except thought ... People came running from all directions. Constables appeared ... Meanwhile, I had not lost consciousness for an instant ... I am told that from the time I was struck down to when I was lifted into a taxicab was perhaps five minutes, but although I was in no way stunned, my physical sensations were so violent that I could not achieve any continuous mental process. I just had to endure them.[1]

Transfer to Lenox Hill Hospital

Churchill recalled that an ambulance was passing, and the crowd stopped it and demanded that it should take him to the nearest hospital but the ambulance, which had a serious case on board, refused. Thereupon a taximan offered to take Churchill to the Lenox Hill Hospital on 76th Street.

Accordingly I was lifted by perhaps eight or ten persons to the floor of the taxicab. I now discovered that my overcoat had been half torn off me and trussed my arms back. I thought both shoulders were dislocated. My right shoulder dislocates chronically, and I asked repeatedly that care should be taken in lifting me by it. Eventually the constable and two others got into the cab and we all started, jammed up together ... At last we arrive at the hospital. A wheeled chair is brought. I am carried into it. I am wheeled up steps into a hall and a lift. By now I feel battered but perfectly competent. They said afterwards I was confused; but I did not feel so. 'Are you prepared to pay for a private room and doctor?' asked a clerk. 'Yes, bring all the best you have … Take me to a private room' … 'We shall have to dress that scalp wound at once. It is cut to the bone'.[1]

Churchill's care at the Lenox Hospital was supervised by a German-born surgeon, Dr Otto Pickhardt (see p. 444), and a neurologist, born in Belfast, Dr Foster Kennedy (p. 439). The latter charged a fee of $250 (equivalent to $4,620 in 2019).[7] Churchill was taken to the operating room and anaesthetized using nitrous oxide/oxygen and his lacerations were sutured and he was X-rayed. Churchill brought some of the X-rays back to London but two skull X-rays were sold subsequenly by Christies New York on behalf of the Pickhardt estate.[8]

Churchill sent his son, Randolph, a telegram on 15 December 1931 which indicated his temperature was 100.6°F (38.1°C), that his head scalp wound was severe, that he had suffered two cracked ribs, had pleural irritation on the right side and was very bruised.[9]

In fact, according to his surgeon, Churchill's injuries included:

multiple bruises and abrasions particularly of both shoulders and right elbow;

a three inch jagged laceration of Churchill's forehead from the bridge of his nose up deep to bone;

a laceration of the nose and right nostril;

fractures of both nasal bones with dislocation of Churchill's nose to the left;

traumatic pleural haemorrhagic (bloody) effusion of the right lung;

fractures involving the distal phalanx of the first toe of the right foot and the middle phalanx of the second toe of the right foot with no displacement of fragments;

possible linear fractures of the 8th and 9th ribs without displacement.[8]

Pickhardt considered that Churchill would have a permanent scar on the forehead and on the right side of his nose and residual pain in the region of the right lower chest and in both shoulders and upper limbs.[8]

In a radio interview on 9 March 1932 Churchill said: 'It's not a jolly thing to be cut down by a motor car at 30 miles an hour. I think it would have knocked the life out of a great many people of my age. I was very lucky in the way it hit me.'[2]

Despite the accident and admission to hospital, Churchill cabled the Honourable Esmond Harmsworth, son of Lord Rothermere, owner of the London *Daily Mail*, on 16 December 1931 to offer two articles in quick succession (being the third and fourth of his series) on how it feels to be run over by a motor car. The London *Daily Mail* had agreed to pay Churchill some £8,000 (equivalent of £547,856 in 2019) for a series of articles whose sale in the United States he was still free to negotiate. While in the United States, Churchill agreed to write a series of articles for *Collier's* for $9,000 (equivalent to $151,967 in 2019).

Churchill informed Harmsworth: 'Have complete recollection of whole event & believe can produce literary gem about 2,400 words. Consider this will be unique feature. Expect be able to cable during week of 27th. Am of course marketing here also & will synchronise publication. Pray cable your view. Am steadily recovering from terrific impact.'[10]

21–30 December 1931: Discharge from Hospital and Recuperation in New York

Churchill was discharged on 21 December to his suite at the Waldorf Astoria. The *Daily Mail*'s own correspondent (Walter Bullock[11]) interviewed Churchill in his suite. The newspaper reported in its edition of 24 December that Churchill was 'still very weak from the shock of the accident last week'. Churchill said that he realized 'that I have had a miraculous escape from death, the curious thing is that I never once lost consciousness'. The reporter observed that Churchill's forehead and nose were still elaborately bandaged and, though able to walk a few steps, on the advice of Dr Otto C. Pickhardt, he would spend the next eight or ten days in bed.

Pickhardt was quoted by the *Daily Mail* as stating that: 'His condition, on the whole is very satisfactory, and it can now be safely said that he will suffer no serious after-effects of his injuries. But he must have rest, as he has been badly shaken up.' Churchill himself stated he would rest at the hotel during the Christmas holidays, and then, if well enough, pay a brief visit to Nassau in the Bahamas, returning to New York in time to deliver his first lecture on 14 January 1932.

Churchill learned from Mr William Bernau of Lloyds Bank, who had arranged his insurance policies with the Phoenix Assurance Company, that the policies did not cover his medical expenses. Compensation would be payable, however, at a rate of £60 per week (equivalent to £4,153 in 2019) 'in respect of the time that Mr Churchill is totally disabled as certified by his medical attendants'.[12]

Churchill also cabled his longstanding friend Professor Frederick Lindemann ('The Prof'; later Lord Cherwell), Professor of Experimental Philosophy (Physics) at the University of Oxford on 24 December asking him to calculate the impact or shock to a stationary body of 200 lb of a motor car weighing 2,400 lb travelling 30 or 35 miles per hour? 'This shock I took in my body being carried forward on the cowcatcher until brakes eventually stopped car when I dropped off. Brakes did not operate till car hit me. Want figure for article. Think it must be impressive.'[13]

On 28 December Churchill cabled Dr Hartigan (see p. 438), his London general practitioner, to enquire about his 'normal blood pressure',[14] presumably because it had been found to be raised in New York. On the same day, Churchill had completed the article of 3,600 words of which he thought highly as he so informed Harmsworth and proposed: 'You can make three of it if you like. Important publications should be successive.'[15]

Churchill cabled Harmsworth again on 30 December 1931: 'Hope you have received and read article. Paragraph about mathematical calculation of impact will have to be adjusted if information does not arrive in time ... Am quite all right and getting stronger every day but have a long way to go.'[16]

Lindemann responded on 30 December 1931 from the Hotel Continental, Nice, France:

Collision equivalent falling thirty feet onto pavement equal six thousand foot pounds of energy. Equivalent stopping ten pound brick dropped six hundred feet, or two charges buckshot point blank range. Shock probably proportional rate energy transferred. Rate inversely proportional thickness cushion surrounding skeleton and give of frame. If assume average one inch, your body transferred during impact at rate eight thousand horsepower. Congratulations on preparing suitable cushion, and skill in taking bump.[17]

The *Daily Mail* published Churchill's account in two parts on 4 January 1932 (*My New York Misadventure*[1]) and 5 January 1932 (*I was conscious through it all*[1]). Harmsworth sent a telegram to Churchill on 1 January 1932: 'Thanks for brilliant article … delighted [at] your recovery.'[18] Churchill told his son: 'I rather plumed myself upon having had the force to conceive, write and market this article so soon after the crash.'[19] The articles were syndicated all over the world and earned Churchill more than £600 (equivalent to £41,100 in 2019).

2–22 January 1932: Nassau, Bahamas

On 31 December 1931 the Churchill party sailed from New York to Nassau, Bahamas, arriving on 2 January 1932. The party stayed at the Polly Leach Hotel, at a rate of $10 (equivalent to $180 per person per day), until a new Governor, Sir Bede Edmund Hugh Clifford, arrived on 10 January 1932 and invited Churchill to move into Government House.[6]

On arrival in Nassau, Churchill sent a telegram to Alber:

Deeply regret unable to comply request. Doctor Graham of Nassau certifies as follows. Improving daily unfit to begin lecturing before end of month. Mental as well as physical rest imperative. Am sure Dr Pickhardt will confirm from previous knowledge of case. Would gladly help … if I possibly could but must regather my life and strength.[20]

Dr Graham's account for professional services was £9 12 shillings (equivalent to £657 in 2019).[21]

On 3 January Churchill sent a telegram to Pickhardt: 'Although improving daily am convinced unfit begin lecturing before February one. Doctors here concur must regain vitality. Kindly cable your advice.'[22] Pickhardt responded on 5 January 1932: 'Heartily endorse postponement of lecturing to February first. Remember forceful impact with shock and shaking of brain cells. Repeat real rest mental as well as physical imperative in building for your future and present usefulness.'[23]

Churchill wrote to his son, Randolph, on 5 January:

Here lead the life as nearly as possible of a vegetable. The air is delicious, mild and cool but we have been unlucky these five days in having so little sunshine and too much wind, however I hope the weather will now be improving to its normal condition of perfection. The water is about 73 [°F] and I hope next week to be able to bathe ... Tonight both branches of the Legislature are giving me a banquet and I have to make a short speech which I am very unfit to do ('it went off all right').[24]

Unfortunately for Churchill the *New York Times* reported his attendance at the dinner and that he gave a speech.[25] It also stated that though he had come to Nassau for a week Churchill had liked it so much he had decided to stay until later in January despite his health improving rapidly.[25] In these circumstances it is not surprising that Alber telegraphed Churchill:

we are finding rising tide of criticism with statements that if you could attend function there last night you could attend one here week and half later. Doing all possible to keep newspaper men quiet but Associated Press man said he anticipated unfavourable editorial comment that would destroy fine impression already made. Therefore earnestly urge you to return January 12 ... Will arrange for you to be seated while speaking. Such procedure would bring widespread favourable comment your sportsmanship and gameness in preventing rather heavy losses falling upon those who have been most friendly. Please cable here ... before noon tomorrow.[25]

On 7 January Churchill sent a telegram to Pickhardt and requested him to kindly supply Phoenix Assurance Company with 'necessary certificate disablement to twenty-eight instant. Phoenix will apply to you.' Clementine Churchill also sent a telegram to Pickhardt on 7 January confirming that Churchill was 'not well enough to resume lecturing until end of month. Much undue pressure being put on him to start Fourteenth. Please see Alber [at] Hotel Vanderbilt.'[26] Pickhardt telegraphed the same day: 'Agree with you. Long conversation Elliott Partner Alber. Emphasized possibility of breakdown in midst of western trip. Agreement reached health demands postponement first lecture to January 28 in Brooklyn. Shall attend Phoenix certificate.'[27]

Churchill sent a further telegram to Pickhardt on 8 January: 'Thank you very much am intensely relieved.'[28] Churchill also wrote at length on the same day:

I arrived here physically very weak but with considerable mental energy, then all of a sudden I felt a great deal of nervous re-action and lassitude. Although my physical energy becomes each day much greater and I can walk and swim for short distance quite all right, I found a great and sudden lack of power for mental concentration and a strong sense of being unequal to the tasks which lay so soon ahead of me. In addition to this both my arms and right side are plagued with a kind of neuritis which makes them at times in each day almost as sore as two or three days after the accident.[29]

Churchill continued:

I have to take a quarter dose of sleeping medicine almost every night and from time to time have had depression of spirit. When they started worrying me to begin on the fourteenth as planned, I felt absolutely sure I could not do it. The doctor here, a very capable man, Dr Graham, took exactly the same view.[29]

Churchill responded to Alber on 11 January:

I am sure it would have been madness for me to try to address large audiences before I am myself again. I have made great progress here, but the shock I received was grave and deep. I have developed very painful neuritis in both arms which so interferes with my sleep that I still have to employ a night nurse. I am growing in strength every day but am still astonishingly feeble; even the act of dressing or shaving tires me. I spend eighteen out of twenty-four hours in bed. I am pretty sure that if I stay here until the 22nd or 23rd, sun-bathing and sea-bathing every day and leading the life of a convalescent I shall be able to give you six solid weeks of work in February and March. It is only in the last two days I have ceased to totter as I walk. How foolish indeed it would have been to compromise the whole of your February engagement by courting a serious break-down through making a premature effort now. The wonderful thing is that I am alive at all ... I am getting better every day and find swimming especially beneficial. I still feel very weak and debilitated and am incapable of any serious physical or mental exertion. My mind is, however, becoming very active again and I have great hopes that the next fortnight may restore me to something of my old vigour.[30]

Not only did Churchill employ Mrs Maura as a night nurse for a week at a cost of £8 and 8 shillings (equivalent to £609 in 2019) but also Mrs Sype,[31] a US nurse, for three weeks for her expertise as a masseuse.[32]

Clementine Churchill wrote to Randolph on 12 January:

> Papa is progressing but very slowly. I am sure he will be again as well as before, but he is terribly depressed at the slowness of his recovery and when he is in low spirits murmurs 'I *wish* it hadn't happened'. He has horrible pains in his arms and shoulders. The doctors call it neuritis but they don't seem to know what to do about it. I think the sunshine and bathing are doing him good, but of course what is really needed is 3 or 4 months complete relaxation. Papa is worried about the lectures and feels he may not be able to stay the course … Last night he said he was very sad that he had now in the last 2 years had 3 heavy blows. First the loss of all that money in the crash, then the loss of his political position and now this terrible physical injury. He said he did not think he would ever recover completely from the three events … I had hoped he would paint here but he does not seem to have the strength or energy to start.[33]

Pickhardt wrote on 13 January to the Phoenix Assurance Company in New York City describing Churchill's injuries.[8] The Insurance Company was informed by Pickhardt that Churchill was on his way to Nassau, Bahamas for a complete mental and physical rest before his first lecture on 28 January.[8]

Bernau wrote to Churchill on 14 January indicating he had 'nearly upset the apple cart' by writing the articles for the *Daily Mail*.[34] As a result, Phoenix Insurance Company had taken the view that as Churchill was well enough to follow his 'profession of occupation' of writing he was no longer totally disabled and therefore the weekly allowance of £60 would cease.[34] Bernau argued successfully that during the currency of the policy Churchill's occupation was 'a lecturing tour in the USA' whatever his occupation or profession in Great Britain. Fortunately, Phoenix Assurance continued to pay Churchill £60 weekly.[34]

While in Nassau, Thompson records that Churchill narrowly missed being knocked down again by a young driver going too fast. Churchill leapt out of the way, grabbing the top posts of a board fence. 'He shivered and shook. Sweat poured down his face and darkened his cream coloured shirt

... it left him weak and shaking.'[5] Thompson recalled Churchill looked at him and said: 'They almost got me that time Thompson.'[5]

Churchill left Nassau on SS *Statendam*, a ship of the Holland America Line on 22 January and arrived in New York on 25 January.[35]

25–30 January: New York

On arrival Pickhardt provided Churchill with the now infamous letter dated 26 January so that Prohibition did not impair his enjoyment of the lecture tour: 'This is to certify that the post-accident convalescence of the Hon. Winston S. Churchill necessitates the use of alcoholic spirits especially at meal times. The quantity is naturally indefinite but the minimum requirements would be 250 cubic centimeters.'[36] Churchill worked on his lectures for three days at the Waldorf Astoria before giving the first lecture at the Brooklyn Academy of Music on 28 January 1932; Cantasano was also present.

The ninth Duke of Marlborough, Churchill's close relative, received a delayed response to his letter of 27 December 1931; Churchill did not reply until 26 January 1932.

> I was indeed nearly killed. In fact, I don't know how I could have been cut down frontally by a vehicle going that speed and have yet survived. I had a bad secondary reaction of nervous and muscular pain when I got to Nassau, but with plenty of bathing and sunshine and complete mental stagnation I have recovered a great part of my usual health. I hope to be able to carry out my tour and be back in England by the third week in March.[37]

31 January–9 March 1932: Lecture Tour

Before the lecture tour got underway, Pickhardt provided Churchill with a list of physicians in all the cities he was to visit.[38] Churchill wrote to Pickhardt on 14 February informing him that he had 'broken the back of the lecture-tour without feeling any ill effects'.[39] Churchill explained that despite the travel and speaking and fatigue of seeing people every day, and an attack of acute tonsillitis lasting three days, he was now able to do a very good day's active work.[39]

Thompson has written that audiences at the lectures averaged 4,200 people (range 3,000 to over 8,000 people)[5] but, despite this good attendance, rearrangement of the lecture tour following Churchill's accident, meant he earned some $23,000 (equivalent to $429,360 in 2019) less than hoped for initially.[40] He also received $1,000 (equivalent to $18,329 in 2019) for a 15-minute radio interview on 10 March 1932.[41] But there was some opposition. Churchill received 700 threatening letters during the tour,[5] his car was stoned twice in Detroit and filth was dumped at his hotel[5] and in Chicago, an East Indian tried to kill Churchill and Thompson had to intervene with gun drawn.[5]

11 March 1932: Home to Chartwell

Churchill left New York on 11 March onboard the White Star liner *Majestic*, which docked in Southampton on 17 March.[4] On his arrival several friends presented him with a new Daimler car, a gift organised by Brendan Bracken.[4]

On 1 April 1932 Churchill wrote to his Publisher, Thornton Butterworth: 'I am much better, but feel I need to rest and not to have to drive myself quite so hard. You have no idea what I have been through.'[42]

Correspondence between Churchill and Pickhardt

Later in April 1932, Pickhardt asked Churchill if he could use his article in the *Daily Mail* as part of a publicity drive among residents to bring in financial support for the Lenox Hill Hospital which had been hard hit by the general recession.[43] Churchill readily agreed and apologised that the article did not contain a direct reference to Pickhardt.[44] In a letter dated 4 May 1932 Churchill explained to Pickhardt that he had regained his full mental and physical vigour but tired more easily. 'Especially I feel the nerves in the small of the back ache … I have also a very strange feeling of pins and needles, but I think it is going off. I have not seen any doctor since I returned so you can see I am fairly competent.'[44]

Pickhardt wrote to Churchill again on 12 April 1957, asking him ('our most eminent patient') to provide 'a few words' to celebrate the centenary of the Lenox Hill Hospital on 13 May 1957 where 'due to your tenacity for life, with excellent care and treatment, you recovered. Since then, the best part of the world has thanked God for your being saved and, of course, for saving the world.'[45] Churchill responded with good wishes for the Hospital's continued success. 'I well remember the admirable care and attention I received during my enforced visit to the Hospital in 1931.'[46]

Financial Aspects

Some comment about Churchill's financial difficulties is needed. The lecture tour was planned at least in part to ameliorate these, and the accident threatened the viability of the tour and the income to be derived from it. We have described Churchill's obvious financial concerns and the sums involved in some detail here in order to illustrate the scale of his difficulties and the way in which he dealt with them in the aftermath of the accident. By any standards, he must be admired for resuming the tour so soon after this accident. Churchill's lecture audiences were huge, between 4,000 and 8,000, and were, without doubt, a measure of his reputation and international standing in the inter-war years. His lecture fees were substantial, even by today's standards. We doubt that the amount paid (equivalent to $18,329 in 2019) for a 15-minute interview on the radio on 10 March 1932[41] could be matched today.

Medical Aspects

Churchill's accident on 13 December 1931 was clearly serious and potentially fatal, and it is remarkable that he recovered without any lasting ill-effects. Given the nature of the blow, and Lindemann's calculation of the force of the impact, it is astonishing that there was no brain injury of any severity. Indeed, although Churchill later mentioned 'concussion',[1] his own detailed description of the event indicates that he essentially avoided a head injury. The accident '... blotted out everything except thought ...'[1] and '... although I was in no way stunned ...'[1] And on or about 24 December Churchill stated '... the curious thing is that I never once lost consciousness'. Furthermore, the title of the second of his two articles published in the *Daily Mail* on 5 January 1932 was *I was conscious through it all.*

His recollection of events immediately before the impact, and of the impact itself are perfectly clear and detailed, and described by Churchill with his characteristic linguistic flair and clarity of expression. Likewise, his memory of events immediately following the accident was both clear and continuous. However, there is some apparent inconsistency with Churchill's later description 'although I was in no way stunned, my physical sensations were so violent that I could not achieve any continuous mental process. I just had to endure them'.[1] Perhaps it is appropriate to best interpret these words as referring to the immediate psychological trauma of the accident.

In his cable to Harmsworth, of the *Daily Mail*, on 16 December 1931, just three days following the accident, Churchill used the phrase 'how it feels to be run over by a motor car'. However, the description of the impact and the injuries sustained indicates that Churchill was facing the oncoming car, which hit his legs (thighs), lifting him and leading to a forceful impact of his head on the bonnet (hood) of the car, causing the nasal bone fractures and deep lacerations of the nose and forehead. There is, however, no description of the damage done to the car from the collision, which might have provided additional corroborating evidence for the nature and mechanism of the impact.

Churchill's major injuries were cutaneous, musculoskeletal and a haemorrhagic pleural effusion, as described here. Churchill recalls his arms being 'trussed back' and thought [that his] 'shoulders [were] dislocated'.[1] This may have implications for some of his lasting symptoms, as we consider below. Perhaps surprisingly, the accident did not lead to obvious cervical spine injury. The likely mechanism of the impact makes it probable that there would have been a sudden forced flexion of the cervical spine at the moment of the impact, before contact of his face with the bonnet of the car.

Recognising the opportunity provided to report the accident to the press, in his own words, and to benefit financially by doing so, Churchill consulted his old friend Lindemann concerning the calculation of the force of the collision impact. Lindemann responded appropriately, with some startling figures. In his communication to Churchill about this on 30 December 1931, Lindemann's reference to Churchill's body habitus and its contribution to the mitigation of the effects of the impact is priceless.

Churchill was remarkably resilient from a psychological point of view following the accident, but there clearly was some effect, which seems entirely appropriate to the severity of the event. Approximately three weeks after the injury, Churchill referred to difficulty sleeping and 'depression of spirit' and later to general fatigue and lassitude, though the interpretation of these latter symptoms as being of either psychological or physical origin is neither appropriate nor helpful.

In a communication to Pickhardt on 8 January 1932, almost four weeks after the accident, Churchill referred to a number of persistent symptoms, including:

A great deal of nervous re-action and lassitude … lack of power for mental concentration and a strong sense of being unequal to the tasks which lay so soon ahead of me. In addition to this both my arms and right side are plagued with a kind of neuritis which makes them at times in each day almost as sore as two or three days after the accident.[29]

Some of these symptoms may reflect the psychological impact of the accident. Without further direct enquiry, it is impossible to know what Churchill meant by 'neuritis', but the rest of that sentence suggests that he may have been referring principally to pain. Clementine Churchill, in a letter to her son Randolph dated 12 January 1932, mentioned that Winston had 'horrible pains in his arms and shoulders. The doctors call it neuritis but they don't seem to know what to do about it.'[33]

One could speculate that the arm pain might either have been referred from the shoulders (clearly involved to some extent in the accident), or possibly the cervical spine. On 11 January 1932 Churchill, in a letter to Alber, said that 'it is only in the last two days I have ceased to totter as I walk'.[30] We do not have access to the medical notes from this time and particularly those of the neurologist, Dr Kennedy, and can therefore not reach a conclusion concerning the possibility of a cervical spinal cord lesion (contusion) that could explain the nature and distribution of these symptoms. There is no record of the cervical spine being investigated at the time.

Professor (later Sir) Herbert Seddon (see p. 451) recorded in December 1960 that: 'Golding [Dr Frederick Campbell Golding (p. 437)] took superb pictures and they showed an old lesion of the 4th and 7th cervical vertebrae which were all fused. There was no change in the state of the 5th thoracic. I then recalled a serious accident the young Churchill had suffered on 10 January 1893 when he jumped from a bridge at [Branksome Dene, near] Bournemouth.'[47] It is possible that a second cervical spine injury, occurring in the accident on 13 December 1931, contributed to the radiological changes noted later in 1960. Furthermore, the presence of an abnormal structure of the cervical spine resulting from the 1893 accident would probably have increased the risk of sustaining a cervical spinal cord contusion in the accident in 1931. However, without additional clinical details available to us now, this must remain a matter of speculation.

The accident in December 1931 might well have ended Churchill's contributions to public life, and indeed might have proved fatal. We cannot but be grateful that he did not sustain a head injury of any severity or with lasting effects, and can merely speculate on the likely progression of subsequent world events had the outcome not been so favourable.

Chapter 7

An Attack of Enteric Fever in September 1932 in Austria

In time of war, soldiers, however sensible, cared a great deal more on some occasions about slaking their thirst than about the danger of enteric fever[1]

Following his recovery from an accident in New York (see p. 31) and a subsequent extensive US lecture tour, Winston Churchill committed himself to research for the biography of his ancestor, *Marlborough*, the first volume of which was published in October 1933. This feat could never have been achieved without the efforts and expertise of Maurice Ashley, whom Churchill had recruited in June 1929 at a half-time salary of £300 per year. Churchill had made the appointment on the advice of a senior history Fellow, Keith Feiling, then Student at Christ Church, Oxford, and later Sir Keith Feiling, Chichele Professor of Modern History at Oxford. In the event Ashley stayed for four years until summer 1933.[2]

Subsequently, in 1932, Churchill recruited more research assistance from Lieutenant Colonel (later Major General) Ridley Pakenham-Walsh, who made copious suggestions on military matters relating to Marlborough's campaigns, and Feiling who provided expert advice on matters of historical controversy.[3] Feiling arrived at Chartwell on 12 August 1932 and stayed eight days.[3] During this time he helped Churchill improve several chapters for the forthcoming biography and make plans to visit the battlefields on which Marlborough had fought in Belgium, Holland and Germany.[3]

However, in summer 1932 Churchill was not totally focused on *Marlborough* as he had had agreed on 1 August 1932, at the behest of Lord Riddell, to produce a series of six articles for the *News of the World* on the World's greatest stories, for a fee of £2,000 (equivalent to £139,000 in 2019). He had been promised a further £500 expedition fee in a telegram from Riddell 'if copy provided by end of year'.[4] In addition to the *News of the World* fee, Churchill also sold the US syndication rights for these six articles to the *Chicago Tribune* for £1,800 (equivalent to £125,000 in 2019).[5]

27–30 August 1932: Visit to the Battlefields

The Churchill party set off from Dover on 27 August on the 11 am 'auto carrier boat'.[6] Churchill was accompanied by his wife, Clementine, daughter, Sarah, and friend, Professor Frederick Lindemann, Professor of Experimental Philosophy (Physics) at the University of Oxford and Director of the Clarendon Laboratory.[3] The plan was that Lindemann would drive the party in his car to Bruxelles arriving in time for dinner at the Hotel Astoria, 101–3 Rue Royale.[6]

Churchill had asked Pakenham-Walsh to make the necessary arrangements with the hotel ('just the ordinary good first class accommodation will suffice').[6] Specifically, Churchill asked for two rooms and two bathrooms adjoining and a sitting room for his wife and himself, one room and a bathroom for Sarah, and a good room and a bathroom, not necessarily en suite, for Lindemann.[6] Churchill invited Pakenham-Walsh and his wife to join them as their guests, and he reserved 28–30 August for the battlefields.[6] Pakenham-Walsh wrote to Churchill from the Hotel Astoria on 24 August confirming these arrangements had been made with the Manager and informing Churchill that the 'hotel is very comfortable and the cuisine so far is excellent', which is not surprising given the reputation of the hotel at the time.[7]

Churchill wrote to Feiling: 'The battlefields were wonderful. Packenham-Walsh presented them admirably and I was able to re-people them with ghostly armies. A surprise was their great size. Ramilies [Ramillies, Belgium], Oudenarde [Oudenaarde, Flanders] and Blenheim [Blindheim, near Höchstädt, Bavaria, Germany] all seemed to me bigger than Austerlis or Gettysburg, and far bigger than Waterloo.'[8] Churchill concluded: 'I was deeply moved by all these scenes and feel sure I can interpret them for the first time. We spent whole days on the fields picnicing there.'[8]

September 1932: Paratyphoid Fever in Salzburg

Following the battlefield visits, Churchill left Germany to drive south through the Austrian Alps to Venice and there to combine a family holiday with writing up the first draft of *Marlborough*. However, as he set out on the last lap of his journey, he developed a persistent fever which began about 2 September. While staying at the Hotel Österreichischer Hof Salzburg,[9]

Salzburg's most luxurious hotel, Churchill's condition deteriorated and he was first assessed by Professor Dr Ludwig Petschacher, a specialist in internal medicine and head of the St Johann Spital, Salzburg, on 7 September.[10] He was admitted on 12 September[11] to Sanatorium Dr Gebhard Hromada, 11 Franz-Josef-Straße in Salzburg, named for its director and chief surgeon.[12] Churchill remained under the care of Petschacher while in the Sanatorium.

The villa in which the Sanatorium was situated had been a sanatorium since the days of the Habsburg monarchy but had been purchased in 1928 by the Weissensteins, a wealthy Jewish family.[12] Elisabeth Weissenstein's husband was Dr Hromada.[12] As there was no Jewish hospital in Salzburg the city's Jewish people relied on the Hromada Sanatorium in the Andrä-quarter until the violence of 1938.[12] Hromada emigrated to Brazil in 1935, returning to Salzburg in 1956.[9]

Petschacher confirmed the diagnosis was paratyphoid fever and an unnamed source reported by *The Times* stated that the cause of the illness was thought to be the drinking of contaminated water, probably in Bavaria.[13] On 13 September Churchill's temperature was 101°F (38.3°C) but was lower than it had been on the previous two days.[14] Mrs Churchill was spending the greater part of each day with her husband who it was reported had had a good night on 12 September.[14] Churchill had been well enough to read the newspapers during the day on 13 September.[14] Petschacher was quoted as saying that Churchill's robust constitution ought to see to see him through his illness much more quickly than might otherwise be expected.[14]

On 15 September 1932, *The Times* reported that Churchill's temperature was almost normal on the evening of 14 September[15] and on 16 September Churchill's temperature had only been slightly higher than the previous day. Churchill had been feeling 'quite bright', and Petschacher was satisfied with his condition.[16] Despite his illness, Churchill felt well enough to begin work again on 17 September on the series of articles for the *News of the World*. One of these articles, *The Count of Monte Cristo*, drafted by Edward Marsh, private secretary to Churchill in many Cabinet posts, for an honorarium of some £25 (£1,700 in 2019) per article, reached him in Salzburg where he worked to polish it. Churchill wrote to Marsh the same day regarding his approach in the draft article and declared: 'I am throwing off this foul attack and planning to travel home Thursday if all well. Shall finish convalescing at Chartwell, and you can come to see me there.'[17]

By Sunday, 18 September 1932 Petschacher stated that Churchill was free of fever and on the road to complete recovery.[18] He declared that if his patient suffered no relapse, he would be able to leave next Thursday (22 September) for England.[18] Anticipating his discharge, Churchill had sent a telegram to London to indicate that he hoped to be present at the annual conference of the National Union of Conservative and Unionist Associations at Blackpool on 6 October 1932 and to support the resolution on the Indian policy.[18] Churchill had also written to Feiling on 19 September 1932: 'I am recovering fast and hope to return on Thursday.'[8] Churchill settled his account with the Sanatorium and Petschacher on 21 September 1932 for 1,910 Austrian Schillings and 1,240 Austrian Schillings respectively.

The Times reported that Churchill left Salzburg for England on 22 September[19] and had arrived home at Chartwell on the evening of 23 September.[20] On reaching home Churchill said that although he was feeling very much better, he had still some way to go to complete recovery.[20] *The Times* report implied that Churchill was discharged from the Sanatorium, but Gilbert states that he discharged himself against medical advice.[21] Gilbert has written that the doctors had insisted that Churchill remain in bed for several weeks.[21] However, as Churchill was impatient to return to Chartwell, to continue both his work and convalescence amid familiar surroundings, he discharged himself from the Sanatorium, and took the train for Calais.[21]

Mrs Churchill met a British doctor on the train, whom she had known in England, and asked whether he could help with Winston. She explained that her husband had just discharged himself, against the doctor's advice, from the nursing home in Salzburg where he had suffered 'bad bleeding' and was now insisting on eating a full lunch with salad, wine etc. 'Will you kindly give him your advice as a doctor?' Whereupon the doctor went over to Churchill and talked to him like a 'Dutch uncle'; Churchill was said by the doctor to have taken it quite well.[21]

On 25 September 1932 Churchill wrote to the Duke of Marlborough: 'I am back again, rather battered, but in another week I shall be quite all right.'[22] On the following day, Churchill wrote to Lord Riddell in a similar vein: 'I am back again, rather battered, and must stay in bed for most of the day. But I have got a long way on in my mind with your work and hope to have the first two articles finished by the middle of October.'[23]

Sir Charles Mendl, Head of the press section in the British Embassy in Paris, wrote to Churchill on 26 September 1932 enclosing multiple cuttings from the French press following an interview Churchill had given.[24] Mendl also gave Churchill some medical advice based on a friend of his who was recovering from paratyphoid infection: 'Paratyphoid is a long job and you ought to be more careful than the English doctors sometimes recommend'.[24]

27 September 1932: Relapse in London

Mendl's concern proved accurate. When Churchill returned to Chartwell, he began a punishing schedule of writing. Much of this work had to be done in bed. As Ashley sat on one side with the documents, Mrs Violet Pearman, his personal secretary,[25] sat on the other side with her notepad, taking dictation.[3] Impatient to make progress, Churchill insisted, however, on walking with Ashley up and down the lawns at Chartwell, to discuss the meaning of the latest discovery of Marlborough's early and tortuous career. By 27 September, 90,000 words had been written for *Marlborough*.[3]

Ashley later recalled that while he and Churchill were sitting in the garden and Churchill was talking with his usual animation about history, he started to 'look pale and distraught'.[2] A doctor was called, and it transpired that Churchill was bleeding internally, the result of a paratyphoid ulcer. As Churchill left Chartwell on a stretcher, he perceived Ashley's anxiety and said: 'Don't worry, Ashley, I am not going to die.'[2] Churchill was driven on 27 September to the Beaumont House Nursing Home, 8–10 Beaumont Street, London.[26]

The Times reported on 28 September that Churchill had suffered a relapse, accompanied by some haemorrhage and had to be admitted to a London nursing home and would be unable to do any public work for several weeks.[27] Churchill was reported to be 'very weak' and 'very ill' but that his condition was not dangerous.[27] The statement said that Churchill was 'up and about too soon after his recent illness, and was working rather hard. He should have had more rest.' A later statement indicated that Churchill 'was resting and rather more comfortable'.[27]

On 1 October 1932 *The Times* reported that Churchill's progress was maintained.[28] Mrs Pearman, Churchill's personal secretary,[25] wrote to CR Everitt of his literary agents, Curtis Brown, on the same day: 'We hope he will recover shortly, in his usual marvellous way.'[29] In early October Churchill received a visit from Marsh. It was resolved that Marsh would write the Preface that the Publisher, Thornton Butterworth, required urgently for a new collection of newspaper articles which he had written over the previous twenty years.[30] Although the Preface to *Thoughts and Adventures* was signed by Churchill and dated September 1932, it was neither written by Churchill nor written that month.[30] The Preface was written by Edward Marsh.[30] So well did Marsh counterfeit Churchill's style that Churchill wrote: 'Rather good pastiche!' on his copy of the typescript.[30] Marsh wrote to the Publisher: 'Mr Churchill has read the preface and thinks it is delightful. All that is needed is his name, the date and Chartwell to add to it.'[30]

As a result of his relapse, Churchill missed the Conservative and Unionist Party Conference in Blackpool, though he told Sir James Hawkey, Vice-Chairman, Epping Division Conservative Association, he was anxious to go to Blackpool in an ambulance.[3] Stanley Baldwin, Lord President of the Council, sent Churchill a handwritten letter:

My dear Winston, so far I have refrained even from good words, but I do want you to realize with what profound sympathy I see you laid up and rendered immobile for the time being. No greater trial could there be to your ardent spirit … For all our sakes you must devote yourself to regaining your strength, and no one will be more glad to hear you from your corner, invoking once more blessings or curses on our heads as may seem good to you on occasion.[21]

Churchill dictated a response to Mrs Pearman and reported to Baldwin that as a result of his haemorrhage he had lost about 'two fifths of my blood' and that it would be at least six weeks 'before I have my ordinary vigour back'.[21] Churchill wrote to a friend: 'I am recovering and recruiting red corpuscles at about 100,000 a day. At present, though increasing in numbers rapidly, they are still rather a raw militia and I do not feel that I could wisely commit my army to any first-class operations.'[21]

The Times reported that Churchill was discharged from the nursing home on 10 October and moved to his private residence (11 Morpeth Mansions, London SW1), and that he would be confined mainly to bed for some time and was in need of rest and quiet.[31] The cost of Churchill's care at Beaumont House was £55 and 2 shillings (equivalent to £3,800 in 2019)[26] and nurses were hired for several weeks from the Nurses Co-operation, Langham Street, Portland Place, London to look after Churchill during his convalescence.[32]

Churchill wrote to his Publisher, George Harrap, on the day he left the nursing home (10 October) and enclosed four chapters of *Marlborough* which he hoped could be galley proofed (six copies) within ten days.[33] Harrap replied the next day:

> It is surprising to see your hand-writing this morning. I hope that I can take this as evidence that you are feeling as though complete recovery is not far away ... I think I can assure you that you will have the galley proof of all within the next ten days ... My secretary observes that she thinks you must be a very bad and unreasonable man, in the face of what your doctors have said![34]

Churchill was unable to attend a dinner on 14 October 1932 to celebrate the 50th anniversary of his Publisher entering the family publishing company,[35] but sent a message to be read by George Harrap's son: 'Every good wish to Mr Harrap on this occasion in the hope that his future as a publisher will not be unworthy of a long and distinguished past.'[36]

On 18 October Churchill wrote to Esmond Harmsworth of the *Daily Mail*: 'I am here now almost bedridden but improving rapidly and it would be splendid if you could come over and lunch or dine on either Saturday, Sunday or Monday.'[37] On 20 October, Mrs Pearman wrote to Nancy Pearn of Curtis Brown: 'Mr Churchill is steadily improving, though progress is rather slow, but as usual nothing can keep him from work, and he busies himself for a good many hours each day and gets through a lot. It will be some time I think before he really gets as strong as before.'[38]

Grace Hamblin[39] recalls being interviewed by Churchill to be his personal secretary when he was recuperating at Chartwell:

> He was sitting up in bed looking very frail and quite small – not at all the big bear I'd expected. He said, 'Good morning, good morning, do bring up a chair.' I brought a chair up, fairly close to the bed – a respectful distance, I thought. 'Oh, do come closer!' So I pulled it a bit closer. 'Do you use a typewriter?' Yes. 'Can you do shorthand writing?' Yes. 'Oh.' Then a long, long stare. I think everyone who knew him knew that look. He would look at you for a long, long time, not really meaning anything, just thinking. But to a new, quite young person, it was rather embarrassing. However, I sat it out and finally he said,

'So you wish to come to me?' Yes, Sir. 'Never call me Sir!' That was how it all started.... I was very fortunate because after his illness he wasn't working so hard as was his usual habit. He could only dictate 100 words a day [a minute presumably], which was very slow. So I made an easy beginning. Also, he couldn't raise his voice so much, which was a great help, I must say![40]

Churchill considered that he was still too weak on 10 November to travel up to London from Chartwell to attend the House of Commons when European disarmament was discussed in the face of the ominous rise of the Nazi Party. However, he was able to attend the House on 23 November when he expressed his fears for the future.[41]

Despite his illness, between October and December 1932, Churchill not only continued substantial work on *Marlborough*, with galley proofs arriving every few days and being corrected by return, but he also wrote six articles for the *Daily Mail*, one for *Collier's*, one for the *Sunday Dispatch*, revised the twelve articles drafted by Marsh for the *News of the World* on the World's greatest stories and three on unemployment for both *Collier's* and the *Sunday Chronicle*.[3]

Medical Aspects

Enteric fever is a systemic infection caused by Salmonella bacteria, including *Salmonella paratyphi A, B, and C and Salmonella typhi*.[42] Although the most common cause of enteric fever worldwide is *Salmonella typhi*, the same clinical syndrome can be caused particularly by *Salmonella paratyphi A*, with complications occurring in about the same percentage of patients. Historically, paratyphoid fever was considered less severe than typhoid fever, though current evidence suggests that infections caused by *Salmonella typhi* and *Salmonella paratyphi A* are clinically indistinguishable and equally severe.[43] Globally, paratyphoid A is more common than types B and C, but in Europe, paratyphoid B is most common. Paratyphoid C is rare and occurs principally in the Far East.

It is uncertain how Petschacher made the diagnosis of paratyphoid fever. He may have cultured *Salmonella paratyphi* from Churchill's blood, faeces or urine or have made the diagnosis following the use of a serum agglutination test. It is unlikely given his reputation and that of his patient that he based this solely on the clinical features.

After ingestion of *Salmonella paratyphi*, the bacteria invade the wall of the small bowel from where they spread to the blood. An asymptomatic period follows ingestion that typically lasts a week, with a range of three to sixty days. Larger bacterial inoculums tend to cause disease with a shortened incubation period. The onset of paratyphi bacteraemia is marked by fever, malaise, a dull frontal headache, anorexia, nausea and abdominal pain but with few physical signs, though an enlarged liver and spleen may be present. Maculopapular spots (Rose spots) seen on the abdomen and chest in typhoid fever are rare in *Salmonella paratyphi* infection. Fever often occurs in a stepwise fashion with five to seven days of daily increments in maximal temperature of 0·5–1° C, with the height of fever usually occurring in the afternoon. There follows a period of ten to fourteen days of sustained fever of 39–41 °C.

More serious complications, for example gastrointestinal bleeding and intestinal perforation, are seen rarely, but usually arise after the third week of the illness, as in Churchill's case. His symptoms indicate an intestinal haemorrhage that was not trivial. It is unclear how the diagnosis of this complication was made, but presumably he became anaemic and there may have been blood in the stool, but contemporaneous medical records are not now available.

The risk of death is between 10 and 15 per cent without treatment.[39] Modern treatment is with either ciprofloxacin, cefotaxime or azithromycin, but these antibiotics were, of course, not available in 1932. Although TAB vaccine (triple typhoid saline vaccine) with antityphoid, antiparatyphoid A and antiparatyphoid B fractions was available before 1920, there is no evidence that Churchill availed himself of the vaccine despite his knowledge of the disease acquired by residing in endemic areas and in his political appointment as Secretary of State for War (1919–21).

Although Churchill told his cousin Sunny, the Duke of Marlborough, that it was 'an English bug which I took abroad with me and no blame rests on the otherwise misguided continent of Europe',[22] this is unlikely to be true given the relatively short incubation period in most cases. More likely is the fact that Churchill spent 'whole days on the (battle) fields picnicing there'.[8] Precisely how Churchill became infected remains a matter of conjecture. Infection may have occurred as a result of food preparation by an individual who was infected or who was a carrier; transmission by an asymptomatic carrier who prepared food for one of the picnics is possible, though the drinking of water contaminated with faeces in Bavaria was thought the most likely at the time. There is no record of anyone close to Churchill having also been unwell with enteric fever. Poor sanitation and poor crowded populations are known risk factors, but Churchill was not exposed to these.

In conclusion, Churchill clearly suffered an episode of enteric fever in 1932, probably due to *Salmonella paratyphi*, complicated by intestinal haemorrhage. With rest, he made a full recovery.

Chapter 8

Chest Pain During Christmas 1941 at the White House

I had a dull pain over my heart[1]

On 7 December 1941, the Japanese attacked the US base at Pearl Harbor. Germany and Italy declared war on the United States on 11 December 1941 and, by this declaration, the United States was brought into the war in Europe.[2] Immediately following the Pearl Harbor attack, Churchill made plans to travel to Washington to meet President Roosevelt to review 'the whole war plan' during ARCADIA, the code name for the Conference.[2]

13–22 December 1941: A Voyage Amid World War[3]

The details of Churchill's journey to Washington are explained in considerable detail by Lavery.[4] Churchill left London by night train on the evening of 12 December[2] and reached Gourock, on the Clyde, on the morning of 13 December. He was then taken by boat to the *Duke of York*, sister ship of the *Prince of Wales* which had been sunk off Malaysia three days earlier.[2]

The party included Admiral Sir Dudley Pound (First Sea Lord), Air Marshal Sir Charles Portal (Chief of the Air Staff), Field Marshal Sir John Dill (Chief of the Imperial General Staff until December 1941), Lieutenant General Sir Gordon Macready (Assistant Chief of the Imperial General Staff), Brigadier Leslie Hollis (Senior Assistant Secretary, War Cabinet), Lieutenant Colonel Ian Jacob (Military Assistant Secretary, War Cabinet), Lord Beaverbrook (Minister of Supply and member of the War Cabinet), John Martin (Principal Private Secretary), Commander Thompson RN (Churchill's aide-de-camp) and Sir Charles Wilson (later Lord Moran; see p. 443).[5]

Wilson had been Churchill's personal physician since 24 May 1940, but this was the first voyage on which Wilson had accompanied Churchill.[3] Churchill later wrote: 'To his unfailing care I probably owe my life. Although I could not persuade him to take my advice when he was ill, nor could he always count on my explicit obedience to all his instructions, we became devoted friends. Moreover, we both survived.'[3]

The Atlantic crossing was so rough that passengers were confined below decks for much of the journey. Churchill self-medicated with Mothersill's Seasick Remedy (hyoscine, chlorobutanol, caffeine) twice on the first day.[2] The *Duke of York* dropped anchor off Hampton Roads just after 4 pm on 22 December.[4] Roosevelt originally intended that Churchill and his party should transfer to a destroyer then steam up the Potomac to Washington, but time was too short because of delays incurred during the sea voyage. The Americans had therefore laid on a special train.

However, Churchill was impatient to end his journey after nearly ten days at sea, and arrangements were then made to fly Churchill from Hampton Roads to Washington.[6] Churchill landed at Washington National Airport where the President was waiting in his car. 'I clasped his strong hand with comfort and pleasure,' wrote Churchill.[6] The party, which included Wilson,[7] soon reached the White House where they were 'welcomed by Mrs Roosevelt, who thought of everything that could make our stay agreeable'.[6]

Accommodation at the White House

Mrs Roosevelt showed Churchill to the Lincoln bedroom, which he turned down claiming that the bed did not suit him. He then looked over the others available. Alert as ever to opportunities, Churchill chose the Rose room (Plate 4) on the second floor across the hall from Harry Hopkins' (Roosevelt's chief diplomatic adviser) almost permanent room.[8] This room was also known as the Queens' room, as this was where Queen Elizabeth slept during her 1939 visit with King George VI.

22–3 December 1941

Dinner at the White House on 22 December was at 8.30 pm for seventeen people. At its end, the President proposed a champagne toast to 'The Common Cause'. After dinner, Churchill had a meeting with the President and conducted the 2-hour conversation with great skill, according to Beaverbrook.[1]

At nearly midnight, Wilson received a message in his room at the Mayflower Hotel that Churchill wanted to see him[1] and he set out for the White House in one of the President's cars. He waited in his patient's bedroom for an hour and a half before Churchill emerged from a meeting with President Roosevelt.[1] Churchill apologised for keeping Wilson waiting, though Wilson surmised that Churchill had forgotten that he had sent for him.[1] Wilson asked, 'Is there anything wrong?'[1] Churchill replied, 'The pulse is regular.'[1] As Lovell[9] later commented: 'Churchill's immediate reference to his pulse could mean only that Churchill's pulse already had significance for both of them.' Churchill asked if he could take a sleeping pill.[1] Wilson agreed that he could take 'two reds [secobarbital 200 mg,[10] a barbiturate hypnotic]'.

At dinner on 23 December, Percy Chubb (husband of a grandniece of the President), noted that while the President was 'in a buoyant mood', Churchill was 'subdued and looked tired'[7] as they discussed the Boer War. The President, a Boer sympathizer while at Harvard, 'kept needling' Churchill about being on the wrong side.[7]

Christmas Eve

'Simple festivities marked our Christmas,' wrote Churchill.[6] The traditional Christmas tree was set up in the White House garden having been moved from Lafayette Park out of wartime caution. So, he and the President went on to the White House's South Portico balcony for the traditional ceremony of lighting the tree.[8] After singing carols, both made brief speeches to crowds of some 20,000–30,000.[1,6] Churchill's began: 'I spend this anniversary and festival far from my own country, far from my family, yet I cannot truthfully say I feel far from home …'.[7] Wilson had been detained from attending the ceremony because Beaverbrook (also his patient) had a sore throat.[9]

After coming in from the balcony, Churchill told Wilson that he had suffered palpitations during the ceremony[1] and made Wilson take his pulse.[1] 'What is it, Charles?'[1] Wilson tried to be reassuring by saying: 'Oh, it's all right.'[1] 'But what is it? Churchill persisted.[1] On being told it was 105 per minute, Churchill responded: 'It has all been very moving.'[1]

Christmas Day

On Christmas morning Churchill invited Wilson to go with him to Ottawa in a few days, adding that he was not afraid of being ill but that he 'must keep fit for my job'.[1] Churchill then went with the President to the Foundry Methodist Church on 16th and P Streets. 'I found peace in the simple service and enjoyed singing the well-known hymns, and one, *O little town of Bethlehem*, I had never heard before. Certainly there was much to fortify the faith of all who believe in the moral governance of the universe.'[6]

After sharing in the Roosevelt family celebrations, including the turkey dinner, at which the President carved,[5] Churchill spent a good part of Christmas Day preparing his speech to Congress.

26 December 1941

On 26 December Wilson went to the White House to pay his daily visit on Churchill. Martin told him that the Prime Minister was still working on his speech to Congress, so he did not see him until later when he joined Churchill at the Capitol and heard the now-famous speech.

Churchill recalled that the President wished him good luck when he set out in the charge of the leaders of the Senate and House of Representatives from the White House to the Capitol. Churchill had never addressed a foreign parliament before, so it was with 'heart-stirrings' that he fulfilled the invitation to address the Congress of the United States. He felt a 'blood-right to speak to the representatives of the great Republic' as he claimed unbroken male descent on his mother's side through five generations from a lieutenant who served in George Washington's army.[6]

'Inside the scene was impressive and formidable, and the great semicircular hall, visible to me through a grille of microphones, was thronged [Plate 5].'[6] Churchill began:

> I feel greatly honoured that you should have invited me to enter the United States Senate Chamber and address the representatives of both branches of Congress.[7] The fact that my American forebears have for so many generations played their part in the life of the United States, and that here I am, an Englishman, welcomed in your midst, makes this experience one of the most moving and thrilling in my life, which

is already long and has not been entirely uneventful. I wish indeed that my mother, whose memory I cherish across the vale of years, could have been here to see. By the way, I cannot help reflecting that if my father had been American my mother British, instead of the other way round, I might have got here on my own.[7]

Churchill spoke for 35 minutes but was so impressive that one correspondent said it seemed like just 5![11]

Chest Pain

There is considerable doubt about the date on which Churchill experienced chest pain. According to Wilson, it occurred on the night of 26 December 1941,[1] whereas Churchill and Dr (later Sir) John Parkinson (see p. 444) date the incident in early January 1942. Wilson recorded that on 27 December, he decided not to call upon Churchill as he seemed preoccupied.[1] However, on returning to his hotel after a morning walk, he found an urgent message requesting he go at once to the White House.[1]

Wilson took a taxi, and when he arrived, Churchill told him that he had got up in the night to open a window as it was hot, but he had to use considerable force to open it and became short of breath.[1] 'I had a dull pain over my heart. It went down my left arm [this radiation was not mentioned at the consultation with Parkinson, see below]. It didn't last very long, but it has never happened before. What is it?'[1] Churchill indicated that he had thought of calling Wilson at the time but the pain had passed off. Wilson examined his patient but found nothing wrong.[1]

'I had no doubt … his symptoms were those of coronary insufficiency,' wrote Wilson later.[1] Naturally, after Wilson had listened to his chest twice, Churchill enquired: 'Well is my heart all right?' Wilson replied: 'There is nothing serious. You have been overdoing things.'[1] Churchill was adamant: 'Now Charles you're not going to tell me to rest. I can't. I won't. Nobody else can do this job. I must.' Churchill believed that he had strained one of his chest muscles when he tried to open the window. 'I used great force. I don't believe it was my heart at all.'[1] Wilson explained to Churchill: 'Your circulation was a bit sluggish. It is nothing serious. You needn't rest in the sense of lying up, but you mustn't do more than you can help in the way of exertion for a little while.'[1]

Then there was a knock at the door, and Harry Hopkins came in. Wilson slipped away and began to think things out more deliberately. 'I did not like it, but I determined to tell no one. When we get back to England, I shall take him to Parkinson, who will hold his tongue.'[1]

Churchill himself wrote that this episode occurred on 3 January 1942: 'The night before I started (for Florida) the air conditioning of my room in the White House failed temporarily, the heat became oppressive, and in trying to open the window, I strained my heart slightly, causing unpleasant sensations which continued for some days. Sir Charles Wilson, my medical adviser, however decided that the journey south should not be put off.'[12] Parkinson recorded that the chest pain occurred on 7 January 1942. Although Parkinson obtained this information from Wilson on 6 February 1942,[13] it cannot be correct because of the date of the visit to Florida (see below). In all probability, Churchill's chronology is correct.

Irrespective of the date this pain occurred, Churchill carried on with his punishing schedule. This included seeing the President for several hours every day, lunching with him and often with Harry Hopkins as a third. 'We talked of nothing but business, and reached a great measure of agreement on many points, both large and small.'[6]

28–31 December 1941: Ottawa

Churchill left Washington in Roosevelt's private railroad car for Ottawa on 28 December at 2.15 pm.[14] Churchill asked Wilson to accompany him to the station and as they drove out of the grounds Churchill opened the window of the car. He was short of breath.[1] 'There seems no air in this car.'[1] Then Churchill put his hand on Wilson's knee saying: 'It is a great comfort to have you with me,' the second time he had used these words in four days.[1]

Churchill slept well on the train and reached Ottawa on the morning of 29 December and drove through streets banked with snow. After a hot bath, he 'seemed his usual self', Wilson recorded. Churchill then lunched with the Canadian War Cabinet and in the evening attended a reception and dinner at Government House. In spare moments Churchill continued to work on the speech he was to give to the Canadian Parliament. So far, Wilson had observed nothing untoward in his patient, though when they were alone, Churchill repeatedly asked Wilson to take his pulse. 'Once, when I found him lifting something heavy, I did expostulate,' wrote Wilson.[1] At this, Churchill remarked: 'Now, Charles, you are making me heart-minded. I shall soon think of nothing else. I couldn't do my work if I kept thinking of my heart.'[1]

The speech to the Canadian Parliament was delivered on 30 December, and on the morning of 31 December, Churchill gave a press conference at Government House before returning to Washington for further talks with Roosevelt. His train left Ottawa at 3 pm on 31 December reaching Washington at noon on 1 January 1942.[7]

1–4 January 1942: Washington

Later on New Year's Day, Roosevelt and Churchill sat together in George Washington's pew at Christ Church in Alexandria to commemorate the World Day of Prayer for Peace. They sang 'The Battle Hymn of the Republic'. Later they visited George Washington's tomb at Mount Vernon. That evening at the White House, Roosevelt, Churchill and the Soviet and Chinese envoys signed *A Declaration by the United Nations*, affirming that the Allies were fighting because they were convinced that 'complete victory over their enemies is essential to defend life, liberty, independence, and religious freedom'.[11]

Churchill claimed his 'American friends thought [he] was looking tired and ought to have a rest'[12] and Edward Stettinius, Special Assistant to the President, placed his small villa 'in a seaside solitude near Palm Beach at my disposal and on 4 January [Gilbert[14] and Martin[15] both state it was on 5 January] I flew down there.'[12] Martin[15] has suggested that the main reason for the visit to Pompano was to provide a break for the President, exhausted by Churchill's late nights and flow of talk!

5–11 January 1942: Pompano, Florida

On 5 January Churchill flew in General Marshall's plane from Washington to West Palm Beach Airport to stay in the bungalow at Pompano, Florida.[15] During the flight, he and General Marshall had some 'very good talks'. They were accompanied by Wilson, Martin and Commander Thompson.[15]

Five days we passed in the Stettinius villa, lying about in the shade or the sun, bathing in the pleasant waves, in spite of the appearance on one occasion of quite a large shark. They said it was only a 'ground shark'; but I was not wholly reassured. It is as bad to be eaten by a ground shark as by any other. So I stayed in the shallows from then on.[12]

Wilson noted that 'the blue ocean is so warm that Winston basks half-submerged in the water like a hippopotamus in a swamp'.[1]

Although this was a time of much-needed relaxation, the work was considerable.[14] Churchill dealt with papers flown down from Washington, sometimes twice daily, telephoned his private office and rewrote four papers on the future of the war in the light of the decisions made in Washington.[14] On 10 January Churchill had lunch with Consuelo Balsan, former Duchess of Marlborough, whom he had known for forty years and who remarked that he looked so well and that this was due to Wilson, who had given up everything to be his physician.[9]

After five days at Pompano, the party returned to Washington by train on 10 January.[15] Further meetings followed with Roosevelt and the combined Chiefs of Staff.

14–16 January 1942: Bermuda

Churchill flew to Bermuda from Norfolk, Virginia, on 14 January and for 20 minutes of the 4-hour flight took the controls of the Boeing 314 flying boat RMA *Berwick* (Plate 6).[14] The intent had been to return from Bermuda to England on the *Duke of York* but the worsening situation in Malaysia persuaded Churchill to fly to England. However, the entire party could not be fitted in, and Churchill suggested to Wilson that he should return by sea. Wilson was appalled.[1] Medically he would be responsible if anything happened to Churchill in the air.[1] Furthermore, as Wilson had been subjected to criticism for attending to Churchill while President of the Royal College of Physicians, he would be in difficulties if he returned to England a week or more after Churchill, for he had argued that looking after Churchill's health was even more important than undertaking his duties as President.[1]

Wilson broke into a meeting of the Chiefs of Staff making plain that he could not agree.[1] Whatever arguments Wilson used were effective for he left with the Prime Minister and his immediate entourage (Beaverbrook, Pound, Portal, Hollis) in the flying boat, *Berwick*, captained by Captain Kelly Rogers.[15, 16] The 18-hour flight was uneventful medically and shortly before

10 am on 17 January the aircraft set down at Plymouth.[16] A special train took the party to Paddington.[15]

17 January–6 March 1942: London

Oliver Harvey, Private Secretary to Anthony Eden, Foreign Secretary, found Churchill in the 'highest spirits and most truculent mood' when he got back.[17] On 9 February Eden informed Harvey in the greatest secrecy that Churchill was considering going to India the following week to meet Chiang Kai-shek and consult with Indian leaders about forming an assembly to work out a constitution for after the war.[17] Eden explained that Churchill would stop in Cairo on the return journey and 'clear up the mess there'.[17] Harvey advised Eden that while there were others (including Eden) who could take on some of these roles, only Churchill could do them all.[17]

The problem, Eden explained to Harvey, was that the doctors had told Churchill that 'his heart is not too good and he needs rest'.[17] Eden asked Churchill what he felt himself and he said he would go if the Cabinet wanted him to go but confessed that he did feel his heart a bit.[17] He had tried to dance a little the other night but found that he 'very quickly lost his breath'.[17]

10 February 1942 and 7 March 1942: Assessments by Dr John Parkinson

No doubt based on what Churchill himself or Moran had said, the understanding of Eden and other senior officials in the Foreign Office in February/early March 1942 was that Churchill was suffering from clinically significant heart disease. So, what was the expert cardiological view?

Parkinson (see p. 444), Physician to the Cardiac Department at the London Hospital, was first consulted by Wilson about Churchill on 6 February.[13] Parkinson's medical notes state that Wilson explained that on about 7 January 1942, some four weeks previously, while Churchill was staying at the White House, he had found his bedroom too hot in the night, got up and lifted the window.[13] He then had pain across his chest and thought he had strained a muscle.[13]

It is clinically significant that Moran did not mention that the pain radiated down Churchill's left arm. This feeling of 'strain' was present the next day, and Churchill noticed that he was somewhat short of breath, but he was well and about.[13] After a day or two (this implies that Churchill was correct about the timing of the chest pain), Churchill flew to Florida and enjoyed some surf bathing, though he noticed some shortness of breath, perhaps no more than was natural.[13]

Before the Atlantic flight home, he felt slight palpitation, and his pulse was 110/min before embarking and the same after one hour in the air at a height of 9,000 ft.[13] It was decided to proceed, and Churchill's pulse fell to a normal rate. Wilson considered the fast heart rate was 'psychological'.[13]

Wilson showed Parkinson two ECGs taken on 7 January 1941 and 6 February 1942 (Plate 7), which Parkinson interpreted as demonstrating a normal heart rate and rhythm with left axis deviation. The axis of the ECG is the major direction of the overall electrical activity of the heart. If leftward it is referred to as left axis deviation. Parkinson considered that the two ECGs were similar except that lead II was not quite so high in the latest record, that of 6 February 1942.[13]

On 9 February Wilson again called on Parkinson and told him that on the evening of 6 February Churchill indulged in a jig after dinner and experienced some discomfort below the left breast and some shortness of breath.[13,18] The next day Churchill complained of some tenderness along the ribs in that region. Wilson told Parkinson that Churchill took no exercise, but could walk quickly and for distances, for example, on inspecting factories. 'But stress was being felt; he was more restless. His one real desire was to see the war through.'[13]

Parkinson examined Churchill on 10 February; Wilson was in attendance.[13] Churchill told Parkinson that some twenty years previously he recalled being told that his heart was 'a little strained'.[13] He knew that he had dropped beats ('intermissions') in his pulse. Parkinson recorded that he had seen an extrasystole (extra beat) on one ECG, but told Churchill it was better not to feel his own pulse.[13] Parkinson found Churchill's pulse was 80/min, his blood pressure was 160/85 mmHg, the heart sounds were normal and there were no murmurs. His abdomen was normal on examination.[13]

A further ECG undertaken by Parkinson that evening again showed left axis deviation and there was inversion of the T-wave in lead III.[13] T waves are a part of a normal ECG and represent the electrical recovery (or repolarization) of the ventricles, the lower chambers of the heart, after a contraction, or heartbeat. The T wave is normally upright in leads I and II, and variable in lead III.

On radioscopy (X-ray screening of the heart), the diaphragm (the muscle separating the chest and abdomen) was high but, allowing for this, the heart and aorta were of normal shape and size. Churchill began to talk about coronary thrombosis, but Parkinson begged him not to use the term as it was inapplicable.

He had nothing of the kind. There might have been a temporary embarrassment in the circulation of the heart at Washington a month ago, though there was nothing material to prove this. Besides his blood pressure was normal and his heart was of normal size. Still, he ought to avoid extreme tests on long journeys for the next 2 to 3 months and even long walks on quays and inspections.[13]

On 13 February Parkinson wrote a formal report to Wilson which read:

Here is the electrocardiogram of your patient, taken on the 10th, at our consultation here. Apart from left axis deviation with T3 inversion [inversion of the T-wave in lead III], not unusual with his build, it may be considered normal, and it is almost identical with the earlier one of 7 January 1941. The Clinical Research Association ECG [6 February 1942] showing extrasystoles seemed to suggest some flattening of T in lead II, but this is not suggested by my record. Provided the next ECG proposed for about 10 days hence, is unaltered, I would be of the opinion there is no graphic evidence that anything material occurred a month ago. Clinically I believe there was a temporary embarrassment of the coronary circulation which produced the pain under stress, and the subsequent slight dyspnoea [breathlessness]. No doubt he will keep you informed if any further symptoms do appear, but we will hope there are none.[13]

On 6 March, Churchill told Eden that he was contemplating meeting with Stalin either in Tehran or in Russia. Harvey considered: 'This from a man afflicted with heart who may collapse at any minute. What courage and what gallantry, but is this the way to do things?'[17]

Parkinson reviewed Churchill on 7 March at Chequers, the Prime Minister's country residence.[13] Churchill was said to be worried by the bad war news and adverse criticism, and a few days before he had a brief lapse of memory, repeating the same anecdote twice. After Parkinson had undertaken a clinical examination and taken an ECG in Churchill's bedroom, Churchill asked him if the 'hump in the record was all right'.[13] Parkinson explained that he did not think there was an abnormality, but wished to make sure. More significant were Churchill's symptoms in Washington, the pain followed by some shortness of breath. These were a hint and constituted a reason for care in the next few weeks, especially until there was warmer weather.[13]

Churchill mentioned that last night in bed he had slight tenderness above the left breast, noticed on deep breathing.[13] This Parkinson said was purely muscular and had nothing to do with the heart, and Churchill agreed. Similarly, Churchill spoke of his extrasystoles, 'sometimes 1 in 4', but accepted Parkinson's view of their insignificance.[13]

When Churchill's projected trip by air to Egypt was discussed, Parkinson indicated that he would much prefer that it should be postponed some weeks.[13] Meanwhile, Churchill declared that holiday or rest was out of the question. He explained that he could not relax and would find most relief from a train tour of inspection of troops. Churchill agreed not to hurry upstairs or walk any long distance. Parkinson said there was no danger in this, but that if he provoked shortness of breath, it would be detrimental. Parkinson told Churchill that he did not believe in medical orders, but opinion and advice. The normal blood pressure and normal-sized heart were sufficient to prove that his cardiac risks were minimal.[13]

As Churchill had mentioned it, Parkinson affirmed that there had been no suggestion of coronary thrombosis in Washington.[13] The symptoms had suggested a temporary embarrassment in the circulation in the heart – 'a sluggishness' according to Wilson.[13] Parkinson explained that Wilson and he desired to take the simple precaution of avoiding an exhausting experience in the several weeks following that event. At this consultation, Parkinson recorded that Churchill was cheerful and friendly and displayed no undue interest or concern about his condition.[13]

Parkinson wrote to Wilson twice on 10 March 1942:

Here is a further electrocardiogram of the Prime Minister taken at Chequers on Saturday, 7 March 1942. It is similar in every respect to that we took on February 10, in particular the T wave in Lead II is of the same size, shape, and direction. The inference is that there is no evidence of any change taking place in the heart muscle.

Further, the record compares favourably with the early electrocardiogram of 6 February 1942, and even with that taken more than a year ago, on 7 January 1941. Though the graphic evidence shows that no material change occurred in the heart at Washington or since, I believe that there was a transient embarrassment of the coronary circulation which evoked the pain under stress, and the subsequent slight dyspnoea. The simple precautions advised that our consultation should ensure that things go well.[13]

In a second letter Parkinson wrote:

I think the enclosed expresses my reading of the electrocardiograms, and also our joint opinion on the Washington episode. You will judge whether it should be shown to your patient or not. I hope he will not begin to take too much interest in his health. If, later, you care to talk it over with me, I am always at your service.[13]

On 21 January 1960, Parkinson visited Wilson (Lord Moran from 1943) at 25 Bryanston Square, London to discuss the precis of the notes he had sent Moran a few days earlier. Moran then told Parkinson for the first time that the pain Churchill had experienced in Washington had 'extended down the left arm'. The omission of such a vital clinical clue for some twenty years is difficult to explain given that Moran had consulted Parkinson about Churchill on many occasions.

Parkinson concluded:

In view of the absence of any subsequent electrocardiographic changes and of the rapid clinical recovery I had always thought that this attack might have been purely muscular (thoracic). This becomes most unlikely when we know that the pain affected the left arm during the attack. It is therefore my present view that the P.M. on that occasion had an isolated attack of angina pectoris, or as it was described in my letter of February 13, 1942 a 'temporary embarrassment of the coronary circulation'.[13]

Medical Aspects

Wilson recorded that Churchill told him that he had developed transient dull pain over (his) heart (the precise location was not stated by Wilson[1]) which went down his left arm, whereas Parkinson subsequently obtained the history from Churchill (and Wilson) four weeks later that he had developed a pain across his chest which persisted until the next day and was associated with some shortness of breath.

Did Wilson make the correct diagnosis? Though he did not document the precise location of the chest pain in his published record,[1] the most obvious causes to be considered in a 67-year-old man were myocardial infarction (coronary thrombosis), angina and musculoskeletal pain, the diagnosis Churchill himself favoured. Critical to the clinical diagnosis is whether Churchill told Wilson that the pain radiated down his left arm. If it did, this would support a cardiac cause. It is clear from Parkinson's clinical notes that this radiation was not mentioned to him by Wilson (or Churchill) in 1942. We find this inconceivable if it did occur, given its clinical significance.

Wilson did not doubt that Churchill's symptoms were due to a 'heart attack', a phrase he used twice.[1] Angina describes a pain in the centre of the chest, which is induced by exercise and relieved by rest and which may radiate to the jaw and arms. Although angina cannot be completely ruled out, the fact that Churchill never suffered a further attack is strongly against this diagnosis. Oesophageal spasm (spasm of the gullet) and gall bladder disease can both give rise to central chest pain and are also therefore possible explanations, given Churchill's long history of dyspepsia. Churchill's indigestion, which was often severe, usually came on during the night or when painting ('I always paint standing up, otherwise the indigestion would be very severe').[19] Regardless of where in the chest the pain was experienced, and whether or not it went down the left arm, it came on as considerable effort was being expended and was associated with breathlessness. The latter, however, a later recurring feature, may only be the effect of exertion on the 'hippopotamus' that was Churchill.

Three weeks after Churchill's return to the UK, Wilson arranged for Parkinson to assess Churchill. After a careful clinical, electrocardiographic and radiological assessment, Parkinson's opinion was that Churchill had not suffered a coronary thrombosis. Parkinson observed left axis deviation with T-wave inversion in lead III on Churchill's ECG. Parkinson concluded that these changes were 'not unusual with his build', and considered that the series of ECGs performed on Churchill could be considered normal. Given that Parkinson had established with Evan Bedford the criteria for the diagnosis of coronary thrombosis,[21,22] his opinion must be considered definitive. It is surprising that Wilson's published record[1] does not mention Parkinson's opinion, particularly given that Wilson stated he would take Churchill to see Parkinson on his return from Washington.

So, what may be said of Wilson's management? Obtaining an ECG in the White House would certainly have been difficult without drawing unwanted attention to Churchill's health. Should he have sought the expert advice of a US-based cardiologist via the British Embassy or even had Parkinson flown out to Washington? Wilson was in a quandary. If he did nothing and Churchill had another and more severe attack, it might be said that he had killed Churchill through not insisting on rest.[1] At least six weeks' bed rest was the standard treatment for myocardial infarction at the time.[1] 'Right or wrong, it seemed plain that I must sit tight on what had happened, whatever the consequences.'[1] To do otherwise would have meant 'publishing to the world' that Churchill was 'an invalid with a crippled heart and a doubtful future'.[1] The effect 'could only be disastrous'.[1] Wilson's explanation to Churchill that his 'circulation was a bit sluggish. It is nothing serious' could be interpreted as being a less than full account of the episode, but Wilson was certain that, if told what he did not doubt was the correct diagnosis, Churchill's 'work would suffer'.[1]

Wilson considered that he had to balance political considerations, his own professional reputation and above all what was best for his patient who considered rightly that no one else but himself could fulfil his role as Prime Minister, duties which he must continue to undertake. Was he correct in doing so? Baron has written: 'Moran took it on his own head to lie to Churchill about his heart attack in Washington because this diagnosis would have crippled Churchill and wrecked American esteem of Britain as an ally. Did this reason of state justify a physician concealing the truth from his patient and the public?'[20] Subsequently, Baron wrote: 'The many doctors who have written about the major illnesses of world leaders concurred that the public is entitled to full disclosure of candidates' medical data. I agree. However, it is only fair to point out that ... when I sought the opinions of senior London physicians in private practice of the great and the good they too held that doctors had a duty of confidentiality to their distinguished patients and no duty to the political health of their country.'[21]

At a time of enormous importance in Anglo-American relationships and at a critical stage of the war, during which, in all respects, Churchill wished to be seen and act as a strong and effective leader, Wilson's decision to play the clinical importance down clearly carried some risk. It is obvious that Wilson agonised over this. 'I felt that the effect of announcing that the PM had had a heart attack could only be disastrous.'[1] But as well as recognising differences in clinical practice between the 1940s and the present era, we should remember that by this time, Churchill and Wilson had formed a trusting relationship with a high level of understanding.[3]

It seems likely that Churchill did indeed appreciate that Wilson had concluded that his symptoms were of cardiac origin. If Wilson's chronology is correct, Churchill's remark to Wilson a few days later in Ottawa indicates Churchill's recognition that focusing too much on his heart would detract from his ability to get on with his work. In the context of the unusually close relationship between the two men, Wilson's approach may be interpreted as both shrewd and appropriate.

Chapter 9

Pneumonia in February 1943 in London

Am I as ill as that? You certainly are.[1]

Churchill returned from Algiers to Britain on Sunday, 7 February 1943, a flight of 8½ hours; he reached London at 1 o'clock. Later that day Churchill presided over his first War Cabinet in four weeks.[2] Following his return, Churchill maintained his customary work output and gave a 2-hour speech[3] in the House of Commons on 11 February 1943 on the war situation, specifically the Conference at Casablanca.[4] 'I thought I had a good tale to tell,' Churchill wrote later.[3]

However, when Churchill addressed the Commons, he was 'far from well, with a heavy cold and a sore throat,' noted Commander Thompson RN, his aide-de-camp.[5] Harold Nicolson MP reported that Churchill had 'a slight cold, looks less well than he did on arrival, but is in tearing spirits'.[6] Churchill's daughter, Mary, also recorded that: 'He was already suffering from a cold and a sore throat.'[7] Churchill admitted later that 'I was more tired by my journeying than I had realised at the time, and I must have caught a chill. A few days later a cold and sore throat obliged me to lie up.'[3]

12 February 1943

Mary Churchill recorded on 12 February 1943 that her father had 'developed a temperature'.[7] John Martin, Principal Private Secretary, wrote: 'PM in bed with a cold.'[8] General Sir Alan Brooke, Chief of the Imperial General Staff, recorded: 'Went round to the Annexe [No. 10 Annexe above the Cabinet War Rooms] at 3 pm ... PM in bed with fever ... I had intended to discuss other questions of command, but did not like to worry him when he had this fever'.[9]

13–16 February 1943

'PM still in bed,' Martin recorded on both 13 and 14 February.[8] Brooke noted that Churchill was present at the Cabinet meeting at 6 pm on 15 February and had a 'very bad sore throat and cold'.[9]

While dining alone with his wife on 16 February, Churchill felt very unwell and found his temperature had soared.[7] Sir Charles Wilson (from 8 March Lord Moran; see p. 443), Churchill's personal physician, was summoned and recorded that: 'during the evening of February 16 his temperature shot up, and, after examining his chest, I had to tell him that he had a patch at the base of the left lung'. 'What do you mean by a patch? Have I got pneumonia? asked Churchill.'[10]

Churchill himself recorded that on the evening of 16 February: 'my temperature suddenly rose, and Lord Moran, who had been watching me, took a decided view and told me that I had inflammation of the base of a lung. His diagnosis led him to prescribe the drug called M and B [May and Baker, manufacturers of sulfonamides].'[3] In fact, we know from the nursing notes that M&B 760 (sulfathiazole) was prescribed (see below).

Dr (later Sir) Geoffrey Marshall (see p. 442), Senior Physician, Guy's Hospital, London and Physician-in-Charge, Brompton Hospital, London, was invited by Wilson to give a second opinion. On being asked on his return how he had got on, Marshall described his entry into the Prime Minister's bedroom filled with important men and tobacco smoke.[1] Winston was chesty and feverish, and Marshall had difficulty in clearing the room before he diagnosed pneumonia. 'You will have to relinquish the conduct of affairs for a fortnight,' Marshall pronounced. 'How dare you,' retorted Churchill, 'the war is at a critical stage.' Marshall replied: 'Very well, but you know what we call this illness, we call it old man's friend because you fade away so gradually that you arrive in the next world before you know you have left this one!' 'Am I as ill as that?' asked Churchill. 'You certainly are.' Churchill acquiesced: 'Very well, then I will do as you say.'[1]

This anecdote is confirmed by Churchill himself. 'They then said I had pneumonia, to which I replied, "Well, surely you can deal with that. Don't you believe in your new drug?"' Dr Marshall said he called pneumonia "the old man's friend".'[3] Churchill asked Marshall why this was the case. 'Because it takes them off so quietly.'[3] Wilson recorded: 'He [Marshall] was soon established high in the P.M.'s favour.'[10] Churchill recalled that on this day 'elaborate photographs' (X-rays) were taken and confirmed the diagnosis.[3]

Churchill also recalled that:

Up to this point all my work had come to me hour by hour at the Annexe, and I had maintained my usual output though feeling far from well. But now I became aware of a marked reduction in the number of papers which reached me. When I protested the doctors, supported by my wife, argued that I ought to quit my work entirely. I would not agree to this. What should I have done all day?[3]

Churchill wrote that he reached an agreement with Marshall that he was only to have the most important and interesting papers sent to him and to read a novel.[3] 'On this basis I passed the next week in fever and discomfort, and I sometimes felt very ill.'[3] When Churchill finished *Moll Flanders* he gave it to Marshall 'to cheer him up'.[11]

17–19 February 1943

Wilson was so concerned about Churchill that he moved into the Annexe for the duration of Churchill's illness.[12] Although Churchill was too ill for his regular lunch with King George VI on 17 February,[2] no medical bulletin was issued until 18 February. This stated that the Prime Minister had been suffering from a feverish cold and was confined to bed.[13]

On the evening of 18 February Wilson telephoned Dr (later Sir) John Parkinson (see p. 444), Churchill's cardiologist, for advice and at 8 pm on the same evening Wilson visited Parkinson at his consulting room at 1 Devonshire Place, London.[14] Parkinson had last reviewed Churchill in March 1942 (see p. 65). Wilson told Parkinson that Churchill had suffered a sneezing bout on 5 February 1943 and that a week previously he had developed a sore throat and a palpable cervical gland on the left side.[14] His temperature had increased and was explained by an infection of the upper air passages.[14] Various blood tests were negative.[14] This morning he had taken Churchill's pulse and found it to be 84 per minute but his hands were noticeably cold, as were his feet and nose.[14] Wilson sought Parkinson's advice as to the clinical implications of these observations.

Parkinson said that it did not imply that Churchill had a 'sluggish circulation', a phrase used in February 1942 after Churchill had suffered chest pain in Washington.[14] Parkinson advised that Churchill should be told it was merely the local circulation in the periphery which was disturbed by the infection.[14] Parkinson recommended that if there was no improvement a portable X-ray should be arranged which might show some local patch of pulmonary consolidation (in the lung).[14] Meanwhile, Churchill should at least use a commode at the bedside and not walk to the adjoining lavatory.[14] A nurse is really necessary.[14] Wilson stated that the 'PM is alive to his symptoms, and rather introspective and difficult regarding his health at present.'[14]

'Do hope that you are feeling better,' Harry Hopkins, President Roosevelt's chief diplomatic adviser, telegraphed on 19 February.[15] Churchill replied the same day: 'Thank you so much. I expect a week more of this sort of thing but the situation is pronounced under control. Must keep Eden [Foreign Secretary] back for at least a week as I had planned to do his work in his absence.'[15] Cadogan, Under-Secretary of State, Foreign Office, wrote in his diary: 'P.M. still has a temperature of 101 [°F; 38.3°C] so our trip, fixed for Monday, is put off.'[16] Harvey, Private Secretary to Eden, also made the same observation.[17]

Churchill was assessed again by Wilson and Marshall, and a medical bulletin was signed by them. It stated: 'The Prime Minister is confined to bed with an acute catarrh of the upper respiratory passages.'[13]

On 19 February Wilson hired two staff nurses from the private wing at St Mary's Hospital to attend Churchill: Doris Miles and Dorothy Pugh. Nurse Pugh has recorded that she received a telephone call from her Matron at 7.30 pm. 'Am to go out on a case tomorrow. Doris M as the night nurse. All very exciting.'[18] Nurse Pugh (Plate 8) had trained at St Mary's Hospital and now worked as a nurse on the Private Wing at St Mary's. She was not allowed to work on the general wards because she had married in 1942. Her husband, Roger, had qualified as a doctor at St Mary's in 1940 and was serving in the RAF as a Squadron Leader in the Mediterranean. Nurse Pugh's unpublished diary to which we have had full access provides considerable clinical information.

Nurse Miles arrived at the No. 10 Annexe that evening and was met by Wilson who said: 'Glad to see you nurse. I must warn you that the Prime Minister does not wear pyjamas.'[12] Nurse Miles wrote later that Churchill wore a silk vest, velvet jacket and velvet slippers embroidered with PM on the front.[12]

Nurse Miles (née Clayton Greene; Plate 10) had also trained at St Mary's Hospital, where her father had been Senior Surgeon and Dean.[19] She was described as a 'cultivated and charming nurse' and had won the Gold Medal for Excellence in Nursing. In 1942 she married Roger Miles who was also a St Mary's graduate (1940).[19] Interestingly, it was after Wilson saw Miles give a riveting performance (in Greek) as Clytemnestra in the school play at Bradfield College that he offered him a place to study medicine at St Mary's; such offers were usually confined to rugby players![19] Jill Rose, Doris Miles' daughter, has now published her mother's letters to her father, though generously we were granted access to these before publication.[20]

The temperature chart (Plate 9) was commenced by Nurse Miles at 9 pm when Churchill's temperature was 102.8°F (39.3°C), his pulse rate was increased to 112/min, and his respiratory rate was increased to 30/min. Nurse Miles observed that Churchill was drowsy, had a slight cough and complained of a headache. She gave him a tepid sponge to try and reduce his temperature. Churchill took great interest in this nursing technique and fortunately for the reputation of Nurse Miles his temperature fell to 100.8°F (38.2°C) at 4.30 am.[12] She also administered sulfathiazole 2.0 g, a sulfonamide antibiotic, at 8.50 pm and 12.50 am.[21]

20 February 1943

Nurse Pugh also met Wilson on arrival the following morning who introduced her to the Prime Minister and Mrs Churchill. 'Both of them very nice indeed.'[18] Later that day she met Lord Beaverbrook, a great friend of Churchill, a newspaper publisher and former Cabinet minister.

Elizabeth Layton, Churchill's personal secretary, remembered Churchill's illness well:

> For some days we wondered whether or not he would live. We were all utterly miserable; he was in his room at the Annexe, and most of the time we hung forlornly about the flat feeling quite lost. On the rare occasions when he dictated, and it could only be on a matter of major importance, his voice was so weak and his manner so gentle that we longed for the old stamp and bark, the quiet word of scorn, the snort of impatience and the final twinkle of forgiveness. The flat was stiff with specialists, and two hospital nurses took up regular abode in the study.[22]

John (later Sir John) Peck, Churchill's Private Secretary, recalled being summoned to his bedroom on 20 February: 'The Prime Minister was sitting up in bed, looking sulky.'[23] Wilson was 'trying to look at ease and master of the situation … A row of some magnitude was evidently in progress.'[23] Wilson had told Churchill that he would have to issue a bulletin, and Churchill had instantly demanded to see it.[23] Wilson had not yet drafted the bulletin, but when he did so Churchill said it was 'alarmist', which would cause confusion and despondency and was, in any case, untrue.[23] Churchill, therefore, dictated his own bulletin. 'On seeing it in type he [Churchill] was hugely pleased with his first effort in a new genre', but Wilson said it was inaccurate and misleading and he could not possibly sign it.[23]

Peck was given the task of rewriting the bulletin.[23] Peck took the view that it was for the doctor to say what was the matter with his patient and for Churchill to pronounce on the political implications.[23] So Peck tried reversing the phrases in Wilson's bulletin, in the hope that the substance would remain the same but that the nuance could meet the Prime Minister's objection.[23] Peck later recalled: 'It worked and after some minor negotiations on drafting and medical niceties'[23] the medical bulletin was issued. The medical bulletin was signed by Charles Wilson MD and Geoffrey Marshall MD and read: 'The Prime Minister has had a comfortable day. There is a small area of inflammation in one lung [the right], but the fever is lower, and his general condition is not unsatisfactory.'[21]

Nurse Miles wrote to her husband: 'The Patient is all he is cracked up to be … We have a congestion of the right base and a haemolytic strep infection – not so good at all, and of course obstinate as a mule. Will sleep with one pillow, and keeps popping out of bed to go to the bathroom, watch me put a stop to that!'[12]

21 February 1943

Nurse Miles returned to St Mary's Hospital this morning to obtain a bedpan, bottle, a long macintosh for the tepid sponges Churchill required and a sputum pot.[12] Churchill thought the 'bed bottle' was an improvement and a 'great comfort'.[12]

Nurse Pugh recorded in her diary on 21 February: 'P.M. had a better night … Saw Sir Charles [Wilson] … A. Eden [Anthony Eden, Foreign Secretary] came just before lunch. Talked to Dr Marshall re visitors. General Ismay [Secretary of the Imperial Defence Chiefs of Staff Committee and

Deputy Secretary of the War Cabinet] arrived ... Mr Churchill [probably Churchill's brother, John ('Jack')] came to see WSC.'[18]

Brigadier (later Professor Sir) Lionel Whitby (see p. 453), an expert on sulfonamides, came up from Bristol to assess Churchill.[12] 'Consultation at 6 pm with Sir Charles [Wilson], Dr M[arshall], Lionel Whitby and Dr Bratton [probably Dr Allen Bratton MC DSO, Senior Assistant Pathologist at Archway Hospital, London]. All very interesting. Met Mrs Sands [Diana Sandys, Churchill's daughter] and Miss Mary [Mary Churchill] ... Am going to live in as it is a rush to get here in the morning.'[18]

The nurses took over Churchill's study as their quarters. Following the clinical assessment of Churchill at 6 pm,[18] sputum cultures and a blood count were taken. A medical bulletin was signed by Charles Wilson MD, Geoffrey Marshall MD and Lionel Whitby MD. It stated: 'The condition of the Prime Minister has improved. There has been no extension of inflammation in the lung.'[24]

Nurse Miles later recalled how during Churchill's treatment with sulfonamides he asked how the drug worked.[2] This same question was also asked of Wilson.[12]

Mary Soames wrote that her Mother was 'not seriously worried about Papa – but he is pretty ill. I was shocked when I saw him. He looked so old and tired – lying back in bed.'[7] Churchill's temperature at 9 pm was 101.6°F (38.7°C), and after a tepid sponge, this fell to 99.6°F (37.6°C) at 1 am. Churchill told Nurse Miles that she deserved a bar for her gold medal for bringing his temperature down.

Churchill was given sulfathiazole 1.5 g at 9 pm and secobarbital 100 mg, a barbiturate hypnotic, at 9.50 pm. Churchill slept from 10.15 pm until 5 am, waking once at 1 am for some cold consommé. Nurse Miles recorded that she had received a further bar to her gold medal for finding the consommé without having to wake anyone up! Churchill slept again from 5.30 am to 7.30 am. Nurse Miles wrote to her husband: 'The trouble is that feeling a bit better he thinks he is cured, and will probably walk down the corridor to have a bath with only a towel round him in the morning.'

22 February 1943

On 22 February 1943, Nurse Pugh wrote in her diary: 'Fairly busy day. PM kept his finger on the bell pretty well all day. Better day on the whole – temp even all day. Now up slightly tonight. [6 pm] 101°F [38.3°C]. Much consternation in the camp. Met Mr D. Sands [Duncan Sandys MP] ... PM told me that Tunisia will be O.K. now.'[18]

Nurse Pugh wrote in her diary that Churchill had been X-rayed and that sulfathiazole 1.5 g had been given at 9 am and 3 pm.[21] Thompson recorded that Churchill was protesting that 'his temperature was only 100 degrees and that he really felt very much better, but Brooke, who had not seen him for a week, thought he still looked very ill. It was not until the beginning of March that the Prime Minister was his old vigorous self again.'[25] Harvey recorded that 'P.M.'s health still stationary. He is taking no papers.'[17] Churchill had to cancel the following day's lunch with King George VI. 'PM's health is still stationary.'[25]

Churchill was in bed with a temperature of 102°F (38.9°C) when the King's three-page handwritten letter reached him. The King wrote: 'I am very sorry to hear that you are ill and I hope that you will soon be well again. But do please take this opportunity for a rest. And I trust you will not forget that you have earned one after your last tour, and you must get back your strength for the strenuous coming months.'[3]

Churchill dictated his reply at once, and at length, the first part a strong defence of Anglo-American policy in North Africa. Churchill replied:

> Sir, it is very good of Your Majesty to write with your own hand to me. I do not feel seriously disturbed by the course of events in North Africa, either political or even military, although naturally there is much about both aspects which I would rather have different. I have been reading all the key telegrams with attention up till two days ago, when I must admit I have fallen a little behind.[3]

Churchill's final paragraph reiterated this. 'Although, I have been hampered by a high fever from reading all the telegrams, I think I have the picture truly in my mind, and I wish indeed that I could have given this account to Your Majesty verbally at luncheon. I send this instead.'[3]

Churchill's temperature and pulse at 10 pm were 100.2°F (37.9°C) and 92/min; at 6.30 am they were 100.4°F (38.0°C) and 92/min.[21] Nurse Miles dispensed secobarbital 100 mg at 10.15 pm, and Churchill slept from 10.30 to 3 am.[21] He received secobarbital 50 mg at 3.15 am and slept again until 6.30 am.[21] Churchill had the top of his head rubbed with methyl salicylate, a potent solution of aspirin (see below).[21]

Nurse Miles reported on Churchill's fluid balance to her husband: Champagne 10 oz (284 mL), brandy 2 oz (57 mL), whisky and soda 8 oz (227 mL) and orange juice 8 oz.[12] Clearly, Churchill was on the mend!

23 February 1943

On 23 February Nurse Pugh recorded: 'PM seems better. Mrs Sandys and Pamela [Pamela Digby, Churchill's daughter-in-law] came in ... this morning. PM had a fair day on the whole – a little restive at times. Usual consultation at 6 pm. Seemed much longer today. Bed bathed PM with Bevir [Anthony Bevir, Churchill's Private Secretary] and Mrs C as an audience – not a very pleasant job – still all was well. PM very sweet.'[18] Sulfathiazole 1.5 g was administered at 9 am at 3 pm. A combination of potassium and sodium citrate were administered during the day, in order to try and ensure Churchill's urine was alkaline (see below).

'I can see for myself,' Mrs Churchill wrote to her daughter Mary on 24 February 'that he is better. His face looks quite different. He has lost that weary look.'[7] Churchill was of the same view when he wrote to Hopkins, 'Have had a bad time and might easily have been worse. Am feeling definitely better now.'[15]

Nurse Miles recorded that methyl salicylate was again applied to Churchill's head to relieve head pains. 'This became something of a ritual every evening and he would sing an old music-hall song while I was doing it:

> Wash me in the water
> Which you washed your dirty daughter in
> And I will be whiter
> Than the whitewash on the wall.[2]

Sulfathiazole 1.5 g was given by Nurse Miles at 9 pm and 3.30 am, secobarbital 100 mg was administered at 10.30 pm and again at 4.15 am after Churchill had been awake from 3 am to 4 am.

24 February 1943

Nurse Pugh recorded on 24 February: 'Condition of PM improved. T[emperature] coming down very nicely. Saw B[rendan] Bracken [close friend of Churchill's and Minister of Information]. Usual consultation at 6pm. Not quite so long this time.'[18] She recorded that sulfathiazole 1.5g was given at 9am and at 3pm. Potassium citrate mixture was administered at 9.30am, 11.15am, 12.15pm, 2.15pm, 5.45pm, 6.30pm and 7.40pm in an attempt to keep the urine alkaline and to prevent sulfathiazole-induced crystal formation; despite this measure, the urine remained acid. Nurse Pugh also applied methyl salicylate to Churchill's head again.

Following this consultation, a medical bulletin was issued signed by Charles Wilson MD, Geoffrey Marshall MD and Lionel Whitby MD, the first to make mention of pneumonia. It stated: 'There is general improvement in the Prime Minister's condition. The pneumonia is clearing, but the temperature has not yet settled.'[26] In fact, Churchill was well enough to watch a film on the Battle of Alamein, *Desert Victory*, a copy of which he sent to President Roosevelt.[3]

25 February 1943

Eden called on Churchill on his way to the House of Commons on 25 February. 'He [Churchill] looked flushed and clearly had a fever.'[27] After referring to one or two matters of business, Eden added: 'By the way, about that telegram you thought of sending last night to Algiers.' 'Thought of sending? What do you mean? I sent it,' said Churchill. Eden replied: 'No, it hasn't gone yet. I wanted to talk to you about it first.' Churchill gripped the counterpane with both hands and growled: 'By what right do you interfere with my private correspondence?'[27] Eden retorted that the message was not private and that the Foreign Secretary sees all important messages.[27] 'As his temperature was clearly mounting by leaps and bounds I said, "All right, we'll talk about it later".'[27]

On leaving Churchill's bedroom, Eden adjured the Private Secretary to send for Wilson and Brendan Bracken MP and to ask them to persuade Churchill not to send any more telegrams until his temperature was normal again.[27] At length, after the House rose, Eden called in to see Churchill, who was reclining benignly in bed with the telegram on the counterpane.[27] 'He asked after my day in the House … before at last he glanced at the telegram and added: "Oh, by the way, you remember that message I intended to send? Perhaps we had better not send it".'[27]

Eden added in his diary: 'This was characteristic of Mr Churchill and of something very lovable in him. First the indignation sparked by fever, then reflection and a generous acceptance expressed without half-tones or hesitation; these were the successive stages which endeared him to those whom he berated.'[27]

Churchill's temperature was down to 97.2°F at 9 am on 25 February 1943 and his condition was 'good'.[18] A medical bulletin was issued by Charles Wilson MD, Geoffrey Marshall MD and Lionel Whitby MD. It stated: 'The Prime Minister's condition continues to improve.'[28]

Wilson had himself developed a 'slight temperature' and had been told off by Churchill,[18] because he had spent most of the day at the Royal College of Physicians in his presidential role.[12] Churchill told Marshall to examine Wilson's chest and send him off to bed. Nurse Miles wrote: 'So I have got three patients now [Churchill, Wilson and Mrs Churchill].'[12] Mrs Churchill had 'burnt her hand two nights ago and I dress that for her every night'.[12]

26 February 1943

Churchill was in 'very good form' on 26 February and Wilson was better too.[18] A further chest X-ray and blood count were performed on Churchill. The usual medical consultation took place at 6 pm.[18] Nurse Pugh noted that this would be the last of Brigadier Whitby's professional visits and that he was a 'very nice person'.[18] A further medical bulletin was issued later that day by Charles Wilson MD, Geoffrey Marshall MD and Lionel Whitby MD. It stated: 'There has been a further improvement in the Prime Minister's condition, and there has been no fever for 24 hours.'[29]

27 February 1943

Churchill was in very good form on 27 February and had slept well.[18] The medical consultation involving Wilson and Marshall took place at 6 pm.[18] A medical bulletin signed by Charles Wilson MD and Geoffrey Marshall MD stated that: 'The Prime Minister's condition continues to be satisfactory, and no bulletin will be issued until Monday [1 March 1943].'[30] Churchill wrote to President Roosevelt who was also unwell: 'I hope you are all right and that the fever will soon go. I have got rid of mine, which was heavy and long, I hope for good.'[3]

28 February–2 March 1943

A medical consultation took place at 6 pm on Sunday, 28 February when Churchill was again observed to be in 'very good form'.[18] A medical bulletin was issued on 1 March 1943 by Charles Wilson MD and Geoffrey Marshall MD which stated that: 'The Prime Minister's condition is improving daily. He is getting up, and no further bulletins will be issued.'[31]

Nurse Miles learned today that she was to go with Churchill to Chequers, the country house of the Prime Minister, while he recuperated.

3–15 March 1943

On 3 March 1943 Churchill was well enough to go to Chequers. Clementine Churchill wrote to their daughter Mary after a few days: 'Papa is progressing very slowly, but (I hope & believe) safely through his convalescence to his normal strong state of health.'[7]

President Roosevelt wrote to Churchill:

Please, please, for the sake of the world, don't overdo these days. You must remember that it takes about a month of occasional let-ups to get back your full strength. Tell Mrs Churchill that when I was laid up I was a thoroughly model patient, and that I hope you will live down the reputation in our Press of having been the 'world's worst patient'.[15]

Nurse Miles explained her daily nursing programme at Chequers to her husband:

My day really begins at 7.00 pm when I'm called with a cup of tea … I have a bath and dress … and by 8 I am all set for dinner. If I can persuade the Patient to do his breathing exercises before he gets up for dinner I do, but his usual excuse is that he is too tired or too busy (too lazy really). At 8.30 a large and very scrumptious dinner in housekeeper's sitting room with two secretaries. This goes on till about 9.30, when I lay a tray with a glass of water and two minute radiostoleum capsules on a large glass plate, and march with them into the dining room.[32]

These capsules contained high doses of vitamin A and D and were marketed as a preventive against infection and also in the prophylactic and curative treatment of rickets and osteomalacia and dental caries. Nurse Miles told Gilbert[2] in 1982 that at other times: 'I had to march into the dining room after dinner (all male) and present him with a red capsule [presumably the barbiturate hypnotic, secobarbital] on a large silver tray – I was then told: "The price of a good woman is above rubies".'[2]

Nurse Miles also told Gilbert that while she was at Chequers Churchill prepared his speeches:

Often in the bath (he was proud of being able to turn the taps off with his toes). He took immense pains with them, walking around in his bath towel, and going through them with Charles Wilson or Lord Cherwell [Churchill's scientific advisor]. I was very struck by his immense vigour and enthusiasm, his determination to get over his illness as quickly as possible. He told me that he ate and drank too much (roast beef for breakfast), and took no exercise at all, but was much fitter than 'old so-and-so who is two years younger than me.[2]

Nurse Miles recorded that after dinner every night there would be a film to watch with all staff in attendance, which hardly ever finished before midnight because it rarely started until 10 pm. Miles recalled that Churchill 'loved watching films particularly newsreels, and was delighted if he featured in them: "Look Pug [General Ismay], there we are"!'[32]After the film Churchill would begin 'solid work, and there is much telephoning and rushing up and downstairs with dispatch boxes'.[32]

Churchill wrote to his friend Lord Camrose, Proprietor of the *Daily Telegraph*, on 5 March 1943: 'I am much better, but I am staying in the country for a few days. Of course I work wherever I am and however I am. That is what does me good.'[11]

On 7 March Churchill was well enough to be driven over to Ditchley Park for lunch hosted by Lady Diana, wife of Duff Cooper.[2] He was accompanied by Elizabeth Layton, who took dictation in the car.[2] Churchill returned to Chequers at 4 pm.[2] On 8 March King George VI was driven to Chequers to lunch with Churchill, in place of their usual weekly lunch at Buckingham Palace.[8] Elizabeth Layton wrote: 'The two of them talked hard in the room next to the office, and we could hear the tongues wagging like mad! But I fear my boss still holds the floor!'[2] When the King was ready to return to London, Churchill went to the door to see him off in spite of instructions to the contrary,[2] presumably from Wilson.

Nurse Miles wrote of Churchill: 'I've got awfully fond of him in spite of his occasional tantrums and rather overbearing ways. He's very sweet to me, and always thanks me so nicely when I do anything for him.'[32] She also wrote: 'He was very kind to me – interested to know that my husband was a Surgeon Lieutenant in a destroyer on the Russian convoys.'[2]

Churchill remained at Chequers until 15 March.

Churchill was interviewed by the Editor of *The Times*, Robin Barrington-Ward, on 29 March 1943 who noted in his diary that Churchill showed no signs of his recent illness, describing him as 'pinky, fresh in colour, hardly a wrinkle, voice firm, all his usual animation and emphasis'.[33]

Medical Aspects

Churchill was 68 years old in February 1943. While the overall mortality from pneumonia in the early 1940s with sulfonamides was 10 per cent, the mortality was 20 per cent in those aged 60–9 years of age.[34] It is of interest that Captain Fitzroy, the Speaker of the House of Commons, who was five years older than Churchill, had been taken ill with pneumonia on almost the same day,[3] but died two weeks later.

Moran records only that Marshall was invited to give a second opinion, though the fact that Whitby signed three medical bulletins (on 24, 25 and 26 February) suggests otherwise. Furthermore, Nurses Pugh and Miles both confirm Whitby's involvement. Hence, Churchill's illness was managed by Moran with the assistance of two nurses and with the advice of a distinguished respiratory physician (Marshall), as well as a pathologist (Whitby) who was also an acknowledged expert on the treatment of infections with sulfonamides.

What treatment did Churchill receive for pneumonia? The 1943 edition of the National War Formulary[35] included only three sulfonamides (sulfanilamide, sulfapyridine and sulfathiazole). We know from the nursing records that Churchill was treated with sulfathiazole for pneumonia due to haemolytic streptococci, initially in a dose of 2 g 4-hourly, decreasing to 1.5 g 6-hourly. Poorly soluble sulfonamides, such as sulfathiazole, when given in high dose readily form crystalline concretions in the renal tubules and ureters, resulting in renal tubular irritation, temporary or permanent kidney damage and death.[36] Although it was traditional to attempt to alkalinize the urine with potassium or sodium citrate mixture, alkalinization was not only difficult to achieve but rarely had much impact on sulfathiazole-induced crystalline concretions.[36] We know from the nursing observations that crystals were present in Churchill's urine on several days and the urine remained acid on pH testing, demonstrating that urine alkalinization was not achieved.

Churchill regularly had the top of his head rubbed with methyl salicylate (oil of wintergreen) by Nurses Miles and Pugh. Methyl salicylate is absorbed through the skin to give high concentrations of salicylate in the blood. Similarly, when aspirin (acetylsalicylic acid) is ingested this also produces salicylate in the blood. However, methyl salicylate is so concentrated that the *ingestion* of as little as 30 mL in an adult would lead to severe salicylate poisoning. The application of methyl salicylate would have relieved Churchill's head pain and helped to lower his temperature. No doubt Churchill also found the rubbing of the aromatic oil into his scalp soothing.

Moran wrote that, 'It is one of Winston's foibles to pretend that he never allowed any of his illnesses to interfere with his work.' Thompson observed, 'Since he [Churchill] regarded even temporary capitulation to any ailment as a sign of weakness he was an impossible patient. In a high fever he would sit up in bed reading State papers and drafting memoranda.'[25]

Churchill claimed that initially he had maintained his 'usual output', though feeling far from well.[3] Churchill later reached an agreement with Marshall that: 'I was only to have the most important and interesting papers sent me.'[3] Churchill admitted there was a blank in his flow of minutes from 19–25 February,[3] and this is confirmed by the *Churchill Documents*,[11,15] though his letter to the King was a notable exception.[3] Although the flow of documents which reached the Prime Minister's bedside was drastically curtailed, not a day passed when Churchill did not put in several hours' work.[25] Thompson recalled that even at the height of his illness Churchill was cabling Hopkins about the progress of Tube Alloys (codename of the clandestine research and development programme to develop nuclear weapons during the Second World War), dictating far-sighted minutes on post-war planning, and keeping a watchful eye on developments in North Africa, where General Anderson's First Army had just sustained a severe mauling.[5] From his sick bed, he sought to placate Stalin, now complaining about the delay in launching Operation HUSKY (the Sicilian invasion).[5]

Chapter 10

Pneumonia and Atrial Fibrillation in December 1943 in Carthage

It was probably will power and adrenaline alone that had sustained him through his high-powered meetings with Roosevelt and Stalin, but by the time of his collapse in Carthage it was clear that Churchill was running on empty[1]

I am afraid I shall have to stay with you longer than I had planned. I am completely at the end of my tether, and I cannot go on to the front until I have recovered my strength[2]

At noon on 12 November 1943 Churchill left London by train for Plymouth and for the battleship HMS *Renown*, in which he was to set sail for Gibraltar at 6 pm that evening.[3,4] It had been decided to use *Renown* for the first part of the journey to Gibraltar, as it was considered that autumn flying conditions across the Bay of Biscay were likely to be difficult. Churchill planned to be away for two months.

Churchill was accompanied by the US Ambassador in London (JG 'Gil' Winant), the First Sea Lord (Admiral Sir Andrew Cunningham), the Secretary of the Imperial Defence Chiefs of Staff Committee and Deputy Secretary of the War Cabinet (General Hastings 'Pug' Ismay) and the Senior Assistant Secretary in the War Cabinet (General Hollis).

In addition, Churchill's own staff were in attendance: John Martin (Principal Private Secretary), Desmond Morton (intelligence advisor), Commander CR 'Tommy' Thompson RN (aide-de-camp), Captain Pim (in charge of the travelling map room), Inspector Walter Thompson (bodyguard),[5] and Lord Moran (see p. 443), his personal physician. Churchill's son, Randolph, and daughter, Sarah, were also part of the entourage.[3,6–8] In addition, there were fourteen WRNS signal officers and five typists on board.[9]

During the first part of the voyage, Churchill spent most of the time in his cabin[4] being nursed by his daughter, Sarah.[10] On his own admission and that of Moran, Churchill was suffering from a heavy cold, exacerbated by a mild fever caused by the recent administration of typhoid and cholera vaccines.[4,6] However, Moran was also unwell as he had fallen getting into the tender taking the party to the ship and he suffered from seasickness for the first 24 hours of the journey.[9]

The *Renown* reached Gibraltar on 15 November 1943, and Harold Macmillan MP, Minister Resident in the Mediterranean, came on board and noted in his diary: 'The P.M. was in excellent form and asked a great deal about the French situation.'[11] Macmillan and Churchill continued talking until 1.30 am in Churchill's cabin.[11] Their conversation continued for 3½ hours the following morning; Churchill had sent for Macmillan at 9 am while eating breakfast, and they continued talking until 12.30 pm.[11] Macmillan recorded: 'It was a fascinating performance. The greater part was a rehearsal of what he [Churchill] is to say at the Military Conference [in Cairo on 22 November].'[11]

Although it had been intended that Churchill would fly from Gibraltar to Cairo, this plan had to be changed as the weather was poor and Churchill's Avro York had been delayed for two days by bad weather at RAF Northolt. *Renown*, therefore, continued via Algiers and Malta to Alexandria, from where Churchill took a short flight to Cairo.[9]

16–19 November 1943: Algiers and Malta

At 1 pm on 16 November *Renown* reached Algiers and Churchill received Admiral Sir John Cunningham (Commander-in-Chief, Mediterranean Fleet), US General Bedell Smith (Chief-of-staff at Allied Forces Headquarters) and General Whiteley (British Deputy Chief of Staff, Allied Forces Headquarters).[11] *Renown* left Algiers after dark on 16 November making 29 knots and reached Grand Harbour, Valetta, Malta on the night of 17 November[12] at about 7.30 pm.

Meanwhile General Sir Alan Brooke, Chief of the Imperial General Staff and Chairman of the Chiefs of Staff Committee, had flown to Malta from London via Gibraltar and had dinner with Churchill at 8.30 pm.[13]

Churchill wrote later: 'I arrived in Malta quite ill with a new cold and temperature, but I had sufficient strength to attend the dinner at the

Governor's [Lord Gort] war-time palace, the real one being uninhabitable from bombardment.'[4]

Gort had placed his bedroom at Churchill's disposal. However, this bedroom overlooked a street which was the favourite promenade of the Maltese and which so disturbed Churchill's rest that he bawled out of the window, 'Please go away and don't make so much noise.'[6] Ismay had decided to remain on board *Renown* where he had his office and personal staff,[12] but reported to Churchill the following morning. Churchill was in bed with a feverish cold and finding Gort's spartan regime a 'trifle unsatisfying'.[12] Churchill asked Ismay: 'Do you think you could bring me a little bit of butter from that nice ship?'[12] Churchill had also experienced a shortage of hot water for his bath.[12] Ismay suggested that he had made a mistake in leaving the *Renown*.[12]

Churchill ignored this observation and went on to say that as Alexander (General, Commander-in-Chief of Middle East Command), Tedder (Air Chief Marshal, Commander of Mediterranean Allied Air Forces from December 1943) and Cunningham were all on the Island, he would like to have a meeting with them and the three Chiefs of Staff as soon as they could be collected.[12]

Ismay wrote in his diary: 'Even if he had been at death's door, he would not have forgone the chance of a talk with the commanders in the Mediterranean. We all managed to squeeze into his none too large bedroom, and the topics discussed included the progress and prospects of the campaign in Italy, plans for the capture of Rhodes, and guerrilla operations in Yugoslavia.'[12]

Churchill was still in Malta on 18 November. He telegraphed Anthony Eden, the Foreign Secretary: 'I am laid up with a sore throat for the moment and am remaining here today and probably tomorrow.'[14] Later Churchill wrote: 'Although I continued to conduct business without cessation I had to remain in bed all the time I was in Malta, except for a Staff conference and a final tour of the frightfully battered dockyard.'[4] Moran thought Churchill was 'still mouldy; a cold in the head has dragged on; he will not take any precautions, but expects me, when summoned, to appear with a magic cure'.[6]

At midnight on 19 November, *Renown* sailed to Alexandria and arrived on the morning of 21 November. Churchill flew immediately from there by Dakota to a desert-landing ground near the Pyramids, a flight of 40 minutes.[4]

21–6 November 1943: Cairo

The Cairo Conference (Codename *Sextant)* began on 23 November and took place at the Mena House Hotel, close by the Pyramids, though the Principals (Churchill, Roosevelt, British and US Chiefs of Staff) were staying in various villas in the vicinity. Churchill also met Chiang Kai-Shek, Premier of the Republic of China. The Conference ended on 26 November, and Churchill had been well throughout until the morning of departure (27 November) when Eden noted in his diary: 'W had lost his voice, I think from too much talk last night, and was sorry for himself until he had a stiff whisky and soda at 8.45 am. He appeared on aerodrome as Air Commodore in khaki drill and amazed me by translation into blue before we touched Tehran. His travelling wardrobe must be prodigious.'[15] Churchill and Eden (plus Martin, the Thompsons, Moran, Kinna and Sawyers) flew in his Avro York, *Ascalon*, to Tehran and arrived that afternoon after a 5½ hour journey.[9]

27 November 1943–2 December 1943: Tehran

On reaching Tehran, Sir Alexander Cadogan the Permanent Under-Secretary recorded in his diary that Churchill had 'lost his voice entirely (of course), so the dinner of the three great ones was off, and they all dined separately (P.M. in bed)'.[16] Sarah Churchill wrote:

> Everything a bit miserable, with my father really very tired and his voice almost completely gone … my father wanted to start the conference there and then. Charles Moran and I, however, went into action – at the risk of getting our heads bitten off – to get him better. Finally, luckily he agreed there should be no immediate meeting and he had dinner in bed like a sulky boy.[10]

After that Churchill was able to participate fully in the first 'Big Three' meeting with President Roosevelt and Marshal Stalin, Chairman of the Council of Ministers of the Soviet Union. On 30 November Churchill's 69th birthday was celebrated, and on the following day, there was a small birthday parade for Churchill, made up of British and Indian troops and employees of the Anglo-Persian Oil Company.[17] Churchill wearing one of 'his indomitable uniforms walked down the single rank of this very small parade and accepted his presents with tears streaming down his face'.[17]

2–10 December 1943: Cairo

At 8 am on 2 December Churchill left Tehran in *Ascalon* for Cairo. During the flight, Churchill was in good form sitting for part of the time in the co-pilot's seat for a better view. During the 6-hour flight, they passed over the Tigris, Euphrates, Jordan and Nile. They landed mid-afternoon at Cairo West Airport, and Churchill dined with Roosevelt that evening, though both were tired after the flight. The following day Churchill inspected his old Regiment the 4th Hussars, gave a speech and watched a tank display.[10] Moran was not content, however, and considered that: 'Winston seems to be sickening for some malady. His exhaustion is very disturbing. But he keeps insisting he must go to Italy without delay to see Alex[ander] … I told him it was madness to set off on a journey when he was under the weather like this.'[18]

Churchill participated in a punishing series of meetings each day during the eight days he was in Cairo.[19] These included difficult meetings with the Turkish President, Ismet Inönü, who after three days still declined to bring his country into the war.[19] By the morning of 10 December Moran considered that he had persuaded Churchill not to go to Italy, at any rate for the present.[20] 'I have never before been so blunt with the P.M., rating him for his folly, but I take no credit for his change of plans. He knows that without my help that he is at the end of his tether. Tehran seems to have got him down. It is plain that he is riding for a fall.'[20]

11 December 1943: Flight to Tunis

Churchill left Cairo in *Ascalon* [2,21,22] at 1 am to fly to Tunis, a flight of 8½ hours. The journey to and from Tunis are described by Lavery[23] and by the navigator on both flights, Squadron Leader Mitchell.[24,25] Mitchell has described how 15 minutes short of landing time the corrected estimated time of arrival was sent by Wireless Telegraphy and acknowledged by Tunis Air Traffic Control with the message that El Aouina was closed to all traffic.[24] Wing Commander HB Collins, the pilot, was told to divert to *Whipsnade* (the code name for an airstrip some 10 minutes flying time away) but queried these instructions and continued to El Aouina. The Avro York overflew the airfield and lowered the undercarriage to indicate the desire to land. Tunis Air Traffic Control was adamant that El Aouina was closed and the pilot must proceed to *Whipsnade*. Mitchell recalls that the plane sailed over the heads of the assembled VIPs awaiting the PM's arrival.[24] The crew assumed that last-minute unserviceability or obstruction of the only long runway was the explanation. The Avro York landed at a 'half-deserted airstrip inhabited by a Beaufighter squadron'.[24,26] Hasty telephone calls established that El Aouina was indeed closed to all aircraft, except Churchill's Avro York![24,27]

While arrangements were made to fly to El Aouina, where Eisenhower and Tedder were waiting, Churchill himself admitted that: 'As I sat on my official boxes near the machines I certainly did feel completely worn out.'[2] Brooke recorded in his diary: 'They took him [Churchill] out of the plane and he sat on his suitcase in a very cold morning wind, looking like nothing on earth ... he was chilled through.'[22] Churchill 'looked ghastly' noted Commander Thompson.[27] Moran reported that Churchill's face 'shone with perspiration'.[20]

It was about an hour before the Avro York took off again. Moran recalled that: 'As the P.M. walked very slowly to the aircraft, there was a grey look on his face that I did not like.'[6] Once at the correct airfield, some 40 miles away according to Churchill's own account,[2] where General Eisenhower had waited 2 hours to greet him 'with imperturbable good-humour',[2] Churchill told Eisenhower that: 'I am afraid I shall have to stay with you longer than I had planned. I am completely at the end of my tether, and I cannot go on to the front until I have recovered my strength.'[2]

Churchill was accommodated in a house at La Marsa, near Tunis, mainly occupied by Eisenhower and his staff. It was known as the White House, and was a 'large and beautiful villa at sea level',[28] guarded by the 2nd Battalion Coldstream Guards.[28] Moran observed that Churchill collapsed wearily into the first chair when he arrived,[20] which was at about 9 am, according to Captain Grey-Turner, Medical Officer of the 2nd Battalion Coldstream Guards.[28] After breakfast, Churchill rested until lunch and spent most of the afternoon also resting and sleeping.[22,27] Churchill wrote later that he slept all day.[2] Moran noted that Churchill did not seem to have the energy to read the usual telegrams.[20] Churchill wrote: 'So here I was at this pregnant moment on the broad of my back amid the ruins of ancient Carthage.'[2] However, that night Churchill was able to dine with Eisenhower, Brooke, Moran, Tedder, Commander Thompson, Martin (Principal Private Secretary to Churchill) and his children, Randolph and Sarah.[19]

Churchill had originally planned to spend one night at Eisenhower's villa and to fly the next day to Alexander's and then Montgomery's [Eighth

Army] headquarters in Italy.[2] It is not surprising that Brooke believed that a trip to Italy in December would adversely affect Churchill's health when there would be snow and seas of mud.[22] Brooke believed that living in cold caravans would finish Churchill off.[6] Brooke had discussed the matter with Moran, who agreed entirely.[22] Brooke therefore tackled Churchill in the evening and told him that he was wrong in wanting to go to Italy.[22] Granted that the troops would be delighted to see him and that he would enjoy the trip, but Brooke said that he did not think that he had any right to risk his health in this way when he had more important matters in front of him connected with the war.[22] Brooke was beginning to make a little progress, and then foolishly said: 'And what is more, Moran entirely agrees with me.'[22] In response, Churchill 'rose up on his elbow in his bed, shook his fist in my [Brooke's] face and said: "Don't you get in league with that bloody old man!!!"'[22] Brooke wrote in his diary: 'Thank heaven, God took a hand in the matter and the next day he [Churchill] was running a temperature!'[22]

12 December 1943

Brooke recorded that he was 'sleeping like a log' when at 4 am he was woken by Churchill in his dragon dressing gown with a brown bandage wrapped round his head.[22] Churchill said he was looking for Moran and that he had a bad headache.[22] Brooke led him to Moran's room and retired back to bed.[22]

Moran records that he went to bed early, but woke to find Churchill standing at the foot of his bed.[20] Churchill complained of pain in his throat (just above his collar bone). Moran observed that Churchill's skin was hot and that his temperature was 101°F [38.3°C], pulse 105/min, though there were no abnormal clinical signs on examining Churchill's chest.[20] Churchill's temperature chart is shown in Plate 12.

Brooke discussed the diagnosis with Moran, who said that as far as he could judge it might be pneumonia or a case of the flu.[22] Sarah Churchill also discussed the possible diagnosis with Lord Moran, 'He is sickening for something, but I do not know what.'[26]

Not surprisingly, Moran considered that Churchill was 'in poor shape to face an infection'.[20] 'If he is going to be ill we have nothing here in this God-forsaken spot – no nurses, no milk, not even a chemist.'[20] Brooke asked Moran what he would require if the diagnosis were pneumonia. Moran replied that in addition to a pathologist and two nurses he would require a portable X-ray set, probably from Algiers.[22] Brooke explained to Moran that these would take some time to get and that they should wire at once for them.[22] To Brooke's surprise, Moran begged him not to wire as this might be a false diagnosis.[22] 'It is fortunate (adds Brooke) those wires were sent to Cairo.'[22]

Commander Thompson also records that signals were sent to Algiers and Cairo requesting that Brigadier Evan Bedford and Brigadier Lionel Whitby should be flown immediately to Tunis,[27] though Whitby did not travel to Carthage to assess Churchill. Professor (Lieutenant Colonel in 1943) Guy Scadding commenting in 1993 wrote that Moran was apparently unaware that there was an RAMC General Hospital in Tunis and summoned up medical and nursing help from Cairo probably because he knew who was stationed there and not who was in North Africa.[29]

Churchill wrote to his wife, 'I am laid up here at Carthage with a temperature of 101 [°F; 38.3°C] and rather violent neuralgic sore throat, due, I think, to a draught in the airplane. I shall therefore stay in bed and recover for two or three days.'[30]

Churchill's temperature remained high that night.[20] Moran states that as there was no bell in Churchill's room, he left Inspector Thompson sitting outside Churchill's bedroom door when he went to bed at about 1 am.[20] Thompson recalls that Moran had told him to listen to the tempo of Churchill's breathing, and if there was any sudden alteration, he was to call Moran immediately. Thompson remembers hearing Churchill's 'fast, stertorous breathing' and that at about 2 am the sound ceased.[31] Fearing the worst, Thompson crept into Churchill's room and found that he was 'breathing quietly and steadily'.[31] Thompson then reported this episode to Moran.

Moran stated that Churchill 'felt poorly and his pulse was shabby [weak]'.[32] After Moran had turned out the light, thinking Churchill was asleep, Churchill said: 'Don't go away, Charles. Is my pulse all right?'[20] Writing to his wife, Moran confided, 'I sat with him [Churchill] 2–3 am. Then he went to sleep, and the temp is now 100 [°F; 37.8°C].'[32]

Inspector Thompson recalls that subsequently, Churchill asked for his sleeping tablets. Thompson played for time, pretending to look for them, knowing they had been removed.[31] Churchill said to Thompson: 'I am tired out in body, soul and spirit ... (but) all is planned and ready.'[31] Thompson quotes Churchill as then saying, 'In what better place could I die than here – in the ruins of Carthage?'[31] a sentiment also expressed in writing by Churchill himself[2] and verbally to his daughter, Sarah, at the time: 'Don't worry, it doesn't matter if I die now, the plans for victory have been laid, it is only a matter of time.'[26]

Later that evening in Cairo, Lieutenant Colonel Pulvertaft (see p. 445), Assistant Director of Pathology, Central Laboratory, housed in the 15th (Scottish) General Hospital in Cairo, was in a nightclub conversing with his hospital's Padre when a Brigadier arrived searching for him. 'You are to follow me immediately. Orders from London. This is a message from the C.I.G.S [Chief of the Imperial General Staff].'[33] Pulvertaft was driven to the General Hospital where the General told him that, 'You are to go immediately to Tunis with two nurses. Go and choose your nurses and take some equipment'. At about 4 am Pulvertaft was told to report immediately to Brigadier Halliday with two nurses (Miss Clark and Mrs Haselden[34]) at the front gate. They drove into the desert and took off for Tunis at dawn. Pulvertaft, as a trained pilot, took control of the aircraft for part of the journey.

13 December 1943

Grey-Turner noted in his diary, 'Strong wind today.'[28] At breakfast time, Macmillan, who was in Algiers, had been asked to arrange for a portable X-ray machine and to come to Tunis with Morton as soon as possible. After spending the morning telegraphing, Macmillan discovered there was 'a perfectly good apparatus at a hospital in Tunis'.[35] Moran noted that at 11 am Churchill's temperature was 99 [°F; 37.2°C] and he felt better.[20]

Pulvertaft later wrote:

Tunis aerodrome was still littered with smashed German planes and there were bomb craters and bullet holes. Two American sergeants with automatic rifles saw us out of the plane. We were led to a large Yank staff car, and the two sergeants stood on the running boards. One aimed his rifle disconcertingly at me, the other at the outside universe. They remained silent. We drove quite a way to what turned out to be Carthage, and then out to the coast to a large villa, once the American H.Q. At the door, I found Lord Moran, whom I knew fairly well from London days. He was very much concerned.

On discovering that Pulvertaft and the nurses had arrived, Churchill said to Moran: 'Now, Charles, what have you been up to? I'm not ill, and anyway what's wrong with me?'[20]

Moran told Pulvertaft: 'I've got Churchill here. He's gravely ill, I want you to examine him'.[33] Pulvertaft had brought with him his professional bag, a travelling laboratory he had specially designed in his civilian days and a microscope and lamp.[33] Pulvertaft was 'led to a small room opening off the large one, and saw Churchill in bed. He looked desperately ill; I thought he was dying. I prepared to examine his blood.'[33]

Pulvertaft took a drop of blood from Churchill's ear. 'That sir was competently done', Churchill said,[33] gratified that sampling was painless.[19] Pulvertaft found that Churchill's total white cell (leucocyte) count was 9,900 per cubic millimetre (9.9 x 10^9/L; normal range 4.0–11.0); sampling was repeated by Pulvertaft daily after that for seven days, partly at Churchill's request[19,20] Churchill was interested in the normal white cell count and how the white cells are mobilised in an infection.[20] Churchill also asked Pulvertaft, 'What are eosinophils for?'[36] Churchill had the blood-count results typed out on large cards in giant letters and figures. 'I will now review my troops', he said to Pulvertaft.

Pulvertaft continued:

When I had finished, I spoke with Moran and told him something of the resources of British medicine in North Africa, and its deficiencies. It was decided that Churchill had pneumonia and a very wonky heart. But the British Army had no portable X-ray apparatus, or electrocardiograph and no modern, up-to-date drugs – and I had finished all my penicillin … I suggested that Evan Bedford, a top heart man should come from Cairo and that Buttle [see p. 431] should be got hold of, as he had all the available penicillin.[33]

Pulvertaft described Buttle as 'perhaps the most remarkable doctor in the medical service during that war. Completely unselfish, utterly dedicated and extremely unconventional he was the despair of authority. He was in charge of blood transfusion in North Africa, Italy and later during the European invasion; he also pioneered many new drugs.'[33]

A portable X-ray apparatus and electrocardiograph (ECG) were acquired by Pulvertaft within 12 hours from from No. 37 American General Hospital,

La Marsa in Tunis.[33] Most importantly, sulfadiazine was also obtained and most probably digitalis too. Pulvertaft states, 'It is a remarkable fact that, so far as I know, no credit was ever claimed by any American for their service on that occasion, without which it is not likely that Churchill would have survived.'[33] Commander Thompson did write, however, to the Commanding Officer of the No. 37 American General Hospital on 3 February 1944 to thank him for the services of Captain Gregorio and the use of the ECG machine (personal communication from Christine DeSalvo, Captain Gregorio's great granddaughter).

Pulvertaft's next task was to find a bedside commode for Churchill.[36] Tedder was able to locate one made from packing cases stencilled 'Dried Milk' in an RAF mobile hospital unit about 70 miles away. It had been made by the RAF sister in charge and was collected personally by Pulvertaft.[33]

The portable X-ray apparatus arrived, and the chest X-ray showed a diffuse opacity at the left base, in keeping with the clinical examination findings of left lower lobe consolidation (pneumonia).[34] After reviewing the X-ray, Moran concluded: 'At least I know where I am now … It means we can begin giving him M. & B. [May and Baker, the manufacturer of some sulfonamides] straight away.'[20] In fact, treatment with sulfadiazine 1 g every 4 hours was not commenced until 2.30 pm on 14 December 1943.

Macmillan and Morton left Algiers at 2.30 pm. 'The weather was very bad, pouring rain and cloud everywhere. By taking the sea route, we managed to get through. We arrived about 5.30 pm.'[35] Macmillan and Morton motored to the White House and found Sarah Churchill, Moran, Martin and Francis Brown (private secretary to Churchill) who 'seemed very fussed about the PM's condition'.[35] Churchill insisted on seeing Macmillan when he arrived, but 'seemed weak and drowsy. I escaped as soon as I could, as I felt sure he was seeing too many people.'[35] Despite his illness, Churchill continued to work 'at an alarming pace' from his bed as Patrick Kinna, Churchill's stenographer, later recalled to Gilbert: 'The doctors present "protested about the volume of work being done by the PM – but to no avail".'[19]

14 December 1943

Macmillan wrote in his diary that 'Moran seems very worried. He is telegraphing all over the place for specialists.'[35] It is not surprising Moran was concerned. Churchill's temperature, pulse and respiratory rate were rising, the white blood cell count blood was higher and there were clinical and radiological signs of pneumonia at the base of the left lung.[20,37]

Moran reported to his wife that Attlee, Deputy Prime Minister, had telephoned and asked whether he would like Marshall (see p. 442), Senior Physician to Guy's Hospital, London and Physician-in-Charge at the Brompton Hospital, London sent out. Marshall had provided a second opinion on Churchill's pneumonia in February 1943,[38] and was to do so again in 1944.[38] Moran declined this offer and sent a message to Mrs Churchill that: 'If I myself were ill in London I would not change this team.'[32] The Deputy Prime Minister and Cabinet were not reassured (see below).

Moran wrote later that after rejecting Cabinet pressure exerted locally and directly through Martin that Parkinson and Marshall should be sent out from England, he was aware that if he arrived back in England without Churchill 'they will remember this against me. I will be another Morell Mackenzie.' Sir Morell Mackenzie had failed to make a diagnosis of cancer in Crown Prince Frederick William of Germany in 1887.[20] Moran wrote to his wife in similar terms at the time: 'Yesterday I was doubtful if he would come through and I saw myself arriving alone at Paddington with Mrs C reproachful and public incensed!'[32]

Although there has been controversy over which sulfonamide was prescribed,[39,40] the records of Pulvertaft [33] and Bedford[34] make clear it was sulfadiazine. Treatment was commenced at 2.30 pm. Pulvertaft measured Churchill's white cell count again and this had risen to 14,500 per cubic millimetre (14.5 x 10^9/L; normal range 4.0–11.0).

On 14 December 1943 Bedford has recorded that while dining with General Biggam, consultant physician to the Army, preparatory to a tour of the Middle East hospitals starting next day, he received orders from General Hartgill, Director Medical Services, to travel to Tunis by air that night on a highly secret mission.[37] 'No names were mentioned and I was simply told that I should be met at the airport on arrival. I was due to leave at midnight, but owing to heavy mist the flight was delayed until 8 am the next day, and I spent an uncomfortable night in the airfield NAAFI waiting to take off. Navy, Army and Air Force Institutes (NAAFI) provide retail and leisure services to the British Armed Forces.

Macmillan recorded in his diary that: 'PM is definitely worse, and has got pneumonia, and they fear pleurisy.'[35] Churchill asked Macmillan to discuss with General Sir Henry Maitland 'Jumbo' Wilson, the general organisation of the Mediterranean command to which he was about to be appointed Supreme Allied Commander, and write him a report.[35] Macmillan recorded that in spite of Churchill's temperature (101°F; 38.3°C) he dealt with the report in the evening and wrote a long telegram to the Cabinet about it.[35]

15 December 1943

'Another damp windy day' according to Elston-Grey.[28] Macmillan reported that Moran had told him that he thought Churchill was going to die last night. 'He thinks him a little better as regards the pneumonia, but is worried about his heart.'[35]

Bedford wrote:

> Eventually I arrived at Tunis at 5:30 pm [on 15 December] and had great difficulty in contacting anyone concerned with my mission in this huge American airfield, but in the course of time I found Lt Col Pulvertaft from the Central Pathological Laboratory, Cairo, and Commander Thompson, one of the Prime Minister's ADCs, who had been waiting for me for some hours.[37]

Bedford was then informed by Pulvertaft that Churchill had been taken ill at Eisenhower's Villa at Carthage, and Pulvertaft was much alarmed at the state of affairs there where 'he said there was much talk of coronary thrombosis, no definite diagnosis, and great anxiety and gloom'.[37]

Later Churchill stopped Pulvertaft as he left the room after further blood sampling. "'I'm dying, am I not?" [he] asked. Pulvertaft responded: "No sir, you are not. I thought you were, but you are on the way up". Churchill said: "I don't believe you. Pneumonia, I've got, Osler said it was the old man's friend".[33] Pulvertaft reassured Churchill that: 'Osler had not got sulfadiazine. It's a better friend'. Churchill said: 'Carthage. Not a bad place … to die.'[33]

Churchill wrote to his wife: 'There seems to be no doubt I have got another touch of pneumonia, but I am being well looked after and have faith in my M. and B.' Later the same day there was a further message from Churchill to his wife sent by Martin, who wrote: 'I should however warn you that Lord Moran does not agree with the first sentence. I thought it better not to trouble patient with argument on point.'[30] Churchill wrote:

'The blood tests this morning were considered satisfactory as indicating healthy but not serious reaction. Temperature between 101 [°F; 38.3°C] and 102 [°F; 38.8°C]. Doctor Bedford a high London consultant on circulation and chest is arriving this afternoon, having been summoned by Moran two days ago. We certainly are not short of any of the talents.'[30] Later in the same telegram Churchill wrote, 'In case I go to convalesce at Marrakech it might be worthwhile to send out a modest package of painting materials ... The days are long and weary.'[30]

Churchill developed atrial fibrillation (an irregular heart beat) at 6 pm. Churchill informed Moran that: 'My heart is doing something funny – it feels to be bumping all over the place.'[20] Moran observed that Churchill was very breathless and on examination found that his pulse was racing and very irregular and that the bases of his lungs were congested and the edge of his liver could be felt below the ribs.[20] Bedford arrived at the villa at 6.30 pm and at once saw Moran, who was tired and anxious. Moran related to Bedford:

at some length the story of the Prime Minister's attacks of dyspnoea, the first at Washington two years previously after which Sir John Parkinson had seen him and excluded a coronary thrombosis. Several lesser attacks had occurred since and recently the Prime Minister had seemed breathless and very fatigued following strenuous conferences in Cairo and Tehran where he had caught a cold. On 11th of December, he reached Tunis, landing at the wrong airfield, where he had to wait feeling cold and tired. On 12th December he complained of pain in the upper chest, the temperature rose to 101 [°F; 38.3°C] and the pulse to 105 [/min].[37]

According to Moran no cause for the pain had been found, and the question of coronary thrombosis was discussed.[37] On 13 December, radiographs of the chest showed an opacity (shadow) at the base of the left lung, fever persisted and the blood showed leucocytosis (a rise in the white cell count demonstrating infection) on 14 December when sulfadiazine was started.[37] On 15 December the white cell count was 11,000 per cubic millimetre [11×10^9/L] and thereafter it fell to normal.

Bedford recorded that Pulvertaft had not exaggerated the state of affairs.[37] Bedford noted in his diary that Moran and Pulvertaft were present for his examination at 6.30 pm on 15 December 1943.[34]

I found the Prime Minister lying on his bed in his underclothes, the bedroom door open, and the secretaries and others strolling in and out with gloomy faces. The patient was drowsy and interrogation unfruitful. My examination showed obvious clinical signs of consolidation of the left lower lobe, atrial fibrillation with a heart rate of 130/min, [systolic] blood pressure 120 mmHg and dyspnoea but no pain. The fibrillation had started at 6 pm, and Lord Moran had sent for digitalis [Moran had sent to Tunis for digitalis earlier in the day[20]] which had not yet been given. The right base was congested and the liver was palpable.[37]

Although Moran recorded that Bedford had 'not suggested any change in the treatment, but his presence will keep the people at home quiet,'[20] Bedford prescribed digitalis leaf 3 grains 6-hourly. The first dose was given at 10 pm on 15 December 1943. Bedford also increased the dose of sulfadiazine to 1.5 g six times daily.[37] Macmillan noted that: 'Bedford seems sensible and gives us comfort.'[35]

Bedford was clear that a decision must be made quickly about suspected coronary thrombosis, that some semblance of order must be established in the sick room and that as far as possible morale must be restored to the entourage. 'I was not impressed by the evidence of previous or present symptoms of coronary thrombosis and decided that an official diagnosis of pneumonia ought to be made forthwith, giving my opinion that the Prime Minister had not had a coronary thrombosis and that the chest pain and fibrillation could be explained by pneumonia in a man of the Prime Minister's age.'[37]

Bedford recorded that the ante-room to the Prime Minister's bedroom was turned into a nursing office with instructions that no visitors were allowed without permission.[37] The atrial fibrillation ceased at 11 pm when the pulse became regular, rate 120/min, temperature 102 [°F; 38.9°C].[37]

The episode of atrial fibrillation lasted some 4 hours, and by the following morning the heart rate had fallen to 96/minute.[32] Moran noted that: 'A man feels pretty rotten, I imagine when he fibrillates during pneumonia, but the PM was very good about it.'[20]

Moran composed a medical bulletin which he had countersigned by Bedford and Pulvertaft on 15 December. 'The Prime Minister has been in bed for some days with a cold. A patch of pneumonia has now developed in the left lung. His general condition is as satisfactory as can be expected.'[20]

This statement was not read to the House of Commons by Attlee until the end of Questions on 16 December 1943.[41]

At about 5.30 pm on 15 December 1943 Scadding was informed that orders had come that he was to prepare to move by air in half an hour and that a Lockheed Lodestar was taking off at 11 pm to take him to Tunis.[29] Scadding was flown through the night, arriving in Tunis at 7 am on 16 December. He was conveyed the 7 miles to Carthage in a large American car.[29]

Churchill sent a telegram to Roosevelt: 'Am stranded amid the ruins of Carthage, where you stayed, with fever which has ripened into pneumonia ... I hope soon to send you some of the suggestions for the new commands.'[2] Roosevelt responded on the 17 December 1943: 'I am distressed about the pneumonia, and both Harry [Hopkins] and I plead with you to be good and throw it off rapidly ... The Bible says you must do just what Moran orders, but at this moment I cannot put my finger on the verse and the chapter.'[2]

Churchill later wrote in his account of the Second World War: 'The doctors tried to keep the work away from my bedside, but I defied them.'[2] Nonetheless, as his account makes clear, Churchill did work very hard with others on the plans for OVERLORD with a substantial number of telegrams being exchanged between all those involved, despite him lying 'prostrate'.[2,42]

Meanwhile, in London, Dr (later Sir) John Parkinson (see p. 444) received a telephone call from Anthony Bevir, private secretary to Churchill, who said:

Some friends wished to talk with me about a patient I had seen. No name was given and I agreed to go in the War Office car which was sent. The following message 'Most secret' was brought by the driver: 'You may be wanted to fly tonight to the PM. The car will bring you here: but you would have time to return to pack. A Bevir'.[43]

Parkinson returned with the driver to Whitehall. There Bevir explained that the Prime Minister after his recent Tehran and Cairo conferences had been very tired. Five days ago he had a feverish cold and since had a pneumonic condition (the opposite side to his attack of some months ago). Temperature 100 (°F; 37.8°C) and later 102 (°F; 38.9°C). He was in a villa near Carthage, and with Lord Moran, Dr Scadding (lungs) and Dr (Brigadier) Bedford (heart) in attendance. The patient's general condition was good but the last report of Lord Moran said the heart was irregular and gave him as much anxiety as the lungs. This led to Parkinson's opinion being sought by

Cabinet ministers because he had seen Churchill before. During most of this conversation Marshall was present. He had been invited to Downing Street also to examine Mrs Churchill, who was flying to North Africa that night.[43]

Clement Attlee, Deputy Prime Minister, and Anthony Eden, Foreign Secretary, joined Parkinson and Marshall.[43] Attlee briefly outlined the position and asked about Scadding. Marshall said he was excellent and had worked and written upon pneumonia. Then he asked Parkinson about Bedford, who said he was first-rate and that his name was well known in the United States and Canada.[43] Marshall explained that second attacks of streptococcal pneumonia were in general relatively favourable. Eden thanked Parkinson and Marshall for their 'disinterested advice' and were informed that no public announcement was to be made. As they were not asked, Parkinson and Marshall said nothing, though privately they both thought something should be announced, perhaps from North Africa.[43]

John Colville (formerly Assistant Private Secretary to Churchill) wrote in his diary that: 'On December 15th, 1943 ... I received an urgent summons to return to No. 10 in uniform [he was a pilot in the Royal Air Force Volunteer Reserve] ... I discovered that Churchill was seriously, perhaps mortally, ill with pneumonia at Carthage and that I was to escort Mrs Churchill to his bedside.'[44]

16 December 1943

The first person Scadding met when he arrived at 7 am was Bedford whose house physician (junior doctor) he had been thirteen years earlier.[29] Bedford told Scadding that they had been summoned from Egypt at Moran's request.'[29] Moran recorded that: 'Scadding arrives tonight. To placate the Cabinet, I had asked the people at Cairo to send him.'[20] In fact, as Scadding wrote in 1993: 'I arrived early in the morning of that day.'[29] Martin reported to his wife following Scadding's arrival: 'We have quite an assembly of medical talent.'[19]

In London Parkinson was telephoned by Leslie Rowan, Private Secretary to Churchill, at 8.15 am and asked about auricular (atrial) fibrillation.[43] He explained its nature. Rowan asked Parkinson whether Churchill had suffered from it previously when Parkinson saw him.[43] He had not.[43] Parkinson explained that he and Marshall wished to raise another issue verbally.[43] At 10.15 am Rowan telephoned again and asked if Parkinson would come and speak to the Deputy PM (Attlee) on this matter, which he did.[43] Parkinson explained that he and Marshall felt it was unwise to postpone any longer the public announcement of the PM's illness, especially now that auricular (atrial) fibrillation was mentioned as a complication. Attlee said at once that it had now been so decided following a bulletin (the first) received this morning from North Africa, which he read to Parkinson and which he was about to communicate to the House [of Commons]. Parkinson agreed that it seemed 'exactly right', and took his leave.[43]

Henry 'Chips' Channon MP described the scene in his diary (16 December):

At the end of Questions, Attlee rose and in his usual monotonous tone announced that the Prime Minister was ill, and that pneumonia had set in in his left lung. The House, taken completely by surprise, gasped, for the immediate and important eventualities which this may mean occurred to everybody. A few minutes later I saw Anthony Eden and John Anderson [Chancellor of the Exchequer], the two rival claimants to the succession, deep in grave conversation in a lobby.[45]

Attlee's statement read:

The House will be sorry to learn that the Prime Minister is in this condition. It will be the desire of us all that we should send our best wishes for his recovery. I may add that highly qualified specialists are in attendance. The House will observe that the bulletin is signed not only by Lord Moran but also by Brigadier Bedford and Lieutenant Colonel Pulvertaft, who are Consulting Physician and Director of Pathology respectively to the Middle East Forces. I can assure the House that every modern facility is available on the spot.[45]

A statement was also issued from 10 Downing Street at 7pm: 'The Prime Minister has had a good night. There is some improvement in his condition.'[41]

Parkinson was asked to see Mrs Churchill, whose departure by plane had been postponed for operational reasons.[43] Mrs Churchill received Parkinson in her bedroom and told him about her proposed journey, and asked him about auricular fibrillation.[43] Parkinson explained its nature, 'not dangerous but serious, a not uncommon complication of pneumonia, adding some risk naturally'.[43] 'Was it the sort of thing people used to go to Nauheim for?' Mrs Churchill asked.[43] Nauheim baths were 'effervescent' and named after Bad Nauheim, 22 miles from Frankfurt Am Main, Germany. Parkinson explained that treatment with digitalis was necessary and that the complication might lengthen the illness and convalescence; 'one had to think in weeks'.[43] Asked about Bedford, Parkinson said: 'No one could be better.'[43]

Due to a thick blanket of fog all the airfields close to London were out of action by the afternoon, so at teatime Mrs Churchill, Miss Hamblin (private secretary),[46] and Colville set off for Lyneham in Wiltshire, a 4-hour journey, where the airfield was still clear.[47] The original plan had been to use a heated aircraft, but an hour before take-off a fault was discovered and instead they had to travel in an unheated Liberator (AL 514), which left at 11.30 pm. There were no seats, but some rugs and RAF blankets had been placed on the floor.[47] Colville wrote in his diary that the party spent most of the night sitting up, talking, playing backgammon and drinking coffee as Mrs Churchill could not sleep.[44] It was still dark on 17 December when they landed at Gibraltar. After breakfast they took off again for Tunis.[44]

According to Pulvertaft, the whole resources of the Army, Navy and Air Force had failed to locate Colonel Buttle.[33] He was, in fact in Tunis and on his way to Italy. He arrived, covered in mud, having had a terrible flight in vile weather in a Mosquito.[33] Had he brought the penicillin? 'Obviously, Bulgy [Pulvertaft's nickname], old man,' he said.[33] Macmillan was relieved that: 'At last a Colonel Buttle – the great M. & B. [sulfonamide] specialist – arrived from Italy. He is an expert on how to give the stuff. He seems clever, determined, rather gauche and rude – just the chap we need.'[35] Macmillan begged Buttle to be firm with Churchill and forbid telegrams or visitors.[35] However, Pulvertaft records that although Churchill took an enormous fancy to Buttle, he (Buttle) insisted on flying back that evening to Italy. 'There's a war on there.'[33]

Bedford confirmed that:

Col Buttle arrived from Cairo bringing a supply of penicillin which was not then available in the Middle East forces ... None of the physicians present had ever given penicillin and as we knew that his previous pneumonia had responded well to sulfonamides, it was decided not to experiment with an unknown remedy but to increase the dosage of sulfadiazine.[37]

The dose of sulfadiazine was increased from 1.5 g 4-hourly to 2 g 4-hourly at 2.30 pm.

It is probable that Bedford was referring to the *systemic* use of penicillin as Pulvertaft had experience of its topical use and it is likely Buttle had as well. Penicillin first became available in very limited quantities in the Middle East in August 1942.[48] Pulvertaft, who played the most important role in both trialling and producing the drug in the Middle East, had reported its use up to March 1943 in *The Lancet* in September 1943 as local treatment for infected wounds, with beneficial results in several patients.[49] In this paper, Pulvertaft also noted that the calcium salt of penicillin had been given intrathecally to two patients, with 'severe reactions', though the clinical details of these two patients are not provided. Among the fifteen case reports in this paper, penicillin was instilled into the cavity of a brain abscess in one patient. There is no mention of systemic treatment with penicillin in any patient in this series.

Churchill wrote to his wife: 'Although yesterday we had a new complication in some heart flutterings, I am able to say today that there is a quite definite improvement at all points and by all tests. My own feeling is that I am at the top of the hill.'[30] This is confirmed by Randolph and Sarah when they wrote to their mother: 'Papa had an excellent night and his condition is much improved.'[30] In a similar vein, Martin noted in his diary, 'PM distinctly better.'[21] Macmillan also recorded that, 'P.M. much better today ... The experts seem to think he is through the crisis.'[35] Macmillan saw Churchill before returning to Algiers. 'He was cheerful, though rather weak.'[35]

A further medical bulletin was issued and signed by Moran, Bedford and Pulvertaft, 'The Prime Minister has had a good night. There is some improvement in his general condition.'

Pulvertaft recalled his time in Carthage:

I spent only a fortnight in that millionaire villa; it was a bewildering experience and what I saw was of course greatly distorted by the ominous likelihood of disaster and death. What impressed me most about Churchill was his capacity for instant and apparently exclusive concentration on the interest of the moment. In my case it was haematology; and he focussed on all the minutiae, technique, the differential diagnosis – a most embarrassing searchlight. He was, at first, most unwilling to accept me at all; once accepted it was very difficult to disengage myself. He was incapable of light conversation. Each sentence was as carefully constructed as a paragraph from Gibbon, of whom I was constantly reminded. But it was quite spontaneous and the devastating criticisms and comments were, however polished, instantaneous.[33]

17 December 1943

Bedford recorded that Churchill's temperature was falling.[37] Moran discontinued sulfadiazine;[20] the last dose was at 2.30 pm on 17 December. The medical bulletin stated: 'There has been no spread of the pneumonia, and the improvement in the Prime Minister's general condition has been maintained.'[20]

Colville records that he and Mrs Churchill landed at 3 pm in Tunis being met by a large party including Sarah Churchill, Tommy Thompson, Martin and Tedder. Churchill himself recalls: 'One morning [presumably one afternoon] Sarah was absent from her chair … I was about to ask for my box of telegrams … when in she walked with her mother. I had no idea that my wife was flying out from England to join me.'[2] This was because Clementine Churchill had asked Sarah not to tell her father: 'I am flying to you tonight … I am telling you this so that you are warned in advance, but on no account tell your father before I arrive as details of the journey may cause him anxiety.'[30]

Mrs Churchill informed her daughter Mary (based on second-hand information) that because Churchill felt so well ('happy as a lark') on the morning before her arrival, he had begun to smoke again. She quoted Moran as stating that it is not so bad for Churchill as it would be for most patients.[47]

Churchill also sent for Colville, 'and I found instead of a recumbent invalid a cheerful figure with a large cigar and a whisky and soda in his hand'.[44]

Clementine Churchill records that: 'After my arrival I stayed with him until six, when he slept for two hours and I rested too. I then had dinner with him.'[47] At 11 pm Moran came in to say goodnight to Churchill and intimated he wanted Mrs Churchill, Sarah and Randolph to leave so Churchill could sleep. However, when Mrs Churchill made attempts to go to bed, Churchill would not let her go and 'showed no signs of fatigue'.[47]

It is noteworthy that Bedford recorded that when Mrs Churchill arrived on 17 December 'at once a more orderly atmosphere prevailed in the villa with regular meals and a noticeable improvement in morale'.[37] Bedford also recorded that against his wishes, Randolph Churchill entered the sick room that evening smoking a cigar and carrying two glasses of whisky.[37]

At 1 am in the morning as she was passing Churchill's door, Mrs Churchill observed that his light was on and the night nurse suggested she should join Churchill, who was enjoying beef tea and 'feeling very cheerful'.[47]

18 December 1943

Bedford 'was not entirely surprised' that after Churchill's consumption of whisky the previous day that he 'was summoned at 3.30 am to find a second paroxysm of fibrillation, though thanks to full digitalisation, the heart rate was only 100/minute. Regular rhythm returned the next day when the patient was much better, temperature normal, pulse regular, 80/minute, blood pressure 130/70 mmHg, though signs of consolidation at the left base persisted.'[37]

Moran himself recorded that Churchill fibrillated for an hour and a half and that the episode did not distress Churchill as it did the first time.[20] Moran recorded further that: 'After six days' fever the temperature is normal, but when I suggested to the P.M. that there was no longer any necessity for a daily blood count he demurred.'[20] Churchill had insisted every day that he be told not only the total number of white cells, but the percentage of the various kinds.[20] Bedford reported that each morning Churchill scrutinised his blood counts, remarking that he wished his armies were doing as well as his leucocytes to combat the enemy.[37]

Mrs Churchill joined Churchill for breakfast at 8.30 am. When she entered her husband's room, Moran was there and explained that Churchill had suffered another attack of atrial fibrillation.[47]

Brooke landed at Tunis at 1.45 pm and was first briefed by Moran. He then saw Churchill, who informed him that he would be promoted to Field Marshal on 1 January 1944.[22] Churchill told Brooke that his temperature had returned to normal, but that his heart was now the trouble. Churchill was keen to hear all the details about Brooke's visit to Italy. In his diary Brooke states that he told Churchill nothing about the depressing impressions he had gained in Italy as Churchill 'would only want to rush into some solution which would probably make matters worse'. They then settled the details about military Command. Churchill had definitely decided that 'Jumbo' Wilson should be Supreme Commander Mediterranean.[22]

Churchill then instructed Brooke to get Martin to draft the wire to Roosevelt to that effect.[22] Churchill was very upset when Brooke informed him he was off in the morning as he was hoping he would stay for a few days. After dinner that evening Brooke came to bid Churchill goodbye. Mrs Churchill was sitting on the bed and Randolph was also there. 'He was in very good form, but objecting to having to spend a week in bed before going on to Marrakesh for a fortnight's recuperation.'[22]

Churchill sent a telegram to Roosevelt: 'Thank you so much for your telegram. I have hearkened unto the voice of Moran and made good progress, but I am fixed here for another week.'[2] Churchill also explained to Roosevelt that he had given much thought to remodelling the commands in consultation with Eisenhower, Alexander, Tedder and Brooke and would now place before Roosevelt the proposals.[2] Macmillan wrote in his diary: 'I judge that he [Churchill] is recovering, because telegrams are beginning to arrive – some rather disturbing!!'[35]

Bedford was outside his own command and recognized that Major General Ernest Cowell, Director of Medical Services of the Allied Armies which invaded North Africa, must be aware of his presence.[37] 'I was not under anyone's orders, but realised that secrecy and security were imperative, as the Prime Minister was generally supposed to be in Cairo. I pointed out to Lord Moran that we might well need help in the way of more nurses or medical supplies, and eventually Moran agreed to my calling.'[37] Bedford called on Colonel Spencer Cox, the Assistant Director Medical Services, who was very glad to see him and to tell him that General Cowell wished to offer all necessary medical help.[37] Bedford was able to send a message of thanks and to add that all was going well.[37]

19 December 1943

Grey-Turner wrote in his diary, 'Better weather today, though the gale still blows.'[28]

Brooke prepared to fly to Gibraltar in the Liberator which had flown Mrs Churchill to Tunis. But before doing so he had breakfast with Moran, who told him the PM had had a good night, that he could now be considered as safe from pneumonia, but that his heart was the only danger.[22] He had had during the last few days two goes of heart flutter with a pulse of 130, and that as a result of such a flutter a clot might form that would affect his brain. He must therefore be kept quiet, but was proving troublesome![22]

While he waited to take off Brooke also recorded that it was a 'very wild blustery day' at the airfield.[22]

Clementine Churchill reported to her daughter Mary that Churchill had, 'consented not to smoke, and to drink only weak whisky and soda'. She also commented that while Churchill enjoyed his lunch and dinner, his appetite was not very good.[47]

After tea, Grey-Turner was invited to the White House to see a film and 'had a talk with Lord Moran', who was writing a report on the PM's illness, possibly for the King, Grey-Turner surmised.[50] Subsequently, he had a long talk with Bedford who suggested that Churchill had 'had a fairly narrow squeak, and he [Bedford] didn't seem too happy about Churchill's health in the future'.[28]

20 December 1943

Moran wrote in *Struggle for Survival* that: 'Now that the P.M. is beginning to be convalescent he is very difficult – on two occasions he got quite out of hand … he has been savaging Bedford and Scadding, who know their job and have been helpful'.[20] This account has been challenged by Scadding: 'I did not keep a diary of these events, but I am sure that I should not have forgotten the experience of being "savaged" by Churchill.'[29] Scadding's recollection is that the conversation recorded by Moran did occur but without the emotional overtones. He was of the view that Moran's account of it was unfair to Churchill, 'representing him as being discourteously overbearing'.[29] Scadding explained many patients with heavy responsibilities demand to be told the evidence on which doctors gave their advice.[29] 'Bedford and I made the usual replies, in which Moran supported us; but the suggestion that he had to rescue us from Churchill's rage must be, to say the least, exaggerated.'[29]

Mrs Churchill also reported that Churchill was 'much better and in very good spirits'.[47] The Churchills breakfasted, lunched and dined together in his bedroom and had 'lovely talks'.[47] The last dose of digitalis was administered at 10 am.

As the Avro York in its standard UK camouflage could have suggested to Luftwaffe reconnaissance aircraft that Churchill was in Tunis, a cover plan was devised in which a VIP villa was rented and ostentatiously guarded by British troops on the outskirts of Cairo at Helwan.[24] As a part of this plan, Churchill's Avro York was despatched back to Cairo West with no attempt to conceal its arrival. The Axis (Germany, Italy, Japan and their allies) press and radio promptly reported that Churchill was in Cairo![24]

In fact, the Avro York's only passenger was Scadding.[24] Scadding later wrote that he had the privilege of returning in the Avro York 'by day ... sitting at Churchill's desk in his comfortable chair ... I felt that I was getting the VIP treatment, especially as my orders were to report to the Commander in Chief, British Troops in Egypt, in Cairo, and refuse to answer questions from anyone else.'[29] Having carried out these orders, Scadding went back to Fayid and continued his 'humdrum function in charge of the medical division of No 19 General Hospital'.[29]

Churchill arranged for Wing Commander Collins and Squadron Leader Fraser, who was shortly to succeed him as captain of the Avro York, to return to Carthage from Cairo in time for a planned Christmas party (see below).[51]

21 December 1943

Mrs Churchill reported that the night nurse had informed her that Churchill had had a very good night.[47] She had been unable to see her husband as Churchill had sent for Patrick Kinna to dictate a paper.[47] Moran reported that Churchill sat by his bed for an hour today.[20] Churchill's recovery is also attested to by Macmillan. 'The P.M. is recovering – rather too rapidly!'[35] Macmillan explained that Randolph Churchill was getting irritated with the French, 'which is bad for his [Churchill's] health, and looks like leading to much trouble'.[35] This was confirmed by Colville: 'Winston almost had apoplexy and Lord Moran was seriously perturbed.'[44]

When Mrs Churchill returned to the villa after a sightseeing tour of the Tunis battlefields with among others Moran, she found her husband sitting up in bed looking 'very pink and mischievous' after a hot bath which he had taken with Bedford's consent.[47] Clementine added when writing to her children: 'Your father has taken a great deal of trouble to seduce Dr. Bedford, and Lord Moran is quite jealous.'[47]

22–4 December 1943

Macmillan noted in his diary that Churchill was telephoning him in Algiers almost hourly.[35] Martin recorded: 'PM out walking on the terrace.'[21] The medical bulletin, signed by Moran and Bedford, read: 'The Prime Minister continues to make steady progress.' Mrs Churchill recorded, 'very good progress'.[47]

Colville wrote in his diary on 24 December that: 'There was a great influx of Generals and others to discuss Operation SHINGLE ...'.[44] Bedford also recalled the assembling of senior military, naval and air force commanders and others at Carthage, including Generals Eisenhower, Spaatz, Alexander, Maitland Wilson and Gale, Admiral Cunningham, Air Marshal Tedder and Harold Macmillan.[37] As a result, his task of protecting Churchill from too many visitors became more difficult, but Generals Brooke and Alexander were most helpful and Bedford was able to discuss the Prime Minister's illness and the imperative need for rest and convalescence if or when he recovered as was now expected.[37] Despite Bedford's best efforts, Churchill rose from his sickbed to hold a conference in the dining room.[44]

An X-ray still showed an opacity at the left base, though this was less than in the previous film.

Christmas Day 1943

Churchill began the day with a 2-hour conference involving British and US senior military staff in his bedroom. It was then time to celebrate Christmas. Macmillan flew in from Algiers, arriving at 1.30 pm. He drove to the White House and found Churchill and assembled guests sitting down to a magnificent Christmas dinner, with soup, turkey, plum pudding and champagne![35] Mrs Churchill wrote to daughter Mary: 'We had a most interesting Christmas luncheon party with all these notabilities assembled, and your father at the end made a charming speech about his distinguished guests and their new functions. This was his first meal outside his bedroom.'[47]

Macmillan recalls that Churchill presided at the festive gathering clothed in a padded silk Chinese dressing gown decorated with blue and gold dragons (Plate 11)[35] and Commander Thompson recalls the striking pair of bedroom slippers which bore Churchill's initials in gold across each foot.[51] Churchill proposed a series of toasts 'in the best Russian style, with a short speech in each case'.[35] Macmillan was gratified that Churchill proposed his toast 'in most eulogistic terms'.[35] Martin also noted in his diary: 'Festive lunch with toasts à la Russe.'[21]

Beasley[52] states that Churchill's son Randolph also proposed a toast: 'Ladies and gentlemen, let us rise and drink to my father's health and his remarkable recovery, which is entirely due (turning first to Lord Moran and then to Dr. Bedford) to M & B.' As Churchill himself expressed similar sentiments on some other occasions,[53] and given the nature of the other speeches made by Churchill after the Christmas Dinner, it would seem more probable that it was Churchill himself who made the toast. This is confirmed in a letter Moran wrote to his wife, quoted by Lovell: 'P.M. in great form. Proposed health of Bedford and me (M & B). I replied that when in difficulty we had another consultant at hand, himself (much appreciated by everyone who knows his interfering nature).'[32]

Colville wrote in his diary that in the evening there was a large cocktail party hosted by Sarah Churchill which Churchill attended 'as if in perfect health'.[44] This merged into a cold, stand-up dinner and 'everybody finished the day feeling the merrier for Christmas'.[44] According to Mitchell, 'Churchill was in sparkling form, working the room in his dressing gown and slippers.'[24]

26 December 1943

Colville noted that 'the P.M. dined in the dining-room for the first time'.[44] Moran had agreed that Churchill could leave Carthage after Christmas but insisted that he must have three weeks' convalescence. 'And where could be better than the lovely villa at Marrakesh, where the President and I had stayed after Casablanca a year before?' wrote Churchill later.[54] In fact, the decision to leave Carthage was also taken for security reasons. 'It was also thought that I had been long enough at Carthage to be located.'[54]

A briefing conference for the flight to Marrakech was held. Moran and other medical advisors believed Churchill's plane should not fly above 6,000 ft for medical reasons. However, Tedder was concerned that the Avro York, a four-engined aircraft strange to the area, would be assumed by Royal Navy convoys to be a Luftwaffe Focke-Wulf Condor with hostile intentions if it flew over the Mediterranean at 6,000 ft. An inland route was chosen by Wing Commander Collins, with as an additional precaution a BOAC

Liberator aircraft flying ahead to radio back the weather conditions found. Tedder confirmed the Captain's choice but decreed that Air Commodore Kelly MC, Principal Medical Officer of the RAF in North Africa, should accompany Churchill with a portable oxygen kit.

Kelly arrived at the White House at midday with a portable oxygen apparatus to instruct the Prime Minister in its use. Kelly later recalled that when he arrived Churchill was propped up in bed, surrounded by documents. Churchill asked Kelly to explain how the oxygen apparatus worked.[55] Following the explanation, Churchill asked Kelly: 'Will you do a trial run on me now?' which Kelly did.[55]

Bedford left Tunis with two nurses, Miss Clark and Mrs Haselden, at noon, bound for Cairo.[34]

Medical Aspects

In a press communiqué issued on 30 December to all newspapers before Churchill left for Marrakech and which Elizabeth Layton remembers typing,[53] Churchill wrote:

> I had planned to visit the Italian front as soon as the conferences were over, but on December 11 I felt so tired out that I had to ask General Eisenhower for a few days rest before proceeding. This was accorded me in the most generous manner. The next day came the fever, and the day after, when the photographs [X-ray] showed that there was a shadow on one of my lungs, I found that everything had been foreseen by Lord Moran. Excellent nurses and the highest medical authorities in the Mediterranean arrived from all quarters as if by magic. This admirable M and B, from which I did not suffer any inconvenience, was used at the earliest moment, and after a week's fever the intruders were repulsed. I hope all our battles will be equally well conducted. I feel a good deal better than at any time since leaving England, though of course a few weeks in the sunshine are needed to restore my physical strength.[56]

In the account recorded in *Closing the Ring*,[2] Churchill added: 'Although Lord Moran records that he judged that the issue was at one time in doubt, I did not share his view. I did not feel so ill in this attack as I had the previous February.'[2]

Churchill's illness was characterized by fever that lasted six days, the development of left lower lobe pneumonia (confirmed radiologically), and two episodes of atrial fibrillation lasting 4 hours and 1½ hours respectively. A total of 26 g of sulfadiazine was given over four days for the pneumonia and fibrillation was treated with digitalis leaf for five days.[34,37]

The overall mortality from pneumococcal pneumonia in the early 1940s in those aged 70 years or over (Churchill was 69) was 40 per cent even with sulfonamides.[57] Furthermore, as Churchill's pneumonia was complicated by atrial fibrillation, the morbidity and mortality would be higher. The association between pneumonia and atrial fibrillation has long been recognized. Acute bacterial pneumonia stresses the heart by increasing myocardial oxygen demand at a time when oxygenation is compromised by ventilation-perfusion mismatch.[58] Pneumonia also raises circulating concentrations of inflammatory cytokines, which suppress ventricular function and lead to cardiac arrhythmias, predominantly atrial fibrillation.[58] Atrial fibrillation develops in up to 7 per cent of cases overall,[59] though 4 per cent is more typical,[58] and occurs predominantly in elderly patients.[59]

Churchill was managed in a private villa by Moran with the practical assistance of two nurses and with the advice of a cardiologist (Bedford) and respiratory physician (Scadding), as well as a clinical pathologist (Pulvertaft). Buttle, though an expert on antibacterial drugs, spent only a few hours in Carthage because he believed he had more pressing priorities on the battlefield. Scadding had extensive clinical experience of using sulfonamides and Bedford had the necessary expertise to optimize digitalis therapy, which he initiated. Churchill recovered from serious illness due to their combined efforts.

There was clear evidence by 1943 that sulfadiazine was superior to sulfathiazole and sulfapyridine in treating pneumococcal pneumonia.[57] In addition, sulfadiazine was also generally preferred as nausea, vomiting and other central nervous system side effects were much less. In addition, sulfadiazine-induced mechanical obstruction of the kidneys by crystalline concretions was also much less frequent and more amenable to control by alkalinization.[57] Conventionally, an initial bolus dose of sulfadiazine 4 g was given, to be followed at 4-hour intervals with 1 g for six doses. The dosage schedule was then changed to 1 g every 6 hours and is so continued until the patient's temperature has been normal for 72 hours.[60,61] Moran does not appear to have received, or at least followed, advice as regards dosing from his US Army colleagues who would be very familiar with the drug.

At the time of Churchill's pneumonia in December 1943, systemic treatment with penicillin was still very limited. This explains why as Bedford[37] and Scadding[21] have recalled there was a consensus against the idea of trying penicillin on Churchill. At that time, the only available preparation was a yellow injectable solution, of which the usual dose was about 50,000 units. Scadding wrote: 'I recall commenting that our patient was progressing well on accepted treatment, and that one does not make therapeutic experiments on the Prime Minister.'[21]

Although we know that digitalis leaf was prescribed by Bedford, we do not know which of the two most likely preparations available (digitalis folia BP/digitalis USP; digitalis pulverate BP and USP) on the market were given as Moran obtained supplies from the US Army in Tunis. Digitalis leaf was first prescribed for Churchill on 15 December 1943 and a total of 16 grains were prescribed.[34] These doses are in keeping with clinical practice at the time: tablets containing 1 grain of the powdered leaf were given either twice, three times or four times a day, according to pulse rate control.[62]

Churchill dictated a press communiqué to the people of Britain in which he stated that as he had with him a 'highly efficient nucleus staff and am in full daily correspondence with London ... I have not at any time had to relinquish my part in the direction of affairs, and there has been not the slightest delay in giving the decisions which were required of me. I am now able to transact business fully.'[56]

At the outset of Churchill's illness, Moran noted on the 11 December that Churchill did not seem to have the energy to read the usual telegrams.[20] Despite his illness, Churchill continued to work 'at an alarming pace' from his bed as Churchill's stenographer recalled to Gilbert.[19] On 14 December Macmillan recorded in his diary that Churchill had asked him to discuss with General Wilson the organization of the Command and write him a report.[35] Macmillan records that despite Churchill's high temperature, he dealt with the matter and wrote a long telegram to the Cabinet about it.[35]

Certainly by 18 December, Churchill explained to Roosevelt that he had given much thought to remodelling the commands in consultation with Eisenhower, Alexander, Tedder and Brooke and would now place before Roosevelt the proposals.[2] It is clear that although his doctors 'protested about the volume of work being done by the PM – but to no avail,'[19] Churchill continued to work very hard with others on the plans for *Overlord* (Battle of Normandy) with a substantial number of telegrams being exchanged between all those involved, despite him lying 'prostrate'.[2] This is confirmed by Ismay who must have seen much if not all of the output: 'He [Churchill] had been away for two months and had been unwell the whole time. But temperature or no temperature, he had got through more work than most men could do in two years.'[12]

Although Churchill's claim that he did not at any time relinquish his part in the direction of affairs can be accepted, it is incorrect for him to state there was not the slightest delay in giving the decisions which were required. It is remarkable, however, that despite the severity of his illness, he was able to continue to direct the affairs of State from his bed.

Chapter 11

Recuperation in January 1944 in Marrakech

Physical weakness oppressed me at Marrakesh following my illness at Carthage. All my painting tackle had been sent out, but I could not face it[1]

For the first time since his illness began in Carthage, Churchill dressed in his Royal Air Force uniform (Honorary Air Commodore of 615 (County of Surrey) Fighter Squadron, Royal Auxiliary Air Force) and Clementine Churchill 'very sweetly fastened the belt for him'.[2] Churchill then inspected a 'magnificent guard of the Coldstream'.[1] As Churchill later recalled: 'I had not realized how much I had been weakened by my illness. I found it quite a difficulty to walk along the ranks and climb into the motor-car.'[1] Lord Moran (see p. 443), Churchill's personal physician, confirmed that when Churchill inspected the guard: 'It was only very slowly and rather hesitatingly that he passed along the ranks. I was relieved when they helped him into his car.'[3] Churchill was no doubt cheered, however, by the telegram reporting that the German battlecruiser, *Scharnhorst*, had been sunk.

Moran wrote: 'I wondered a little if the P.M. would find himself short of breath in the air after his illness, but the pilot assured me we need not go higher than five thousand feet … I knew there was nothing for it but to await developments. However, none came.'[3]

Churchill, his wife Clementine, daughter Sarah, Moran and Sawyers (Churchill's valet) left Tunis at 8.15 am on 27 December 1943 in the Avro York *Ascalon*;[4] Air Commodore Kelly, Principal Medical Officer of the RAF in North Africa, also accompanied Churchill with the oxygen apparatus (see p. 115).[5] After breakfasting, Churchill read papers for a while, then rested on his bed.[6]

John Colville (Assistant Private Secretary) and General Leslie Hollis (Senior Assistant Secretary to the War Cabinet) had flown ahead in the BOAC Liberator which was to provide advance information on the weather to Squadron Leader Mitchell, the navigator of *Ascalon*.

Inspector Thompson, Churchill's bodyguard, reported that 'at each stage of the flight Churchill asked that his pulse be checked and on being told that it was all right he roared, "Of course I am all right! I don't need to be told this! I'm announcing it!"[7] Thompson also reported that for a brief spell Churchill persuaded the pilot to let him take over the controls,[7] though this is not corroborated by others present on the flight.

After some 3½ hours of flying below 6,000 ft, the aircraft approached the main Atlas mountain. Mitchell reported that his own meteorological observations, strengthened by the Liberator's radioed reports, made it clear that the Taza Pass was in deep cloud.[8] The Liberator had gone through perilously close to the high ground on its passage.[8] The decision had to be made whether to turn north and come out over the Mediterranean or to climb for 15 minutes and clear this section of the Middle Atlas range at 11,500 ft. The pilot chose the latter option and so informed Churchill and the other passengers. Churchill said: 'Don't worry about me, consider the safety of the aircraft first.'[9]

It is probable that the discussion was not as simple as the pilot coming to a decision and informing Churchill of his intentions. Kelly reported to Gilbert that Churchill began sending frequent messages to the pilot as to the plane's height and position, and the weather reports received from the Liberator.[6]

> A message came back that the weather was very bad and bumpy. The Prime Minister said: 'If I were not on this aircraft it would be flying at 19,000 ft. It is ridiculous keeping it low, it will crash into the mountains.' He told Sarah [Churchill] to go and tell the captain to go higher, but as he was leaving the cabin he said to her, 'It is my wish but do not give an order'.[6]

There is no corroborating evidence to suggest as Mitchell does that Kelly 'nearly had a fit' at the proposal that they fly at a higher altitude.[8]

Churchill later wrote: 'in order to keep under six thousand feet [it] seemed to me an unfair proposition for the others in the plane. I therefore sent for the pilot and told him to fly at least two thousand feet above the highest mountain ... Lord Moran agreed.' Moran also noted this conversation.[3]

As the Avro York prepared to climb to 10,500 ft, Kelly prepared the apparatus and began to give Churchill oxygen.[6] 'I set the oxygen at about 10,000 ft. We climbed gradually. The Prime Minister's colour became perfectly normal, and he went on taking oxygen. When we were at 10,500 ft.

I pushed the regulator up higher.'[6] On reaching 12,000 ft, and with Kelly sitting at the end of Churchill's bed, *Ascalon* entered a cloudless region.

Moran was content when he saw that Churchill was 'quite happy playing with his oxygen apparatus' and fell asleep in his chair.[3] The aircraft then descended slowly to 5,000 ft, whereupon Churchill wanted to discontinue the oxygen, but Kelly advised Churchill to continue it as he was afraid that if the oxygen was discontinued suddenly, it might have a bad effect on Churchill's heart.[6] At 1 pm the oxygen was turned off, and, 10 minutes later, Churchill and Kelly had a very good lunch. 'The PM was in great form,' Kelly recalled later.[6]

Ascalon landed at Marrakech at 4 pm and Churchill made his way to Villa Taylor, built by a wealthy American, Mrs Moses Taylor. Mrs Taylor used the estate as a winter retreat until the Second World War, when it served for a time as the American headquarters in Morocco. From its Berber tower, it commanded a magnificent view over the rooftops of Marrakech to the plain and the mountains beyond. Commander Thompson RN, Churchill's aide-de-camp, later described the villa:

> The house and garden had been created in local style, with a central courtyard, orange trees, and fountains, and the interior decoration, with its lavish use of painted wood, mosaics, and rich furnishings, was exotic in the extreme. The tiled bathrooms were striking and the baths were sunk into the floor and were fed by water gushing from the mouth of lions.[10]

Churchill had stayed there with President Roosevelt after the Casablanca Conference in 1943.

Inspector Thompson wrote that on arrival Churchill was very tired and went straight to bed.[7] Churchill appeared for dinner, however, as Kelly recalled later.[6] As Churchill was leaving the dining room, he put his hand on Kelly's shoulder and said: 'Kelly, you have rendered me a great personal service today, I am very grateful to you.'[6]

28 December 1943

Churchill sent the following signal to the Medical Directorate, Middle East Forces marked 'Most Secret' personal to Brigadier Bedford from Colonel Warden (Churchill's code name): 'Perfect journey – no ill effects although we flew at 12,000 feet.'[5,11] Lord Beaverbrook, Lord Privy Seal, arrived unannounced but expected.[4]

New Year Celebrations

Generals Eisenhower and Montgomery arrived for a 'pow-wow' on 30 December.[12] Both joined the Churchills for an early dinner on New Year's Eve, so that Montgomery could go to bed. Punch was brewed, Churchill made a little speech, the clerks, typists and some of the servants appeared and they sang 'Auld Lang Syne'.[4] Colville was linked arm-in-arm with Montgomery and the American barman.[4]

Churchill, using his codename, Colonel Warden, sent a Most Secret personal telegram to Roosevelt:

I am so sorry about your influenza. I earnestly hope you will defer to McIntyre's [the White House physician] advice and show that attitude of submission to the medical faculty which you have so sedulously enjoined on me. Flower Villa is perfect. The doctors want me to stay here for the next three weeks. The weather is bright though cool. The cook is a marvel. We go for picnics to the mountains. Last night Eisenhower was with us on his way to you and I had a long talk with him. Montgomery is here now on his way to England. I think we have a fine team and they certainly mean to pull together ... Accept all my best wishes for a New Year which will not only be marked by triumph but will open wider doors to our future work together.[13]

Clementine Churchill reported to her family that Churchill was 'gaining strength every day', though Churchill was disappointed that his recovery was slow.[12] 'When in the end he is quite well, the slowness of his convalescence may be a blessing in disguise, as it may make him a little more careful when he has to travel.'[12] A similar assessment was made by Moran.[3] Specifically, according to his wife, Churchill was not staying in bed 'more than in normal life'[12] and was also enjoying the sunshine (Plate 13), but the air was 'sharp and cold'.[12] Commander Thompson recalled later: 'Churchill worked in bed in the mornings; whenever possible they went off for a picnic lunch and spent the afternoon in the foothills of the Atlas Mountains.'[14]

Churchill wrote: 'Physical weakness oppressed me at Marrakesh following my illness at Carthage. All my painting tackle had been sent out, but I could not face it.'[1]

On 31 December, Churchill told his wife, 'I am not strong enough to paint.'[12] However, his energy must have returned as Commander Thompson later recalled that Churchill and Margaret Nairn, the wife of the Vice-Consul, an accomplished artist, often painted together.[14]

Churchill wrote: 'I could hardly walk at all. Even tottering from the motorcar to a picnic lunch in lovely weather amid the foothills of the Atlas was limited to eighty or a hundred yards. I passed eighteen hours out of the twenty-four prone. I never remember such extreme fatigue and weakness in body.'[1] There is support for this incapacity. Moran and Commander Thompson both described how on one such picnic Margaret Nairn and Diana Cooper (née Lady Diana Manners; wife of the British Representative with the French Committee of National Liberation and from 1944 Ambassador to France) used a tablecloth folded like a rope and placed it around Churchill's middle and hauled him unceremoniously up the plateau. John Wilson (Moran's son on leave from the Royal Navy) and Inspector Thompson dragged Churchill up the last few yards, while Moran pushed from behind and another member of the party carried his cigar.[3,14]

Churchill continued his recollections:

On the other hand, every temptation, inducement, exultation, and to some extent compulsion, to relax and lie down presented itself in the most seductive form. The Taylor villa was a perfect haven, lacking nothing that comfort could require, or luxury suggests. I was utterly tired out and here was the most attractive bed of repose, not only offered by gracious hosts, but enjoined by Lord Moran, the President and the War Cabinet.[1]

3–13 January 1944: Meetings with Generals

A chest X-ray was performed on 3 January 1944 which showed no evidence of remaining consolidation, but there was thickening of the pleura along the left axillary line. As Churchill's health improved, he began planning military operations. He became so absorbed in the plans that the picnics had to be cancelled twice.[3]

Generals Gammell, Bedell Smith, Gale and Devers arrived from London on 5 January on their way to theatre. On 7 January, Generals Devers and Bedell Smith returned with General 'Jumbo' Wilson, General Alexander and Admiral John Cunningham to meet Churchill for an Operation SHINGLE (Allied amphibious landing prior to the Battle of Anzio) Conference.[4]

Clementine Churchill wrote to her daughter Mary: 'I think Papa is now really quite himself again. Every day sees an improvement. He simply loves the picnics.'[12] In conversation with Diana Duff Cooper before dinner, she said: 'I never think of after the war. You see, I think Winston will die when it's all over.'[12]

14 January–18 January 1944: Return Home

On Friday, 14 January the Churchill entourage flew to Gibraltar in four planes where the battleship HMS *King George V* was waiting to take the party home. At Gibraltar there was a further SHINGLE Conference.[4] Anxious to reach home with the least delay, Churchill made enquiries about the possibility of a return by air.[14] This was opposed by Moran.[14] The weather deteriorated, however, so Churchill returned by ship escorted by the cruiser HMS *Mauritius*.[14] On the evening before they reached Plymouth Sound Churchill brought all the midshipman into his Map Room and gave them a lecture on the war situation.[14] Shortly before midnight on 17 January the *King George V* dropped anchor in Plymouth Sound, Churchill disembarked and went by King George VI's personal train to London. The Cabinet awaited his arrival at Paddington Station at 10 am.[14]

Sir Alan Lascelles, private secretary to the King, told Harold Nicolson MP that when Churchill had been to see the King that morning Lascelles had met him at the Palace door. Lascelles asked after his health. 'I'm quite all right ... Only I'm a little groggy still on my pins [legs].' Lascelles asked Churchill whether he would like to take the lift. 'Lift,' said Churchill and proceeded to run up the stairs two at a time. When he reached the top, he turned round to Lascelles and cocked a snook.[15] Two hours after arrival at Paddington Churchill was in the House of Commons for Prime Minister's Question Time.

Harold Nicolson MP wrote in his diary:

We were dawdling through Questions and I was idly glancing at my Order Paper when I saw ... a gasp of astonishment pass over the faces of the Labour Party opposite. Suddenly they jumped to their feet and started shouting, waving their papers in the air. We also jumped up and the whole House broke into cheer after cheer while Winston, very pink, rather shy, beaming with mischief, crept along the front bench and flung himself into his accustomed seat. He was flushed with pleasure and emotion, and hardly had he sat down when two large tears began to trickle down his cheeks. He mopped at them clumsily with a huge white handkerchief. A few minutes later he got up to answer questions ... I should like to say that he seemed completely restored to health. But he looked pale when the first flush of pleasure had subsided, and his voice was not quite so vigorous as it had been.[15]

After Churchill had answered Questions, he held a Cabinet meeting in his room at the House leaving at 1.28 pm for lunch with the King at 1.30 pm![4]

19–21 January 1944: Assessment by Dr John Parkinson

Churchill told Colville that his heart was giving him trouble. He ascribed it to indigestion.[4] After Churchill's return from convalescence in Marrakech, Moran telephoned Dr John Parkinson, Churchill's cardiologist, on 21 January about Churchill's latest electrocardiogram taken by the Clinical Research Association, which was said to show a change, and which had been sent to Parkinson that morning.[16] Parkinson informed Moran that it showed only a slight change, and that it should be repeated in the sitting and lying posture. Parkinson agreed to do this at 1 Devonshire Place, Parkinson's consulting room, and screen the heart at the same time.[16]

Churchill came with Moran on 11 February at 9.15 am for Parkinson's assessment. ECGs were taken by Miss Mickleburgh, his technician and secretary, with the patient sitting, then lying.[16] With Moran present, Parkinson examined Churchill by radioscopy and noted that the dome of the right diaphragm was rather flat, a little high and perhaps not moving quite so well as the left.[16] The recent pneumonia had affected the left lower lobe, whereas the pneumonia in February–March 1943 had involved the right lung.[17] There was no cardiac enlargement. Churchill remained at Parkinson's consulting room for some 20 minutes. The BP (blood pressure) was not taken as it was known to be normal.[16] The heart sounds were normal and there were no murmurs. In appearance Churchill's colour was 'a good pink, he looked and sounded as if he felt the burden of his position, but conversed freely and pleasantly'.[16]

Churchill did not complain of any symptoms other than slight flatulence, and said he had felt in general better in the last fortnight.[16] Three weeks ago Churchill experienced more frequent extrasystoles (extra beats) but 'not fibrillation and I felt all right'. Parkinson recorded that Churchill 'can and does lie flat with one or two pillows only and sleeps on his stomach'.[16] 'He gets up at 10.00 am or 11.00 am, takes a customary nap on his bed about teatime, and works evenings till about 2.30 am.' Meanwhile, the ECGs had been developed.[16] 'Lead IV.R [AVR] was perfectly normal. Lead T2 was almost flat (isoelectric) or diphasic or perhaps bifid as once before and change in posture had not affected this. In other respects the electrocardiograms were like those of 1941 and 1942.'[16]

Parkinson told Churchill that 'the electrocardiogram had changed a little, perhaps as a result of the pneumonia or the accompanying fibrillation, or it might be due to no more than the passage of time – two years since the last ECG. However that might be, it had no serious significance.'[16] Parkinson's concluded: 'I would regard his heart as normal for his age (69), and he was fortunate having always a normal blood pressure. To speak freely, he might sometime in the future have a recurrence of the fibrillation; and if so he should not be perturbed, it would not be dangerous or very serious, but would require treatment.'[16] Churchill said at once: 'I would send for him [Lord Moran]. No. I would not be anxious.'[16]

Parkinson hoped that after these experiences Churchill would take more care to retain his health. Churchill claimed that he did avoid physical exertion and hurrying, but he 'must fly'. It was suggested that his flying trips abroad entailed fatiguing work under varying conditions, even though not much physical exertion. His general strength and health were tested by them.[16]

Chapter 12

Pneumonia in August–September 1944 in London

A sudden attack of my former malady with a temperature of between 103 and 104 degrees[1]

At the start of August 1944, Winston Churchill decided that he must undertake a morale-boosting tour of Field Marshal Alexander's Fifth Army in Italy. He also wished to concern himself with two problems of a political nature: the internal Italian situation and Yugoslavia. Rome had been captured by the Allies on 4 June 1944. On 10 August 1944 Florence would be captured. However, despite Churchill's pleas, it had been decided that troops should be moved from Italy to the South of France to advance the Allied Armies in the north. Alexander's Army had been reduced by 7 divisions, some 100,000 men, but Alexander still sought to continue offensive affairs.[1]

Churchill later wrote:

I now decided to go myself to Italy, where many questions could be more easily settled on the spot than by correspondence. It would be a great advantage to see the commanders and the troops from whom so much was being demanded, after so much had been taken … Alexander, though sorely weakened, was preparing his armies for a further offensive. I was anxious to meet Tito [Marshal Tito, Yugoslav communist revolutionary and leader of the Partisans], who could easily come to Italy from the island of Vis, where we were still protecting him … Finally there was the Italian political tangle of which Rome was now the centre.[2]

Churchill had initially intended to visit Alexander at the start of August, but 'the days were so crowded with Cabinet business that my dates receded'.[2]

The Need for Mepacrine

As Lord Moran (see p. 443), Churchill's personal physician, wrote later:

> Now that we are going to Italy in August, there is the question of
> malaria. I had a presentiment that the battle for mepacrine would have
> to be thought all over again. I determined to get my facts right – it
> avoids a massacre. I went for them to Millbank [Army Medical College,
> Millbank, London]. 'Whatever else he does in Italy' they said, 'he must
> take mepacrine as a safeguard against malaria'.[3]

So next morning, 7 August 1944, Moran 'went to the Annexe [No. 10
Annexe, a flat directly above the Cabinet War Rooms] soon after nine o'clock,
knowing by experience that I was likely to find him alone at that hour. When
I had said my piece, he glowered at me. Mepacrine, he was told, made people
quite ill. And, anyway, he thought it was quite unnecessary. I stuck to my
point, leaving him to think it over.'[3]

After Moran had left the Annexe, Churchill telephoned Buckingham
Palace to enquire whether King George VI had taken mepacrine on his
recent tour of Italy. He had not. Unbeknown to Moran, Churchill had sent
a Personal and Top Secret telegram to General Alexander on 3 August 1944:

> What is the danger of malaria if I pay you a visit? Have you much of it
> on your staff? They want me here to eat for a fortnight and thereafter
> apparently continuously for six weeks a ferocious kind of yellow pill
> which I believe is synthetic quinine. Do you all do it out there? Should I
> be in malarious districts? I do not want of course to be laid up just now.
> I will give you firm dates in a day or two. All good wishes. The House
> [of Commons] was most cordial on every occasion when I spoke of your
> affairs yesterday.[4]

General Alexander sent a telegram in response on 4 August also marked
Personal and Top Secret:

> My doctors tell me that these yellow pills do not prevent malaria but
> only suppress it temporarily. They upset some people considerably.
> Whilst I cannot guarantee you immunity from malaria, I think you may
> regard the risk as slight. Neither I nor my staff take pills and we had

virtually no malaria at my Headquarters. I suggest you tell the doctors to keep their pills. If you have Mess wellingtons or mosquito boots, bring them with you for evening wear.[5]

Churchill showed the telegram from Alexander to Moran. Moran explained that during the first two months of the Sicilian campaign the previous year the Army had lost the effective strength of two infantry divisions from malaria.

Those in command agreed that this wastage from malaria could have been avoided, for if mepacrine were taken regularly there was little or no malaria. It was simply a question of discipline, of a drill for the administration of mepacrine. The principle was laid down that commanders would be held personally responsible for the malaria wastage. As for Alex, when he proclaimed to the Prime Minister that neither he nor any of his staff set an example to their men by taking the pills themselves, he may not have known that it was a court-martial offence in the Army in Italy under his command to omit mepacrine drill.[3]

Moran concluded:

General Alexander suggests the doctors keep their pills. I venture to wonder if General Alexander's views on medical matters have the same value as mine on military affairs. The P.M. lost no time in replying to this blast: 'Most immediate. Secret. Telephone message 6th August from the Prime Minister to Lord Moran. In view of your salvo, all surrender unconditionally and hoist the yellow flag'.[3]

Moran commented in his later record: 'After that sally, how could anyone be out of temper?'[3]

Churchill took mepacrine until 12 September when Moran agreed to discontinue the medicine.

10 August 1944: to Italy via Algiers

Churchill requested that Anthony Eden, Foreign Secretary, designate someone from the Foreign Office to go with him to Italy as much of his work would be political. Eden chose his Principal Private Secretary, Pierson Dixon, 'since I knew the work and the P.M. knew my face'.[6] At lunchtime on 10 August Dixon was informed that 'Tonight's the night'.[6] Dixon spent a busy day liquidating his affairs, collecting briefs and getting decisions on a number of outstanding points. He had supper, packed and drove to RAF Northolt at 9.30 pm.[6] 'A delicious warm summer's evening, but the flying bombs are still going strong. We waited about a quarter of an hour in the gathering dusk on the aerodrome, then the P.M. arrived. His aeroplane took off immediately,'[6] and the rest of the entourage, including, Dixon followed in a second Avro York a few minutes later.

Churchill (using the codename Colonel Kent) flew in his usual York, LV 633 *Ascalon*, to Maison Blanche Airport, Algiers and arrived at 8.45 am on 11 August. Churchill was accompanied by Moran, Brigadier Jacob (Military Assistant Secretary to the War Cabinet), Commander Thompson RN (aide-de-camp), Leslie Rowan (Private Secretary), John Peck (Private Secretary), Sawyers his valet and a detective.[7] Duff Cooper, the British representative to the newly formed French Committee of National Liberation, met Churchill at the airport[8] and 'took me to his house, which his wife had made most comfortable'.[2] Churchill was driven to Duff Cooper's villa accompanied by his son, Randolph,[8] who had been injured recently in an aircraft crash. Churchill and Cooper sat talking for about an hour before Churchill took his bath and had lunch.[8] Cooper recorded that Churchill was 'most optimistic about the war in general and on the whole was in excellent form'.[8]

Just before dawn Dixon looked out of the port window of the second York and saw the faint outline of the Rock [Gibraltar] and its signal station.[6] At 10 am the York landed at Maison Blanche. 'This aerodrome is usually a sea of mud, but today it was dry under the hot summer sun. Drove to the Admiral's villa, had breakfast and bath.'[6]

Churchill, Randolph and Duff Cooper were driven back to the aerodrome at about noon.[8] Churchill then flew to Pomigliano Airport, Naples, where he landed at 5.15 pm, wearing a light tropical suit and an enormous sun-helmet.[9] He 'emerged from his plane to find rain falling in torrents – so heavily, indeed, that none of the motorcyclists escorting his car got as far as Naples. Blinded by the downpour two fell off at a level-crossing, and the rest retired with engine trouble.'[9]

Churchill was met at the airport by Harold Macmillan, Minister Resident in the Mediterranean.[10] Macmillan recorded that it was a very hot and thundery afternoon.[10] Churchill was 'installed in the palatial though somewhat dilapidated Villa Rivalta, with a glorious view of Vesuvius and the bay'.[2] Here General Sir Henry Maitland 'Jumbo' Wilson, Supreme Allied Commander in the Mediterranean, explained to Churchill that all arrangements had been made for a conference next morning with Tito.[2] Macmillan joined Churchill for dinner that night, and he considered that the PM looked very tired.[10]

12–13 August 1944: Meetings and Some Relaxation

On 12 August 1940 Macmillan recorded that Tito arrived at noon and a conference took place between Churchill and Tito, at which Dixon was present;[6] this was followed by lunch which Macmillan attended.[10] On the afternoon of 12 August Churchill went out in a motor launch to bathe off the island of Ischia.[6]

Churchill and Dixon visited Capri late morning on 13 August using the motor launch Rear Admiral Morse, Flag Officer Northern Mediterranean, had requisitioned from the Prince of Piedmont, heir to the throne of Italy. Dixon recorded that Churchill was 'in holiday mood' and that after a swim they had a huge lunch in a rustic restaurant.[6] Churchill and Dixon steamed back along the line of an outgoing convoy – American vessels with transport and six escorting British destroyers. The convoy was sailing to the South of France for the invasion starting on 16 August. As they passed each destroyer, Churchill stood up in the prow of the motor launch and saluted.[6]

Further meetings took place between Churchill and Tito later that afternoon [6] and Macmillan and his wife dined with Churchill.[10] Macmillan recorded that Churchill: 'Was in excellent humour, very pleased with the Battle of Normandy. Most of the evening was taken up in the Map Room where the progress of the battle was explained in great detail.'[10]

Churchill wrote later of these days in Naples:

On all these three days at Naples I mingled pleasure with toil. Admiral Morse, who commanded the naval forces, took me each day in his barge on an expedition, of which the prime feature was a bathe. On the first we went to the island of Ischia, with its hot springs, and on the return we ran through an immense United States troop convoy sailing for the landing on the Riviera. All the ships were crowded with men, and as we passed along their lines they cheered enthusiastically.... We also visited Capri. I had never seen the Blue Grotto before. It is indeed a miracle of transparent, sparkling water of the most intense, vivid blue. We bathed in a small, warm bay, and repaired to luncheon at a comfortable inn ... These days, apart from business, were a sunshine holiday.[2]

14–20 August 1944: Military Manoeuvres

On 14 August Churchill left for Corsica in General Wilson's Dakota[2] to be present at the landings in the South of France (Operation DRAGOON).[10] Churchill wrote:

We had a pleasant flight to Ajaccio, in the harbour of which General Wilson and Admiral Sir John Cunningham [Commander-in-Chief, Mediterranean Fleet] had posted themselves on board a British headquarters ship. The airfield was very small and not easily approached. The pilot was excellent. He had to come in between two bluffs, and his port wing was scarcely fifteen feet from one of them. The General and the Admiral brought me aboard, and we spent a long evening on our affairs ... We were five hours sailing before we reached the line of battleships bombarding at about fifteen thousand yards. I now learned from Captain Allen [Later Commodore GRG Allen who advised Churchill on his Second World War memoirs] that we were not supposed to go beyond the ten-thousand-yard limit for fear of mines ... Here we saw the long rows of boats filled with American storm troops steaming in continuously to the bay of St. Tropez. We then returned to Ajaccio.[2]

Thompson[9] has recorded that DRAGOON opened with a tremendous combined bombardment of the French coast by aircraft and warships, and the dropping of 14,000 parachutists. In the early hours of 15 August the landings were made along a 50-mile stretch of the Riviera running from Cannes towards Toulon. By 10.30 am came news that the whole of the central sector had been taken with few casualties.[9]

Churchill returned to Ajaccio 'in a distinctly disgruntled frame of mind. He complained that he not been allowed within six miles of the coast, he had seen no opposition of any kind – and to make matters worse he had run out of cigars.' Churchill had become so bored that he had borrowed a novel from HMS *Kimberley's* captain and retired to his bunk to read it.[9] Churchill wrote on the flyleaf of the borrowed book 'This is a lot more exciting than the invasion of Southern France.'[9]

On 16 August Churchill reached Naples from the South of France. He dined with Macmillan again that evening who recorded that Churchill 'did not much enjoy his trip. The trouble was he did not see enough shooting and fighting. However he seemed to be in a merry mood.'[10]

On the morning of 17 August Churchill:

> ... set out by motor to meet General Alexander. I was delighted to see him for the first time since his victory and entry into Rome. He drove me all along the old Cassino front, showing me how the battle had gone and where the main struggles had occurred ... On August 19 I set out to visit General Mark Clark at Leghorn [Livorno]. This was a long drive, and everywhere we stopped to visit brigades and divisions. Mark Clark received me at his headquarters. We lunched in the open air by the sea. In our friendly and confidential talks I realised how painful the tearing to pieces of this fine army had been to those who controlled it.[11]

21–7 August 1944: Rome and More Military Manoeuvres

As Alexander's offensive could not start until 26 August Churchill flew to Rome on the morning of 21 August and arrived in time for lunch and was in 'excellent form'.[10] While in Rome Churchill stayed '... at the Embassy, and our Ambassador, Sir Noel Charles, and his wife devoted themselves to my business and comfort. Guided by his advice, I met most of the principal figures in the *débris* of Italian politics produced by twenty years of dictatorship, a disastrous war, revolution, invasion, occupation, Allied control, and other evils.'[11]

On 23 August Churchill had an audience at 11 am with His Holiness, Pope Pius XII. He held a press conference at noon, had a lunch meeting with Crown Prince Umberto, the Prince of Piedmont, and met with the Italian government from 3.30 pm to 4.30 pm. Macmillan recorded:

> He [Churchill] thus saw in one day all forms of power – spiritual, regal, governmental – and the fourth estate of the realm. His versatility is

extraordinary and he was clearly very pleased with it all. It was a good idea to see *all* the members of the Government and thus overcome an incipient attack here and at home based on his only seeing the political 'right'.[10]

Churchill wrote: 'Early on 24 August 1944, after my short visit to Rome, I returned by air to Alexander's headquarters at Siena, living in a château a few miles away. The offensive was now fixed for the 26th. I took the opportunity of visiting the New Zealand Division.'[12] Churchill was in regular communication with President Roosevelt over these military developments.[12,13]

28 August 1944: Return to England

Churchill flew to Naples on 28 August.[12] A large dinner was held at Villa Rivalta on Churchill's return from manoeuvres and on his last night in Italy. Macmillan went to Pomigliano aerodrome to see Churchill off on 28 August: 'He was in excellent spirits, especially with the latest news from the battlefronts.'[10] Churchill left Naples in *Ascalon* but, at about 5.30 pm, the plane ran into a thunderstorm. After 7 hours in the air, the Avro York landed at Rabat, Morocco. Thompson recorded that Churchill was so ill after the flight from Naples that Moran advised him to stay in Rabat for the night.[9] Sawyers indicated to the flight crew that his Master was not best pleased and soon after Wing Commander Collins was summoned to explain himself, which he did in forthright terms.[14] Furthermore, further thunderstorms were reported on the route.[1] The enforced rest in Rabat refreshed Churchill, and the next day they flew on to Northolt.[9]

29 August 1944: 'Sudden Attack of My Former Malady'

After about 6 hours in the air on 29 August, and some 2 hours from Britain, Churchill developed a 'sudden attack of my former malady with a temperature of between 103 and 104 degrees [F]'.[1] Clementine Churchill wrote that the Avro York 'made a lovely landing [at 6 pm] and taxied right up to where everyone was waiting … Lord Moran emerged and ran across the tarmac to the car where I was sitting and said: "He has a temperature of 103. We must get him back quickly and get him to bed".'[15]

The Chiefs of Staff, John Colville (Assistant Private Secretary) and special newspaper correspondents were also there to meet Churchill.[16] Admiral Sir Andrew Cunningham (First Sea Lord) noted: 'The PM was hurried to his car by Moran. He certainly looked ill.'[1] Colville recorded that Moran emerged from the aircraft 'looking agitated and we found that the P.M. had a temperature of 103 degrees [F], developed since luncheon'.[16] Churchill 'emerged looking crumpled and feverish'[15] and was rushed to London leaving everyone stunned and astonished.[15]

The War Cabinet had been fixed for 6.30 pm on 29 August, in order that Churchill should have time to get there.[17] Eden walked into Churchill in the 'passage as I was leaving for Cabinet. He seized my hand. "Ah, there you are, dear Anthony, come into my room, I want to talk to you".'[17] This was followed by Mrs Churchill informing Eden that Churchill had a temperature of 103°F. Eden recorded that while Churchill was undressing and tumbling into bed, he told him that he had developed a sudden chill a few hours from home.[17] 'Extracted myself as soon as I could for he [Churchill] showed every desire to discuss all our problems and I felt the whirl of approaching doctors, etc.'[17] Eden left and sent Moran in and went down to Cabinet.[17]

Moran recorded that Churchill was chesty for some days after developing the temperature and that the chest X-rays revealed a shadow at the base of the lung.[18] He described the illness as the 'third dose, though a very mild one, of pneumonia'.[18] The other episodes of pneumonia treated by Moran were in February 1943 (see p. 73)[19] and December 1943 (see p. 88).[20] The mildness of Churchill's pneumonia may explain why no medical bulletins were issued, and only the 'smallest circle of people knew he [Churchill] was ill'.[15]

Dr (later Sir) Geoffrey Marshall (see p. 442), Senior Physician, Guy's Hospital and Physician-in-Charge, Brompton Hospital, London, was again invited to give a second opinion.[15] Marshall took blood tests and X-rays and gave a sulfonamide,[15] probably sulfathiazole as this sulfonamide was prescribed in February 1943 (see p. 74). 'It is a slight attack – there is a small shadow on one lung, but in himself he is well.'[15]

Nurse Dorothy Pugh had again been recruited from St Mary's Hospital, at Churchill's specific request (personal communication Dr Robert Pugh). Nurse Pugh recorded in her diary: 'Call from Matron. Am to go to Storey's Gate – PM just landed – slight chill – I hope nothing more. Welcomed by them all – as an old friend.'[21]

Moran also consulted again the cardiologist, Dr (later Sir) John Parkinson (see p. 444).[22] What should be done if during the fever Churchill again developed atrial fibrillation, as he had done previously in Carthage in December 1943?[20] Parkinson recommended tab. digit. folia (digitalis folia BP) 1 grain, 4-hourly, though an ECG should be performed first to confirm the abnormal rhythm.[22]

30 August 1944

On 30 August Churchill was better, his temperature had fallen and he did a certain amount of work in bed.[16] He was assessed by Moran, Marshall and Colonel (later Lieutenant General Sir) Robert Drew RAMC, medical officer to the War Cabinet Offices (see p. 434).[21] Field Marshal Sir Alan Brooke, Chief of the Imperial General Staff, was sent for by Churchill at 7 pm and Brooke 'found him looking ill'.[23] Churchill also saw General Eisenhower, Supreme Allied Commander of the Allied Expeditionary Force, about the change in command in Normandy and Eisenhower 'stayed very late'.[21]

'A very marked improvement' in Churchill's condition was noted by Colville[16] on 31 August, and Nurse Pugh stated that he was 'in very good form'.[21] It was agreed that the arrangements for OCTAGON, the coming conference with the US President, should be allowed to stand. King George VI came for an hour to see Churchill,[16,21] and he signed a submission creating General Montgomery a Field Marshal. Brooke, Eden and Lord Camrose, Editor-in-Chief, *Daily Telegraph*, also visited.[24]

31 August–4 September 1944: Recovery

Clementine Churchill wrote to her daughter Mary:

It is a slight attack – there is a small shadow on one lung, but in himself he is well & this morning, now 7 a.m. the temperature is normal. I was sick with fright Tuesday night [29 August] & yesterday. We hope it will not be necessary to publish bulletins & strange to say Lord Moran says that in about 5 days he can go to Canada by sea. I shall go with him now, Sarah too. I do wish you could but your job is essential.[15]

Churchill was assessed by Moran and Marshall on 1 September. Churchill's temperature was normal, and he was 'in tearing form'[16] having entirely emptied his box (red boxes used by ministers to carry their documents). Churchill gave Colville a survey of the road to D-Day, and beyond.[16] Brooke recorded that 'Winston is improving rapidly and it looks as if we should all be starting for Quebec on Monday [4th September] evening.'[23] Churchill saw the Polish Prime Minister in the evening.[25] Churchill telegraphed President Roosevelt: 'I am much better though still eating masses of M and B [May & Baker, manufacturer of sulfonamides].'[24]

On 2 September Churchill was assessed again by Moran, Marshall and Brigadier (later Sir) Lionel Whitby (see p. 452), an expert on sulfonamides.[21] Although Churchill was 'much better' on the 3 September and was 'up for lunch and supper',[21] he was unable because of his illness to attend the War Cabinet, which met in his absence.[26] As Whitby had left London, Churchill was assessed only by Moran and Marshall.[21]

Churchill still had a high temperature on 4 September, but he lunched alone with Eden and they spoke of various problems and plans and also of the political situation.[27] Churchill insisted on getting up to attend a Cabinet meeting at 5.40 pm on the Warsaw crisis.[23, 26] Eden wrote in his diary: 'W. was I think tired and did not look at all well.'[17] Nurse Pugh was told by Moran at 6.30 pm (presumably following the usual 6 pm consultation) that she was required to go on the trip to Canada with Churchill.[21]

Harvey[25] has reported that Eden had insisted on five doctors signing a note that Churchill 'was fit to travel, and that if he went, he should take an M & B specialist with him'. Churchill had said it was quite unnecessary. 'He would have the ship's surgeon!'[25] Harvey[25] quoted Moran as stating that he 'would not have allowed anyone else to travel, but he might pick up on the sea voyage'. Eden had apparently persuaded Admiral of the Fleet Sir Andrew Cunningham, First Sea Lord, to make the ship take a day and a half longer.[25]

Moran wrote: 'There had been some doubt whether he [Churchill] would be fit to set off on another trip so soon. I decided at the last moment to ask Lionel Whitby and a nurse to come with us.'[18] Moran thought that Churchill believed that a pathologist was an essential part of the team to deal with an attack of pneumonia.[18] 'I thought it would comfort him to have one on board.'[18] The presence of Whitby and Nurse Pugh was to be kept secret Downing Street informed the British Secretariat in Quebec: 'For your information only, Whitby is a specialist and colleague of Moran but it is most important this should not be known nor any deductions drawn. Mrs Pugh is a nurse. This also is not to be made known.'[24]

5–10 September 1944: to Halifax on the *Queen Mary*

Churchill's special train left Addison Road Station (Kensington Olympia), London at 9.40 am and reached Greenock, Scotland at 7.30 pm. The party consisted not only of the Churchills, the three Chiefs of Staff, Colville, Commander Thompson and Martin, but also Moran, Whitby and Nurse Pugh. Churchill thought he had developed a temperature on the journey and Moran could not find a thermometer. Churchill said: 'I am sure Nurse Pugh has one.' She did (personal communication Dr Robert Pugh)!

Colville recorded in his diary:

> Travelled in the P.M.'s train ... After a luxurious journey we reached Greenock at 7.00 p.m. and were transferred by tender to the *Queen Mary*. I found a large and spacious cabin and devoured an even larger and more spacious dinner (oysters, champagne, etc.) in the P.M.'s dining-room. There were just eight of us, the P.M., Mrs C., their immediate entourage, Lord Moran, Lord Leathers [Minister of War Transport] and Lord Cherwell [Churchill's scientific advisor].[16]

After dinner Colville played three games of bezique with Churchill.[16]

Churchill himself wrote later: 'On Tuesday, September 5, we sailed once again from the Clyde in the *Queen Mary*. All the Chiefs of Staff came with me, and met daily, and sometimes twice a day, during our six days' voyage. I wanted, before meeting our American friends, to harmonise and grip the many plans and projects which were now before us.'[27]

Churchill spent 6 September in his cabin on the *Queen Mary* reading *Phineas Finn*.[16] Colville recorded:

> A quiet day, the P.M. being still rather under the weather as a result of the substantial doses of M. & B. [sulfonamides] he has been given during the last week. I lunched and dined with the P.M. and Mrs C., lunch being a small *en famille* affair, and General Ismay and Brigadier Whitby ... being invited to dinner. Both meals were gargantuan in scale and epicurean in quality; rather shamingly so.[16]

Churchill was in 'low spirits and not very well', Mrs Churchill wrote to her daughter Mary. 'I hope it is just the M & B working off and perhaps some anti-malaria tablets [mepacrine].'[24]

Colville recorded in his diary on 7 September:

Another quiet day, devoted by the P.M. to *Phineas Finn* and by me to walking about the deck and swapping 'lines' with Liberator pilots on their way home. I also ploughed through the many files, political and economic, we have brought with us … Lords Cherwell and Moran were invited to dine. The P.M. produced many sombre verdicts about the future, saying that old England was in for dark days ahead, that he no longer felt he had a 'message' to deliver, and that all that he could now do was to finish the war, to get the soldiers home and to see that they had houses to which to return. But materially and financially the prospects were black and 'the idea that you can vote yourself into prosperity is one of the most ludicrous that ever was entertained'.

The menu for dinner was: Oysters, consommé, turbot, roast turkey, ice with cantaloupe melon, Stilton cheese and a great variety of fruit, petit fours, etc.; the whole washed down by champagne (Mumm 1929) and a very remarkable Liebfraumilch, followed by some 1870 brandy: all of which made the conversation about a shortage of consumers' goods a shade unreal.[16]

Colville wrote that due to the Gulf Stream the weather on 8 September was very hot, sticky and cloudy like the Equator.[16] Churchill felt 'the heat acutely … Lords Leathers and Cherwell dined. The P.M said he thought the Joint Planners etc., were being too optimistic about an early victory.'[16]

On 9 September, Colville recorded:

The P.M., feeling more or less himself again, did a considerable amount of work, mostly connected with the strategic questions at the coming conference. He has not yet given his mind to the complicated problems connected with finance and the future of Lease-Lend, and Lord Cherwell is in despair. The Gulf Stream heat, which the P.M. has found quite overpowering, persisted until midday when there was a sudden fall of about 20 degrees in temperature, accompanied by clear skies and a fresh breeze … The P.M. had a slight temperature again and was highly irascible.[16]

Mrs Churchill also recorded that Churchill's temperature went up again at 3 p.m.[24] According to Moran, Churchill became 'thoroughly rattled and bad-tempered, until Whitby restored morale by finding that he had a normal blood count.'[18]

Brooke recorded that the Chiefs of Staff were to have met Churchill for dinner this evening 'but he started another temperature and had to remain in bed cancelling an invitation for us to dine with him! I am afraid he is very definitely ill and doubtful how much longer he will last. The tragedy is that in his present condition he may well do untold harm.'[23]

That night, Colville discussed Churchill's rise in temperature with Moran, who 'does not think seriously of it, probably it is the heat'.[16] Moran told Colville 'that he does not give him [Churchill] a long life and he thinks that when he goes it will be either a stroke or the heart trouble which first shewed itself at Carthage last winter'.[16] Colville commented: 'May he at least live to see victory, complete and absolute, in both hemispheres and to receive his great share of the acclamations. Perhaps it would be as well that he should escape the aftermath.'[16]

The *Queen Mary* reached Halifax at midday on 10 September. Churchill disembarked and boarded a Canadian National Railways train that would take him to Quebec, a 20-hour journey. 'While the luggage was being put on the train the P.M. stood on the balcony at the rear of his "car" while the crowd sang patriotic songs, very well in tune. He made them a short speech.'[16] Churchill reached Quebec at 10 am on 11 September.[16] President Roosevelt's train had arrived on an adjoining track 10 minutes earlier.

Moran discontinued Churchill's mepacrine on 12 September, even though he had been advised that Churchill should continue it for a month after leaving Italy to ward off malaria.[18] 'The P.M. makes very heavy weather about the tablets; he ascribes to them his bad turn on the ship. Besides, mepacrine gives you a yellow cachectic look, as if you had cancer, and people like Brendan [Bracken MP] say to him: "You ought to stop that stuff; it's making you ill".'[18]

Clementine Churchill wrote to her daughter Mary on 8 September that: 'I noticed that everybody who has taken them [mepacrine] is turning yellow – Lord Moran, Tommy [Thompson] – Papa less than the others because he has a natural pink complexion.'[13] It is not known whether Moran continued to take mepacrine himself!

It is of interest that Colville records that he used Churchill's supply of penicillin when he developed a 'feverish cold' on 15 September.[16]

Thompson[28] recorded that as the Churchill party were about to embark again on the *Queen Mary* in New York they learned that Lord Moran, who had lost his pass, had been turned away by the guards when he tried to board the ship. He had been found by a member of the Mission sitting disconsolately on his suitcase at the foot of the gangway.

Churchill wrote to Whitby from Moscow on 16 October thanking him for sending a copy of the Hippocratic Oath: 'My confidence in the members of the medical profession, already high, is enhanced by the knowledge that they are bound by such undertakings. I was most grateful to you for your kindness in so readily accompanying me on my journey ... to Quebec.'[29]

Medical Aspects

Churchill was 69 years old in August 1944. While the overall mortality from pneumonia in the early 1940s with sulfonamides was 10 per cent, the mortality was 40 per cent in those aged 70 years or over.[30]

What treatment did Churchill receive for pneumonia? It is not known with certainty with which sulfonamide Churchill was treated in August 1944, though in February 1943 he received sulfathiazole and in December 1943 sulfadiazine, which was supplied by the US Army in Tunis. Sulfadiazine was the preferred sulfonamide by August 1944, though it was not available generally in the UK. The 1943 edition of the National War Formulary[31] included only three sulfonamides (sulfanilamide, sulfapyridine and sulfathiazole). It is probable, therefore, that Moran again prescribed sulfathiazole.

Moran only records that Marshall was invited to give a second opinion,[32] but Nurse Pugh confirms Whitby's involvement.[21] Moreover, it is unlikely Moran would have invited Whitby to accompany Churchill to the Quebec Conference in September 1944 unless he had also been involved in treating Churchill's illness. Pugh also records that Drew was present on 30 August.

Based on Churchill's work output in August/September 1944,[13] there is reasonable evidence that overall, and despite his illness, he was able to maintain his 'usual output', almost certainly because his illness was shorter and less severe than the episode of pneumonia in February 1943.[19]

Churchill was concerned about Moran's prescription of mepacrine. Mepacrine had been introduced in 1943 by the British Army both as a prophylactic measure to suppress malaria during and subsequent to exposure to infected mosquitos and as a treatment for vivax malaria and falciparum malaria.[33] It was recognized, however, that mepacrine caused adverse effects which could be incapacitating. It often stained the skin yellow,[34] which Clementine Churchill observed in Moran and Thompson. Mepacrine regularly caused nausea and vomiting, colic and diarrhoea, though additional fluid often ameliorated these gastrointestinal features, and less commonly psychiatric disturbances attended its use.[33,34] Mepacrine is no longer used as an antimalarial.

Chapter 13

A High Temperature in January 1945 on the Way to Yalta

He's always like this after those pills![1]

I t had been agreed that ARGONAUT, the conference between Marshal Stalin, President Roosevelt and Prime Minister Churchill, would take place in Yalta in the Crimea early in February 1945. Churchill was anxious that the British and American Staffs should have talks in Malta before travelling to Yalta. John Colville, Churchill's Assistant Private Secretary, wrote in his diary:

> The conditions there sound ghastly and I am glad not to be going ... Churchill invited me to go, but it would have upset office arrangements in London and John Martin [Principal Private Secretary] (to my disappointment) dissuaded him. This saved my life, for there was no more room in the Prime Minister's C-54 and I should have been in the York which crashed off Pantellaria [in the Strait of Sicily], having lost the way to Naples, killing all but one of the passengers.[2]

29 January 1945: Flight to Malta

It had been Churchill's intention to fly to Malta at midnight on 29 January using his personal aircraft, the Douglas C-54 Skymaster, in order to arrive at Malta after daybreak. However, while Churchill was attending a Cabinet meeting on 29 January 1945, Commander CR Thompson RN, his aide-de-camp, received a telephone call from the Air Ministry warning that snow was on the way and unless they were in the air by 9.30 pm they would not be able to get away that night. Fortunately, Lord Moran (see p. 443), Churchill's personal physician, was at his cottage at Uxbridge, close to RAF Northolt. Thompson left a cryptic message with Lady Moran, which fortunately she interpreted correctly and she drove her husband to the airport.[3] Moran wrote later: 'There is bad weather coming in from the Atlantic, and snow is expected at Northolt. This might make taking off difficult, so we are to be in the air by 9 o'clock. The idea is to fly before the gale.'[4]

Churchill was accompanied on the flight to Malta by his daughter, Sarah, Martin, Moran, Sir Edward Bridges (Secretary to the Cabinet), Thompson and Frank Sawyers (Churchill's valet).[5] Anthony Eden, Foreign Secretary, and the Chiefs of Staff had preceded the main party by flying out earlier that day and 'flew high and were not given oxygen with the result I [Eden] arrived with a headache, not feeling too good'.[6]

Sarah Oliver (née Churchill) later recalled: 'At about 9.30 on a bitter night, January 29th, our party clambered aboard a Skymaster which had been given to us by the President [as part of the Lend–lease arrangement] and had been fitted out by the RAF. It was extremely comfortable and seemed as silent as a ghost. It had a specially designed interior so that emergency conferences could be held.'[1]

Before departure Thompson wrote out a signal for General Hastings 'Pug' Ismay, Secretary of the Imperial Defence Chiefs of Staff Committee and Deputy Secretary of the War Cabinet, giving him the new ETA in Malta of 4.30 am and informing him that Churchill would remain in bed in the aircraft on arrival; he did not wish anyone to stay up to meet him.[3] Alas this signal was not sent or at least did not arrive!

Sarah also remembered that: 'though my father had an amazing constitution the heavy injections before these trips sometimes made him feel ill, and once again he was to start out on a journey not feeling his best'.[1] She continued:

> The trip there was quite miserable. The plane itself was perfect, a wonder of comfort, and it seemed silent as a ghost, but no sooner were we on board all puffing and blowing and out of breath, than worry set in. We had a delicious dinner but as usual, since the plane was cold at first, all the heating was turned on as my father sat huddled in his greatcoat. Then it began to get hot and we were all turning pink as tomatoes. Despite adjustments, my father began to look like a poor hot pink baby about to cry … It was about one o'clock before we settled in for the night, but nobody slept much.[7]

Churchill's Illness

Moran wrote that:

> I turned in soon after we were in the air to get some sleep, as we were to land at Malta between four and five in the morning; an hour later Sawyers pulled my curtain back and said that the P.M. had a temperature – a good beginning to a winter journey of three thousand miles. The P.M. blames my sulfaguanidine tablets, which he has been taking during the day.[4]

Sarah recalled that her father took his own temperature and found it was above normal and thought: 'Here we go again!'[7]

Churchill was 'restless', and Moran soon gave up any attempt to sleep.[4] Churchill asked Moran if he would like to send for Sir Lionel Whitby (see p. 453) and '... what about Clemmie? – The Moscow performance over again. He has developed a bad habit of running a temperature on these journeys'.[4]

30 January 1945: Arrival in Malta

As the Skymaster approached Luqa Airfield at 4.30 am Thompson got up and put on a monkey jacket over his pyjamas. He wanted to leave the aircraft on arrival to explain to Air Commodore Whitney Straight, who was in charge of the RAF arrangements, that Churchill would need transport to the dockyard at 8 am.[3] When the Skymaster stopped on the tarmac Thompson left the plane and was blinded by floodlighting.[3] As his eyes became accustomed to the glare he saw to his horror that every high-ranking officer and civilian from the Governor downwards was standing to attention in front of me.[3] To make matters worse at least three signals had come in during the night, all giving different times of arrival.[3] The final one had announced that Churchill would land at 3.30 am, but this was Greenwich Mean Time not the time in Malta.[3] Thompson recorded that: 'Surrounded by this bunch of near explosive VIPs, I thought I was lucky to regain the Skymaster without being torn limb from limb.'[3]

Sarah wrote later:

> I found it impossible to sleep in the silence of the grounded aircraft, where every rustle and sigh could be heard, so I dressed in my bunk

– a feat to test any contortionist. Somehow the long hours crept by. I pulled back the blackout from my window and saw the sunrise over the hangars of the airfield. The pale blue sky grew warmer and the grass was emerald green. There was no snow.[1]

Sawyers, Churchill's valet, 'a paragon of devotion',[1] told Sarah: 'He's always like this after those pills.'[1] Moran, despite the comment on his drugs, 'remained calm, but still thought it wise for my father to see a specialist before he left the aircraft. It remained "touch and go" for a few hours whether it would not be better for him to go to the hospital instead of to the harbour of Valetta, where HMS *Orion* was waiting to accommodate us.'[1]
Martin recorded that:

The Prime Minister gave us all rather a fright by running a temperature, and the night was much disturbed by the comings and goings of Lord Moran and his consultations with local medical opinion. A bed was prepared in the military hospital and we had all but summoned Sir Lionel Whitby when fortunately the Colonel [Churchill] took a turn for the better, and a little after breakfast time it was decided to proceed to our cruiser.[5] Moran recorded that: 'Winston stayed in bed in the plane till noon, when he was taken to H.M.S. *Orion*.'[4]

HMS *Orion*

Martin wrote that the party were: 'immediately installed in most comfortable quarters and overwhelmed by the characteristic hospitality of the Royal Navy. All concerned, from the Captain down, left nothing undone for our convenience, giving up the best cabins in the ship. Colonel Kent [Churchill] spent most of his time at CRICKET [Malta] aboard and chiefly in bed.'[5]

Sarah recorded that the bed in her father's cabin was the wrong way round.[1] 'Sawyers knew all about it and carefully redesigned his cabin. Bed, hot water bottles – my father fell asleep. We lunched without him, and when late in the afternoon Lord Moran decided to wake him his temperature was down. He then immediately set to work.'[1]

Sarah asked her father whether he would like to add something to a letter she was writing to her mother. 'Indeed I would,' he replied. 'Tell her my temperature's down, my tummy-ache has gone. My functions have resumed their norm – in fact I'm in the best of form.'[7] Churchill himself wrote about his illness in a letter to his wife dated 1 February:

I had a serious alarm coming over lest I was going to have another attack, for my temperature went to 102½°F [39.2°C] in the night. But it all passed off agreeably the next day and now I am in my usual health. I think it must have been connected with all those things which I was taking or possibly was the reason which made me take them.[8]

Eden recorded in his diary:

Went across to see Winston at 6.30 pm on his summons. Brookie [Field Marshal Sir Alan Brooke] and I went into his cabin and was staggered when he told us that he had had a temperature of over 102°F last night. Perfectly normal now. Alec [Sir Alexander Cadogan, Permanent Under-Secretary for Foreign Affairs] told me that he was sure it was all due to excitement. W[inston] and I and Brookie had talk over work of combined Chiefs of Staff so far, prospects on the Western Front, Alex's [Field Marshal Sir Harold Alexander] future etc.... Alec and I dine with Winston, Harriman [Averell Harriman, President Roosevelt's special envoy to Europe, coordinator Lend-Lease programme and US Ambassador to Russia] also there.[6]

Cadogan recorded in his diary on 31 January that Churchill: '... felt ill on the way out, and proved to have a temperature of 102.4°F. But was quite all right yesterday evening, cheerful and eating and drinking everything within reach. Personally, I think it's simply excitement! Our dinner consisted of Harriman, Moran, Anthony [Eden], Martin, Sarah and the Captain of the *Orion*. And we *did* get away soon after 10.30.'[9]

Martin reported to the Private Office that Churchill was able to have:
... long and useful conversations with Alexander [Supreme Commander of the Allied Forces Headquarters], General Marshall [Chief of Staff US Army], Admiral King [Commander in Chief, United States Fleet], Harry Hopkins [President Roosevelt's chief diplomatic adviser] and 'Ed' Stettinius [United States Secretary of State] ... The Colonel [Churchill] did not make any public appearance ashore, but one evening we went to dinner with the Governor at San Anton Palace.[5]

Moran summarised his patient's illness thus:

> Only this morning he was in the doldrums when, turning his face to
> the wall, he had called for Clemmie. Surely this bout of fever should
> put sense into his head. But Winston is a gambler, and gamblers do
> not count the coins in their pockets. He will not give a thought to
> nursing his waning powers. And now, when it was nearly midnight, he
> demanded cards and began to play bezique with Harriman. Damn the
> fellow, will he never give himself a chance?![4]

Medical Aspects

Churchill himself described fever and 'tummy-ache' as the features of his
illness.[7] He explained to his wife: 'I had a serious alarm coming over lest I
was going to have another attack, for my temperature went up to 102½°F
in the night. But it all passed off agreeably the next day and now I am in
my usual health. I think it must have been connected with all those things
which I was taking or possibly was the reason which made me take them.'[8]
Churchill and his valet blamed Moran's prescription of sulfaguanidine, a
sulfonamide antibiotic, for his high temperature but Moran noted that 'the
P.M. has views on everything, and his views on medicine are not wanting in
assurance'.[4]

But why was Churchill prescribed sulfaguanidine? In all probability it
was prescribed prophylactically to prevent dysentery and other intestinal
infections in Yalta. Sulfaguanidine was used in the 1940s to treat acute
intestinal infections including bacillary dysentery and there are reports of
its effectiveness,[10, 11] though benefit was not always demonstrated.[12] Based
on his extensive clinical experience, Scadding,[13] who treated Churchill in
December 1943,[14] has advanced the observation that small doses of readily
absorbable sulfonamides, which for other infections would be regarded
as prophylactic rather than therapeutic, give as good results in acute mild
bacillary dysentery as larger ones, and possibly better results than very much
larger doses of the poorly absorbable compounds (such as sulfaguanidine).[13]
We are not aware of any contemporaneous evidence indicating a therapeutic
benefit from the prophylactic use of sulfaguanidine prior to Churchill's
arrival in Yalta. However, one can sympathise with Moran's caution, given
Churchill's medical history and propensity to develop potentially serious

infections, and the imperative to keep the 'Great man' in good health may have influenced his decision to prescribe sulfaguanidine.

Bunting and Levan[15] reported in 1944 that sulfaguanidine can cause febrile reactions with oral temperatures ranging from 100.0°F to 103.8°F in some 10 per cent of soldiers treated in the convalescent phase after recovery from shigella dysentery. Fever was observed in eleven of eighteen casualties on days three to five of treatment (sulfaguanidine 3.5 g three times daily) in this study, though others have suggested that fever at 7 days is more typical.[16] On withdrawal of the drug, the temperature returned to normal within 24 hours in all cases.[15] Seven patients were re-challenged and all became febrile in 4–8 hours.[15] In some patients a more serious condition (sulfonamide hypersensitivity) arises which is characterized not only by fever, but by a generalized maculopapular rash and variable damage particularly to the liver and kidney. This reaction usually develops seven to fourteen days after initiating therapy and usually resolves seven to fourteen days after discontinuation of the antibiotic.[17] It is fortunate that Churchill did not develop these additional features.

There was controversy in the 1940s as to whether second or multiple courses of sulfonamides resulted in a higher percentage of febrile reactions than the first course.[16] As Churchill had received sulfonamides at least in February 1943,[18] December 1943,[14] and August 1944,[18] a drug-induced cause for his high temperature is most likely. The absence of any specific symptoms in association with the fever and its rapid resolution are also in support of a drug-induced reaction. We conclude that Churchill was almost certainly correct in his diagnosis!

Chapter 14

Diagnosis of Inguinal Hernia in September 1945 at Lake Como

When I was very young, I ruptured myself and had to wear a truss. I left it off because I went to Harrow ... Now however in the last 10 days it has come back ... I shall have to wear [a truss] when not in bed for the rest of my life[1]

At the General Election in 1945, the Conservatives (213 seats) were defeated heavily by Labour (393 seats), though Winston Churchill retained his seat at Woodford with a majority of 17,000 over his one opponent. He demitted office as Prime Minister on the evening of 26 July 1945. The Second World War ended on 14 August 1945 when Japan accepted the Allied terms. Despite his obvious need for a rest, as Leader of the Conservative Party, Churchill could not avoid the demands of his Party. On 21 August 1945 he addressed its backbench 1922 Committee. Henry 'Chips' Channon MP who was present recorded in his diary: 'He seemed totally unprepared, indifferent and deaf, and failed to stir the crowded audience. I came away fearing that the Tory party was definitely dead.'[2]

A Villa on Lake Como

Mary Soames, Churchill's daughter, has written that it was decided in family conclave that her father, 'bereft of office and – temporarily – of occupation', though he remained an MP and Leader of the Opposition, would be better out of the way while her mother, Clementine, wrestled with the refurbishment of the two houses (Chartwell and 28 Hyde Park Gate, Kensington). So a 'long painting holiday was prescribed' for her father.[3] In fact, it was Churchill's intent also to begin work on his war memoirs as well (see below). There is no truth in the suggestion that Churchill's real purpose in going to Como was to retrieve the incriminating but forged 'Mussolini file' containing overtures to the Il Duce (Benito Mussolini).[4]

At this time, Field Marshal Alexander, Supreme Allied Commander of the Mediterranean Forces, offered Churchill the use of a villa on Lake Como to which the British Army had access. Lieutenant Colonel Cunningham, Military Assistant to Alexander, wrote to Sarah Oliver, Churchill's other daughter, on 18 August 1945:

> We were delighted to have your father's telegram this morning, saying that he will be coming out to stay at Como. I have not seen the villa yet … but I believe it is very lovely. I have written today to Major-General Nares who commands that part of the world, and to whom the villa really belongs, asking him to make all the arrangements. The house is completely staffed by the same chaps who looked after your father when he stayed with us at Siena last summer and who know the form very well indeed. I have asked General Nares to provide two motor cars (open and closed), a motor launch, and an A.D.C, if possible from your father's own Regiment. The A.D.C. can look after all the details so that I hope you will have no work at all to do.[5]

These arrangements were confirmed in a further telegram marked *Top Secret* from Alexander (but sent by Cunningham) to Brigadier Jacob, Military Assistant Secretary to the War Cabinet, which confirmed that Alexander's aircraft No. 722 would proceed to the UK two days before departure to bring the party out.[6] Churchill sent a telegram to Alexander on 26 August 1945: 'I most grateful to you for all your arrangements. I should like to start September 1 or earliest good weather day thereafter. Party consists of self, Sarah, one lady secretary, valet and one detective. I hope this is not too many and that a fortnight's stay will not be too long. Please let me know. Winston'[7]

Alexander sent a message by telephone to Chartwell on 27 August 1945: 'I am so glad you are coming to Italy and am much looking forward to seeing you. I am sending my airplane to fetch you and it is entirely at your disposal. You must stay as long as you like.'[8]

Alexander also wrote Churchill a handwritten note on 30 August 1945:

> My dear P.M. This is just a note to welcome you on your arrival in Italy – I hope you will forgive me for not being here to meet you in person, but I am attending a big Polish ceremony at Monte Cassino which I have promised for a long time to attend. But, I shall come up

on the 6th and if I may I should like to spend a couple of nights with you and then to go on to Trieste where the VIII Corps are holding a Tattoo from 9th–11th. If that would amuse you, they would love to see you – however, we can discuss this when we meet. I hope you had an enjoyable journey from England and I hope you will be comfortable and happy in the villa. You must ask for anything you want. With best wishes to you and your party. Yours ever Alex[9]

Cunningham arranged that Major JLE Ogier MC from the 4th Queen's Own Hussars should act as Churchill's aide-de-camp. Churchill had himself been a junior officer in the 4th Hussars and he had been the Honorary Colonel of the Regiment since 1941. Ogier was joined by Lieutenant Colonel Anthony Barne, Commanding Officer, and by Lieutenant ADD 'Tim' Rogers MC from the same regiment, together with a guard of twenty-four men.[10] Barne and Rogers had driven for two days from Austria and had been involved in a serious accident but were not hurt.[10] Rogers had first acted as an aide to Churchill in 1942 when he was visiting Egypt. Churchill was so favourably impressed with Rogers that he insisted on having him back as his aide on all his subsequent visits to the Army in Africa and Italy.[11] Churchill informed Clementine that all three officers were 'particularly smart and intelligent' and all were 'picked men, but very keen to come'.[1]

Villa Le Rose, Moltrasio, has been identified as the most likely location for Churchill's stay, though Brigadier Edwards[12] stated he went to Villa d'Este, another villa on the shore of Lake Como and now a luxury hotel, to give his surgical opinion. Cunningham and his future wife, Delia Holland-Hibbert, a Wren (member of the Women's Royal Naval Service), were asked by Alexander to ensure that the villa was prepared for Churchill's arrival. Cunningham and Delia Holland-Hibbert both kept a record of this visit and Mrs Cunningham revisited Villa Le Rose in 2014 with her daughter, Lavinia Winch.

Cunningham recorded that the villa:

Is in the most beautiful situation on a steep hillside about a hundred feet above the lake; inside it is the very apotheosis of luxury with inch deep carpets and attractive lighting. Out of doors, formal gardens sloped steeply downwards to a tiny blue swimming pool just above the lake, and, on the lowest level, we found a boathouse and changing rooms – and in the boathouse there were three motor launches, one of which was reputed to be the fastest on the lake. We dined quietly in the very modern but strangely attractive dining room and then listened to some of John Ogier's gramophone records and watched the last light fading from the lovely lake and the twinkling reflections from the lights on the farther shore [personal communication Jeremy Cunningham].

2 September 1945: Flight to Milan

On the morning of 2 September Churchill flew from London to Milan in Field Marshal Alexander's Dakota, a flight of 5½ hours.[13] Churchill was accompanied by his daughter, Sarah, Lord Moran, his personal physician (see p. 443), Elizabeth Layton, his secretary, Sergeant Davies, his detective, and Frank Sawyers, his valet. Churchill spent the flight to Italy reading his wartime minutes.

Moran wrote:

All the time Winston remained buried in a printed copy of the minutes which for five years he had sent out month by month to the Chiefs of Staff and the Cabinet. Even during luncheon he went on reading, only taking his eyes from the script to light a cigar. I drove with him to the house on Lake Como that had been prepared for him. 'People say my speeches after Dunkirk were the thing. That was only a part, not the chief part … They forget I made all the main military decisions. You'd like to read my minutes, Charles.'[13]

Cunningham recorded that Churchill:

Duly arrived on time, accompanied by Lord Moran, a secretary, detective, a valet and more baggage than I had believed our aircraft was capable of carrying. Winston himself was in tremendous form and not at all tired by the journey although Sarah was definitely piano [subdued]. The first thing the old boy said was: 'What about a bathe?' and on being asked whether he would like some tea said: 'No, I never eat between meals…. but I'll have a whisky and soda' and helped himself to an enormous one [personal communication Jeremy Cunningham].

Churchill also described the villa to Clementine in a letter dated 3 September 1945:

This is really one of the most pleasant and delectable places I have ever struck. It is a small palace almost entirely constructed of marble inside. It abuts on the lake, with bathing steps reached by a lift. It is of course completely modernized, and must have been finished just before the War, by one of Mussolini's rich commerçants who has fled, whither it is not known ... Every conceivable arrangement has been made for our pleasure and convenience. Sarah and I have magnificent rooms covering a whole floor, with large marble baths and floods of hot and cold water ... the weather is delightful, being bright and warm with cool breezes.[1]

Yesterday we motored over the mountains to Lake Lugano, where I found quite a good subject for a picture. I made a good beginning and hope to go back there tomorrow, missing one day. I have spotted another place for this afternoon. These lakeshore subjects run a great risk of degenerating into 'chocolate box', even if successfully executed. I have been thinking a lot about you. I do hope you will not let the work of moving into these 2 houses wear you down. Please take plenty of rest.[1]

3 September 1945: Inguinal (Groin) Swelling

On the morning of 3 September, though Moran recorded that it was on 5 September, Churchill sent for Moran.

He had discovered a swelling in his groin. He was keyed up and waited anxiously while I made my examination. When I told him he was ruptured, he seemed relieved it wasn't anything worse, but he immediately fired at me a stream of questions. Was an operation necessary? Would it be strangulated? Would it get worse? How long would it be before he got used to a truss? Why should he get a rupture at his age, when he hardly took exercise?[13]

Following the examination by Moran, Churchill went painting. The first picture was a success, according to Sarah Churchill – 'a luminous lake and boats, backed by beetling crag, with a miniature toy village caught in the sunlight at its foot'.[14] Sarah also reported to her mother that the aide-de-camp (Major Ogier) had got on with her father 'like a house on fire. Charles [Moran] and I sit back comfortably while the two boys fight the battles from Omdurman to Alamein.'[14] Churchill continued to forge his relationship with Lieutenant Rogers who was to lease Churchill a racehorse in 1955 and to purchase two horses from Churchill for his own stud.[11,15] 'High Hat' was purchased by Rogers from Churchill for £80,000 (approximately £2 million in 2019).[11]

Sarah wrote that while the battles were fought, Moran 'was lost in a coma of philosophical meditation with himself about how many bugs the Italian water he was about to drink contained and whether they would prove fatal or not'.[14]

4 September 1945: Examination by Brigadier Edwards

On 3 September, Brigadier Edwards (p. 436), the consulting surgeon for the Army in Italy, and in peacetime a surgeon at King's College Hospital, London, received a telephone call from Moran asking him to come to Como urgently to see Churchill.

A Fairchild plane was put at my disposal. We reached Milan early afternoon on the 4th, having refuelled in Rome. There I was met and taken to Villa d'Este, a beautiful house on the shore of Lake Como. The journey had taken seven hours and throughout it I had been in a fever heat of anxiety as to what I might find. I was under the impression that Churchill was seriously ill. Arrived at the house I was met by Lord Moran who told me that Churchill was out painting. What a relief! What had happened was that Churchill had suddenly developed an inguinal hernia.[12]

Edwards recorded that Churchill:

Had just returned from a painting expedition, and when I entered his large bedroom in the villa, he was lying on his bed, dressed in his famous blue battle suit which later I saw to be finely cut and of nice soft material. I noted (and was thereby able to answer a question I had often asked myself) that his eyebrows were rusty red, and his remaining hair was that non-descript colour between ginger and grey. His pale blue eyes were tired, and that famous chin, and that nose, and straight mouth (inclining from the horizontal) made up the portrait one had seen so often in print and in colour[12]

He got up from the bed to shake hands and to thank me for coming, looking directly into my eyes, but not smiling. He started to answer a few questions about himself, but he was far more interested in showing Lord Moran and me the results of his labours with the brush. There were two canvases, quite large, perhaps 4 ft x 3 ft. Both were in watercolour – one which was near completion, painted at Lake Lugano and one here at Como. The latter had been done today at a three hour sitting. It seemed a lot of painting for three hours.[12]

Not being anything of the painter, I could not dare be critical, and as I was averse to fulsome praise, I said very little, or turned his questions as to my opinion of the mountains, or the water, with evasive answers. I reminded him of the article he wrote in the *Strand Magazine* perhaps 20 years ago which he wrote after he first tried his hand at painting. He then had said that painting up to a reasonable standard was easier than he had imagined.'[12]

Finally, after perhaps 20 minutes, we returned to the physical infirmity of Winston Churchill – and this time to some purpose. He was very patient with my examination, and having finished it, and made by diagnosis, I was subjected to a cross-examination – which was surely a search for knowledge and performed in a kindly way – which for detail and directness would have done credit to a member of the Court of Examiners [of the Royal College of Surgeons of England]. It was then that I had an insight into that extraordinary brain (I had much more reason later in the evening to admire it more fully). It was fortunate for me that I knew the subject well.[12]

When we had finished, he twice thanked me for my kindness in coming to see him. I was quite speechless the second time. I felt I owed him so much (as do so many thousands, nay millions) and as he must have endured so much sycophantism I was fearful lest anything I said should be mistaken by him for anything having the slightest flavour of that detestable trait. But thinking back I need not have worried, for anything I said would have been too sincere to have been mistaken for anything but what I really felt: and now he is a private gentleman, axes had no grindstone on which to sharpen.[12]

Edwards's son, Professor AWF Edwards FRS, has recorded that after his father had:

> Advised Churchill against a hernia operation he went to Milan with his army technician to get a truss made. They found a surgical outfitter opposite the Cathedral and tried to order a truss for delivery the next morning. The owner said it that was quite impossible. Father (a Brigadier) explained that unfortunately, he would therefore have to commandeer the shop so that his technician could make the truss himself. Ah, said the owner, is it for the famous man staying on Lake Como? Then it will be ready first thing in the morning.[12]

Following the announcement of Churchill's operation (see p. 177), Edwards wrote to Churchill on 12 June 1947 to wish him a 'speedy recovery from operation, with a minimum of discomfort'. He also explained that:

> The astute Italian instrument maker gathered from my rank, and insistence I made about urgency, that the patient was of supreme importance – and finally asked outright if the truss was for you. Just imagine the glory that would have been his – 'instrument maker to Mr Winston Churchill' in large print over his door! But I managed, not without some difficulty, to convince him that he was mistaken.[16]

On 5 September 1945 Churchill wrote to his wife, Clementine, from Lake Como, explaining what had happened:

> Darling a tiresome thing has happened to me. When I was v[er]y young, I ruptured myself & had to wear a truss. I left it off because I went to Harrow & have managed 60 years of rough-and-tumble. Now however in the last 10 days it has come back. There is no pain, but I have had to be fitted w[ith] a truss wh[ich] I shall have to wear when not in bed for the rest of my life – Charles [Lord Moran] got a military surgeon from Rome [he came from AFHQ, Caserta] who flew & has been w[ith] us for the last 3 days.[1]

Mrs Churchill responded on 11 September: 'My darling I'm so distressed about the truss – I hope it is comfortable & does not worry you. Did you strain yourself or stretch unduly – And will you now be able to do your exercises which are so potent a preventative of indigestion? Please take great care of yourself.'[1]

4–7 September 1945: Dinner with Churchill

Edwards remained at the villa for four days.

> Dinner after dinner was to me wholly entertaining. I was fascinated by three things – what he said, how he said it, and his changes of expression. He talked freely of the war – the atom bomb, Stalin (pronounced *Starleen*), *Mister* Bevin [Minister of Labour in the war-time Coalition government], Alex [Field Marshal Alexander] and Monty [Field Marshal Montgomery]; Vienna, Greece, Australia; the advantages of a monarchy, of Republican America; of casualties in relation to firepower. Of how he would have used gas were England invaded, and of the 'humanity' of gas as a weapon of war. He has a flair for exactness (he was troubled by my remarks about the depredations of the royalists in Greece) and a supreme gift of saying exactly what he means.[12]

Edwards recalled:

> The glorious hesitancy while he waited to search his mind for the right word, and with which we became familiar in our time of danger, is constantly noticeable. He has the knack of emphasising differences between things by using a qualifying adjective for each, which has an opposite inference ... He is a great European (he confesses – rather prides himself on this) and a monarchist rather than a Tory. 'The Crown separates pomp from power'. He made the remarkable – but to me wholly understandable – statement that he would prefer to be enslaved (? was that the word – dominated perhaps) by the Germans than the Russians. And thank God, he said, that the secret of the atom was in the right hands. It will take Russia three years to discover and act upon the discovery.[12]

Edwards remembered:

> Churchill has the most fascinating chuckle, and his face, when he is
> pleased with a thought of his, or a situation conjured up by remark of
> someone else, wrinkles up like a baby's – like Puck's. His eyes are dull
> – and the conjunctivae a little red, as though he had had conjunctivitis.
> They can be hard as he looks at you – or as tender as a woman's –
> they can weep easily. I believe now the story of how he cried – of how
> he wept – as described by M. Herriot when he realised all was lost in
> France. He is emotional – not 'Irishly' so. I think the right descriptions
> that he allows himself to react fully and without restraint and without
> troubling himself about what impression he makes on the onlooker. He
> is no actor, no poseur.[12]

Edwards wrote to Churchill on 15 September 1945: 'I hope you are not too
uncomfortable. Thank you for your gracious hospitality at the Villa. It was a
wonderful experience for me.'[17] Churchill responded on 2 November 1945:
'Thank you so much for your letter of September 15. It seems a long time
ago that I was basking in the sunshine of the Riviera, but I am toiling on with
treatment. It was good of you to write.'[18]

Barne also only stayed four nights with Churchill before returning to
his Regiment.[19] He spent the days picnicking, boating and accompanying
Churchill to various spots where he would spend hours painting watercolours
of the lakes.[19] Barne later reminisced:

> We had a speedboat and a police launch so could evade the Italians.
> Once he wanted a swim and nearly swamped our light craft when
> getting overboard. I could then not get him back onboard though we
> both struggled hard so I towed him into the shallows and signalled to
> Sarah. She waded out to help him. He looked like a great pink baby
> emerging from the water.[19]

Barne wrote to Churchill on 10 September 1945:

> I greatly enjoyed my stay with you. It was a very great honour for me.
> The Regiment is very proud to be allowed to provide your Guard. I
> greatly appreciate the honour paid us by the Field Marshal in facilitating

this movement of troops, enabling us to maintain this Guard. I trust the weather remains fine for you to continue with your painting.[20]

Churchill responded on 17 September:

We have had wonderful weather, and I have eight large paintings in an advanced state of decomposition. We have been a very happy party, and I have formed a great regard for John and Tim, whose kindness has been unfailing. We've had no visitors at all since the Field Marshal left except Monsieur Montag, the art critic, who has been very helpful and brought a most magnificent present of paint colours from Zürich. Sarah has deserted the arts since you departed, and Tim is too shy to plunge in with the brush. It has been a great compliment to me being guarded by my own Regiment, and I am touched by the sentiment which inspired the action of my great friend, who has led you to so many victories.

Yours very sincerely

W.S.C.

P.S. I shiver when I think of your escape. All's well that ends well.[21]

3–19 September 1945: Painting

Churchill wrote to Clementine on 5 September 1945:

We have had three lovely sunshine days, and I have two large canvasses underway, one a scene on the Lake of Lugano and the other here at Como. The design is I think good in both cases, and it has been great fun painting them ... I cannot describe to you the luxury of this small palace. It is the last word in modern millionairism ... It has done me no end of good to come out here and resume my painting. I am much better in myself, and am not worrying about anything.[1]

Clementine received a further letter on 8 September: 'I have now four pictures, three of them large, in an advanced state, and I honestly think they are better than any I have painted so far ... Charles [Moran] plays golf most days ... His devoted care of me is most touching.'[1]

Alexander arrived at the villa on 6 September 1945 and he and Churchill painted together for a day.[22] The two pictures now hang alongside each other at Chartwell. Alexander's picture has a note on the reverse side: 'Painted with Winston Churchill September 1945'.[22]

Churchill wrote to his daughter Mary on 10 September 1945: 'Here is sunshine & calm. I paint all day & every day & have banished care & disillusionment to the Shades. Alex came and painted too. He is v[er]y good. Monsieur Montag is coming to comment & guide me in a few days. I have three nice pictures so far, & am now off to seek for another.'[23] Churchill first met Charles Montag in 1915. Montag was known principally as a landscape painter in his early career, but subsequently he became the organiser of important exhibitions of French art in Switzerland and an adviser to individual art collectors including Churchill. In 1921 Churchill exhibited several works in Paris at the Galerie Druet under the pseudonym Charles Morin. On this occasion Montag stayed for four days.[23]

On 11 September 1945 Churchill wrote to Alexander in the hope they could paint together again: 'Montag comes Thursday 13th. I hope for heavy concentration on the pigmentorial front, preliminary bombardment beginning 14th and general assault 15th–16th. Essential you should be present on the battlefield and encourage troops to further victories. Weather conditions favourable and supplies of all kinds ample, especially now that Swiss communications [Montag] can be opened.'[23]

Churchill explained to his wife in a letter on 13 September 1945 that: 'It takes an hour to an hour and a half by motor-car through winding roads, or speed-boat across the lake, to reach the painting grounds, so we take our lunch with us and have picnics nearly every day. I have six pictures in all, but some are not quite complete.'[23]

Churchill confirmed that Sarah, Moran and Elizabeth Layton would be returning on 18 September 1945 in Alexander's Dakota and that he himself would leave Como between 18 and 20 September and probably then motor along the Riviera.[23] He would be accompanied by Ogier, Rogers, Sawyers and Davies.

On 18 September 1945 Churchill wrote to Clementine:

I plan to go to Genoa tomorrow, and stay two nights there, so as to get two afternoons at a picture, then on via Nice or Cannes to Marseille, hoping to get another picture by the way. I'm arranging to fly home on the 24th, so as to give plenty of time for the plane to return to bring Alex to England on October 1. I really have enjoyed these 18 days enormously. I have been completely absorbed by the painting and have thrown myself into it till I was quite tired. I have therefore not had time to fret or worry, and it has been good to view things from a distance. I think you will be pleased with the series of pictures, eight in all (now nine!) which I have painted. I am sending them home by Sarah, who will give you all our news.... I am confident that with a few more months of regular practice I should be able to paint far better than I have ever painted before. This new interest is very necessary in my life.[23]

Churchill continued:

Montag has just left, having been with us for four days. He was most helpful in his comments. I do not entirely agree with his style, and when he paints himself it is disappointing, but he has a vast knowledge and one cannot paint in his presence without learning. I'm quite embarrassed by the magnificent outfit of colours and brushes which he brought with him. They must have cost him £50 at least, and he is not at all a rich man.[23]

In fact Churchill had written to Montag on 29 August 1945 asking whether any 'good supplies of paints & brushes can be obtained in France or Switzerland. My stock is somewhat depleted'.[24]

On 19 September 1945 Churchill and his party left Lake Como for the Villa Pirelli on the Mediterranean Coast, 18 miles east of Genoa, where he stayed for several days. Churchill then travelled westwards first to Monte Carlo for two days then to a villa at Antibes (Villa Sous le Vent) placed at his disposal by General Eisenhower.[10] He then returned to Monte Carlo.

Villa Pirelli Genoa

Churchill described the journey in a letter to Clementine:

We motored in four hours to Genoa through lovely country with a particularly striking view of Pavia over the Ticino River and arrived after dark to find the local British colonel in charge of the district installed in the marble palace which belonged to Pirelli [Italian engineer and entrepreneur] ... There it stands on a rocky bluff overlooking the sea and the bathing place where I got a beautiful clear water of the palest green to try to paint. I worked hard for two days at the illusion of transparency and you shall judge when you see the result how far I have succeeded.[23]

Colonel Wathen, Commander of the Genoa Sub-Area, later recalled to Gilbert:

I had never seen him before and the following points struck me. He looked much less tired than one would have expected after six years of war and the fact that he was over 70 years of age. Although his hair was thin it was not entirely grey, he had a boyish pink and white complexion and a merry twinkle in his eyes. He was active in his movements. He was full of thanks for my hospitality and hoped that I had not been inconvenienced. He soon put one at one's ease. On arrival he was *not* smoking a cigar. During his stay he usually did have one stuck in his face, but as often as not it was out and he used as many matches as a pipe-smoker. He did not smoke more than five or six cigars a day. As regards drinks he might have had six or seven small whiskies a day, with lots of soda; a brandy after lunch and two after dinner. Field Marshal Alex had given him 100 bottles of Veuve Clicquot; by the time he came to us, four bottles were left and he was very generous at passing them around at dinner. Incidentally, he told me that the Government had allowed him £200 [approximately £8,500 in 2019] for his holiday expenses.[10]

Wathen also recalled that he and Churchill went bathing:

To my surprise and considerable apprehension the morning after his arrival, Mr Churchill said that he was going to bathe and would I accompany him. We did our best to dissuade him, as there was a bit of a swell and the bathing place was rocky. However, he was quite adamant. We had to go down some 75–100 steps to reach the sea. The cavalcade was headed by Mr Churchill wearing his California hat, a silk dressing gown and bedroom slippers and smoking a cigar. I followed, then came Ogier, Rogers, Sgt Davies, Mr Sawyers (carrying an enormous towel) and finally two military policemen … He thoroughly enjoyed himself, frisking about like a porpoise. Getting him out was a bit of a problem, owing to the swell and the rocks; we managed, by me pushing from the water and Ogier pulling from the land.[10]

Rogers went to Monte Carlo in Alexander's yellow armour-plated Mercedes to make reservations at the Hôtel de Paris which was just reopening after the war. Having succeeded in the mission, Rogers returned to Genoa.[11]

21–22 September 1945: Monte Carlo

Churchill continued his letter to Clementine dated 24 September 1945:

> The weather was delightful and it seemed to me very foolish to go home on the 24th. We, therefore, sent Tim Rogers (Lt) and Major John Ogier on ahead to reconnoitre the neutral State of Monaco. Their report was highly pleasing and the manager at the hotel which is only half full was delighted to receive us on reasonable terms. We motored there on the 21st along the coast road which you will remember we traversed together on our return from the Cairo conference in 1921 … Every important bridge over the valleys leading down to the sea has been smashed to pieces by bombing or naval artillery and all kinds of deviations had to be made. Nevertheless in five hours we came through and arrived in the lap of luxury at Monte Carlo … The Monagesques gathered in crowds and welcomed me on every occasion with the greatest fervour.[23]
>
> We had our meals on the veranda facing the Casino but I did not transgress the 80 paces which separated me from that unsinkable institution. Instead we sent Tim in with two milles to try his luck on strict instructions how to play and after he prepared himself by two days of intense thought. After a half-hour he returned bringing two other milles with him.[23]

Churchill did not tell his wife the whole story! Churchill, Rogers and Ogier 'settled down to a pleasant and leisurely routine in the Hôtel de Paris. Churchill would work at his correspondence in bed until 11.30, when he would get up, have an early lunch, and spend the rest of the day painting'.[11] Rogers had received a message from Mrs Churchill enjoining him at all costs to prevent Churchill gambling in the casino. 'Then you shall go and gamble for me' was Churchill's rejoinder. Rogers played with great circumspection the whole evening and ended up £250 to the good.[11] 'That's not the way to gamble; I shall have to go down myself tomorrow and show you how to do.'[11] The next night Churchill won £3,000 but the night after that he lost it all and on the final night he lost £7,000 (approximately £300,000 in 2019).[11] Churchill arranged that Rogers would speak to the casino manager with the request that the debt would not be presented until Churchill sent word because foreign exchange controls made immediate payment awkward. Flourishing the cheque above his head, the manager answered in theatrical terms, 'Pray tell Mr Churchill that this cheque will never be presented.' 'That's much more agreeable,' said Churchill. 'We'll have a bottle of champagne.'[11]

23 September 1945: Arrival at Villa Sous le Vent, Antibes

In the same letter dated 24 September 1945 Churchill explained to Clementine that:

> General Eisenhower sent his aide-de-camp to see me on arrival, asking me to come on to his villa at Antibes which was vacant and fully staffed I therefore moved in here after two days at Monte Carlo. My two young officers and I are now in this beautiful place surrounded by every comfort and assistance. In four or five days I propose to return to Monte Carlo and stay there until the 5th or 6th of October when I shall be back to have a few shadow Cabinet meetings.[23]

Churchill also explained to Clementine that:

> I went back to Cap Martin, where I painted a picture which you will remember and had another go at olive trees with a brightly coloured background gleaming in the sun, but I must return there a third time as yesterday afternoon there was no sunlight – only warmth and brightness but not enough to cast a shadow which I need for my effect.

Churchill had painted the previous picture of an olive grove at La Dragonnière while he and Clementine were staying at a villa owned by Lord Rothermere. The villa was now owned by a relation:

> and his small children who are very nice came out and bought the picture which I painted eight years ago. It is not a patch on what I can do now, although, as you know, I have hardly touched a brush in the interval. Apparently they had been brought up on the picture and were tremendously excited to see the painter.[23]

Churchill concluded:

> Meanwhile this rest and change of interest is doing me no end of good
> and I never sleep now in the middle of the day. Even when the nights are
> no longer than 5, 6 or 7 hours, I do not seem to require it. This shows
> more than anything else what a load has been lifted off my shoulders.[23]

In a further letter dated 24 September 1945 from Antibes Churchill confirmed
the arrangements to stay at Eisenhower's villa: 'I shall stay here about one
week & then go back to Monte Carlo Hotel for a few days. I may not be home
until the 5th or 6th October. Why sh[oul]d I not stay here in the sunlight &
have a little rest & detachment after all these years of unrequited struggle.'[23]

Churchill sent a telegram to Eisenhower: 'My visit to your villa was
delightful and I am most grateful to you for your hospitality and also for the
arrangements for my homeward journey on October 5th. Trust I shall see
you if you pass through England.'[25]

On 24 September Moran wrote to Churchill in his role as President of
the Royal College of Physicians inviting him to be present and speak at the
Harveian Dinner to be held on 18 October 1945 at the Dorchester Hotel as
the College building in Pall Mall had not yet been repaired following damage
by a bomb during the war.[26] The engagement card for October 1945 has not
survived, and no response to Moran's letter can be found in the Archive.
We do know, however, that Churchill had suffered from a cold and sore
throat for a week prior to 21 October, which had prevented him attending
Parliament.[27] In all probability he did not attend the dinner.

Medical Aspects

Churchill acknowledged that his loss of office as Prime Minister had
resulted in a substantial load being lifted off his shoulders. Nonetheless,
there is little doubt that by August 1945 after 'all these years of unrequited
struggle' Churchill was in need of a long holiday for physical, emotional and
psychological reasons. Furthermore, his wife Clementine was finding life
with Winston a 'misery' and his son Randolph fell out with his father again
during dinner at Claridge's in late August 1945.[28] The family were in no
doubt that a holiday was essential.[3] The first part of the holiday, brokered by
Alexander, was based at Villa Le Rose, Moltrasio, on Lake Como.

At the start of the holiday Churchill suffered a recurrence of a longstanding medical problem, an inguinal hernia, which was manifest as a swelling in the groin, or rupture. A sac of peritoneum containing fat or part of the bowel, bulged through his abdominal wall, resulting in the hernia. Churchill was fortunate that an expert opinion could be obtained rapidly. Edwards's contemporaneous record of his consultation with Churchill on 3 September 1945 reveals the characteristic intellectual clarity, penetration and relevance of Churchill's enquiry about the hernia and the treatment necessary for it.[12]

More than that, Churchill acquired a guest for four days who provided much-needed interest and stimulation after a day's painting. In addition, because Alexander had made arrangements for Churchill's Regiment (4th Hussars) to provide two officers, Ogier and Rogers, this stimulus and excellent support continued after the return of Edwards to his clinical duties and Barne to his Regiment. That the holiday was convivial is supported by the consumption of ninety-six bottles of Veuve Clicquot, donated by Alexander, over sixteen days during the stay on Como. There can be little doubt that this enjoyment continued in Genoa and Monte Carlo, even if it involved only two individuals after the return of Sarah and Moran to London.

Churchill's 'rest and change of interest' and 'detachment' did him 'no end of good' and he no longer required sleep in the middle of the day. Although Churchill had intended to make a start on his memoirs, his main focus was on painting and he was pleased with the pictures he had painted which he considered were amongst his best. As he explained to Clementine: 'This new interest is very necessary in my life.'

Churchill flew back to London in the first week of October 1945 after painting fifteen pictures during twenty-five days of sunshine. His daughter Mary has written:

Those weeks of beautiful and changing scenes, of balmy air and good companionship, had restored him in body, mind and spirit. They had distanced the humiliation he had suffered, and put it in proportion. They had afforded him a physical rest he sorely needed after the stupendous and long drawn-out-trial of the war years; and his right to remind ourselves that he was now in his seventy-first year. But above all he had re-established his 'brush skill' and discovered again his passion for painting.[3]

Chapter 15

Repair of Inguinal Hernia in June 1947 in London

Wake me up soon, I've got lots of work to do.[1]

In 1891 Winston Churchill saw Sir William MacCormac KCB KCVO (1836–1901), Surgeon at St Thomas' Hospital, London, on several occasions because he had developed a hernia.[2] On 5 September 1945 Churchill wrote to his wife, Clementine, from Lake Como, explaining that: 'When I was v[er]y young, I ruptured myself & had to wear a truss. I left it off because I went to Harrow & have managed 60 years of rough-and-tumble.'[3] We have described in the previous chapter, the fitting of a truss by Brigadier Harold Edwards (see p. 150) in September 1945 on Lake Como.

One of Churchill's surgeons, Professor (later Sir) James Paterson Ross (see p. 449), Head of the Professorial Surgical Unit at St Bartholomew's Hospital, London, later recalled that Churchill had suffered troublesome symptoms from his hernia for several years and that during the war he sometimes had to leave important meetings so that he could lie down and reduce his hernia.[4] There is no confirmatory history that Churchill was troubled by a hernia during the Second World War.

However, according to Lord Moran (see p. 443), Churchill's personal physician from May 1940, the search for an effective truss had gone on:

Ever since [presumably from 1945], with small success. Lately, the hernia has got much larger, it is increasingly difficult to control with the truss, and is hardly ever out of his [Churchill's] mind. He seems to look on it as a particularly humiliating hint – anyway to those who can read – of the impermanence of things. The very integument which confines his vital organ has, he protests, given way; it can, of course, be patched, stitched and strengthened to hold for a little longer, but only for a time.[5]

Referral to Sir Thomas Dunhill KCVO

Moran invited Sir Thomas Dunhill (see p. 435) to operate on Churchill.[5] This referral has surprised some who considered that Dunhill might not have been the best choice, because of his age (he was in fact 71 not 81[6]) and because he did not have the necessary expertise.[6]

What are the facts? Within a few years of appointment in 1920 to the professorial surgical unit at St Bartholomew's Hospital, London, Dunhill had established himself as the leading thyroid surgeon in England and in the opinion of Sir Geoffrey Keynes, a distinguished surgical collegue, he was 'a general surgeon in the true sense, exceptionally competent at all forms of surgery, whether abdominal or orthopaedic',[7] and was considered by many as the best general surgeon at St Bartholomew's Hospital.

Dunhill retired from the staff at St Bartholomew's Hospital in 1935 on his 60th birthday, thereafter engaging in what was for some years a very flourishing private practice at 54 Harley Street. By 1949, however, Dunhill had only three patients left: George VI, Queen Mary and Churchill. In 1949 Queen Mary gave Dunhill a beautiful silver porringer ('With much gratitude and best wishes Mary R'), which is now in the possession of the Royal Australasian College of Surgeons.[8] In 1939 Dunhill was awarded an Honorary FRCS (Eng), the first time this Honorary Fellowship had been bestowed on a surgeon who was in active practice.

We also know from the clinical notes of Sir John Parkinson (see p. 444), Churchill's cardiologist, that Dunhill had assessed Churchill in summer 1941: 'Dunhill was satisfied as to the prostate, and the urine was normal.'[9] Following this professional encounter Churchill sent Dunhill the four-volume set of his *Marlborough: His Life and Times* in gratitude. Dunhill replied on 21 May 1941:

Dear Prime Minister
You have given me a very great pleasure. I never dreamed that I should possess a set of the *Marlborough* volumes inscribed by you. To meet and serve you was its own reward – and the two sentences spoken by you this morning have made me chuckle many times since.
Thomas P Dunhill[10]

In May 1942 arrangements were made to pay Dunhill's out-of-pocket expenses for the nurse, dressings etc of 10 guineas (£10 10 shillings).[11] The nature of the surgical intervention is unknown, but when pressed, rather than a fee, Dunhill requested either an electric shaver (he had been impressed by Churchill's), or if this was unobtainable, another book by Churchill to add to his library. Although attempts were made to obtain an electric shaver via the American Embassy, it was Vice Admiral Lord Louis Mountbatten who procured for $17.50 (equivalent at the time to £4 7 shillings 4 pence) a Remington® electric razor from McReynolds Pharmacy, 18th & G Streets, on his next visit to Washington on 4 June 1942.[12] Miss Hill, Churchill's secretary, then had to procure a transformer in England.

Dunhill wrote to Churchill on 14 July 1942:

Dear Mr Prime Minister
You have given me an entertaining and most useful instrument. The first try has been quite successful, even with corners usually difficult. As my eye lights on the soap, brush and hitherto faithful Gillette, I say 'goodbye to all that'. May I give you my fervent wishes in your great job and tell you how honoured I have been to help a little.[13]

On 29 December 1942 Churchill asked Dunhill to come and see him the following day, which he did, and he was accompanied by Sir Charles Wilson (ennobled as Lord Moran in 1943).[14] Dunhill and Moran also saw Churchill at noon on 29 September 1943.[15] Julian Ormond Smith, Past President of the Royal Australasian College of Surgeons, has written about this 1943 professional encounter. According to Beasley, Churchill's medical biographer, Dunhill 'was more than Orm's [Smith] old boss, more than Orm's mentor, almost his surrogate father' (personal communication). Referring to Moran's book, Smith wrote that at least Moran 'had the good taste to refrain from citing another operation which Dunhill performed on the Prime Minister, as he then was in 1943'.[16]

Although it has been suggested that this operation was a prostatectomy,[17] there is no evidence that Churchill was away from wartime duties for several weeks for a major operation in 1943, though he suffered from pneumonia in February 1943 (see p. 73)[18] and December 1943 (see p. 88).[19] Beasley (personal communication) speculates that the operation would probably have been something 'undignified', such as an anal fistula.

There is much correspondence between Churchill and Dunhill that suggests that further surgical opinions were provided and minor surgical procedures undertaken by Dunhill. On 10 April 1946, Dunhill wrote to Churchill:

Thank you for your letter. It is entirely due to you that I, as an individual, and we as a nation exist. I count it a great privilege to have been permitted to contribute in some small way to this end by keeping you fit and it is that I simply could not accept remuneration. I realise you may wish to feel independent. May I therefore suggest that you give me one of your books. I would value that for I have so thoroughly enjoyed those I have read.[20]

Churchill sent a telegram to Dunhill the following day: 'Thank you so much for your charming letter.'[21] On 16 May 1946, Dunhill suggested via Miss Sturdee,[22] Churchill's secretary, a further consultation with Churchill for the following week (this took place on 22 May 1946) when 'he could also explain his opinion about the Belt [presumably for the treatment of the inguinal hernia]'.[23] In August 1946 Dunhill himself underwent a minor operation and recuperated in the country. Churchill sent him some 'beautiful gladioli'. Dunhill wrote: 'More especially I appreciate your thoughtfulness- with all your commitments – in taking time to have this done.'[24]

On 30 September 1946 after a holiday in Switzerland Churchill wrote to Dunhill:

I have been meaning for some time to send you some of my books as a mark of my thanks and appreciation of all the care and attention you have shown me in my ailments. I am having a copy of the Malakand Field Force bound for you, which may take some weeks. Meanwhile I send you the books of my pre-war speeches and of the Secret Session Speeches I made during the war, which I hope may interest you. Pray accept these books from me with my best wishes. I am so glad you are restored.[25]

Given that Dunhill had provided Churchill with regular surgical opinions since at least 1941, it is hardly surprising that Dunhill was invited to operate on Churchill on this occasion. Churchill himself may well have insisted on the referral in the light of Moran's rather patronising views on Dunhill. Moran wrote:

Rather funks an operation on a man of his [Churchill's] age and eminence. He is a simple soul, though a fine craftsman, and regards Winston with awe and reverence as the man who saved this country from defeat. He won't hear of any question of payment whenever I have called him in to see Winston; he sees him at any time of day which suits the patient, scratching all his other appointments without a word, and he cut his summer visit to Norway by nearly a fortnight to fit in with Winston's arrangements. It is an attractive side to his character, but I am not sure it is a sound attitude for doctor towards a patient. The only safe role is to treat Winston exactly like any other patient.[5]

Moran had written earlier in *The Times* following Dunhill's death:

which is another way of saying that he was a great physician, who would use a knife only when he must. For many years I used to go to him when in difficulties and I do not recall that he ever led me wrong. Others who put themselves in his hands felt like that about Dunhill: from the moment he spoke to them in his earnest, subdued way they felt secure in his care. They were right, for his judgement was immaculate.[26]

Moran concluded: 'His friends will remember him as a very gentle soul, very humble, and very unworldly who had in him, as it seemed to us, some of the elements of greatness.'[26] This final comment particularly aroused controversy, with Smith stating that it was 'an affront to the memory of his distinguished life … was ever such a qualified and reluctant tribute simply wrung from a man!'[27]

Sir Geoffrey Keynes, a long-time surgical colleague of Dunhill, has written:

Lord Moran has insisted that Dunhill was not only an exquisite human carpenter, but also had a quite outstanding gift for observation. He was a naturalist practising the art of surgery, which is another way of saying that he was a natural physician who would only use his instruments when he knew he must. In this way he gained the confidence of his medical colleagues and his patients alike. Through association with Lord Dawson of Penn he attended a Royal patient and so came to be appointed Surgeon to the Royal Household, Sergeant Surgeon to King

George VI, and extra surgeon to the present Queen. Though he was the least pushful and self-seeking of men, he came to be greatly trusted in the highest quarters. He was a perfectionist in ordinary life as in surgery.[28]

Moran was still referring Churchill to Dunhill in 1953,[29] despite his stated opinion on Dunhill.

Preparation for the Operation

Churchill's engagement card for May 1947 indicates that Moran, Dunhill and a surgeon (presumably Paterson Ross) assessed Churchill on 9 May 1947.[30] Although Moran does not mention this in his published record, Parkinson, the cardiologist, who had assessed Churchill on several occasions previously, also saw him with Moran on 3 June 1947 at his consulting room at 1 Devonshire Place.[9]

The consultation was proposed as a preliminary to the hernia operation, and not because of any cardiac symptoms. Churchill complained of an occasional slight ache above the left breast lasting for an hour or two after some nervous upset (the last time after a discussion with his son, Randolph), and unrelated to exertion.[9] Churchill told Parkinson that he 'could not hurry, but could go any distance at his own pace'.[9] He had reduced his weight by 3lb. Churchill remembered that he had seen a heart specialist in 1903 who told him he had a strained muscle of the heart and advised Nauheim baths, no effervescing drinks and no smoking,[9] advice that Churchill had clearly ignored! A Nauheim bath is taken in water through which carbon dioxide is bubbled and is named after the town of Bad Nauheim, Germany.

In a letter to Moran, Parkinson wrote:

He looked to me younger and better than in February 1944 when the war was still in progress. The heart sounds are normal and no murmurs are heard. The blood pressure is 140/80. Radioscopy shows a heart of normal shape and size. The right dome of the diaphragm is flattened as if from an old plural adhesion, and yet the diaphragm moves fairly well. The electrocardiogram is normal and almost identical with previous ones ... A single auricular extrasystole [extra beat] is recorded.[9]

Parkinson recorded Churchill telling him: 'You were a great comfort to me during the War in regard to my heart and heart consciousness.'[9] Parkinson's conclusion was 'that there was no evidence of depreciation in the cardiovascular system and I believe that he is as good as ever. There is nothing to suggest that there is any particular cardiac risk at operation.'[9] On 12 June Churchill sent Parkinson a signed photograph with his good wishes.

Moran was also in discussion with Dunhill:

I had at last to put a blunt question to Dunhill: was there any real chance that he [Churchill] will be able to live the rest of his life without an operation? Dunhill thought it was most improbable, and I decided forthwith to push Winston to a decision, so that the operation might be done while the going was good. If he must have it done, now is the time. So, after months of indecision, a date has been fixed.[5]

Churchill vacillated nonetheless. He told Moran he would make a last determined effort to get used to the truss and put up with the skin irritation.[5] Moran tried to persuade Churchill that he would get a good dividend for the small risk he was taking.[5] However, with his liability to contract pneumonia, the surgeons were understandably apprehensive of complications after the anaesthetic; they jibbed at Churchill smoking cigars.

Moran recorded:

At last they screwed up their courage to tell him that in men over 70 statistics proved that pulmonary complications were seven times more common in smokers than non-smokers. Winston declared positively he could give up smoking whenever he liked; he would certainly not smoke for a fortnight before the operation if that was what the doctors wanted. It is true that he did make a feeble and abortive attempt to keep his word; then he decided to cut down the number of cigars to half; finally, he contrived to see Dunhill alone, and soon persuaded him to say that if Winston didn't mind the extra risk he, Dunhill, didn't.[5]

Moran has also recorded that there was a skirmish over the 'place where the operation was to be performed; Winston made a strong plea for his own house, but this time the surgeons stood their ground'.[5] Fife Nursing Home,

23 Bentinck Street, London (Matron: Princess Arthur of Connaught, Duchess of Fife) was chosen.

Despite Dunhill's reputation as a surgeon it is improbable that he had performed an inguinal hernia repair in recent years. Wisely, he made arrangements to practise with Paterson Ross, who probably was also out of practice. In the summer of 1947, Dunhill and Paterson Ross attended 'a sprawling redbrick, slate roof Victorian lunatic asylum'[31] at Hill End, St Albans, to where St Bartholomew's Hospital had been evacuated as its bomb damage from the Second World War had still not been repaired.

The house surgeon to Paterson Ross in 1947 was Mr Martin Birstingl FRCS.[4] He recalls that Paterson Ross told him to put two inguinal hernias on the list because Dunhill wanted to come and see 'how we are doing them nowadays'.[4] 'Ross did the first operation and it went fairly well. Then Dunhill started the second hernia, slowly and in a rather tense atmosphere, which further degenerated when he began the repair and his third suture neatly pierced the femoral vein and the wound filled with blood.'[4]

Dr Richard Gordon, author and sometime anaesthetist, also recalls that:

One morning that June, when I was a young doctor administering anaesthetics, a pleasant-looking grey-haired visitor appeared in our operating theatre corridor, accompanying the professor of surgery. A nurse whispered that he was Sir Thomas Dunhill KCVO CMG Sergeant Surgeon to the reigning King George VI and former surgeon to King George V, now retired from Barts and aged 71 ... To our surprise, he shortly scrubbed up and assisted the professor with the repair of an inguinal hernia. I was flummoxed. Why was the Kings surgeon – or even the professor – performing an operation of such boring straightforwardness it was usually left to the juniors? Sir Thomas repaired all the hospital's hernias for a week.[31]

The Times announced on 7 June 1947 that Churchill would shortly undergo 'an internal operation which may keep him away from his public duties for about a month. It is understood that the operation is not of a very serious character.'[32]

Moran went down to Chartwell on 8 June to see if anything was wanted, and had to submit to a close cross-examination. 'What anaesthetic would be given? Would it be injected into his veins? How long would it be before he went off? I said before he could count fifteen. Whereupon he at once asked: how did the anaesthetic cause unconsciousness? Would he be very uncomfortable afterwards, and if so for how long? Would he have much pain?'[5]

11 June 1947: Pre-operative Assessment and Operation

Churchill arrived at the Fife Nursing Home using the cover name of Mr Spencer,[33] 'with two big volumes of Macaulay's essays as a solace'.[5] Moran found Churchill immersed in them on the morning of the operation. They soothed him Churchill said. Churchill asked Moran to pass him the other volume, when he began to read from Macaulay's review of Ranke's *History of the Papacy*.[5]

> He went on reading savouring the opulence of the language, so much of it pure Winston, while Thomas Dunhill leant over the end of the bed to catch the words, his lips parted with pleasure, not so much in Macauley's measurement of the achievement of the Catholic Church, as in pure joy at his fortune in hearing a great historic figure talk and pay tribute to another master of words. 'A fine piece of English writing … a fine piece of word painting'.[5]

Kelly, a barrister who had joined Churchill's literary team first as an archivist then as a literary assistant, recalls Churchill telling the anaesthetist: 'Wake me up soon, I've got lots of work to do.'[1]

The operation notes have not survived. Moran recorded, however, that Churchill was on the table for more than two hours. 'Adhesions, the legacy of the operation for appendicitis years ago [1922; see p. 20)], made technical difficulties.' The abdominal scar was 8 in long.[2] 'I could see that Dunhill, his assistant and the anaesthetist were engrossed in their job; but I was only an idle spectator.'[5]

In fact Dunhill's 'assistant' was none other than Paterson Ross and the anaesthetist was the distinguished Dr Christopher Langton Hewer (see p. 438), who has related with piquant relish that Ross was treated by Dunhill as though he was still a house surgeon![34]

Birstingl has written that 'most people believe that although officially done by Dunhill, the actual surgeon was Ross'.[4] Professor John Connelly, junior registrar to Paterson Ross in 1952–3, recalls seeing a signed framed photograph of Churchill in Ross' study.[4] Connelly was told that it was given to Patterson Ross because he assisted Dunhill at Churchill's hernia operation and undertook daily afternoon follow-up visits at Churchill's home (see below).

The official bulletin issued on 11 June 1947 stated: 'Mr Churchill had an operation for hernia this morning. His condition after the operation is satisfactory.' The bulletin was signed by Thomas P Dunhill, J Paterson Ross, C Langton Hewer, KLS Ward (Churchill's GP at Chartwell[35]) and Moran. *The Times* reported that Churchill would be 'absent from his duties as Leader of the Opposition for at least a month'.[36]

11–16 June 1947: Post-operative Recovery

Mrs Langton Hewer sent flowers from her garden to Churchill on 12 June. 'May a humble admirer send you these few flowers from the garden in token of the great respect and affection we have for you. We thank God for giving you to our country and trust that you will shortly be restored to your full health.'[37]

Mrs Churchill wrote on 16 June to Lieutenant Commander Frank de Vine Hunt RNVSR, a former member of Churchill's Map Room staff:

> How good of you to send me the 'Legend' which you have prepared with so much thought and care for my husband. I know he will be so much pleased. He is coming home tomorrow in an ambulance and will have to spend another fortnight in bed. He will find the 'Legend' by his bedside. The operation has been most successful and I believe that it will give him a new lease of life.[38]

The 'Legend' was designed to provide Churchill with 'a ready reference when writing his War Memoirs, and in this way to save him a certain amount of trouble'.[39]

On 17 June Mrs Churchill wrote to her daughter, Sarah: 'Papa is getting on splendidly and comes home this afternoon. He will be in bed for another 10 days.'[1]

17 June–7 August 1947: Home and Recuperation

Churchill returned home probably to Chartwell (though the engagement card states he returned to 28 Hyde Park Gate[30]) where he was looked after by Nurse Helen Blake.[1] Dunhill visited Churchill on 22 June and 23 June.[30]

On 1 July Denis Kelly delivered a broadside to Churchill, even though he was still supposed to remain in bed for medical reasons, over his habit of 'rummaging' among the documents. His concern was that the cataloguing and indexing of the archive for the War Memoirs, which was almost complete, would be wrecked by Churchill.[1] Kelly proposed a solution which kept both parties content.

On the same day Dunhill requested a copy of the poem about the aurora borealis, which Churchill had quoted to him, to put up in his fishing hut in Norway.[40] In the absence of Dunhill in Norway, Paterson Ross reviewed Churchill on 9 July and 17 July.[30]

On 12 July Dunhill wrote to Churchill from Norway:

> The black band [sleep mask] and the poem arrived yesterday – a calendar month from the day of the operation. It was good of you to send them. I hope you have made progress and regained strength and agility – although I observed no lack of either after the first post-operation day. The band is a great comfort. No longer do I fear the aurora borealis turning itself about, and most inconsiderately becoming an unnecessarily bright sun at 2.30 am. The members of the party chuckle over Dan Leno's poem and are more amazed than ever at your versatility and charm. The salmon are giving good sport, and the mosquitos are not unduly penetrating.[41]

Dan Leno was the stage name of George Wild Galvin (1860–1904), a leading English music-hall comedian.

Dunhill wrote to Churchill immediately on returning to England on 1 August. 'First may I congratulate you on what I read and hear. You have been a remarkable patient ... the salmon accompanying this was caught by my host and smoked by a Norwegian admirer for you ...'[42] Churchill sent a telegram to Dunhill by return. 'So glad you are back. Hope you have enjoyed yourself we must meet next week. Thank you so much for the salmon.'[43] Dunhill reviewed Churchill on 6 August.[30]

As soon as Churchill was allowed out of bed, work on Churchill's War Memoirs reached a high pitch of activity. Kelly has explained in detail the intense process involved: 'The day began at 7 o'clock at night. I had to go straight up to his bedroom because he could hear the taxi arrive and was impatient for the latest proofs from London.'[1] At dinner, Churchill and Kelly ate at opposite ends of the table each with their own copy of the current text:

> Sherry with the soup; champagne with the main cause; port with the cheese; brandy with the coffee; each with our pen and scribbling pad, then back to his study … A woman secretary would arrive with the evening letters … Then down to the real work of the evening. Silent typewriter behind us to our right; long, hesitant, brilliant dictation; corrections with a red pen; retype.[1]

Kelly explained that:

> Each chapter was drafted, printed, redrafted and reprinted at least half a dozen times, and circulated to a group of experts for criticism and comment … A chapter was usually between five and eight thousand words; the rule was 'chronology is the key to narrative, but subjects break-in'; the commandment:- 'Say what you have to say as clearly as you can and in as few words as possible'.[1]

Writing occupied the morning. After lunch, there was a walk round the estate. While Churchill took his afternoon sleep, Kelly and others toiled 'to give him enough work for the evening until 2 o'clock the following morning'.[1]

Churchill summarized these various stages of literary production when he was awarded the *Sunday Times* Annual Literary Award for 1949 and Commemorative Gold Medal following the publication of the first two books in his series on *The Second World War*:

> Whilst writing, a book is an adventure. To begin with it is a toy, then an amusement, then it becomes a mistress and then it becomes a master and then it becomes a tyrant and, in the last stage, just as you are about to be reconciled to your servitude, you kill the monster and fling him to the public.[44]

The hard, literary work was interrupted on 7 August 1947 when Churchill joined his son-in-law, Christopher Soames, for a rabbit shoot. His personal detective, Ronald Golding, recalled:

> About noon, I drove WSC up in a Jeep, by which Mr Churchill always used to get around the farm. We stopped at a field which was almost harvested, with just a small square of wheat in the middle. Mr Churchill clambered slowly out of the Jeep … Just as he got his feet on the ground, there was a shout from the others and the rabbit darted from the centre of the field. In a flash Mr Churchill raised his gun and fired one barrel. The rabbit keeled over dead. It was a wonderful shot, and the usual Churchill luck. The others had been waiting hours for the opportunity.[45]

It is an indication of Churchill's regard for Dunhill that he is on a very short list of 'Personal friends' who were to receive a copy of *The Gathering Storm* on publication in 1948,[46] and of all subsequent volumes in the series on *The Second World War*. The last volume was received by Dunhill on publication in 1954.

> My dear Prime Minister
> It is very good of you to send me the final volume of your *Second World War*. I regard the series as a very valued possession as I have regarded my occasional associations with you as the purple patches in my life. May I wish Lady Churchill and you health and vigour to continue to carry on.[47]

20 October 1947: Assessment by Dr John Parkinson

On 20 October Churchill was re-examined by Parkinson following an episode three days previously when he had felt some discomfort at the left costal margin for some 2 to 3 hours. Churchill described the discomfort as like flatulence and palpitation, with the heart 'missing' frequently e.g. 1, 2, 3, stop. On examination Parkinson found Churchill's blood pressure to be 150/90 mmHg. Radioscopy [X-ray] showed no cardiac or aortic enlargement. The electrocardiogram (leads I, II, III only) was normal; two atrial extrasystoles (extra beats) were recorded. Churchill was urged by

Parkinson to ignore the extrasystoles as they had no clinical significance and they were not worth treating by drugs. Parkinson told Churchill that his heart was healthy.[9]

Medical Aspects

This account of Churchill's hernia repair, assembled from a number of contemporaneous medical and non-medical sources, demonstrates several notable features.

First, the concern and reverence for Churchill's health. The medical and surgical personnel and expertise recruited by Moran and Dunhill were impressive, and it is clear that no one wished to be responsible for any mistake in the care of a man whose importance was ranked on a par with members of the Royal Family.

Second, the good judgement and humility of the very distinguished surgeons concerned. They recognised their limitation in performing an apparently 'simple' operation.

Third, the skill of the anaesthetist Langton Hewer, and the post-operative care of Churchill, who was an overweight smoker then in his 70s, and well-known to be prone to the development of pneumonia.[18,19,48]

How successful was the operation? Two US surgeons commented in 2003: 'The results speak for themselves: tissue repair, probably under tension (no mesh, no preperitoneal approach, no laparoscopy), of a large and long-standing hernia in an obese patient who suffered from chronic obstructive lung disease, with no recurrence on prolonged followup.'[17] As judged by the absence of any further mention of the hernia during the remainder of Churchill's life, either by Churchill himself or by his personal physician Moran, the operation was indeed successful.

Finally, it is clear that Dunhill established with Churchill a relationship not only of professional trust but also of personal understanding, mutual respect and friendship extending back to 1941. The witty correspondence between the two men, cited here in part, and Dunhill's presence on Churchill's list of personal friends leaves no doubt about this, and sets Dunhill apart from Churchill's many other medical advisers, with the possible exception of Professor Sir Herbert Seddon.

Chapter 16

First Stroke in August 1949 in Monaco

What has gone wrong, Charles? Have I had a stroke?[1]

On 26 May 1949 Winston Churchill was re-examined by Sir John Parkinson (see p. 444), his cardiologist, in the presence of Lord Moran (p. 443), his personal physician.[2] On this occasion Churchill complained again of intermittent extrasystoles (extra heart beats) and flatulence and admitted on direct questioning that he had felt slight shortness of breath on waking with the symptoms.[2] Identical symptoms had been reviewed by Parkinson in October 1947 (see p. 180) and Churchill had been reassured.[2] Parkinson noted during this repeat examination that Churchill looked well. His pulse was 70/min and regular. The heart sounds were normal and his blood pressure was 145/90 mmHg.[2] The electrocardiogram was normal.[2] Again Parkinson insisted that the extrasystoles were without clinical significance. Parkinson recorded that Mrs Churchill had once told him that the extrasystoles had been present since the Churchills were first married.[2]

Parkinson emphasised to Churchill, however, that everything should be done to prevent any recurrence of the atrial fibrillation he had suffered in December 1943 (see p. 88).[3] He must take more care and arrange to rest more. Parkinson's conclusion was that Churchill's heart was in 'good condition'.[2]

25 July–9 August 1949: Holiday in Italy

In the summer of 1949 Winston Churchill and his wife Clementine spent the first part of their summer holiday on the shores of Lake Garda. The Churchills flew to Bergamo in a Dakota of Silver City Airways on 25 July and first stayed with their entourage in an apartment with twelve rooms, on the third floor of the new wing of Grand Hotel Gardone Riviera, Lombardy, Italy. Despite being on vacation, Churchill remained in continuous contact with London via a special phone line managed by two secretaries,

Miss Lettice Marston[4] and Miss Cecily 'Chips' Gemmell.[5] In addition to political work, Churchill combined 'hours of painting with hours of writing' his War Memoirs.[6] However, as the Churchills found the temperature and humidity in Gardone unbearable, they continued their holiday at the Grand Hotel Carezza, Nova Levante, in the Dolomites, which was much cooler than Gardone and had 'more paintable scenery'.[7]

10–18 August 1949: Council of Europe, Strasbourg

On 10 August the Churchills went to Strasbourg where Churchill was to attend the Inaugural Session of the Consultative Assembly of the Council of Europe.[6] Churchill led the Opposition section and Herbert Morrison, Deputy Prime Minister, the government section of the British delegation at Strasbourg. The first meeting was held on 12 August and on 15 August, applauded by large crowds, Churchill received the Freedom of the City.[8] Churchill was under the impression that the public holiday was in his honour;[8] he had not realised it was for the Feast of the Assumption of Mary into Heaven!

On 17 August Churchill gave a speech (Plate 14) which Harold Macmillan MP (Minister Resident in the Mediterranean 1942–5 and future Prime Minister) 'ranked in its effect with those in Fulton and at Zurich'.[8] While Mrs Churchill flew home, Churchill left Strasbourg by air the next day for Monte Carlo to continue his holiday and left Macmillan in command of the Opposition group.

August 1949: La Capponcina at Cap d'Ail

The Churchill party were staying at La Capponcina at Cap d'Ail, across the bay from Monte Carlo. The villa was owned by Lord Beaverbrook, newspaper proprietor and Lord Privy Seal, 1943–5. For almost a week Churchill painted, worked on revising volume 4 of his War Memoirs, and swam turning somersaults in the sea to amuse Merle Oberon, the actress and house guest.[7]

On the evening of 23 August Churchill played cards (gin rummy) with Beaverbrook, Wardell (vice-chairman of the Beaverbrook organization) and others. Wardell has recorded: 'At one o'clock in the morning we stopped for soup and cigars. Presently we resumed playing.'[9] Churchill began to lose, and he moved his father's multi-band signet ring from his right hand to his left. 'It's never been off my finger. I'll change my luck.'[9] At about 2 am, Churchill complained of cramp in his right hand, the hand from which he had removed the ring. Nonetheless, he went on playing, giving his attention to the game.[9]

At the end of the game, Churchill said he had a most peculiar sensation and must go to bed. He added up the score and wrote in a clear hand an IOU. Churchill and Wardell walked up the stairs and Wardell carried Churchill's cigars. As Churchill slowly mounted the steps he paused, turned to Wardell and said: 'The dagger is pointing at me. I pray it may not strike. I want so much to be spared, at least to fight the election. I must lead the Conservatives back to victory. I know I am worth a million votes to them ... Perhaps two million.'[9] Churchill entered his room.[9] Churchill said: 'I still have cramp ... I've a strange sensation I have never had before.'[9] Wardell wrote that Churchill was in full possession of all his faculties and took a pill.[9] 'My sleeper [hypnotic], I'll give you one, if you like.'[9] Churchill undressed. Wardell went downstairs to lock the door and turn out the light. As Wardell came up the stairs, Churchill was closing his door, standing naked. He waved his hand and said: 'Goodnight.'[9]

Churchill then asked Denis Kelly, a barrister who had joined Churchill's literary team as an archivist then became a literary assistant, to sit with him while he took a bath. Kelly later recalled that this was the only time in ten years he had been asked to sit with Churchill while he had a bath.[7]

When Churchill awoke at about 7 am on 24 August, the cramp was still present.[7] A little later Churchill found he could not write as well as usual. Beaverbrook summoned Dr Gibson (see p. 437), a local practitioner, and telephoned his son, Max Aitken, in London who arranged for Lord Moran to come out immediately.[7,9]

Gilbert[7] wrote that Moran was contacted by Dr Roberts but this is probably incorrect as Churchill later told Dr Russell (later Lord) Brain (see p. 431) he had been seen by the local doctor 'a Scotsman',[10] whereas Roberts was a Welshman.[11] In all probability, therefore, it was Gibson who telephoned Moran: 'I think Mr. Churchill has had a stroke. I would like you to see him as soon as you can.'[1] Moran arrived at Nice with his golf clubs, to suggest nothing was amiss with Churchill,[7] and was met by Beaverbrook, also Moran's patient, and informed of the previous night's events.

On entering his bedroom, Churchill said to Moran: 'I am glad you've come; I'm worried.'[1] Moran recorded: 'I could find no loss of power when I examined him; his grip was strong. Later, when he squeezed paints out of their tubes, he could not do it as well as usual.'[1] Churchill himself was certain that his speech was not affected and Moran could detect no abnormality.[1] Moran asked Churchill about his writing.[1] Reaching for his pen, and steadying a bit of paper against a book, Churchill wrote very slowly and carefully: 'I am trying to do my best to make it legible. It is better than it was this morning. W. Churchill.'[1] Churchill was particularly concerned about his signature. Miss Gilliatt, personal secretary,[12] later recalled: 'He kept on practising it, asking one again and again, is it all right?'[7]

'What has gone wrong, Charles? Have I had a stroke?'[1] Moran explained that when people speak of a stroke, they mean that an artery has burst and there has been a haemorrhage into the brain. 'You've not had that. A very small clot has blocked a very small artery.'[1]

Churchill enquired:

Will I have another? There may be an election soon. An election in November is now more a probability than a possibility. I might have to take over again. It feels like being balanced between the Treasury Bench [the front bench in the House of Commons occupied by the Prime Minister and the Chancellor of the Exchequer], and death. But I don't worry. Fate must take its course.[1]

Moran recorded that Churchill's memory was not impaired.[1] Churchill said: 'there seems to be a veil between me and things. And there's a sensation in my arm that was not there before … it's like a tight feeling across my shoulder-blade.'[1]

Although Mrs Churchill was kept fully informed about her husband's condition, she remained at home. Although anxious about his illness, she concluded that her sudden arrival would certainly have aroused suspicions that Churchill was suffering from something more than a chill,[6] which was the diagnosis announced in the press on 26 August 1949. Even his daughter Sarah was not informed of the correct diagnosis. She wrote from New York: 'My darling Papa, I was so terribly relieved to hear that it was only a cold and that you are alright again.'[7]

Macmillan recorded that on 25 August he had received the shattering news of Churchill's illness.

We got the most exaggerated stories – he had pneumonia, he had had a stroke, he was gravely ill. However, Duncan Sandys [former Member of Parliament and Churchill's son-in-law] came in to me early in the morning, to say that he had talked with him on the phone and he seemed in good form. It seems that he has certainly got a chill, and since Moran is with him, it is probable that he will not be allowed to return here [Strasbourg] – at least for some days. Naturally, the rumours spread throughout the day, and were not altogether dispelled by a reassuring bulletin.[8]

The truth of Churchill's stroke remained a secret known only to the doctors, and to those staying at Beaverbrook's villa. At the urging of Moran, Churchill stopped work for three days, but felt well enough on the fourth day to dictate a few letters.[7] Churchill ended his letter to Field Marshal Montgomery on 27 August with reference to his health as the public had been informed of it: 'I am laid up here for a few days as the result of a chill, but am making good progress.'[7]

Macmillan wrote:

In fact, as I was afterwards to learn, Churchill had suffered from one of those minor attacks which were to threaten him for the rest of his life. This one, happily, proved slight, and by careful control of the news was effectively concealed. This indomitable old man was still destined to fight two General Elections and form another Government which was to last nearly four years. As soon as he began to recover, the telephone began to ring with increasing urgency.[8]

Churchill invited Kelly to dine with him in Monte Carlo.

We sat at a balcony table overlooking the street. A French lady in full evening dress passed by, stopped, gasped and curtsied. She could not believe her eyes. Churchill bowed from his chair … I realised he intended to show the world he was fit and well and had deliberately chosen this most public yet normal way of proving it.[7]

Moran also recalled:

When some days later he [Churchill] lunched at the Hotel de Paris, and everyone rose to their feet as he entered, and no one noticed anything, he gained confidence.[1]

31 August–4 October 1949: Return to England

Churchill returned home on 31 August and his aircraft landed at Biggin Hill. When Churchill saw all the photographers with their cameras, he was certain they would notice that something was wrong with his gait, and 'he waved them away with an angry gesture'.[1]

On 3 September, Churchill felt well enough to go to Epsom Downs Racecourse to see his horse Colonist II run.[7] Churchill went to 11 Downing Street on 18 September to be told by Sir Stafford Cripps, the Chancellor of the Exchequer, of the imminent devaluation.[7] Later Churchill told Moran at Chartwell: 'I'm not the man I was before this happened. I had to see Cripps at No. 11 about devaluation. It was an act of courtesy on his part. He was cool and debonair, but I was in a twitter.'[1]

As a gesture of thanks to Moran, Churchill now executed a second seven-year Deed of Covenant in favour of Moran's wife, Dorothy, for £500 a year (approximately £17,500 in 2019), free of tax. Churchill wrote to Moran: 'I hope you will not forbid me to do this and I have taken the necessary steps with the Bank.'[7]

5 October 1949: Assessment by Dr Russell Brain

Brain, a distinguished neurologist and soon to succeed Moran as President of the Royal College of Physicians, saw Churchill at Chartwell for the first time as a patient on 5 October,[10] though this encounter is not recorded by Moran in his published record. Moran had informed Brain that some years previously while Churchill was in the United States, he had had an attack of vertigo and unsteadiness, the latter taking some weeks to settle down, and which was attributed at the time to a labyrinthine (inner ear) lesion.[10]

In addition, Moran described the episode of chest pain which Churchill suffered while staying in the White House in December 1941 (see p. 57).[13] Moran feared Churchill had suffered a coronary thrombosis but owing to the circumstances, could not get an electrocardiogram done, and Churchill carried on as usual, though complaining of some dyspnoea.[10] On his return to

London Churchill was assessed by Parkinson who did an electrocardiogram, and according to Moran 'refused to commit himself'.[10] In fact, Parkinson did commit himself and did not support the diagnosis of coronary thrombosis (see p. 65).[13]

In the summer of 1949, before Churchill went abroad, he asked Moran to feel his pulse after bathing, and Moran thought it poor volume.[10] Moran said Churchill smoked thirteen cigars a day and took a fair amount of alcohol – three brandies after dinner – but was never the worse for it.[10]

When Moran and Brain went into the room, Churchill handed his partially smoked cigar to his valet.[10] Brain recorded that Churchill was in his bed, which carried a shelf full of proofs, which he was correcting.[10] On his left was a double-decker locker on which amongst other things stood a whisky and soda, while on the floor nearby was a white enamel bucket into which he shook his cigar ash.[10] Churchill was wearing a dark red and gold bed jacket and a nightshirt which reached just below his waist, and had a division down the middle behind because as he explained to Brain he wrote a good deal in bed.[10]

Churchill began by saying: 'You reconnoitre first, and then we'll have the history of the campaign,' by which he meant that he wanted Brain to examine him before he gave his history. However, as this was bad medicine, Brain explained to Churchill that he must have the history first. Churchill reported that on 28 August (in fact it was 23–4 August) he had been bathing and painting during the day and was sitting up at 2 am playing gin rummy. Suddenly, he felt his right leg go numb to above the hip, and also in the region of the shoulder, and when he tried to write down the score, he could not write properly. The next morning Churchill's leg was still numb, and he sent for the local doctor (Dr Gibson). Moran arrived at 11 am. Churchill explained that it was thought his speech was a little affected, but Churchill claimed it was very slight: 'as if I was between asleep and awake'. In fact, at the time, Churchill himself was certain that his speech was not affected and Moran could detect no abnormality.[1]

Churchill said there was a sensation like lumps in the upper part of the right thigh, but nothing to be seen. Churchill's writing difficulty, which Brain recorded as being motor in origin (see explanation below), lasted three days and he had slight difficulty in walking. He was still unsteady on reaching England, but not now. He still got an occasional tight feeling in the right leg, right shoulder and the right side of the back near the spine. 'Occasionally I get the twitters – a momentary feeling of giddiness.'[10]

Brain's examination revealed that Churchill's speech and articulation were normal.[10] The optic discs were normal, but there was some retinal arteriosclerosis. Pupils and ocular movements were normal, and the visual fields were full. The remaining cranial nerves were normal. There was no weakness or ataxia of the limbs; the tendon reflexes were present and equal but the ankle jerks were a bit sluggish. The right plantar reflex was recorded as '? extensor' (a physical examination sign consistent with a recent or previous stroke) in Brain's original note, the left was flexor. To demonstrate something, Churchill made Brain sit on his bed while he pressed on Brain's back. 'It was like the hug of a bear!'[10] recorded Brain. The abdominal reflexes were absent. There was no cutaneous anaesthesia. Pinprick was felt slightly less acutely on the right forearm than on the left. There was no postural loss. Vibration felt less acute on the right shin than on the left. Romberg's sign was negative and the gait normal. In this test the patient is asked to stand upright. Romberg's sign is positive if the patient is able to maintain his posture when his eyes are open, but sways and loses balance when his eyes are closed. There were frequent extrasystoles (extra beats), and the blood pressure was 160/90 mmHg.[10] Brain recorded that Churchill looked little more than 60 at 74.[10]

Brain explained to Churchill that his symptoms were due to a temporary impairment of the circulation through a part of his brain. Churchill's response: 'I may be worth a million votes to the party. I must warn you that whatever advice you give me, I mean to go on. I am not afraid to die.'[10] Churchill then began to wander around in his little bed jacket and nightshirt, bare from the middle thighs downwards.[10] 'You must see me walk.'[10] Churchill then did a kind of goose-step and stood still with his eyes closed to show how steady he was.[10]

Churchill then insisted on Moran and Brain having a drink. 'I diagnose that you would like some sherry!'[10] Moran, however, was anxious to get away as the Duke and Duchess of Westminster were coming to dinner, and it was essential for political reasons that no one should know that Brain had seen Churchill. Moran and Brain drank a hasty glass of sherry and left Churchill splashing in his bath.[10]

13–21 October 1949: Speeches

Churchill was well enough by the middle of October to make two substantial speeches in London. The first to the Conservative Trades Union Congress was on 13 October, the second on 14 October was to the Conservative Annual Conference.

On 20 October Churchill gave the Chancellor's address at the University of Bristol's annual honorary degree-giving ceremony and on the following day spoke to several thousand veterans at the fourth Alamein Reunion ('Up till Alamein we survived. After Alamein we conquered').[7]

15 October and 8 December 1949: Assessments by Dr Russell Brain

Brain assessed Churchill again on 15 October when he recorded that: 'there was no substantial change in his condition'.[10] When Brain told Churchill that the postponement of the election would give him four months' respite, Churchill responded: 'Yes, but in four months' time, I shall be four months older. That I think is incontestable.'[10]

Brain assessed Churchill again on 8 December at Hyde Park Gate.[10] Churchill was in bed with his cigar and whisky and soda. He described his symptoms as follows: 'It is a quiet and agreeable, warm, India-rubbery, velvet feeling in the right groin and a stiffness around the shoulder. The first sensation was a lump which did not exist. There is no pain and no disability. It is like a sheet of warm material one-sixteenth of an inch thick and one inch from the surface, spread out over it.'[10] Pointing to a Sorbo pad, Churchill said: 'It feels like this, but only half as thick and frayed at the edges.'[10] Churchill had had no subjective anaesthesia and there had been no difficulty in writing. He had been painting during the last few days.[10] Examination revealed no loss of light touch, pinprick or appreciation of passive movement. The knee and ankle jerks were sluggish but equal, and the plantar reflexes were both now flexor.[10]

On 29 December 1949–12 January 1950: Holiday in Madeira

Churchill flew to Madeira on 29 December for a working holiday with his wife, daughter Diana, literary assistant Bill Deakin, and personal private secretaries Miss Sturdee[14] and Miss Gilliatt.[15] The party stayed at Reid's Hotel and were surrounded by Churchill's War Memoirs materials. Churchill had intended to stay in Madeira for several weeks but, while he was away, Clement Attlee, the Prime Minister, announced that a General Election would be held on 23 February 1950. Churchill flew back to London on 12 January to commence electioneering.[15]

Medical Aspects

There is no doubt that Churchill suffered a stroke in August 1949, at the age of 74. Brain found a mild neurological deficit when he first examined Churchill in October that year, some seven weeks after the onset of symptoms. The abnormal signs were subtle and almost exclusively sensory, comprising disturbance of some primary modalities of sensation on the right side. However, the right plantar reflex was equivocal, the only sign of pyramidal tract involvement (the motor pathway from the brain, also known as the corticospinal tract). There was no good evidence of speech involvement, and the contemporaneous remarks concerning Churchill's speech, quoting his exact words, indicate no impairment of his extraordinary linguistic ability, and his characteristically pithy and witty powers of expression.

From the descriptions recorded by witnesses to the event and by Churchill himself, he experienced transient mild impairment of his ability to write. This seems to have been a problem of legibility, rather than a specific dysphasic-dysgraphic deficit (speech and writing). Brain did not record any deficits of cortical sensory function, but by that time, seven weeks after the onset of the stroke, Churchill's sensory symptoms were minimal and intermittent.

Churchill's transient writing difficulty was interpreted by Brain as being of motor origin, and Brain's original note, verbatim, states that: 'Writing difficulty which was "motor" lasted three days only.'[10] He probably reached this conclusion because of the finding of an equivocal right plantar response, indicating the involvement of the corticospinal tract. However, Churchill's prominent sensory symptoms clearly indicate thalamic involvement (the main sensory relay in the brain), and it is most likely that the lesion affected the ventral posterior sensory nucleus of the thalamus and the adjacent posterior limb of the internal capsule (a thalamo-capsular infarct).

The onset and progression of the symptoms over several hours are now considered to be typical of small vessel occlusion, possible mechanisms including haemodynamic factors, propagation of thrombosis, excitotoxicity due to neurotransmitter release, inflammation or conduction block. A small haemorrhagic stroke cannot be entirely excluded, and small deep haemorrhages may exactly mimic a lacunar infarct due to vessel occlusion.

Could hypertension have been a factor? Sir John Parkinson recorded Churchill's blood pressure on four occasions prior to this stroke: 160/85 mmHg (6 February 1942); 140/80 mmHg (3 June 1947); 150/90 mmHg (20 October 1947); 145/90 mmHg (26 May 1949).[2] The blood pressure of 160/90 mmHg, recorded seven weeks after the onset of the stroke by Brain, would have been regarded at the time as borderline normal for a man of 74, though now would be considered to be high. This and Churchill's steady alcohol intake were risk factors for either occlusion or haemorrhage.

Churchill's pulse was in sinus rhythm, with frequent extrasystoles, but crucially, the cardiac rhythm was not atrial fibrillation, so a cardiac embolus is unlikely. Churchill had suffered two episodes of atrial fibrillation in December 1943 when being treated for pneumonia (see p. 88)[3] and was to do so again in 1958 (see p. 273).[16] Finally, it is worth reflecting that the early days of computerised tomography (CT brain scans) were still some twenty years ahead, and even then, in the early days of CT scanning, the resolution would quite possibly have missed a small capsular lesion of the sort likely to have been responsible for this stroke.

One might wonder why Brain was invited by Moran to see Churchill only at such a long interval following the onset of the stroke (about seven weeks). However, when viewed in the context of the limited approach to the investigation of stroke possible at the time, and the largely expectant management, taken together with the rapid improvement of Churchill's mild symptoms, this is understandable.

In the light of later neurological events, it is relevant to consider whether there might have been any abnormal emotional or behavioural change at the time of this first stroke, which might indicate the presence of more widespread cerebrovascular disease already present at that time. It is clear from the descriptions of Brain and the non-medical witnesses to the event that Churchill's command of language, his unconventional dress and his longstanding habits were unchanged. His colourful description of his symptoms matched his characteristic linguistic command and expressive succinctness. His request of Brain to 'reconnoitre first, and then we'll have the history of the campaign' supports this and moreover reveals that he wished to remain in complete control even at a time of serious personal vulnerability.

The visits of Brain to Churchill on 5 and 15 October and 8 December 1949 are not mentioned by Moran in his book *Winston Churchill: the Struggle for Survival 1940–1965*,[17] which records Brain's first consultation as taking place on 25 May 1950. The reasons for this are not clear.

Brain received a pre-publication copy of Moran's book which was inscribed 'Russell from Charles, April 29 1966.'[18] Brain was upset that he had been quoted without his knowledge and permission. On 9 May 1966 Brain wrote a letter to *The Times* which was published the following day.[19] After acknowledging that Moran had sent him a copy of the book, he went on to write:

Since Lord Moran has already alluded to me in one of the published extracts, I must point out that these confidential matters have been published without my knowledge. To put matters in perspective, my notes show that I was first asked by Lord Moran to see Sir Winston in October, 1949, and that I saw him on 20 occasions, the last being during his final illness. Sometimes for various reasons I saw him alone, once, at least, at his request. During these 15 years I came to know him well, and I cannot accept the accuracy of all that Lord Moran says about the consultations which he reports ... I hope that this unhappy controversy will not be allowed to obscure Lord Moran's great services to Sir Winston. Over the years I saw his devotion at first hand, and I know that it was given at great personal sacrifice.[19]

Chapter 17

Cerebrovascular Disease January 1950–March 1952 in London

I couldn't think of the words I wanted. Wrong words seemed to come into my head, but I was quite clear what was happening[1]

Churchill suffered his first stroke in August 1949 (see p. 182).[2] On 29 December 1949 Churchill had flown to Madeira for a working holiday.[3] Churchill had intended to stay in Madeira for several weeks but, while he was away it was announced that a General Election would be held on 23 February 1950. Churchill flew back to London on 12 January 1950 to commence electioneering.[3]

24 January–6 February 1950: Assessments by Lord Moran

On 24 January Churchill sent for Lord Moran (see p. 443), his personal physician since May 1940, who visited his patient at once. Churchill explained to Moran: 'About an hour ago everything went misty. There was no warning. I could just read, with difficulty. What does it mean, Charles? Am I going to have another stroke?'[4] Moran reassured Churchill: 'You seem to get arterial spasms when you are very tired.'[4] Churchill's response: 'You mustn't frighten me.'[4]

Moran next visited Churchill on the morning of 5 February. The previous night Churchill had spoken to 5,000 people at an election meeting in Leeds. 'I felt invigorated by the meeting, brutalized as I am by fifty years of it. Of course, when it was all over I was tired.'[4]

Moran went to see Churchill again on 6 February because Miss Sturdee, Churchill's personal secretary, had informed him that Churchill was taking on more speeches. After a speech in Manchester, Churchill planned to speak at Oldham and for his son, Randolph, at Plymouth.[4] Moran attempted to persuade Churchill, without success, that it was unnecessary for him to stump the country making speeches when broadcasting was an option.[4]

Moran wrote: 'I begin to see that we must let things take their course. I must be sensible. After all, if anything does happen, he would prefer to go out fighting a general election, with plenty of cheering and booing and heckling.'[4]

Although Churchill was re-elected as MP for Woodford on 23 February 1950 with a majority of 18,000, it was clear by noon on 24 February 1950 that although the Conservatives had won 298 seats (up from 213), they had failed to win the election as there was a Labour majority of 6.[3]

25 May 1950: Assessments by Lord Moran and Dr Russell Brain

Moran assessed Churchill again on 25 May because the tightness over his shoulders had increased. 'He can't get the stroke out of his mind,' Moran wrote.[4] To reassure Churchill Moran again invited Dr Russell Brain (see p. 431), his neurologist, to give a second opinion. Brain recorded that Churchill's symptoms were unchanged, and there were no abnormal physical signs.[5] Brain has written that he had no further record of this meeting.[5]

However, Moran quoted Brain as stating to Churchill: 'The cells in your brain which receive sensory messages from your shoulder are dead. That's all. It's a bit of luck that sensation only is affected.'[4] Beasley, a medical biographer of Churchill, has challenged the accuracy of Moran's written record of Brain's comments as he considered it inherently unlikely that an eminent neurologist would phrase his explanation in these terms. 'It is difficult to imagine that dead sensory cells would transmit the sensation of tightness or anything else.'[6]

11–25 October 1951: Assessment by Lord Moran and Churchill is Elected Prime Minister Again

Churchill was assessed by Moran on 11 October. Churchill told Moran that he had a muzzy feeling in his head. 'Oh, it's nothing to do with alcohol; it comes on generally before luncheon. Aspirin helps it. If it's due to circulation in my head, can't you think out something, Charles, that would be more effective than aspirin?'[7] Churchill went on: 'I am not so sure as I was that I shall be able to see things through … I'm not afraid to die but I want to do this job properly.'[7] Moran advised Churchill there was no treatment that would rejuvenate the circulation in his head. If Churchill wanted to stay the course, he must cut out things; he could not do everyone's job as he had done in the war.[7]

The Conservatives won the General Election on 25 October by 17 seats (Conservatives 321; Labour against 295; Liberals 6; others 3), and Churchill was again Prime Minister.

29 November 1951: Advice of Sir John Parkinson Sought

Moran telephoned Sir John Parkinson (see p. 444), Churchill's cardiologist, for advice after Churchill had experienced a 'muzzy feeling' on several occasions before lunch.[8] Moran had found that Churchill's pulse was 72/minute and regular and his blood pressure was 150/80 mm Hg. Parkinson's opinion was that this muzzy feeling was not cardiac in origin.[8]

6–15 February 1952: Death and Funeral of King George VI

On 6 February King George VI died. When John Colville, Churchill's Joint Principal Private Secretary, went to the Prime Minister's bedroom that morning, Churchill was sitting alone with tears in his eyes reading neither his official papers nor the newspapers.[9] Colville recorded that he had not realized how much the King meant to Churchill.[9] Churchill summoned a Cabinet that morning.[9]

The King's funeral was held at St George's Windsor on 15 February.[9] Following the funeral the postponed foreign affairs debate took place and Churchill 'made a good but much interrupted speech, discrediting Attlee and Morrison and dumbfounding his attackers'.[9] The following week Churchill gave a further speech in the defence debate which was followed by a 'clever budget, slashing food subsidies but providing new incentives for hard work and overtime by lowering the bottom rates of income tax'.[9] All of this Colville considered had been a severe strain on Churchill.[9]

21–9 February 1952: Assessments by Lord Moran

On the evening of 21 February Moran received a telephone call from Churchill. 'Where are you, Charles? I'd like to see you.' Moran got into a taxi and went to 28 Hyde Park Gate immediately.[1] On arrival, Moran was told: 'This is the Cuban Embassy, sir. The Prime Minister left here some time ago.'[1] Churchill had in fact leased his home to Robert Mendoza, the Cuban ambassador. Moran proceeded to No. 10 (the Prime Minister's formal residence) where he found Churchill sitting on his bed in his boiler suit.[1]

> I am glad you have come. I took up the telephone when I woke an hour ago, and I couldn't think of the words I wanted. Wrong words seemed to come into my head, but I was quite clear what was happening and did not say them. This went on for about three or four minutes. Then the operator asked, 'Do you want the Private Office?' What does it mean, Charles? Am I going to have a stroke? If this happened again I'd have to pull out. It might come on in a speech. That would be the end.[1]

Moran said he would get some trinitrin medicine (glyceryl trinitrate, a vasodilator). 'What will that do?' Churchill enquired. Moran explained that it would dilate the blood vessels and bring 'more blood to the spot'.[1] 'Will it do me any harm? It won't burst an artery?' Churchill enquired.[1] 'Tell me, Charles, what happened? Why couldn't I find the words I wanted?'[1] Moran explained that some of the small vessels in Churchill's head had gone into a state of spasm, contracting so that the circulation to the speech centre was diminished.[1] Moran told Churchill: 'You'll have to pull out or arrange things so that the strain is less.'[1] Churchill listened attentively and then said: 'I keep having to make important decisions, terrible decisions. It never stops. It is worse than the war.'[1]

'What shall I say if I run into Clemmie?' Moran asked.[1] 'Oh, come, we'll go and tell her everything. She's in bed with a cold,' responded Churchill.[1] Churchill told his wife what had happened; 'she was grave but quite composed'.[1]

Moran recorded: 'I wanted to do a little hard thinking. In the past I have taken great risks when I let him carry on at Washington after the heart attack [Churchill did not in fact suffer a heart attack (see p. 57)[10]], and again at Monte Carlo, two and a half years ago, when he had a stroke[2] [see p. 182]. But now something must be done.'[1]

Moran considered these symptoms might be the first warning of another stroke.[1] If they were he could not help as events would settle themselves.[1] In a few days if no clot formed and it was only spasm of the arteries, in a man whose cerebral circulation was no longer what it was, a difficult decision would have to be faced.[1] Ought Churchill to resign, or could anything be done to patch him up for a little?[1] With a vote of censure hanging over Churchill, and the prospect of a row in the House over the Budget, Moran knew Churchill would hate pulling out at this moment.[1] Aneurin Bevan MP, a left-wing member of the Labour Party, and his gang would say that Churchill had run away from trouble, as there was, in Churchill's words, a lot of venom about.[1]

Moran knew, too, that Churchill had set his heart on seeing the young Queen crowned before he gave up office. That it was a bad time for Anthony Eden, Foreign Secretary, to take over was clear to Churchill; he would be held responsible for the unpopular austerity measures.[1] Was Churchill more likely to have a stroke in the next six months if he carried on? No doctor could tell; it was mere guesswork. Moran recognized that if he went to Churchill and said: 'You must get away from this grind or you will have serious trouble,' it would have little impact as Churchill was not easily frightened off his course.[1] Moran concluded: 'I was beginning to see that it was not the moment for him to go.'[1]

Moran wrote that after he had slept on things there seemed only one course to take. If Churchill came safely through the next few days he had got to square up to him after the Budget and persuade him to be sensible.[1] 'I don't overrate my chances, but it is my job as his doctor. I think I know the turn of his mind as no one else does. I shall hate doing it, but it's the only thing I can do for him.'[1]

It was in that frame of mind that Moran called upon Churchill on the morning of 22 February. Churchill had had a good night and was in the mood to look upon the incident as closed.[1] 'Anyway, I saw that he didn't want to talk about it and I got away in a few minutes.'[1]

Moran sought out Colville with the news that on the previous evening Churchill had suffered 'a small arterial spasm' which he considered might be the precursor of an immediate stroke; if not, it was at least a plain warning that if the pressure was not relaxed on Churchill dire results would follow in six months or less.[9] Moran wanted political advice and so Colville and Moran went to see Lord Salisbury, Lord President of the Council, 2 hours later.[1,9] Moran wrote that: 'My first care must be not to put sharp weapons into the hands of anyone who might use them to hurt him [Churchill].'[1] Moran wanted to hear from someone in the Cabinet whether the duties of Prime Minister could be cut, and he considered that Lord Salisbury was the most appropriate person to advise as 'his complete detachment and single-mindedness, with his lack of personal ambition, give me a comfortable sense of security'.[1] Colville recalled Salisbury suggesting that Churchill might go to the Lords, leaving Eden to manage the Commons and thus Churchill would remain PM till after the Coronation in May 1953.[9] Moran's account is that Salisbury said: 'A Prime Minister cannot shed his responsibilities.'[1]

Moran and Colville saw Sir Alan Lascelles, Private Secretary to the Sovereign, that afternoon at Buckingham Palace. Moran began by admonishing Lascelles: '… that if, when I had done, he felt that the P.M. ought to retire, he must forget what I had said; for if I could not help my patient I must see that nothing I said did him hurt. With that prelude I told my story.'[1] Lascelles followed carefully what Moran explained and said:

> Well, listening to what you have told me, I would say at once the Prime Minister ought to resign and be content to be the elder statesman in the Commons or the Lords – better perhaps in the Lords. I have been expecting for some time to see you in this room. It is true that sometimes the Prime Minister is all on the spot, and then I say to myself: Why am I worrying? But at other times he doesn't seem able to see the point of a discussion.[1]

Colville intervened and explained that Churchill had told him a few days before that he would like to hang on until the Coronation in May of next year.[1] After that, he would resign. Lascelles appeared to agree that if we could bring him through this year, it would be the best plan.[1] It was concluded that nothing should be done until the Budget was over. Then Moran would deliver a medical ultimatum that Churchill cannot go on at the present pace, that he must either throw in his hand or in some way cut down his work.[1] Lascelles wanted Moran to go to Churchill and say outright that he must go to the Lords.[1] Moran maintained, however, that while Churchill would listen to him on the medical argument, he would switch off when he began on politics.[1] Colville agreed. Moran said he would try and get Churchill into a state of mind so that he saw something must be done: it was for others to suggest that something. Lascelles agreed reluctantly.[1]

Moran called on Churchill at Chartwell on 23 February. 'I did my stuff and was out of his room in five minutes. I knew he did not want to talk about what had happened, but I knew, too, that it was there at the back of his mind; he had been warned – and Winston is still quick enough to take his leads. He was subdued.'[1]

Moran found Churchill 'chastened, but still uncommunicative' on 25 February.[1] Churchill eventually said: 'I knew something had happened when I could not get my words on the telephone. I didn't like it. I was frightened. Oh, not frightened … I'm not frightened of anything. But I'm all right now. Why, you couldn't tell by examining me that anything had happened.'[1] Moran responded: 'But the fact remains you've had notice to go slower.' 'I don't mind dying in harness' replied Churchill. Moran responded: 'That won't help anyone … You've got a certain stock of energy, mental energy, and you can either spread it out over a period of time or just use it up recklessly – and in that case it won't last long.'[1]

After Churchill had replied to Herbert Morrison's speech (a vote of censure) on 26 February he went to his room in the House, and Moran joined him.[1] Churchill told Moran: 'I was alarmed at lunch-time; I seemed to have no wits, and I was very tired and shaky before getting up to speak, but I felt stronger as I got under way. Now I feel quite all right.'[1] As Gilbert commented:

On February 26 the powers of recuperation and the extraordinary determination of this man of seventy-seven were made abundantly clear to those who had known of his arterial spasm and discussed how to send him to the House of Lords. For it was only five days after the attack that Churchill spoke in the House of Commons on Foreign Affairs.[11]

Moran advised Churchill to go home and have a bath and dine before returning to the House. But Churchill said he would return to the House for a short time. 'He really wanted to know what people thought of his speech. He was excited. His pulse was 112. I have a feeling that the chance of translating him to the Lords is gone.'[1]

Moran called at No. 10 at 5.30 pm on 27 February, hoping to see Churchill before he retired for his rest. 'I found him animated, very different from the subdued Winston whose future has never been out of my mind since the difficulty with the telephone.'[1] Churchill explained: 'You know, Charles, yesterday was a great success; the papers have been most kind.'[1]

Moran next visited Churchill on 29 February 1952 after breakfast.[1] Churchill said: 'Since the speech I have felt better and more cheerful about things. During luncheon that day I was stupid, dull and muzzy, and I wondered if I could make a speech at all. But we put them on their backs.'[1]

Moran enquired whether a long Cabinet tired him. 'Oh, no, I get excited; my appetite thrives on what it feeds on. I get muzzy in the head about lunchtime, and then I get better as the day goes on.'[1]

6–23 March 1952: Further Assessments by Lord Moran

Moran called at No. 10 at nine on the morning of 6 March. Churchill was full of the debate in the House and told Moran:

> You ought to read the papers. They are very interesting, if you like politics. The Bevan group sat all together in one part, and Attlee's supporters were gathered together in another group. There they were, glowering at each other ... The split might deepen and lead to a coalition. I should not be against it. I would retire if necessary.[1]

Moran asked him if he had been less tired. Churchill answered: 'If I don't get my sleep in the afternoon I cannot sit up late and work. I get muddled and tired.'[1]

Although on 1 March Churchill had handed over his Defence portfolio to Field Marshal Alexander, which would reduce his own workload considerably, it did not satisfy his doctor. Moran wrote to Churchill on 12 March as follows:

> My dear Prime Minister, I have given careful thought to the significance of the little disturbance when you went to the telephone on February 21st. It was of the same nature as the sudden mistiness which you had within a fortnight of the Leeds speech in the 1950 election, namely due to spasm of the cerebral arteries. And these were first cousins of the blocking of a little artery at Monte Carlo in August, 1949. All three point to some instability in the cerebral circulation, which must be increased by excessive mental effort. On the other hand if it were possible to lighten the load without giving up being Prime Minister, which on medical grounds would not be wise at the moment, then you ought to be able to carry on more or less indefinitely. Of course if you would like confirmation of my interpretation of events, we could get Russell Brain at any time, but they are really capable of no other explanation. If there is any point that I have not made clear, I will of

course come at any time you want. I feel sure that you would like the medical facts put down for your consideration. When I saw Clemmie about your deafness I told her my view. Charles'[1]

Moran also explained to Mrs Churchill in writing what he had done.[1] Mrs Churchill telephoned Moran subsequently and explained that her husband '... was not angry when he got your letter; he just swept it aside. I mentioned the Lords, but he would not consider it. Charles, I'm glad you wrote. It may do good. Instead of going to the House this afternoon and listening to Mr. Thorneycroft [President of the Board of Trade], he has gone to bed.'[1]

Churchill himself raised the letter with Moran. 'I got your letter. I don't want you to worry. You really needn't. One has got to die sometime.'[1] At that moment Dr RMB MacKenna, Consultant Dermatologist at St Bartholomew's Hospital, London (see p. 441), came into the room to advise Churchill on his chronic skin condition (see p. 359), and that was the end of Moran's attempt to translate Churchill into the House of Lords.[1] Moran commented in *Winston Churchill: The Struggle for Survival 1940–1965* that: 'I am under no illusions. We have failed.'[1] Colville wrote in his diary that Churchill 'took it, so I gather, with sang-froid; but he does not know that anyone apart from Mrs C knows of this matter'.[9]

On 23 March at 4 pm Moran visited Churchill as he was about to lie down for his afternoon rest, but the Prime Minister invited Moran to come to his room. As Churchill undressed, he said to Moran:

I have noticed a decline in mental and physical vigour. I require more prodding to mental effort. I get a good deal of prodding. I forget names. I might even forget yours – people whose names I know as well as my own. I'm as quick at repartee in the House as ever I was. I enjoy Questions there. Do you think I ought to see Brain?[1]

Moran replied that it was no use seeing Brain unless Churchill was ready to take his advice.[1] Churchill said he thought it would be a bad thing if he retired now.[1]

Moran said Brain would certainly advise cutting down what he had to do. Churchill protested that he already devoluted a good deal of work.[1] 'I'm halfway in my seventy-eighth year, and one can't expect to live forever. I really don't think you need to worry. I soon get tired physically; when I have fed the robin and the swans, and perhaps walked three-quarters of a mile, I have had enough. I dislike standing, except when making speeches.'[1]

Medical Aspects

In the period January 1950 to March 1952, Churchill suffered two definite acute cerebrovascular episodes, and reported intermittent symptoms indicative of cognitive deficit, though without obvious acute onset. In the first of the two acute episodes, occurring on 24 January 1950, Churchill's description of his symptoms indicates either a visual problem ('... everything went misty') or perhaps less likely, a dyslexic deficit ('I could just read with difficulty'). No examination findings were recorded by Moran, but the symptoms were apparently transient. On balance, it seems most likely that this was a transient ischaemic (interruption of blood flow) episode affecting either part of the visual radiation or the visual cortex (the visual pathway), but without further details of exactly what Churchill meant when describing the symptom, this remains speculative. It is worth noting that Churchill was not seen by Brain in the immediate aftermath of this episode.

Brain was summoned by Moran in May 1950, at a time when Churchill reported increased tightness over his shoulders. Brain felt that his symptoms had not changed and a neurological examination was normal. Churchill was concerned about further strokes, but these bilateral symptoms at this time seem more likely to have had a musculoskeletal basis.

It is worth noting that Churchill's speech at the Royal College of Physicians on 10 July 1951 (see p. 206), accepting his Honorary Fellowship of the College, was amusing, witty and entirely appropriate, and demonstrated no impairment of language function or any other cognitive problem. It was vintage Churchill!

It is difficult to place an interpretation on the nature of Churchill's complaint of a 'muzzy head' in October 1950, and the same complaint reported much later to Moran on 29 February 1952. From the information available now, it is not clear whether this symptom occurred on a daily basis nor whether Churchill experienced it for days, weeks or possibly longer. Without the benefit of further documentation, one could speculate that this might have been a symptom of cognitive decline, but equally that it was non-specific. Support for the latter view is that the symptom was transient and stereotyped in its timing and duration, occurring recurrently at about lunchtime, and then resolving later in the day.

On 21 February 1952 it is clear that Churchill experienced an episode of expressive dysphasia lasting 3–4 minutes. This was due to left cerebral hemisphere ischaemia, most likely cortical in location with a thrombo-embolic basis. Moran's explanation of the underlying pathology being likely to be arterial spasm would not be today's preferred view. No mention is made of Churchill's cardiac rhythm or blood pressure at the time of the transient neurological disturbances occurring on 24 January 1950 and 21 February 1952, and we should therefore assume that both were normal. Cerebral haemorrhage is a much less likely pathological basis for these mild transient neurological symptoms.

Brain had examined Churchill in May 1950, some four months after the earlier transient ischaemic attack (TIA) in January 1950, and did not remark specifically on the presence or absence of a carotid bruit, but as a famously meticulous and thorough clinician he would almost certainly have made this examination. It should be remembered that imaging of the carotid artery bifurcation with ultrasound was still some years away.

It is of interest that Brain was not invited by Moran to see Churchill between 25 May 1950 and 24 June 1953, and specifically, not at the time of the transient episode of dysphasia in February 1952 described here. As with the delayed involvement of Brain by Moran following the stroke in 1949,[1] it reflects the limited investigation of stroke possible and accepted clinical practice at the time.

Thus, by February 1952, Churchill had suffered a small completed stroke (the first, right-sided hemisensory disturbance in 1949;[2] see p. 182) and two TIAs. One of the TIAs affected the circulation to the left cerebral hemisphere, but the localization of the episode of 'misty' vision is uncertain.

In February 1952, Churchill remarked to Moran: 'I keep having to make important decisions, terrible decisions. It never stops. It is worse than the war.'[1] It is a matter for speculation that Churchill was finding things more difficult either because he was by then some ten years older, or that he had thrived particularly as a wartime prime minister, or that his cerebrovascular disease was already more widespread than was clinically obvious by that time; or perhaps a combination of all of these.

Although the episode of dysphasia on 21 February 1952 appeared to last only 3–4 minutes and resolved completely, Lascelles noted: 'At other times he doesn't seem able to see the point of a discussion.'[1] Furthermore, Churchill told Moran on 23 March 1952 that he had noticed 'a decline in mental vigour… I forget names'.[1]

Taken together, the evidence indicates that Churchill had acquired some permanent, and increasing neurological deficit due to cerebrovascular disease between 1949 and March 1952. The fact that he was able to continue in public and political life at the highest level of functioning is a tribute to his remarkable pre-morbid abilities and what might be identified as considerable cognitive reserve, even in the face of advancing cerebrovascular disease.

Chapter 18

Churchill Unveils a Portrait of Lord Moran in July 1951

Just right Moran: makes you look like a medieval poisoner.[1]

W inston Churchill was present for the unveiling of a portrait of Lord Moran (Plate 15), his personal physician since 1940, at a dinner held in the Library at the Royal College of Physicians in the presence of a large number of Fellows on 10 July 1951. The portrait was painted by Professor Pietro Annigoni. Churchill received the first Honorary Fellowship of the College from Dr Russell Brain (see p. 431), his neurologist, and now President of the College in succession to Moran.[2]

Brain explained to Fellows:

When I came to consider who should present Lord Moran with his portrait it was obvious that the ideal person would be Mr. Churchill. As a Fellow he could speak on behalf of Fellows and say better than any of us how much the College owes to the Past-President for his single-minded and devoted service through nine difficult and strenuous years. And he could also speak as a patient about his doctor ... We share the whole nation's debt to Lord Moran for his professional care of Mr. Churchill. Well, when I invited Mr. Churchill he said at once that he would come and we are all very grateful to him. Tonight we are honouring leadership, the nation's leader and the leader of this College. A leader needs many virtues, but two pre-eminently – courage and imagination. The great leader is not a mere man of action: he is a man whose actions are informed by the sensibility of the artist. So in honouring Mr. Churchill we honour at the same time the statesman, the author and the artist, one whose words enliven our tongue and whose deeds will ever adorn our history.[2]

Churchill gave the oration:

First of all I must thank you for according me an Honorary Fellowship of the Royal College of Physicians. I also had the honour to be made a surgeon eight years ago, and now I can practise, in an honorary fashion, the arts of surgery and medicine. Unless there is a very marked shortage of capable men in both these professions, I shall not press myself upon you. No doubt in these difficult times it will be a comfort not only to the profession but to the nation at large that you have me in reserve.[3]

Churchill continued:

I have not yet taken any final decision as to which of these beneficent branches I should give priority to (in case an emergency arises). Being temperamentally inclined to precision and a sharp edge, it might be thought that I should choose the surgeon's role. At any rate you can be sure of having something to show, and I have been told that this was the view of many young medical students. However, all comes out even at the end of the day, and I am assured that latterly an entirely new phase has come over the art of medicine. It has become much less a process of emphasizing or mitigating, or correcting tendencies, and making grave and luminous pronouncements upon them, than of taking hard and quick decisions. Science, progged on by the urge of the age, has presented to us in the last decade a wonderful bevy of new and highly attractive-medicinal personalities. We have M and B [sulfonamides made by May & Baker], penicillin, tetramycin [probably Terramycin, that is oxytetracycline], aureomycin [chlortetracycline] and several others that I will not hazard my professional reputation in mentioning, still less in trying to place in order. And medical science has presented to you an ever-increasing growth of decisions as rapid and as refined as ever presented to the surgeon.[3]

Churchill also spoke about Moran:

It is my duty to pay your tribute to Lord Moran and, when the time comes, to present him with the portrait which has been painted by Professor Pietro Annigoni. Well, I know Charles Moran I would say almost as well as he knows me. He was for nine years President of your illustrious College. His war record is magnificent. In the first World War he won the MC and was mentioned in many dispatches and has Italian decorations all gained under the hard fire caused by the mistakes of our military experts in the first great struggle with which our generation has been afflicted. In the last war, Charles came with me wherever I went. That puts me in the position of the man who said one night, 'I think my companion here ought to have the VC because he has been everywhere I have been.' At any rate, we went for a good many long journeys by air at a time when the comforts of air travel had not been developed to the almost perfect state they have now … I am deeply indebted to him. He was for twenty-five years Dean of St Mary's Hospital. He is a great figure in your life, for nine years head of the College, a man deeply versed in his profession and in all its most profound characteristics, a man who apart from his profession stands out as a leading figure in the public life of Britain. I must now mention Lady Moran, who sustained him as only a wife can, and I know all about that.[3]

Moran responded:

There are so many circumstances which contribute to the pleasure of my wife and myself. In the first place this is no common routine, for it has never been the custom of the College to have the portrait of every President painted. On the contrary, in the last fifty years only two Presidents have been hung on these walls. Again, when a whisper reached me what was afoot I wondered doubtfully whether there would be many subscribers … And yet more fellows have combined to make this gift, 364 in all, than were present at that record attendance [356 Fellows were present at the Comitia at which Brain was elected President in 1950]. Then, of course, it adds greatly to our delight that you have chosen to present this portrait on your behalf our most distinguished Fellow, Mr. Churchill.[2]

After the presentation of the portrait, Churchill was overheard saying to his physician, 'Just right Moran: makes you look like a medieval poisoner.'[1] The opinion of one Fellow was that Annigoni had 'created an arresting tour-de-force. Moran appears to stand out as a vivid lively personality as indeed he was in life and as President of the College.'[4]

This was the second time that Churchill had visited and spoken to the Fellows of the Royal College of Physicians. On 2 March 1944, he had proposed the Toast of the College at a luncheon.

I am very grateful to my cherished friend, Lord Moran, for all the kind expressions he has used, in commending this toast to you, about me and about the conclusions which his naturally close and intimate investigations have enabled him to form. He has been my companion on the various journeys I have had to take in the course of public business about the world during this war, and always a devoted and comforting friend. We get on very well together. As you can see from the excellent speech to which you have just listened, we divide our labours; he instructs me in the art of public speaking, and I teach him how to cure pneumonia.[5]

On 8 March 1944, Moran sought the advice of Dr (later Sir) John Parkinson (see p. 444), Churchill's cardiologist, on another matter and mentioned that he considered Churchill's recent speech to the College suffered from a lack of time and preparation only, and he did not see any sign of depreciation in his mental capacity.[6]

Chapter 19

Acute Stroke in June 1953 in London

Unless – as is just possible – there is a miraculous recovery in the next forty-eight hours … his office will have to be abandoned.[1]

In the last week of May 1953, all of Britain had begun celebrations for the Coronation of Queen Elizabeth II.[2] On 27 May, Sir Winston Churchill aged 79 years, spoke at a luncheon given before the Commonwealth Parliamentary Association and that evening gave a pre-conference dinner party at 10 Downing Street. The Coronation took place on 2 June, and Churchill attended though he was very tired when the day came,[2] according to Jane Portal, his personal secretary.[3] On 3 June Churchill was in the Chair at the opening meeting of the Commonwealth Prime Ministers; Churchill also chaired the second meeting on 4 June.[2] In the absence of the Foreign Secretary, Anthony Eden, who was awaiting a further operation, Churchill and his wife were hosts to the Queen at a banquet at Lancaster House on the evening of 5 June.[2] The following day Churchill was at the Derby Stakes at Epsom Downs Racecourse and on 8–9 June he chaired the fourth and fifth meetings of the Commonwealth Prime Ministers.[2] On the evening of 9 June there was a 'vast Commonwealth dinner at No. 10 for the visiting Prime Ministers, followed by a reception'.[4]

12–21 June 1953: Preparations for the Bermuda Conference

On 12 June Churchill went to Chartwell for the weekend and telegraphed President Eisenhower regarding the forthcoming Bermuda Conference. Sir Pierson Dixon, Deputy Under-Secretary of State, Foreign Office, met with Churchill on 20 June and wrote: 'Mentally, he is more alert than he was towards the end of the war. As always, he did all the work himself in the sense of dictating the telegrams himself after reaching the decision.'[2] On 21 June Churchill sent Eisenhower a note of those who would accompany him to Bermuda.[2] Two days later Churchill telegraphed Eisenhower again regarding the meeting.[2]

23 June 1953: Assessment by Lord Moran

Yet, when Lord Moran (see p. 443), Churchill's personal physician, saw Churchill on 23 June, he concluded that Churchill was 'played out – as he was at Cairo before the Carthage illness [see p. 91[5]]'.[6] 'I thought his speech was slurred and a little indistinct. Twice I had to ask him to repeat what he had said … I told him I was unhappy about the strain, that it was an impossible existence and that I hoped he would find he could do something about it.'[6] Before leaving No. 10 Moran sought out David Pitblado, Joint Principal Private Secretary to Churchill, to tell him that he was worried.[6]

23 June 1953: Dinner for the Italian Prime Minister

That night Churchill was host at No. 10 for a dinner for thirty-eight people in honour of the Italian Prime Minister, de Gasperi. Sir Kenneth Clark, Chairman of the Arts Council, wrote of the events:

> Although I can remember very few of our own parties, I do remember one dinner party at No. 10 Downing Street, which I may describe, as it has a certain historical interest … I had been looking across at Mr Churchill somewhat apprehensively, but when the time came he made an excellent speech about Italy, and one could feel a wave of relief passing over the guests. The men left the table immediately after the ladies, and we got as far as the door of the drawing-room when Mr Churchill slumped into the first chair. I saw Jane [Lady Clark] standing nearby, and told her to sit beside him. He took her hand and said 'I want the hand of a friend. They put too much on me. Foreign affairs …', and his voice drifted away. I discovered Mary [Churchill's daughter]. There was no doubt of what had happened. Mary and Christopher [Soames MP, Churchill's son-in-law and Parliamentary Private Secretary] got him to bed.[7]

John Colville, Joint Principal Private Secretary to Churchill, recorded in his diary:

> On June 23rd Meg [his wife Lady Margaret] and I dined at No. 10 for a big dinner in honour of the Italian Prime Minister, de Gasperi …
> At the end of dinner W[inston Churchill] made a little speech in his

best and most sparkling form, mainly about the Roman Conquest of Britain! After dinner, he had a stroke, which occurred while he was in the pillared room among the guests. He sat down and was almost unable to move. After the guests had left, he leant heavily on my arm but managed to walk to his bedroom.[1] Colville wrote in his diary that nobody seemed to notice that Churchill did not stand up to say goodbye to de Gasperi or any of the ladies.[1]

Mary Soames, Churchill's daughter, has also recorded the details of dinner:

When alerted, I hastened to his side; Christopher told me to try and guard him from the people, as he was having difficulty with his speech. I did my best, but it was not very easy – my father looked unhappy and uncertain and was very incoherent. Christopher managed to convey to Signor De Gaspieri that Winston was very much overtired, and the Italian Prime Minister, with kind understanding, soon took his leave, the other guests following his example. A few had noticed the slur in Winston's speech and his unsteadiness, but attributed it to his having had a little too much to drink; nobody guessed the real reason – that he had sustained a stroke. Meanwhile Jock Colville tried, unsuccessfully, to contact Moran, but finally had to leave a message asking him to come to No. 10 in the morning. We escorted my father upstairs to his bedroom, and there he seemed to feel, and to be, much better.[8]

Although repeated attempts were made to contact Moran, it was not until half an hour after midnight that the No. 10 switchboard was able to contact Moran and to ask that he see Churchill at 9 am the following morning.[9]

24 June 1953: Assessments by Moran and Brain

The following morning, Moran spoke with Colville and Christopher Soames before seeing the Prime Minister.[9] Moran went in to see his patient. Churchill said: 'Ah, Charles, I thought you would never come.'[9] Moran observed that the left side of Churchill's mouth sagged; it was more noticeable when he spoke. Moran asked Churchill to walk. Although he was able to do this unaided, he was not very steady on his feet, and at one point Moran thought he would fall and jumped to Churchill's side. Churchill said: 'I would not like to walk to my seat in the House of Commons with members watching. What has happened, Charles? Is it a stroke?"[9]

Moran then examined Churchill and found there was no loss of power of the hand or leg.[9] Moran explained to Churchill that the circulation in his head was sluggish; there was spasm of a small artery. It belonged to the 'same family' as the incident at Monte Carlo in August 1949.[9,10] Churchill responded that he thought that was the trouble.[9] Moran asked Churchill if he would like to see Sir Russell Brain (see p. 431), Churchill's neurologist, again, but received no answer.[9] Moran said he would return in the afternoon.[9]

As soon as Moran's back was turned, Churchill got up, dressed and presided at the Cabinet for 2 hours.[11] When Colville escorted Churchill to the Cabinet Room he felt sure the telltale droop of his mouth on the left side and his slurred speech would betray the secret. In the event no member of the Cabinet noticed anything wrong![11] For example, Macmillan wrote: 'I certainly noticed nothing beyond the fact that he was very white. He spoke little, but quite distinctly, I remember that he called to me "Harold, you might draw the blinds down a little, will you?" I also noticed that he did not talk very much.'[12] RA 'Rab' Butler, Chancellor of the Exchequer, later told Colville that nobody at the Cabinet table noticed anything strange except that the Prime Minister was more silent than usual.[1]

Fortunately, as Churchill was extremely tired, there were no guests for luncheon. Churchill dined with his wife and Christopher and Mary Soames. Once more Churchill had difficulty in getting up from his chair. After lunch, Churchill telephoned Moran, who noticed no speech deficit, and asked Moran to bring Brain with him.[9]

Brain recorded that Moran asked him to go and see Churchill at 10, Downing Street.[13] 'He did not give any reason for this ... but when I got there, I found that Churchill had had a stroke.'[13] Brain recorded that Churchill had slept after the Cabinet meeting and his secretary mentioned that she thought there was some drooping of the left side of his face.[13] This was apparent when he spoke and also when he smiled, and his speech was at first somewhat slurred, but there was at no time any evidence of aphasia (the loss of the ability to express himself or understand speech).[13] There was a slight weakness of the left lower face on voluntary and emotional movement, and his tongue deviated slightly to the left.[13] There was no weakness of the limbs and no change in sensation, but the left plantar reflex was extensor (a subtle sign consistent with a small stroke) while the right was flexor (normal).[13]

Churchill walked about the room with only a slight trace of unsteadiness.[13] Churchill said he had no headache but felt as though there was something in his head.[13] He was put on trinitrin (glyceryl trinitrate, a vasodilator) night and morning. After his examination was finished, Churchill gave Brain an address on foreign policy![13]

Churchill had intended to answer questions in the House of Commons that afternoon, but Mrs Churchill and Christopher Soames persuaded him not to do so,[8] adding their weight to Moran's warning that he might risk breaking down completely if he did.[9]

25 June 1953: Recovery at Chartwell

On Thursday, 25 June 1953 the effects of the stroke were rather more pronounced according to Mary Soames.[8] When she saw her father that morning, she found him very despondent. Moran also assessed Churchill.[9] He noted no improvement in his speech and that if anything Churchill was more unsteady in his gait.[9] Churchill said: 'I don't feel like managing the world and yet never have they looked more like offering me it. I feel, Charles, I could do something that no one else can do. I was at the peak of my opportunities, exchanging friendly messages with Malenkov [Chairman of Council of Ministers, USSR] and Adenauer [Chancellor of the Federal Republic of Germany].'[9] Moran asked Churchill: 'You meant to send the messages?'[9] 'No I have done already,' replied Churchill.[9]

Moran noticed that Churchill's speech was becoming slurred and more difficult to follow.[9] Churchill lay back on his pillow as if he were too tired to go on.[9] Once more Moran pressed him not to attend the Cabinet, and when he became obstinate Moran said that the left side of his mouth drooped and that he did not want him to go among people until he was better.[9] They would notice things, and there would be talk.[9] After Moran had gone, Soames attempted to influence his father-in-law. In the end, Churchill gave up the idea and left about noon for Chartwell.[9] It was thought better that Churchill went down to Chartwell where privacy could be more easily achieved.[8] Fortunately, Churchill had been able to walk unaided to his car at Downing Street but by the time he reached Chartwell he needed considerable help getting out of the car.[8]

Colville recorded in his diary: 'When I drove down to Chartwell alone with the Prime Minister (Lady Churchill having gone on ahead to prepare the household), he gave me strict orders not to let it be known that he was temporarily incapacitated and to ensure that the administration continued to function as if he were in full control.'[1] Colville realised that however well he knew Churchill's policy and the way his thoughts were likely to move, he had to be careful not to allow his own judgment to be given Prime Ministerial effect. To have done so would have been a constitutional outrage. 'It was an extraordinary, indeed perhaps an unprecedented, situation.'[1] Colville was aided by 'the down-to-earth intelligence of Churchill's son-in-law, Christopher Soames, Member of Parliament for Bedford ... the shrewdness of his comments, combined with his ability to differentiate between what mattered and what did not, was of invaluable help in difficult days'.[1]

Colville recognized that he could not obey Churchill's injunction to tell nobody.[1] The truth would undoubtedly leak to the press unless he took immediate defensive action. So he wrote urgently and in manuscript to three particular friends of Churchill, Lords Camrose (proprietor of the *Daily Telegraph*), Beaverbrook (proprietor of the *Daily Express*) and Bracken (proprietor of the *Financial Times* and *Economist*), and sent the letters to London by despatch rider. All three men immediately came to Chartwell and paced the lawn in earnest conversation. They achieved the all but incredible, and in peace-time possibly unique, success of gagging Fleet Street, something they would have done for nobody but Churchill.[1]

Not a word of the Prime Minister's stroke was published until Churchill himself casually mentioned it in a speech in the House of Commons a year later.[1] Colville also prepared briefs for Butler and Salisbury, Lord President of the Council and Leader of the House of Lords.[1] Colville also wrote to Lord Cherwell, Churchill's scientific advisor, the 'Prof':

His articulation and his movements are seriously affected and unless – as is just possible – there is a miraculous recovery in the next forty-eight hours ... his office will have to be abandoned. His courage is beyond praise and Clemmie's too; but it is heart-rending to be here and to see the physical deterioration that has asserted itself. He finds great difficulty in speech and since this morning he has all but lost the use of his left arm.[1]

Colville stayed at Chartwell nearly a fortnight supervising matters.[1]

26–30 June 1953: Assessments by Moran and Brain

Brain went down with Moran to see Churchill at Chartwell on 26 June. Brain recorded that Churchill had obviously deteriorated.[13] His speech was more dysarthric (slurred), and his left hand was becoming weaker and his gait more unsteady.[13] At times he would choke and cough when swallowing.[13] There was considerable clumsiness of the left hand, but his left grip was still fair and movements of the arm at the elbow and shoulder good.[13] The main weakness was in the small muscles of the hand. Power was little diminished in the left leg, but he tended to stagger to the left when he walked.[13] There was no impairment of appreciation of pinprick or postural sensibility. The tendon reflexes were brisker on the left side than on the right, and as before, the left plantar reflex was extensor (a physical examination sign consistent with a recent or previous stroke) while the right was flexor (normal).[13]

Moran also recorded his assessment on 26 June but did not mention that Brain was present.[9] Churchill told Moran as he entered his room that 'my hand is clumsy'.[9] Transferring his cigar to his left hand, he made a wavering attempt to put it to his lips. Moran examined Churchill's left hand and arm and observed some loss of power in the left grip – and this had developed since yesterday, three days after the onset of the trouble.[9] Moran wrote: 'I do not like this, the thrombosis is obviously spreading. He knew that his hand was weaker.'[9] Churchill complained: 'I am having great difficulty in turning over in bed. Two days ago I wanted to take the Cabinet. Now I couldn't. I have scratched Bermuda. It will not come out until Ike [President Eisenhower] replies to my telegram.'[9]

Brain has written that Christopher Soames asked him:

In Moran's presence what I thought were the prospects of Winston making a reasonably complete recovery. I had to think quickly. I was not too hopeful and certainly did not expect that he would make the almost complete recovery as far as his physical condition was concerned which he did, but I thought that in the circumstances, it was worse to give a prognosis which turned out to be too bad than one which events would show to be too good. So I put his chances of a reasonably complete recovery at 50/50.[13]

Moran recorded this prognostic comment on 24 July 1953, when Brain was not present (see below).[9]

Moran and Brain prepared a first medical bulletin[14] which read:

The Prime Minister has had no respite for a long time from his very arduous duties and there has developed a disturbance of the cerebral circulation which has resulted in attacks of giddiness. We have therefore advised him to abandon his journey to Bermuda and to have a month's rest. *Sir Winston had a similar though less serious attack in August 1949 when staying in Cap d'Ail* [The words in italics do not appear in *The Struggle for Survival*[9]].

Moran has stated that after he had left, Butler and Salisbury altered the Bulletin and persuaded Churchill to agree to their wording.[9] The National Archive[14] contains the revised version signed 'WSC 25.VI' which reads:

The Prime Minister has had no respite for a long time from his very arduous duties and is in need of a complete rest. We have therefore advised him to abandon his journey to Bermuda and to lighten his duties at least for a month.

Macmillan wrote that:

Butler and Salisbury took a heavy responsibility in agreeing to what was undoubtedly the wish of the Prime Minister and the members of his family that the medical bulletin should be issued in a comparatively helpful form. However, I felt they were fully justified. It was only fair that Churchill should have a few weeks to make up his mind.[12]

Moran concluded that Butler and Salisbury:

May well be right, that is of course if he comes through. For if he recovers and wants to carry on as Prime Minister, then the less we say about a stroke, the better for him. But will anyone who knows the P.M. credit that he is willing to take a month's rest merely because his doctors thought he was overdoing things? And besides, if he dies in the next few days will Lord Salisbury think his change in the bulletin was wise? It is a gamble. [Note: Moran's original notebook entry read 'In the long run it is wisest to be honest with the public.'[15]]

On 26 June 1953 the Queen sent Churchill a letter in her own hand:[9]

My dear Prime Minister, I am so sorry to hear from Tommy Lascelles that you have not been feeling too well these last few days. I do hope it is not serious and that you will be quite recovered in a very short time. Our visit here is going very well and Edinburgh is thrilled by all the pageantry. We have been lucky in having fine weather, but I fear that it is now raining after a thunderstorm.

With all good wishes
Yours very sincerely
Elizabeth R

Churchill replied at once and informed Her Majesty that he was not without hope that he might soon be about and able to discharge duties until the autumn, when he thought that Anthony Eden would be able to take over.[9]

Churchill also sent a telegram to Eisenhower on 26 June: 'You will see from the attached medical report the reasons why I cannot come to Bermuda.'[16] Eisenhower replied by return:

I am deeply distressed to learn that your physicians have advised you to lighten your duties at this time and that consequently you will be unable to come to Bermuda for our talks. I look upon this only as a temporary deferment of our meeting. Your health is of great concern to all the world and you must, therefore, bow to the advice of your physicians.'[16]

On 26 June 1953, Butler was summoned to Chartwell. On arriving he was handed a letter from Colville dated 25 June 1953 which read:

I write, very sorrowfully, to let you know quite privately that the PM is seriously ill and that unless a miracle occurs in the next 24 hours there can be no question of his going to Bermuda and little, I think, of his remaining in office ... he's been left with great difficulty of articulation although his brain is still absolutely clear. His left side is partly paralysed and he's lost the use of his left arm. He himself has little hope of recovery. *His courage and philosophic resignation are beyond praise and admiration and Lady Churchill, too, is heroic* ...[17]

Butler wrote: 'The family and Christopher Soames were in tears; but quite soon the mighty constitution prevailed, and I remember sitting at dinner whilst Winston with his good arm carried to his lips a beaker of brandy.'[17] Although it was officially conveyed to Butler that Eden was the rightful deputy, given that he was recuperating from a serious illness, Butler was by a tacit understanding expected to perform as the head of the government, with Salisbury taking charge at the Foreign Office in place of Eden. Butler and Salisbury returned to London together.[17]

Mary Soames saw her father on 27 June. 'There are nurses now, and he cannot walk, or use his right [presumably left] hand much. In the afternoon he had a fall – but beyond the jolt – no damage.'[8] Churchill told Moran that morning:

I'm getting more helpless. I shall soon be completely paralysed on my left side. I don't mind. But I hope it won't last long. Will the other side be paralysed? Why it might last for years. Tell me, Charles, is there no operation for this kind of thing? I don't mind being a pioneer. Anyway, it is clear now that we made the right decision in abandoning Bermuda.[9]

Moran got Churchill out of bed, but he could hardly stand and recorded that there was now some obvious loss of power so that Churchill's left foot drops and his toes catch the carpet. Churchill could not walk without two people helping him, though in the wheelchair provided by Brendan Bracken he could propel himself from room to room. Churchill paused before his portrait in the blue drawing room. 'It is a picture of a very unhappy man painted after the Dardanelles by Orpen [Sir William Newenham Montague Orpen]. He thought I was finished.'[9]

On 28 June 1953, Mary Soames recorded: 'Today he is gayer.... Lord M says there is a distinct improvement.'[8] Brain recorded, however, that there was 'no substantial change'.[13] At luncheon Churchill was well enough to sit at the head of the table and to entertain Beaverbrook as the main guest. During lunch, Moran could see that Churchill was becoming tired and Churchill asked Moran to take him to bed. Churchill insisted on getting out of his chair, and he was helped into his room, 'his good foot coming down on the passage with a noisy stump, while the toes of his left foot dragged along the carpet'.[9] When Churchill and Moran were alone, Churchill said, 'A week ago I was thinking of running the world – and now –.'[9]

By 29 June 1953, instead of being dead, Churchill was feeling very much better. Churchill told Colville he thought 'probably that this must mean his retirement, but that he would see how he went on, and that if he had recovered sufficiently well to address the Tory party at their annual meeting in October at Margate, he would continue in office'.[16]

The Cabinet meeting was held at noon on 29 June. In the absence of the Prime Minister and Foreign Secretary, Butler presided and told his colleagues of the visit that he and Salisbury had made to Chartwell on 26 June. Macmillan wrote: 'He revealed to us what we had only surmised – the nature of his illness. It was a terrible shock to us all. Although the story was told simply and discreetly, many of us were in tears or found it difficult to restrain them.'[12]

On 30 June 1953, Sir Norman Brook, Cabinet Secretary, and Colville dined with Churchill alone. Brook wrote later that Churchill was:

in a wheelchair. After dinner, in the drawing-room, he said that he was going to stand on his feet. Colville and I urged him not to attempt this, and when he insisted, we came up on either side of him so that we could catch him if he fell. But he waved us away with his stick and told us to stand back. He then lowered his feet the ground, gripped the arms of his chair, and by tremendous effort – with sweat pouring down his face – levered himself to his feet and stood upright. Having demonstrated that he could do this, he sat down again and took up his cigar.

Brook commented: 'It was a striking demonstration of will-power. In defeat: defiance … he was determined to recover.'[18]

2–23 July 1953: Assessments by Moran and Brain

Macmillan was 'summoned' to dine at Chartwell on 2 July 1953.[12] Moran told Macmillan that he was more than satisfied at Churchill's progress but that he thought he might be shocked at Churchill's appearance.[12] 'My first impressions were of astonishment that a man who had suffered such a calamity could show such gaiety and courage. During dinner, and until he went to bed, just after 11 pm, his talk seemed much the same as usual. The atmosphere was not oppressive, but almost lively.'[12]

Butler recounts that he went down to Chartwell again while Churchill was still convalescing. Churchill's nurse wheeled him to look at his beloved goldfish pond. On one side of it are some stepping-stones leading to the other end and, without saying anything, Churchill started to try to negotiate these. Butler plunged into the water on one side and held Churchill up while the nurse came along behind. Butler and the nurse got Churchill over safely and wheeled him back to the summer-house where they sat, Butler drenched, discussing English history as depicted in the Weald of Kent![17] Butler wrote: 'Very few men can have got over such a paralysis in so lion-hearted a manner.'[17]

Brain saw Churchill at Chartwell again on 3 July 1953.[13] The previous night Churchill had had an attack of jerking of the left leg involving the flexor muscles of all joints and slight jerking of the left hand. This went on for a quarter of an hour or more.[13] Brain recorded:

Since I last saw him, he had become still weaker in the arm and leg, and was unable to walk, but now he was improving and his speech was better. There was still weakness of the left lower face and left half of the soft palate, but his tongue deviated slightly to the right. The left grip was fair and there was moderate weakness of all movements of the left upper limb. There was general weakness also of the left lower limb in which plantar flexion was fair and the power of dorsiflexion and inversion of the foot was just returning. As before, the tendon reflexes were brisker on the left side than on the right, and the plantars were left extensor [a physical examination sign consistent with a recent or previous stroke], right flexor [normal], and there was no sensory loss. He was now able to use his left hand to propel his wheel chair, and to walk unaided a few steps. I noted that the right carotid pulse was still much smaller in volume than the left.[13]

Moran recorded that 4 July 1953 was 'a good day. Full of spirits.'[19] Churchill could walk a short distance and said that each day he would do a little more.[19] During dinner, Churchill's retirement in October came up. 'I shall do what is best for the country' and with a whimsical smile, 'Circumstances may convince me of my indispensability.'[19] Moran wrote: 'There it is: he has no intention of retiring if he can help it.'[19]

Churchill could walk unaided on 5 July 1953,[19] but the next day he did not feel 'on top of things', but was able to recite without difficulty Longfellow's *King Robert of Sicily*.[19] Moran wrote that Churchill:

Means to carry on if he is able, and the question whether he will be able is hardly ever out of his head. This is his secret battle. There are moments when he does not want to do anything, when a dreadful apathy settles on him and he nearly loses heart. But he always sets his jaw and hangs on.[19]

Moran recorded on 8 July 1953 that there was some gain in the strength of Churchill's left foot and an obvious improvement in Churchill's attitude to life.[19] Moran told Churchill on 10 July: 'You are supposed to be a bad patient, but you have behaved very well in the last fortnight.'[19] Churchill replied, 'I feel I have done my bit.'[19]

Churchill demonstrated to Moran on 11 July 1953 that he could lift his left arm above his head and turn on the switch of the reading lamp which he could not do the previous day.[19] Churchill invited Moran to walk in the garden with him and observe 'what I can do'.[19] After the walk Churchill said: 'I'm better but I'm not entirely recovered yet. I get very weary. You must give me some strength, Charles, before I can do anything. At present I keep dropping off to sleep.'[19]

Churchill's nurse telephoned Moran on 12 July 1953 and explained that the Prime Minister did not feel so well when he woke this morning. He was much stiffer, particularly in his back muscles. Moran explained to Churchill that this was due to the extensive walk in the garden yesterday when he used muscles he did not generally use. Churchill again complained of '… immense fatigue. Can't you give me a tonic, Charles? Something to get rid of this horrible sense of exhaustion?'[19] Moran recorded on 13 July 1953 that Churchill was in good form, though his leg twitched for an hour last night.[19]

On 17 July 1953 Churchill sent a telegram to Eisenhower which ended: 'I have made a great deal of progress and can now walk about. The doctors think that I may well be well enough to appear in public by September. Meanwhile, I am still conducting business. It was a great disappointment to me not to have my chance of seeing you.'[20]

Butler was Churchill's dinner guest at Chartwell on 19 July 1953. Colville, who was also present, noted that Churchill was 'much improved in powers of concentration' and 'sparkled at dinner'.[1] Butler had brought the speech he intended to make in the Foreign Affairs debate. After dinner, Churchill 'went carefully and meticulously through Rab's speech'.[1] Moran was told the following morning that Butler was astonished by the progress Churchill had made in the course of the week. Butler did not rule out a comeback.[19]

On 22 July 1953 Moran found Churchill 'in poor form. Speech very slurred, and he is walking badly.' Camrose joined Churchill to discuss Volume VI of *The Second World War* and told Moran Churchill would never go back to the House [of Commons].[19]

Churchill handed Moran a message on 23 July 1953 that had appeared in the French and American press. 'Monsieur Bidault [French Foreign Minister] told the Council of Ministers that the P.M. is suffering from complete paralysis, and that though he retains his intellectual lucidity, he is incapable of moving without assistance. Mr Eden is cutting short his convalescence in order to fly home.'[19] Churchill jumped out of bed and, walking across the room, climbed on to a chair and stood erect without holding on to anything![19]

Churchill was well enough on 24 July 1953 to travel from Chartwell to Chequers.

24 July–11 August 1953: Assessments by Moran and Brain

On reaching Chequers, Churchill invited Moran to accompany him on a possible visit to Moscow. Moran wrote: 'Sir Russell Brain, a careful, prudent physician, puts the PM's chance of coming back alive from a trip to Moscow as low as fifty-fifty. Excitement might bring on another stroke or at any rate leave him unable to play his part when he got there. But if he knew the odds I am sure he would take them.'[19]

This statement is strongly disputed by Brain:

This prognostic comment of mine has somehow been transposed by Moran to a consultation a month later, and it now appears under date July 24th 1953 on p. 442 of his book. By July 24th, Churchill was much better... I was not asked what his prospects were of coming back alive from a trip to Moscow, nor if I had been, should I have put it as low as 50/50 ... Moreover, this remark of mine appears under July 24th 1953, which is a day on which I did not see Churchill.[13]

Brain reviewed Churchill again on 25 July 1953 at Chequers, when he recorded that Churchill was much improved, and his speech more normal.[13] There was no dysphagia (difficulty swallowing) now. He had a little weakness of the left lower face. In the upper limb, there was now little weakness at any joint. He could brush his hair and move his fingers individually.[13] In the lower limb, all movements were good against resistance. He walked with a slight limp.[13] He could do a 'knees-bend' twice and had climbed on to a chair and stood on it. He walked well and quickly, but with slight ataxia (incoordination) of the right lower limb at the ankle. The reflexes were as before.[13] There was no sensory loss, but subjectively Churchill complained of two numb areas on the outer side of the left lower limb above and below the knee.[13] Churchill said the right side of the body (which had previously been affected) felt more abnormal than the left. His blood pressure was 170/90 mmHg. There were occasional extrasystoles (additional heart beats), but his pulse did not become rapid even after considerable exertion. Churchill still had some frequency of micturition and some precipitancy (urgency) and had noticed the loss of emotional control. He wept if moved, for example, by poetry.[13]

Moran noted: 'Brain thinks he may recover 90% physically. But he is less certain about his ability to concentrate. He doubts whether he will be alive in a year's time.'[19] On 2 August 1953 Churchill had an audience of the Queen. He informed Her Majesty that he would decide in a month as to his fitness to continue as Prime Minister.[1]

Churchill met with Salisbury, Butler and Sir William Strang, the Head of the Foreign Office, on 8 August 1953 to discuss the Soviet reply to an invitation to a conference of Foreign Ministers. This was the first meeting Churchill had chaired since his stroke. Colville, who was present at the meeting in the Hawtrey Room, wrote in his diary: 'Apart from his unsteady walk, the appearances left by his stroke have vanished, though he still tires quickly. However Lord Moran told me he thought there might be another stroke within a year. Indeed it was probable.'[1]

12–23 August 1953: Assessments by Moran and Brain

On 12 August 1953 Churchill returned to Chartwell via 10 Downing Street so that he could be assessed by Brain; Moran was also present. When they arrived, Churchill was in the Cabinet Room sitting in the Prime Minister's chair with the usual extinct cigar and a whisky and soda. Churchill invited his doctors to take their seats at the Cabinet Table.[13] Subsequently, Churchill lay on his bed and Brain found that he had 90 per cent recovery of power in the left face and upper and lower limbs.[13] On walking, Churchill did not swing his arm and tended to catch his toe. His left plantar reflex was still extensor (a physical examination sign consistent with a recent or previous stroke).[13] Churchill still suffered occasional twitching of his left leg, but his emotionalism was very much less. 'I've got more bite,' Churchill said, clenching his teeth.[13]

Against Moran's advice, Churchill chaired his first Cabinet meeting since his illness on 18 August 1953 at 5 pm.[8,20] The meeting went well. Norman Brook told Moran that he did not think any of Churchill's colleagues had noticed anything different from an ordinary Cabinet.[20]

24 August 1953: Assessment by Sir John Parkinson

Churchill was reassessed by Sir John Parkinson (p. 444), his cardiologist, on 24 August at his rooms at 1 Devonshire Place, in the presence of Moran. Parkinson had first assessed Churchill in February 1942 (see p. 65).[21,22] Moran reported to Parkinson that Churchill was more breathless on effort since his stroke two months ago and his pulse was a little quicker.[20,22] Parkinson noted that Churchill was taking one or two secobarbital tablets to sleep at night. On examination, Parkinson found some deafness and doubtful slurring of speech. Churchill's pulse was 70/minute and regular and his blood pressure was 145/90 mmHg.[22] His urine showed a trace of albumin (protein).[22] Radioscopy (X-Ray) showed a normal heart and the electrocardiogram was also normal with one extrasystole (extra beat).[22] Churchill told Parkinson that although the family wanted him to retire, he felt that he still had things which he could best do. [22] Mentally he seems less responsive but is clear in mind and speech. At the end of the consultation, Parkinson noted that Churchill was chatting in his 'old interesting and friendly fashion'.[22]

Moran recorded that Parkinson told Churchill that 'his heart was years younger than his age, and more in that key, until the P.M. must have wondered why I had taken him to a heart specialist'.[20] 'Well, Charles, we need not bother about my pump any more.'[20]

25 August 1953: Assessment by Brain

Brain saw Churchill at 10 Downing Street on 25 August 1953.[13] Brain recorded that Churchill took Cabinet last week and was very tired afterwards, and both legs twitched for an hour and kept him awake. 'He complains that his walking varies and he seems loose at the knees. He was walking badly yesterday but not much wrong today. There was no change in his physical signs. I think the trouble is variability in the collateral circulation [remaining blood supply to the area affected by the stroke], influencing the highest levels of control.'[13] Churchill's pulse was 84/minute after exercise, falling in half a minute to 76/minute.[13]

Moran reported Brain as stating that he doubted whether Churchill would ever be able to make speeches in public or to answer questions in the House of Commons. 'Even if I am wrong and he resumes his duties in the House, I believe that in a few weeks the effort would be too much. His walking, which is still unsteady, might get worse, and he might be so fatigued that he could no longer carry on. In any case, probably a month from now his gait will be much the same, at any rate when he is tired.'[20] Brain agreed that Churchill's willpower had no doubt helped him. Brain agreed with Moran that if Churchill retired now, he would probably be dead within the year. 'On the other hand, if he decided that he can still do a useful job of work for the country it is for his doctors to help if they can, and certainly not to hinder.'[20]

Moran spoke with Norman Brook as to how Churchill had weathered his second Cabinet since the stroke.[20] The Cabinet had lasted 2 hours and 40 minutes and Brook reported that the Prime Minister was quite fresh at the end of it.[20] Churchill had had no difficulty in concentrating as long as the discussion lasted.[20] After the Cabinet, Churchill had been in close discussion with other colleagues in the delicate task of the reorganisation of the government.[20]

At 7 pm that evening Churchill went to his room and worked on the proofs of *Triumph and Tragedy* until dinner time when he was joined by Lord Swinton, Secretary of State for Commonwealth Relations, and Butler, and they did not leave him until 1 am in the morning.[20] Moran then told Brook that at 9 am the following morning Churchill was breakfasting and right at the top of his form.[20]

Medical Aspects

Churchill's second stroke threatened to end his time in office as Prime Minister and indeed his political career. The onset of his neurological symptoms on 23 June 1953 was followed by improvement, though not complete resolution, within 24 hours. It then worsened, the neurological deficit from the stroke probably reaching its maximum extent some three days after the onset. There then appears to have been some fluctuation in the severity of the symptoms until about ten days after onset, followed by gradual improvement. When Brain examined Churchill on 25 July 1953, four weeks after the onset, he was in no doubt that there had been considerable improvement. It was on this day that Brain recorded Churchill's symptoms of emotional lability, but these had improved by the time Brain saw him again on 12 August 1953. We comment further on this feature below.

On 18 August 1953 Churchill presided over a long meeting of the Cabinet at which, apparently, none of his political colleagues realized that he had experienced any new medical problem. Indeed, Churchill's ability to work on the proofs of his book, *Triumph and Tragedy*, following this Cabinet meeting, before a working dinner finishing at 1 am the following day, clearly indicates restoration of his characteristic energy and stamina.

The stroke consisted of a left hemiparesis (weakness of the left side of the body). The dysarthria (slurring of speech) was probably in proportion to the observed facial weakness, rather than indicating a cerebellar deficit (a motor coordination centre of the brain). No sensory signs were recorded acutely, and there was no disturbance of higher cerebral function. The progressive and fluctuating onset is now recognized as being typical of a stroke due to small vessel disease, as discussed in our paper concerning Churchill's first stroke in 1949.[15] Thrombosis *in situ* in a lenticulostriate perforating branch of the right middle cerebral artery, causing a small infarct (lacunar stroke) in the posterior limb of the right internal capsule, in the region of the corticospinal projections, seems the most likely pathological basis for this pure motor stroke. A small subcortical haemorrhage cannot be absolutely excluded, but the slow progression and fluctuation make this much less likely.

Parkinson's later cardiac examination was essentially normal, and no mention was made in the examinations earlier in the course of this illness of any abnormality of cardiac rhythm which might indicate the possibility of a cardiac embolus (blood clot) as the cause of the stroke. Churchill's excellent recovery is also consistent with a small lacunar infarct as the pathological basis for the stroke.

This stroke in 1953 indicated that by then Churchill had bilateral cerebrovascular disease, the earlier episodes in 1949[10] and 1950–2[23] having affected the left cerebral hemisphere. The clinical features suggest small vessel (arterial) disease. With this in mind, it is interesting to comment on Churchill's symptoms of 'emotionalism', as recorded by Brain when he saw

Churchill on 25 July 1953.[13] Emotional lability is a recognized feature of focal frontal cerebral lesions and widespread small vessel cerebrovascular disease when it is often associated with some impairment of cognitive function. However, it may also occur as a transient feature of many acute severe illnesses, both cerebral and systemic. The fact that Churchill's 'emotionalism' had improved so substantially and rapidly between Brain's examinations on 25 July 1953 and 12 August 1953, suggests that it may well have been a non-specific effect of the acute illness.

Churchill's ability to function at a very high level in Cabinet on 18 August 1953, to the extent that other members of the Cabinet, ignorant of the fact that Churchill had recently had a stroke, felt that he was functioning normally, supports this conclusion. Churchill's will and drive to recover from this episode and return to his full responsibilities as Prime Minister were indeed impressive, and one can but speculate about the influence this may have had on both the rapidity and completeness of his recovery. It is clear that he confounded the more cautious and entirely appropriate prognoses of both Moran and Brain. But this was Churchill!

Chapter 20

Churchill's Triumph at the Conservative Party Conference in October 1953 in Margate

What does it matter if anything does happen to me? There is no disgrace in going out trying to do one's job[1]

Sir Winston Churchill, while Prime Minister, suffered an acute stroke on 23 June 1953 (see p. 210),[2] after his earlier stroke in 1949 (see p. 182)[3] and cerebrovascular episodes occurring between 1950 and 1952 (see p. 194).[4] The last chapter followed Churchill's recovery until the end of August 1953 when he had chaired his second Cabinet meeting since his stroke.

On 26 August 1953 Lord Moran (see p. 443), Churchill's personal physician, wrote: 'It is now my job to try to persuade the P.M. to be sensible about his health. I do not look forward to the task. He is a poor listener unless you agree with him ...'[5] Moran recorded that he told Churchill: 'We have taken a good many risks together. But now it's my job as your doctor to warn you bluntly that if you are not willing to think out a new way of being Prime Minister, you would be wise to resign before October.'[5] Churchill replied: 'I've been troubled a good deal, my dear Charles, with this decision. I'm not sure the effect of giving up everything all at once would be very good for me.'[5]

31 August 1953: Dinner with Harold Macmillan

Harold Macmillan, Housing Minister, and Anthony Eden, Foreign Secretary, were invited by Churchill to dine at Chequers on 31 August 1953. Macmillan had not seen Churchill alone since he had dined with the Prime Minister on 2 July 1953, though of course he had been present at two Cabinet meetings.

But in the open, and moving, is a more severe test. His recovery has certainly been remarkable. He walks pretty well, although he still drags the left leg slightly. The arm seems recovered; the face shows no or little sign. The speech is as clear as before … On the other hand, if you happen to look towards him when he is off guard, he looks – as he is – a very old man.[6]

1–2 September 1953: Further Discussions with Macmillan and Assessment by Moran

On the following morning Macmillan had further discussions alone with Churchill. He concluded:

(a) The P.M. intends to remain P.M. as long as he can 'face' the Party Conference and the House of Commons. 'Face' means, of course, meet the physical strain. He is what he calls 'bad on his pins' still – but this is improving. If he maintains the progress he has made since I last saw him, he thinks he can do it.

(b) His purpose is not merely (or so he protests and no doubt persuades himself) to prolong his tenure of office. He thinks he can contribute something – perhaps something vital – in the next six months or so to the world situation.[6]

Moran found Churchill in bed at Chequers correcting proofs when he arrived at 7.30 pm that same day.[5] Churchill told Moran: 'I was frightfully well this morning quite like old times. Now I feel flat. I have had to make a lot of small corrections in the book.'[5] After Moran got dressed for dinner he returned to see Churchill still in bed and seemingly too tired to make the effort to get up, though dinner was waiting for him.

When Churchill did get out of bed, his gait was very unsteady.[5] Moran asked Churchill at what time he had gone to bed. He admitted he had talked to Macmillan and Eden until 1.45 am.[5] Moran remonstrated with Churchill: 'It won't do.' Churchill responded: 'Now, Charles you must not fuss me.'[5] Moran said: 'Well if you want to be fit for the party meeting you are not going the right way about it. I don't think you've got hold of the way Brain and I are thinking.'[5] Moran said he would put it on paper. 'Oh, don't do that,' said Churchill peevishly, 'I know what's bad for me. I must get into bed by midnight.'[5]

After dinner Moran found Churchill dictating to a secretary and told Churchill that he was overtired and ought to go to bed. After a few minutes

Churchill rose wearily, swayed as if he might fall, and walked unsteadily to his room.[5]

The following morning (2 September 1953) Moran recorded that Churchill was rested after 'nine hours "beautiful sleep"'[5] Churchill got out of bed to demonstrate to Moran how well he could walk when he gave his mind to it. Churchill had nothing on but a silk vest, so that as Moran followed him along the passage and out into the Great Hall, Moran could see how much more steadily Churchill walked now that he was rested. 'But why was I so unsteady last night? Can you explain that, Charles?' Moran replied: 'Probably a combination of fatigue and alcohol.' Moran explained to Churchill why he thought alcohol affected his gait since his stroke. When Churchill was tired, alcohol made his walk very unsteady. Churchill did not think there was much in this.[5]

Churchill invited Moran to see how he got into his bath.[5] Churchill stepped in, and grasping both sides of the bath, slowly sat down. Churchill then found he could turn the tap even with his left foot. Moran asked Churchill if he had noticed any difference since the stroke. Churchill hesitated, then said: 'Yes my memory is not so good. I sat between two people last night during dinner and I could not remember their names, though I knew them quite well. I find it very embarrassing.'[5]

8–11 September 1953: Further Assessments by Lord Moran

On 8 September Churchill said to Moran: 'I have taken a step forward, Charles. This morning's Cabinet was a considerable advance on the first two ... Of course, I am tired now. Come and see the Chancellor [of the Exchequer].'[5] Churchill addressed RA Butler: 'I thought that I was all right this morning. Did you think so?'[5] Butler agreed that he felt the Prime Minister had 'really done the Cabinet well'.[5]

The Queen had invited the Churchills to be her guests at Doncaster Races on 11 September 1953 for the St Leger, and then to travel with her and Prince Philip on the Royal Train to Scotland and to spend the weekend at Balmoral.[7] Churchill had accepted this invitation immediately but as the date drew near Moran and Mrs Churchill thought the expedition would be too tiring and indeed might jeopardise his recovery.[7]

On 3 September Lady Churchill wrote to her husband:[7]

I would like to persuade you to give up Doncaster and Balmoral.

First Doncaster You will be watched by loving but anxious & curious crowds – It would be rather an effort to keep up steady walking – It may be a longish way to the Paddock and there would be much standing about. Altho' you sit in the Queen's Presence in intimate Court Circles – if you sat in public when she was standing it would be noticed. Then Balmoral – You are improving steadily though slowly, but I think you are not up to a night in the train and so on yet. And you don't want to have a setback before the Margate speech; but rather you must husband your strength for that important event, & for Parliament.[7]

For this reason Moran warned Churchill on the 8 September to be careful about alcohol when he joined The Queen in the Royal Box at the Doncaster Races and then at Balmoral.[5] Churchill told Moran: 'I promise I will be on my best behaviour.'[5]

Before Churchill left for Doncaster on 11 September, Churchill's first public appearance since his stroke, he was assessed by Moran. Churchill was in good form. 'I'll give you an exhibition.'[5] In his vest and reading jacket Churchill proceeded to walk very carefully across the room with a 'determined, concentrated expression on his face'. As he turned he swayed, but repeated the movement. When Churchill reached his bed, he stood on his right leg, and then on his left, when he was a little unsteady. Then he bent both knees, dropping down until he nearly sat on the floor.[5] 'I'm pretty steady don't you think, Charles? There is a longish walk at the station, but I think I can manage it.'[5]

Churchill then sat on the edge of the bed and picked up his slippers, embroidered with the letters WSC in red, using his left big toe and second toe.[5] Churchill said proudly: 'Not everyone can do that even if they were all right.'[5] Churchill reported that Lord Camrose had visited the day before and saw a great improvement in his condition and particularly that Churchill was less emotional.[5] Churchill arranged for Moran to assess him again on his return from Balmoral on 15 September 1953 at 5 pm after the Cabinet meeting.[5]

11–15 September 1953: Churchill at the St Leger and at Balmoral

At the Doncaster Races the Queen invited Churchill to appear in the Royal Box before the crowds: 'They want you,' Her Majesty said.[5] 'I got as much cheering as she did,' Churchill reported.[5] From Doncaster, Churchill travelled in the Royal Train with the Queen and Prince Philip to Balmoral, the Scottish home of the Royal Family. While Churchill was staying at Balmoral, he went to Crathie Church, which he had last visited forty-five years before when he was President of the Board of Trade. Churchill claimed to have walked for ¾ mile in the heather.

On his return from Balmoral on 15 September 1953, Churchill inspected the guard of honour when he got out of the aircraft and shook hands with those present.[5] Later that day Moran assessed Churchill again as planned. After getting out of bed and walking across the room a little unsteadily Churchill said to Moran: 'You see, I am a little shaky, but I am tired now; I have done a very long day … You see I am not behaving like an invalid. I am doing everything I should normally do.'[5]

16 September–30 September 1953: Holiday at La Capponcina, Cap d'Ail

On the morning of 16 September 1953, Churchill chaired the Cabinet and, after lunch with the Irish President, Eamon de Valera, he chaired a further Cabinet meeting. He informed Moran later that day: 'I was on top of the Cabinet business.'[5] The Queen had told Elizabeth Gilliatt,[8] Churchill's personal secretary and daughter of Sir William Gilliatt, Gynaecologist to the Royal Household, that the improvement Churchill had made since she last saw him was 'astonishing'.[5]

Churchill flew to Nice on 16 September 1953 to stay at La Capponcina at Cap d'Ail, across the bay from Monte Carlo, for a recuperative holiday. The villa belonged to Lord Beaverbrook, newspaper proprietor and Lord Privy Seal (1943–5). Churchill was booked on the flight under the name 'Mr Hyde'.[9] A French journalist who had discovered the flight details was barred from the flight by British European Airways, at the request of Special Branch.[9] She had sought an interview with Churchill the previous day and when her request was declined she informed a colleague that she planned to confront the Prime Minister on the flight.[9]

Churchill was joined by Mary, his daughter, and her husband Christopher Soames and later by John Colville, Churchill's Joint Principal Private Secretary, and his wife, Lady Margaret.[10] Churchill's supporting team were also present including Jane Portal, Churchill's personal secretary,[11] and Sergeant Edmund Murray, his bodyguard. Murray has written that the holiday: 'passed peacefully and uneventfully, the Old Man [Churchill] wishing to do nothing else but paint for most of the time, which meant that I was much in demand setting out his easel, paints and brushes, and discussing subjects and the state of the weather, and going out to find suitable sites'.[9] Churchill smiling said: 'If only you could order and arrange the weather as you do my painting material, it would be wonderful.'[9] According to Murray, the highlight of the holiday was a magnificent firework display staged one evening at the Sporting Club of Monte Carlo when the Churchills were dining there.[9]

Churchill's first handwritten letter while on holiday was to the Queen, the second to his wife.

Madam

I must express to Y[ou]r Majesty the keen pleasure which my wife and I derived from our Northern journey, and still more for the kind and gracious thought that led to its being planned. Balmoral was indeed a happy scene of youth and joy – all the brighter on the background of Premonition [the horse had won the St Leger] … I am now here in warm sunshine and the delightful villa built by the dressmaker, Molyneux, with much taste and care, and I shall not often leave its garden where I am installing my painting tackle … The sense of crisis in Security and Finance which oppressed me when two years ago I was asked by your dear Father to form a Government has subsided into a tangle of detail in which there lie many difficulties, tho[ugh], if my judgement is right, no grave immediate dangers.[12]

On 21 September Churchill wrote to his wife a handwritten letter:[7]

My darling one,

The days pass quickly & quietly. I have hardly been outside the garden, and so far have not had the energy to paint in the sunlight hours. [Somerset] Maugham [the author] who lunched yesterday said that we had left it late in the year to come here. But the climate is mild and cheerful, but for one downpour and thunderstorm. I do not think I have made much progress, tho[ugh] as usual I eat, drink & sleep well. I think a great deal about you & feel how much I love you. The kittens [Mary and Christopher Soames] are v[er]y kind to me but evidently they do not think much of my prospects. I have done the daily work and kept check on the gloomy tangle of the world, and I have dictated about 2,000 words of a possible speech for Margate in order to try & see how I can let it off when it is finished to a select audience. I still ponder on the future and don't want to decide unless I am convinced.[7]

Mary Soames wrote to her mother on 22 September 1953: 'Papa is in good health – but alas, low spirits – which Chimp [Christopher] and I are unable to remedy. He feels his energy and stamina to be on the ebb tide – He is struggling to make up his mind what to do. I'm sure you know the form – you have been witnessing it all these months.'[7]

Colville flew out to join the party on 24 September 1953. Colville recorded that Churchill, spent hours 'painting the rocks and pine trees'.[10] He also recorded two amusing anecdotes: one involved Churchill dispatching Colville to play Chemin de Fer at the Casino at Monte Carlo in his stead and the other a visit to a restaurant at San Remo with Churchill that turned into a disaster![10] On a more serious note Colville also recorded that Churchill could not make up his mind whether or not to go on as PM:

On the whole he inclines to do so or at any rate to see what he can do. He certainly wants to, but is a little doubtful of his capacity to make long speeches. He thinks he will take the big one he has to make on October 10th, at the Conservative Conference Margate, as the test. His conversation at Cap d'Ail was of little else.[10]

In a similar vein, Jane Portal wrote to her uncle, RA Butler:

The P.M. has been in the depths of depression. He broods continually whether to give up or not. He was exhausted by Balmoral and the Cabinets and the journey. I sometimes feel he would be better engaged on his *History of the English-Speaking Peoples* which is already very remarkable. He greatly likes your messages telling him all the news and you are in high favour. He is preparing his speech for the Margate conference, but wonders how long he can be on his pins to deliver it. He has painted one picture in tempera from his bedroom window.[13]

On 26 September 1953 Clementine Churchill wrote to her husband: 'I think much about you Darling & your problem, so difficult to resolve. I have faith that you will know best.'[7]

Churchill found the time to reread the draft of his book *A History of the English-Speaking Peoples* following comments about restructuring the book received from Alan Hodge, editorial assistant on the project. Churchill returned from the South of France on 30 September 1953, the day he approved the final preface to the final volume (Volume 6) of his War Memoirs, entitled *Triumph and Tragedy*.[12] This was published in the United States on 30 November 1953 (60,000 copies) and in the UK on 26 April 1954 (200,000 copies).[12]

1–9 October 1953: Preparation for the Conservative Party Conference

On the morning of 1 October Churchill saw Eden,[14] who had been away from his post since an operation on 12 April 1953 to remove gallstones. Eden's bile duct had been damaged, leaving him susceptible to recurrent infections, biliary obstruction and liver failure.[15,16] The meeting was to discuss both Eden's own future and the future of Churchill's initiative for a great-power summit.[14] Eden wrote in his diary: 'Made it clear to W[inston] that I was ready to serve in any capacity, but he made it evident he wanted me to stay on at F[oreign] O[ffice]. Asked about plans and he said he wanted to try himself out, first in Margate and then in the House. Have some doubts as to how that will go physically.'[17]

That evening Churchill dined with Eden, Lord Salisbury (Lord President of the Council and Leader of the House of Lords), who had acted as Foreign Secretary in Eden's absence, and Butler.[17] The talk was almost entirely on foreign affairs as Eden noted in his diary.[17]

On 2 October Churchill presided at the first Cabinet meeting since his return from France. That evening he wrote to Eden:

It was a great pleasure to me to see you in your place today and I'm sure it was right that you should resume your high office on Monday as we have arranged ... The important thing for you (and me) is to make a good impression on the Margate Conference and upon Parliament when we meet. I hope you will give first place in your thoughts to your speech next Thursday, and I should myself much like to see any draft beforehand so as to shape my remarks accordingly. I also think when Parliament meets there will have to be a Foreign Affairs debate which

Brighton School, 29 and 3(?) Brunswick Road, Hove, in the celebration of Queen Victoria's Golden Jubilee on 20 June 1887. Winston Churchill attended the school for three years. (© *Churchill Archives Centre, Churchill College, Cambridge* (*The Papers of Lord Randolph Churchill, DCH 09 001 027*))

2. Winston (right), brother Jack (middle) and Bertie Roose (the son of the Churchill family doctor on the left) in 1887. (© *Churchill Archives Centre, Churchill College, Cambridge* (*The Papers of Lord Randolph Churchill, RDCH 09 001 027*))

3. Winston Churchill campaigning in Dundee and speaking seated; Mrs Churchill is sitting next to him. (© *Alamy* (*HRAC8P*))

4. Rose room (Queens' room), White House. (© *National Park Service, Abbie Rowe, Courtesy of Harry S. Truman Library*)

Winston Churchill MP addresses a joint session of the US Congress on 26 December 1941 in ʹashington DC. (© *IWM* (*NYP 54898*))

6. Winston Churchill at the controls of the Boeing 314 flying boat, RMA *Berwick*. (© *IWM* (*H 16637*))

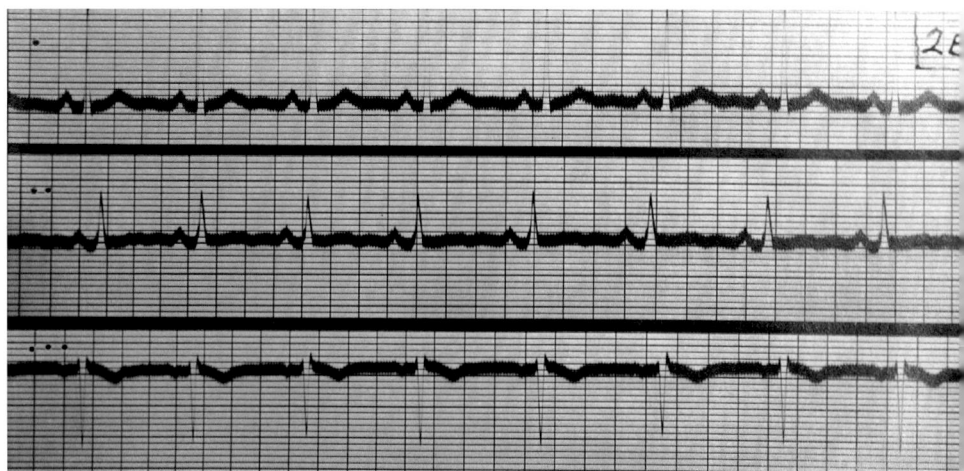

7. ECG performed on Winston Churchill 6 February 1942. (*Reproduced by permission of the Royal College of Physicians*)

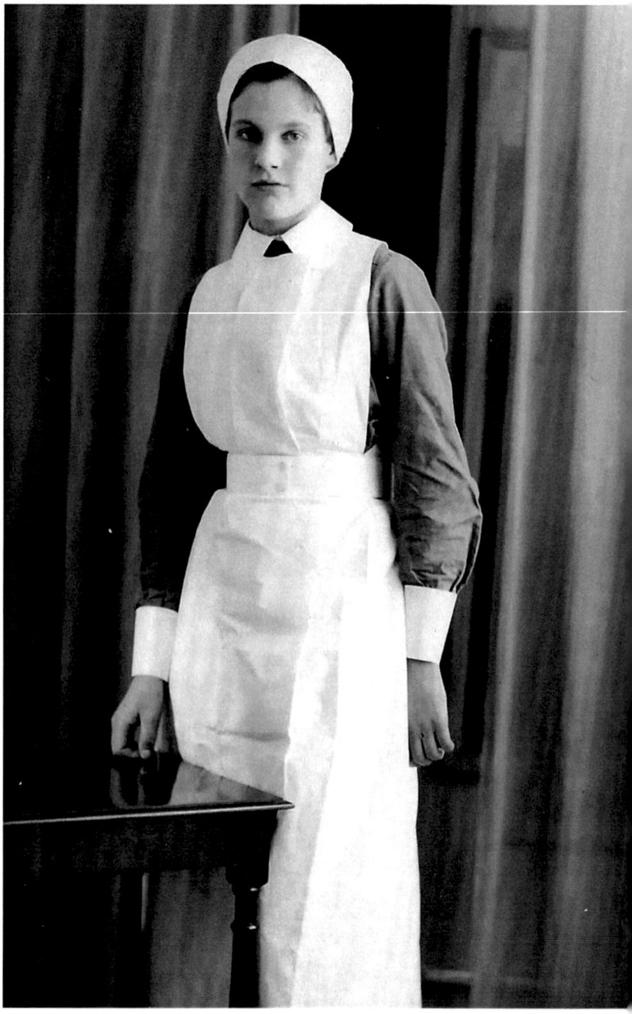

8. Nurse Pugh who nursed Churchill in February 1943 and August/September 1944.

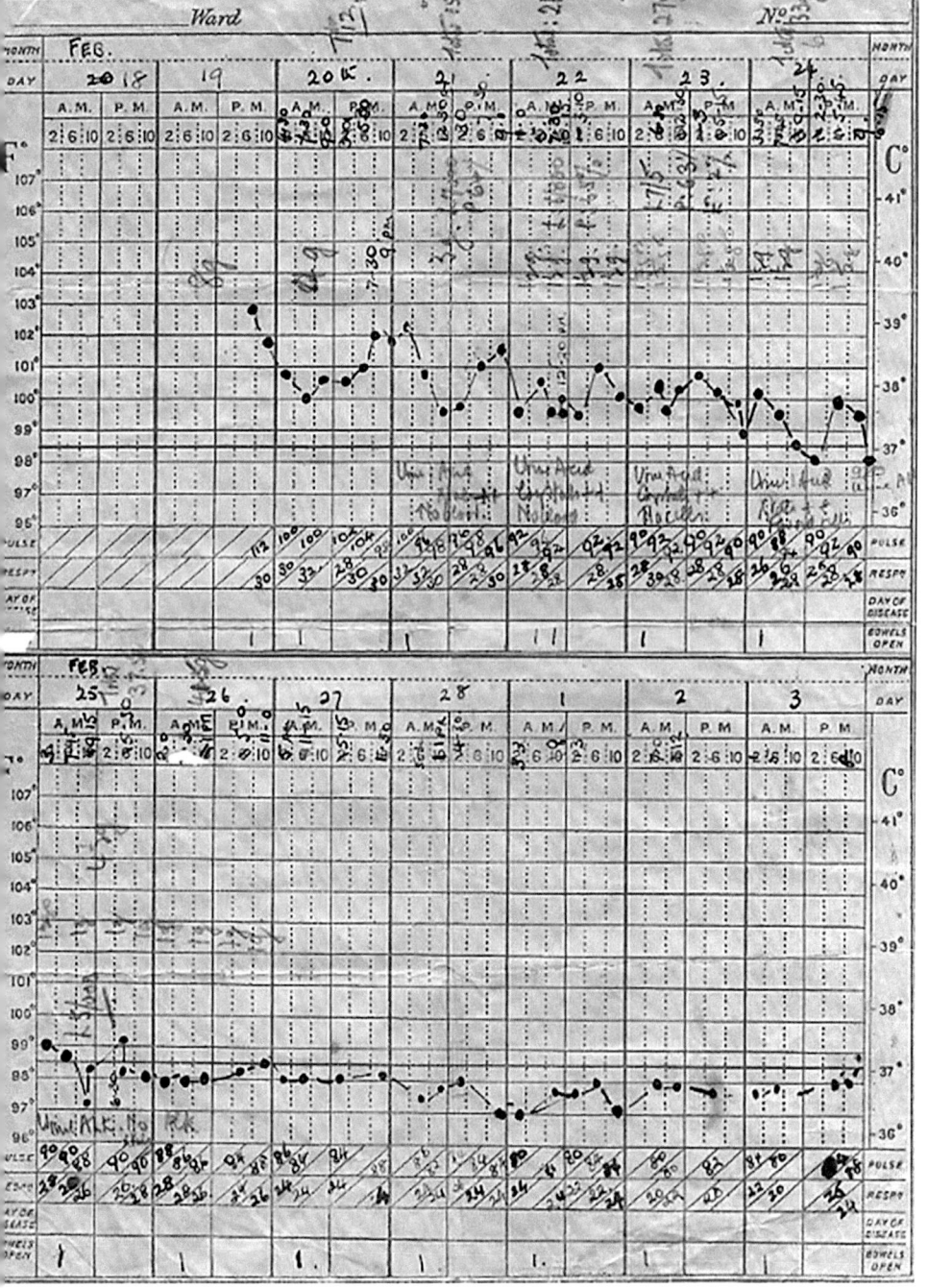

Churchill's temperature chart when he developed pneumonia in London in February 1943. (© *Jill* *ose*)

10. Nurse Doris Miles who nursed Churchill in February 1943 receiving the Gold Medal for Excellence in Nursing. (© *Jill Rose*)

11. Churchill, dressed in his siren suit and dressing gown, stands beside General Eisenhower on Christmas Day 1943. (© *IWM* (*NA 10074*))

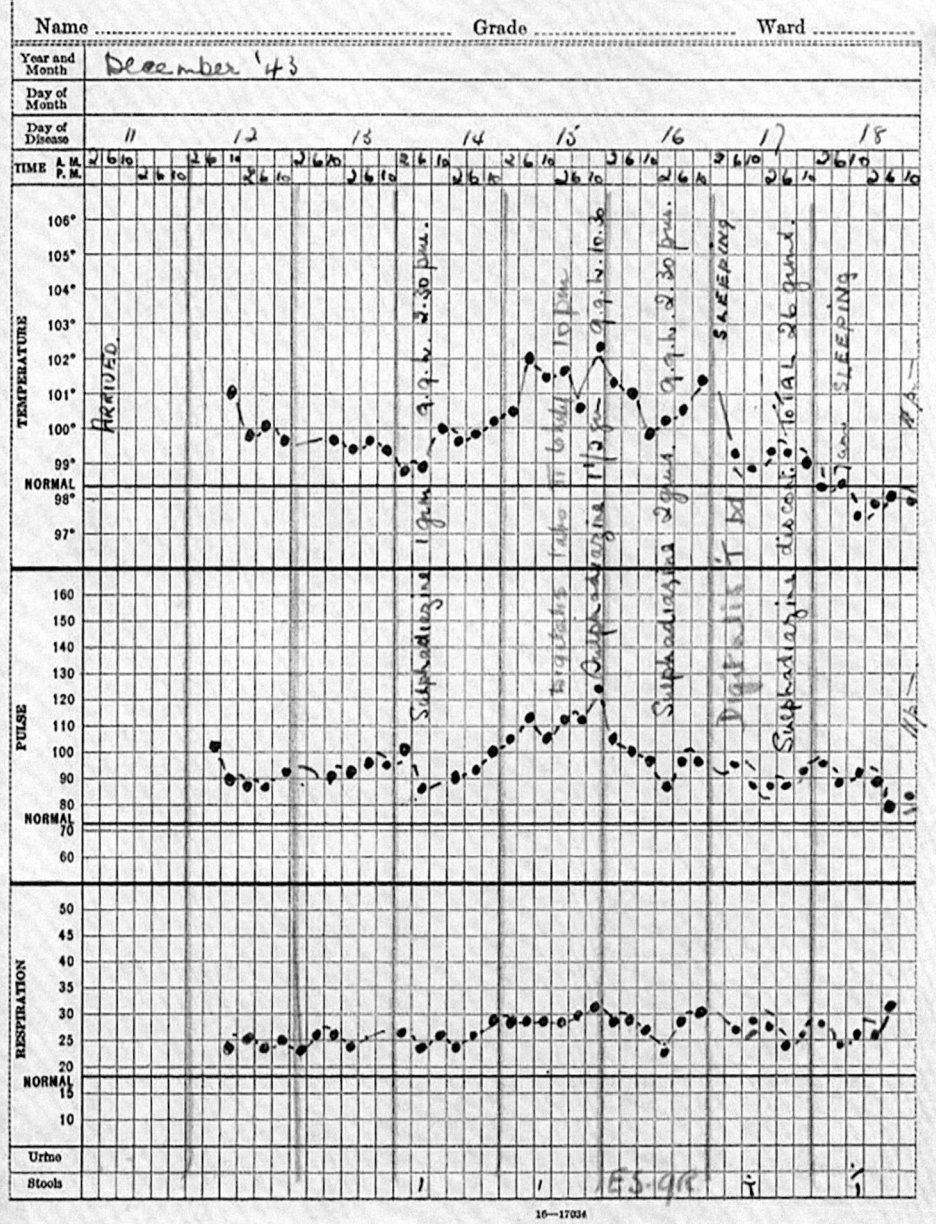

. Churchill's temperature chart when he developed pneumonia in Carthage in December 1943.
) *Lord Moran*)

13. Churchill sits in the sunshine in Marrakech, Morocco, in January 1944 during a period of convalescence after falling ill with pneumonia. (© (*IWM K5870*))

14. Churchill speaking at the Council of Europe on 17 August 1949. (© *Council of Europe*)

15. Portrait of Lord Moran painted by Professor Pietro Annigoni and unveiled by Churchill on 10 July 1951 at the Royal College of Physicians. (© *Royal College of Physicians*)

. Sir Winston Churchill's triumphant speech at the Conservative Party Conference 10 October 53 after recovering from a stroke. (© *Getty Images* (*613494280*))

17. Sir Winston Churchill disembarking after flying back from Nice on 3 April 1958. (© *Alamy* (*E0R5MH*))

18. Sir Winston Churchill, Anthony Montague Browne and President Eisenhower on a Marine helicopter on 6 May 1959 while visiting Washington DC. (© *Alamy* (*F2B5Y6*))

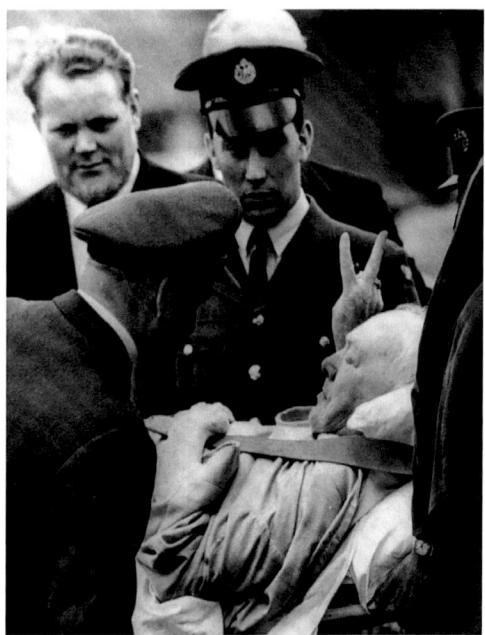

9. Lord Moran arrives with a present at
8 Hyde Park Gate to celebrate Sir Winston
Churchill's 86th birthday on 30 November
1960. (© *Alamy* (*E0W132*))

20. Sir Winston Churchill being admitted to the
Middlesex Hospital on 29 June 1962. (© *Alamy*
EOWD8E)

1. Lord Moran reads a medical bulletin to the press outside Sir Winston Churchill's home in January
1965. (© *Alamy* (*E0X327*))

22. Dr Davis Evan Bedford CBE (1898–1978). (© *Cambridgeshire Collection, Cambridge Central Library*)

23. Lord Brain Bt FRS (1895–1966). (© *NPG* (*164682*))

24. Viscount Dawson GCVO KCB KCMG (1864–1945). (© *NPG* (*167038*))

25. Lieutenant General Sir Robert Drew KCB CBE (1907–91). (© *NPG* (*175191*))

26. Sir Thomas Dunhill GCVO CMG (1876–1957). (© *NPG* (*167313*))

27. Harold Edwards CBE (1899–1989). (© *NPG* (*170454*))

28. Sir Crisp English KCMG (1878–1949). (© *Valerie Herbert*)

29. Dr Thomas Hunt CBE (1901–80).
(*Reproduced by permission of the Royal College of Physicians*)

30. Sir Geoffrey Marshall KCVO CBE.
(© *NPG (186506)*)

31. Lord Moran MC (1882–1977). (© *Yousuf Karsh, Camera Press, London*)

32. Sir John Parkinson (1885–1976). (© *Elva Carey*)

. Professor Robert Pulvertaft OBE (1897–1990).
Rosalind Davies (née Pulvertaft))

34. Lord Richardson Bt LVO (1910–2004).
(© *Sybil Richardson by courtesy of Anne Stafford and Clare Wales*)

. Dr EC Robson Roose (1848–1905).
W & D Downey)

36. Sir James Paterson Ross Bt KCVO (1895–1980). (*Courtesy of Barts Health NHS Trust Archives and Museum (SBHX8/977)*)

37. Professor John Guyett Scadding in 1943 (1907–99). (© *John Scadding*)

38. Professor Sir Herbert Seddon CMG (1903–77). (© *NPG (185200)*)

39. Professor Sir Lionel Whitby CVO MC (1895–1956). (© *NPG (92681)*)

may well take a couple of days. In this case I would speak either the first or the second day as you wish.[14]

For the next week Churchill continued to work on his speech and he practised it in front of 'a looking-glass, watching myself speak as I did in bygone days, long ago'.[18]

2–9 October 1953: Moran's Assessments and Prescription of Amfetamine

Moran reviewed Churchill on 2 October 1953.[18] Churchill told Moran he had written 4,000 words, 'enough for an hour's speech'.[18] Moran recommended a 50-minute speech and Churchill did not demur.[18]

Churchill requested that Moran should prescribe a medicine to ensure that he gave a successful speech at the Conservative Party Conference, on which his Premiership depended. 'You must give me something to take before my speech at Margate.'[18] This was requested primarily because of 'muzzy feelings' in the head,[18] which followed Churchill's second stroke on 23 June 1953.[2] As Lovell[19] has reported, Moran prescribed either Edrisal (amfetamine sulfate 2.5mg, aspirin 160mg, phenacetin 160mg; 'minors') or Drinamyl tablets (amfetamine sulfate 5mg and amylobarbital 32mg; 'majors'); in all probability it was the 'minor'. This opinion is based on Moran's statement in a letter to Churchill in May 1959: 'So far we have used the "minors" only before speeches etc.'[20]

On 8 October 1953 Churchill had a dress rehearsal. He ate a dozen oysters, two mouthfuls of steak and half a glass of champagne at noon. Moran had prescribed a test dose of an amfetamine-containing drug for Churchill at 1 pm.[18] At 2 pm Churchill got on his feet and gave the speech in 36½ minutes, without a pause. His wife sat behind him. '... I had not the stimulus of an audience. But I know now that I can stand that time. I feel it is alright.'[18] The amfetamine 'cleared my head and gave me great confidence'.[18]

10 October 1953: Conservative Party Conference

Colville accompanied Churchill to Margate on 9 October 1953. The second dose of amfetamine was administered an hour before Churchill's speech on 10 October.[18] Mr CP Wilson, a Consultant ENT Surgeon at the

Middlesex Hospital, London and Churchill's regular otolaryngologist, was in attendance to spray his throat before the speech.[18]

Churchill spoke for 50 minutes without losing his place or his concentration, standing throughout (Plate 16). Churchill concluded his speech by saying:

> One word personally about myself. If I stay on for the time being bearing the burden at my age it is not because of love for power or office. I have had an ample share of both. If I stay it is because I have a feeling that I may through things that have happened have an influence on what I care about above all else, the building of a sure and lasting peace. Let us then go forward together with courage and composure, with resolution and good faith to the end which all desire.[21]

Colville recorded in his diary that Churchill made the speech:

> With complete success. He had been nervous of the ordeal: his first public appearances since his stroke and a fifty minute speech at that; but personally I had no fears as he always rises to occasions. In the event one can see but little difference, as far his as his oratory went, since before his illness.[10]

Macmillan wrote:

> How would Churchill come through this ordeal? The answer was really magnificent. He spoke for 50 minutes, in the best Churchillian vein. The asides and impromptus were as good as ever. His voice seems sometimes still weak, and once or twice flagged. But this happens to everybody in the course of a long speech. Altogether, the old man has triumphed once more by sheer persistence; and the public, in and out of the conference hall, shared almost ecstatically in his triumph.[6]

Butler recorded:

> Winston got over the Conservative conference at Margate magnificently. After his speech he sent for me in the Green Room of the Hall and ordered me away for a week's change and holiday. He said, 'You have

been doing too much and I am now finding my strength again.' Very few men can have got over such a paralysis in so lion-hearted a manner.[13]

Jane Portal (later Lady Williams) recalled: 'It was a terrific ordeal. Everyone was watching him for frailty. It was a triumphant achievement to get through that.'[14]

That evening Moran returned by train from Bath and called at No. 10 after 10 pm.[18] He found Churchill, his wife and their daughter Diana, son-in-law Duncan Sandys and Colville listening on the radio to the account of the day's events at Margate.[18] A glance at Churchill's face told Moran that 'it had come off'. Churchill greeted Moran affectionately.[18] Churchill said:

The pill was marvellous. What was in it? Did you invent it? Now, Charles, I know you don't like medicines, but you see what good they can do. You must have given a lot of thought to this pill. I won't ask for it often, I promise. Perhaps once a month when I have a difficult speech in the House ... I owe a great deal to you, my dear Charles.[18]

Later in the conversation Churchill said: 'Now I can sit back and get others to do the work.'[18]

Mary Soames wrote that her father's speech:

Was an unqualified success: *The Times* wrote of a 'triumphant return to public life'; doctors, closest colleagues, loving relations – all others had been confounded. As we looked back over the harassments and anxieties of the past months, it seemed miraculous. There was no more talk, for the present, of resignation or retirement, as Winston once more took up the normal load of his work as Prime Minister. But Clementine, deeply thankful though she was at the return of his health and strength knew that he was working, if not living, on borrowed time, and that any moment he might be struck down again.[7]

11 October 1953–4 November 1953: Nobel Prize and House of Commons Again

On 11 October 1953 Colville dined with Churchill at Downing Street. 'W[inston] was elated by his success, but more tired than one might have hoped.'[10] On 16 October 1953 Churchill learned that he had been awarded the Nobel Prize for Literature 'for his mastery of historical and biographical description as well as for brilliant oratory in defending exalted human values'. He wrote to his wife: 'It is all settled about the Nobel Prize. £12,100 [approximately £355,000 in 2019] free of tax. Not so bad!'[14] Churchill was unable to collect the Prize personally in December as he was attending the Bermuda Conference. Churchill was represented by his wife and daughter Mary who stayed at the Palace at the request of King Gustav Adolf and Queen Louise.[7] Lady Churchill read Churchill's speech of thanks for this exceptional honour at a banquet for over 900 people.[7]

On 20 October 1953 Churchill went to the House of Commons for the first time since his stroke to answer Prime Minister's questions. Prior to his attendance he took a 'Moran', presumably a 'minor' (amfetamine sulfate 2.5 mg, aspirin 160 mg, phenacetin 160 mg). Moran recorded that he asked Churchill whether jumping up and down for nearly a quarter of an hour answering supplementary questions tired him. 'Oh, no, not at all; but it did make me rather short of breath ... You hit the bull's eye with the pill.'[22]

Henry (Chips) Channon MP wrote in his diary on 20 October 1953: 'We saw Winston's long-awaited (and some prophesied never-to-be) return acclaimed. He seems self-confident, though a touch deaf in spite of his hearing aid, but apparently more vigorous than before. But I doubt whether he can carry on for long. The added strain of the House of Commons will be too much.'[23]

Clementine Churchill spoke to Moran on 23 October 1953:

He [Churchill] promised me that he would retire when Anthony [Eden] was fit to carry on, and now when Anthony is perfectly fit he just goes on as before ... You know, Christopher [Soames MP and son-in-law] is very fond of Winston, and he has promised to tell me if his stock falls in the House of Commons. He has given me his word that I should be told if they want to get rid of him. But the trouble is, Charles, that his stock has actually risen ... They cannot make it all out, Charles. They have heard all kinds of rumours about a stroke and paralysis, and now he seems in better form than ever. They described how he strode up a long corridor in the House of Commons, swinging his arms as if he was 20.[22]

On 3 November Churchill prepared to make his first major speech in the House of Commons since his stroke in June 1953. Moran observed that Churchill was sitting up in bed turning over the sheets of his speech and that he was cheerful and in good heart. Miss Portal said that the speech had taken much less out of Churchill than the Margate address. He had taken trouble over it of course but he did not get worked up preparing it, and seemed happy about the way it would be received.[24] Moran wrote: 'The fact is that he is greatly changed since his illness … Even his secretaries can relax, for when things go wrong they can tell him without a scene.'[24] Lord Woolton, Conservative Party Chairman, exclaimed: 'Winston is positively good-tempered these days.' A Labour member of the House of Commons asked Moran: 'What have you done to Winston? There is something serene about him.'[24]

Channon described the scene:

In the house, Winston, who had not been present at the opening of Parliament this morning, rose amidst cheers, and it was immediately clear that he was making one of the speeches of his lifetime. Brilliant, full of cunning and charm, of wit and thrusts, he poured out his Macauley-like phrases to a stilled and awed house. It was an Olympian spectacle. A supreme performance which we shall never see again from him or anyone else. In 18 years in this memorable house I have never heard anything like it … then he sought refuge in the smoking room and, flushed with pride, pleasure, and triumph sat there for two hours sipping brandy and acknowledging compliments. He beamed like a school-boy.[23]

Macmillan recorded:

His performance on November 3rd was really remarkable. It was the first speech he had made in the HofC [House of Commons] since May 11th. He was far more confident than at Margate. Indeed, he was complete master of himself and of the House. It seems incredible that this man was struck down by a second stroke at the end of June. I would not have believed it possible at any time during the summer or even in the early autumn.[6]

After the speech Moran found Churchill in his room, tired but in good heart. 'Your pill cleared my head. Now I can turn my mind to other things.'[24] Moran noted:

His face was grey. I wanted him to go back to No. 10 to rest. But he was worked up and was all agog to hear what they were saying in the lobbies about his speech. 'The house like it I think' ... He emptied his glass and, rising with an effort from his chair, tottered out into the Lobby.[24]

The following day Churchill said to Moran: 'What does it matter if anything does happen to me? There is no disgrace in going out trying to do one's job.'[1] Later Churchill said:

> I am getting better every day, Charles. Don't you think it is a remarkable recovery? Have you ever seen any similar case? I take things for granted now which even a fortnight ago worried me. I still become lachrymose at times, and if some of the thoughts in my speech had occurred to me for the first time in the house I should have been tearful. But I'd been over it all before, so I wasn't troubled.[1]

Churchill then discussed with Moran when he might go to Washington. 'I don't want to go to Washington as long as there is a waddle in my walk. I have decided to walk a thousand yards every day, in the garden or in the park. I think if my muscles were toned up I might walk better. I couldn't deal at present with all the reporters in Washington.'[1] Churchill arranged to meet President Eisenhower at Bermuda on 4 December 1953.

9 February 1954: Assessment by Sir John Parkinson

After his return from Bermuda, Churchill was assessed again on 9 February 1954 by Sir John Parkinson (see p. 444), his cardiologist, at the request of Moran who considered that Churchill had been rather more breathless on exertion in recent months.[25] Churchill admitted that this was the case and also said that he had noticed his heart beating irregularly (though his heart missing beats was a long-standing complaint).[25]

When Parkinson examined Churchill he found that his pulse was 60/minute, regular and with extrasystoles (extra beats). The heart sounds were normal and there were no murmurs. Churchill's blood pressure was 140/85 mmHg.[25] The urine showed albuminuria [proteinuria]. Radioscopy of the heart and aorta were normal, though the diaphragm was slightly raised. The electrocardiogram was normal except for the presence of extrasystoles.[25] Parkinson recorded that at this visit Churchill undressed and dressed himself without assistance. Parkinson advised Churchill to ignore the slight palpitation (due to the extrasystoles) and to walk as little as possible to avoid any shortness of breath.[25] Parkinson suggested to Moran that only if the Prime Minister became more breathless than at present should he consider giving him one tablet of digoxin each morning for a trial period.[25]

Medical Aspects

Summarising these events, Brain wrote:

In 1953, when he was Prime Minister, he had a left hemiplegia – 'my stroke' – as he later called it in a speech in the House. This occurred in the latter part of June and in October he spoke at the Annual Conference of the Conservative Party. I well remember watching it on television and wondering what would happen. His stroke had not been made public and I don't think anyone who did not know could have guessed what his condition had been four months previously. All he was left with was a slight limp with the left foot, which he called 'a halt in my gallop'.[26]

By all accounts, Churchill's recovery from the stroke, at the age of 78, was indeed remarkable. Examination of the acute features of that stroke provides some rationale for this. Churchill suffered a pure motor stroke on 23 June 1953, most likely due to a small internal capsule thrombotic lesion.[2] Sensory function was not disturbed, nor was there speech or other cognitive deficit. Recovery of his motor function is well documented both by Brain and in several non-medical accounts, though Churchill's self-report of a walk of ¾ mile in the heather at Balmoral might be interpreted as somewhat over-optimistic, in the context of these other more objective observations. It perhaps emphasises his determination and wish to persuade both medical and non-medical people close to him that he was capable of carrying on as before the stroke.

Churchill's cognitive function and emotional state require comment. On 2 September 1953, some nine weeks after the stroke, in response to questioning by Moran, Churchill stated that he had had difficulty in remembering the names of two people he knew 'quite well'. Many would regard this observation by Churchill, seen in the context of his large circle of friends and acquaintances and the particular circumstances, as being quite normal.

Much has been made of Churchill's emotional state at this time. We believe that there has probably been over-diagnosis of the establishment of persistent emotional lability at that time. On the day following his speech in the House of Commons on 3 November 1953, Churchill remarked to Moran that he still became lachrymose at times, implying an increased recent tendency, perhaps following the stroke four months previously. Again, we feel it is not justifiable to read too much into this symptom as Churchill had a long history of tearfulness, with well-documented episodes occurring in 1897, 1921, 1930 and on several occasions during the Second World War.[27] This tendency was clearly part of Churchill's personality, and one could speculate that it reflected his deep sense of caring and commitment to personal friends and matters he regarded to be of great importance.

In this context, the change in Churchill's mood in the period following the stroke, observed by Moran, Churchill's secretaries and the Labour member cited by Moran, following the great Commons speech on 3 November 1953, is insufficient to indicate a 'pseudobulbar affect', as suggested by some.[28] So-called pseudobulbar affect, as produced by bilateral cerebral hemisphere vascular disease, is accompanied by dysarthria, dysphagia and very commonly if not invariably, some degree of cognitive impairment. These additional features were not present in Churchill. It seems at least equally likely that the emotional and behavioural change resulted from a shift in Churchill's outlook, on the background of his longstanding characteristic pattern of emotional response to certain situations, following the further reminder of his own mortality, leading to a less combative, more reflective and more benign outlook.

Churchill complained of a 'muzzy head', as recorded by Moran prior to the Conservative Party Conference speech on 10 October 1953, but he had reported this intermittent symptom some three years previously.[3] Again, it is difficult to put a causative interpretation on this symptom, without further description. It is perhaps too easy to attribute it to the transient effects of either alcohol intoxication or hangover in a habitual drinker. Churchill reported it to Moran again in 1953, possibly partly in order to get Moran to prescribe a stimulant to be taken before his speech. It would be facile to ascribe Churchill's barnstorming and much-admired performance at the

Conference to the amfetamine prescribed. Moran's approach to Churchill's request was admirably cautious: a test dose, probably of amfetamine sulfate 2.5 mg, given on 8 October 1953, accompanied by oysters, steak and a little champagne, led to an excellent dress rehearsal of the speech, and does not appear to have caused adverse effects. It was probably this dose that Churchill took before giving the Conference speech on 10 October 1953.

The regular administration of amfetamines shortly after a stroke, at much higher doses than those employed by Moran, has not been shown to be of benefit in improving motor function, disability or cognition.[29,30] However, Moran's use of amfetamine sulfate 2.5 mg as a single dose before major speeches seems to have been successful in clearing Churchill's 'muzzy head' and giving him confidence. Evidence for the effectiveness of single low dose treatment of amfetamine on cognitive function in subjects of Churchill's age is lacking. Cognitive improvement has been demonstrated in much younger subjects with single doses of amfetamine some seven-fold larger than the dose in Churchill's 'minors'.[31] It is also worth noting that in a recent double-blind crossover trial in healthy young subjects, no significant cognitive enhancement by amfetamine was demonstrated, though participants believed their performance had improved, perhaps reflecting in part the difficulty of adequate blinding in such a study.[32]

The accounts of Churchill's scintillating performances at the Conservative Party conference on 10 October 1953 and in the House of Commons on 3 November 1953, described here, can leave no doubt that he continued to be capable of functioning cognitively at an extremely high level. We conclude that it is most unlikely these outstanding presentations, from an accomplished orator, were attributable to amfetamine treatment.

Although the use of daily aspirin would be expected to be of benefit in the secondary prevention of stroke, the administration of aspirin 160 mg as a constituent of a 'minor' would not have been of benefit except in acute ischaemic stroke.[33,34]

Following his stroke in June 1953, Churchill undoubtedly recognised that he was teetering on the brink and knew that his days in high office were numbered. Nevertheless, with his characteristic sense of duty, combined with intellectual and linguistic brilliance, style, panache and the ability to rise to the occasion, he confounded the less optimistic forecasts of his medical advisers, family and colleagues.

Chapter 21

Acute Ataxic Stroke in June 1955 in London

It is wonderful that you have kept me going for so long.[1]

At noon on 5 April 1955 Sir Winston Churchill held the last Cabinet meeting of his career, almost fifteen years after the first Cabinet of his wartime administration, and almost fifty years since he had first sat in Cabinet.[2] Churchill told the Cabinet that he intended to submit his resignation to Her Majesty at an audience that afternoon.[2]

Anthony Eden, who was soon to succeed Churchill, spoke the valedictory words at the Cabinet:

> The Foreign Secretary said that his Cabinet colleagues had asked him to speak on this occasion on behalf of them all. It therefore fell to him to express their sense of abiding affection and esteem for the Prime Minister and their pride in the privilege of having served as his colleagues … If in a succeeding Government they met with success, this would be largely due to the example which he had shown them: if they did less well, it will be because they had failed to learn from his experience and skill as a statesman. They would remember him always – for his magnanimity, for his courage at all times and for his unfailing humour, founded in his unrivalled mastery of the English language. They would always be grateful for his leadership, and for his friendship, over the years that had passed; and they would hope to enjoy in future his continued interest and support in their endeavours.[2]

On the morning of 6 April 1955, Churchill received his last document at 10 Downing Street, a note written by Anthony Montague Browne, his Private Secretary. That afternoon Churchill gave a tea party for about 100 staff at No. 10, including the private secretaries, the telephonists, the messengers, the drivers – so that he and Lady Churchill could thank them before taking their leave.[3] Churchill was cheered away by his staff, who lined the long corridor leading from the Cabinet Room to the front door.[3] Churchill drove from Downing Street to Chartwell accompanied by Ms Gilliatt,[4] his personal secretary since 1945.[2] 'I was very sad. I had wished he could die in office,' she later recalled.[2] Lady Churchill remained behind as she had many things to arrange.[3]

6 April 1955–11 April 1955: Chartwell

When Churchill arrived at Chartwell, there was a small crowd at the gates to welcome him back.[3] Mary Soames wrote: 'Christopher and I both dined with him; he was in quite good form, and messages were flowing in. So all had been accomplished with fitness – and, as Winston had said to a press reporter on the steps of Chartwell, "It's always nice to come home".'[3]

On 7 April Churchill began to work again on the 1939 proof sets of *A History of the English-Speaking Peoples*. Thus, within 48 hours of his retirement, he had found a new focus of activity.[2] Throughout 1955 Churchill's morale was much dependent on the *History*, as Churchill told Moran on several occasions:

I'm interested in my book, that's all I care for now [17 June];[5]
Any fun I get now is from my book [17 June];[5]
Only my book commands my ability and my interest. All the rest is drudgery. I find the fifteenth century more interesting than the twentieth [21 November].[6]

The revision of the *History* depended principally on Alan Hodge, Editor of *History Today*, with Dennis Kelly (barrister and editorial assistant) chiefly responsible for retrieving and collating the various sets of proofs. Hodge recruited a series of outstanding historians, including Dr AL Rowse (see below), to work on the task.[7] The Preface of Volume 1, *The Birth of Britain*, was dated 15 January 1956.[8]

12 April 1955–20 April 1955: Holiday in Sicily

On 12 April, his sixth day of retirement, Churchill left Chartwell for a two-week holiday in Sicily with his wife. Churchill had declined Lord Moran's repeated offers to accompany him to Sicily. Instead Churchill took two friends: Lord Cherwell (Professor Frederick Lindemann; 'The Prof'), whom he had known for thirty-five years, and John Colville, who had been a member of his private office for more than eight years, latterly as Joint Principal Private Secretary.[2] While the main party travelled by air, Churchill's bodyguard, Sergeant Edmund Murray, and his valet, Jock Kirkwood, had to travel with the baggage by train via Paris and Rome, which took two-and-a-half days.[9]

Mary Soames has written that her parents were away for a fortnight:

> but for Clementine the holiday was a failure. She had little respite from pain [from neuritis], and in addition the weather was cold and grey. Although Chartwell and Hyde Park Gate were both at this moment uninhabitable because of alterations and decorations, she was only too glad to get back to England earlier than planned, and they both stayed for a short time at the Hyde Park Hotel.'[3]

Colville also described in his diary that it rained almost solidly for a fortnight.[10] Churchill painted one of the caves and entertained Harry (publisher of *Time*, *Life*, *and Fortune*) and Clare Luce (US Ambassador to Italy), who arrived from Rome.[10] Churchill and Murray instructed Clare Luce how to paint.[9] Colville wrote:

> The Prof. [Lord Cherwell] talked much of the crying need for higher technological education and I volunteered to try to raise the money for a new institute or college, to be inspired and prompted by Winston. It was thus that Churchill College [Cambridge] had its origins. Our visit, intended for three weeks, was cut short because of the cold and wet and we came home about 20 April.[10]

21 April 1955–2 June 1955: Fighting and Winning the Election at Woodford

While the Churchills had been away, the date of the next General Election had been announced (26 May 1955). Churchill threw himself into fighting for his seat, and he also addressed a few meetings outside his constituency; one of them was in Bedford where he spoke for his son-in-law, Christopher Soames.[3] Churchill was once again elected at Woodford by a large majority

(15,808), and in the Country the Conservatives were returned with an increased majority (59 over all other parties) in the new parliament.

On 31 May, Churchill told Moran that he had spent 3 hours that morning working on *A History of the English-Speaking Peoples*. 'Oh, it was simple, just rearrangement, and picking out an unnecessary passage here and there. It's thinking and composing I find difficult.'[1] On 2 June Churchill sent Alan Hodge and Dennis Kelly his thoughts and instructions about the first volume.

2–6 June 1955: Assessments by Lord Moran

Churchill telephoned Moran on the morning of 2 June 1955 and asked to see him.[1] Churchill told Moran that after dinner the previous night, he had felt light-headed ('felt queer') as if he had drunk too much, though this was not the case as his son-in-law, Christopher Soames, confirmed.[1] However, when he woke in the night, the light-headedness had gone, but in the morning his right hand was 'clumsy'.[1] 'Twice I have knocked over my cup and upset the coffee.'[1] Churchill reached for his pen and wrote his name several times. 'My writing is not good. I know that something has happened.'[1] As he was speaking, his cigar slipped from his mouth. 'Yesterday when I lunched with Max [Lord Beaverbrook] I kept dropping my cigar and Max kept picking it up.'[1]

Moran examined Churchill. When Churchill tried to touch Moran's finger with his right hand, he made a circle round it.[1] Churchill had a good strong grip. When Churchill attempted to walk, Moran was afraid that he might fall, his 'right leg shot out unsteadily in the air, as if goose-stepping'. Moran told Churchill that there had been another spasm of an artery.[1]

At the request of Lady Churchill and Christopher Soames, Moran accompanied Churchill to Chartwell and stayed the night.[1] On arrival at Chartwell, Churchill rejected all attempts to help him up the steps. Churchill 'made his way to the office in a succession of darts, bumping against the wall, first to the right then to the left, so that it seemed he must fall. In the office he flopped into a chair.'[1]

The following morning Churchill was much better and again wrote his name out several times. While Moran was examining Churchill's signatures, his right arm 'made a sudden purposeless and uncontrolled movement, upsetting the cup, so that his fingers ended in the coffee'. That night

Churchill went to bed after taking a 'red' (secobarbital 100 mg) capsule and a 'green' one (promethazine), washed down with a little whisky.[1]

On the morning of 4 June Churchill told Moran: 'I think I am definitely better.'[1] Once again Churchill wrote out his name several times. 'Yes, the first signature is almost normal. I am better, definitely better.'[1] Later in the day, while watching a film, Christopher Soames reported to Moran that Churchill had retired to his room because his heart was 'pounding'. When Moran examined him, he found that his pulse was rapid and irregular. However, when Churchill woke up the following morning: 'I felt master. I was on top. I was in good health again.'[1]

On 6 June Churchill gave Moran one of his pictures and told him: 'It is wonderful that you have kept me going for so long.'[1] Churchill was now sufficiently recovered that he made plans to see as much of Alan Hodge and Dennis Kelly as possible to move forward with *A History of the English-Speaking Peoples*. Churchill now re-read Chapter 7 which had lain unaltered for nearly twenty years, and he was not completely satisfied with what he read.

8–9 June 1955: Opening of Parliament

On 8 June Churchill was well enough to be driven to London for the Opening of Parliament. On the following day, Churchill received rapturous applause both from Members of Parliament and the public gallery. Moran recorded:

> Mr Attlee rose from his seat and, quickly crossing the floor, took Winston by the arm pushing him forward in front of him towards the table. Sir Winston must take the oath before him; while the whole House, seeing what was being done, rose to applaud ... Then he [Churchill] signed the role of Members, writing his name for the thirteenth time in the roll of the Parliaments of Great Britain, very carefully, very deliberately – no doubt he had in mind what had happened at Chartwell.[5]

Churchill took the place he had habitually occupied in the 1930s – the first seat below the gangway on the Government side.[3]

Churchill attended the Trinity House Dinner that evening; Trinity House is a charity dedicated to safeguarding shipping and seafarers since 1514. As he did regularly, Churchill also attended The Other Club dinner on 9 June 1955. The Other Club had been founded by Churchill and FE Smith, subsequently Lord Birkenhead in 1911. On being asked by Moran how the latter dinner went, Churchill replied: 'I don't think anyone noticed anything unusual … I'm not so well as I was before this happened. I wonder if I shall get back where I was.'[5] Moran recorded against an entry dated 12 June 1955 that Churchill had been dreading another stroke 'almost from hour to hour' and had wanted to see Moran every day.[5] On this day Churchill proclaimed: 'I'm writing better, much better. I think I'm over this turn.'[5]

15 June 1955: Assistance from Anthony Montague Browne

On 15 June Churchill learned from Harold Macmillan, Foreign Secretary, that he could use the services of one of his former private secretaries, Anthony Montague Browne, who had returned to the Foreign Office. Macmillan wrote to Churchill:

> I have had a talk with Montague Browne and I am glad to hear he is being of service to you. Please make all use of him you can for as long as you wish … I leave tonight on the first lap of the great journey on which you started us [Meeting in New York to discuss the proposed Summit]. It is sad to think that you will not be at the 'top level' meetings yourself, but you have the satisfaction of being the pioneer. I have asked Montague Browne to show you one or two telegrams.[11]

This was generous of Macmillan as Churchill had already summoned Montague Browne to help him at Lord Beaverbrook's villa, La Capponcina, at Cap d'Ail, before formal arrangements were made.[12]

16–21 June 1955: Assessments by Lord Moran

On 16 June 1955, Moran found Churchill in the rose garden at Chartwell. 'What is my pulse like? It was very quick yesterday afternoon.'[5] Moran has not recorded an assessment. On 17 June Churchill discussed his forthcoming speech at the Guildhall with Moran. Moran reassured Churchill that: 'We'll get you through Guildhall without any trouble.'[5]

Churchill had been invited to spend the weekend of 18–19 June at Hatfield House, the home of Lord Salisbury, Leader of the House of Lords. Moran recorded that Churchill had rather dreaded his visit to Hatfield, but it had been arranged that he should not get there till 7 o'clock on Saturday and return on Monday morning. That only left the midday hours on Sunday and with a 'minor' (amfetamine sulfate 2.5 mg, aspirin 160 mg, phenacetin 160 mg) Churchill expected to get through lunch. Churchill informed Moran on his return that he thought the weekend had 'gone all right though he was walking badly'.[5]

21 June 1955: Speech at the Guildhall at the Unveiling of Churchill's Statue by the Lord Mayor

On 21 June Churchill gave a speech at the Guildhall when his statue was unveiled.[13]

I regard it as a very high honour that the City of London should decide to set up a statue of me in this famous Guildhall, which I have so often visited and spoken in during the last half century. I must admit that I think that the House of Commons has made a good rule in not erecting monuments to people in their lifetime. But I entirely agree that every rule should have an exception. The fact that you have done so in my case will both prove the rule, and emphasize the compliment. I greatly admire the art of Mr Oscar Nemon whose prowess in the ancient realm of sculpture has won such remarkable modern appreciation. I also admire this particular example, which you, my Lord Mayor, have just unveiled, because it seems to be such a very good likeness. But on this point, as indeed in any other part of this ceremony, I cannot claim to be either impersonal or impartial. I am indeed an interested and biased party ... It is to the future that we must turn our gaze. I confess that, like Disraeli, I am on the side of the optimists ... Whatever is the outcome, we must persevere in the maintenance of peace through strength ... Let us go boldly forward and play our part in all this.[13]

That evening Churchill told Moran that his performance at the Guildhall had restored his confidence. 'It was a formidable ordeal. Did you like my speech? It would be easy on such an occasion to say foolish, conceited things.

I carefully avoided that.'[5] After Churchill had explained to Moran that he had slept for more than an hour after his return from the Guildhall, Moran recorded that sleep did Churchill almost as much good as a 'minor'.[5]

22 June 1955: Assessment by Sir Russell Brain Bt

Brain assessed Churchill at the invitation of Moran at 9.15 am on 22 June 1955. He learned from Churchill and Moran that two weeks ago (in fact it was three weeks previously on 1 June) while dining at Chartwell, on getting up Churchill felt as if he was drunk – swimmy.[14] After this, Brain recorded, Churchill had difficulty in controlling his right hand, misjudged distances and knocked things over. His writing got very bad, and he became a bit unsteady on his feet.[14] Moran stayed with him for five days, and he had steadily improved. Moran said that his speech became worse at the time. He is still somewhat dysarthric, his speech not always intelligible.[14] Otherwise, there was no change in his physical signs except that now both plantars were extensor (a physical examination sign consistent with a recent or previous stroke). There was no ataxia, nystagmus or new sensory loss. His gait was fairly good with an effort. He was said to be well in the mornings and unresponsive at lunchtime unless he took a 'minor'.[14]

Moran also recorded this assessment by Brain.[5] Churchill explained that three weeks ago: 'I bumped up against the wall. I thought I was drunk, but in the morning my writing was bad. I put my signatures in an envelope, but I have left it at Chartwell.' Churchill reached for his pen and wrote his name several times and handed them to Brain.

This is like my normal writing, whereas that morning my hand lingered so that I upset things – I cannot sprinkle sugar as well even now. I wondered if it would get worse as in 1953, when I did things the day after my stroke, and I was not paralysed until the following day. But this time the other channels opened up. I'm getting rather good at that. And Charles watched me like a cat, day and night, for five days. I can walk all right if I set my mind to it. He flung off the bed–clothes and stalked across the room. Then he stood and lifted first one leg and then the other. I'm still not very steady.[5]

Moran recorded that Brain made a careful examination, then sat back in his chair and said nothing.[5] 'Charles is right', Brain said at last. 'It was a spasm, and now the artery has opened up again. I see no reason why you should not in a short time be as good as before.'[5] 'You mean before I resigned?' asked Churchill.[5]

> Of course, putting down responsibility is a very relaxing affair. My whole psychological position had to be changed. After my return from Sicily I had to begin my election address. The quality of thought, such as it is was, was not diminished, but I had become very slow. I got it out all right in the end, but I dislike original composition. I am not ambitious any more. I really want not to make an ass of myself. I began my Guildhall address on Monday. I did 300 words in the car coming up from Chartwell, another 300 between 10 o'clock and midnight. In the morning I finished it off only just in time. My bad time is from noon until 4:30. I am embarrassed by the midday blur.[5]

Churchill went on to complain of his poor memory, particularly for names. He looked at the glass of whisky by his bed. 'I keep it by me all day. Oh, it is only weak, and I only sip it. It is more a companion than a stimulant.'[5] Brain listened attentively to Churchill's story but offered no comment, according to Moran.[5] 'Winston waited impatiently for suggestions, but they did not come. He told Brain the whole story that he might get his help. He wanted to be told that his mind was not giving way. He wanted to do something.'[5] Brain said, 'There is nothing I can add to the treatment.'[5]

Moran summarised Brain's assessment as follows:

> Brain is an honest man, he has no patter. He told me, when I saw him to the door, that he noticed Winston a good deal changed. But of course he had not seen him for a year. There was really nothing to be said. He did not try to say comforting things. He would be more popular with Winston if he did.[5]

Brain[15] was offended by the two comments made about his seeming failure to communicate adequately with Churchill. These observations were disturbing to Brain as he thought that if Moran's book was widely read, the comments might be detrimental to his clinical practice.[15] Legal advice was sought, but wisely the issue was not pursued.[15] Although Brain's son concluded that the remarks about the lack of patter rang true, he considered their publication showed a gratuitous insensitivity to the feelings of a loyal and very supportive colleague.[15]

30 June 1955–15 August 1955: Visit of Dr AL Rowse and Further Assessments by Lord Moran

On 30 June 1955 Churchill wrote to Macmillan, 'AMB [Montague Browne] is a great help to me in my official and semi-official aftermath.'[16]

Moran assessed Churchill again on 6 July 1955: 'My mind works as well as ever, but I dislike the effort when I have to use it,' Churchill told his doctor who thought this statement was 'generous'.[5] Churchill told Moran that he was spending 4 or 5 hours a day on corrections and alterations to the *History*.[5] Moran noted in his records that he must ask Hodge whether this involved 'mental effort'.[5] As Moran was leaving Churchill told him that two of his fingers had gone numb before he went to bed.[5] 'It doesn't mean anything, Charles? I'm not going to have another stroke … Tomorrow Henry Luce's people will be here about business in connection with the book. I want to be in good form.'[5]

Rowse has written of an encounter with Churchill on 11 July 1955 at Chartwell.[17]

> Before lunch I was summoned up to his bedroom, and there, and last, was the so familiar face, much aged: that of an old man who gone back to his baby looks. The eyes a cloudy blue, a little bloodshot, spectacles on snub nose, a large cigar rolled round in his mouth. He had been at work. 'I like work'. Beside the bed a small aluminium pale for cigar-ash; before him, stretching right across the bed, a tray-desk on which were the long galleys of his *History of the English-Speaking Peoples*.[17]

Churchill welcomed Rowse with a touch of old-fashioned exaggerated courtesy as if the honour were his that the professional historian had come to see him. Rowse returned the compliment by stating that Churchill had beaten the professionals at their own game, that his *Marlborough* was an historical masterpiece along with Trevelyan's *England Under Queen Anne*.[17] Churchill said that now that he had some time, he was re-reading the *History* he had written before the war, but he wasn't satisfied with it.[17] Rowse then read the revised chapters on Henry VII and Henry VIII while Churchill got dressed. 'The figure all the world knew then entered: striped blue zip suit, blue velvet slippers with WSC worked in gold braid, outwards, in case anybody did know who was approaching.' Over lunch, Churchill told Rowse of the severe stroke he had suffered, so that he couldn't feed himself – and yet managed to hold onto office.[17] Having said his goodbyes, Rowse noted: 'It was infinitely sad and touching. One may never see or hear him again. At any moment the last stroke may come.'[17]

On 13 July 1955 Churchill sent a specially designed silver V-sign to 113 former members of his staff and the establishment at 10 Downing Street, including the cleaners, electricians, telephonists, messengers and carpenters. The recipients also included Colville who wrote on 17 July 1955:

I treasure the silver V-sign, commemorating your Second Administration, and am placing it on my watch chain as an object to be very especially prized. I hope that during the last week of July or at any time in August you will let me know if you feel the need of either companionship or bezique, and I will be at your disposal.[18]

Churchill attended The Other Club dinner on 14 July 1955 from 8.45 to 11.45 pm. Although most of the diners had left by then, Churchill stayed to the end. 'There was some good fun. I got home [Chartwell] at a quarter to one, tired but not unduly tired.'[5]

President Eisenhower wrote to Churchill on 15 July 1955:

Soon Anthony [Eden] and I will be meeting with the French and the Russians at Geneva ... Personally I do not expect, and I hope the people of this country and of the world do not expect, a miracle. But if we can inch a little closer to the dream that has been yours for these many years, if together at the meeting table we can create a new spirit of tolerance and perhaps, in concert, come to the realization that force and the threat of force are no longer acceptable in dealings among nations, we shall gain much that will help us in the long and complicated process that must come after the Summit meeting. As I leave Washington, my thoughts are with you.[19]

Churchill replied by return on 18 July 1955:

My dear friend, I am deeply grateful to you for your letter and the thought that prompted you. I was touched by what you said when I resigned, and I had two of your letters with me at the time which I had not answered ... It is a strange and formidable experience laying down responsibility and letting the trappings of power fall in a heap to the ground. A sense not only a psychological but of physical relaxation steals over one to leave a feeling both of relief and denudation. I did not know how tired I was until I stopped working. I cannot help, however, feeling satisfied with the way things have turned out.[20]

August 1955: Macmillan Visits Chartwell and Arranges for Montague Browne to be Seconded Full-time

Macmillan wrote in his diary on 5 August 1955:[21] 'I made a pilgrimage to Chartwell where I found Churchill alone. He was very grateful for the smaller attentions which I have been able to show him. Montague Browne goes to see him two or three days a week. He helps him with his immense correspondence and also brings a selection of foreign telegrams for him to see.'[21] Macmillan reported to Moran at lunch on 10 August 1955 on his conversation with Churchill. 'Of course Winston is older but when I took the conversation back to Lloyd George his memory was surprisingly good.'[5] Macmillan asked Moran how long Churchill would go on like this. Moran replied that was guesswork.[5]

On 12 August 1955 Moran visited Churchill at 6 in the evening. Although Churchill had just gone to bed, he had spent the day painting a portrait of Lady Churchill from a photograph taken twenty years previously.[5]

Moran visited his patient again on 14 August 1955 and found Lady Violet Bonham Carter was staying at Chartwell.[5] Lady Violet was a longstanding friend of Churchill's and daughter of Herbert Henry Asquith, Prime Minister at the time of Churchill's close association with him. Lady Violet told Moran that she was shocked by the deterioration in Churchill. She had made a point of speaking about the past, but all Churchill said was: 'I can't remember.'[5]

Macmillan wrote to Montague Browne in early August 1955:

Many thanks for your note of August 2. I dined with Winston on Friday night [5 August 1955]. I thought him in good form – better than I expected. He is extremely grateful for all the work you gave him, and I hope you will be able to go on doing so … I do not know what you are doing for leave, but if you are in the Foreign Office on Monday, August 15, you might look in for a moment and see me.[12]

The Foreign Secretary told Montague Browne:

Winston needs you. He's going to travel extensively and as you know he is already deep in correspondence with Ike, with Adenauer, de Gaulle and I don't know who else. Moreover, the Middle East Department is not one that one can flit in and out of like a weekend cottage – I know it's not your fault. So I'm going to second you to Winston. You will continue to be a full member of the Service, and will pay you as before. Winston will reimburse the Treasury. In the nature of things it will be two years at the most.[12]

In fact, for nearly another ten years Montague Browne was to be Churchill's constant and devoted private secretary to the very end.

7–27 September 1955: Presentation of the Portrait of Sir Winston Churchill as Warden of the Cinque Ports and his Holiday in the South of France

On 7 September Churchill spoke at the presentation of his portrait by Bernard Hailstone as Lord Warden of the Cinque Ports in Hastings.[22]

I take great pride in holding the office of Lord Warden of the Cinque Ports. When you approach the end of a long life there is a comfort in looking back on the past, and belonging to an institution of such age and dignity … I am most grateful, Mr Speaker, for your many compliments. It is quite true that I was called upon to play a part in the War, and, oddly enough, that this entailed many visits to the Cinque Ports … We now have to look forward, and not back, we now have to think of the perils of the future, and not those of bygone years.[22]

On 15 September Churchill travelled to the South of France to stay at Lord Beaverbrook's (newspaper proprietor and Lord Privy Seal, 1943–5) villa, La Capponcina at Cap d'Ail, across the bay from Monte Carlo. Churchill was joined there by Lady Churchill, daughter Mary and son-in-law, Christopher Soames. He painted in the warm autumn sunshine and wrote to Moran on 26 September 1955 as follows: 'My dear Charles, I have been very well, and lived an idle life except at the Book and painting. I have taken one minor so far since arriving, in two parts. Memory lags and tickles tease. I eat, drink and sleep well. I am sorry about Ike. He will be a great loss.'[23] Although President Eisenhower had suffered a myocardial infarction on 24 September 1955, he lived until 1961. Moran wrote to Churchill in response: 'I was most delighted to hear from you and to get such an excellent report. It is most encouraging … If I were in Ike's shoes, I should count it no more than a provisional notice to quit.'[16]

On 6 October 1955 Churchill wrote to Beaverbrook: 'My dear Max, We have had a very pleasant three weeks here, and Clemmie is better. The chef is excellent, the garden lovely. I have painted another picture, and so far I have not spoiled it, which is something.'[16]

November–December 1955: Speeches and Memory Loss

Following his return from France on 15 November 1955, Churchill had speeches to prepare for his Constituency (18 November 1955), Harrow School (24 November 1955), the Young Conservatives (5 December 1955), Drapers Hall (7 November 1955) and the Mansion House dinner (16 December 1955). Most of these speeches had been drafted by Colville. On the 13 December 1955 Churchill told Moran: 'I keep losing my memory. I could not remember Anthony's [Eden] name today. And now I have forgotten the name of Sir …'[6]

Churchill celebrated his 81st birthday on 30 November 1955.

Medical Aspects

Churchill clearly suffered a further stroke on 1 June 1955. His symptoms of light-headedness, followed within hours the next morning by clumsiness of the right hand and poor writing, together with Moran's examination findings on 2 June 1955 of target imprecision of the right hand in the absence of weakness, ataxia of the right leg and gait ataxia suggest an acute cerebellar infarct.

Brain did not see Churchill until 22 June 1955, three weeks following the onset of the stroke. Brain had not assessed Churchill since 25 August 1953, almost two years previously, when Churchill was recovering from his acute left hemiparesis (partial paralysis of the left side of the body).[24] At their consultation on 22 June 1955, Churchill told Brain that his speech had also been affected at the onset and that his gait was still not very steady. Brain found that there was dysarthria, his gait was 'fairly good with an effort' and both plantar responses were extensor (a physical examination sign consistent with a recent or previous stroke). No other abnormal signs were recorded, but this examination took place three weeks following the onset of the stroke, by which time the neurological deficit would be expected to have improved. Indeed, there had been steady improvement during this period, as documented by Moran. Churchill was able to return to editing his book by 6 June 1955, and he was well enough to make a speech at the Guildhall on 21 June 1955.

Brain does not suggest a localization for this stroke and indeed, his clinical note for 22 June 1955 is fairly brief. However, the dizziness, dysarthria, limb and gait ataxia, in the absence of limb weakness or focal brain stem signs, suggests that this was a cerebellar stroke, most likely an acute infarct. There were no clinical features to indicate that this was a cerebellar haemorrhage. The persistent dysarthria and gait ataxia, when the right limb ataxia had resolved, suggests a predominantly centrally placed cerebellar lesion, but also affecting right cerebellar hemisphere function, though nystagmus was not recorded at any stage.

However, an alternative anatomical localization of Churchill's acute ataxia was a deep lacunar infarct in the pons or internal capsule, producing a so-called ataxic hemiparesis, a syndrome originally described by Miller Fisher in 1965 and more recently reviewed with clinical and radiological correlations.[25] Features of the lesions in these extra-cerebellar sites include dysarthria, gait ataxia (features that were present in Churchill), nystagmus, ipsilateral facial weakness and ipsilateral hemisensory loss involving the face, body and limbs (features that were not present in Churchill). Taking all this into consideration, but of course without the benefit of either CT or MR imaging at the time, we conclude it is more likely that Churchill's acute presentation was the result of an acute cerebellar infarct. The prodromal light-headedness would perhaps also be more in keeping with a cerebellar lesion.

Moran noted a rapid irregular pulse on 4 June 1955, possibly atrial fibrillation, but this appears to have been transient, and it occurred three days following the onset of the stroke. A cardiac embolic basis for the stroke seems less likely than thrombosis *in situ* as the pathology of the stroke.

This stroke occurred in the context of symptoms indicating gradual cognitive decline. On the day before the onset of the stroke, Churchill had noted that while he could edit his book, 'It's thinking and composing I find difficult.' And on 22 June 1955, he remarked that his memory was poor, particularly for names. However, his exceptional speech and language skills were objectively largely maintained, as evidenced by his successful electioneering between April and the end of May 1955, his Guildhall speech on 21 June 1955, only three weeks following the onset of this most recent stroke, and his letter to Eisenhower, following the cerebellar stroke, on 18 July 1955.

A change in Churchill's mood was noted by Brain,[15] as reported to him by Lord Woolton (Chancellor of the Duchy of Lancaster, 1952–5) towards the end of 1955. Woolton referred to Churchill while he was still Prime Minister, remarking to Brain: 'I can't think what you doctors have done to him. Before, he used to stick his chin out; now he is genial and humorous, even on serious matters.'[15] This could be seen as an indication of a change in personality, reflecting the advance of cerebrovascular disease. However, we should remember that Churchill was by then 80 years old and knew that his days as Prime Minister were numbered. A little mellowing of his mood at that time should perhaps not be over-interpreted.

Nevertheless, it is very likely that Churchill was indeed becoming gradually cognitively impaired, his symptoms being the most reliable indication of this. However, all the evidence suggests that any modest impairment of Churchill's intellect still left him with greater cognitive skills at the age of 80 than most could hope for in the prime of their lives. He was certainly not stuck for words.

Chapter 22

A Further Stroke in October 1956
in the South of France

I've just had one. It was the real thing, you know. The real thing. But I'm all right now.[1]

Sir Winston and Lady Churchill celebrated their forty-eighth wedding anniversary on 12 September 1956. Four days later Lord Moran (see p. 443), Churchill's personal physician, visited the Churchills and 'found Winston playing bezique with Clemmie, a happy picture.'[2] Churchill had planned to re-visit La Pausa, a villa in Roquebrune-Cap-Martin, in the Alpes-Maritimes, for a working holiday, for some time. Churchill had confirmed to his hostess on 4 September 1956 that:

On Monday, therefore, the 17th of September, I will re-visit Pausaland [Churchill's name for La Pausa]. I hope I may bring Montague Browne [Private Secretary] with me, and I shall indeed look forward to finding you and Emery safely ensconced in the villa. The only thing that might alter my plans will be WAR [this was at the time of the Suez crisis]. In that case I should have to attend Parliament, and whatever sittings may be necessary.[3]

On 17 September Churchill flew to the South of France to stay at La Pausa. Churchill had suffered his first stroke in 1949 (see p. 182),[4] further cerebrovascular episodes in 1950–2 (see p. 194),[5] a second stroke in 1953 (see p. 210)[6] from which he recovered[7] and an acute ataxic stroke in June 1955, again with excellent recovery (p. 246).[8]

La Pausa

The villa, some 6 miles east of Monte Carlo, stands high on the shoulder of the mountainside above Cap Martin and commands sensational views towards Menton on one side and Monte Carlo on the other.[9] It was designed and built by the French fashion designer Coco Chanel in the early 1930s and owned by Chanel until 1953 when she sold it to the Hungarian publisher Emery Reves, Churchill's long-time literary associate, who with his future wife Wendy, were to be Churchill's hosts once again.

Sergeant Murray, Churchill's bodyguard, has explained why Churchill found the villa so attractive, though he had some personal reservations:

> Its setting, in green and well-tended gardens full of Mediterranean flowers and lavender, shaded by olive trees, was quite superb. It was perched several hundred feet above sea-level, adjacent to the mediaeval village of Roquebrune, a noted tourist attraction, with to the east a fine view towards the Italian mountains ... it was a house furnished with an eye to taste of the high order, but, despite this and the Rodin statues and the highly valuable paintings, a sense of coldness, or soullessness was always present, to me, at least.[10]

17 September–19 October 1956: Working Holiday

Churchill wrote to Lord Cherwell on 19 September telling him 'the weather is beautiful – sunny yet cool' and inviting him to come to La Pausa.[11] Churchill also wrote to his wife on the same day, 'Dr Roberts has examined me and finds me in very good health. I have started resolutely on the Baruch [Bernard Baruch, friend and financier] hearing aid, and am getting very used to wearing it. I can even hear the bird talk when I am alone.'[11] Roberts (see p. 447) was to become Churchill's regular doctor in the South of France.

Churchill wrote again to his wife on 24 September after learning that she would not be joining him at La Pausa:

> Here all is peaceful and I am glad to say that the whole book team [this included Alan Hodge, Editor of *History Today*, and Maurice Shock, Politics Fellow, University College, Oxford] is hard at work. I am wearing Bernie's [Baruch] hearing aid every day when in company and I find it a great relief. It is complete and in perfect order and I think I should get used to the habit of using it. I quite agree that it is a necessity. I have not tried any painting yet, although there has been plenty of sunlight ... I had a letter from Anthony [Eden, Prime Minister] thanking me for the cigars, and incidentally showing a robust spirit. I am so glad they are going to the Security Council immediately ... I must say I am very

glad the burden does not rest on me ... I am very glad with the way the book [*History of the English-Speaking Peoples*] is getting on, and I think you will be both pleased and surprised at the way the work is going.[12]

Churchill wrote again to his wife on 2 October:

I have done a great deal of work at the book and not painted yet. Mr Shock, who brings this letter this afternoon, has done me a very good note on the first Gladstone and Disraeli chapter, and I look forward to receiving another fertile wodge in a fortnight ... There are only three more chapters in the last book to be composed after which there will be only bits and pieces of final revise. I am keeping the printers and my whole outfit very busy. The Prof [Lord Cherwell] arrived last night. It was nice of him to face the journey.[11]

In the second week of October Churchill wrote a further letter to his wife indicating that he planned to return home on 22 October. 'I'm so glad you and Mary are going to see the horse run on Saturday. I hope it will not rain and that Le Pretendant will fulfil our hopes.'[12] In fact, Le Pretendant defeated the Queen's horse.[11]

Churchill wrote again to his wife on 15 October:

The time has passed v[er]y quickly & I am now within a week of coming home – five weeks to a day it will be. It has been a v[er]y pleasant spell, quiet and peaceful. I wish you had come for a week or so ... I have begun painting one picture – a large long one of the view to the Eastward; and have progressed so well that after three days it is still an attraction to me ... I hope the Queen was not too vexed at being beaten. It was just as well I wasn't there as there w[oul]d have been embarrassing cheers and counter-cheers.[11]

20 October 1956: A Further Stroke

Murray recalled:

At about 8:30 am, Sir Winston got out of bed to go to the bathroom. A few minutes later, the male nurse who had been on hand since his illness a year or more earlier, went into the bathroom and found him sitting on the floor, blue in the face and unable to move. The nurse quickly got him back into bed, piled hot water bottles round him and administered the prescribed treatment [nikethamide] decided on by his doctor, Lord Moran, at the time of the earlier stroke. The nurse immediately telephoned Dr David Roberts the English doctor who attended Lord Beaverbrook when he was at La Capponcina, and who was also one of the doctors in attendance on Prince Rainier and his family in Monaco. Sir Winston very quickly returned to his usual self, and when I went in to see him I found him sitting up in bed, a grave look on his face, but reasonably well.[1]

Churchill said: 'I've just had one. It was the real thing, you know. The real thing. But I'm all right now.'[1] Murray told Churchill that no one could possibly imagine that half an hour earlier he had had 'one of those things' and that he hoped he would be up and about soon.[1] Murray told Churchill: 'I get very bored when I am out on my own.' Churchill smiled and said: 'I shall have to stay in bed for three or four days, I'm afraid.'[1]

On 20 October Moran was staying with the Lieutenant Governor of the Isle of Man, Sir Ambrose Dundas Flux Dundas. Dundas told Moran: 'France wants you on the telephone.' Moran could not hear what Churchill said and so spoke with Roberts. 'Roberts was guarded on the telephone, but I gathered Winston had some kind of black-out this morning. No, he did not think it was necessary for me to see him. He was already much better. All day I have had a feeling of disquiet. When Winston telephoned, did he want to see me?'[2]

Roberts wrote to Moran on 25 October:

As you will know from my telephone conversation with you, Sir Winston has had an attack of cerebral spasm. During the attack he lost the use of right leg, right arm, left side of face and Broca's area [the area of cerebral motor cortex responsible for the initiation and control of speech]. After an injection of 3 cc's [mL] of Coramine [nikethamide] the signs of spasticity passed off. I put him on a fat-diminished diet, vitamin pp [niacin; vitamin B3], papaverine and aminophylline. He has made very good progress, and has even been out in the garden. Today I have taken blood tests for cholesterol, urea and coagulation time, and

I shall forward the results of these tests to you with Sir Winston on his return.[13]

On 26 October Moran recorded: 'I hear from France that Winston has had an attack of cerebral spasm. During the attack he lost the use of his right leg, right arm, left side of face and Broca's area. It appears that he fell down and lost consciousness for about 20 minutes.'[2]

21–8 October 1956: Recovery

Murray records the challenges during Churchill's recovery:

Life with the Old Man himself was almost as difficult, because, frankly he was not cut out to be an ideal patient. Luckily his diet was only slightly restricted by his illness, but at lunchtime on the first day, when his doctor was just playing safe, his meal consisted of nothing but a piece of cheese, and he reacted strongly. 'Only cheese for lunch. Only cheese for lunch.'[1]

After that, however, Churchill insisted on eating much more normally and even went downstairs like everyone else, so the male nurse and Murray had the task of carrying him up and down the stairs several times each day. Fractious as his illness sometimes made him, Churchill was always appreciative of the help Murray gave, and never failed to thank him for it.[1]

The stroke delayed Churchill's return to England by more than a week, and the illness drew the inevitable reaction from the press all over the world. Murray wrote: 'Life became tiresome as we contended with hordes of international reporters and constantly ringing telephones. I did my best to cope with my side, but it was impossible to stop bits of idle gossip, much of it incorrect, appearing in the newspapers.'[1]

The Times reported inaccurately on 22 October that:

Sir Winston Churchill who is on holiday on the Riviera has a slight cold but is going on well, it was learnt at his London home yesterday. Lady Churchill is flying out to join him today. It is expected that she will travel from London Airport. Sir Winston Churchill has been on the Riviera for a month. He is staying at Roquebrune, Cap Martin.

According to messages from Reuter and Associated Press on Saturday [20 October], he cancelled a booking to fly back to England today.[14]

Lady Churchill arrived at Nice Airport on 22 October on her way to join Sir Winston Churchill at Roquebrune-Cap-Martin. 'She said her visit was connected with her husband's health and she did not know yet how long she would stay. Sir Winston Churchill has suffered from a chill since Friday, but today he was reported to be "very well."'[15]

Montague Browne later recalled these events:

On 20 October he had suffered a stroke, or more accurately, perhaps, a 'spasm', in the South of France, where he was staying with Wendy and Emery Reves. He recovered sufficiently rapidly to travel home a few days later, and just four days after the incident he was walking in the garden. He seemed to have these 'spasms', minor strokes in effect, as other people catch colds, and to suffer extraordinary little harm from them, though one must suppose that the cumulative effect, after the stroke of 1949 and the much more severe one in 1953, must have been considerable. Certainly on this occasion WSC's intellectual powers seemed none the worse and his interest in the development of the Suez crisis remained lively.[16]

28 October 1956: Return to London

The Churchills returned to London on 28 October in an Elizabethan airliner on a scheduled British European Airways flight. 'Sir Winston Churchill … looked well when he arrived at London Airport. He was driven to his London home.'[17]

1 November 1956: Assessment by Sir Russell Brain Bt

Brain recorded that Churchill was seen with Moran on 1 November, though Moran did not record this assessment.[2]

Twelve days ago while in the South of France, he got up to go to the lavatory, found his right leg was weak and fell down, and does not remember anything more for twenty minutes. He thinks he was alright after this, but Dr Roberts, who saw him, reports that he had loss of speech, and weakness of the right arm and leg. He also mentions weakness of the left face, but that is probably a relic of the previous attacks. He complains of no symptoms now. I thought he was slightly dysarthric, but there was no weakness of the face or tongue or limbs. Both plantars [reflexes] were extensor [a physical examination sign consistent with a recent or previous stroke]. It was difficult to feel any carotid pulse on either side of the neck.[18]

2–4 November 1956: Return to Political Activity

Montague Browne wrote:

I was the more surprised when, on 2 November, WSC said that he felt too tired to draft a public message of support for the Government's action over Suez. The Private Office at Number 10 had asked me to convey this request from the Prime Minister. Did WSC not wish to support the operation? Yes, he said, he definitely did want to support it. Would I please draft in that sense?[16]

The letter addressed to the Chairman of Churchill's Constituency Party, Alderman Donald Forbes, was published on 3 November. The Prime Minister wrote: 'My dear Winston, I cannot thank you enough for your wonderful message. It has had an enormous effect, and I am sure that in the US it will have an even greater influence … These are tough days – but the alternative was a slow bleeding to death.'[16]

Lady Churchill wrote to Roberts on 3 November: 'Since our return, Winston seems really on the whole well. He is being very good about the diet. I want you to know the gratitude I feel for all you have done for him, not only for your professional skill, but for your infinite kindness and patience.'[19]

4 November 1956: Assessment by Lord Moran

In an entry dated 4 November, Moran records that Churchill was still breakfasting at Chartwell when he entered his room, though it was after 10 am.[2] Churchill began a sentence then lost the thread. Churchill said: 'I find it difficult to write letters. I mean to compose them. I find it difficult to do anything.' Moran recorded, 'I noticed that he was drowsy and apathetic. He gazed at me blankly, so that I was not sure whether he had heard what I had said, but when I told him it looked as if Dulles had cancer he woke up.' 'What makes you say that?' Churchill asked.[2]

Moran discussed Churchill with his daughter and son-in-law, Mary and Christopher Soames.[2] Mary Soames said: 'I know there is nothing to be done.' She had noticed a marked deterioration in her father when he came back from France. 'What I find sad, Charles, is that he doesn't seem interested in anything any longer. He doesn't want to do things ... Of course, he varies a good deal. Last night, though we all bellowed, it seemed as if he heard nothing. And then – not very often now – he will perk up and for a short time take an interest in the conversation.'[2]

Murray recorded: 'Pretty soon he [Churchill] was back in action, making his way regularly to his special seat in the House of Commons, immediately below the Treasury Bench, after Question Time each day. But despite this activity, his latest stroke had thrown a shadow of doubt across his path, as I realised soon afterwards from an incident at Chartwell.'[1]

Churchill asked Murray to collect the painting he had been working on immediately before his illness. When Murray returned with the painting Churchill said to him: 'It will probably be the last one I shall ever do.' Murray commented: 'Happily that gloomy prophecy proved incorrect, and he managed to paint at least half a dozen others before advancing age sapped his ability and interest.'[1]

Shortly after this Churchill was having an extension to his studio built. Murray found Churchill placing a foot on the first rung of the ladder the builders were using. Murray told Churchill: 'You can't go up there, Sir Winston.'[1] Churchill remonstrated with Murray. 'You know this is not the first time I have gone up a ladder.' Without further ado Churchill began to ascend slowly but with great determination. At the top he walked around a narrow plank and complimented the workmen on the way they were tackling the job. For the next two days Churchill repeated his climb to inspect the progress of his new building.[1]

Medical Aspects

Churchill suffered either a further left cerebral hemisphere stroke on 20 October 1956 consisting of a right hemiparesis and dysphasia, or a focal epileptic fit. By the time Roberts saw Churchill on the day of the onset of this stroke, his dysphasia had largely or completely resolved. When he saw Churchill on 1 November 1956, Brain recorded that the mild weakness of the left side of the face noted by Roberts was probably a residual sign of the previous acute left hemiparesis (left-sided stroke), though this sign was not found by Brain in his own examination. Indeed, Brain found no weakness, but did record bilateral extensor plantar responses (a physical examination sign consistent with a recent or previous stroke). Improvement from this cerebral event was rapid, and although it was recorded by Murray that, for a time between 21 and 28 October, Churchill needed to be carried down the stairs, he was walking independently in the garden four days after the acute onset.

There was a period of 20 minutes following the acute ictus during which Churchill apparently could not remember events, and this was interpreted by Moran as a period of 'unconsciousness'. However, amnesia for events following an acute event of this sort, in the absence of any objective examination findings, does not necessarily equate to loss of consciousness. Piecing together the sequence of events now from the evidence available, it seems most likely that Churchill suffered an acute small left cerebral hemisphere cortical ischaemic attack, with rapid though incomplete resolution within 24 hours, thus probably amounting to a small completed stroke. Infarction due to thrombosis *in situ*, in keeping with small vessel disease, was the likely pathology. As in some of Churchill's previous cerebrovascular episodes, cerebral arterial 'spasm' was invoked by his doctors, but this mechanism would not be today's preferred likely mechanism.

An alternative explanation of the event is that Churchill suffered a focal epileptic fit, with a subsequent Todd's paresis (transient paralysis of a part of the body which has been involved previously in a focal epileptic seizure). However, the extensor plantar response found by Brain twelve days following the episode probably indicates a new deficit resulting from this episode, and this would be in favour of a small completed stroke rather than a focal fit. Against this is the 20-minute period of amnesia, and the rapid recovery. It is interesting that Brain did not commit himself to a diagnosis of this episode.

At any rate, Churchill's recovery was rapid, leaving little residual deficit. Nevertheless, it is clear from Moran's observations when he saw Churchill on 4 November 1956, two weeks after the stroke, that Churchill's cognitive state was notably variable, and this was substantiated by Mary Soames' account of her concerns about her father. In keeping with his remarkable resilience to such events, Churchill resumed some activity in the House of Commons following this probable stroke. His determination to recover in the aftermath of the stroke was also alarmingly demonstrated to his bodyguard, Murray, by his insistence on climbing a ladder to assess the progress of building works at home, much to Murray's concern. And finally, Churchill's artistic creativity was clearly also not at an end at this time, despite his own prediction shortly following the small stroke.

Roberts prescribed nikethamide, papaverine, aminophylline, niacin and a fat-diminished diet. With the exception of a low-fat diet, none of these treatments is employed routinely today following a stroke, though intraarterial papaverine is used occasionally. Niacin is an essential vitamin but there is no evidence that Churchill's diet was deficient. Nikethamide was a widely used respiratory stimulant and analeptic in 1956, but has no current role in the treatment of acute stroke. Papaverine produces relaxation of involuntary muscle throughout the body and causes a decrease in cerebral vascular resistance and an increase in cerebral blood flow.[20] In a small study intra-arterial infusion of papaverine for the treatment of cerebral vasospasm was found to be effective after mechanical thrombectomy in acute ischaemic stroke.[21]

Aminophylline was used in the treatment of stroke because it was believed that this drug was a cerebral vasodilator. However, it was later demonstrated that cerebral blood flow decreased after aminophylline due to a local action on the cerebral vessels.[22] A Cochrane review[23] identified only two small trials[24, 25] using aminophylline, neither of which found any benefit in acute stroke.

In a double-blind trial conducted by Geismar et al.[25] intravenous aminophylline was compared with placebo in seventy-nine patients with acute cerebral infarction. Immediate improvement in the neurological evaluation score was significantly more frequent in patients receiving aminophylline (38 per cent) than in those on placebo (15 per cent); only patients with mild or moderately severe strokes responded to the injection. After three weeks, however, the treated patients did not fare significantly better than the controls in terms of neurological score and residual disability. Survival rate, length of stay in hospital, and social readaptation were similar in the two groups. The authors concluded that intravenous aminophylline in patients with ischaemic strokes can bring about an immediate symptomatic relief, but without appreciably influencing the ultimate recovery.

Forty-six patients with a mean age of 75 years were randomised into two groups: twenty-two received aminophylline (a bolus dose of 230mg followed by 0.5mg/kg/h in dextrose 5.5 per cent) and twenty-four received placebo (dextrose 5.5 per cent) over 72 hours.[24] The groups were comparable in all aspects at the outset of the trial. Serum theophylline concentrations were kept within the therapeutic range recommended for patients with asthma. No significant difference in outcome was noticed between the groups during the hospital period when repeated neurological assessments by two different scores and mortality were compared.

In defiance of advancing cerebrovascular disease, at the age of 81 years, Churchill bounced back yet again!

Chapter 23

Pneumonia, Jaundice, Rigor and Atrial Fibrillation February–April 1958 on the Riviera and at Chartwell

In the past three weeks you have had two attacks of basal pneumonia, the first with pleurisy, the second without.[1]

Sir Winston Churchill, aged 83 years, planned to have a recuperative holiday in January and February 1958 in the South of France at La Pausa, a villa in Roquebrune-Cap-Martin owned by the Hungarian publisher Emery Reves, Churchill's long-time literary associate.

The villa commands sensational views towards Menton on one side and Monte Carlo on the other.[2] Sergeant Edmund Murray, Churchill's bodyguard, wrote: 'Its setting, in green and well-tended gardens full of Mediterranean flowers and lavender, shaded by olive trees, was quite superb.'[3]

13 January–16 February 1958: Holiday

On 13 January 1958, Sir Winston Churchill flew to Monte Carlo together with Anthony Montague Browne, his Private Secretary, and Murray. On 18 January Churchill wrote to his wife Clementine explaining that a fur muff she had given him was a great success in keeping his hands warm: 'I use it at all meals, and on the whole it achieves its purpose. It is v(er)y cold.'[4] When Churchill wrote again to his wife on 23 January he told her that he had started painting again '*indoors* for the snow is on the hills all around. Flowers arranged by Wendy is the subject'.[5]

At the end of January, President Eisenhower invited Churchill to visit the United States and to stay at the White House. Churchill hoped that he could accept and he pressed his wife to join him.[5] On 13 February Dr Adenauer, Chancellor of the Federal Republic of Germany, paid a visit to Churchill at

La Pausa.[6] Montague Browne described an altercation in the local press over whether Churchill should call on Adenauer or the other way round. In fact, Churchill had said that as he was a private citizen, he should go to see the Chancellor, and the latter with his usual perfect courtesy, insisting on calling on the older man.[7]

17 February 1958: An Extended Lunch on a Yacht

On 17 February Churchill was invited to lunch on the yacht belonging to Aristotle Onassis, a Greek shipping magnate who lived in Monaco. After lunch, at about 3 pm, Churchill expressed a wish to go to the Rooms at Monte Carlo to gamble.[8] Reves suggested that they might play chemin de fer on the yacht instead.[8] They played for high stakes and drank more alcohol than usual. As the afternoon wore on it was noted that Churchill was very white and tired.[8] At about 7 pm Reves reminded Churchill that they had been invited for lunch. Was it not time to go home? Winston grumbled that Reves was breaking up the party.[8] Nonetheless, the party broke up, and Churchill returned in an unheated Rolls-Royce driven by his host to La Pausa.[9] Churchill seemed 'all in'[8] and had a sleepless night.[9]

18 February 1958: Assessment by Dr Roberts: Fever and Cough

Churchill was not well enough to be driven to Nice Airport to meet his wife, arriving from London for a planned visit.[9] Lady Churchill was met at the airport by Montague Browne and Churchill's daughter, Sarah, who had arrived ten days earlier.[2] During the day Churchill developed a fever and cough and was assessed by Dr David Roberts (see p. 447), his local doctor on the Riviera, who prescribed penicillin. In fact, Churchill was not even fit enough to leave his bed and 'outdoors staff' were told that he had a stomach chill.[9] Roberts spent most of the day at La Pausa, and a telegram was sent to Lord Moran (see p. 443), his personal physician, asking him to come and assess Churchill.[9] At the same time, Montague Browne issued a bulletin announcing that Churchill was indisposed and must stay in bed.[9] 'The press are asked not to telephone to the villa. Another bulletin will be issued tomorrow.'[10]

Murray has written that:

Such a bulletin was bound to arouse doubts and fears, so it was not surprising that the next day, like vultures scenting prey, the Press began to congregate once more from most parts of Europe. Before long they had made their HQ in the Hôtel de Paris in Monte Carlo. Mr Montague Browne was issuing daily reports at impromptu press conferences in the Hotel.[9]

19 February 1958: Bronchopneumonia

Moran flew out on 19 February and stayed for two weeks. On arrival, he examined Churchill and made a diagnosis of bronchopneumonia. A medical bulletin issued on 19 February by Moran and Roberts stated: 'Sir Winston Churchill is suffering from pneumonia at the base of the lung and pleurisy. He had a good night and has passed a comfortable day.'[11] Roberts added that 'We are very pleased with Sir Winston's condition. He is responding to treatment marvellously, but it will take some time.'[11] Montague Browne stated that: 'Sir Winston was in good spirits and spent the day seeing members of his family and dealing with his correspondence.'[11]

20–7 February 1958: Rigors

On 20 February Moran entered Churchill's room about noon and found him shivering violently, his teeth chattering.[8] Moran concluded that a rigor on the third day meant the infection was spreading.[8] Moran decided to change the antibiotic to oxytetracycline and get a blood count.[8] The arrival of a French bacteriologist led to a protest by Churchill about the potential pain the blood test would cause.[8] Moran and Roberts issued a further medical bulletin which stated: 'Sir Winston's condition is not greatly changed since yesterday. He is comfortable, his strength is maintained, and his fever is a little lower.'[12] Roberts said later that Churchill was 'bearing up well'.[12]

The medical bulletin issued on 21 February stated that Churchill's pneumonia was clearing up and his condition was showing 'very definite improvement'.[13] The bulletin said that Churchill had had a good night and was more comfortable and that his 'progress is so far satisfactory'.[13] Churchill kept a thermometer by his bed and took his temperature at all times of the day and night, showing alarm at any irregularity.[9]

In keeping with his usual practice, Churchill had demanded to see the medical bulletins.[8] 'I would be more candid and less revealing,' he complained.[8] Churchill told Montague Browne he was keen to stir up his doctors: 'If I don't push them along, nothing at all would happen.'[8] He was bent on returning to England in time for The Other Club dinner on 27 February,[8] a club founded by Churchill and FE Smith KC (later Lord Birkenhead) in 1911.

Montague Browne told reporters that Churchill was in bed but had dealt with considerable correspondence and was in excellent spirits.[13] He said that the Queen had made enquiries about Sir Winston's health and that there had been many enquiries from all over the world.[13] Churchill had sent a telegram to Her Majesty: 'My wife and I are deeply grateful to Your Majesty for your most kind enquiries.'[14]

President Eisenhower also sent a telegram on 21 February: 'Mrs Eisenhower and I have been delighted to hear the reports each day of your steady recovery from your bout with pneumonia. We now know you will continue to get well and we are looking forward to your visit with us in April. With affectionate regards to Clemmie and as always the best to yourself, as ever. IKE[15]

Churchill replied on 22 February: 'I am most grateful for your warm-hearted message. I think I am making good progress. Clemmie joins me in affectionate good wishes to you both. WINSTON.'[16]

Lady Churchill said that her husband was 'very well'.[13] Lord Evans, the Queen's Physician, had arrived in Nice on holiday on 21 February and said he would make a courtesy call on Churchill in the next few days.[13]

Moran recorded on 22 February that: 'I am not really anxious about Winston, but at 83 it is all guesswork. Perhaps if he felt ill he would be more amenable. This morning he announced that he intended to go downstairs to luncheon, although he has not yet been out of bed. Dr. Roberts, in order to dissuade him, said something about his heart.'[8] Churchill raising his voice said: 'It has been a comfort to me that my heart is sound and that I shall not lurch into the next world without warning. And now you talk about my heart as if it were diseased … I know a great deal. I'm not dependent on my doctors. I know what I can do.'[8] Murray recorded that the doctor's orders that Churchill must stay in bed 'left him restless and fractious, despite the humouring bestowed upon him by his staff and friends'.[9]

By 23 February Churchill's temperature was normal.[17] The medical bulletin signed by Moran and Roberts stated that: 'Certain laboratory investigations of a routine nature which were carried out this morning are all normal. Sir Winston's progress continues to be satisfactory.'[17] A further bulletin was issued on 24 February which stated that the 'pneumonia continues to resolve and the pleurisy is causing him less discomfort'.[18] Churchill's general condition was stated to be satisfactory. During the day Churchill received M. Pierre-Jean Moatti, Prefect of the Alpes-Maritimes Department, and Mme. Moatti. Mr Moatti, an old friend, brought the greetings and good wishes of President Coty, the French government and the Alpes-Maritimes Department.[18] These were Churchill's first visitors apart from members of his family since he fell ill.[18]

Vice-President Richard Nixon wrote a letter to Churchill on 24 February:

My dear Sir Winston,
Along with your countless admirers throughout the world, I was pleased to learn that you are recovering so nicely from your recent illness. This is the kind of encouraging good news all of your friends want to hear! In a recent letter from Mr Joyce Hall he told me about the enthusiastic reception your exhibit received at the Nelson Gallery in Kansas City [Churchill had selected thirty-five of his paintings for the exhibition]. The fact that all previous one-day attendance records were broken on the opening day is, I am sure, indicative of the way your work will be received everywhere in the United States. It was a great disappointment to me not to be among those present on the first day of the showing. Both Mrs Nixon and I hope to have an opportunity to see your canvases before they leave our country, and we look forward with pleasure to welcoming you to Washington again soon. Our kindest regards to you and Lady Churchill.[19]

Churchill replied to Vice-President Nixon on 4 March: 'I am touched that with your many burdens you should have taken the time to write such an agreeable letter. Thank you so much. I too am looking forward to our meeting. With warm regards to Mrs Nixon and yourself.'[20]

The medical bulletin of 25 February stated that Churchill: 'Continues to gain in strength and his progress is satisfactory.'[21] Montague Browne said that so far as he knew tomorrow's bulletin would be the last one.[21] Roberts said: 'The bout of pneumonia is well on its way out and we are now concentrating on the last touch of pleurisy.'[21] Evans told reporters that he 'thought the whole illness could resolve itself in a couple more days. Pneumonia normally should clear itself in a week to 10 days, but this was a remarkable recovery in so short a time.'[21]

A portable X-ray machine was procured[9] and permitted Churchill's doctors to state in the final medical bulletin issued on 26 February: 'An X-ray of Sir Winston Churchill's lung taken yesterday is very satisfactory. There are no abnormal shadows and there is no fluid in the pleural cavity. It is not our intention to issue further bulletins.'[22] Montague Browne told reporters: 'So far nothing is changed in Sir Winston's plans to visit President Eisenhower in Washington in April.'[22]

On 27 February the Prime Minister, Harold Macmillan, and Hugh Gaitskell, Leader of the Opposition, in the name of the House of Commons, sent Churchill a telegram: 'At the end of Questions today the whole House asked that a message of congratulations should be sent to you on your recovery, conveying the warm good wishes of us all.'[23]

The reply from Churchill dated 28 February was read to the Commons by RA Butler, and stated: 'I am deeply honoured that the House of Commons should send me a message as you have done. I hope soon to be once more in my seat. Meanwhile please accept my grateful thanks.'[24] While the message was read, Churchill's customary seat on the front row below the gangway was carefully left untenanted.[25]

Brendan Bracken (Viscount Bracken; former MP and great friend of Churchill who died from oesophageal cancer in August 1958) wrote on 27 February:

I am pleased and relieved beyond all telling by the news of your rapid recovery. If you were to write a book on Health without rules it would outsell all your other books and would soar above the fantastic sales of Mary Baker Eddy's *Science and Health with Key to the Scriptures*. It is claimed by Christian Scientists that this book has already sold 50 million copies but as Madam Baker Eddy only attained the trifling age of 62, your book would be a much more authoritative guide to the best means of attaining long life! As the Inland Revenue would take away any profits you derive from such a masterpiece, this must remain one of the great unwritten books of our age.[26]

On the day that Churchill was able to leave his bedroom for the first time, he was helped downstairs by his detective. Churchill said: 'You have not seen very much of me for a month now,' then with his old chuckle … 'but you have stopped everyone else from seeing me in a very poor state as well.'[9]

Before Moran left La Pausa, he had developed a temperature. On the balcony, after dinner, Moran was not looking very happy. Churchill advised him: 'Now you get off to bed and take your temperature. Use my thermometer if you like. And let me know if there is anything else I can get you!'[9]

7–23 March 1958: Lord Moran Departs and Dr Roberts Provides Continuing Care

Moran recorded on 7 March that Churchill felt that his troubles were at an end. He hoped to go home for a week, 'partly because he is getting bored – there is nobody exciting out here – and partly because he wants to go to The Other Club.'[8] Moran flew back to England on the afternoon of 7 March.

Pol Roger dispatched a case of twelve bottles of Pol-Roger EXTRA DRY 1934 to Churchill on 13 March.[27] Churchill wrote to Odette Pol Roger on 15 March: 'How charming of you to send me the case of delicious champagne. It is making my recovery most cheerful and pleasant. I am much better now, and shall be returning to England soon.'[28]

Field Marshal Lord Montgomery, Deputy Supreme Commander, Europe, arrived at Nice Airport on 15 March on his way to spend the weekend with the Churchills.[29] During the day Sir Winston and Lady Churchill left the grounds of the villa for the first time since his illness began and took luncheon at their favourite restaurant in Nice.[29] Montgomery departed on 18 March, and Lady Churchill described Montgomery's visit 'as a great tonic'.[2]

On 16 March Churchill developed the signs of a left-sided basal pneumonia and Roberts instituted treatment again and by 19 March Churchill's temperature was normal. Roberts communicated this to Moran in a letter dated 20 March.

On 17 March, the final volume of Churchill's *History of the English Speaking Peoples*, was published entitled *The Great Democracies*.[30] Churchill inscribed a copy to 'David Myrddin Roberts from Winston S. Churchill, March 1958.'

Roberts informed the press on 19 March that Churchill had to stay indoors today, but reported that Sir Winston was doing very well.[31] 'People should stop worrying about his health. If he is confined indoors it is because of a bit of strain and bad weather on the French Riviera.'[31]

In fact, Roberts was so concerned about his patient that he wrote to Churchill on 19 March:

Dear Sir Winston,

In the past three weeks you have had two attacks of basal pneumonia, the first with pleurisy, the second without. The second attack was a relapse owing to tiredness of effort. The fertile soil of this type of pneumonia is a wetness of the lower parts of your lungs in which a low grade infection has been able to thrive.

From this you will see that in order to avoid another relapse we must wait until your lungs are dry before we can allow you to do too much. The lower part of your left lung is dry this morning, but you must still take care not to do too much. I know that this convalescence is tedious for you, but a lasting result can only be obtained by waiting a little longer before returning to your normal mode of life. D M Roberts[32]

Although no medical bulletin was issued on 20 March, a member of the household informed the press that Churchill was 'very well'.[33] On 22 March, Roberts gave a press conference and announced that Churchill had a 'slight recurrence of his old illness' but refused to elaborate further.[34] Roberts spent an hour with Churchill both on the morning and afternoon of 23 March.[34] At a press conference the same day Roberts stated that the 'recurrence of the illness had been successfully checked. In spite of a general weakness, Sir Winston Churchill looked very much himself – rosy and cheerful.'[34] A member of the household reported that it was pneumonia that had recurred during the weekend.[34] While Churchill's condition had given rise to anxiety on Saturday, 22 March Churchill 'was now making steady progress and his condition was satisfactory'.[34]

24–31 March 1958: Obstructive Jaundice

Moran was staying with the Freybergs in the Norman Tower at Windsor Castle. Lieutenant General The Right Honourable The Lord Freyberg VC was Deputy Constable and Lieutenant Governor of Windsor Castle. Moran was telephoned by Montague Browne on the evening of 23 March and informed that Roberts wanted to speak to him.[8] Roberts reported that since Moran's return to England, Churchill had suffered two bouts of fever.[8] Moran said that he thought he ought to see Churchill again and after explaining this to Lady Churchill, he flew to Nice again on the morning of 24 March.[8] Mary Soames travelled with Moran from London and joined her mother at La Pausa.[35] Her sister, Diana Sandys, had arrived the previous night while on a tour of the continent and was staying at a hotel in Monte Carlo.[35] On arrival at Nice Airport, Moran told reporters: 'There is nothing alarming that I know of.'[35]

After examining Churchill Moran wrote: 'Winston hardly looked at me as I entered his room. He said not a word. I took no notice of this wintry reception and began questioning him. He admitted grudgingly that he had been very worried on Saturday, and had wanted to see me; but now it was too late, his illness was all over.'[8] It had been noticed that Churchill was yellow, but this was thought to be due to the antibiotic Moran had prescribed. 'In fact, he is suffering from obstructive jaundice, caused either by a stone or by an infection of the bile passages. I shall be glad when we get him back to England.'[8] Moran reviewed blood tests arranged by Roberts before his arrival.

Moran and Roberts nonetheless told reporters that 'all is well'.[35] Moran said that 'Sir Winston Churchill may now have to stay on the Riviera for a little longer.'[35] Montague Browne told reporters that Churchill was still weak after the weekend recurrence of pneumonia, but he was eating well and making good progress.[35] It was not intended at present to issue any further bulletins.[35]

A member of the household told reporters that on 31 March Churchill had strolled in the garden of the villa and will do so each day until he returns home.[36] Moran returned to London later in the day.[36] At Nice Airport he told reporters that: 'Sir Winston who is 83 had made a remarkable recovery and was now perfectly fit.'[36] Churchill was 'going fine'.[36]

Lady Churchill's 73rd birthday was on 1 April, and a small party had been arranged at La Pausa. A birthday cake in the form of a large Easter egg had been flown out from London.[36]

Roberts examined Churchill on 2 April and judged him fit to fly back to London. Lady Churchill sent a handwritten note dated 2 April to Mrs Riley, Roberts' mother-in-law, which read: 'We are so grateful to Doctor Roberts, not only for his great professional skill, but for his kindness & understanding.

He has been wonderful in getting my husband through this troublesome and dangerous illness.'[37] The Churchills entertained President Coty at dinner at La Pausa later that day.[38]

3 April 1958: Return to Chartwell

The Churchills returned from the South of France on 3 April (Plate 17).[25] *The Times* reported that this was in a Viscount airliner of British European Airways,[39] though Murray has claimed that the plane belonged to Olympic Airways, which was owned by Onassis.[9] At Nice Airport, Churchill met Lord Beaverbrook.[5] 'I saw Winston for fifteen minutes or more. He was certainly clear in mind and I do hope that by this time he is strong in body.'[5] Lady Churchill sent a telegram to Roberts: 'Winston stood the journey very well and is in good spirits. Thank you so much for all you have done.'[40] Churchill began his convalescence at Chartwell on Maundy Thursday.

Roberts submitted his professional fees for twenty-seven days attendance of Fr 55,000 (approximate equivalent in 2019, £7,400).[41]

4–11 April 1958: Jaundice and Fever

Moran saw Churchill twice in the first week following his return from France:

> On each occasion he poked fun at me as a prophet. I had urged him to get back to England in case he was stricken by a third attack of jaundice. 'Pray, at what moment may I expect this mysterious malady to appear?' He said this with an assumption of gravity, and I am bound to admit that he has not seemed so alert and free from symptoms for a long time. But when I went to his room this morning he looked glumly at me. He had a pain over his lower ribs on the right side.[8]

Churchill admitted: 'Yes, it might be the same pain that I had in France.'[8]

On 10 April Churchill informed President Eisenhower that he considered it inadvisable to undertake the journey at present.[42]

Churchill had planned to watch an important gallop that had been arranged for one of his horses on 10 April. Moran told him that the wind was bitter and that judging by the course of events in his first two attacks: 'I thought he might well be running a temperature by teatime. I said this not as if I were opposed to his going, but just to bring before him a few relevant facts. Then I left him. About five o'clock [Nurse] Wright telephoned that Sir Winston's temperature was 100°F [37.8°C]. He had stayed in bed all day.' Moran again prescribed oxytetracycline. By the next morning (11 April) Churchill did not seem to take in what Moran said, and he was 'feverish all day'.[8]

12–22 April 1958: Jaundice and Atrial Fibrillation

Nurse Shepherd telephoned Moran before breakfast on 12 April to inform him that Churchill was jaundiced and his pulse had gone up from 64 to 110 per minute. Moran wrote:

As I pulled aside the curtain that separates his room from the study, [Nurses] Wright and Shepherd were removing the bedclothes to get him into his vest and bed-coat. Winston sleeps naked, and I noticed that his chest and belly were bright yellow. Nurse Wright said Sir Winston had been talking rubbish; he was sure he was wandering. When I sounded him his heart was fibrillating [atrial fibrillation; an irregular heart rhythm]. It looks as if we may be in for trouble.[8]

Moran invited Dr Thomas Hunt (see p. 439), Senior Physician at St Mary's Hospital and Churchill's previous personal physician, to review Churchill. Hunt assessed Churchill on the 12 April at 11 am at Chartwell.[43] He found Churchill to be jaundiced, confused, with a fibrillating pulse of 102/minute, a blood pressure of 110/70 mmHg and a temperature of 103°F (39.4°C). Churchill complained of a right-sided lower chest pain. He noted the history of pale stools and dark urine. The lack of bilirubin in the intestinal tract is responsible for the pale stools typically associated with biliary obstruction.

In addition to 45 fluid ounces (1,278 mL) of water and glucose orally, digoxin 0.25 mg twice daily was instituted to control the atrial fibrillation, together with neomycin 250 mg four times daily for two days to sterilise the gut, and Synkavit (acetomenaphthone; vitamin K) to counteract the vitamin K deficiency found in obstructive jaundice. Sodium and potassium concentrations were also measured and were normal.[43]

That night Moran dined with Lady Churchill but 'found it difficult to keep my mind on the conversation. When Clemmie left the table I crept into

Winston's room in case he was asleep. He has held his own all day, and is perhaps a little more alert tonight.'[8]

Nurse Wright reported to Moran at noon on 13 April that Churchill 'was jibbing at the treatment'. Churchill had refused to take the prescribed glucose and had not drunk anything but a cup of coffee since dinner time yesterday. Churchill was assessed by Hunt on 13 April who observed that Churchill's temperature was normal and his pulse 72/minute. Churchill was 'talking well', and his urine was lighter.[43] Hunt noted that Churchill had drunk 60 ounces (1,704 mL) of oral fluids and put out 43 oz (1,222 mL) over the previous 24 hours. Hunt recommended an intake of 50 oz (1,421 mL) per day henceforth.[43] Churchill was not keen on the oral fluids and told Hunt: 'I'm not going on drinking a bucketful of water like this for the rest of my life.' Hunt told Churchill he could get up in two days' time and have a glass of champagne, if he felt well.[43]

When Moran saw Churchill on the same day he burst out: 'I've got my temperature down below normal. What more do you want?'[8] Moran explained: 'You are still yellow.' Churchill requested a mirror and gazed at himself for some time. Moran recorded: 'He is still a little muddled, but there is a noticeable all-round improvement since yesterday. Only the jaundice persists.'[8]

Hunt reassessed Churchill on 15 April.[43] Churchill no longer had a fibrillating pulse (76/minute regular), but extrasystoles (extra beats) were present. Rales [crepitations; extra lung sounds] were heard at the bases of the lungs on examination. Hunt recommended that digoxin could be discontinued and that Churchill could have a bath and get up for a meal on 16 April.[43]

Churchill announced that evening (15 April) that he was planning to go to London and the House of Commons next Tuesday (22 April).[8] Moran explained to him that he 'might manage London on that day, but I didn't know about the House'.[8] Churchill responded 'with heat': 'I am going to the House. I am not going to be prevented.' Moran held his peace. Then Churchill looked up and said, 'I am sorry. My temper is not as good as it ought to be.'[8]

On the morning of 16 April, Churchill was still complaining of pain: 'I have still got the pain. It's no better.'[8] Moran recorded that: 'I am pretty sure that there must be a small stone holding up the bile. Anyway, at his age no one is keen on surgery. Besides, he is not so yellow, and is following the

Budget debate as if it really interested him.'[8] Churchill came down to dinner for the first time since his illness. Moran recalled to Churchill how after his stroke in 1953 he had recited the first fifty lines of *King Robert of Sicily* with only two mistakes. He tried to repeat the feat but only succeeded in recalling a line or two. 'My memory is much worse; in the last nine months it seems to have deteriorated.'[8]

Hunt made a further assessment on 19 April.[43] He recorded that Churchill had been out in the garden and had walked 100yd. He had no pain or fever. His lungs were clear, his pulse was 72/minute, and his blood pressure was 125/80mmHg. His urine was positive for bilirubin.[43]

23 April 1958: Return to the House of Commons

On 23 April Churchill returned to the House of Commons, his first appearance in the Chamber since 20 December 1957.[44] 'A sudden tumult of cheering burst on the chamber in the middle of question hour today,' *The Times* reported.[44]

It was the Commons' spontaneous, affectionate welcome to Sir Winston Churchill. The acclaim bore him in swelling volume to his seat below the gangway and echoed afresh through the House when Mr Selwyn Lloyd, the Foreign Secretary, who had been about to reply to a question, expressed the delight of everybody at seeing their right honourable friend with them again. Sir Winston Churchill, a little paler and slimmer than when we last saw him, but as alert and twinkling as ever, beamed happily around him and bowed his acknowledgement of Mr Bevan's [Shadow Foreign Secretary] gesture of greeting. The house later staged a noisy scene almost as if for his special delectation, with Mr Bevan a leading figure.[44]

Churchill stayed up until 11pm playing cards, Hunt recorded.[43]

24–30 April 1958: Assessments by Lord Moran and Dr Hunt

Hunt and Moran assessed Churchill again on 24 April at noon.[43] Hunt recorded that Churchill was well and was not jaundiced. He recommended to Churchill that X-rays should be postponed (see below), he should eat small meals, drink only moderate amounts of alcohol, avoid chills and fatigue.[43]

Churchill went out to dinner in London on 24 April (The Other Club) and on 29 April (Royal Academy).

On 28 April Hunt wrote to Moran summarising the medical course since 12 April:

> As we discussed I feel sure that the three attacks of pain followed by fever and jaundice must with little doubt have been due to the passage of one or more small stones down the common bile duct. The very good response to increased fluid intake and antibiotics, means I think, that there is no biliary obstruction remaining now, and I hope that the stone or biliary sludge must have passed and not become impacted at the ampulla of Vater. I do not think we can tell for certain whether there are any stones still present in the gallbladder, or whether the recent attacks were possibly only due to bile inspissated in the hepatic ducts themselves. I think the former is the most likely, but I doubt if a straight X-ray would give us more than 25 per cent chance of deciding, as any calculi will probably be non radio-opaque. I admit I am nervous of advising intravenous biligrafin or even an oral cholecystogram with dye in case of possible reactions, and even if we found definite stones in the gall bladder I doubt if we should wish to consider surgery in the present case. As agreed I feel, therefore, that the best hope of preventing further attacks is to keep up a good fluid intake and avoid fatigue, chill and any excess of alcohol. If further attacks occur I think we shall have to rely, as before on antibiotics and extra fluids.[43]

Moran replied on 30 April: 'Many thanks for your letter and for the notes. He is in very good form at present, and went to the [Royal] Academy dinner last night and is none the worse to-day. For the moment we could do no more than cross our fingers and await events.'[43]

Medical Aspects

Churchill's recuperative holiday in France turned into a disaster! This was Churchill's fourth episode of pneumonia in adult life, previous bouts having occurred in February 1943 (see p. 73),[45] December 1943 (see p. 88)[46] and August 1944 (see p. 127).[45] Churchill suffered a third episode of atrial fibrillation; two previous episodes occurred in December 1943 (see p. 88),[46] and short-lived episodes had occurred on several other occasions.

This was, however, Churchill's first episode of obstructive jaundice, though he was to suffer a further attack of jaundice in June 1962 (see p. 333). Roberts was of the opinion that this was due to the antibiotic prescribed by Moran, whereas Moran believed correctly that this was due to a gall stone or infection of the bile passages.[8] Hunt was of a similar opinion to Moran and believed that the three attacks of pain followed by fever and jaundice were due to the passage of one or more small stones down the common bile duct.

An oral cholecystogram performed in 1936 by Dr H Courtney Gage, Radiologist to St Mary's Hospital, London, at the behest of Hunt had shown no gall stones and barium studies of Churchill's stomach and duodenum undertaken at the same time had revealed no ulcer.[47] Hunt was strongly of the view that neither a repeat oral cholecystogram or an intravenous cholangiogram, particularly the latter, should be performed because of the risk of an adverse event to the iodine-containing dye used for the procedure. Furthermore, the intravenous cholangiogram may not have been diagnostically helpful as Churchill was jaundiced. In addition, as surgery was not contemplated in the short term, investigation with an iodine-containing dye was not warranted at this time. These were sensible clinical decisions.

Penicillin and oxytetracycline are not known to cause obstructive jaundice and there is no evidence that erythromycin was prescribed, which can result in cholestatic hepatitis.[48] The only possibility is that erythromycin was prescribed by Roberts on 16 March 1958 but, if so, he did not mention this to Moran who investigated whether the other antibiotics could cause jaundice.

As a result of this illness Churchill was absent from his usual seat in the House of Commons for some thirteen weeks.

Chapter 24

Two Strokes: April 1959 at Chartwell and October 1959 in London

Damnation! Is it a stroke, Charles?[1]

Despite Sir Winston Churchill's severe illness in spring 1958 while holidaying in the South of France (see p. 273),[2] he planned a four-week visit to Roquebrune-Cap-Martin, a two-week sail to the Canary Islands on the yacht belonging to Aristotle Onassis, a shipping magnate and owner of Olympic Airways, and a five-week visit to Morocco early in 1959, as well as a visit to the United States.

12 January 1959–18 February 1959: Morocco

On 12 January at 11.30 am Sir Winston and Lady Churchill flew to Marrakech in an Olympic Airways Douglas DC 6, arranged by Aristotle Onassis, for his sixth and final visit to that city. The Churchills were to spend their holiday in Morocco at the Hotel Mamounia during which time Churchill painted two pictures, one from the hotel terrace and one in the gardens.[3] The Churchills were accompanied on the flight by John Colville (former Joint Principal Private Secretary) and his wife, Lady Margaret, Lady Monckton (Conservative Peer and wife of Sir Walter who had been Churchill's Minister of Labour and National Service in his last government), Anthony Montague Browne (Private Secretary) and his wife Nonie, Miss Doreen Pugh (personal secretary), Sergeant Edmund Murray (Churchill's bodyguard), Mr and Mrs Ivan Shepherd (nursing attendants), Ms Frieda Abraham (Lady Churchill's maid) and two valets.[4]

Careful advance arrangements had been made to ensure that Churchill received ten daily newspapers and five Sunday newspapers. In addition, six-dozen bottles of Pol Roger and six-dozen bottles of hock and five-dozen bottles of spirits were also imported with the support of the British Embassy in Rabat; Miss Pugh was responsible for keeping Churchill informed of the amount drunk during the extensive entertaining.[5]

Colville recalled that: 'When we arrived there was an enormous Guard of Honour provided by the King of Morocco, but Winston, aged 84, pulled himself together, strode down the steps of the airliner and inspected the whole Guard of Honour without showing any signs of age or illness.'[6] Among the welcoming party was the British Ambassador, Sir Charles Duke, and the Governor of Marrakech, in whose Lincoln Churchill was driven to his hotel.[3] While the Churchills were relaxing at Hotel Mamounia, Murray had to deal with the potential abduction of Churchill by the Berbers who were dissatisfied with their treatment by the new King of Morocco and his government and who wished to focus world attention upon their plight.[7]

The Colvilles and Lady Monckton returned to London on 23 January 1959.[8] Colville wrote to Churchill on 26 January: 'Meg and I loved our stay at Marrakech, every minute of it, and are more than grateful to you for including us in such an agreeable party ... and are still pining for that delectable view of the Atlas, for our nightly games of poker and for the pleasure of your company.'[6]

Lady Churchill wrote to her daughter, Mary:

The first ten days were enlivened by Jock [Colville], Meg and Biddy Monckton ... As for Meg, she and Papa flirted outrageously and almost romped ... When they all went away poor Papa fell into the doldrums – he is better now & has started a picture from the terrace outside his bed-room ... Thank God Papa is blooming in his health. His memory fails a little more day by day & he is getting deafer. But he is well.[9]

19 February 1959–1 March 1959: Canary Islands

On 19 February the Churchills left Safi, the port of Marrakech, and joined Aristotle Onassis's yacht, *Christina*, for a cruise to the Canary Islands and along the Moroccan coast.[7] Murray recalls that Churchill was in great form and had a very healthy appetite. 'Most of the time he had an Edwardian approach to meals and often had a sort of mixed grill for breakfast, and possibly a glass of champagne on special occasions.'[7] Murray also painted the portrait of Christina, Onassis's daughter.

2–5 March 1959: London

Churchill returned to London on 2 March.[6] Churchill then had a very busy four days including a dinner of The Other Club on 5 March, the principal reason for his return to England.[6] Additionally, he spent the afternoon and evening of 3 March at the House of Commons; he visited the House of Commons again on 4 March to see Harold Macmillan, the Prime Minister. Churchill met his solicitor twice on 3 March and 5 March.

On 4 March Churchill had appointments with his dermatologist, Dr RMB MacKenna (see p. 441), and Lord Moran (see p. 443), his personal physician. In addition, Churchill visited the Royal Academy for the one-man show of his paintings[9] and attended a meeting of the Trustees of Churchill College, Cambridge on 4 March. At the invitation of the Colvilles he attended a performance of Gilbert and Sullivan's *The Gondoliers* on that evening. Field Marshal Viscount Montgomery was also in the party at this performance by the D'Oyly Carte Opera Company. Montgomery was a Director of Portsmouth Football Club and had arranged privately for the theatre to pass him the result of the game. Churchill also knew that he was facing a three-line whip (mandatory attendance at a House of Commons vote) that evening and when he saw a note being passed along the row he stood up – assuming it was his summons to the House – and trooped out, followed by the whole party, including a mystified Lord Montgomery for whom the note had been intended![7]

6 March 1959–5 April 1959: South of France

On 6 March Churchill flew at 10.45 am on a British European Airways flight to Nice in the South of France to stay at La Pausa, a villa in Roquebrune-Cap-Martin some 6 miles east of Monte Carlo. Churchill's hosts were again to be Emery Reves, his long-time literary associate and publisher, and his future wife Wendy.

6–15 April 1959: Return to London and Assessments by Lord Moran and Sir Russell Brain Bt

Churchill returned to London on 6 April and was reviewed routinely by Dr MacKenna and Lord Moran.[6] He then began to prepare for a considerable ordeal, a speech in his constituency on 20 April.

Moran had visited Churchill at Chartwell on 13 April on his way to London.[1,10] After his visit Lady Churchill had telephoned Moran at 8 pm and informed him that after Winston had gone to bed (for a rest), he rang his bell and when Shepherd, his valet and trained nurse, answered it he noticed that Winston was not speaking properly. Shepherd reported this to Lady Churchill. Although her husband wanted to stay the night at Chartwell, Lady Churchill had to explain to him that as there were no servants at Chartwell, they had to return to Hyde Park Gate.[1]

Lady Churchill explained to Moran:

Winston is usually very silent in the car, but on the way to London he kept trying to say something. I was not sure whether he wanted to tell me things or whether he was experimenting to find out for himself what he could say and what he could not. When he failed to get the words he exclaimed: 'Damnation! Is it a stroke, Charles?'[1]

Moran examined Churchill at about 10 pm.

When I asked Winston how he was I could not understand what he was trying to say to me. He knew what he wanted to say, but he could not say it. I gave him my pen and he wrote something very slowly and very carefully. I took the paper from him, but I could not read what he had written ... I went back to his room and reassured him. He had been like this before, and it had all cleared up. I told him that in a day or two he will be all right. He said he was worried.[1]

After examining Churchill on 14 April Moran concluded that it was impossible:

To detect that there is anything wrong with his speech ... A few days ago I noticed that the pupils of his eyes did not react to light, and now there is this speech defect and the little finger; there seems no end to these wandering clots. I keep wondering what will happen next. But Winston has made up his mind to go to The Other Club on Thursday [16 April].[1]

Moran invited Brain's (see p. 431) opinion again. Brain and Moran reviewed Churchill on 15 April at 5 pm.[8] Brain recorded in his clinical notes:

Seen with Lord Moran. The previous day he had a sudden attack of
speech difficulty. Could say very little for an hour or two, then rapid
improvement. Now he made only occasional mistakes with words, and
slight slurring. About the same time, his right little finger felt dead
and became cold. No change in neurological signs. Slight expressive
dysphasia. Right little finger was cold and blanched. There have clearly
been two small emboli, presumably from an atheromatous plaque in the
aorta. WC was due to speak the next day in his constituency which was
very important because his adoption as a candidate might depend upon
it. He insisted on going and got through it.[11]

Moran recorded:

When Brain had examined Sir Winston he told me that a small artery
had been blocked, cutting off the circulation to his speech centre for a
time. But the circulation had been re-established. I had advised Russell
to ask Winston if he had made any plans, and if he had, to urge him
to cancel them. Winston said that he was speaking to his constituents:
'I cannot cancel it without giving a reason. I should have to tell them
about this, and I could not then take part in the election. Macmillan has
asked me to take some part. What does it matter if I do break down?' He
broke out impatiently: 'I am quite content to die'.[10]

According to Moran, Brain 'could think of nothing to say. He sat looking
at Winston for quite a time. Then he half turned to me as if he would say:
"Cannot you do something to put an end to this visit?"'[10] Lady Churchill
awaited the physicians in the library.[10] 'Did you persuade him not to speak
on Monday?' Brain told her what had happened. He then asked: 'Does
Sir Winston worry?' Lady Churchill replied:

No Winston isn't a worrier. But he is profoundly depressed. The days
are very long and very dull. It was never like this in the past. He found
a hundred things to do. He reads a lot, but he does not enjoy what
he reads. He cannot paint now. He painted two pictures in five weeks
at Marrakech. He wants to stay in bed. Today an agreeable, amusing
woman came to luncheon. Winston likes her, but at the last moment,
he decided to lunch in bed. He has given up America, thank God. But
what about this speech? Cannot you do anything, Charles?[10]

16 April 1959: Forthcoming General Election

Churchill invited his constituency chairman, Alderman Forbes, to lunch. Forbes later recalled: 'Being eighty-four Sir Winston wished to make sure that he was correct in offering himself as a candidate at the forthcoming General Election. He graciously asked me to reassure him that by so doing he was not blocking any aspirations I had in that direction. He received that assurance.'[6] Moran assessed Churchill again at 3.15 pm.

Churchill dined at The Other Club at 8.15 pm which Gilbert described as 'a tenacious gesture, even a defiant one, for someone so recently in pain and unable to speak properly'.[6] Sir Hartley Shawcross (Barrister, Labour MP and former Attorney General) told Moran on the following day that Churchill scarcely spoke to the man on his left and when something was said to him he seemed to connect for perhaps one or two sentences and then rang off.[1]

17–20 April 1959: Appointments with Dr Roberts and Lord Moran and Constituency Speech

The engagement card for April indicates that Dr Roberts, Churchill's doctor in France, came at 10 am and Moran at 2.30 pm on 17 April.[8]

Only a week after his further stroke, Churchill was driven to Woodford to speak in his constituency. 'It is a long time since I have made a speech in public,' he began.[6] The speech which had been prepared for him by Anthony Montague Browne was delivered in a voice at times barely audible[1,6] and dealt with the Cold War.[12] At the end of his speech, which lasted for 22 minutes, Churchill told his constituents that he was ready once again to offer himself as a candidate. This announcement was received with 'tumultuous applause'.[9] As Churchill came off the platform he turned to Montague Browne with the words: 'Now for America.'[13]

Later that day Churchill told Moran: 'It needed nerve.'[1] 'You mean you were nervous,' asked Moran? 'Oh no. But if you are uncertain whether you will break down, it needs nerve.'[1]

3 May 1959: Assessment by Lord Moran

Although on 20 April Churchill had apparently been keen about his forthcoming visit to the United States, by 3 May he confided to Moran:

I wish I was not going. I would rather stay in bed and read.' Moran wrote later: 'I think it is beginning to dawn on him that to fly across the Atlantic for a few days as things are with him is a bit of a gamble. I told him he was mad to take the risk. But his mind is made up. Anything, I fancy, to break the purgatory of these interminable days. He will not take me. He cannot bear that people should think that he needs a nurse to look after him. When I said 'Goodbye' he said: 'You agree to my going?' 'Under duress,' I answered. At this Winston gave me a faint smile.[1]

Moran was clearly disappointed not to be accompanying Churchill to Washington, as a letter he wrote that day makes clear. Montague Browne wrote: 'Lord Moran addressed a long, persuasive letter to his Eminent – and by now almost only – Patient, explaining why he should accompany him. WSC was vexed: 'No, I don't want that bloody old man,' he said. Actually he was rather fond of Moran, but he would have been an encumbrance on this journey.' Churchill later apologized for this remark.[13]

Moran wrote to Churchill:

I was rather sad when you said this morning that you wished that you were not going on this trip. I expect you feel that this visit is only worthwhile if you can do it really well. But I believe that this is still possible. Any doubts I have had are not concerns with any vascular accident or emergency; after all, it is good odds against anything of that kind happening. I only wonder if you will be in such good form that people in the States will say: 'I'd like to remember him like that.'[14]

I am sure it is possible to tune your circulation so that you will be in such form. I say this because your circulation still responds to 'Minors' [amfetamine sulfate 2.5 mg, aspirin 160 mg, phenacetin 160 mg[15]] if used at the right time, and when it is safe to use them judging from the pulse tension – perhaps using more 'Minors' than we had done hitherto. So far we have used the 'Minors' only before speeches etc. But I had it in mind to use them to keep you in top form throughout your visit (which is short enough to make that possible). I was pretty certain that 'Minors' so used would make a difference between your visit being an outstanding success and merely one where your form might be compared sadly with what they remembered in former times.[14]

That is why I was very sorry when you decided not to take me. I have learnt so much about your circulation in the last 19 years and what can be done to tone it up that I believe I could have made the difference. I wanted you so much to bring off this trip so that people would talk of it as a wonderful thing in itself and not just talk of your former visits. I wanted them to say how marvellous it was that in your eighty-fifth year you were so much 'on the spot' and plainly in a state when you give Ike [President Eisenhower] the advice he so obviously needs.[14]

Planning for the Visit to the United States

Churchill intended to fly to Washington on 4 May 1959 and to stay at the White House initially at the invitation of the President before transferring to the British Embassy, to go to New York on 8 May to see his friend Bernie Baruch (financier and Presidential adviser) and return to London on 10 May. Montague Browne, Murray and Shepherd were to accompany Churchill.[13] Montague Browne wrote that Churchill:

Prepared himself meticulously for his talks with the President. He had suffered a further, if minor, deterioration in his health, and his family and I feared both that the strain of the trip could have serious consequences and that he might leave a tragically diminished memory with his American friends. But as he was adamant to make this political effort for Anglo-American relations, which proved to be his last, I set out on a damage limitation exercise. WSC was persuaded not to make any major prepared speeches: he was bound to address the dinner or luncheon parties he attended, but this would be impromptu, or impromptu from a draft, and infrequent. I briefed the White House, the Embassy and Baruch appropriately and they were all wonderfully helpful, even the White House suppressing its endemic tendency to leak.[13]

4–10 May 1959: Stay at the White House and British Embassy

Montague Browne has described the journey:

Churchill flew in a jet for the first time, a de Havilland Comet. Given the steepness of climb immediately after take-off … I thought that

WSC would be disconcerted. Not so; just annoyed at having to put his cigar out. We had headwinds and had to land in Iceland to refuel ... At New York, we transferred to the Presidential aircraft, the Constellation *Columbine*, waiting with a very welcoming number of officials. The occasion was slightly marred by a scruffy customs man who pushed his way through the dignitaries, shouting that he must ask 'Mr Choichill poisonally what he'd got in his baggage.' Two very large and silent plain-clothes figures picked him up under the shoulders and removed him, his feet paddling furiously.[13]

Stag Dinners had been arranged by President Eisenhower at the White House for the evenings of 5 May (fifteen guests) and 6 May (fifty guests);[8] Churchill spoke briefly at both from a prepared script.[13] During this stay at the White House, Eisenhower and Churchill visited the President's farm near Gettysburg,[7] taking a Marine helicopter to do so (Plate 18). Churchill gave the President one of his paintings, *The Valley of the Ourika and Atlas Mountains*, which he had painted in 1948.

On the morning of 7 May Churchill transferred to the Embassy. A luncheon party took place at which the former President Harry S Truman and his wife, former Secretary of State Dean Acheson and his wife and General Maxwell Taylor (Chief of Staff of the Army) and his wife were the guests.[8] A Stag Dinner for thirty people took place at 8 pm at which the President was the chief guest.[8]

Churchill travelled to New York once again on the *Columbine* on the morning of 8 May and the pilot took the party on a rooftop-high tour of Manhattan Island in perfect weather.[13] Churchill stayed with his friend Bernie Baruch.[13] Churchill left New York to fly home by Comet at 9 pm on 10 May.[8]

22 October 1959–21 November 1959: Assessments by Sir Russell Brain Bt and Lord Moran

On the evening of 22 October Montague Browne was talking to Churchill when he 'yawned twice, went white, face and hands, and became unconscious ... I thought he was dying'. As Moran could not be contacted immediately (he was in Bath for a series of meetings in the West Country), Montague Browne telephoned Sir Russell Brain and told him that Churchill 'had suddenly become unconscious. Lord Moran was in Bath and would [he] go at once?'

Montague Browne was later able to contact Moran. Moran asked him how long it was before Churchill came round:

Oh, I suppose it was not more than a few minutes. When he did come round, he seemed dazed. He said he felt very ill, as if he had been turned upside down. I don't know if I did right, but when I couldn't get you I telephoned Sir Russell Brain, and he'll be here any minute. I will ring again when Sir Russell has seen Sir Winston.[1]

Brain recorded in his clinical notes:

I got to Hyde Park Gate in about twenty minutes, by which time they had got him upstairs and into bed. Mr Browne said that they had both been sitting in the same room when Sir Winston said he felt ill. He looked very pale, and his eyes turned up. He was unconscious. There was no convulsion. Sir Winston was in bed; he looked rather pale. His pulse and respiration were normal. He could be roused to speak and at my request, moved both arms and legs and grasped my hands. There was no paralysis, and I concluded that he had had a minor epileptic attack. I stayed for an hour or more and had tea with Lady Churchill, who said that they had lunched at the Savoy with Randolph and Sir Winston had seemed normal then but perhaps a little silent. He was more conscious when I left but drowsy. No paralysis had developed, and the plantar reflexes were flexor. I rang up later to find that he was sitting up having some dinner.[11]

Moran decided that: 'I must see him tonight. It doesn't sound too good.'[1] On reaching Hyde Park Gate, Moran found that Churchill could not answer his questions. Churchill was 'propped up in bed looking at his dinner on the bed-rest; he was not interested in food. He had a quiet pulse, his colour was good, and he was falling asleep as we left him. I do not think anything will happen.'[1]

Brain assessed Churchill again with Moran at 9.15 am on 23 October. Churchill told his doctors: 'that he had had a good night, and felt quite normal. He was sorry to have caused so much trouble. He did not remember much about the attack but said it felt as if he were being turned upside down. He seemed as usual. He is to take 3/4 grain of sodium phenytoin [phenytoin sodium 50 mg] each morning.'[11]

Moran recorded that:

> When Russell and I saw Winston he seemed much as usual. He did not feel ill. Russell thought his attack was due to petit mal ... it was not uncommon as a sequel to a sluggish cerebral circulation. Even if there were was a recurrence, the risk that he would die in one of these attacks was small, but Russell did not think that he would be alive in six months time.[1]

Moran observed on 24 October that Churchill was playing bezique with his wife. Lady Churchill said that 'he is much better'. Churchill himself, when questioned by Moran, admitted that he felt 'worse' because of 'muzziness'. Churchill told Moran that he had put Tolstoy aside to read the second volume of Alan Brooke's autobiography. Churchill then apologized for forgetting that he had called Moran 'a bloody old man'.[1]

Churchill returned to Woodford on 30 October for the unveiling by Montgomery of his statue, generously donated by his constituents. It was not to Churchill's liking![7]

Lady Churchill telephoned Moran on 17 November to tell him of her concerns regarding Winston. After lunching with Beaverbrook, he 'got out of the car [and] lurched to the right; he would have fallen but for Bullock [chauffeur]'.[1] Moran telephoned Beaverbrook and was informed that during lunch Churchill 'could not get the words he wanted'.[1] When Moran saw Churchill an hour later 'he still had difficulty in finding his words'.[1] Moran asked Churchill how he felt: 'Frightfully stupid.'[1] Churchill had planned to see Adenauer, Chancellor of Germany, that afternoon, but Moran told him that he would not be able to do so as he might use wrong words and it might be very noticeable.[1] However, Churchill told Montague Browne not to cancel any of his appointments for the moment.

Moran again invited Brain to assess Churchill. Brain's clinical notes state:

> Moran telephoned me in the afternoon and asked me to come at once. I got to Hyde Park Gate in a quarter of an hour. Churchill had come up from Chartwell that morning and went to lunch with Beaverbrook.

When he tried to get out of the car, he had to be supported, and he had sat through lunch looking pale and saying little. When I got there, he was sitting in the library, drowsy and yawning. He could be made to respond, but his speech was slurred, and he had some expressive aphasia. Adenauer was due at six o'clock. Moran wanted me to persuade Churchill that he was not fit to see him. This was not difficult, and the Adenauer visit was cancelled. Churchill was got up to bed while Moran and I had tea with Lady Churchill. After that, he seemed to be reviving. He said that he would like to play cards. Lady Churchill said she wished he would play something other than six pack Bezique. She added: 'Winston is now starting to cheat!'[11]

Lady Churchill told Brain that Winston was very disappointed that he could not see Adenauer: 'You see, Sir Russell, there will not be many of these occasions in the future.'[1] Brain confided in Moran that he thought one day Winston would be found in bed unable to speak. The right carotid artery had been blocked before, and it looked now as if the left was affected. 'You mean he will have a stroke in the night?' Moran enquired? Brain nodded in agreement.[1]

Lady Churchill told Moran on 18 November: 'You wouldn't know anything had happened.' Adenauer had expressed a great desire to see Churchill and this had been arranged. Later Moran was told how well the encounter had gone. 'The first quarter on an hour he was hesitant, and his voice was not very strong, though his answers were all sensible. Then he blossomed. His voice got stronger, and he asked a lot of intelligent questions … I think Charles it went off very well.'[1] Moran saw Churchill an hour after Adenauer's visit. 'I saw … I saw … that man'. Adenauer, Moran asked? Churchill nodded.[1]

Moran had gone to Oxford, leaving Brain in charge of Churchill's care. Brain was rung up at lunch time on 19 November and went along at 3 pm to see Churchill.[11] Churchill:

had got up as usual, but while waiting for lunch, they found him with several volumes of Edgar Allan Poe, and he said he wanted to know what happened to Marie Antoinette. He did not believe she was executed. He slept through most of lunch, and then ate some, but was still preoccupied with the problem. Eventually, Lady Churchill got an encyclopaedia to convince him. She was catechised and remembered most of the details. I found him drowsy but recovering. Blood pressure 110/70. He had had a bad night with confusion, exhausted by the Adenauer visit which took place yesterday. Bed and then better.[11]

Brain recorded in his notes:

Talking these episodes over with Moran, I suggested that we ought to think of the possibility of a cardiac origin for these episodes, and as a result, he asked John Richardson [see p. 445] to see Churchill. I wrote to Richardson on January 28th 1960, giving him an account of what had happened, and ended my letter as follows: I am sure all of these episodes have been circulatory, and I thought that the cerebral ones were probably due to a fluctuating blood supply through thickened cerebral vessels. It was the attack of syncope which made me suggest to Moran that a cardiac dysrhythmia might be at the bottom of it.[11]

Richardson wrote back on 1 February 1960:

I enclose the electrocardiogram as I think it might interest you with its highly variable pace-maker. I would like to have it back as it is the only one I have got the other I sent to Moran. I think the finding is important as it would obviously be better for him not to be on digitalis unless the indications are extraordinarily strong.[11]

Moran went to see Churchill again on 21 November, and he was reading Zweig's *Marie Antoinette*, but Moran was not sure how much Churchill had taken in, particularly as Miss Pugh [personal secretary] had shown Churchill some papers and 'he did not seem to take them in as he usually does'.[1]

30 November 1959: Sir Winston Churchill's Birthday

Churchill celebrated his 85th birthday by attending the House of Commons where the Leader of the Opposition, Hugh Gaitskell, and the Leader of the House, RA 'Rab' Butler, proposed their warmest and most heartfelt good wishes.[6]

Medical Aspects

This account, assembled from medical and non-medical sources, describes two further mild strokes, in April 1959 and in November 1959. In the first of these, with onset at around 8 pm on 13 April, although there was rapid improvement of acute expressive dysphasia within 2 hours (Churchill was able to tell Moran at 10 pm that same evening that he was worried), there was still mild nominal dysphasia when Brain examined him on 15 April. We conclude that this was a small completed stroke rather than a transient ischaemic attack (TIA), but with minimal residual neurological deficit.

In the second episode on 17 November, Churchill lurched to the right on getting out of a car and again developed expressive dysphasia. Brain examined Churchill within hours of the onset, when he recorded expressive dysphasia and some slurring of speech. Although this had improved by 19 November, Churchill was unable to find Adenauer's name. This was probably within 24 hours of the onset, and because there is no specific comment about Churchill's speech in the days that followed, it is possible that the dysphasia had recovered fully within 24 hours and was by definition a TIA.

The first of these episodes coincided with signs of ischaemia affecting the little finger of the right hand (see p. 303), leading Brain to propose that both the cerebral and digital events were due to emboli arising from the aorta. However, as we have discussed already in relation to Churchill's numerous previous strokes,[16–21] it seems at least as likely that the left cerebral ischaemia in April 1959 was also due to cerebral small vessel disease.

The episode of loss of consciousness on 22 October 1959 requires comment. We do not have a complete account of this episode, which was preceded by pallor and a sensation described by Churchill as being 'like being turned upside down'. Churchill's posture at the start of this episode is not known for certain, but it seems likely that he was sitting in a chair and was thus semi-erect. If so, it is reasonable to assume that he probably remained seated during the period of unconsciousness, during which no convulsion occurred. Brain's account does not clarify whether Churchill was subsequently in bed when he examined him. According to Montague Browne, unconsciousness lasted not more than a few minutes and Churchill seemed dazed when he came round. When Brain arrived, probably within an hour or so of the onset, Churchill was conscious, drowsy and 'very pale'. The pulse was normal, but there is no record of the blood pressure. Churchill had recovered sufficiently to eat his dinner later that evening.

Brain concluded at the time that this was a 'minor epileptic attack' and Churchill was treated with a small dose of phenytoin. However, in November 1959, following the second episode of left cerebral hemisphere ischaemia, discussed above, and 'some confusion' during the night of 18 November, Brain referred to the episode on 22 October as 'syncope'.

On 28 January 1960, Brain wrote to Richardson, questioning whether there might be a cardiac basis for this episode and possibly some other recent symptoms. Richardson performed an ECG and wrote, with some concern, explaining the finding of a 'highly variable pacemaker', advising avoidance of digitalis treatment. From this limited evidence, it seems possible that Churchill had developed what would now be recognised as sick sinus syndrome. This could well have been the basis for the episode of syncope, and the later period of confusion, the latter on the basis of reduced cardiac output and an already chronically compromised cerebral circulation. Churchill's presumed sitting, rather than recumbent, posture during the attack might have been responsible for prolongation of the episode if it was indeed due to bradycardia (slow heart rate) and hypotension (low blood pressure). On the balance of the evidence now available, syncope seems more likely than epilepsy as the explanation of this episode.

There is little doubt that Churchill's cognitive function was gradually deteriorating, most probably on the basis of increasing cerebrovascular disease. Memory impairment, boredom, periods of apathy, mood swings and loss of interest in matters at times, including in painting, were all noted by Lady Churchill and others during this period, as described here. But despite this, at the age of 84, Churchill's schedule of public and private engagements was at times hectic and would have been challenging even at a much younger age. As previously, Churchill demonstrated that he could rise to the occasion and that when he really wanted to do something, he still could, most notably at this time his visit to Washington, which was clearly a great success.

Chapter 25

Right Finger Gangrene in May 1959 in Washington

I don't care what's wrong with my bloody finger![1]

When Lord Moran (see p. 443) assessed Sir Winston Churchill on 13 April 1959 at about 10 pm following his loss of speech,[2] he noticed that Churchill's little finger was 'white and cold'.[3] When Moran asked Churchill if it was painful he nodded.[3] Moran records no further details about Churchill's finger so it must be presumed that the features he experienced (pain and colour change) were transitory.

Despite suffering a small completed stroke with minimal residual neurological deficit on 13 April 1959 (see p. 288), it was still Churchill's intention to fly to Washington on 4 May 1959 and to stay at the White House initially, at the invitation of the President, before transferring to the British Embassy, to go to New York on 8 May 1959 to see his friend Bernie Baruch, financier and presidential adviser, and return to London on 10 May.[2]

Moran wrote: 'I hear he went off in good heart. He has a feeling that for the moment he is on the map again. Perhaps, after all, life is not quite over. But I am full of forebodings. I cannot get the thought out of my head that I may not see him again.'[3]

4–10 May 1959: At the White House and British Embassy

Montague Browne, Churchill's Private Secretary, recorded that:

Halfway through the visit, I was sitting by WSC's bedside while he finished his breakfast. 'Look at this,' he said suddenly, holding out a finger. A small area at the tip was jet black. 'I burnt my finger the other day while I was lighting a cigar, and now it has gone numb.' The first doctor to see it look concerned. After we had left the room, he told me that it was gangrene. I asked if it would spread. It might, he replied;

the patient's circulation was obviously bad. Here was a pickle. WSC was as brave as you could be, but he was something of a hypochondriac, and the word gangrene would conjure up terrible visions of the deadly First World War gas gangrene. Should he fly home at once, cutting short his programme? I communicated with Lord Moran in London, who was neutrally reassuring, but the matter was taken out of our hands by WSC himself: 'I don't care what's wrong with my bloody finger,' he said, 'I feel very well and I won't have my programme changed.' And that settled it.[1]

When Montague Browne telephoned Moran to inform him, Moran impressed upon the doctor to whom he spoke 'the need for secrecy'.[3] Moran drove to Chartwell on 9 May to inform Lady Churchill of the medical news before Churchill returned. 'What is the worst that can happen?' Before Moran could answer her daughter, Diana said: 'Oh, of course, Papa might have his hand off for gangrene.'[3]

11–24 May 1959: Assessments by Lord Moran and Professor Rob

Churchill landed at Heathrow at 10.15 am, and Moran saw him just before noon, but he was so tired after the flight he could hardly keep awake.[3] On reflection, and despite her previous misgivings, Lady Churchill concluded: 'I am very glad Winston went to America, though I was against the journey at first. He loved the visit. I think he wanted to go to America before he died, because of his mother.'[3]

Moran invited Professor Charles Rob (see p. 446), vascular surgeon at St Mary's Hospital, London, to give an opinion on Churchill's finger on 12 May. Rob proceeded to explain 'very clearly and even a little bluntly' that there had been a clot in the artery of his little finger. There was a black spot because not enough blood could get to the finger. If Churchill rested, he would probably lose only a bit of the finger. The black spot was dead tissue; it might take months – even a year – to dry up and come away. Churchill responded: 'A year! A year! You are asking too much. I have an appointment tomorrow. I am not going to deny myself this.'[3]

Rob again reviewed Churchill's finger at 9 am on 13 May.[3] Churchill was still asleep, but when he awoke he gave Moran a 'sour look'[3] as he was sure he intended to try and prevent him lunching with the Prime Minister, Harold

Macmillan.[3] 'Rob said there was a risk if he went, but that risk was small.'[3] 'What is it?' demanded Churchill. 'If you don't rest you might lose the hand,' Rob told him.[3] Churchill attended lunch with Macmillan!

On 14 May Churchill announced his intention of attending Lord Beaverbrook's annual dinner.[3] He asked Rob what were the odds that this would make his finger worse. Rob replied fifty-fifty.[3] Churchill arrived at the dinner in a 'bad temper; he sat silent, brooding'.[3]

Although Moran had given Churchill a finger-stall to hide the black spot, he proceeded to show it to everyone, even exciting the interest of Macmillan who wanted to know its significance.[3] Rob reviewed Churchill again on 21 May at 6.30 pm. On 24 May Churchill removed the finger-stall and said to Moran; 'It's a poor sight. I have never seen anything like it before.'[3]

At the behest of Lady Churchill, Rob wrote to Churchill on 1 June 1959:

As you know, we believe that the cause of the discoloured area of skin at the finger tip is the blockage of the blood vessels to that finger and when I saw it immediately after your return from America there was a possibility that the process might spread to involve the hand. Fortunately this has not occurred and now we have a localised abnormality confined to the fingertip. In my view the normal skin will slowly grow in under the discoloured area and over a period of several months this discoloured area will be replaced with rather thin and somewhat sensitive skin, but this will gradually thicken and about a year from now I think the finger will be relatively normal, although there may be a slight change in shape at the tip. As regards the fingernail, I think there is a strong possibility that you may lose this and grow a new one, but I am not certain that this is going to occur. On the whole I think the finger has done very well indeed and progress has been much better than I expected. I would like to stress again that I think from now on things will be rather slow and you may occasionally get spasms of pain or peculiar feelings in the fingertip as the fresh nerve endings are growing into the part at the tip where they have been destroyed.[4]

Rob later recalled his visits to Churchill: 'He was, I thought, an alert, very interesting and somewhat deaf man … [he] was in good health and mentally still exceptional. I thought he was bored by his retirement.'[5]

22 July–13 August 1959: Sailing in Greek and Turkish Waters

On 22 July, the Churchills set sail again on *Christina* as a guest of Aristotle Onassis, a Greek shipping magnate who lived in Monaco, for a cruise of Greek and Turkish waters. Moran, Montague Browne and Sergeant Murray, Churchill's bodyguard, were among the passengers.[5,6] In Capri, Gracie Fields, the singer, came on board and sang several songs, and on departing sang *Come back to Sorrento ... or I die*.[6] She was a great success and Lady Churchill 'clapped her hands repeatedly, and her eyes shone with an enthusiasm I had rarely seen in her' recorded Murray.[6] Throughout the cruise Moran would not let his patient swim: 'Oh no, you might get a chill.'[5]

The cruise involved sailing through the Dardanelles at night. Murray surmised this had been intentional to spare Churchill's feelings.[6] As Nonie Montague Browne later recalled: 'they knew it would upset him'.[5] In fact, Churchill instructed his nurse to fetch Murray and together they watched the distant outline of the shore for 2 hours on the night of 4 August.[6] '... judging from Sir Winston's reactions then and immediately after, it was an experience which had considerable impact upon him, and during the next two or three days, he was in silent, retrospective mood' recorded Murray.[6]

13–30 August 1959: Monte Carlo

On 13 August the *Christina* berthed at Monte Carlo, and Churchill went to La Capponcina, Lord Beaverbrook's villa at Cap d'Ail, across the bay from Monte Carlo. Montague Browne flew back to London on 14 August but returned to La Capponcina on 19 August.

On 15 August Churchill showed Moran his finger tip 'with a touch of pride'. The black tip had come away. 'You could not tell that anything was wrong. It took three months, and they talked about a year!'[3] So within four months the necrotic black tip had come away and the rest of the finger remained healthy.

Lady Churchill flew to London on 20 August to undergo an operation on her eyelid at Queen Victoria Hospital, East Grinstead by Sir Benjamin Rycroft, consultant ophthalmic surgeon; the eyelid droop was the result of a prolonged attack of shingles.[7]

Churchill transferred to La Pausa on 23 August, a villa in Roquebrune-Cap-Martin, in the Alpes-Maritimes, some 6 miles east of Monte Carlo, where Emery Reves, Churchill's long-time literary associate, was to be Churchill's host yet again.

Churchill returned home on 30 August.

29 September–21 October 1959: Adoption at Woodford as the Conservative Candidate and General Election on 8 October 1959

Churchill went for his adoption meeting at Woodford on 29 September. He had left Chartwell at 5.00 pm, given his adoption speech on arrival, dined with his Constituency Chairman, Alderman Donald Forbes, at 6.30 pm and gave a major speech at Hawkey Hall at 8 pm.[8] Churchill reminded his constituents at his adoption that: 'I am much touched by your action, Ladies and Gentlemen, in doing me the honour of adopting me as your candidate for the ninth time. We have had eight victories running, and I am sure that if everyone plays his part as you have always done, we shall increase our score on 8 October.'[9] The major speech, written by Montague Browne, told his constituents of the way out of the deadlock caused by the confrontation of the nuclear and conventional capacity of the Great Powers.[10]

In the General Election on 8 October, the Conservatives were returned with an overall majority of 100 seats, but Churchill's majority though substantial (14,797) was down. Later his daughter Mary suggested that: 'It may well be that the feelings of discontent among some of his supporters were reflected in this result.'[7] For some time Parliamentary Questions on behalf of Churchill's constituents had been raised in the House of Commons by the Conservative Member for the neighbouring seat of Walthamstow, John Harvey MP, and Constituency correspondence was dealt with by Churchill's secretariat and Agent, Colonel Hugh Barlow-Wheeler.[7]

17 October 1959: Planting of an Oak Tree at Churchill College, Cambridge

Churchill flew from Biggin Hill airfield to Cambridge, accompanied by Lady Churchill and Montague Browne, a flight of 30 minutes which saved a journey of more than 3 hours by road, to plant an oak tree to mark the foundation of Churchill College.[5] After lunch at King's College, Cambridge, the party proceeded to the site designated for the new College for the tree planting, and Churchill gave a speech drafted by Montague Browne but much edited by him.[11] After his speech, Churchill attended a meeting of the College Trustees and was informed that just over £3 million (equivalent in 2019 of some £69 million) had been raised, enough to enable the Trustees to proceed with the building of the College.[5]

Medical Aspects

Although Churchill's right little finger was noted by Moran to be pale and cold on 13 April, it was not until 7 May that Churchill noticed that the tip was black, drawing Montague Browne's attention to this and attributing the appearance to a burn sustained as a result of lighting a cigar. The lesion was apparently painless. This was some three weeks after the finger was first noticed to be blanched and cold. Ischaemic changes of the digits caused by embolic phenomenon are rare. When they do occur, the nidus for emboli include the heart, proximal atherosclerotic occlusive and aneurysmal disease. Moreover, an embolic occlusion at the onset would have been likely to have produced a more rapid line of demarcation between viable and non-viable tissue.

Thus, it seems more likely that the digital ischaemia resulted from local digital artery stenosis and subsequent occlusion rather than embolism. This, in turn, throws doubt on Brain's conclusion concerning an aortic source of emboli. Rob later referred to a 'clot' in the finger artery, without committing himself to any more specific pathological causation. At any rate, the digital ischaemia was minor and seemed to trouble Churchill very little, resolving satisfactorily with loss of only a small amount of tissue from the tip of the finger within four months.

Chapter 26

Fracture of Fifth Thoracic Vertebra and Stroke in November 1960 in London

How long have I to go on like this, waiting for death?[1]

Sir Winston and Lady Churchill had been out to dinner with Lord and Lady Salisbury on the night of 15 November 1960, returning to Hyde Park Gate about midnight.[2]

Before retiring Churchill went into his wife's room to say goodnight, leaving Nurse Roy Howells outside the bedroom door. Howells recalled more than a decade later: 'I heard a thud and Lady Churchill called out: 'Howells come quickly!' I ran in and found Sir Winston lying near the wardrobe in Lady Churchill's dressing room which led off the bedroom.'[2]

Apparently, having kissed his wife goodnight, Churchill had half-turned to tell her something as he was going out of the door, somehow losing his balance and falling against the side of the wardrobe.[2] The corner caught him between the shoulder blades.[2] At that time Churchill relied heavily on a walking stick[2] following the effects of a stroke in 1953,[3,4] and he had a habit of pivoting on his left foot which meant that sometimes he was caught off balance.[2] Although Churchill had been warned on many occasions that this was an unwise thing to do, 'with usual Churchillian pugnacity he paid little attention to medical advice'.[2]

Following the fall Churchill lay on the carpet in great pain. Howells made him comfortable and wrote that he telephoned Lord Moran, though Moran claimed he was contacted by Lady Churchill.[1] While Moran was on his way, Howells checked to make sure no limb was broken, then fetched the policeman (Constable Clarke[5]) on duty outside the house to help roll Churchill on to a rug. Using this as an improvised stretcher Howells and the policeman carried him to his bed. The policeman was called in because at that time there was no butler in the household and the only other person in the house was Lady Churchill's maid.[2]

Moran recorded that he had been telephoned by Lady Churchill 'about Midnight' on 12 November 1960.[1] This is incorrect; it was the night of 15–16 November 1960. Lady Churchill explained that: 'Winston had come to her room to say Goodnight. He had kissed her, when stepping back he lost his footing and fell backwards; his head struck the wall, and then he fell heavily to the ground.'[1] Moran recorded that when he got to the house 'Howells said that he found Sir Winston lying on the floor; he looked like marble; he had no pulse; he thought he was dead.'[1]

According to Howells, Moran arrived and put Churchill under 'light sedation'.[2] Churchill then spent 'a fitful night' with Moran sleeping in the room above.[2] Howells recalls that Churchill was in such pain that his physician could not carry out a proper examination until the next morning.[2] Moran noted that Churchill 'seemed to understand what I said and there were no signs of shock. I decided to stay with him for the night.'[1]

Moran invited the opinion of Professor (later Sir) Herbert Seddon (see p. 451), Clinical Director of the Royal National Orthopaedic Hospital.[1] Seddon arrived at Hyde Park Gate at 11.45 am and found Churchill propped up in bed and very comfortable:

There was a small swelling on the back of his head but nothing else. A little tenderness at the upper part of the thoracic spine but no other abnormality either there or elsewhere. I telephoned Campbell Golding who told me that X-rays of the upper thoracic spine taken with a portable machine would be useless. We would have to go to his consulting room. Trying to wrap up Sir Winston produced such violent pain in the upper thoracic spine that we had a bit of a game getting him down the stairs and into the ambulance.[6]

Seddon arranged for Churchill to be taken by ambulance to 64 Harley Street to be examined radiologically by Dr Campbell Golding (see p. 437), Consultant Radiologist at the Middlesex and Royal National Orthopaedic Hospitals.[6]

Seddon recorded in his notes:

I held Sir Winston's head firmly during the journey, but he still had a good deal of pain. Golding took X-rays of the thoracic spine and of the pelvis, and we found a crush fracture with no displacement of T5.

I would have liked pictures of the cervical spine too, but Golding said that it would be necessary for him to sit on a stool; this was out of the question because it would have hurt him so much. Anyway there was nothing to suggest a fracture in the neck. Lord Moran and I agreed to nurse him at home with day and night nurses from St Marys Hospital.[6]

In addition to Howells, Churchill was attended by Nurses Thomson, Wood and Hutton,[7] the latter two being seconded from St Mary's Hospital, London.

The formal report by Golding stated:

There is a wedge deformity of the body of thoracic 5, and there is a minor deformity of the disc plates of thoracic 8 and 9. There is some osteoporosis of all the vertebrae. I have no sure way of telling whether these changes are recent or old. In the lateral film one can imagine that the condition has been present for some time, but in the antero-posterior film the deformity of thoracic 5 looks more recent. There is a little lipping of all the vertebral margins and some narrowing of the disc of thoracic 9–12. The film of the pelvis shows some degenerative changes in the lower lumbar vertebrae, but none in the hip joints. There is no evidence of an injury. There are arterial changes in several regions.[6]

Seddon considered '… that we should probably make an earnest effort to get lateral films of his cervical spine, if there is any clinical indication injury in this region. One could hardly do this lying down since he has a short neck and high shoulders.'[6]

Seddon wrote when drafting the bulletin for Montague Browne at 4.30pm on 16 November that: 'We must not talk about a fracture of the spine because this conjures up the idea of permanent paralysis in the lay mind. Sir Winston has a fracture (of the 5th thoracic vertebrae) but it is not a serious or disabling affair and there is no paralysis. If pressed we may honestly add, there is no cause for anxiety.'[8] The first bulletin stated: 'Sir Winston has fallen and broken a small bone in his back. He was seen today by Lord Moran and Mr Seddon, and will have to remain in bed for a little time.'[9]

Moran wrote: 'When a man is in his eighty-seventh year and fractures his spine anything may happen, but in the bulletin we were content to record that Sir Winston had fallen and broken a small bone in his back. Seddon's sound judgement and good sense are a great comfort. I do like a man who knows his job.'[1]

The Times reported that Churchill had fallen and broken a small bone in his back:

He is in bed and must remain lying on his back for the present. Professor HJ Seddon … said last night: 'He will be in bed a little while, but it is nothing serious' … It was learnt last night that he [Churchill] is in some discomfort and the only easy position for him is on his back in bed. Lady Churchill was with him, and he was said to be 'quite cheerful'. Sir Winston's secretary said that there was no cause for anxiety.[10]

17 November 1960

The nursing records state that Churchill was 'awake at 9.15 am. Very difficult.'[7] Seddon recorded that Churchill had been fairly comfortable sleeping on his back:

Lord Moran told me that this position would almost certainly be fatal; his chronic bronchitis made his chest like a musical box. He must be sat well up. So I ordered a hospital bed that we could crank up. It was higher and narrower than his own bed and Churchill did not take kindly to it at all, grumbling incessantly about the discomfort it caused.[6]

Seddon recorded:

Later in the day [3 pm] Philip Yeoman [Senior Registrar] and I – purposely avoiding saying to Sir Winston what we had in mind – lifted him smartly into the sitting position and moved him to the new bed. The patient expressed his views about this in the strongest possible terms, ending with a growl 'Narrow bed – narrow minds'. We could not have avoided hurting him, but the pain soon subsided and we never had another cross word.[6]

Churchill was reviewed again by Seddon and Moran at 5.20 pm.

After seeing Churchill on 17 November, Moran told *The Times* 'Things are going very well.'[11] A bulletin stated that 'Sir Winston had a very good night and is resting in bed.'[12]

Churchill received many telegrams and cables as soon as news of the accident became known. Her Majesty the Queen sent a telegram to Churchill: 'I am so sorry to hear about your accident and send you my best wishes for a speedy recovery. Elizabeth R'[13] Churchill replied by return: 'I am most grateful to Your Majesty for your very kind message. Winston S. Churchill'[14]

President Eisenhower cabled Churchill:

Dear Winston,

All the people in America are distressed to learn of your accident none more so than I. I do trust that the whole business is not too painful and while I know you will not enjoy the enforced period in bed, I hope you will do exactly what the doctors say. Do take care of yourself. Mamie joins me in affectionate regard to Clemmie and yourself.

As ever IKE[15]

Churchill responded by return: 'Thank you so much dear Ike. You have been much in my thoughts and I will be writing to you soon. Winston.'[16]

The nursing records state that a codeine compound tablet [codeine phosphate 8 mg, aspirin 260 mg, phenacetin 260 mg] and a Disprin™ tablet [soluble aspirin 300 mg] were given at 10 pm. Churchill slept from 10.15 pm until 12.50 am.

18 November 1960

Churchill slept again from 1 am to 5.15 am when he awoke complaining of pain in his right shoulder radiating to the sternum.[7] 'Sir Winston was extremely apprehensive – colour good with pulse volume quite good – perspired freely.'[7] A codeine compound tablet was given at 5.15 am and repeated at 5.30 am.[7] Seddon was informed at 5.55 am and told nursing staff: 'Will visit later to examine and decide whether the pain is from fracture, right shoulder or chest infection.'[7]

Churchill slept for short periods from 6 am to 10 am.[7] Churchill was examined by Yeoman at 10 am. The day nursing records state that Churchill was still complaining of some pain in the *left* (not right) shoulder extending down the left arm.[7] Breathing exercises and leg massage were carried out by Miss Martin-Jones, the physiotherapist.[7] 'Patient not unduly distressed during treatment but very drowsy after. Slept for three-quarters of an hour.'[7]

When Moran saw Churchill, he recommended that the physiotherapist should concentrate on deep breathing exercises rather than leg massage.[7] The shoulder pain was still present at 6 pm when it was observed that Churchill was 'slightly cyanosed around the lips. Breathless on slightest exertion.'[7] At 7 pm the nursing records state: 'Pulse irregular at times. Volume varies.'[7]

Seddon wrote:

> A very busy day starting with a telephone call at 6 am to the effect that Sir Winston had wakened with pain in the right shoulder radiating to the sternum. One or other of us made visits during the day, and the last one was by Lord Moran, John Richardson and myself at 8.45 pm …
>
> [Later Lord] Richardson [see p. 445] did an ECG. Fortunately, he had one that had been made in June. He found no change at all and the physicians concluded there had been no serious cardiac episode during the night. However, the patient was still bothered by pain in the neck and in both shoulders. I knew he had dislocated the right one when he was young, and it would not abduct beyond 90°.[6]

Seddon continued:

> At one point, Lord Moran, John Richardson and I found ourselves standing in a row before Sir Winston, telling him what we had found. His little budgerigar was flitting about the room and settled on Lord Moran's shoulder, then he moved on to John Richardson and looked as though he was going to peck his ear. So I put out my finger, and the little bird hopped onto it. So I stood there with my index finger as a perch looking pretty silly. Winston chuckled so much that I don't think he paid any attention to what the physicians said.[6]

Richardson also recalled the event: 'I had the unusual experience of taking the cardiogram of the most famous man on earth with his beloved budgerigar "Toby" sitting on my right wrist.'[20]

Richardson also recalled another earlier consultation at Chartwell:

Winston did not wish to see any doctor and did not say a word to me except in answer to direct questions during my whole detailed examination including of course his electrocardiogram. I packed up and walked to the door in silence. 'Aren't you going to tell me what you think Sir John'. 'No Sir, I'll tell Lord Moran.' 'Well, I'm very much obliged to you' was said with a wicked smile and I was across the room and on a stool at his feet in seconds, telling him. I saw him quite often after that, including one long night at Hyde Park Gate, and he was always grateful and courteous, but I was rather pleased at having experienced his wrath and to have survived.[20]

The nursing records state that Seddon did not think the pain was from the fracture but from internal bruising.[7] Churchill's temperature at 10.45 pm was 99.4°F [37.4°C]. He was given a codeine compound tablet at 10.15 pm 'with little effect'.[7] Churchill subsequently became 'confused and restless'. Moran was informed at 12.35 am.[7]

Today's bulletin stated that Churchill 'has had a rather disturbed night, but his spinal injury is progressing satisfactorily and is giving no anxiety.'[18] *The Times* reported that Churchill's daughter, Mary Soames, had 'travelled from Scotland overnight. She spent nearly two hours with her father. "He is bored with being in bed, but he seems fine and in good spirits. There is no cause for worry … now he is quite well. He was able to eat his lunch".'[19]

Dr David Roberts (see p. 447), Churchill's doctor in the South of France, wrote to Churchill: 'I am very grieved to hear of your most unfortunate accident. I have heard the news today while on a short holiday in Central France. Please accept my best wishes for a speedy recovery.'[20]

19 November 1960

Secobarbital 100 mg was ordered and given at 1.45 am.[7] Churchill slept for short periods until 2.50 am.[7] Then he became 'extremely restless and confused. Continuously trying to get out of bed. Restrained with some difficulty. Refused to have TPR [Temperature, Pulse, Respiratory rate] taken and was altogether uncooperative. Eventually went to sleep at 4.30 am. Slept well since.' 'Intake [presumably over the previous 24 hours]: Champagne 8 oz, coffee 3 oz, soup 9 oz, brandy 1 oz and sips of water.'[7]

Churchill was seen and assessed by Moran and Seddon. Today's bulletin stated: 'Sir Winston did not have a very good night but the pain of his injury is less.'[21]

The nursing records state that Churchill's temperature was 98.0°F [36.7°C] at 1 pm and that at 2.45 pm he was sponged and his pressure areas received attention.[7] 'Patient objected most violently to being moved and washed. Settled down eventually. Complaining of ? severe pain in left shoulder at 4.00 pm.'[7] Churchill was stated to be 'rather quiet this evening though not complaining of any pain.'[7] A codeine compound tablet was given at 10.15 pm. 'Churchill slept from 10.30 pm until 1.45 am.'[7]

20 November 1960

Churchill was awake from 1.45 am to 4.20 am.[7] 'Confused but quiet and resting well.'[7] 'Sir Winston has a rash over right hip and upper right leg. The spots are small and red almost "pinhead" in type. Sir Winston denies they are irritating but has been seen to scratch them.'[7] Calamine lotion was applied, and Churchill was said to be very cooperative by his nurses.[6,7] Churchill had his usual breakfast of coffee, fruit and orange juice at 9.30 am.[7]

Yeoman reviewed Churchill at 10.15 am, and the patient ate a small lunch after sleeping from 12 midday until 1 pm after physiotherapy.[7]

Today's bulletin stated: 'Sir Winston had a better night and his condition continues to improve.'[22]

Churchill was reviewed by Moran at 3 pm and recommended a codeine compound tablet as night sedation.[7] The nurses recorded that Churchill was able 'to move around very well in bed. Able to turn his head without pain.'[7] Although Churchill was given a codeine compound tablet at 10.30 pm, secobarbital 100 mg was also administered at 2.15 am despite Moran's earlier stipulation.

21 November 1960

Churchill slept until 6.10 am. Nursing staff observed that Churchill was 'mentally extremely confused at times. Extremely difficult.'[7] Calamine lotion was applied to the rash, and cortisporin™ [neomycin, bacitracin, polymyxin B and hydrocortisone] ointment was applied for anal irritation.[7] At 9 am Moran telephoned Seddon to say that Churchill had had a disturbed night with some mental confusion and had had angry words with Howells.[6]

Howells later wrote, probably about this incident:

On one occasion I remember we had a blazing row over the bed rest and I'm afraid we swore at each other. Afterwards we made it up. Sir Winston, his bottom lip jotting, said: 'You were very rude to me, you know.' I told him: 'Yes but you were rude too.' Then with just a hint of a smile, he looked up and said blandly, 'Yes, but I *am* a great man.' There was no answer to that. He knew, as I and the rest of the world knew, that he was right.[2]

Moran also recorded the same incident (though he dated it 17 November 1960):

Last night he shouted at Howells till at last the poor man's patience gave out and he answered back. This morning Winston told me that Howells was mad; he would have to leave. I asked Howells what Winston had said. 'Oh, he just shouted abuse at me. You see, sir, even when Sir Winston is well he never says anything to me, unless, of course, he has to ask me for something.'[1]

During the morning Churchill announced to his nurses that: 'He would be getting up this afternoon!! Seems quite happy at the prospect.'[7]

Seddon and Moran both visited Churchill.[7] Seddon recorded: 'At 3:30 pm two nurses got Churchill into a chair without any difficulty, and he took three steps himself. He remained up for 12 minutes, perfectly comfortably, but his head slumped forward, and he seemed afraid to hold it straight.'[7] Churchill slept from 5 pm to 6.30 pm, but was 'rather cross on awaking'.[7]

Moran told reporters, 'There is not going to be a bulletin today. The position is the same as before – there is nothing to add. No news is good news.'[23]

Churchill finished dinner at 9 pm and had a visitor (Christopher Soames, Churchill's son-in-law) until 10.30 pm.[7]

Secobarbital 100 mg was given at 10.45 pm and repeated at 2.50 am. Soluble aspirin 300 mg was given at 1.40 am.[7]

22 November 1960

Churchill was observed to be very confused in the early hours of the morning. 'His facial expression showed distress, cause not known. Pulse 100/min.'[7] At 2.50 am Moran was informed of his patient's condition.[7] Secobarbital 100 mg was ordered at 3 am and Churchill slept from 3.45 am to 7 am.[7] He settled quickly again and was still sleeping at 2 pm, so was awakened.[7] Moran telephoned at 8 am and told the nurses he would review the question of night sedation later.[7]

At 3 pm Churchill was observed by the nurses to be 'very cooperative and cheerful. Sitting up in bed reading newspapers.'[7] Churchill was seen by Yeoman, Seddon's Senior Registrar, at 3.15 pm, by Moran at 3.30 pm and by Seddon at 6.30 pm. Moran decided that secobarbital 100 mg could be given on 'settling' and that the barbiturate could be repeated 3 hours later if necessary. Soluble aspirin 300 mg could also be given between the doses of secobarbital.[7]

Churchill was helped out of bed and sat in the chair from 4.10 pm to 5.10 pm.[7] 'Not complaining unduly of any pain ... Would not use the electric shaver himself.'[7] Churchill was able to walk the short distance from chair to bed.[7] Seddon examined Churchill at 6.30 pm. He put Churchill's 'neck through a full range of movements with no difficulty and no discomfort. Sir Winston was most cooperative.'[7]

At 7 pm Churchill was visited by his dermatologist Dr RMB MacKenna (see p. 441), who recommended that Churchill's usual prescriptions ('lotions and ointments') for his skin diseases should be continued.[7] Following this assessment Churchill 'decided to have a wash and clean his teeth!'.[7] His ablutions were followed by a four-course dinner![7]

The Times reported that Churchill had:

> Got up for a time yesterday sitting in a chair ... Earlier yesterday Mrs Duncan Sandys [Churchill's daughter, Diana], had said he was getting better all the time. He is sitting up in bed and keeping very cheerful ... Lord Moran said 'The position is the same as before-there is nothing to add. No news is good news.'[23]

Later that night Churchill had 'complained of pain in the left shoulder and arms with numbness in the left thumb which was painful on movement'.[7]

The pain had developed immediately after Churchill's position had been changed.[7] Churchill later said his thumb had been numb for some days.[7] Nursing staff thought there was some diminished use in his left hand.[7]

Churchill was given soluble aspirin 300 mg at 10.15 pm and secobarbital 100 mg at 10.35 pm and though he 'settled down' he did not sleep.[7] A further tablet of secobarbital 100 mg was given at 2.15 am.[7]

23 November 1960

Overnight Churchill was 'restless and confused at times'.[7] However by 12.45 pm he was sitting up and reading newspapers and was most cooperative.[7] Moran assessed Churchill at 12.55 pm. He recommended that one tablet of secobarbital (presumably 100 mg) should be given initially followed by a quarter tablet (presumably 25 mg), then a further quarter if required. Churchill then 'ate a good lunch'.

At 1.45 pm Moran telephoned Seddon to say that Churchill had complained of a little loss of sensitivity over the left thumb and that he had found the left grip week. This suggested to Moran a mild hemiplegia (stroke).[6] Churchill walked to the bathroom with assistance. He appeared to 'drag' his left foot more than usual … walked back to his chair and remained out of bed until 4.35 pm.

After lunch Churchill was introduced to Piers Dixon who had just become engaged to his granddaughter, Edwina Sandys. Dixon wrote in his diary:

Winston was smoking a cigar, half sitting up in bed, winding and unwinding his hands. Edwina was I think very shocked by his condition. She said later that he had never looked so ill. She left almost immediately. She was very worried … I tried hard to think of non-platitudinous but suitable things to say; that I was exactly ten years older than Edwina. Winston replied that 'I am ten years older than my wife.'[24]

Seddon reviewed Churchill himself at 3.45 pm.

Patient sitting comfortably in his chair, holding his head well up, but apathetic and mis-communicative. Upper limbs: cannot raise left more than 90° (full active movement on 18 November 1960), grip about one-third of that on the right and the hand lay on his lap in the pen holding position. The biceps jerks were brisk bilaterally, the triceps jerk was brisk on the left but absent on the right and the supinator jerk was brisk on the right but absent on the left. There was no spasticity and cutaneous sensation in the left forearm and hand was normal. The nurses had noticed he had dragged his left foot. Some drooping of the left corner of mouth and sagging of the naso-labial fold but no demonstrable weakness of the facial muscles.[6]

For an interpretation of these clinical signs, see below.

Moran reviewed his patient again at 4.15 pm and encouraged frequent head and shoulder movements.[7] Although Churchill was tired in the evening, he ate a fairly good dinner.[7]

At 10 pm it was recorded that Churchill's 'left arm was still painful. Unable to apply very much pressure with left hand.'[7] Later in the night the nursing notes stated: 'Left arm painful, some loss of movement/poor grip. Quiet and cooperative, rather confused.'[7] Secobarbital 100 mg was administered at 10.30 pm, but Churchill remained restless until 1 am.[7]

The Times reported that Lord Moran had stated that Churchill is 'going on all right'.[25]

24 November 1960

Further sedation was declined by Churchill, but he slept from 1 am to 4 am.[7] Thereafter, he slept intermittently until 9 am. 'Rather cross and uncooperative during bed changing,'[7] nursing staff recorded. Seddon recorded during his assessment at 10 am that Churchill had been incontinent at 4 am and 9 am. On examination, Seddon found Churchill's 'grip as yesterday. No spasticity. Upper limb reflexes unchanged except the biceps and triceps are less brisk. Lower limbs possibly a little diminution of power below the left knee. No spasticity. Reflexes unchanged.'[6]

Moran assessed Churchill at 3 pm and recommended that the usual night sedation regimen be continued (secobarbital 100 mg on retiring, followed by a 25 mg tablet, repeated if necessary).[7] Churchill 'sat out in a chair from 3.30 pm until 5.00 pm with no ill effects' and was alert when he had a visitor for one hour at 5.45 pm; both Lord Beaverbrook and Mr Aristotle Onassis were listed on the engagement card for the early evening.[7,26] At 7.45 pm

Churchill 'had a wash and was very cooperative. Says he is very hungry. Ate a good four course dinner. Appears a little vague.'[7] Later that evening Howells noted that Churchill was able to turn the pages of his book with his left hand, implying some improvement in the power in his left arm.[7] Secobarbital 100 mg was given at 10.55 pm, and Churchill slept very well but was 'confused at times'.[7]

25 November 1960

Churchill 'woke up at 8.45 am, rather vague but cooperative. Had a small amount of breakfast. Slept for 1.5 hours until 12.50 pm. Visited by Lord Moran – no change in treatment ordered.'[7] Seddon also assessed Churchill and recorded:

Left arm reported to be a little stronger but some pain in the shoulder. *Evidence in favour of left hemiplegia is*:

(1) dragging of left foot said to have been present on 23rd November;
(2) Slight weakness of the left leg muscles that I found on 24th though I could not be certain of it.

Against a hemiplegia: No change in lower limb reflexes at any time. If it is not a hemiplegia it is a lower motor neurone lesion at the level of C5 – C7. But on the 23rd the biceps and triceps were brisk, and the grip was weaker than it is today. Yet the pain and vague sensory disturbance in the hand suggests a radicular lesion.[6]

Churchill sat out in a chair from 3.45 pm to 4.45 pm.[7] 'Quite cheerful but rather tired by 8 pm.'[7] Secobarbital 100 mg was administered at 10.30 pm, and secobarbital 25 mg at 12.50 am.[7]

26 November 1960

'Awoke at 9.20 am. Seemed rather depressed. Had usual breakfast of coffee and fruit. Complaining of a lot of pain in the left arm when he was first raised up in the bed. The pain did not ease during the morning.'[7] Soluble aspirin 300 mg given at 11.15 am, and the pain was much easier at noon.[7] Churchill was sat out in the chair for 1½ hours, with no ill effects, and walked to the toilet.[7] Churchill 'entertained visitors with no apparent tiredness',[7] including daughter Diana, Edward Heath (Lord Privy Seal) and a longstanding friend, Lady Violet Bonham Carter.[26] He also 'ate a good dinner, and was very co-operative'.[7]

The Times reported that Churchill was 'still going on nicely'.[27]

27 November 1960

Churchill woke at 10.45 am, when he was observed to be 'rational but drowsy', and sat out between 3 pm and 4.30 pm.[7] He also walked to the toilet with assistance.[7] Moran examined his patient at 4.45 pm.[7] It was agreed that Moran and Seddon would discuss on 28 November whether it was appropriate for Churchill to sleep again in his own bed.[7] Nursing staff recorded that Churchill was cooperative but 'rather low in spirits' in the afternoon, but was moving his left arm more freely.[7] Churchill ate a 'fairly good supper' and was reading quietly at 9.15 pm.[7] Secobarbital 100 mg was given at 10.30 pm

28 November 1960

Churchill slept until 2 am, passed urine and then slept 'restlessly' until 4.30 am.[7] He passed urine again and slept until 7.30 am.[7] He spent the morning reading newspapers, but got up for lunch from 1 pm to 2.30 pm.[7] Churchill walked to the toilet twice. 'Right eye is discharging and both eyes look reddened … eye drops instilled'.[7]

The Times reported that Churchill was sitting up in his chair and is still visited daily by Lord Moran.[28] Churchill was given secobarbital 100 mg at 10.15 pm after which he slept for long periods, though he was 'confused at times'.[7]

29 November 1960

Churchill had a 'quiet morning. Some confusion for short periods then quite rational.'[7] 'Very cooperative. Sat out of bed at 12.30 pm. Walked to toilet.'[7] 'Requested to go back to bed at 1.10 pm. Rather breathless … had lunch in bed.'[7] Churchill was 'very vague most of the afternoon. Appears to know what he wants to say but finds difficulty in completing a sentence. His inability to remember things tends to upset him more. Visited by Lord Moran at 2.15 pm. Lord Moran saw Sir W[inston] in this confused state.'[7] Seddon recorded that Churchill was 'incoherent during the afternoon. Lord Moran found him confused at 2.15 pm. Better in the evening.'[6] Churchill had a better evening. 'Fairly good dinner. Patient slow but coherent this evening – contentedly smoking a cigar.'[7] Moran visited again at 9.30 pm and found Churchill 'quite lucid'.[7] Secobarbital 100 mg was given at 10.15 pm, but Churchill had an unsettled night initially but then slept from 2.30 am until 8.15 am.[7]

30 November 1960

On 30 November Churchill celebrated his 86th birthday. The day began with him eating a 'good breakfast. Very cheerful and rational. Read newspapers.'[7] He slept from 11.30 until 12.15 pm.[7] Moran delivered his birthday present personally (Plate 19) and then assessed Churchill with Seddon who agreed that Churchill's time out of bed should be directed by Churchill's own wishes. Churchill got up for lunch, and close relatives (daughters Mary and Sarah, son Randolph, grandson Winston) joined him for lunch. His daughter Diana came after lunch and Viscount Montgomery of Alamein at 4 pm. Most importantly, as far as Churchill was concerned, was that he was allowed to transfer back to his own bed![7] Although Churchill was stated to be 'extremely tired' after celebrating his birthday, he still 'ate a fair supper'.

Moran reported: 'He is getting on very well.'[29] Churchill issued the following statement: 'I am very grateful to all those who have so kindly sent me messages of good wishes for my health and for my eighty-sixth birthday. There are so many I cannot acknowledge all of them personally, but I would like to express my warm thanks to the senders for the thought which has given me much pleasure.'[29]

A spokesman said that Churchill had spent a happy day with his family and had received a birthday message from the Queen. He returned to bed in the afternoon after luncheon but 'he will probably enjoy a cigar tonight'.[29]

Secobarbital was given as usual at 10.15 pm, but Churchill 'did not sleep for some time'.[7]

1–2 December 1960

The nurses recorded that Churchill had only slept for 3 hours the previous night. He woke up at 9.30 am when he was observed to be 'fairly cheerful'. After breakfast, Churchill had a 'quiet morning'.[7] Moran attended at noon.[7] Churchill got up for lunch in Lady Churchill's room and retired to bed at 2.30 pm to read.[7] Churchill semi-dressed for dinner. Moran saw Churchill again at 10 pm. Secobarbital was given at 10.50 pm, but Churchill 'slept restlessly' until 2.00 am.[7]

After passing urine at 2 am, Churchill slept until 8 am.[7] He then ate a good breakfast, slept for 30 minutes and then spent the rest of the morning reading quietly.[7] Churchill was semi-dressed for lunch and up for 1½ hours. 'No apparent tiredness afterwards.'[7] Churchill also semi-dressed for dinner and there was 'no apparent tiredness afterwards'.[7] Seddon assessed Churchill again and observed Churchill walking.[7]

Howells recorded in the nursing notes that Churchill demanded that the wedge be removed from his bed. It was explained to him that it was Lord Moran's wish that he should not sleep flat. Sir Winston was adamant, so the wedge was removed.[7] This was part of a long struggle between Churchill and his nurses over this issue.

Howells later wrote in his book:

> After a day's battle it was agreed that he could have his own bed back as long as he had fracture boards under the mattress to support his back while he was lying flat on a wooden support at a 45° angle to prop him up during the day. He agreed to all this and it was generally thought to be a good compromise and that he would settle down to the business of getting well again. He had other ideas however. The next day he announced that he did not intend using the back support and that he was going to take a bath. From that time onwards, it was 'open warfare' between Sir Winston and the nursing team. Every morning there was a struggle to get the angle wooden support into his bed. He firmly resisted all attempts to do this but it was always installed after a rather exhausting struggle.[2]

Churchill retired at 9.30 pm. 'Pressure areas treated. Ointment applied to groins and around anus.'[7] Secobarbital 100 mg and a vitamin B compound tablet were administered at 10 pm.[7] 'Churchill had a better night and slept flat on two pillows from 10.30 pm to 5.00 am.'[7]

3–4 December 1960

Moran agreed after visiting Churchill at 1 pm that he may have the back rest (the wedge) removed at night but that he must be kept propped up as much as possible with pillows.[7] Churchill got up for lunch and played cards afterwards, a total of 2½ hours out of bed.[7] Churchill dressed for dinner, but requested to go back to bed after an hour.[7] Secobarbital was administered at 10.45 pm. Churchill slept from 11 pm until 2.10 am when he requested and was given secobarbital 25 mg at 2.20 am.[7]

At 2.20 am Churchill awoke. Howells wrote:

[Churchill] was quite rational and alert but finding no one responded to his 'cries of help' proceeded to 'bang on the wall' with a urinal [bottle] although his bell was at hand and he had already turned on the light, used a bottle, replaced it selecting an empty one with which to strike the wall. This went on for about two minutes. Sir Winston was extremely abusive for about 15 minutes. I may say that Sir Winston when asked said he did not require anything and refused to say why he was cross. Abusive again at 9.00 am. Uncooperative!!![7]

Churchill calmed down after one hour and ate breakfast. 'Rather subdued for the rest of the morning.'[7]

Seddon saw Churchill at 1.45 pm. 'Very comfortable and cheerful. During the night he had an unexplained outburst of rage and banged a urinal (empty) against the wall so hard that this dented the plaster. He was grumpy this morning and again for no apparent reason.'[6] Moran also recorded this incident.[1]

Seddon also recorded that there was: 'A most disturbing development, a definite angular deformity at the cervico-thoracic junction which looked rather more than what one sees fairly often in old people. Had there been a second fracture? I telephoned Moran (in Stafford) and then Golding.'[6]

Churchill dressed for dinner, and Seddon visited again at 7.45 pm.[7] It was agreed again that while the bed was to remain elevated by the wedge during the day, at night two pillows could be substituted.[7] Secobarbital was given at

10.15 pm, and Churchill slept until 1.45 am when he requested more night sedation; secobarbital 25 mg was given.[7]

5 December 1960

Seddon recorded:

> We went by ambulance to Golding's rooms. Golding took superb pictures and they showed an old lesion of the 4th and 7th cervical vertebrae which were all fused. There was no change in the state of the 5th thoracic. I then recalled a serious accident the young Churchill had suffered on 10 January 1893 when he jumped from a bridge at [Branksome Dene, near] Bournemouth [see p. 6].[6]

Moran recorded: 'Seddon tells me that without this protective block it is probable that one of the cervical vertebrae would have been fractured in his fall, and then we should have been in real trouble. Winston, as I have said before, seems to have nine lives.'[1]

The Times also reported this radiological examination:

> Sir Winston Churchill went from his home in Hyde Park Gate, London, by ambulance to Harley Street for an X-ray examination. Sir Winston was examined by Dr Frances Campbell Golding, a radiologist. He returned home after an hour and 40 minutes. It was his second X-ray examination since his accident. Lord Moran ... said the X-ray 'was very satisfactory. He is making good progress'.[30]

6–31 December 1960

The Times reported that Moran had visited again on 6 December and that Churchill 'is still making progress'.[31] Seddon recorded on 12 December that Churchill was 'very confused during the previous evening and in the night'.[6] Moran recorded on 19 December:

> A bad day. Winston knows what he wants to say but cannot say it; he cannot get the words he wants. To make matters worse, the Prime Minister chose to visit him today ... I gather the meeting was rather a

flop, and they are afraid the Prime Minister will talk. Winston asked: 'How long have I to go on like this, waiting for death?'[1]

Seddon's notes indicate that Churchill was able to get out of bed without assistance on 21 December and he walked up and down the room with fair confidence, holding his head much stronger.[6]

Churchill left Hyde Park Gate on 23 December to spend Christmas at Chartwell with his family. Just before Churchill set off, two men arrived with four green steel boxes.[2] They contained the first four reels of *The Valiant Years*, the twenty-six-part film made by the American Broadcasting Company and based on Churchill's Second World War Memoirs. The reels were especially tailored to fit the projector in Chartwell's basement cinema. It was a series which gave Churchill hours of pleasure.[2]

The Churchills entertained the Prime Minister, Harold Macmillan, to dinner at Chartwell on 29 December.[32]

Churchill and Seddon

Seddon wrote to Montague Browne on 31 January 1961:

Lady Churchill was good enough to speak to Lord Moran and you to my secretary about my fee for attending Sir Winston. Sir Winston returned to the House of Commons last Thursday. That I was able to help towards this is a sufficient reward, and if he and Lady Churchill have no objection, I would prefer to leave it that way. May I take this opportunity of thanking you most warmly for many acts of kindness during what was, for a while, rather an anxious undertaking.[33]

Montague Browne responded: 'I would just like to add, if I may, what a comfort it was to us all to know that you were in charge. I think that Sir Winston's present good health is a wonderful tribute to what you did.'[34]

Churchill wrote to Seddon on 2 February 1961:

Montague Browne has shown me your letter of 31 January. Please allow me to express to you my gratitude for all your skill and care during my illness, and my warm thanks for the graceful terms in which you phrase your letter. It was indeed fortunate for me that I should have been attended by you and I am well aware of the trouble you took. I hope you will accept a photograph and a copy of my biography of *Marlborough* which I have signed for you.[35]

Before Seddon responded he sought Montague Browne's advice:

Will you please read the enclosed letter. I have no means of knowing how Sir Winston would regard an expression of an opinion on the writing of history from someone who is no more than an enthusiastic dabbler. But he could not have sent me a more welcome gift and that is why I have written more than a simple letter of thanks ... I was greatly touched by your personal note: I too hope that we may meet again though I trust on a sunnier occasion.[36]

In fact, in June 1962, Seddon led the surgical team that dealt with Churchill's fractured hip (see p. 333).[37]

Seddon wrote to Churchill on 6 February 1961:

I am grateful to you and Lady Churchill for your extremely kind letters. And may I say how delighted I am to have this excellent photograph and the signed volumes of your biography of *Marlborough*. May I dilate a little on the last. I have not yet read all your books – *The River War* was to be the next – but of those I know *Marlborough* is my favourite ... I have not yet come across a picture of it that can compare with yours. And when the subject of a biography is a hero, and Marlborough was in all conscience, I applaud the writer who brings out the heroic lineaments; when this is done the faults, the human failings, are usually faithfully dealt with too ... I shall not forget the great kindness of Lady Churchill and of yourself that so greatly lightened Lord Moran's and my task.[38]

Montague Browne wrote on 8 February 1961: 'Many thanks for your letter. Sir Winston was very pleased to see what you had written – and much interested too. He seems well, and we are off to Monte Carlo on Saturday. Au Revoir.'[39]

18 May 1961: Review by Sir Russell Brain Bt

On 18 May 1961 Churchill was reviewed by Brain:

> Some little time previously, Churchill had had a fall in his bedroom which had resulted in a crush fracture of one of his dorsal vertebrae. I was asked to see him again because he was complaining of painful numbness of the left index finger which seemed to have troubled him since his fall. I found some analgesia over the finger. There was no muscular weakness, but the left triceps jerk was diminished. It appeared to be a lesion of the 6th cervical root which I thought was due to cervical spondylosis, exacerbated by the fall. He had had his spine X-rayed and when I saw the X-rays, I found they showed gross changes: marked lordosis from the 1st to the 5th cervical vertebrae, while the 5th, 6th, and 7th were kyphotic; their bodies appeared fused together, C5 and C6 at an angle leading to the kyphosis, with wide separation of the tips of the spinous processes of these two vertebrae, apparently due to old trauma. This is the cause of the characteristic posture of his head on his shoulders.[40]

The fracture probably dated from 10 January 1893 when Churchill was unconscious for several days after a severe fall (see p. 6).

Medical Aspects

The clinical history and radiological evidence indicate that Churchill sustained a partial crush fracture of the T5 vertebra in the fall which occurred on 15 November 1960. This was initially very painful, but the pain had substantially improved within a week of the accident, as he was able to get out of bed, with the help of nurses, on 21 November, and take three steps. As to the cause of the fall, it seems likely this was due to Churchill's already unsteady gait, necessitating regular use of a walking stick, and probably acutely provoked by him turning, while walking, to speak to his wife.

Churchill complained of pain in the shoulder and left arm on several occasions over the next few days. Seven days following the fall, he reported numbness of the left thumb with pain on moving the thumb. The latter suggests a local musculoskeletal cause, while the cause of the former was not established with certainty. Subsequent X-rays of the cervical spine, which Seddon had been much concerned about obtaining, showed changes attributable to Churchill's neck trauma in earlier life, together with age-related degenerative changes. It seems probable that the fall may have exacerbated the longstanding cervical spine disease, leading to pain in the shoulder and arm and possibly also the transient sensory impairment in the thumb.

It was not until eight days after the fall, on 23 November, that Moran detected weakness of grip in the left hand, and on the same day, Seddon confirmed this and also found weakness of elevation of the left arm at the shoulder, together with a mild left facial droop, though without demonstrable weakness. On the same day, the nurses noted that Churchill was dragging his left foot.

Seddon did not find any change in the left arm reflexes, nor any increase in muscle tone in the left arm. It is noteworthy that Seddon performed his neurological examination on this day and on the following day with Churchill sitting in a chair, not an ideal posture for detecting subtle signs of neurological deficit. On 24 November, Seddon recorded that the left biceps and triceps tendon reflexes were less brisk, and there was possibly some weakness below the knee. The plantar reflexes were 'impossible to elicit because the soles of the feet are extremely ticklish'.[6] On 25 November, Seddon recorded that the left arm was stronger, but with weakness of the left shoulder girdle; he did not find left leg weakness.

On 25 November, Seddon weighed up the evidence in favour of, and against, a hemiplegia. It seems that he came down on the side of nerve root lesions as the major pathological basis of the physical signs found.

By 28 November, Churchill was walking to the bathroom, with no obvious left-sided weakness. Seddon recorded that all reflexes were present, though there was puffiness and tenderness in the left anatomical snuffbox, raising the possibility of a scaphoid fracture in Seddon's mind. On 2 December, Churchill's gait was shuffling, but 'symmetrical', according to Seddon.

Putting all this together, in retrospect there seems little doubt that, eight days following his fall, Churchill sustained a mild left hemiparesis (partial paralysis of the left side), which had substantially resolved within five days. Under the prevailing circumstances, clinical assessment was understandably difficult, and this new stroke occurred in the context of the acute crush fracture of the T5 vertebra and exacerbation of longstanding post-traumatic and degenerative cervical spine changes.

One might question why Moran did not involve Sir Russell Brain, the neurologist, in the acute stages of this episode, particularly as Brain had examined Churchill on many occasions previously. Brain was not asked by Moran to see Churchill until some six months later (5 May 1961), on account of painful numbness of the left index finger. Brain's examination revealed no weakness, a reduced left triceps jerk and reduced pin-prick sensation in the left index finger, signs which Brain concluded were due to a lesion of the sixth cervical root due to cervical spondylosis exacerbated by the fall in November 1960.[35]

We may conclude now that Churchill already had multiple medical problems and that, as events unfolded, and in the context of difficult conditions for detailed neurological assessment, it was not obvious either to Moran or Seddon that a small acute stroke had indeed occurred. It is very likely that this new stroke was again due to small vessel cerebrovascular disease, in line with Churchill's previous strokes.[3, 41–3]

Features of Churchill's ill health following the fall included periods of confusion, irritability and behavioural change including an uncharacteristic outburst of aggressive behaviour, and several episodes of incontinence. Three factors are likely to have contributed to these symptoms. First, his age: Churchill was 86 on 30 November 1960. Second, small vessel cerebrovascular disease: Churchill had already had several symptomatic cerebrovascular episodes.[3, 42, 44] In the modern era of CT and MR scanning, it is often the case that in people of Churchill's age and with similar history, imaging shows evidence of widespread small vessel disease, with multiple lesions, not all attributable to documented clinical episodes of neurological deficit.

And third, even though Moran regularly reviewed the regimen for secobarbital, Churchill was prescribed this hypnotic during his illness on a regular, probably nightly basis, often with more than one dose per night. The medical[6] and nursing[7] notes both confirm that secobarbital, a barbiturate hypnotic, was prescribed by Moran as night sedation.

The British National Formulary (1957)[45] mentions only two secobarbital (then known in the UK as quinalbarbitone) strengths, whether dispensed as a tablet or capsule: 50 mg and 100 mg. Lovell[46] described Moran's prescriptions and stated that Moran prescribed 'reds', which contained secobarbital 100 mg in tablet form, 'baby capsules' which contained secobarbital 15 mg and 'midget capsules' which contained secobarbital 7.5 mg. However, the nursing notes[7] are explicit and state repeatedly that Churchill was administered either a whole tablet or a quarter tablet, presumably therefore 100 mg or 25 mg. Of course, barbiturates are now never used as hypnotics, but their use in Churchill reflected standard prescription practice at the time. Long-term use of barbiturates can cause confusion, dizziness, depression and ataxia with an increased tendency to fall, especially in the elderly, who may suffer a fracture as a consequence.[47] Alcohol may exacerbate these adverse effects, as may opioids such as codeine which Churchill was also prescribed for pain; Churchill continued to imbibe alcohol throughout his illness.

In support of our conclusion that secobarbital was an important contributory factor to Churchill's episodic confusion, behavioural disturbance and incontinence, is the relative preservation of his cognitive function and wit, evident during this illness. His reaction to Seddon and Yeoman moving him unexpectedly to a new bed ('Narrow bed – narrow minds'), and his quip, in annoyance, to Howells on 21 November ('Yes, but I *am* a great man') both indicate that his intellect was remarkably well preserved, given his difficult circumstances. As Howells later recalled: 'It was an extraordinary performance for a man of his age.'[2]

On 27 January 1961 Seddon wrote: 'We have been disturbed by certain abnormalities of behaviour, sudden bursts of rage, periods of apathy and sulkiness, with intervals of cheerfulness. What bothered me was whether this injury had caused an acute ageing, as fractures sometimes do with old folk. But at the finish that is to say nine weeks after the injury, Sir Winston was in Lord Moran's view back to where he had been before.'[6]

And so it was that Churchill recovered once more to fight another day. In considering these events afresh now, the title of Anthony Montague Browne's account of Churchill's later years, *Long Sunset*,[48] seems highly appropriate.

Hip Fracture in June 1962 in Monte Carlo, Femoral Vein Thrombosis and Jaundice in London

I think I've hurt my leg[1]
Remember, I want to die in England.[2]

In Sir Winston Churchill's later years, the Mediterranean warmth and light, particularly that of the South of France became more and more important to him.[3] Aged 87, on 26 June 1962 Churchill flew from London to Nice for a fortnight's holiday in an eighth-floor suite at the Hôtel de Paris, Monte Carlo. Churchill was accompanied by Celia Sandys, his granddaughter, Anthony Montague Browne, his Private Secretary, two nurses (Roy Howells and Miss Robin Powell) and Sergeant Edmund Murray, his bodyguard.

The accident happened shortly before 6 am on 28 June.[4] Nurse Powell was on duty and was sitting outside Churchill's room reading a book when she heard a crash and a thud in the bedroom.[1] She ran in and found Churchill lying on the floor.[1] The crash Powell heard was the noise of the anglepoise lamp being knocked off the glass-topped bedside table; the thud was Churchill hitting the floor.[1]

Powell telephoned Howells who was asleep on the third floor.[1] Howells told her to telephone Montague Browne and Dr Roberts (See p. 447), Churchill's general practitioner in Monte Carlo, who lived at Cap d'Ail, 2 miles away.[1] Howells ran upstairs to Churchill's suite. He found Churchill lying on the floor in his bedroom covered by a blanket with his head propped up by a mound of pillows. 'He seemed reasonably calm and, smiling benignly, said, "I think I've hurt my leg".'[1] Howells has written: 'A great wave of depression swept over me as I realised the possible repercussions of the accident. Sir Winston, despite all the constant care and attention to see that he came to no harm, had fallen and broken his left leg. I knew what this could lead to; further complications which did not bear thinking about.'[1]

Montague Browne recorded that Howells woke him up and told him that Churchill had had a fall and was seriously injured.[2] 'I found WSC lying silently on the floor, propped up on pillows. He was conscious and dignified, but obviously in pain. The rather trite analogy of a wounded stag crossed my mind.'[2]

Roberts arrived at the hotel and after a brief examination telephoned the Princess Grace Clinic just outside the town and asked them to bring over a portable X-ray unit.[1] It was set up in the bedroom half an hour later, and Dr André Fissore took a series of X-rays.[1] The X-rays confirmed that the fracture was in the upper third of the femur. Churchill, still lying on the floor, was made as comfortable as possible. Roberts put his leg in a splint and by the time the ambulancemen got up to the eighth floor the whole of the hotel knew about the accident.[1] As Churchill was wheeled on a trolley to the hotel lift, dozens of maids and hotel staff gathered in the corridors. The lift was too small to accommodate the stretcher, so Churchill had to be carried down to the ground floor. Howells has written: 'He was quite a weight and the stretcher-bearers and I had to take rests on the stairs.'[1]

Churchill was carried out of the rear door of the hotel and smiled and waved to a small crowd. He was driven to the Princess Grace Clinic and was taken up in the lift and wheeled into a private side room (Room 102).[1]

An hour later Churchill was taken to the operating theatre and given an injection. A temporary immobilising plaster was applied under the direction of Dr Chatelin, the senior surgeon at the Princess Grace Clinic, to prevent movement of the fracture. After about an hour Churchill was wheeled back to his room.[1]

Celia Sandys has recalled that:

I went down to the hotel lobby and was immediately struck by the heavy atmosphere of doom and gloom. My cheerful *bonjours* were received with astonished glances, prompting me to ask what had happened. I was told that my grandfather had had an accident, and was in hospital … The hordes of reporters outside the hospital were a clear indication of the anxiety that had been engendered by the news.[3]

Montague Browne has recorded that when Churchill:

had recovered from the application of a huge plaster cast, I went to see him. I thought he was dozing, but after a minute he greeted me with a smile. I sat in silence and after a further interval he asked, quite courteously, that the others present should leave the room. He told me in an almost inaudible voice to make sure that they had gone, then said in a strong tone: 'Remember, I want to die in England. Promise me that you will see to it.' I gave the required promise unhesitatingly, but privately wondered if I would be able to carry it out, for he seemed mortally stricken.[2]

Lady Churchill was telephoned in England and the doctors responsible for Churchill's care announced that Lord Moran has said the operation should be carried out in London, where he would be in attendance.[1] 'Loud was the fury of the local doctors, with the notable exception of Dr Roberts,' Montague Browne recorded. 'Did I realise that the move might kill WSC, a man of eighty-seven who had suffered many strokes? Yes, I realised only too clearly; but I also knew that it was the only course to take, and CSC [Lady Churchill] concurred on the telephone without hesitation.'

Howells recalls another aspect of Churchill's recovery from the anaesthetic. Churchill 'roared in typical Churchillian fashion, "You monsters! You monsters! Leave me alone. Get out of here – all of you!"'[1] Churchill was furious when he discovered that he was in plaster.[1] At 7 pm that evening he had a light meal, a brandy and a cigar which the French doctors had advised against.[1] These supplies had been brought in by Howells. The 'British' (though Nurse Powell was from New Zealand) nursing team completely took over from the French hospital staff in looking after Churchill's immediate needs, not least because so few of the French nurses spoke English.[1]

Celia Sandys remembers 'how vulnerable my grandfather looked in his hospital bed with his leg newly plastered'.[3]

28–9 June 1962: Preparation for Churchill's Return Home

Montague Browne telephoned No. 10 (the Prime Minister's Office and residence) on 28 June, and within a very short time, Harold Macmillan, Prime Minister, had ordered an RAF Comet ambulance, based at RAF Lyneham, Wiltshire, to fly to Nice to bring Churchill home on 29 June. The Comet of No. 216 Squadron, Transport Command, left Lyneham at 7 pm on 28 June for Nice.[4]

Montague Browne read a bulletin to journalists in the Hôtel de Paris on 28 June: 'Sir Winston Churchill is suffering from a simple fracture of the shaft of the femur. He will return to London by air on June 29 for further treatment. His general condition is good. Sir Winston has been attended by Dr David Roberts, Prof Chatelin, head surgeon at the Princess Grace Clinic, Dr André Fissore [radiologist] and Dr Gramaglia [anaesthetist].'[4]

Montague Browne wrote to thank Roberts on 24 July: 'I should like to take this opportunity once again of expressing to you all our very warm thanks for your devoted and skilful help, and the speed with which you anticipated difficulties. I literally do not know what we should have done without you'[5] Churchill himself wrote on 24 August: 'Now that I have returned home, I should like to express to you my warm thanks for the speedy and effective care you gave me when I broke my leg. I am really much indebted to you for all the trouble you took. I look forward to seeing you again soon.'[6]

Accounts were sent from Roberts,[7] Fissore,[8] and Gramaglia[9] for NF 500 (equivalent to £660 in 2019) and from Chatelin for NF 1,500 (equivalent to £1,980 in 2019).[10] Fissore and Chatelin also requested on their fee notes a cigar 'Churchill'![8, 10]

Other reports from Monaco said that Churchill's resistance was 'remarkable – positively Churchillian'.[4] Chatelin said Churchill was given an anaesthetic, and his left leg was encased in plaster from hip to ankle and that he was 'doing very well and is resting comfortably'.[4] Lord Moran (see p. 443), Churchill's personal physician, released a statement in London stating that he was keeping in touch with the situation and had received a bulletin from Monaco saying that this 'was not a life-and-death matter'.[4] He would be waiting at London Airport to meet Churchill.[4]

The first messages of sympathy came from Prince Rainier, Ruler of the Principality of Monaco, and the Queen and Duke of Edinburgh.[4] The Prime Minister, Harold Macmillan, spoke in the House of Commons of the regret at news of the accident.[4] The Speaker of the House of Commons, Sir Harry Hylton-Foster QC, sent a 150-word telegram to Churchill containing the verbatim passage from the proceedings in which Mr Macmillan, Mr Gaitskell, Leader of the Labour Party, and Mr Grimond, Leader of the Liberal Party, sent him their good wishes.[4] Churchill replied: 'I am deeply obliged to the House for the solicitude with which it has honoured me. May I ask you, Mr Speaker, to convey my gratitude.'[11] The Prime Minister spent half an hour with Lady Churchill at Hyde Park Gate after he had an audience with the Queen.[4]

29 June 1962: Transfer to the Middlesex Hospital

Howells recorded that Churchill left the Princess Grace Clinic on a stretcher, with one of his cigars wedged in his mouth.[1] The hospital staff crowded at the windows to watch the departure of Churchill who waved and smiled at them. 'He was in fine form and showed no signs of the pain he must have been suffering,' wrote Howells.[1] The crowd clapped when they saw Churchill carried out and there were cries of 'Bon voyage!'[1]

Roberts sat in the back of the small ambulance with his patient and Howells sat in front with the driver.[1] As they drove the 13 miles of twisting Riviera road to the airport a French TV camera team drove in front of them shooting a film from the top of the van.[1] Churchill gave his famous V-sign on departing Nice Airport at 11 am, and a team of RAF nurses looked after Churchill during the flight.[12]

Squadron Leader Yetman, Captain of the Comet, said they had flown across Europe at 28,000 ft, 10,000 ft lower than was customary.[12] This made it possible to reduce the cabin pressure considerably, and so make it easier for the patient to breathe. The weather was excellent, and there were no more than 10 seconds of turbulence during the whole journey.[12]

Celia Sandys wrote that 'strapped into the stretcher bed in the body of the Comet, he looked even more fragile. I sat and held his hand, and could only hope and pray that he would make it home.'[3] Churchill was given pethidine 100 mg by intramuscular injection at 12.40 pm. On the journey home, Churchill is said by Montague Browne to have made only one remark to him: 'I don't think I'll go back to that place, it's unlucky.'

Celia Sandys told reporters in London that her grandfather had had a comfortable flight.[12] His only refreshment during the 2-hour trip was a whisky and soda, described by one of the crew as a 'very weak one'. Churchill read newspapers carrying reports of his accident and talked to his secretary and the medical staff. He appeared to be cheerful and in good spirits.[12]

Lady Churchill, son Randolph, Lord Moran and Mr Philip Yeoman, senior orthopaedic registrar, had been waiting at the airport North Terminal for half an hour before the aircraft touched down and taxied to the apron at 1.30 pm.[12] Celia Sandys waved to Lady Churchill from the cabin of the Comet as it came to a halt.[12] Once the cabin door was open, Lady Churchill hurried up the steps accompanied by Moran, Yeoman and Randolph Churchill. She greeted senior RAF medical officers and then moved forward to the specially equipped cabin where Churchill lay on a stretcher immediately behind the flight deck.[12]

On the other side of the aircraft, the door of the forward cabin was opened, and a forklift truck was driven into position.[12] Medical orderlies stepped on to the truck platform and eased the stretcher through the doorway. In the background, a group of onlookers clapped and waved as Churchill raised his right hand to give them the V-sign.[12] Celia Sandys recalls that when Churchill was carried off the plane, he spotted the crowd that had gathered to see him, and 'with characteristic spirit and typical determination raised his hand and gave the V-sign. It was worth the effort. Hugely relieved, they clapped and clapped, and he smiled as he was gently lifted into the waiting ambulance.'[3]

Howells recalls that the journey to London was most touching because every time the ambulance was caught up in a traffic jam, people ran into the road, tapped on the ambulance windows and shouted: 'Get well soon Sir Winston.'[1] On arrival at the side entrance of the Middlesex Hospital, the street was jammed with people and Churchill 'received a fantastic reception when he was carried out giving his familiar V-sign [Plate 20]'.[1] Reuters journalist, Robert MacNeil, recalls the event:

I was outside the hospital as they brought him out. I leaned close to the ambulance window to see his face and judge how ill he was. Two feet away from me, the old boy opened his eyes and smiled. He raised his hand to me to me in the famous 'V' sign of the war years. Evidently history couldn't claim him yet.[13]

29 June 1962: Admission to the Middlesex Hospital

The Middlesex Hospital had made careful arrangements to look after Churchill. He would be accommodated in a room on B floor of the Woolavington Wing, the private wing at the Middlesex. On arrival at 2.30 pm, Churchill found the room was filled with flowers sent by family, friends and admirers.[14]

Apart from Howells, the Middlesex had a team of three sisters, three staff nurses and two other nurses rostered to look after Churchill. Among them was Sister Gill Keefe whose recollections of her special patient are cited below.[15] Murray patrolled up and down the corridor outside keeping a watchful eye on everyone who went into the bedroom.[15]

Before Churchill's arrival, Miss Marjorie Marriott, Matron of the Middlesex Hospital, told Sister Keefe that she was to 'special' Churchill.

> She told me … that I was never to leave Churchill's room when on duty and, if I needed anything, I must ring the bell … I remember Miss Marriott looking at me, with those piercing eyes, and saying, 'When the ambulance arrives, you must go out and greet him, and I will take care of Lady Churchill'.[15]

Sister Keefe found herself trapped in a noisy, jostling crowd and, with difficulty, pushed her way through to the stretcher coming out of the ambulance.[15]

29 June 1962 at 6 pm: Operation Undertaken by Mr Newman and Professor Seddon

Montague Browne has recorded:

> I was much relieved when Prof Sir Herbert Seddon [in fact Seddon was not knighted until 1964] took him in charge [Seddon had treated Churchill in November 1960, see p. 309]. He was considered to be the greatest authority on broken hips, and was additionally a sympathetic and wise man. Determined too. He told me that his colleague Philip Newman [see p. 443] was to carry out the operation. 'Why not you', I demanded rather brusquely. 'Because Newman will do it twice as well as I can,' replied Seddon. 'Now stop fussing and leave us with our patient.'[2]

On arrival, Seddon recorded that Churchill was 'cheerful and not ill' and that 'he has no pain in the back … No food today.'[16] The front half of the hip spica was removed.

> Bladder palpable. Reflexes: R knee +; L knee +; R ankle jerk +; L ankle jerk not examined. Colour of feet normal. Remove rest of plaster under anaesthetic.'[16]

Churchill was prepared for surgery. He was examined by Dr OP Dinnick (see p. 434), senior anaesthetist, at 3.15 pm who documented that Churchill was 'pale but not grossly dyspnoeic. Not coughing. Impossible to examine chest properly because of plaster. Breath sounds heard on left well – less clear on right – râles [crackles] on left. BP140/80, peripheral veins reasonably full. Pethidine 30 mg IV for pain. No fall in BP. Pulse full but occasional ectopic beats on ECG which shows a very prolonged PR interval [first degree heart block] and flattened T waves in some leads ... with atrial premature beats. No immediate bar to urgent surgery as soon as blood is available.[16]

The decision was made to operate at 6 pm. Premedication of pethidine 75 mg and hyoscine 0.3 mg was administered at 4.45 pm.[16]

The X-ray of Churchill's left femur which accompanied him from France was reviewed by Seddon and showed a 'basal fracture of the neck ? some valgus of upper fragment: no displacement. Translucency in the shaft of the femur up to a point 3 ½ inches below the lower rim of the trochanter.'[16] Investigations showed that the serum proteins were normal and no Bence-Jones protein was present to suggest myeloma.[16]

The operation began at 6 pm, and Newman performed the procedure, with Seddon assisting. The general anaesthetic was administered by Drs Dinnick and Cope (see p. 432). Induction was uneventful using thiopentone [thiopental], followed by nitrous oxide/oxygen and halothane.[16] There was some fall in the blood pressure (to 60 mmHg) after Churchill was moved on the table. The blood pressure was restored with blood (1 pint), dextrose saline and switching the anaesthetic to Trilene™ (trichloroethylene) and pethidine.[16] The systolic blood pressure on the trolley at 8 pm was 140 mmHg.[16]

Seddon recorded that the fracture was easily reduced with slight internal rotation. During insertion of the pin, an area of outer cortex of the greater trochanter separated, but a repeat X-ray revealed no displacement of the fracture site.[16] A four-hole plate was connected with the nail and attached to the femoral shaft with 9/64 inch screws. The wound was closed, with suction bottle drainage, after installation of chloramphenicol 1 g, an antibiotic.[16] A dressing was applied, though there was considerable discussion over this because of Churchill's possible sensitivity to Elastoplast™, and Churchill was returned to his room in the private wing of the hospital at 8 pm, 'condition satisfactory'.[16] Lady Churchill returned to the hospital at 7.55 pm with her daughter, Diana; Montague Browne left 40 minutes later.[12]

A bulletin was issued that evening (at 9.05 pm) by the Superintendent of the Middlesex Hospital, Brigadier (later Sir) Geoffrey Hardy-Roberts which stated: 'The fixation of the fracture of the neck of the femur was carried out this evening successfully, and Sir Winston's condition after the operation is at present satisfactory.'[12] The bulletin was signed by Lord Moran, Professor HJ Seddon, Mr PH Newman, Dr OP Dinnick, Dr DH Cope and Dr Campbell Golding (senior radiologist, see p. 437).[12]

29 June 1962–20 August 1962: Post-operative Course

At 8.30 pm on 29 June, the foot of Churchill's bed was placed on 9in blocks as his blood pressure was recorded as 100/50 mmHg; dextran and dextrose saline were prescribed as ongoing intravenous fluids.[16] His respiratory rate was 22/minute. 'Pulse – some fibrillation.'[16] During the night Churchill's blood pressure rose to 150/60 mmHg, and his pulse became 'full and regular'.[16] Pethidine 25 mg was administered for pain relief. For most of the night Churchill slept well.[16]

During 30 June four formal ward rounds took place, and Seddon was present at 10 am, 2 pm and 6.15 pm and stayed the night. Moran noted Churchill's temperature was 99.4°F (37.4°C), that he was coughing well, and arranged a chest X-ray.[16] This showed an area of consolidation (suggesting pneumonia) and some evidence of a slight pleural effusion (fluid collection in the pleural cavity associated with infection) on the left side.[16] Churchill was lifted into a chair at 5.30 pm, 'a manoeuvre not acceptable to the patient, but accomplished without any apparent pain'.[16] The respiratory rate increased and at 10 pm was 30/minute.[16] The day after the operation, Lady Churchill arrived. Churchill was dozing but, when he heard his wife's voice, his face lit up: 'My darling Clemmie, darling!'[15]

Howells recorded that: 'The morning they discovered this, he was propped up in bed smoking one of his giant cigars. When Moran tried to examine him, he found Churchill unwilling to part with the cigar, wedged firmly between his teeth, so that he could listen to his chest with his stethoscope.'[14]

On 1 July Churchill had enjoyed a lunch of soup and fish and had been helped out of bed into a chair by two nurses,[17] where he sat for 2 hours.[18] Lady Churchill and her daughter, Diana, visited for 1 hour 10 minutes in the afternoon.[17] Lady Churchill told reporters that her husband 'is very much better'.[17] A thirty-two-strong Salvation Army Band also played *Onward Christian Soldiers* outside,[17] which Howells states was thoroughly enjoyed by Churchill.[14] The official bulletin issued at 11 am on 1 July stated: 'Sir Winston Churchill has had another good night and his progress is maintained.' The bulletin was signed by Moran, Seddon and Newman.[17]

Lady Churchill visited her husband on two occasions on 2 July, and during one of these visits, Churchill had smoked a cigar.[18] She told reporters, 'He is looking very well today and has been sitting up in bed.' Moran and Newman also visited their patient.[18] A bulletin issued on 3 July stated: 'There have been no complications so far.' Churchill was allowed out of bed.[19] The press representatives added to Churchill's stock of his favourite brand of cigars with the message: 'With good wishes from reporters and photographers downstairs, to whom news of your progress has been of more than purely professional concern.'[20] Montague Browne responded on 3 July: 'Gentlemen, Sir Winston Churchill has asked me to express to you all his very warm thanks both for the excellent cigars and the sympathetic and helpful way in which you have carried out your duties. He sends you his very good wishes, and hopes that you will understand if he does not sign this personally.'[21] A hospital sister told the journalists: 'He thinks it is quite wonderful of you. He is very touched.'[19]

On 3 July Churchill's pulse was 'averaging 90 instead of 68' and he was commenced on digoxin 0.25mg daily.[16] Based on the evidence of his detective, Churchill also became confused and disorientated soon after the operation,[22] and the confusion was still present on 5 July when Dr Evan Bedford (see p. 430) examined Churchill (see below).

When Churchill was being lifted out of bed to be X-rayed, he proclaimed to his doctors: 'I am a member of Parliament. I refuse to allow any more of it.' They asked for Murray's help. On seeing Murray, Churchill said: 'Murray, my dear Murray, I'm a free man. Why are they pushing me about like this? I have never seen anything like it. Look, Murray, I'll leave here before dinner tonight. All we've got to do is get out of here and across the park. I never saw anything like it.'[22] Murray responded: 'They do know what they are doing Sir Winston. They are like everybody else in the streets outside. They want to get you on your feet again. One thing's quite certain – if they say you have to stay, you can't get up and walk out.'[22] Later as Murray helped Newman to lift Churchill back into bed, Murray told Churchill to put his arms around their necks and pull yourself up as we lift you. Churchill said to Murray: 'I never imagined you would become associated with this atrocious manhandling, Murray.'[22]

The fact that it was difficult to persuade Churchill to take the medicines prescribed by his doctors has been recorded both by Howells[14] and Keefe.[15] On 4 July Churchill got up for luncheon.[23] He sat beside his bed and ate from a table. Lady Churchill told reporters: 'He is alright and seems quite cheerful.'[23]

Newspapers were delivered each day, but Keefe suggested that Montague Browne had already pared them down before Churchill saw them.[15] Keefe has written that: 'I pulled up a high stool to help him turn the pages. He started with the *Daily Express* article, with the caption "He comes under watchful eye of nurse Gillian 'Sunny' Keefe, born 1939."'[15] Churchill stabbed the paper with his index finger and said: 'Is that you? Huh – mere baby!'[15] Keefe replied: 'Maybe – but I know how to look after you,' which produced a chuckle and a twinkle.[15]

He did have the sweetest smile – so good to see after the miserable first two days of post-operation depression when, with bottom lip pursed, he had complained, 'I want to go home.' He looked so sad and vulnerable; who wouldn't, in their late eighties, with a leg in plaster, flown from France, now in discomfort and in hospital? Here, I have to admit, I gave him a hug.[15]

Churchill had a light breakfast and then read the newspapers on 5 July. A bulletin issued by the Middlesex Hospital stated: 'Sir Winston is comfortable and has had a good night. There has been some irregularity of the pulse.'[24] In fact the Resident Medical Officer (RMO) had found Churchill's pulse to be irregular and concluded that he was in atrial fibrillation.[16] Moran asked Evan Bedford to review him which he did on 5 July; he had last assessed Churchill in Carthage in December 1943 (see p. 101).[25] Evan Bedford recorded that Churchill 'was confused and disorientated and was taking digitalis in case of a recurrence of atrial fibrillation. However, the electrocardiogram showed partial heart block so that digitalis was stopped'. As the ECG showed sinus (regular) rhythm, not atrial fibrillation, the pulse irregularity detected by the RMO must have been due to extrasystoles (extra beats). Digitalis is contraindicated in the presence of first-degree heart block, identified on ECG.

Lady Churchill told reporters on 5 July: 'Sir Winston is resting well and is very peaceful. He is very quiet today and is looking happy.'[24] A bulletin issued on 6 July stated that a repeat X-ray was satisfactory and Churchill's pulse was more regular.[26]

On 7 July, Seddon recorded that there was an 'obvious femoral venous thrombosis' with swelling and tenderness of the thigh and leg.[16] Bedford was asked to attend again and advise on anticoagulant therapy. Churchill was treated first with heparin then with phenindione, both anticoagulants. The bulletin on 7 July revealed that: 'there are early signs of phlebitis in his left leg, and the appropriate steps have been taken to deal with this condition'.[27] The bulletin on 8 July signed by Moran, Seddon, Newman and Evan Bedford stated that there had been no extension of the phlebitis,[27] though the bulletin issued on 9 July stated that Churchill's left leg was more swollen.[28]

The bulletin issued on 10 July stated: 'There has been no extension of the thrombosis, and the left leg is less swollen.' Churchill read the newspapers and smoked a cigar. Mary Soames, Churchill's daughter, told reporters: 'He is extremely robust. Talking to him he seems in splendid form. We thought he looked remarkably well. He was about to have his supper.'[29]

Keefe has recorded that:

Cigars were the bane of my life. Sir Winston would take two or three puffs, then rest his hand over the ashtray and let the cigar smoulder. The free fingertips would lie in the ash. Lady Churchill had said that she did not want him to drop ash on his silk vests as it made holes. She also asked me to make sure he did not have ash under his fingernails at visiting time.' First thing in the morning, I would put the waste basket outside the door, and the 'vultures' descended for the cigar butts.[15]

On 11 July Churchill's son, Randolph, visited him. He told reporters that his father was 'sitting up in bed, smoking a cigar, sipping a glass of brandy, and wiggling his toes'.[30] Randolph Churchill also recorded his impressions later: 'He was, considering everything, looking well; he was sweetly affectionate, absent-minded and bloody-minded.'[31]

On 11 July, Churchill's respiratory rate increased to 36/minute, and his pulse rose to 108/ minute (suggesting a respiratory infection), and on 12 July many added sounds were heard in the chest again in keeping with a respiratory infection.[16] Tetracycline was commenced.[16] The bulletin issued on 12 July stated: 'Since yesterday, Sir Winston Churchill has had a slight rise in temperature, due to a bronchial infection. There has been some decrease in the swelling of the leg.'[32] The bulletin on 13 July stated: 'Sir Winston Churchill had a comfortable night. His temperature is normal, and he is coughing less.'[33] A fortnight after Churchill's operation he was well enough to have several of the stitches removed from his leg.[14] Lady Churchill told reporters on 13 July that her husband's stitches had been removed that day.[33]

On 14 July Churchill summoned Murray but then could not remember for what he wanted him. 'Never mind Sir Winston, I'll come back when you have remembered, and I shall take some time off when you're out of hospital.' 'I'll never come out of hospital,' said Churchill.[22] Murray responded: 'Don't be silly you're the only one who thinks that. Everyone else thinks you will be up very soon.' 'Out of bed perhaps, but not out of hospital.'[22] On 15 July Moran reported to journalists that Churchill 'is the same as yesterday. All is well.'[34]

The bulletin issued on 16 July stated that Churchill was making satisfactory progress and had been sitting in a chair. By 17 July, the press was informed that Churchill was able to walk unaided and move across the room to a chair on the other side.[35] Howells has written that:

A chair was placed across the room from his bed and gingerly, with a physiotherapist at his side, he walked over to it. The next day he walked 30 yards in the hospital corridor. It was a great credit not only to the doctors and nurses but also to Churchill himself. Once more he had overcome a severe disability by his sheer determination.[14]

Keefe recalls that Churchill hated physiotherapy and wasn't very communicative with the physiotherapist. 'When I encouraged him to do a simple straight-leg-raising exercise, he stared me out. I threatened to tickle his foot. To my delight, he suddenly chuckled and raised his leg. I am not sure who was having who on.'[15]

The hospital carpenter arrived to fix the door window blind.[15] As the carpenter left, Churchill proffered his right hand, saying: 'Thank you, my man.'[15] The carpenter shook hands and said: 'I was at El Alamein with you, sir.' Churchill became enlivened, and they had a brief chat.[15] The carpenter's eyes welled up, and he left fumbling for his handkerchief. 'Me too,' recalled Keefe.[15]

One day Keefe recalls that a small bottle of Pol Roger champagne arrived. 'I had never opened a bottle of champagne and twisted the wire the wrong way. I looked up, straight into the mirror above the washbasin, and saw him watching me with much amusement. I smiled back and was treated to one of those lovely smiles.'[15]

On 20 July Churchill had two non-family visitors. The first was former President Eisenhower, the second, the Prime Minister. Although on three occasions Macmillan declined to say whether he had discussed the government changes with Churchill,[36] Macmillan noted in his diary that: 'He has certainly made a wonderful recovery. He was sitting up, reading a novel of CS Forester. He seemed very cheerful and quite talkative. He strongly approved the reconstruction of the government.'[31] The bulletin issued on 20 July stated: 'Sir Winston Churchill is able to spend a few hours each day sitting at his bedside and he has taken a few steps, with assistance, in his room.'[36]

On 25 July, Lord Avon (Anthony Eden, Prime Minister 1955–7) visited Churchill and told journalists: 'Sir Winston looked far better than I dared hope. He was very cheerful and very talkative.'[37] Moran, Seddon and Newman visited Lady Churchill at Hyde Park Gate 'about several matters',[38] including arrangements for Churchill's discharge from hospital.

Churchill was 'subdued almost apathetic' on 30 July. 'Slight temperature rise this morning' (98.8°F; 37.1°C). 'Conjunctiva yellow and skin of abdomen lemony.'[16] Bile pigment and urobilinogen were present in the urine. Blood tests revealed raised liver enzyme activities (ALT [SGOT] 240 U/L and AST [SGPT] 456 U/L).[16] Dr Walter Somerville, Consultant Cardiologist at the Middlesex Hospital, was consulted and concluded this was: 'Intrahepatic rather than obstructive jaundice … Unlikely to be phenindione jaundice in light of small doses given but possible.'[16] Somerville recommended that phenindione should be tailed off more rapidly. The jaundice had faded by 3 August.[16]

Reports that Churchill had become jaundiced began to circulate on 2 August.[39] The Deputy Superintendent of the Middlesex Hospital, Mr GK Buckley, issued a statement: 'From some newspaper reports it might be inferred that Sir Winston has had an attack of jaundice of the same variety as in the past. This is not so, and he has not had any such attack.'[39] Moran said, 'Sir Winston … has seen visitors every day this week and there have been no grounds for concern at any time.'[39] Churchill had developed jaundice in 1958 probably due to gall stones (see p. 273).[40]

Churchill sent Seddon a telegram on 1 August: 'I am so sorry to hear that you are unwell and do hope you will soon be fully recovered.'[41] Seddon responded on 2 August:

Thank you for your very kind message. It is no more than a trifling upset. I think I should be back to full activity by the time you receive this note and I am looking forward to paying you a visit after lunch on Sunday [5 August]. I shall be particularly interested to learn if you are finding yourself steadier and stronger on your feet … I shall be able to come one evening next week – quite apart from official visits – at about the time when the coffee is brought into your room [see below]. You make me so welcome.[42]

Seddon recorded that the swelling from the femoral vein thrombosis had subsided by 16 August.[16]

Sister Keefe recalls that when the time came to say goodbye to Churchill, he was sitting in a low armchair after lunch. 'I sat on a footstool on the floor beside him, to be at his level so that he could hear better. He stroked my cheek and said: "My pet lamb." He then held my hand and, with complete eye-to-eye contact, said, 'Thank you." It was a beautiful, rewarding moment for me, never to be forgotten.'[15]

21 August 1962: Home Again

Churchill was discharged from Hospital after fifty-four days on 21 August. With a broad smile, a V-sign and a cigar in his hand, Churchill was carried in a chair by four attendants to a waiting ambulance.[43] Hundreds of people filled the streets outside, and nearby office windows were filled with waving workers.[43] For his return home, Churchill was immaculately turned out. He wore his grey homburg, initials WSC on the silver lining, his gold cufflinks engraved with the family crest on one side and his monogram on the other, a cream poplin collar attached shirt and a medium grey Prince of Wales check suit with knife-edge creases in the trousers. He wore a blue polka dot tie and across his six-button waistcoat hung his heavy gold watch chain.[14]

Churchill arrived home in time for lunch and celebrated his return home by calling all the staff into his bedroom for a glass of champagne.[44] The house at Hyde Park Gate was now altered so that Churchill did not have to use the stairs, and a bedroom and bathroom had been created on the ground floor of No. 27. In No. 28 a lift was installed from the ground floor to the dining room on the lower ground floor, which also enabled Churchill to have access to the garden in which he loved to sit, according to Mary Soames.[45]

Churchill-Seddon Relationship

During his convalescence, Churchill and Seddon developed a more personal relationship than the one they had established in November 1960, when Churchill was treated for a fracture of the fifth thoracic vertebra (see p. 309). Churchill told him that he found the evenings burdensome and invited Seddon join him to keep him company. Seddon explained that he was very busy but would attend when he could and that he would have his dinner beforehand and arrive for coffee.

Seddon has written:

When I arrived the coffee, brandy and cigars appeared. Sir Winston poured the coffee himself and always asked whether I preferred white or brown sugar. Then the brandy. Incidentally (I had no idea what he was like in his younger days) I have never met anyone who could make a modest dose of cognac last so long. The big ceremonial was choosing the cigar, about four boxes were placed on his bed tray. Each was opened and he pawed through the cigars to find one that was exactly right; he sniffed them, he rolled them between his fingers and listened to them. What good that did defeated me because he was deafer than me. I think I smoked these great cigars on three evenings. Then I gave up: there were just too big, and I asked if I might light a pipe instead. He agreed but added – about the cigars – you're still young: it's simply a matter of experience. Sometimes we talked. He waxed enthusiastic about Marrakech and painting there. I said I'd been once, and even done a little painting. On several evenings the Rank Organisation sent a man in with a projector and a film that they thought might appeal to him. Maybe I was in on two film sessions but can remember only one: Sink the Bismarck. I think I watched the grand old Warrior as much as the movie. He never took his eyes off it, and they lit up. He sat upright and his usually pale face flushed. His cigar went out: he just held it: his mouth opened in rapt attention. Winston was fighting the battle over again.[16]

Churchill wrote to Seddon on 17 September: 'I think you know how grateful I am for all your devotion and skill, which has enabled me to regain my health. I will not therefore enlarge on the theme beyond saying that I shall always remember what you have done for me. I hope you will accept these momentos of our association.'[46]

Seddon could not respond to Churchill's letter until 12 October (though his wife did immediately) as he was in East Africa:

You thank me most generously. May I, in reply, recall the words of a sixteenth century surgeon, Ambroise Paré, 'Je le pansai, Dieu le guérit [I bandaged him and God healed him]. What a delight it is to possess such a superb piece of silver [antique silver swing-handled basket, 1797[47]], with an inscription perfect in its simplicity [Herbert Seddon. With gratitude. Winston S Churchill[47]] ... How kind of you to add a box of cigars [50 cigars]; I have not yet finished my first supply! In thanking you for these mementos may I also say how grateful I am to Lady Churchill for her patience and understanding and to you, Sir Winston, for your kindness to Philip Newman and me – your faithful servants – which made our anxiety easier to bear.[48]

On the occasion of Churchill's 88th birthday (30 November 1962) Newman and Seddon sent him a telegram: 'Best wishes from two surgeons who hope in the words of the 51st Psalm that the bones which thou hast broken may rejoice.'[16] Churchill replied: 'I am grateful to you for your telegram and thanks to you both Psalm 73 verse 2 [But as for me, my feet were almost gone; my steps had well nigh slipped] no longer applies.'

Medical Aspects

At the age of 87, Churchill fractured the neck of his left femur, a very serious injury at this age, then as now. Apart from his great age, his general health was not good and in particular, he was known to have extensive cerebrovascular disease by this time.[49–53] In addition, there had been previous episodes of pneumonia[25,40,54] and atrial fibrillation.[25,40] Despite these adverse medical factors, his recovery from the femoral fracture was complicated only by postoperative confusion, transient jaundice and a deep vein thrombosis.

It is not known what drug or drugs Churchill was given by injection prior to the application of the plaster cast to the left leg in France, whether this was simply opioid analgesia or whether anaesthetic drugs were given in addition. Montague Browne records a rational conversation with Churchill following this procedure, whereas Howells records a seemingly irrational outburst that could be construed as either frustrated anger at what had happened, or a transient confusional state.

However, following the operative treatment at the Middlesex Hospital on 29 June 1962, there clearly was a period of confusion, and this seems to have coincided with the development of pneumonia. Churchill's recorded resistance to comply with medication almost certainly had a different basis. Churchill, used to being in complete control of events, was immobile, vulnerable and utterly dependent on his carers. He would not be unique in lashing out verbally under these circumstances.

The cause of Churchill's jaundice was probably phenindione treatment, which had been started on 7 July for the deep-vein thrombosis. He was noted to be jaundiced on 30 July. It resolved after withdrawal of phenindione treatment, which is known to induce jaundice and is mainly cholestatic in type, although liver cell damage may also occur.[55] Phenindione-induced jaundice often follows the onset of a rash and pyrexia, though typically not until the fifth week of treatment[56] and eosinophilia is a common association.[57] Although Churchill's jaundice developed earlier than five weeks, there does not appear to have been an alternative cause for the jaundice. Although Type I (mild) halothane-induced hepatotoxicity is marked by mild transient increases in serum transaminase activities, it is not characterized by jaundice and usually occurs 1–2 weeks after halothane exposure.

Churchill's postoperative stay in hospital was long (fifty-four days in all), but he weathered yet another threatening illness with his characteristic dogged determination, and with his prodigious cigar-smoking habit undiminished, perhaps reinforced by the gift of cigars from the press amassed outside the Middlesex Hospital, a well-wishing gesture surely unique in the relationship of a politician and the press!

His daughter Mary considered that although her father:

Made a remarkable recovery from this accident – attending an Other Club dinner on 1 November – yet it marked a definite further stage in his slow decline. A sad remaining witness to this are his letters: from 1961 his handwriting at times is noticeably less confident – and there are fewer, and shorter letters – but after breaking his hip Winston's writing became very wandery. The short notes are full of affection and concern, if occasionally somewhat muddled – but the message shines through.[58]

Chapter 28

Vascular Episode in the Left Leg in August 1963 at Chartwell

Are you going to take my leg off?[1]

On 21 June 1963 Sir Winston Churchill returned to Monte Carlo for his last cruise on *Christina*, the yacht belonging to Aristotle Onassis, a Greek shipping magnate who lived in Monaco. He was accompanied by his son Randolph, grandson Winston, the Colvilles ('Jack' Colville, Churchill's former Joint Principal Private Secretary and his wife Lady Margaret) and the Montague Brownes (Anthony, Churchill's Private Secretary and his wife, Nonie).

Winston recalled that:

Wherever we came into harbour a large crowd would immediately gather and Grandpapa was greeted with waves and heartfelt cheers by the local Greeks, no doubt in recognition not only of the fact that British forces had liberated Greece from the Nazis, but that, thanks to my grandfather's personal intervention when he visited Athens the last Christmas of the war, Greece was saved from Communism and consequent incorporation within the Soviet bloc.[2]

4 July 1963: Return to London

Churchill flew back to London on 4 July 1963 and attended the House of Commons on 29 July 1963, though Members were shocked by his frailty.[3] Colville dined on 1 August 1963 and stayed the night and Field Marshal Viscount Montgomery of Alamein stayed for the weekend of 3–5 August 1963.

12 August–3 September 1963: Assessments by Lord Moran and Professor Herbert Seddon

According to Churchill's engagement cards,[4] Lord Moran (see p. 443), Churchill's personal physician, reviewed him at 6 pm on 9 August 1963, though this must have been a routine visit as Professor Herbert Seddon (see p. 451), Professor of Orthopaedics in the University of London, recorded that it was not until 11.30 pm on 12 August 1963 that Churchill became pale and dizzy for about 10 minutes and sweated a good deal.[1] At 3 am on 13 August, he had a severe pain below the left knee, and the leg was colder than the right. By 4 am the pain was less and on the following day, he had none at all. When Moran reviewed Churchill, the left foot was colder than the right except for the dorsum, and the colour was purplish.[1]

On 15 August 1963 Montague Browne wrote to Lord Beaverbrook, Churchill's longstanding friend:

> Sir Winston has not been very well for 48 hours, with a very minor embolism in one leg, but it is passing and I think that he will get up today. We have kept very quiet about it as the word 'embolism' has a sinister ring and we would have been besieged by those seeking information. Other than this, Sir Winston has been rather apathetic and withdrawn mentally, but every now and then it changes.[5]

It must be presumed that Montague Browne gleaned the diagnosis of 'embolism' from Moran or Seddon.

On 18 August 1963 a prominent vein was observed by Moran along the back of Churchill's calf from a point 8 in below the knee going down to the ankle.[1] The left foot was still abnormally cold, and there was slight pitting oedema (swelling) of the dorsum.[1] When Churchill tried to walk or even put his foot to the ground it became cherry-purple, the veins were congested, and there was some pain.[1] Churchill disliked having a sock put on or removed.[1] When he got back into bed, the foot went white, but in about 10 minutes the colour returned to what it had been before the attempt to walk.[1] There was very little pain during the day, but Churchill had wakened during the night with pain of short duration. Moran telephoned Seddon and informed him of these events and followed up this conversation with a letter.[1]

At Moran's request, Seddon went down to Chartwell on 20 August 1963. Seddon recorded that Churchill looked the same as when he had seen him the year before following his left hip fracture (see p. 333).[1] Churchill complained that his left leg was uncomfortable at the back about a third of the way up from the ankle.[1] Churchill explained that it was when he tried to get out of bed he felt the pain, which radiated from there down to the heel.[1] His hip was comfortable. Nurse Roy Howells said that the two lateral toes had gone a deep purple that morning after Churchill had had his bath and he admitted that the temperature of the water was about 104°F (40°C), because Churchill refused to have anything cooler.[1] Seddon enquired about the use of hot water bottles, but they had not been used at any time.[1]

Seddon examined Churchill and observed that the general colour of the leg was 'about normal' and on pressure over the toes the return of blood was nearly as good as on the other side.[1] However, from a point below the mid-leg, the part was much cooler than on the right.[1] Only a trace of oedema (swelling) was present. Seddon could not find the enlarged vein, but there was slight tenderness of the calf muscle behind the poster-medial border of the tibia in the lower third of the leg.[1] There was no pain on dorsiflexion of the foot, no tenderness over the heel and nothing abnormal in the skin there. Both femoral pulses were easily felt, the pedal pulses were just palpable on the right and absent on the left.[1] Seddon did not attempt to feel the popliteal pulses because he had not been able to palpate them previously.[1] The tendon reflexes were unobtainable, as before. Slight but definite diminution of sensation in the sole of the foot.[1]

Seddon concluded that Churchill had suffered an acute vascular accident, and was getting over it reasonably well.[1] Moran and Seddon agreed that the best treatment would be confinement to bed, keeping the left leg cool and forbidding baths. Seddon informed Dr Ward (see p. 452), Churchill's general practitioner at Chartwell, that the threatening signs would be pallor of the leg, very sharp pain and loss of sensation in the foot and that if this occurred, he would come or, during his absence in Vienna, Mr Philip Yeoman (Seddon's Senior Registrar) would attend.[1] Seddon sent Ward a note on 24 August 1963 suggesting that the urine should be examined for diabetes mellitus.[1]

The situation was explained to Churchill, who asked Seddon if he was going to take his leg off, and then to Lady Churchill.[1] She asked how long it was likely to be before the circulation would be sufficiently good to permit him to walk again. Seddon said a fortnight, more or less.[1]

Churchill's engagement cards[4] suggest that Seddon reviewed Churchill on 23 August 1963 at 5.30 pm with Moran and Ward, but exceptionally Seddon did not make an entry in his notes. Montague Browne wrote to Beaverbrook again on 23 August:

> Sir Winston's state is stationary, which is a little worrying. He showed early signs of improvement, but they have not been maintained, and he cannot get up very much as when his foot is lowered to the ground it becomes discoloured, indicating that the impediment in the circulation is still there … Sir Winston is mentally much better than he was, and it is a great pity that his physical condition does not march with it.[6]

Seddon assessed Churchill again at Chartwell on 29 August 1963.[4] Ward reported that Churchill's blood pressure was 140/90 mmHg; no albumen or sugar was present in the urine.[1] Churchill said his leg was still a little sore, but Seddon could find no tender area anywhere, and when Seddon got Churchill to stand, he felt no pain.[1] There was no pain on forced dorsiflexion of the foot, and active movements were full and painless.[1] The coolness of the left leg was less noticeable than on 23 August, but it still blanched on elevation and was moderately cyanosed when dependent.[1] Nurse Howells said this was better than two weeks ago. With the leg horizontal, blood returned in 15 seconds after pinching a toe.[1] The left hip was normal apart from the absence of internal rotation. Seddon saw an area of redness above the lateral malleolus and warned that pressure should be kept off it; Seddon sent Ward subsequently some spongy rubber and plastic foam sheeting to apply.[1]

Seddon agreed that Churchill could walk to the toilet and his chair and sit in it for 1½ hours a day with the left leg elevated on a stool, putting it to the ground for 4 minutes, say, every 15–20 minutes.[1] Over the next ten to fourteen days, Seddon recommended that Churchill should increase the time out of bed gradually to 3–4 hours and should take no baths for the present because no one can control the time he spends in the bath or the temperature of the water.[1]

Churchill was reviewed by Moran on 1 September at 5 pm and on 3 September at 5.30 pm.[4] Montague Browne wrote to Beaverbrook again on 3 September: 'I thought you would like to know that Sir Winston is making good, though slow, progress, and he is now getting up every day and seeing a film after dinner. Mentally, he continues a great deal better than during the summer.'[7]

10–20 September 1963: Assessments by Professor John Kinmonth, Lord Moran and Professor Seddon

Seddon invited Professor John Kinmonth (see p. 440), vascular surgeon to St Thomas's Hospital, London, to assess Churchill on 10 September 1963 at 4.30 pm.[4] Moran was also in attendance.[4] Kinmonth found little blanching of the limb on elevation and less cyanosis when it was dependent.[1] There was a patch of superficial necrosis of the skin about 4 cm long by 2 cm wide about 8 cm above the lateral malleolus.[1] Kinmonth urged the nursing staff to keep it dry and advised a cradle over the feet as well as the spongy rubber.[1] Churchill was getting about comfortably.

When Churchill woke on 12 September 1963 he found a letter from his wife:

> My darling Winston
>
> Today we have been married 55 years
> September the 12th 1908
> September the 12th 1963
> Your loving
> Clemmie[8]

Seddon reviewed Churchill again with Moran and Ward at 3.30 pm on 16 September 1963.[4] Seddon recorded that there was no blanching of the limb on elevation.[1] The warmth of the foot was almost normal. Toes became pink 4 seconds after being squeezed. Necrotic patch now a dry scab only 1.5 cm x 1.5 cm.[1] It was agreed that Churchill would not have a bath until this necrotic patch had separated.[1] During this attendance, Seddon mislaid his pen which was not found until 23 September 1963. Doreen Pugh, one of Churchill's personal secretaries, wrote to Seddon to explain: 'Apparently it was in Sir Winston's study all the time, and lots of people looked at it and thought it belonged there!!'[9]

Montgomery stayed at Chartwell from 17–19 September 1963 and Moran reviewed Churchill again at 6.30 pm on 20 September 1963.[4] Montague Browne wrote to Beaverbrook on 2 October: 'Sir Winston is still in bed for most of the time. His foot shows no deterioration, but equally, little progress, and he is depressed … I hope that the household will move to London before long, and that this may have a restoring effect.'[10]

25 September 1963: Visit of Harold Macmillan

Harold Macmillan, Prime Minister until 13 October 1963 when he resigned because of ill health, went to see Churchill at Chartwell on 25 September 1963 at 3.30 pm. He wrote:

> I found him much better than I expected. Christopher Soames had told me that since the last seizure (which affected his legs) he was failing very rapidly. He doubted whether he would even know me. But since then his astonishing constitution has served him well. Actually, today was a good day. Montague Browne told me that it was an exceptionally good day. He has some very bad days when he is very moody and speaks to nobody ... He talked about the films of his life; about *The River War*, and the tents where he slept with the Spanish officer, with bullets going by just overhead. About the First World War, and his life in Admiralty House. (He was interested in the move back to No 10). He talked a lot about old friends – Jumbo Wilson, Alex, Montgomery [Field Marshals Wilson, Alexander and Montgomery]. Altogether it was rather wonderful. He remarked that he made me Minister of Housing. 'You were disappointed at the time but it made you PM.'[11]

26 September–18 October 1963: Further Assessments by Lord Moran and Professor Kinmonth

Lady Churchill had been unwell with a stress-related illness for much of the summer and by September 1963 had become 'more and more depressed, exhausted and agitated: it was decided she must have a complete break from Chartwell'.[8] She went to stay with her daughter, Mary, at Hamsell Manor, Eridge, Kent, but after a few days the seriousness of her condition became apparent, and she was 'heavily sedated ... driven up to the Westminster Hospital, where she remained, receiving proper treatment, for over three weeks'.[12]

On 30 September 1963 Lady Churchill wrote to her husband indicating she would join him for the following weekend, presumably 4–6 October 1963. Churchill expressed his delight: 'I am very glad you are about to come here and very pleased that you will select Friday as the day. I shall be delighted to see you again, and hope that it will mark a sign of a truly bright time and give me a few days which, like others in their turn, will be sweet and happy.'[13] After the weekend Lady Churchill returned to the Westminster Hospital.[3] Dr JW Barnett who was responsible for her care wrote to Churchill on 10 October 1963 informing him that Lady Churchill: 'is suffering from severe nervous exhaustion, with consequent depression and agitation'.[14]

Montague Browne contacted young Winston and told him that his grandfather was alone at Chartwell and would appreciate a visit. Winston wrote to his grandfather immediately and sent him copies of the photographs he had taken on their recent cruise.[15]

Churchill wrote:

My Dear Winston,

Thank you so much for the letter and excellent photographs. Your grandmother is unwell and is having a rest cure in the Westminster Hospital, so I am alone, and it would be very nice if you would come and see me as you suggest.

> Your loving Grandpa,
> Winston S Churchill[16]

Winston had dinner with his grandfather and received a 'splendid box of cigars' as a birthday present.[17]

Moran assessed Churchill again at 2.30 pm on 11 October 1963 and on 14 October 1963, and Dr Ward was also present. At noon on 18 October 1963 Kinmonth assessed Churchill in the presence of Moran. No more medical attendances are recorded in Churchill's engagement cards for the remainder of 1963. However, on 28 November 1963, Kinmonth met Seddon who told him he had been to 28 Hyde Park Gate, Churchill's London home, three to four times because Churchill complained of pain in the leg.[1] This was due to overuse not to any fresh circulatory embarrassment![1]

Medical Aspects

Some four hours after an episode of dizziness and sweating at 11.30 pm on 12 August Churchill developed a severe pain below the left knee and a cold left leg from mid-calf downwards. Subsequently, when Churchill tried to walk or even put his foot to the ground it became cherry-purple, the veins were congested, and there was some pain; mild oedema was present after a few days. Seddon concluded that Churchill had suffered an acute vascular accident and agreed with Moran that the best treatment would be confinement to bed, keeping the left leg cool and forbidding baths. Seddon informed Ward that the threatening signs would be pallor of the leg, very sharp pain and loss of sensation in the foot. In these circumstances he should be informed immediately. A month later Churchill had made a full recovery.

Seddon's diagnosis was correct. Acute leg ischaemia presents as a painful, pale and pulseless limb. It can be due either to an embolic event or thrombosis in an atherosclerotic stenosis. The commonest cause of a peripheral embolus in 1963 was rheumatic heart disease in a patient with atrial fibrillation. Although Churchill had suffered three episodes of atrial fibrillation (two in December 1943 and one in April 1958), these were all secondary to pneumonia and he did not suffer from rheumatic heart disease. Other sources of emboli such as aortic aneurysm must be considered. The development of a thrombosis at the site of an atherosclerotic stenosis, either in the superficial femoral artery or popliteal artery, is now the commonest cause of acute leg ischaemia. In patients of Churchill's age, the principal risk factor for peripheral arterial disease is smoking and he certainly smoked several cigars (at least partially) daily. Diabetes mellitus is another important risk factor for peripheral arterial disease but Ward excluded this diagnosis. Other risk factors include hypertension (which Churchill did not have), raised concentrations of plasma fibrinogen and hyperlipidaemia, investigations not routinely available in 1963.

On 29 August Seddon saw an area of redness above the lateral malleolus and warned that pressure should be kept off it; Seddon sent Ward some spongy rubber and plastic foam sheeting to apply. Alas by 10 September there was a patch of superficial necrosis of the skin about 4 cm long by 2 cm wide about 8 cm above the lateral malleolus. This necrotic area was in all probability due to local pressure rather than the ischaemic event.

Although Churchill had recovered physically by the middle of September 1963 he was alone at Chartwell as Clementine had been admitted to Westminster Hospital for rest and sedation. He was cheered by his grandson's visit, that of his friend and successor, Harold Macmillan, and by the visits of Field Marshal Viscount Montgomery of Alamein.

Montague Browne's prognosis was proven incorrect; Churchill bounced back yet again!

Chapter 29

Churchill's Skin Diseases*

*This tickle is quite intolerable. It kept me awake. Yes, a bloody night. The
skin man has given me fourteen ointments or lotions in turn without any
theory behind any of them. Just doling out some potion or unguent to keep
me quiet. It's a disgrace to the medical faculty.*[1]

At the request of Lord Moran (see p. 443), Dr Henry MacCormac
(see p. 441), a distinguished dermatologist, saw Winston Churchill
as a patient for the first time on 19 February 1947. The visit was
described in a letter to Moran as 'hurried from his [Churchill's] point of
view'.[1] Following this brief consultation, Churchill did not use the prescribed
ointment. Indeed he did not even obtain it![1]

MacCormac reviewed Churchill again on 23 April 1947, and on this
occasion, a diagnosis of seborrhoeic dermatitis was made.[1] Seborrhoeic
dermatitis, a red, itchy, flaky rash that particularly affects skin areas with
numerous sebaceous glands, which affected Churchill's left ear, the area
where his inguinal hernia truss (see p. 150) pressed on his abdomen and the
skin folds on his abdominal wall. Churchill was given a tar ichthyol cream
in a water miscible base (Eucerin),[1] that had a cooling effect (see below). On
24 April 1947 MacCormac reviewed Churchill again, and he was encouraged
that 'all was going well'. MacCormac noted that Churchill also complained
of itching in various places which 'I imagine cannot be dealt with by diet or
[by] diminishing his smoking.'[1]

With the forthcoming repair of Churchill's inguinal hernia in mind,
MacCormac wrote to Moran that as certain antiseptics would have to be
applied, it would be appropriate to test out those selected before the operation
on Churchill's skin to be sure that post-operatively an acute eczematous
reaction did not occur.[1] It is not known which surgical skin preparation

---

* Co-authored with Dr Ian White, Consultant Dermatologist, Guy's and St Thomas'
  Hospitals, London

antiseptics were being considered. Tincture of iodine was in regular use at the time and was recognised as a contact allergen. Application to the skin of a previously sensitised individual will cause the development of an allergic contact dermatitis. Povidone iodine and chlorhexidine were not used until the 1950s. The repair of Churchill's inguinal hernia took place on 11 June 1947 (see p. 168)[2] but it is not known whether the antiseptics were tested pre-operatively.

1948: Seborrhoeic Dermatitis, Itching and Eczema

On 22 April 1948 MacCormac was asked to see Churchill urgently as he had suffered a recurrence of the itchy seborrhoea on his face.[1] 'Seborrhoea' means excessive discharge of sebum from the sebaceous glands resulting in an oily skin. Presumably MacCormac meant 'itchy seborrhoeic dermatitis' (seborrhoeic eczema). MacCormac considered that this would settle down satisfactorily following the use of a glycerol lotion applied to the skin, dried off, and then followed by a 'tar cream in a water-miscible base'.[1] Churchill was reviewed again four days later.[1] MacCormac was pleased with Churchill's progress and prescribed vitamin B complex two capsules daily which he believed would help in the treatment of seborrhoeic dermatitis, though he admitted to Moran that he could not offer any rational explanation for the anticipated benefit.[1]

MacCormac wrote to Moran on 8 October 1948 to confirm that he would be reviewing Churchill at 6 pm on 9 October with Dr Ward, Churchill's general practitioner at Chartwell (see p. 452).[1] MacCormac reported that Churchill had developed seborrhoeic dermatitis again, and was most bothered by pruritus (itching), which had been treated in France.[1] Ward had also prescribed sedatives which MacCormac considered might help.[1] Churchill's secretary, Miss Jo Sturdee,[3] wrote to Moran on 15 February 1950 with a list of the drugs prescribed by Ward which were stated to be 'helpful and harmless',[4] though no copy of this list or of MacCormac's letter to Moran on 9 October 1948 can be found.

MacCormac wrote again to Moran on 26 October 1948 when he reported on a professional encounter with Churchill that morning.[1] Churchill had been using a:

Lead lotion [lead and spirit lotion BPC containing lead subacetate 2.5 per cent and methylated spirit] as a sort of douche to the face, which

I did not think desirable. I told him on 20 October only to dab it on over the inflamed areas, and today have prescribed a simple face spray consisting of glycerin [glycerol] with a little spirit of ether and rosemary, made up in water, which should be a mild and agreeable astringent.[1]

Presumably this concoction of glycerol with spirit of ether and rosemary was a personal formulation developed by MacCormac and had some antiseptic properties.

MacCormac continued:

I see no reason why he should not settle down quickly, but in view of the prolonged attack of dermatitis, the skin has of course become rather sensitive and more likely to react to internal and external agents, although I still feel confident that diet, in the ordinary sense, has nothing to do with the eruption. He is continuing to take the gentian and soda mixture, which subject to your views, seems to be helpful and harmless.[1]

Gentian is a typical bitter and has no recognized place in dermatology, even if relatively harmless. MacCormac indicated that he would be reviewing Churchill again on the morning of 27 October 1948.[1]

MacCormac saw Churchill on 16 December 1948 at his request.[1] MacCormac recorded that Churchill's face and hand appeared normal, and although Churchill said he suspected the condition was latent, it neither itched nor gave any abnormal appearance.

On the other hand he has developed a number of superficial patches of dry eczema about the ankles. He is what I call an eczema prone subject, and I have always had in mind the possibilities of some extension of his eruption, which worried me considerably during the war period, as it would have been so easy to convert a simple process into an extensive and severe eruption by injudicious treatment. The lesions on his ankle are largely traumatic – the bath and soap and water – and I think can be cleared up and the skin protected by simple boric zinc ointment.[1]

The word 'irritant' would now be used rather than 'traumatic'. Presumably MacCormac considered Churchill to have developed so-called 'asteatotic eczema'. The eczema often has a distinctive crazy-paving appearance with diamond-shaped plates of skin separated by red bands. Avoiding the irritant factors and regular application of an emollient/moisturiser usually settles the condition without further intervention. Zinc ointments were commonly used. Boric acid has mild antiseptic properties and was used for this purpose at the time.

MacCormac continued:

> I suggested a more complicated procedure, but he took this rather unkindly, although the mood soon passed! I have asked him to continue the gentian and soda, which he does not like, but which it seems to me has really done good. As he is going to France in the near future I have suggested seeing him again if that is possible. I may say in confidence I think the French dermatologists were inclined to over-treat him.[1]

1949: Retirement of Dr Henry MacCormac for Medical Reasons

MacCormac continued to see Churchill on a regular basis, but on 10 March 1949 he wrote to Moran:

> I have sometimes suffered from minor attacks of angina, which have been progressively worse and culminated in a rather more severe upset the other day. I am carrying on my work at my consulting rooms and occasionally elsewhere, which I can do quite well. This letter is about Mr Churchill. As you know he rings me up to go to him, which I can do with pleasure, regarding it as a very great honour. But I do not think I should be able to get over to him at once, as in the past, as it is unlikely that I shall drive my car again, and that will mean a certain amount of readjustment. I hope you will not have any further trouble, but it might be as well to have another dermatologist available, and this of course will be a matter for your decision and choice ... I am making this suggestion on his behalf, as I would not wish to inconvenience one whom I regard as the greatest Englishman.[1]

Moran replied by return:

> I was distressed to hear that you are having this trouble. I trust that the attacks may remain minor in degree and infrequent. About Churchill,

I am most grateful for all you have done in the past, and very loath indeed to lose your valuable advice, but if you really would like me to make other arrangements I do not feel, in the circumstances, that I ought to argue with you. He's going abroad as you know, I think today week, and I propose to do nothing pending his return, in case you feel better and were able to reconsider your decision.[1]

On 27 April 1949 MacCormac wrote to thank Churchill for his very kind letter received the day before. He was particularly touched by a signed copy of one of Churchill's books: 'It will be my most cherished possession.'[5]

Churchill must have been helped by the treatments prescribed by MacCormac because he wrote to Moran on 13 November 1950: 'This face spray, which your friend Dr MacCormac prescribed for me, has done me a lot of good. I have used it for nearly a year and have been able to give up many other condiments and unguents which I used formerly. I should like to know your opinion about it and whether there is anything in it which will do harm if one relies on it for too long.'[6] No response from Moran can be found.

McCormac died on 12 December 1950[7] and Churchill wrote to his widow on 29 January 1951: 'He always attended to me with the greatest skill and courtesy, and this I shall not easily forget.'[8] Mrs MacCormac replied the following day: 'My husband as you know considered it a great privilege to attend you. I shall always remember the day he brought home the copy you so kindly gave him of *Their Finest Hour*. I had seldom seen him so happy, and proud. You were often in his thoughts during the last days of his illness.'[9]

1951–2: Appointment of Dr RMB MacKenna and Assessment for Boils

Dr RMB MacKenna (see p. 441), another distinguished dermatologist, succeeded MacCormac as Churchill's dermatologist and first reviewed him on 30 January 1951.[1]

He complains that the skin of the cheeks is a little itchy but there is less rash visible. The eruption on the lower parts is fading very satisfactorily. I saw no reason to make any change in treatment and explained fully to him that a change might be more disadvantageous than helpful

... May I take this opportunity of thanking you for asking me to see Mr Churchill; it is a very great honour.[1]

Gilbert recorded that MacKenna wrote to Churchill on 5 April 1951, though the letter cannot be found in the Churchill Archive at Churchill College, Cambridge:

I am anxious that you should take the tetramycin [probably Terramycin, that is oxytetracycline, a tetracycline antibiotic], although I realise you may be reluctant to do so, for if boils do form in the armpit they tend to be deep and difficult to cure. The small nodule you showed me this morning is the right phase for the tetramycin to attack it. Supplies of tetramycin are very short.[10]

This may have been a simple boil but it would be unusual to develop such an infection at this site at Churchill's age. A topical antimicrobial such a tincture of iodine and a paste would have been used in addition to oral oxytetracycline.

Three months later Churchill mentioned the use of oxytetracycline in a speech at the Royal College of Physicians on 10 July 1951 at which he received the first Honorary Fellowship and spoke in honour of Moran whose portrait was being unveiled (see p. 206).[11]

On 25 July 1951 MacKenna wrote to Churchill thanking him for his great kindness in giving him four beautifully bound books: ... which I shall read with all the extra pleasure which comes from following the thoughts of an author whom one knows, and with the added epicurean enjoyment of increasing one's knowledge of history by perusing the work in such a superb edition. It is most generous of you to have rated my small services so highly and I find it difficult to discuss appropriate words in which to thank you. Perhaps if I say that the gift comes at a time when I'm in that morbid state – common to all of us – of revising my Will and that I am having a paragraph inserted so that my boys shall each – in their turn – have a share in these treasured possessions, you will realise something of how I value the gift.[12]

On 11 October 1951 Moran recorded that: 'He [Churchill] had been impressed by the X-rays; it was a "wonderful machine". Turning to MacKenna he said: "Immediately I had it I felt the benefit; I believe they will cure the bloody itching over my shoulders. I would like another dose today."'[13] Probably Churchill was given Grenz rays, that is low-energy, non-penetrative electromagnetic radiation, though conventional X-Rays at 10–20 per cent of the skin erythema dose could also have been administered (see below).

On 27 May 1952 MacKenna wrote to Moran:

I have just learned from Mr Churchill that you have been in the hands of the surgeons – a sad fate for an ex-P.R.C.P [President of the Royal College of Physicians], but may be less dangerous than being in the hands of a brother physician, for the surgeons can do things dramatically, and when they succeed the results are excellent. I was glad to learn you will soon be 'fit for duty' again.[1]

The identity of the surgical procedure is unknown. There are no entries in the Moran published record between 19 April 1952 and 1 June 1952 and Moran's biographer, Lovell, does not mention the episode.[14] As regards Churchill's progress, MacKenna continued: 'The PM is much better in regard to boils but the itching on the shoulders is very troublesome and I have given him a small dose of X-rays on a limited area on each shoulder, which should assist. He is now using "the spray" to relieve the itching.'[1]

Moran wrote to MacKenna on 31 October 1952: 'The patient seems in pretty good form, though from time to time he grumbles that his irritation is still there. But when I don't comment, he says no more.'[1]

1954: Seborrhoeic Keratosis

MacKenna saw Churchill again on 27 October 1954.[1] Churchill was:

Still worried about the seborrhoeic wart [seborrhoeic keratosis, 'senile wart'] on the right lumbar area and asked to have it removed. I told him I thought it was most unwise to tamper with this lesion. It is completely innocent at present and likely to remain so. If we remove it either by excision or with a curette he would have a scar which might well become chafed and rubbed by his waistband and be much more of a nuisance than the wart is now. In these circumstances I suggested we try softening the wart by applying an ointment at night containing equal parts of glycerin of starch and Ung. Acid. Salicyl [salicylic acid ointment].

MacKenna continued: 'He asked me to prescribe for a tendency to dryness in the nasal vestibules. He has had this symptom for years and I should think it is probably due to irritation of the mucosa by tobacco smoke. I ordered a little white vaseline to be applied at night.'[1] Vaseline®, a white soft paraffin (petrolatum), remains in widespread use as an emollient.

On 10 November 1954 MacKenna reported to Moran that the seborrhoeic wart was softening and doing well.[1] 'He is quite pleased with the result although of course is not free of the lesion. He seems however to be more comfortable.'[1] By 24 November 1954 MacKenna found the seborrhoeic wart was softening 'very nicely' and so he had increased the amount of salicylic acid in the ointment to 2 per cent. 'The nose is comfortable. He complains of slight itching in the groins. Remembering the trouble with boils etc. we had a few years ago I examined him carefully but could find nothing except slight irritation from perspiration to account for the symptom.'[1] This indicates that scarring from the previous 'boils' was not present.

'I suggested that he should apply a <u>thin</u> smear of Eurax™ [crotamiton] ointment which should relieve itching and after he has done this he is to imply apply some talcum and boric powder which was also ordered.'[1] Crotamiton remains available as a topical antipruritic. Talcum powder applied to the groin area reduces chaffing and is still used for this. Boric acid has a slight antimicrobial effect but is no longer used.

MacKenna found 'little wrong with his skin' when he reviewed Churchill on 15 December 1954.[1]

1955: Carbuncle

On further review on 26 January 1955 Churchill complained of 'slight itching in the armpits'; indicating the axillae were now affected as well as the groin area, though again 'nothing abnormal' was seen on examination and MacKenna again recommended Eurax™ cream.[1]

In April 1955 Churchill was suffering from a carbuncle (a collection of boils with multiple drainage channels) and Moran recorded on 5 April that:

It had been arranged that Winston's carbuncle should be treated with X-rays at MacKenna's house at half-past six, but it was seven o'clock before the P.M. turned up.... While he was taking off his clothes he [Churchill] asked MacKenna whether any microbes had grown in the cultures he had taken from the carbuncle [carbuncles are due to staphylococcal infection]. 'Yes, plenty.' 'What were they like?' persisted Winston. 'Virulent,' answered MacKenna. 'Virulent,' repeated Winston, 'but I trust not malignant. We must use terms with precision. Tell me when you begin the X-rays.' 'They have begun,' responded MacKenna reassuringly ... Then Winston, still smoking his cigar, shuffled to a seat with his trousers round his ankles.[15]

A separate letter from Moran indicated that oxytetracycline had been prescribed for five days.[1]

On 17 November 1955 Churchill was found by MacKenna to have a 'healing septic lesion on the left side of the chest which has been either a boil or carbuncle, and two small pimples on the right arm; for all of these I have ordered neomycin [an aminoglycoside antibiotic still used topically] ointment'.[1] MacKenna recorded that Churchill was still 'plagued with the itching', although there was nothing to see and he advised Moran that if Churchill 'would only keep bath water off his skin especially on the shoulders he would improve, I think, but unfortunately he loves his bath dearly'.[1] On further review on 30 December 1955 MacKenna reported to Moran that Churchill's skin 'seems to be fairly comfortable and he is continuing with his present remedies'.[1]

1956: Itching

MacKenna reviewed Churchill again at Moran's request on 11 February 1956 because the itching was '... a little more troublesome than it was and has been waking him at night'.[1] Two new (unnamed) local remedies were prescribed but MacKenna was not optimistic that they would provide relief.[1]

A further review took place on 26 July 1956 at 28 Hyde Park Gate, Churchill's London home in South Kensington. For itching, Churchill was prescribed chlorphenamine 4 mg three times daily (a sedative antihistamine), one tablet of Bellergal™ (belladonna leaf 100 µg, ergotamine 300 µg, phenobarbital 20 mg) twice daily and diphenhydramine (an antihistamine) cream.[1] Calmitol™ (camphor, menthol, hyoscyamine, chloral hydrate) lotion was also employed.[1]

MacKenna reviewed Churchill again on 13 September 1956 when he complained of 'a little more trouble with the itching which now extends to the hips'.[1] On examination, MacKenna could find 'very little visible'. Chlorphenamine and Bellergal™ were continued and a new astringent spray was initiated containing lead subacetate 2 per cent and phenol.[1] Phenol has anti-septic properties, but low concentrations also have an anti-pruritic affect; it is still used in calamine lotion.

1958–60: Intertrigo

MacKenna reviewed Churchill on three occasions in May 1958.[1] On the first occasion, he observed that there was intertrigo (a superficial inflammation of two moist skin surfaces that are in contact) of the thighs, slight balanitis (inflammation of the glans penis) and a nasty crack in the upper part of the natal cleft (the deep groove which runs between the two buttocks) over the bottom of the sacrum.[1] Microorganisms that are normally resident on flexural skin multiply in the warm moist environments.

At review a week later the balanitis and intertrigo were 'doing quite well but I am worried about the fissure over the bottom of the sacrum. This could easily develop into a bedsore; I am dealing with it with hydrocortisone [a steroid] and neomycin [an antibiotic]'.[1] Hydrocortisone was included for its anti-inflammatory properties. Fortunately, this treatment helped and on 28 May 1958 MacKenna reported to Moran that the 'natal cleft is better in that the redness of the fold has diminished but the small fissure in the skin is still present and I do not like its indolence'.[1] MacKenna prescribed triiodothyronine (a thyroid hormone) ointment which he considered often promoted healing and was also considering a ripple mattress.[1] Experimental data in mice and rats have been published more recently suggesting that topical triiodothyronine stimulates epidermal proliferation and dermal thickening.[16]

In September 1958, Dr David Roberts (see p. 447), Churchill's doctor in the South of France, wrote to MacKenna to explain that during Churchill's stay at La Capponcina at Cap d'Ail, across the bay from Monte Carlo, as the guest of Lord Beaverbrook (Lord Privy Seal, 1943–5 and newspaper proprietor), he had suffered from pruritus and intertrigo, which he considered had been aggravated by hot weather, perspiration and humidity. A lesion on

Churchill's shoulder was the most irritating of all 'and as you will see it is a small keloid scar that I have been treating with sedative applications. I did suggest to Sir Winston that this condition could be completely eradicated by electrocautery.'[1] A keloid is a bulky scar that develops in the skin as a result of injury that spreads beyond the borders of the original area damage. Electrocautery of a keloid/hypertrophic scar may result in recurrence of the scar.

Churchill was assessed by MacKenna on 4 April 1959 and 6 April 1959,[17] though no clinical notes are available. At 7 pm on 22 November 1960 Churchill, who was in bed recovering from a fracture of his fifth thoracic vertebra, was visited by MacKenna who recommended that Churchill's usual prescriptions ('lotions and ointments') for his skin diseases should be continued.[18]

Medical Aspects

Churchill was 72 when the first record of a dermatological complaint is available. He was diagnosed as having seborrhoeic dermatitis, which is a common, relapsing condition consisting of erythematous patches with superficial scaling.[19,20] Areas of skin with a high density of sebaceous glands are particularly affected; these areas include the scalp, face, anogenital areas and large flexures. It is not explicitly stated what part of Churchill's left ear was affected. Retro-auricular involvement is often seen in seborrhoeic dermatitis; otitis externa may be considered a variant. Pruritus (itch) is variable. Ordinary dandruff (pityriasis capitis) is also considered a mild variant.[21] Commensal lipophilic yeasts of the genus *Malassezia* (previously called *Pityrosporum*) are associated with seborrhoeic dermatitis and considered pathogenic through possible immunological mechanisms.

Seborrhoeic dermatitis is not usually linked to any underlying illness but fatigue and 'psychological stress' can sometimes trigger a flare of the condition. Flexural psoriasis and intertrigo may affect the large flexures and have a similar clinical appearance to seborrhoeic dermatitis.

The initial treatment was with an ichthammol-based ointment; this was an established treatment at the time of Churchill's presentation in 1947. Ichthammol is a product obtained by dry distillation of sulphur-rich oil shale, sulfonation of the resulting oil and then neutralization with ammonia. It is a viscous, water-soluble substance with a characteristic bitumen-like odour.

Pharmacologically it has anti-inflammatory, bactericidal and fungicidal properties; it remains in use to the present day though largely superseded by topical steroids.

It is not stated whether the product prescribed contained coal tar in addition to ichthammol or whether the term 'tar ichthyol' refers to the source of the product. However, coal tar has been used for medical purposes since the early 1800s. It is a complex mixture of phenols, polycyclic aromatic hydrocarbons and heterocyclic compounds demonstrating antifungal, anti-inflammatory and anti-pruritic properties. The use of tar preparations remains a useful and effective remedy for seborrhoeic dermatitis.[22]

MacCormac also prescribed glycerol for Churchill's seborrhoeic dermatitis. Glycerol remains widely used as a humectant in skin preparations, that is in moisturisers, for dry skin. As glycerol is hydroscopic, the skin will not 'dry'. MacCormac may have intended the glycerol lotion as a cleansing agent.

MaCormac also recommended the use vitamin B complex, but could not provide an evidence basis. There was a contemporaneous personal view by an American dermatologist that rosacea was caused by vitamin B deficiency. As rosacea and facial seborrhoeic dermatitis can co-exist, this may have led to this recommendation.[23]

Smoking is associated with a number of skin conditions, including psoriasis, hidradenitis suppurativa and palmar plantar pustulosis, but Churchill did not suffer from these conditions. Smokers may be more severely affected than non-smokers by many inflammatory skin diseases,

Although Churchill had been using lead and spirit lotion BPC (containing lead subacetate 2.5 per cent and methylated spirit) on the recommendation of MacCormac, he had been applying it rather generously. In 1948 lead acetate-containing lotions were used externally for bruises, wounds, abscesses, erysipelas, ulcers, skin cancers, whitlows, piles, scabies and to treat poison ivy dermatitis. Although lead acetate can be absorbed rapidly through the skin, such treatment does not cause systemic lead poisoning unless application is prolonged.

Churchill developed pruritus affecting the shoulders and was treated with 'X-rays'. It is not known whether this term refers to Grenz rays, which are part of the electromagnetic spectrum comprising low energy (ultrasoft) X-rays or conventional X-Rays. Grenz rays were so called as it was believed that the biological effects resembled those of UV light and traditional X-rays and hence were on the border between the two (Grenz means 'border' in German). Grenz rays are essentially absorbed within the first 2 mm of skin.

Grenz rays have been used as a treatment of eczema, psoriasis, palmoplantar pustulosis, lichen simplex chronicus and other dermatoses; such use has now been all but abandoned. The mechanism of action is unknown but Grenz rays have effects on the Langerhans cells in the epidermis. Conventional X-rays at 10–20 per cent of the skin erythema dose were also used at this time and resulted in rapid reduction in pain and accelerated healing for the treatment of carbuncles.

Seborrhoeic keratoses are exceedingly common on the trunk but other sites may be affected. They are usually asymptomatic but may be pruritic. They are benign and usually left untreated unless symptomatic or cosmetically unacceptable. There would be no clinical indication for excision unless for diagnostic purpose, such as to exclude malignancy in a pigmented keratosis that may have an appearance suggestive of a melanoma. Curettage continues to be used together with gentle cautery of the base. Cryotherapy using liquid nitrogen was available in 1954. Salicylic acid has a keratolytic effect so the stratum corneum is softened. With such treatment a seborrhoeic keratosis may be soften to the extent that it may be rubbed or picked away.

Churchill may have been susceptible to intertrigo due to his background of seborrhoeic dermatitis. Intertrigo describes an inflammation of the skin in the flexures or body folds, particularly the axillae, groins, under a protruding abdomen and natal cleft where the skin is moist. It is particularly common in people who are overweight. Microorganisms that are normally resident on flexural skin, the microbiome, multiply in the warm moist environments. Although intertrigo can be caused simply by the warm moist environment in a susceptible individual, seborrhoeic dermatitis and a psoriatic diathesis may be a cause.

The presence of flexural seborrhoeic eczema/intertrigo can be considered a fertile ground for the development of boils (furuncles) and carbuncles, which are caused by infection with staphylococcus. One may speculate that Churchill may have been a nasal staphylococcal carrier with his history of dryness of the nasal vestibules.

Over the decade of Churchill's dermatological history, the differences in clinical practice compared with the present are evident. The use of X-rays in dermatology had been largely abandoned by the 1940s but Grenz rays were in use until the 1970s. Antibiotics, topical steroids and antihistamines during the 1950s were novel compared with their widespread use now. The use of bespoke concoctions has all but disappeared as medicine has become evidence-based and not anecdotal.

Chapter 30

Did Churchill Suffer from the 'Black Dog'?[*]

Black Dog: Winston's name for the prolonged fits of depression from which he suffered.[1]

Accrording to the *Oxford English Dictionary* [2] the first use of the phrase 'black dog' to describe melancholy and depression was in 1776 by Dr Samuel Johnson, the creator of the *English Dictionary*, who suffered from depression. Johnson called his melancholia 'the black dog' in conversations and correspondence with his friends, including Hester Lynch Thrale (also known as Piozzi), whose diaries and correspondence are an important source of information about Johnson.

In 1969, the psychiatrist Anthony Storr published an essay *Churchill: the Man*,[3] reprinted in 1980 as the first chapter of his book, *Churchill's Black Dog and Other Phenomena of the Human Mind*.[4] This essay established very firmly in the public imagination that Sir Winston Churchill suffered throughout his life from recurrent attacks of severe depression, or even manic depression (bipolar disease). Indeed, Churchill's depression is now taken for granted as being almost as much a fact of his biography as that he was born in 1874 and died in 1965.

Storr begins his influential and seminal essay as follows: 'The psychiatrist who takes it upon himself to attempt a character study of an individual whom he has never met is engaged upon a project which is full of risk ... psychiatrists who attempt biographical studies of great men are apt to allow theory to outrun discretion.'[3]

He then throws caution to the wind. His hypothesis is as follows: Churchill was genetically predisposed to melancholia, a predisposition that was reinforced by an upbringing peculiarly liable to result in depression. His beloved mother was neglectful of him: she was more interested in the social whirl than in her

---

* Co-authored with Dr Anthony Daniels, Consultant Psychiatrist, and published in part in the *Journal of the Royal Society of Medicine*[5]

offspring. His greatly admired father, Lord Randolph Churchill, was neglectful too, and in so far as he took any notice at all of the young Winston, it was to point out his deficiencies. He did not think much of his son, believing that he was not clever enough for the law and that the army would have to do for him instead. When Winston offered to be Lord Randolph's private secretary, Lord Randolph turned him down with contumely.

Not long afterwards, Storr's hypothesis continues, Lord Randolph died, and his son spent the rest of his life trying to come up to his deceased father's high standards of achievement in order to earn his love and approbation, a futile and impossible task of course because his father was dead. In the absence of demonstrative parental love, then, Winston Churchill was permanently insecure and tried to earn that love by exceptional activity and accomplishment, which caused him to be hyperactive except when it became obvious that such accomplishment would never make up for the absence of love, whereupon he became depressed. He therefore veered between hyperactivity and his Black Dog. Such is Storr's hypothesis. This is a plausible story, but of course much of the hypothesis is undermined if, in fact, Churchill did *not* suffer from serious depression.

Storr concluded:

It is at this point that psychoanalytic insight reveals its inadequacy. For, although I believe that the evidence shows that the conclusions reached in this chapter are justified, we are still at a loss to explain Churchill's remarkable courage.

In the course of his life he experienced many reverses: disappointments which might have embittered and defeated even a man who was not afflicted by the 'Black Dog'. Yet his dogged determination, his resilience, and his courage enabled him, until old age, to conquer his own inner enemy, just as he defeated the foes of the country he loved so well.[3]

The evidence that Storr adduces in favour of Churchill's supposed depression is repeated over and over again in subsequent studies, so that on reading certain passages one has a powerful sensation of déjà lu. As John Ramsden, the historian, has stated: 'Storr's view of Churchill strongly influenced all later accounts, sometimes dangerously so in the more inexpert hands.'[6]

Post and Robins[7] stated categorically: 'The best documented case of depression of a political leader is that of Winston Churchill [the authors reference Storr[3,4] and Moran[8] to support this contention] … He ruefully characterized his depression as "my black dog", a faithful companion, sometimes out of sight, but always returning.'

Lord Owen, a former Foreign Secretary, who was a qualified doctor and senior trainee in clinical neurology, cited Storr as his authority for the statement: 'Throughout his life Churchill suffered from bouts of severe depression.' Owen goes further in his book about the psychopathology of politicians, *In Sickness and in Power*: 'The testimony of those who worked closely with Churchill does imply a manic as well as a depressive side to him'.[9]

Nassir Ghaemi, a professor of psychiatry, in a best-selling book titled *A First-Rate Madness*,[10] cites a lengthy passage from Storr's essay to buttress his argument that Churchill suffered from depression, to his and his country's advantage. It was, according to this author, Churchill's tendency to depression that made him a political realist during his years in the wilderness and during the rise of the Nazis, and he even goes so far as to claim that it was Churchill's depression that caused him to be in the wilderness in the first place.

Ghaemi states:

There is no doubt that he had severe periods of depression; he was open about it – calling it, following Samuel Johnson, his 'Black Dog'. Apparently his most severe bout of depression came in 1910, when he was, at about age 35, Home Secretary … Churchill suffered from more than depression, though. Many historians now acknowledge his depression, but they generally don't appreciate that when he was not depressed, Churchill's mood shifted frequently … Numerous physicians who knew Churchill or studied him have concurred on the view that he likely had a cyclothymic personality, which, as we now know, is biologically and genetically related to Bipolar Disorder. For example, Lord Russell Brain, a famed British neurologist, new Churchill for almost two decades and saw him as a patient for twenty visits. Lord Brain concluded that Churchill 'had the drive and vitality and youthfulness of a cyclothyme'.[10]

Ghaemi continues:

These observations suggest that when he wasn't depressed, Churchill probably had hypomanic (mild manic) symptoms: he was high in energy, highly sociable and extroverted, rapid in his thoughts and actions, and somewhat impulsive. He would routinely stay awake late into the night, with a burst of energy after midnight when in his bathrobe, he would dictate his many books and conduct much of his other work. He was incredibly productive, not only serving as a minister or prime minister for decades, but writing forty-three books in seventy-two volumes (not to mention an immense body of correspondence) ... Churchill was treated for his moods throughout his life. We have no evidence that he received much treatment that was specifically psychiatric, mainly because the first psychiatric medications weren't discovered until the 1950s. However, his doctor, Lord Moran, gave Churchill amfetamines at least in the 1950s, and possibly earlier. Amfetamines are effective antidepressants and were the most commonly used drugs for depression in the 1930s and 1940s; they're sometimes prescribed for depression even now.[10]

The conclusions that Ghaemi has drawn will be challenged below.

In addition, other authors have drawn a similar conclusion without citing Storr. Andrew Solomon, in *The Noonday Demon: An Anatomy of Depression*, states that both Abraham Lincoln and Winston Churchill 'suffered from depression (and used) their anxiety and their concern as the basis for their leadership, but that requires a truly remarkable personality and a particular brand of depression that is not disabling at crucial times'.[11] Andrew Norman, a medically qualified author, has argued in his book *Winston Churchill: Portrait of an unquiet mind*[12] that Churchill should be described as a 'hypomanic-depressive'.[13]

Some, including Best, have accepted that Churchill's 'Most evident recurrent affliction was not physical but psychological: depression ... its importance has been exaggerated' and that 'It never stopped him doing anything he wanted to do.'[14] Most importantly, Attenborough (who has written a detailed rebuttal of the conclusions of Moran, Storr and others in *Churchill and the 'Black Dog' of Depression*[15] and in *Diagnosing Churchill: Bipolar or 'prey to nerves'?*[16]) and Gilbert, Churchill's official biographer, have come to the conclusion that Churchill's 'black dog' was a transient, never significantly disabling, reaction to serious misfortunes for himself or for Britain and was insignificant when compared with Churchill's resilience, courage and leadership at times of major setback or crisis.[15,17]

Gilbert described Churchill as: 'A man often angered and saddened by the bad turn of events, but having unusual resilience to come back fighting within a short time; not someone incapacitated through mental ill-health or through excessive drinking.'[17] This opinion was based on Gilbert's detailed assessment of the 'daily records of the war years' and beyond. But Gilbert's opinion also took note of the views of those closest to Churchill such as his daughter, Mary, and Sir John Colville, Churchill's Joint Principal Private Secretary, 1951–5 (and Assistant Private Secretary 1940–1 and 1943–5). The opinions of Lady Soames and Sir John Colville are discussed further below.

So what is the evidence that Churchill suffered from repeated episodes of 'black dog', that is from a Major Depressive Disorder as defined in the fifth edition of the *Diagnostic and Statistical Manual of the American Psychiatric Association (DSM-5)*[18] or from a Bipolar I Disorder or from a Bipolar II Disorder?

Evidence from Sir Winston Churchill

In none of Churchill's own published writings does the term 'black dog' occur, though the term can be found in a letter he sent to his wife dated 11 July 1911[19] and this is hinted at in a second letter dated 28 January 1916.[20]

The first letter was written as Churchill was about to join his wife at the seaside.[19] Churchill reported that the wife of a cousin had been cured of depression by a doctor in Germany.

> Very nice dinner last night with Ivor & Alice [Guest; later Viscount and Viscountess Wimborne)]. Pretty pleasant friendly people … Ivor considers himself still an invalid for all purposes except pleasure! Alice interested me a great deal in her talk about her doctor in Germany who completely cured her depression. I think this man might be useful to me – if my black dog returns. He seems quite away from me now – it is such a relief. All the colours come back into the picture. Brightest of all your dear face – my darling.[19]

This statement implies strongly that at some time *in the past* ('quite away from me now') Churchill had suffered from the 'black dog', which he equates to depression.

The second letter dated 28 January 1916 was written to his wife Clementine while Churchill was serving as battalion commander on the Western Front during the First World War:

You must not suppose that any of my depressions here have any relation to those terrible and reasonless depressions w[hic]h frighten me sometimes. I sorrow only for real things, for g[rea]t enterprises cast away needlessly—wantonly—for not having the power w[hic]h I c[oul]d use better than any other living Englishman to determine the war policy of Britain. It is painful at times; but it is bearable always. Otherwise my spirits are surprisingly good.[20]

When did Churchill experience the 'black dog' or 'terrible and reasonless depressions'? If Churchill suffered these during the time he was Home Secretary, it is possible this was due in part to the great responsibility he had of taking decisions over death sentences. Churchill had taken thirty-seven such decisions prior to July 1911. On 20 October 1912 Churchill reported to friends with whom he was staying for the weekend: 'How it had become a nightmare to him having to exercise his power of life and death in the case of condemned criminals, on an average of one case a fortnight ... He spoke of these cases with emotion.'[21] At this time Churchill already knew that he was to become First Lord of the Admiralty (24 October 1911).

The memory of these events remained with Churchill for several decades. For example, during a debate in the House of Commons on corporeal punishment on 15 July 1948, Churchill said:

I found it very distressing nearly 40 years ago to be at the Home Office. There is no post that I have occupied in Governments which I was more glad to leave. It was not so much taking the decisions in capital cases that oppressed me, although that was a painful duty. I used to read the letters of appeal written by convicts undergoing long or life sentences begging to be let out. This was for me an even more harassing task.[22]

Many years after his time at the Home Office he would also tell his daughter Diana of the anguish he felt in carrying out these duties.[23]

Lord Riddell (Managing Director of the *News of the World*) who played golf with Churchill twice weekly and met him frequently has offered an alternative explanation. Riddell recorded in his diary in 1911: 'He is a charming companion, full of witty, amusing, unexpected sayings – never dull, never tedious. I find him a most considerate and loyal friend. He is also kind-hearted.'[24] Before the public announcement Churchill had confided in Riddell that 'I am going to the Admiralty'. Riddell also recorded in his diary that Churchill was unhappy at the Home Office and that the recent strikes had caused him much 'anxiety', as he was 'freely criticised by the Press and certain of his colleagues. The situation weighed upon him ... Nevertheless, like all public men, he frequently alleged that, being concentrated on his job, he was not concerned with his critics.'[24]

We deduce from this scanty evidence the possibility that Churchill suffered from non-occupationally disabling mild depression prior to 1911. There is no evidence to support a conclusion that Churchill suffered from prolonged and consistent low mood that interfered with his activities (and what activities!). These features were presumably the fleeting accesses of despair that can overtake anyone and do not constitute a diagnosis any more than accesses of joy constitute a diagnosis.

Churchill also wrote about the worry and mental overstrain in those who have to bear exceptional responsibilities and duties over a long period of time. Churchill proposed an eminently sensible and indeed insightful approach as to the nature of the interest that should be chosen to maintain mental equilibrium. In Churchill's case, of course, it was principally painting, which no doubt explains why the article was republished as the Introduction in *Painting as a Pastime*,[25] after first appearing in the *Strand Magazine* in December 1921:

Many remedies are suggested for the avoidance of worry and mental overstrain by persons who, over prolonged periods, have to bear exceptional responsibilities and discharge duties upon a very large scale. Some advise exercise, and others, repose. Some counsel travel, and others, retreat. Some praise solitude, and others, gaiety. No doubt all these may play their part according to the individual temperament. But the element which is constant and common in all of them is Change. Change is the master key. A man can wear out a particular part of his mind by continually using it and tiring it, just in the same way as he can wear out the elbows of his coat. There is, however, this difference between the living cells of the brain and inanimate articles: one cannot mend the frayed elbows of a coat by rubbing the sleeves or shoulders; but the tired parts of the mind can be rested and strengthened, not merely by rest, but by using other parts.[25]

Evidence from the Churchill Family

Churchill's daughter, Mary (Lady Soames), has written:

A lot has been made of the depressive side of his character by psychiatrists who were never in the same room with him. He himself talks of his black dog, and he did have times of depression, but marriage to my mother very largely kennelled the black dog. Of course, if you have a black dog it lurks somewhere in your nature and you never quite banish it; but I never saw him disarmed by depression.[26]

Storr and many others after him cite a memoir by Sarah, Churchill's daughter, as evidence of his depression. '[At] one of his birthdays a few years before [his death by which time Churchill was out of power and of little importance politically], in answer to my sister Diana's exclamation of wonderment at all the things he had done in his life, he said: "I have achieved a great deal to achieve nothing in the end."'[27]

Evidence from Sir John Colville

Before considering Moran's description of Churchill's 'black dog', it is appropriate to place his comments in perspective. Colville was Churchill's Joint Principal Private Secretary from 1951–5 and had been his Assistant Private Secretary from 1940–1 and from 1943–5. Colville had a particularly close relationship with Churchill and regularly liaised with Moran as Colville's Diaries[28] make clear. He has stated that:

Churchill was frankly sceptical of Moran's constant emphasis on psychology since he liked straightforward and uncomplicated explanations of men and behaviour. Moran was always trying to fathom the workings of his patient's mind, and he sometimes seemed to resent the fact that Churchill's policy was so often proven right. He used on occasion to speak of it with pitying contempt, but it was noticeable that when challenged he was unwilling or unable to propose an alternative. He claims in his book Churchill had none apart from him on whom to unburden his cares. My experience was entirely to the contrary: Churchill was prone to unburden himself, impulsively but never with self-pity, on all with whom he was intimate, and the more worried he was the more he did so, for, indiscreet as he could sometimes be himself, he trusted all too readily in the discretion of others.

I think Moran was baffled because obsessed by his own *Anatomy of Courage* [see[30]], he was always pursuing his favourite analytical researches from a basis which was false as far as Churchill was concerned. The subject had to be made to fit into the accepted framework, and he therefore satisfied himself that Churchill suffered from long fits of depression, was a prey to bad dreams and was deeply apprehensive. There are, I suppose, few if any normal human beings who are never depressed, and, though Churchill was the exception to many rules this was not one of them. But if there were times when he seemed moody and introspective, gaiety and ebullience were far more often the order of the day, and the sun was seldom long behind the clouds.[29]

Colville has given an alternative explanation for Churchill's occasional use of the term 'black dog':

Of course we all have moments of depression, especially after breakfast. It was then that Moran would sometimes call to take his patient's pulse and hope to make a note of what was happening in the wide world. Churchill, not especially pleased to see any visitor at such an hour, might excuse a certain early-morning surliness by saying 'I have got a black dog on my back today'. That was an expression much used by old-fashioned English nannies. Mine used to say to me, if I was grumpy, 'You have got out of bed the wrong side' or else 'You have got a black dog on your back'. Doubtless Nanny Everest was accustomed to say the same to young Winston Churchill.[31]

Evidence from Sir Anthony Montague Browne

In June 1955 Harold Macmillan (Foreign Secretary) decreed that Churchill could use the services of one of his former private secretaries, Anthony Montague Browne, on a part-time basis.[32] In August 1955 this arrangement was made official and Montague Browne was seconded from the Foreign Office.[33] As Lady Soames has stated, 'I think I can say without exaggeration that, Clementine apart, AMB [Montague Browne] saw my father more continuously, both in what remained for him of public life and in private, than any other person.'[34]

Montague Browne summarised this period:

During the ten years of WSC's retirement events in his life worthy of historical record inevitably became fewer ... The reasons for this diminuendo are straightforward. His own health, though erratically resurgent, often to his doctor's surprise, was gradually deteriorating, and he was sadly aware that he had neither the mental muscle, the memory nor the energy to take up any sustained theme. But besides these decisive difficulties lay also his own profound melancholy at Britain's decline and the stormy and forbidding international outlook. This was not the 'Black Dog' of which many of WSC's biographers have written, which in thirteen years I never heard him mention and which allegedly was a subjective mood of deep depression, having little to do with outside events. It was an objective, detached and sadly logical reaction.[35]

Evidence from Cecily 'Chips' Gemmell

Miss Cecily Gemmell[36] was one of Churchill's personal secretaries (1947–51) before becoming personal secretary to Lady Churchill. In the *Oral History* collection of the Churchill Archives Centre, Churchill College Cambridge there is an interview with Miss Gemmell, which was recorded in 1986. She recounted the details of a meal in Morocco during which she and Lieutenant General Sir Henry Pownall, Churchill's military advisor for his Second World War memoirs, 'got on to the subject of committing suicide. I don't know how we did that'. She recalls that Churchill was furious: 'Apparently Churchill suddenly came to and said: "Shut up! Shut up! Don't talk like that!" I think I remember reading somewhere, he got terribly depressed, the Black Dog on the shoulder, and so this was something he didn't like to hear people talking about.'[37] Some minutes later, the interviewer asked: 'You mentioned that he had depressions … What caused that?' Miss Gemmell replied: 'It's all documented … Lord Moran talks about that, the Black Dog …'. The interviewer then asked: 'Did it happen when you were with him?' She replied: 'Perhaps it did, I don't know.'[37]

In 1993 Miss Gemmell gave a further interview for the BBC TV mini-series *Churchill*, which was written and presented by Martin Gilbert.[38] Miss Gemmell again recalled having a meal with Churchill and Pownall and having a 'light-hearted discussion on suicide, if such a thing is possible, and it seemed as if Mr Churchill was deep in his own thoughts and wasn't listening and suddenly jerked upright in his chair and shouted: "Stop it, you mustn't talk like that. It's not right. Once I almost thought of throwing myself under a train".' Miss Gemmell recalled the silence and shock that ensued.[38]

In the first interview Miss Gemmell was uncertain whether Churchill had been depressed when she worked for him. In addition, she stated: 'Apparently Churchill suddenly came to' almost as though she was reporting the story second-hand. In the second interview Miss Gemmell described the discussion with Pownall as 'light-hearted'. Perhaps it was the flippancy of the conversation over lunch which upset Churchill.

We agree with Attenborough: 'Thus there are at least two versions by Cecily Gemmell of an occasion when the subject of suicide was broached within earshot of Winston Churchill. It is impossible to be sure which one is more accurate … They do not … significantly weaken the case that Churchill was never suicidal.'[39]

Evidence from Lord Moran

Moran was the first author to claim that Churchill suffered from the 'black dog'. Moran had a long-term interest in the psychology of fear and courage; he even stated in his book *The Anatomy of Courage*[30] that it was 'but a step to my book on Sir Winston Churchill where I set out to describe the effect of strain on an individual'.[40] Yet, despite this and his detailed descriptions of Churchill's illnesses, there is nothing in the 798 closely printed pages of Moran's book (or in the underlying archive) that remotely resembles the kind of mental state examination which a clinician uses, or ought to use, to establish a diagnosis of depression, even as a retrospective attempt. In addition, there is no evidence from these sources that Moran ever invited a psychiatrist to give a second opinion on Churchill. Nor is there any mention of such a professional encounter in Gilbert's detailed biography or the accompanying *Companion Volumes/Churchill Documents.*

There are in fact only ten references, all of them brief, to the 'black dog', 'black depression', 'depression', 'melancholy' or 'black moods' in *The Struggle for Survival.*[8] The first mention is in the entry for 29 November 1943 during the Tehran Conference when Moran said that Churchill made a great effort to shake off the 'black depression' that had settled on him.[41] The second reference occurs on 14 August 1944 (which also includes a footnote to 'black dog' to explain Moran's use of the term).[1] The third (dated 13 September 1944)[42] is an exposition by Moran of what he considers to have been Churchill's unwillingness to admit any errors. The fourth (8 August 1945) relates to Churchill's feelings expressed to Moran two weeks after losing office.[43] The fifth reference is an undated note that Moran made that follows the entry for 4 January 1946 and relates to a perceived 'state of melancholy'.[44] The sixth reference (6 July 1946) is a description by Moran that Churchill was in 'one of his black moods'.[44] The seventh reference (21 March 1955) is a comment made by Jane Portal (now Lady Williams), Churchill's secretary, to Moran.[45] The eighth reference relates to a discussion Moran had with Brendan Bracken (24 July 1958) on Churchill's personality where it is stated that the condition was inherited ('the inborn melancholia of the Churchill blood').[46] The ninth reference is to events on 4 June 1959 (entry 8 June 1959) when Churchill was considered by Moran to be 'giving way to the Churchill melancholia'.[47] The tenth and final reference (9 June 1959) is to the rhetorical question: 'Is Winston's black dog catching?'[47]

These entries will now be considered in greater detail.

Entry for 29 November 1943
During the Tehran Conference which began on 28 November 1943, Moran made a midnight call on Churchill to see if he needed anything. Churchill was discussing the future with Anthony Eden, Foreign Secretary, and Clark Kerr, British Ambassador to Russia.

The P.M. was talking in a tired, slow voice, with his eyes closed …
[Churchill] stopped. 'Charles hasn't a drink – When I consider the vast
issues, I realize how inadequate we are.' 'You mean a war with Russia?'
I do not think he heard. Then he appeared to make a great effort to cast
off the black depression that had settled on him.[48]

Although Moran expected to find Churchill in 'poor fettle' the following
morning, 'he seems to have dismissed the night's happenings as if they were
only a bad dream'.

This episode does not support a clinical diagnosis of depression or bipolar
disease.

Entry for 14 August 1944 (Probably Relates to 24 September 1944)[1]

Storr relied heavily on the entry for 14 August 1944 in *The Struggle for
Survival*,[1] when Churchill reminisced about his life more than thirty years
before. Before this passage is discussed in detail, it should be recognized
that Moran's book is not a contemporaneous diary record, as it appears
superficially to be. The second Lord Moran acknowledged this in his
Introduction to the first volume of the paperback edition, when he stated:

So many people were unaware that 'my diary' was, in effect, shorthand
for the notes my father jotted down at the time … The rather haphazard
way in which the contemporary passages were assembled and the
constant revision and rewriting … over a period of years sometimes
made it difficult to determine what was written at the time and what
was added later.[49]

Grant who wrote the Introduction to the second paperback volume explained
further that the constant revisions to *The Struggle for Survival* resulted in
the 'dispersal of some of the essay material ['essays on the various aspects of
the Churchill persona'] into the "diary" entries' which helped to 'create a
misleading impression about the nature of the book'.[50]

Detailed examination of the Moran archive by Attenborough[16,51] has
confirmed that much of the passage below can be found in the handwritten
archive in an entry dated 24 September 1944. The words underlined below
do not appear in the handwritten version and words in square brackets
express differently what is in the handwritten draft. The introduction to the

September entry reads: 'He has a long session tonight at dinner. Cunard. White Star. The Prime Minister, Mrs Churchill and guests.'
In the published entry for 14 August 1944 Moran recorded that:

[The PM was in a speculative mood today.] 'When I was young' he ruminated 'for two or three years the light faded out of the picture. I did my work. I sat in the House of Commons, but black depression settled on me. It helped me to talk to Clemmie about it. I don't like standing near the edge of a platform when an express train is passing through. I like to stand right back and if possible to get a pillar between me and the train. I don't like to stand by the side of the ship and look down into the water. A second's action would end everything. A few drops of desperation. And yet I don't want to go out of the world at all in such moments. Is much known about worry, Charles? It helps to write down half a dozen things which are worrying me. Two of them, say, disappear; about two nothing could be done, so it's no use worrying, and two perhaps can be settled. I read an American book on the nerves, The philosophy of fate; it interested me a great deal.[1]

Moran said: 'Your trouble – I mean the Black Dog business – you got from your forebears. You have fought against it all your life. That is why you dislike visiting hospitals. You always avoid anything that is depressing.'[1] 'Winston stared at me as if I knew too much. [He went on to talk] about the folly of repression ...'

The second paragraph above is different in the handwritten entry, as notably it omits the question supposedly posed by Churchill: 'Is much known about worry, Charles?' Instead, the entry reads (underlining indicates the differences from the paragraph in the published version): '*On worry*. It helps to write down half a dozen things which are worrying you. Two of them say disappear, two nothing can be done about so it's no use worrying, and two perhaps can be settled. I read an American book on the nerves, The Philosophy of Faith: it interested me a great deal. Then talked about the folly of repression ...'

That this entry in all probability relates to 24 September 1944 rather than 14 August 1944 is confirmed by an entry in the Colville diaries for the same date.[52] Colville recorded that:

Mrs Churchill gave a cocktail party at 6.30. It was quite beautifully executed by the ship's stewards. This was followed by a domestic dinner party, about which the chef took special trouble and at which the P.M. and Mrs C., Tommy [Lieutenant Commader Thompson RN, Churchill's aide-de-camp], John [John Martin, Churchill's Principal Private Secretary] and myself, Joe Hollis [Colonel Leslie Hollis, Senior Assistant Secretary (Military) to the War Cabinet and Secretary to the Chiefs of Staff Committee], Lord Moran and Brigadier Whitby [Churchill's physicians] were present.

Importantly, Colville wrote:

The PM regained some of his old spontaneous form and did not depend on reminiscences as much as he usually does now. He said that when he was Home Secretary his nerves were in a very bad state and he was assailed by worries in a way he never has been in the war. He then discovered that the best remedy was to write down on a piece of paper all the various matters which are troubling one; from which it will appear that some are purely trivial, some are irremediable, and there are thus only one or two on which one will need concentrate one's energies. Lord Moran said that when deterioration in a man set in the first things that went from him with those he had most recently learnt. Played bezique with the P.M. who was in very mellow mood, till 2:30 a.m.[52]

Attenborough[51,53] has pointed out that the Colville diary entry for 24 September 1944 parallels the contents of Moran's September handwritten passage to a significant extent, save that Colville records Churchill's avowal of having endured a difficult period quite early on his political career, using the words 'nerves' and 'worries', rather than Moran's 'black depression'. There is nothing in Colville's diary entry concerning Moran responding to Churchill's mention of 'nerves' and 'worries' with a pronouncement that his 'trouble – I mean the Black Dog business' is responsible. Colville recalls Moran stating only that when 'deterioration in a man set in the first things that went from him were those he had most recently learnt'.[52]

Both the Colville diary entry for 24 September 1944 and the Moran handwritten note for the same date characterised the occasion in question as a dinner party. In contrast, the published entry for 14 August 1944 is quite different. There is no mention of a dinner with guests and, before John Martin arrived, the passage reads as though Churchill and Moran were alone; Churchill was in 'speculative mood' and 'ruminated' before Churchill. In contrast, Colville describes Churchill holding forth to his guests in characteristic style.

Moran adds a footnote to this entry: 'Black Dog: Winston's name for the prolonged fits of depression from which he suffered.'[1] It should be noted that Moran defines 'black dog' as the 'prolonged fits of depression from which he [Churchill] suffered', not from which Churchill 'had suffered'. In the composition of this entry and footnote, Moran seems to have been untroubled by this inconsistency. In the concluding chapter to *The Struggle for Survival*, Moran wrote: 'But before the first World War he had learnt to disguise his natural apprehension and had managed to extirpate bouts of depression from his system.'[54] Even if Moran had believed this second-hand evidence, should he not more accurately have written: 'prolonged fits of depression from which he had suffered *before 1914*'?

Commentary after 13 September 1944[42]

Following the entry for 13 September 1944, Moran included some comments not linked to the date entry. Moran stated: 'In his early days, as I have already recounted, he was afflicted by fits of depression that might *last for months* [our emphasis]. He called them the 'black dog'. He dreaded these bouts and instinctively kept away from anyone or anything that seemed to bring them on.'[42]

Moran was not Churchill's physician at the relevant time, nor has he provided the evidence for this statement. Moran might have more accurately noted that the 'fits of depression', or 'black dog', which had settled on Churchill was not so black that he was unable to do his work and to sit in the House of Commons, nor was its level of severity such as to put him beyond the assistance of informal counselling from his wife Clemmie. These points suggest that the condition in question, whatever the precise medical diagnosis, was a mild one.

Entries for 2 August 1945 and 8 August 1945[43]

Moran 'found' Churchill in the penthouse suite on the sixth floor of Claridge's Hotel on 2 August 1945 where Churchill was staying temporarily after losing the 1945 General Election.[43] Moran recorded that the sun was streaming into the bedroom. 'It was very cheerful' and attributed the following remarks to Churchill. 'I don't like sleeping near a precipice like that,' pointing to the balcony. 'I've no desire to quit the world' he said with a grin, 'but thoughts, desperate thoughts come into the head.'

In fact, careful research by Attenborough[55,56] has shown that the published account omits the following words from the manuscript book: Shakespeare. Don't tell anyone this.' (Note: the quotation marks are missing from the manuscript book before 'Don't').

In addition, as Attenborough has explained the published entry differs substantially *in tone* from Moran's original manuscript book.[55,56] The engulfing mood of gloom of the published entry is substantially dispelled by the manuscript entry. The manuscript book states that Moran was 'kept waiting an unusual time as he [Churchill] was deep in a business interview'.[55] Churchill then discussed his reception in the House the previous day, when Conservative MPs demonstrated their strong support for him, his troublesome indigestion, for which he had restarted his breathing exercises (Churchill demonstrated these), his 'private worries' over money even though offered £20,000 (equivalent to about £856,000 in 2019) from *Time* and *Life* for four short articles ('I'm not going to work when they take nineteen and six out of every pound I earn') and his concern that if Aneurin Bevan becomes Minister of Health Moran might not be able to look after him as a private patient.

At this point Mrs Kathleen Hill, Churchill's personal secretary, came in and asked if Churchill would take a trunk (long-distance) call that he had put though to Lord Camrose, proprietor of the *Daily Telegraph* and soon to be Churchill's unpaid literary agent. Churchill took the call: 'Is that you Bill' and set up a lunch appointment.[55]

As Attenborough has concluded: 'Churchill's association with Camrose at this date is almost certainly an indication that, regardless of variations in mood following the election defeat, Churchill was looking towards, and working towards, the rewards, material and psychological, of producing a worldwide bestseller, the Labour Government's taxation policy not withstanding.'[55] The manuscript book entry also reveals that Mrs Hill informed Moran that Churchill's post-election letter bag 'was bigger than Attlee's'.[55]

In a Foreword to *The War and Colonel Warden*, Averell Harriman, President Roosevelt's personal envoy, currently the US Ambassador to the USSR and future US Ambassador to Britain, recalled a lunch in July 1945 in the penthouse apartment on the top floor of Claridge's Hotel when only Churchill, Mrs Churchill and Brendan Bracken were present.[57]

Churchill talked about the election. The repudiation by the British people had been a very deep shock to him. He told me that the week since I had seen him in Potsdam had been the longest in his life but that he was now adjusted to these events. In order to make some consoling comment, I pointed to the fact that the Labour Party had not gained a majority of the popular vote, that if there had been proportional representation in Britain as in France, the Conservative and Liberal Parties would have a majority of seats in the Commons and then he would no doubt still be Prime Minister. Churchill indignantly rejected this idea saying: 'I will fight against the evils of proportional representation with all my strength.' He explained that one could not have responsible government with proportional representation. He said it was essential that one Party have responsibility for government so that the people should know whom to hold accountable. Otherwise democracy cannot succeed. To me, it was completely in character that at this time of great personal disappointment he was as vigorous as ever in upholding his basic concept of the great traditions of the British democratic system of government, which he understood so well. I also suggested that his retirement would give him an opportunity to write the history of the war as no one else could. 'Yes,' Churchill replied but there is other work to be done.' I knew then that this turn in events had cast only a passing shadow on his indomitable spirit.[57]

In the entry for 8 August 1945 Churchill explains to Moran that he kept waking about 4 am and had to take a 'red' (secobarbital 100 mg) to get to sleep, or 'futile speculations' filled his mind. 'It's no use, Charles, pretending I'm not hard hit. I can't school myself to do nothing for the rest of my life ... I get fits of depression. You know how my days were filled; now it has all gone. I go to bed at twelve o'clock. There is nothing to sit up for.'[43] In reality, Churchill was still responding to hundreds of letters and planning his future as Party leader: 'In the anxious days that lie ahead we shall need a strong and closely-knitted team.'[58]

Commentary after 4 January 1946[44]
Following the entry of 4 January 1946, Moran appended 'notes in my diary, undated, but written later, at different time'.[44] In one of these undated records in 1946, Moran recorded that Churchill:

Was troubled because he [Churchill] seemed to be sinking into a state of melancholy that I could not fully explain. I knew that he was beginning to feel his years, and that his physical powers were on the decline, which alone can completely change a man's outlook. Winston himself was sure he was despondent because he was nearly spent. 'I'm pretty well played out. I imagine when one folds up like that, this kind of business hit hits one harder. Is anything known about these things, Charles?' But was there not something more behind this despair? Could it be the shock of his defeat had stirred up the inborn melancholia of the Churchill blood? Brendan, I remember, told me Winston's mood in 1915 when he had to leave the Government because he was held responsible for the failure of the attack on the Dardanelles. According to Brendan, Winston kept on saying to him – often several times in a day – 'I'm finished I'm finished.'[44]

Without knowing the date this conversation took place it is difficult to place it in perspective. Churchill was in the United States until 20 March and Moran was not present.[59,60] On 29 March, three days after his return to London, Churchill invited his pre-war literary assistant, Bill Deakin, Fellow of Wadham College, Oxford to deal with the political and diplomatic side of his War Memoirs which he had now decided to write.[61] Other members of the team for this mammoth writing task were assembled including Lord Ismay as military advisor, Denis Kelly and a new personal secretary, Lettice Marston. Meetings were also held with his publisher, solicitor and tax advisor.[61]

Entry for 6 July 1946[44]
Moran recorded that when he called upon Churchill today 'he seemed in poor heart–one of his black moods'. Churchill said, 'I'm fed up. Victory has turned to sackcloth and ashes.'[44]

Entry for 21 March 1955[45]
Jane Portal told Moran, 'You will find the P.M. very depressed. He has given up reading the newspapers and sits about staring into space. They are really kicking him out.'[45]

Entry for 24 July 1958[46]
In a conversation between Moran and Brendan Bracken (former MP, Churchill confidant and close friend) on 24 July 1958 at a time when Bracken

was dying at home from carcinoma of the oesophagus (he died on 8 August 1958), Bracken stated:

Have you read [A.L.] Rowse on *The Later Churchills?* ... He says that of the last seven Dukes of Marlborough five suffered from melancholia ... It has not been easy for him (Churchill). You see, Charles, Winston has always been a 'despairer'. Orpen [Sir William Orpen], who painted him after the Dardanelles, used to speak of the misery in his face.[46] He called him the man of misery. Winston was so sure then that he would take no further part in public life. There seemed nothing left to live for. It made him very sad. Then in his years in the wilderness, before the Second War, he kept saying: 'I'm finished'. He said that about twice a day. He was quite certain that he would never get back to office ... he missed the red boxes awfully. Winston has always been wretched unless he was occupied.[46]

Bracken explained:

This strain of melancholy, a Churchill inheritance, is balanced in Winston by the physical and mental robustness of the Jeromes. There was in his formidable grandfather a touch of the frontiersman. When he had angered the mob he promptly put a machine-gun on the roof, which he himself could operate ... The healthy bright red American blood cast out the Churchill melancholy. But not entirely. Winston has always been moody; used to call his fits of depression the 'black dog'. At other times, as you know, he goes off into a kind of trance. I have seen him sit silent for several hours, and when he is like that only a few people can make him talk.[46]

It should be noted that the focus of this conversation (only a small part of which is reproduced above) about Churchill was really initiated by Moran. Bracken began by stating, 'Now, Charles, I haven't brought you here to talk about my troubles. Let's get down to something more interesting. I want to talk to you about Winston. Where shall I begin?'[46] Moran responded, 'You once told me that Winston was full of apprehension ... what made you say that? The public would think it out of character.'[46]

It seems improbable given the long and close relationship (thirty-five years) between Bracken and Churchill that Bracken would focus on this aspect of Churchill's life without prompting, particularly as Churchill had visited him on three occasions while he was dying (27 June 1958, 18 July 1958, 31 July 1958[62]), when as he was well aware, and as Bracken told Moran: 'That's why as you say, he [Churchill] won't go near a hospital.'[46]

Entry for 8 June 1959 (Relating to 4 June 1959)[47]

The entry for 8 June records that Moran found Churchill 'on Thursday' (presumably 4 June) with a 'glum face, brooding over his bed rest. I taxed him with giving way to the Churchill melancholia. "Why do I get stuck down in the past?" asked Churchill. "Why do I keep going over and over these years when I know I cannot change anything? You, Charles, have spent your life puzzling how the mind works. You must know the answer."'[47]

Entry for 9 June 1959[47]

'Is Winston's Black Dog catching?' This rhetorical question is an opening statement to a discussion Moran had with Sir William Haley, Director General of the BBC (1944–52) and Editor of *The Times* (1952–66), at Marshalls Manor, Moran's home. Moran states that Haley's 'factual talk is the medicine I need when I am getting too introspective'. This comment follows on from Moran's discussion with Churchill the previous day and suggests that their conversation was still on his mind.

Was Churchill ever Treated for Depression?

Moran never attempted to treat depression in his illustrious patient, which suggests he was hardly very concerned about it. Churchill did request that Moran prescribe a medicine to ensure that he gave a successful speech at the Conservative Party Conference at Margate on 10 October 1953 after he had suffered a stroke in June 1953.[63] In all probability Moran prescribed Edrisal (amfetamine sulfate 2.5 mg, aspirin 160 mg, phenacetin 160 mg; 'minors').[64] There is also evidence that Moran prescribed the same dose of amfetamine sulfate before other major speeches which 'completely cleared away the muzzy feeling' in Churchill's head.[65,66]

Evidence from Churchill's Other Physicians

There is no suggestion in the medical records of other experienced physicians responsible for providing opinions on Churchill, notably Lord

Brain, Sir John Parkinson and Dr Evan Bedford, that in their *independent* opinion Churchill suffered from, or required treatment for, depression. However, when Brain assessed Churchill on the first of twenty occasions on 5 October 1949 he recorded, 'I should think from what Moran told me that Churchill is a cyclothyme. Apparently he was subject to depression in his earlier days. He has the drive and vitality and youthfulness of a cyclothyme. He works five or six hours a day at his book. He looks a little more than sixty at seventy-four.'[67]

These comments, written in real time by Brain on his first encounter with Churchill, very much reflect what he had been told by Moran, that is Churchill had a history of depression but was highly productive. There are no further comments by Brain during subsequent examinations that support this conclusion.

Evidence from Violet Bonham Carter

In Violet Bonham Carter's memoir of Churchill between the years 1906 and 1916, she makes no mention of Churchill's supposed depression. Bonham Carter was not just another writer about Churchill: she was the grown-up daughter of the Prime Minister, Herbert Henry Asquith, at the time of Churchill's close association with him. She saw him frequently and was close to him, or at least as close as anyone could be. She says of him, inter alia:

'He too had that irrational certainty about himself ... A world in arms could not have shaken it ...'.[68] And: 'And in spite of his dark moments of impatience and frustration sometimes verging on despair, I was conscious of his own ultimate confidence in himself. He had no doubts about his star.'[69] And: 'His zest, vitality, activity and industry were inexhaustible. He seemed to be endowed by Nature with a double charge of life.'[69]

Bonham Carter clearly implies that these were characteristic, not episodic, traits. Suffice it to say that these are not the traits of a depressive nor, for that matter, of a person in a state of mania. However, Bonham Carter *does* notice Churchill's periods of despair. For example, after the failure of the Gallipoli campaign, following which he had to resign, he told Bonham Carter: 'I'm finished ... No I'm done.'[70] In other words, he thought that his public life was over: and public life, together with writing, was all-important to Churchill.

What is most noticeable, however, is not that Churchill despaired, but that he recovered very quickly from his despair. After his removal from the cabinet, Churchill went to the trenches in France as a Lieutenant Colonel. Of his farewell luncheon, Violet Bonham Carter wrote: 'The rest of us [were] trying to "play up" and hide our leaden hearts. Winston alone was at his gayest and best.'[71]

And indeed, once Churchill got to France, by sheer force of personality and administrative ability, he put new heart into a battalion with reportedly very low morale.

Medical Aspects

We accept that it is generally unwise to speculate on the possible presence or absence of particular mental disorders in a person we have never met, especially when such speculations are heavily dependent upon the mainly theoretical considerations of others, who may also have not met that individual. The observations of family members, valued friends, colleagues or health professionals who have no particular experience or expertise in psychiatry can all be misleading.

Contemporaneous accounts can be affected by inappropriate use of terminology. For example, the terms 'melancholia' and 'rumination' respectively connote a particular condition and mental experience, which are understood rather differently by a clinician and specifically a psychiatrist and a member of the general public. Furthermore, the seemingly insightful self-reflections of an individual may be affected by the passage of time, as the recollection of a prevailing affect at a particular point is known to be questionable after a few months have passed.

However, based on the available medical (and non-medical) sources, we are not persuaded, even if others have been, that Churchill suffered from a Major Depressive Disorder or from Bipolar I Disorder (a manic episode, possibly preceded by or followed by a hypomanic episode or major depressive episode) or Bipolar II Disorder (hypomanic episode and a major depressive episode), as defined in the fifth edition of the *Diagnostic and Statistical Manual of the American Psychiatric Association (DSM-5)*.[18] Equally, there is no evidence that Churchill suffered from a Cyclothymic Disorder as defined in DSM-5.[18] Both Bipolar II Disorder and Cyclothymic Disorder are associated with hypomanic episodes, but in Cyclothymic Disorder depressive symptoms are less severe and do not meet full severity or duration criteria for a diagnosis of a depressive episode. In practice, it may be very difficult to differentiate the two disorders without monitoring the condition for a long period of time and gathering information from other sources such as family members.[72]

It has also been suggested that there may be a multi-generational family history of 'melancholia' in Churchill, but although such a history is common in patients with Bipolar Disorder, it is itself insufficient to make a reliable diagnosis. The psychiatrist would also seek to establish whether other features are present which might support the Bipolar Disorder diagnosis. For example, clear evidence of at least one discrete period of mania with its unusual elation, marked over-activity, increased irritability and enhanced creativity, with observable features such as rapid speech, racing thoughts, distractibility and altered judgement, leading to substantial impairment and the perceived need for hospitalisation. Of course, some bipolar patients do not experience such typical manic episodes, but instead report rather milder and somewhat less impairing 'hypomanic' episodes. However, the accurate distinction of this pattern of recurring affective illness from the quotidian variation in the high-functioning cyclothymic personality can be difficult, and again could only be achieved through detailed interview.

To make the clinical diagnosis of a recurrent Unipolar Depressive Disorder, a psychiatrist would look for evidence of an episodic condition characterized by discrete periods of upsetting and impairing depressive symptoms (particularly persistent and pervasive low mood, troublesome reduced motivation and distressing loss of interests and decreased capacity for pleasure), present for more than two weeks, with intervening and often prolonged periods of relatively good mental health. Episodes of illness can occur either with or without preceding adverse life events or the presence of enduring difficulties, although in most patients there is a strong association between recent adverse experiences or persisting challenges and periods of depression.

Of course, absence of evidence is not proof of absence; but the onus is surely on those who make a diagnosis to provide the positive evidence for it. In reality there are no gaps in Churchill's very heavily documented career sufficiently large to be explained by periods of Major Depressive Disorder or Bipolar Disorder. Specifically, it is preposterous to suppose that Churchill was depressed in any serious sense during a tumultuous time in British politics during which he was President of the Board of Trade (1908–10) or Home Secretary (1910–11) and was instrumental in passing important reforms.

Churchill's reported periods of 'black dog' before 1911 may correspond to the 'prolonged fits of depression' reported second-hand by Moran: but the exact nature of this 'black dog' is uncertain. Churchill notes that relief from these periods is associated with the experience of returning colours in a picture, which suggests the periods were characterised by anhedonia (loss of interest, pleasure and reward), but the duration of this anhedonic experience is not clear. When episodic and distressing anhedonia is reported by a patient, a psychiatrist would carefully establish whether other depressive symptoms (such as low mood, disturbed sleep or suicidal thoughts) occurred at the same time. If Churchill experienced such depressive symptoms pre-1911 any associated impairment appears to have been limited, given his ability to respond effectively to extraordinary challenges then and over subsequent years.

For a man who went through the Battle of Omdurman, escaped as a prisoner of war with a death sentence on his head during the Boer War, had to deal with the siege of Sidney Street, sign death warrants, plan a major amphibious attack, deal with the economic problems of the 1920s, watch the blindness of his peers during the build-up to the Second World War, take over the leadership at a pretty low point, survive crushing reversals during the war, lose an election afterwards and become Prime Minister again at a time of declining powers, to name only a few incidents, not to have experienced periods of transient depression/despair would be remarkable to the point of being pathological.

Throughout his life, in fact, Churchill's despair – always in response to events – was quickly followed by recovery. The normal word for this is resilience, though some have hinted at manic defence. Moran even notes that he went to bed in despair and rose with optimism. If Churchill's thought is to be deemed a psychiatric symptom, then, all thought of whatever stripe, other than the most banal, is likewise to be considered a psychiatric symptom.

Although low doses of amfetamine given continuously may have some benefit in mild depression, intermittent prescribing of amfetamine sulfate 2.5 mg by Moran to clear the 'muzzy feeling' in Churchill's head prior to major speeches would offer no such benefit. Nor is there clinical evidence that the occasional use of amfetamines caused depressive symptoms in Churchill after it had been taken. Moreover, the first dose of amfetamine was not prescribed to Churchill until October 1953. The fact that Churchill had been prescribed a psychostimulant (amfetamine sulfate) and a barbiturate (secobarbital) for short-term management of inertia or insomnia is insufficient to support the diagnosis of a recurrent depressive disorder.

While it is true that some people drink because they are depressed, far more people are depressed because they drink. If Churchill had suffered from prolonged periods of consistently depressed mood, which we doubt he did, the quantity of alcohol that Churchill drank on a daily basis would be of importance. Although Churchill did not show any signs of dependence, his tolerance most probably would have been high. It is therefore very relevant that Montague Browne never saw Churchill drunk for ten years or more at an age at which one might have expected his tolerance already to have declined. 'I never saw him drunk, but enlivened, stimulated, sometimes eloquently impassioned in a theme after dinner.'[33] Surely, Moran would have suggested that Churchill should eliminate or reduce his intake of alcohol if he considered there was a possibility that it was responsible for the 'black dog' which he had diagnosed? After all Moran supported Hunt when he told Churchill to stop drinking when he suffered recurrent bouts of obstructive jaundice in 1958.[73] Based on Moran's published record of his professional encounters with Churchill, the Moran Archive,[74] the case notes of other attending physicians, including Lord Brain,[75] Sir John Parkinson[76] and Dr Evan Bedford,[77] there is no support for the idea Moran would have been too respectful to have said anything about it to his patient.

Our view, then, is that the available evidence suggests that Churchill suffered no major psychiatric disorder, exceptional man as he undoubtedly was. Churchill 'lived a life that was quite human and profoundly inspirational. He was a man with a huge personality who enjoyed life, family and the fulfilment of destiny, without the hobble of a debilitating mental illness. The myth of the "Black Dog" as Churchill's metaphor for severe clinical mood disorder is just that – a myth.'[78]

The question then arises as to why it should so rapidly and almost universally have been accepted that he *did* suffer from psychiatric disorder. In the first place, there is a general desire to pull great men down and give them feet of clay, to diminish them in some way, so that they may more approximate ourselves in size. But there is also a contrary desire, to elevate the psychiatrically disturbed so as to lessen the fear of mental illness and its associated stigma. If Churchill was psychiatrically ill, why fear psychiatric illness? Finally, there is the matter of psychiatric imperialism, which desires that all human conduct become a psychiatric symptom.

Churchill was exceptional, but he was normal.

Chapter 31

Was Churchill an Alcoholic?

I could not live without Champagne. In victory I deserve it. In defeat I need it[1]

The overwhelming evidence is that Churchill loved alcohol, drank steadily by sipping, had a hardy constitution and was only rarely affected by it[2]

In popular language an alcoholic is a person addicted to alcohol, a person having a strong, often uncontrollable, desire to drink, a person showing the effects of habitually drinking alcohol, such as regular inebriation (being drunk). Those suffering from alcohol dependence (now termed Alcohol Use Disorder) will often place drinking above all other obligations, including work and family, and will usually develop a physical tolerance or experience withdrawal symptoms if they stop (see below).

There is the widespread perception that Sir Winston Churchill was often drunk not only when he was socialising, but also when he was the Prime Minister or working as a prolific author. For example, in an opinion column published in the *British Medical Journal* in 1994, Professor Ian Robertson wrote: 'Winston Churchill reputedly put away a bottle of spirits a day and often had to be carried dead drunk from the War Rooms.'[3] After objections from Sir Winston Churchill's grandson, Winston,[4] and former secretary, Grace Hamblin,[5] Robertson apologized,[6] but defended himself by citing three biographies[7-9] as support for his case. However, Charmley[9] was citing Jacob (see below).[10]

Twenty-five years later the *Wall Street Journal* columnist Peggy Noonan wrote an article in June 2019 about Boris Johnson, the British Prime Minister, in which she stated: 'Winston Churchill, a flawed outsider with imperfect judgment but the right man for 1939. But Churchill was an authentic genius who wrote a masterpiece of the English language while drunk and went to war hung over.'[11]

Although Noonan's opinion is held by many, it is not supported by the evidence. As Richard Langworth, Senior Fellow, Hillsdale College Churchill Project, wrote in response:

> He did not write 'a masterpiece of the English language while drunk.' Nor is it true that he 'went to war hung over.' ... No one else served in four wars and wrote five books by age 25, held all but one major office of state, was twice prime minister, wrote fifty books and won a Nobel Prize.[12]

Churchill's Own View of Alcohol

In 1930 Churchill wrote in *My Early Life*:

> The undergraduates of Oxford and Cambridge used to drink like fishes, and they even had clubs and formal dinners where it was an obligation for everyone to consume more liquor than he could carry. At Sandhurst, on the other hand, and in the Army, drunkenness was a disgraceful offence punishable not only by social reprobation often physically manifested, but if it ever got into the official sphere, by the sack. I had been brought up and trained to have the utmost contempt for people who got drunk, except on very exceptional occasions and a few anniversaries – and I would have liked to have the boozing scholars of the Universities wheeled into line and properly chastised for their squalid misuse of what I must ever regard as a good gift of the gods. In those days I was very much against drunkards, prohibitionists and other weaklings of excess: but now I can measure more charitably the frailties of nature for which their extravaganzas originate.[13]

There is little doubt that Churchill enjoyed alcohol. In 1946 when proposing a visit to Mme Odette Pol-Roger in Epernay, Churchill wrote: 'I could not live without Champagne. In victory I deserve it. In defeat I need it.'[1] And again: 'A single glass of champagne imparts a feeling of exhilaration. The nerves are braced, the imagination is agreeably stirred, the wits become more nimble.' Yet, Churchill was well aware of the consequences of excess: 'A bottle [of champagne] produces a contrary effect. Excess causes a comatose insensibility. So it is with war, and the quality of both is best discovered by sipping.'[14] In 1955 Churchill commented to his physicians, Lord Moran and Sir Russell Brain, about a glass of whisky by his bed. 'I keep it by me all day. Oh, it is only weak, and I only sip it. It is more a companion than a stimulant.'[15]

An observation made by Sir John Colville, who worked closely with Churchill for many years first as Assistant Private Secretary and then as joint Principal Private Secretary, is also relevant. He has written:

> After dinner one evening in August 1940 Churchill declared to Desmond Morton and me, as he waved away the brandy and demanded iced soda water: 'My object is to preserve the maximum initiative energy. Every night I try myself by court-martial to see if I have done anything effective during the day. I don't mean just pawing the ground – anyone can go through the motions – but something really effective.'[16]

Such a view probably explains Churchill's remark: 'All I can say is, that I have taken more out of alcohol than alcohol has taken out of me.'[17]

How Much did Churchill Drink?

Andrew Roberts, Churchill's most recent major biographer, has concluded: 'Throughout his life he [Churchill] enjoyed depicting himself as a heavy drinker, but it is remarkable on how few occasions anybody else thought he was drunk.'[2] Churchill often asked Lord Cherwell (Professor Lindemann): 'Prof please calculate the amount of champagne and spirits I have consumed in my life and indicate how much of this room they would fill.' Lindemann then pretended to calculate with his slide rule: 'I'm afraid not more than a few inches, Winston.' 'How much to do, how little time remains,' was Churchill's response.[18]

Sir Robert Rhodes James, Churchill's biographer and former Senior Clerk of the House of Commons and Member of Parliament, has written: 'Churchill's enjoyment of alcohol has created legends – to which he himself contributed – which have assumed startling proportions.' To support this opinion he quoted an unnamed 'reliable source' as to Churchill's drinking habits:

> He never drank the sort of quantities of alcohol frequently ascribed to him at the time, though indeed he drank *somewhat* more than

the average. He was basically a wine drinker – champagne at lunch sometimes and dinner always. But the idea that he drank a whole bottle or more at either meal was untrue … He might or he might not have a glass of brandy as a liqueur afterwards. Infrequently he would have one glass of sherry before the meal. He did not really like sherry. He did not drink port. He would have about three really mild whiskies and sodas – sometimes brandy and soda – as a thirst quencher during the day. Not before 11 am (one, sometimes), one at teatime, and one before going to bed, perhaps one other during the evening … W. was usually most careful never to absorb a lot of mixed drinks … You are of course quite right about the wildly exaggerated stories circulated, and also W's curious humour in enjoying them not contradicting them.[19]

Some of those closest to Churchill during the Second World War have also commented on his alcohol intake. Lieutenant General Sir Ian Jacob, Military Assistant Secretary to Churchill's War Cabinet, considered that Churchill:

Drank a great deal. At breakfast he had coffee and often orange juice, though I have seen him drink white wine for breakfast on occasion. During the morning he would often have a glass of iced soda water by him which he sipped from time to time. He didn't drink cocktails or sherry, but drank a good deal at lunch, often champagne followed by brandy. He didn't have tea, but about teatime or later, according to when he had his sleep, he would start drinking iced whisky and soda. He probably had two or three glasses, not very strong, before dinner, and then at dinner he always had champagne, followed by several doses of brandy. Then during the late evening and night he had more whisky and soda. He had obviously become accustomed to this kind of routine for years, yet he was never the worse for drink in my experience, and as far as I could see, he never felt the slightest ill effects on the morning.[10]

In an interview with Andrew Roberts, Jacob told him that on one occasion in Cairo Churchill had drunk a bottle of white wine at breakfast.[20] Jacob was also interviewed for a BBC documentary by Sir Martin Gilbert, Churchill's main biographer, in which he stated that Churchill always had a bottle of champagne for lunch.[21] The accuracy of this account has been challenged by Sir John Peck, Churchill's Private Secretary from 1940–5, who wrote:

'Ian Jacob hardly ever had lunch with Winston so he could only have been quoting hearsay … even if Churchill had champagne for lunch everyday he would never have got through an entire bottle, and even if he had a glass or two himself, I fear Sawyers the butler would have ensured that none was wasted.'[22]

On 14 May 1981 Colville reflected to Gilbert on Churchill's whisky drinking. 'Winston's whisky was very much a whisky and *soda*. It was really a mouthwash. He used to get frightfully cross if it was too strong.'[23] This observation is supported by Lady Soames who described the 'Papa Cocktail' as a 'smidgen of Johnnie Walker covering the bottom of a tumbler, filled with water and sipped throughout the morning'.[24]

Sir David Hunt, Private Secretary to Churchill during his second premiership, supports Colville's description:

To my mind, and from my own observation, he was remarkably moderate. He certainly drank the weakest whisky-and-sodas that I have ever known. This was brought home to me early on, in fact on 30 November 1951, his seventy-seventh birthday. After his birthday party he came down to the Cabinet Room to work just the same and with his usual thoughtfulness invited me to have a drink with him. 'You've never seen a Prime Minister of seventy-seven before,' he said. 'No, sir, I replied, 'but you have.' [Gladstone] The whiskies had been poured by a messenger, not by one of his own servants; mine tasted normal enough to me, but he was deeply indignant with the messenger for mixing it far too strong. In truth in his normal drink the whisky only faintly tinged the soda.[25]

The historian, AL Rowse, of All Souls College, Oxford, who was assisting Churchill with his literary endeavours, was entertained by him to lunch on 11 July 1955 shortly after Churchill had suffered a stroke.[26] The lunch:

Had been a good one: fried fish, then lamb cutlets and peas, ice cream and fruit. I am really a teetotaller: I did not dare to confess that with Winston: he would not have been able to support so dire a confession. I had some Bristol Milk [sherry] in the library, as ordered, while waiting for him; an excellent hock accompanied the meal. When it came to cheese, I wasn't going to have any – let alone port with it. Port in the middle of the day! Or indeed at any time. I was forced to compromise with a bit of cheese. Then – 'Some brandy?' A lifelong member of the Duodenal Club, I drew the line at brandy. 'Then have some Cointreau with your coffee! It's very soothing.' It was very soothing.[27]

Rowse has written a detailed description of the topics they discussed over several hours at lunch. The afternoon was spent discussing history: a work-session on the typescript Rowse had brought.[27] 'I was utterly tired out, by the fullest and richest experience I have ever had,'[27] wrote Rowse.

Edward Stettinius, former Administrator of the Lend-Lease Program until appointed Under-Secretary of State in 1943 and Secretary of State in December 1944, had lunch and dinner with the Churchills on 9 April 1944. Although there was much important political, financial and military information discussed, Stettinius recorded in his diary that Churchill had 'an extraordinary number of brandies and ports' after lunch.[28]

On 23 August 1941, Mackenzie King, the Prime Minister of Canada for twenty-one years, dined at Chequers Court, the country house used by the Prime Minister of the United Kingdom. In addition to Churchill, his wife and their daughter Mary, General Sir Hastings Ismay (Chief military assistant), Commander Thompson RN (aide-de-camp) and Lord Cranborne (later Marquess of Salisbury; Secretary of State for Dominion Affairs) and Lady Cranborne were present. King wrote in his diary: 'Churchill talked very freely to me at dinner about many topics and also fully with any I brought up. He took a great deal of wine to drink at dinner. It did not seem to affect him beyond quickening his intellect and intensifying his facility of expression.'[29]

Clive Ponting, another of Churchill's biographers, has claimed that in the 1930s when 'Churchill's heavy drinking became a serious problem' his friends were naturally worried and this led Lord Rothermere (newspaper proprietor) to offer Churchill two bets. These were explained in a letter Churchill wrote from Hotel Mamounia in Marrakech to his wife Clementine on 30 December 1935:

First £2,000 if I went teetotal in 1936. I refused as I think life w[oul]d not be worth living, but 2,000 free of tax is nearly 3,500 & then the saving of liquor 500 = 4,000. It was a fine offer. I have however accepted his second bet of £600 not to drink any brandy or undiluted spirits in

1936. So tonight is my last sip of brandy. It was kind of the old boy to take so much interest in Randolph's health and my own. I think you will be pleased.[30]

Ponting offers no evidence for his assertion that Churchill's heavy drinking had become a 'serious problem' in the 1930s after it had begun in the 1920s.[8] Nor does he provide evidence of Rothermere's specific concern for Churchill's drinking habits, though Churchill himself admits that the wagers were offered because of Rothermere's concern for his and Randolph's 'health'. If this interpretation is correct, the fact that Rothermere's father had been a heavy drinker may have been a factor in the offer. However, it is known that Rothermere was not only a strong supporter of Churchill's but also that he liked to place wagers, and this may have been no more than a generous gift to a friend. Certainly, Churchill would have had a hard time winning his bet with Rothermere, as he apparently did, if he was suffering from the Alcohol Use Disorder as defined by the American Psychiatric Association.[31]

Based on the observations above, there is little doubt that Churchill consumed substantial quantities of alcohol on a daily basis, particularly at lunch and dinner, though probably his consumption was little different from the amount imbibed by many of those who moved in the same circles socially and politically at the time. This does not mean that he was suffering from Alcohol Use Disorder.

Was Churchill Ever Drunk?

Professor Warren Kimball, Churchill historian, has written:

> The potentially darker side of Churchill's use of alcohol has been presented, but only in caustic and irresponsible fashion. Neither those accusations, nor the argument that Churchill watered and nursed his drinks, are persuasive to this writer, but such is the fate of iconoclasm. All that said, there is no credible testimony of Churchill being drunk, in the falling down, non-compos mentis sense, while he was Prime Minister, whatever the occasional reports of slurred words.[32]

Grace Hamblin,[33] one of Churchill's personal secretaries, wrote to the *British Medical Journal* in response to Robertson's[3] article: 'I joined Sir Winston's secretarial staff in 1932 and remained with his family until his death in 1965.

In all those years, except for illness or holidays, I saw him almost daily and had a unique opportunity to watch his moods – sometimes sad, sometimes exuberant, but never the worse for drink.'[5]

Peck confirmed to Gilbert: 'Personally, throughout the time I knew him I *never* saw him the worse for drink. The glass of weak whisky, like the cigars, was more a symbol than anything else, and one glass lasted him for hours.'[34]

Sir Anthony Montague Browne, Churchill's principal private secretary for more than ten years until he died, and who spent most days with Churchill, wrote: 'In these circumstances it is possible to suppose that WSC's appreciation of alcohol would be increased, in short that he would drink more. The reverse was the case. It has always irritated me to hear the exaggerated tales of his consumption. I never saw him drunk, but enlivened, stimulated, sometimes eloquently impassioned in a theme after dinner.'[35] Montague Browne recalled a dinner at the Hôtel de Paris, Monte Carlo, one of thirteen consecutive nights that he had dined with Churchill *à deux*:

The night was balmy, the dining room magnificent and the food and wine was *sans pareil*. We drank pink champagne and WSC's conversation was a wonder and a delight … When we returned home [to La Capponcina], we had to negotiate the long flight of Capponcina steps. WSC said: 'Give me your arm, my dear, I'm a bit boozed.' There was absolutely no objective evidence of this.[35]

There is evidence that Churchill was somewhat inebriated on one occasion during the Tehran Conference in 1943 and on the night of 6 July 1944, though on neither occasion was he drunk in the 'falling down, non-compos mentis sense'. Corporal Danny Mander was in charge of security at the British Legation in Tehran when the Tehran Conference took place involving President Roosevelt and Marshal Stalin.[36] He recalls that:

The only time I saw the PM the worse for alcohol was when I helped him walk back to our legation after one of those long dinners with the Russians. It was a fine, clear night and he and Eden chose to walk rather than ride in the limousine. They were still on their feet – just. I put my arm within his to hold him steady and had a corporal do the same for Mr. Eden. Thus they continued straight and upright to the British consulate, talking together (but not carousing!) in proper British fashion.

Mander has made clear that Churchill and Eden need not have walked, because a limousine had been provided, but they decided to do so because it was a fine, clear night.[36]

According to Field Marshal Lord Alanbrooke, on 6 July 1944 Churchill 'was very tired as a result of his speech in the House concerning the flying bombs, he had tried to recuperate with drink. As a result he was in a maudlin, bad tempered, drunken mood, ready to take offence at anything, suspicious of everybody, and in a highly vindictive mood against the Americans'.[37]

This opinion is confirmed by Admiral of the Fleet Viscount Cunningham who wrote in his diary: 'There is no doubt the PM was in no state to discuss anything. Very tired and too much alcohol. Meeting starting unpropitiously by Brooke calling him to order by undermining the generals in command at Cabinet meetings ... This obviously hurt him badly. But he was in a terrible mood. Rude and sarcastic ...'[38]

Lord Avon (Anthony Eden, Foreign Secretary, at this time) also recorded in his diary:

> Sir Alan Brooke reproached the Prime Minister with lack of confidence in his generals. Mr. Churchill was hurt and indignant, since he took pride in his knowledge of strategy and his close relations with the commanders ... I called this 'a deplorable evening' which it certainly was. Nor could it have happened a year earlier; we were all marked by the iron of five years of war.[39]

Clearly, as Andrew Roberts has stated: 'The unimaginable pressures of his job had clearly got to Churchill, and on that occasion – a single one of the 2,194 days of the war – he cracked. Fortunately, no decisions were taken and there were no other accusations of drunkenness against Churchill at any other meeting of the war.'[40]

The Opinion of Churchill's Doctors and Nurses

We have had access to the clinical notes and letters of all of Churchill's doctors who left an archive. Lord Brain (see p. 431), Churchill's neurologist, records in his notes for 5 October 1949 that Churchill drank 'a fair amount, but never the worse for it. Three brandies after dinner.'[41] Lord Moran (see p. 443), Churchill's personal physician from 1940, did not leave a written comment about his patient's alcohol intake. In June 1952, however,

Churchill told Moran: 'I drink a great deal it keeps me going. Oh, not too much, Charles.'[42]

Alcohol does not feature as a clinical issue except in two instances. Firstly, when Moran supported Dr Thomas Hunt (see p. 439), who provided a second opinion in 1958 when Churchill suffered recurrent bouts of obstructive jaundice that were unrelated to alcohol (see p. 273).[43] Hunt recommended that Churchill must avoid 'any excess of alcohol'.[44]

Secondly, after Churchill had suffered a series of strokes and acute cerebrovascular events,[45–8] Moran considered that fatigue and alcohol might be contributing to Churchill's unsteadiness. In July 1953 after a conversation with Moran following which Churchill was in tears:

… he took refuge in levity: I am trying, Charles, to cut down alcohol. I have knocked off brandy … and take Cointreau instead. I disliked whisky at first. It was only when I was a subaltern in India, and there was a choice between drinking dirty water and dirty water with some whisky in it, that I got to like it. I have always, since that time, made a point of keeping in practice.[49]

Moran later commented: 'But since the stroke he has discovered that alcohol does him no good. It makes his speech more difficult to understand and fuddles what is left of his wits; and yet he does not attempt to control his thirst. "Is alcohol a food?" he inquires inconsequently.'[49]

In September 1953 Churchill asked his doctor why he was so unsteady the previous evening. 'Can you explain that, Charles?' Moran responded: 'Probably a combination of fatigue and alcohol.'[50] Moran then explained to Churchill why alcohol affected his gait since his stroke. 'When he was tired it made his walk very unsteady. He did not think there was much in this – but perhaps my warning may bear fruit.'[50]

In November 1953 Churchill told Moran: 'I am thinking of substituting port for brandy. You wouldn't be against that?'[51] Moran answered that: 'It was the lesser of two evils,' whereat Churchill grinned broadly.[51]

Although Moran appropriately recommended a reduction in Churchill's alcohol intake post-stroke, Moran never suggested that Churchill should eliminate or reduce his intake of alcohol during the Second World War or in the post-war period prior to his first stroke in 1949, which suggests that Moran did not consider that alcohol was impacting Churchill's personal and professional life. Based on Moran's published record of his professional encounters with Churchill, there is no support for the idea that Moran would have been too respectful to have discussed this with his patient.

Churchill's nurse for the last seven years of his life, Roy Howells, has written:

> Without any doubt at all, fine old champagne brandy was Sir Winston's favourite drink. Whisky was a close second, champagne third. But he loved to drink wine at meals and took it for both lunch and dinner. It was always white wine; he did not hold with switching to red wine for a meat course. His attitude was one of, 'I *like* white wine and I intend having it *whatever* I eat.' This was typical of the man. He knew what he wanted and most of the time people fell in with his likes.[52]

Did Churchill Ever Suffer from the Alcohol Withdrawal Syndrome?

Heavy regular drinkers who suddenly decrease their alcohol consumption or abstain completely, due to intercurrent illness, family pressure, self-motivation or difficulty in procuring alcohol, may experience the alcohol withdrawal syndrome, the features of which may include sweating, fast heart rate, tremor, irritability, anxiety, agitation, delirium, seizures and hallucinations. Indeed, alcohol withdrawal syndrome is one of the potential criteria that can be used to diagnose Alcohol Use Disorder.

Careful scrutiny of the medical and nursing records, particularly the fluid charts, written during Churchill's illnesses, indicates that despite not drinking alcohol until he was feeling better, he did not develop the features of Alcohol Withdrawal Syndrome.

For example, when Churchill was severely ill with pneumonia in Carthage in December 1943, he did not drink alcohol from the time the illness was diagnosed (12 December) until 17 December at 6 pm; his first drink then was a whisky and soda!

Medical Aspects

The *Diagnostic and Statistical Manual of Mental Disorders, 5th Edition (DSM-5)*[31] defines Alcohol Use Disorder as follows:

> A maladaptive pattern of substance use leading to clinically significant impairment or distress, as manifested by 2 or more of the following, occurring at any time in the same 12-month period:

1. Alcohol is often taken in larger amounts or over a longer period than was intended.
2. There is a persistent desire or unsuccessful efforts to cut down or control alcohol use.
3. A great deal of time is spent in activities necessary to obtain alcohol, use alcohol, or recover from its effects.
4. Craving, or a strong desire or urge to use alcohol.
5. Recurrent alcohol use resulting in a failure to fulfill major role obligations at work, school, or home.
6. Continued alcohol use despite having persistent or recurrent social or interpersonal problems caused or exacerbated by the effects of alcohol.
7. Important social, occupational, or recreational activities are given up or reduced because of alcohol use.
8. Recurrent alcohol use in situations in which it is physically hazardous.
9. Alcohol use is continued despite knowledge of having a persistent or recurrent physical or psychological problem that is likely to have been caused or exacerbated by alcohol.
10. Tolerance, as defined by either of the following:
    a. A need for markedly increased amounts of alcohol to achieve intoxication or desired effect.
    b. A markedly diminished effect with continued use of the same amount of alcohol.
11. Withdrawal, as manifested by either of the following:
    a. The characteristic withdrawal syndrome for alcohol
    b. Alcohol (or a closely related substance, such as a benzodiazepine) is taken to relieve or avoid withdrawal symptoms.

Based on all the clinical evidence available to us, and multiple contemporaneous sources, and notwithstanding Churchill's daily consumption of alcohol (except when he was ill), there is no evidence that Churchill ever met the necessary criteria for the diagnosis of Alcohol Use Disorder. We conclude, to use the familiar lay term, he was not an alcoholic.

Chapter 32

Churchill's Terminal Illness in January 1965 in London

Thus, quite peacefully, on the morning of 24 January 1965, he went out on the ebb tide.[1]

C hurchill went to the House of Commons for the last time on 27 July 1964, more than sixty years since his first attendance. On the following afternoon, the Prime Minister, Sir Alec Douglas-Home, accompanied by the Opposition Party leaders, Harold Wilson (Labour) and Jo Grimond (Liberal), and by the Leader of the House, Selwyn Lloyd, called at 28 Hyde Park Gate to present Churchill with a Resolution which had just come before the House and had been carried *nemine contradicente*.[2] There was no official ceremony in the Commons because there was concern that a farewell speech might prove too much for Churchill.[3] The Resolution read:

That this House desires to take this opportunity of marking the forthcoming retirement of the right honourable Gentleman the Member for Woodford by putting on record its unbounded admiration and gratitude for his services to Parliament, to the nation and to the world; remembers, above all, his inspiration of the British people when they stood alone, and his leadership until victory was won; and offers its grateful thanks to the right honourable Gentleman for these outstanding services to this House and to the nation.[4]

Churchill then spoke a few words of words of thanks after which the visitors were given champagne. Mary Soames, his daughter, was present to witness this 'muted, yet fit ending to a long, long day'.[2] On 15 October 1964 the General Election was held, the first which Churchill had not contested since 1900. The Conservative Party lost narrowly, and a Labour government was formed, headed by Harold Wilson.[4]

On 15 November Churchill's granddaughter Edwina and her husband Piers Dixon asked him to inscribe a copy of his biography for them.[4] Churchill also enjoyed the company of two former Prime Ministers during November 1964: Harold Macmillan (Prime Minister 1957–63) on 19 November and Anthony Eden (Lord Avon; Prime Minister 1955–7) on 27 November. Lady Violet Bonham Carter, a longstanding friend, visited on 25 November.[5]

On the day before Churchill's 90th birthday on 30 November 1964 many people gathered in the street outside Hyde Park Gate, when, 'carefully dressed and looking benevolent, Winston appeared at the open window of the drawing room so that the press could take some birthday photographs'.[6] Churchill's birthday brought an avalanche of good wishes (over 70,000[4]), one of which was inscribed to 'The Greatest Man Alive, WSC, London'. Montague Browne kept repeating: 'We are waist-deep in mail!'[7] The Queen sent flowers (birds of paradise and freesias): 'To Sir Winston with my sincere good wishes and congratulations on your ninetieth birthday, from Elizabeth R.'[7] The BBC showed *Ninety Years On*, a birthday tribute devised by Terence Rattigan and Noël Coward: it was full of Churchill's favourites – songs from the Boer War and the Edwardian music halls to 'Run, Rabbit, Run'.[6]

Churchill's 90th Birthday – 30 November 1964

On his birthday Churchill shaved, bathed and then went back to bed. It had been decided he should have lunch in bed in order to conserve his energies for the traditional large family dinner in the evening.[7] Lady Churchill had arranged for all his secretarial, nursing and domestic staff (ten in all) to gather in his bedroom to drink his health in Krug champagne.[6,7] Everyone individually wished Churchill a happy birthday, and he sat up in bed and beamed at the assembled company and held out his glass. The bedroom visitors sang 'happy birthday to you' then drank a toast proposed by Lady Churchill.[7] Lady Churchill also took this opportunity to thank the staff for their loyal and devoted care: 'I know you do it because you love him so.'[7]

Churchill had lamb cutlets, peas and potatoes for lunch and was joined by his wife and Montague Browne who sat at a small round table at the side of the bed.[7] At 3 pm the Prime Minister (Harold Wilson) called to bring Winston good wishes from the Cabinet. Churchill was resplendent in a red paisley smoking jacket of which he was very proud.[7] It had been given him by his wife on his previous birthday.[7] Lady Churchill and Wilson discussed the garden at Chequers, the Prime Minister's official country residence, before they toasted Winston in brandy. Churchill replied with a toast to the new government.[7]

Over 500 presents were received. Lady Churchill gave her husband a small golden heart enclosing the engraved figures '90'.[6] It was to hang on his watch-chain and joined the golden heart with its central ruby 'drop of blood' which had been her engagement present to him fifty-seven years before.[6] Montague Browne gave Churchill a recording of stirring military marches played by the Grenadier Guards.[7] Lord Moran (see p. 443) gave his patient a set of all the songs sung by the boys of Harrow School.[7] After shaking Churchill's hand, Moran said to Howells: 'If you tell him he ought not to do something he will not listen, but, if you can convince him that it is to his advantage, he will always listen.'[7] Howells noted that he was not sure this was *always* strictly true.[7]

That evening Churchill was again taken to the windows to acknowledge the cheers and singing of the crowd. The curtains were opened and Churchill 'raised his hand in the V-sign'.[4]

There was the 'usual hallowed family dinner party' to celebrate Churchill's birthday.[6] Those present were: his children (Randolph, Sarah, Mary); son-in-law Christopher; grandson Winston and wife Minnie; granddaughter Arabella; grandson Julian Sandys; granddaughter Edwina and her husband Piers Dixon; granddaughter Celia and Lady Churchill's cousin Sylvia (Henley). The only guests not members of the family were John ('Jock' (Joint Principal Private Secretary, 1951–5)) and Lady Margaret Colville, and Anthony (Principal Private Secretary) and Nonie Montague Browne.[7] Lord Montgomery had been invited but was himself ill in hospital.

Mary Soames wrote:

The house glowed with candlelight and flowers, and we were united yet one more time in drinking first Winston's health and then Clementine's. But this birthday evening had for us all a poignant quality – he was so fragile now, and often so remote. And although he beamed at us as we all gathered round him, and one felt he was glad to have us there, in our hearts we knew the end could not be far off.[6]

Churchill dined for the last time at The Other Club, held in the Pinafore Room at the Savoy Hotel, on 10 December 1964, fifty-four years since his first attendance.[4] Coote wrote in the history of the Club that: 'It had become increasingly difficult to awake the spark, formerly so vital; and all that could be said was that he knew where he was and was happy to be there.'[8]

Harold Macmillan spoke at the first dinner after Churchill's death on 18 February 1965:

> We all have this link in common whatever our political views may be. Our finest hour and our greatest moment came from our work with him … There are a great many in this room who have had our conflicts with him. In the end we invariably succumbed to that great charm, when, having shot down all our arguments in flames, he would nevertheless turn to us with a smile and say, 'There is something in what you say'.[8]

At the same dinner, Lord Chandos (formerly Oliver Lyttelton MP who served in three different roles in Churchill's war-time Cabinet) said:

> He enjoyed a good dinner. He made jokes at the expense of all but at the cost of none. He enjoyed a conflict of ideas, but not a conflict between people. His powers were those of imagination, experience, and magnanimity. Perhaps not enough has been made of his magnanimity. He saw man as a noble and not as a mean creature. The only people he never forgave were those, who, in the words he so often used, 'fell beneath the level of events'.[8]

On 6 January 1965, Churchill gave Montague Browne his 1964 Christmas present. It was six beautifully bound volumes of his speeches, edited by Randolph. 'To my surprise, with touching effort, he managed to sign them, his signature diminishing from Winston S Churchill to an exhausted W on the last volume. They were the last documents he ever signed.'[9]

On the evening of Thursday, 7 January 1965 Churchill dined as usual with Lady Churchill in the sunken dining room. They had cold duck, French fried potatoes and peas, and crème caramel. Churchill drank a glass of champagne followed by a brandy and then smoked a cigar before retiring to bed.[10] But he could not sleep and spent a very restless night.[10]

Nurse Howells wrote:

The next day he stayed in bed until evening, getting up for dinner which he sat through in a very subdued mood. He did not say very much, and when offered his cigar and brandy after the meal he said quite emphatically 'No, I don't want it'. He was even reluctant to go to bed. When he finally did go in the early hours of Saturday, January 9, he was not to get up again.[10]

The Final Two Weeks: A Further Probable Stroke

Howells has recorded that it was obvious on Sunday,10 January 1965 that something was very wrong.[10] Churchill had no appetite and was lethargic.[10]

Sir Winston lay in his huge double bed on the ground floor and appeared to be in a very depressed state. On the table at his bedside lay his gold watch, the gold cigar case given him by Onassis [Aristotle Onassis, friend and Greek shipping magnate], the gold clock given by Lord Beaverbrook [friend and minister in Churchill's wartime government] and a special copy of *This Island Race*, beautifully bound in red leather, a present from his publishers. Next to this was a pile of books from Kensington Public Library and a box of assorted cigars.[10]

Howells continued:

Lady Churchill and the family made every effort to try to lift him out of his depression. Flowers, specially brought from his Chartwell gardens, decorated the bedroom and were constantly being changed. Randolph and his son Winston called in, as did his daughter Mary. Sarah, Lady Audley, was abroad. She was informed that her father was not well, but it was not considered serious enough for her to fly straight back at that stage.[10]

The bed was covered with a blue blanket and at night a white counterpane, with handsewn raised red dots the size of sixpenny pieces, was put on.[10] Three radiators in the bay window warmed the room, keeping it at a constant temperature of 70°F.[10] When Sir Winston slept, the long flowered curtains were drawn at the window overlooking the garden. A green night light burned on the large writing desk in the corner.[10]

Lady Churchill was very distressed by her husband's deterioration, and Lord Moran was telephoned. Moran recorded:

At half-past eleven in the morning of January 10 1965 [according to Howells and Sir Russell Brain (see p. 431) it was 11 January] Howells telephoned to me. He did not think Sir Winston was so well. He could not rouse him. I found him propped up by pillows in his bed, his head bent forward, his hands laid out on the sheet, arranged for death. I lifted his left arm, and when I let it go, it fell to the bed. I could not feel a pulse. His hands were cold and he was blue about the mouth. I thought it wise to warn the public in my bulletin that he had had another stroke and that his condition was critical.[11]

On 11 January 1965 Brain recorded in his case notes that he had received another referral from Moran to see Churchill:

Charles Moran telephoned to say that Winston was not well and asked me to go and see him. I went between tea and dinner, picking up Moran on the way. As we drove there, he said that Winston was going down hill and the last few days he had been increasingly drowsy. We went straight to his room. His nurse said that he had deteriorated during the last few days. He could no longer stand unsupported. He had recently had difficulty in swallowing solids and fluids but was still swallowing semi-solids. He was still moving his limbs on both sides normally. He lay in bed with both eyes closed, peacefully. One could get a little response to questions – a grunt only, and he would not put out his tongue for me. He was like someone in a deep sleep. I could not detect any evidence of a fresh cerebral lesion, and both his plantars were flexor. I told Charles Moran I thought this was an episode of cerebral ischaemia and it was terminal. We went in to see Lady Churchill in the sitting room. She said he had been deteriorating recently. He could no longer feed himself, which had been embarrassing, and it meant he had had to have meals in his own room. I said he was seriously ill.[12]

Brain asked Moran how much Churchill took in about his birthday. Moran said it was hard to know. There had been a music-hall broadcast in the evening, and they thought he had appreciated some of it.[12]

Howells wrote that Moran and Brain:

> ... arrived at the house at 5.30 pm and were received by Lady Churchill in the drawing room. She showed them into the bedroom and withdrew. After a lengthy examination, the two doctors returned to the drawing room and gently broke the news to her that Sir Winston had suffered a stroke.[10] That evening Mrs Soames and her husband called to dine with Lady Churchill. All three spent some time at Sir Winston's bedside and were distressed when he did not appear to recognise them.[10] His cat, Jock, still slept on the bottom of the bed, curled up in a ginger ball.[10]

Montague Browne wrote that Churchill:

> ... was deeply unconscious, and even a layman did not need the confirmation of Lord Moran and Sir Russell Brain that this was the end of the road. The family were informed by CSC [Lady Churchill], and I told the Queen's Private Secretary and the Prime Minister. Pressed on how soon death was likely to take place, I can only say that I thought it would be later than one might expect, given WSC's extraordinary vitality, but even I did not guess that he would defy the darkness for another 14 days.[9]

Montague Browne sent the Duke of Norfolk, the Earl Marshal, a prearranged telegram 'Hope Not imminent'. Operation HOPE NOT was the official name for the arrangements for Churchill's State funeral.[9]

On Tuesday, January 12 the effects of the stroke became more obvious. Sir Winston's left side had become paralysed, and he could move his left hand only slightly.[10] He also had difficulty in focusing.[10] He began to develop a bad cough and was put on a course of antibiotics.[10] Brain had advised Moran to institute nasal feeding and an antibiotic, Achromycin™ [tetracycline].[12] The family rejected nasal feeding, however, so Churchill lived without prescribed nourishment for thirteen days after he became unconscious.[12] The news of the stroke was still kept secret.[10] The family and Lord Moran decided this was the best course because they knew that at the first mention of his illness an avalanche of sightseers would pack the quiet cul-de-sac outside.[10]

On 13 January Moran telephoned Brain and told him that Churchill 'Now had weakness of the left arm and leg. How long would he live – two days?'

Brain said it might well be a week. 'A bulletin might become necessary.'[12] In fact, Brain recorded that the weakness of the left arm and leg disappeared after a day or two and was therefore more likely to be due to fluctuating cerebral circulation rather than to a thrombosis as Moran had thought.[12]

By Thursday, 14 January Churchill's condition was causing considerable anxiety.[10] Howells recorded: 'Mrs Soames said she would stay at the house each night to help her mother who was bearing up magnificently under the strain.'[10] At this stage Howells had been on duty for eight consecutive nights and was due for a short rest.[10] However, Lady Churchill asked him to stay on. The entire arrangements for the nursing staff at the house were revised. Two nurses were to be on duty during the day, and two at night. Howells was to work at night with Ann Huddleston, a 23-year-old nurse from Yorkshire who had been trained at St George's Hospital and who had been with Churchill a year and was very popular with the family.[10] The day nurses were Felicity Leeming from Guernsey and Adrienne Knox from New Zealand.[10]

Montague Browne sent Lady Churchill a typewritten note on 15 January:

I am sorry to say that the Press are now aware of Sir Winston's illness. At the moment I have taken the line that we do not comment on his day-to-day health and that the health of a man of Sir Winston's age is inevitably fluctuating. I have indicated however that he is not well. I have spoken to Randolph who agrees we should issue a bulletin, and I will be back from lunch when Lord Moran comes. I suggest we should add to the end of the bulletin: Members of the press are particularly requested to await bulletins, rather than make enquiries of Sir Winston's family, medical advisors or household.[13]

According to Howells, the two physicians, Moran and Brain, Lady Churchill and Mary Soames had a long discussion in the drawing room on the morning of Friday, 15 January.[10] Moran and Brain knew that rumours about Churchill were already beginning to circulate and some had begun to reach Fleet Street. Moran explained that as Churchill was worse, a bulletin would have to be issued. Moran and Brain agreed on its terms.[12] Montague Browne was authorised to make a statement to the press agency saying that Sir Winston was not well following a heavy cold. The headlines in the early editions of the London evening papers were: 'Sir Winston unwell'. It was a tremendous understatement. But no one outside the Churchill family knew the real position.[10]

More than 500 people were jammed round the front door when Lord Moran walked out of the house after lunch on 15 January to read the first bulletin signed by Moran and Brain. Moran stood on the pavement and read from a slip of paper (Plate 21): 'After a cold, Sir Winston has developed a circulatory weakness, and there has been a cerebral thrombosis.'[14] Immediately a buzz ran through the crowd, 'he's had a stroke ... old Winnie's had a stroke'.[10]

Within an hour of the statement being made, the tiny Hyde Park Gate cul-de-sac was packed with newspapermen, photographers and television teams. People passing by saw them and swelled the crowd. 'At last the true position was being made clear,' wrote Howells.[10] But from now on there was to be added strain on the family because they were literally in a state of siege.[10] Huge arc lights shone on the front door whenever anyone entered or left the house, television cables lay across the pavement, dispatch riders constantly revved their motorcycles as they waited for pictures to be rushed back to newspaper offices, a mobile canteen was set up at the end of the street, television commentators seemed to be continually recording or perhaps rehearsing their on-the-spot reports.[10] A Salvation Army band asked if they could play outside the house.[10] They were thanked and reluctantly turned down.[10]

Lady Asquith of Yarnbury (formerly Lady Violet Bonham Carter), a very longstanding friend of Churchill's,[15] was telephoned by Sylvia Henley, Lady Churchill's cousin:

To tell me that beloved W was very ill. They were trying to keep it secret till 7 o'clock news ... I felt stunned ... Murray let me in to the front door [at 4.30 pm[14]] ... Clemmie came down – very brave but looked worn out. She asked if I w[ou]ld like to come & see him & I went into his bedroom. He was propped up on pillows – breathing quite easily and quietly & his beloved face looked at peace ... I sat beside him – longing to exchange one last thought or word ... When he is gone I shall feel 'that there is nothing left extraordinary under the visiting moon'. I left him with a wrench and reeled out into the mob of press & flashlights – the reporters surrounded me 'How did you find him Lady Asquith?' I said 'very peaceful' & evaded a shower of questions by taking refuge in my taxi'.[16]

Other visitors on 15 January included the Prime Minister, Harold Wilson.[14] Moran's second bulletin on 15 January was issued at 9.41 pm after another 45-minute visit. This stated: 'There has been little change in Sir Winston's condition during the day. He is slipping into deeper sleep and is not conscious of pain or discomfort. A further bulletin will be issued at noon on Saturday [16 January].'[14]

Moran called as usual on 16 January, and two bulletins were issued. The first at 11.35 am stated: 'Sir Winston had a peaceful night. There is no material change in his condition.' The second at 9.32 pm stated: 'Sir Winston is a little weaker, but he has slept peacefully throughout the day.'[17] When he left a reporter asked Moran if Churchill was unconscious:

> He refused to comment. He knew his patient had been semi-comatose for the last three days but did not want to spread alarm and despondency. That night hope flickered briefly when Sir Winston appeared to be slightly improving. He seemed to recognise the voices of his visitors and managed to drink some glucose and orange juice. His temperature was down to normal, and a wave of optimism swept through the house. It was not to last long.[10]

Brain records that Moran kept him informed of events up to the time of Churchill's death. At some time during this period, Brain advised injections of phenobarbital for leg twitching that had developed,[11] but these were already being given for Churchill's restlessness.[12] The nature of the leg twitching, not directly observed by Brain, is uncertain. Spasticity had never been a prominent feature of Churchill's multiple strokes, and it seems quite possible that these were myoclonic jerks.

Murray recalled:

> Four days, I was told, was the most that Sir Winston could be expected to survive, but he defied all the expert predictions. For the next nine days, I stood guard, mostly for as long as 18 hours a day, there in front of that house in Kensington where the public and the world press began to congregate in their hundreds. At one time it looked as if he might defy all the predictions, and pull through, from the fourth day he rallied slightly. I had myself been in to see him that morning, as usual, as I stood beside his bed he seemed to be unaware of my presence and made

no response when the nurse Roy Howells, announced me. Then gently I placed my hand in his right hand as it lay on the counter pain, and at once his fingers curved from mine and a firm grip. At that moment the nurse, seeing the rebirth of interest, offered a glass of orange juice to the invalid, and for the first time in four days he sipped from the glass. His complexion improved, losing the bluish tint of past days, and optimism grew. Young Winston came into the room, then followed me into the lounge when I left. 'He'll do it on them yet, Sergeant Murray', he said with a hint of excitement in his voice as he offered me a Scotch.[3]

Churchill's grandson Winston has written that although:

Lord Moran had ordained that he should be given no further sustenance or liquid ... I could not bear to see how parched his lips had become and the way in which they moved involuntarily as if asking for a drink, so, in defiance of the eminent doctor's injunction, I gave him a small sip of orange juice from a jug that was still by the bed.[1]

Montague Browne has written:

At intervals, I went into WSC's bedroom, formerly my office. There was no visible change, and as he lay as though asleep, with a nurse sitting beside him and occasionally moistening his lips. I sat with him briefly and held his hand. His hands were beautiful. Aristocratic is a silly word to describe physical attributes; aristocrats come in all shapes and sizes, but there was something aesthetically appealing about those hands, and the word did seem suitable.[9]

The first bulletin on 17 January was issued at midday after Moran had visited for an hour. It stated: 'Sir Winston had a peaceful night but has had a rather restless morning. There has been some irregularity of the pulse.'[17] The second bulletin was issued at 8.33 pm after Moran's second visit of the day which lasted 30 minutes: 'After a restless start Sir Winston has had a peaceful day, but he has lost ground. There will be a further bulletin tomorrow.'[17]

The first bulletin issued on the morning of 18 January after Moran had visited for 33 minutes stated: 'Sir Winston has had a restful night. He is a little weaker, but otherwise, there is nothing to report.' A crowd of several hundred were held back in near-freezing temperatures by twenty policemen as Moran read out the second bulletin issued at 9.40 pm which stated: 'Sir Winston has had a peaceful day and there is no change in his condition. There will be another bulletin tomorrow about noon.'[18] After Moran read his statement, he was asked if this was a hopeful sign. He replied: 'I think the bulletin is all I can give you.'[18]

At 2.30 am on 19 January Churchill's breathing became erratic, and Moran was called from his bed at 2 am.[10, 18] He arrived at the house, slipped off his overcoat and white silk scarf and hurried into the bedroom.[10] After examining Churchill, Moran talked to Lady Churchill and Mary Soames but advised against calling the family to the house at that stage.[10]

Moran later recalled this night:

The nurse on duty thought he was dying. But when I came to him there was no change. Meanwhile the world seemed to stand still, half incredulous that this man whom they held in reverence for what he had done was about to be taken from them. The narrow street was blocked by reporters. They did not speak to one another; they appeared numb by what was happening behind the great black door. As I came out, there was a shuffling of feet as they pushed forward to catch my words.[11]

Moran visited Churchill on two further occasions that day.[18]

Howells has explained that each day the routine was the same. Moran called, examined his patient, talked to Lady Churchill to decide on the wording of the bulletin, which he then read on the doorstep to the pressmen.[10] Lady Churchill's room was immediately above the front door and the TV arc lights directly faced it. Each night when she retired she could hear the crowds outside and there was the continual strain of the glaring lights, the crowds and the noise.[10]

Lady Churchill asked Montague Browne at 5.30 pm on 19 January to request the press to withdraw, which he did:

Lady Churchill expresses her true thanks to members of the press, who have shown great kindness and restraint. However, she would be most grateful if the press, radio, TV and film representatives could withdraw from Hyde Park Gate. The numbers have grown to such an extent that the cameras, floodlights and inevitable disturbance have become a severe strain, apart from obstructing the street. In future, medical bulletins will be issued over the telephone to the news agencies and not read aloud at the front door.[19]

Within a few minutes the television arc lights went out and camera crews began to pack up their equipment.[19] Lady Churchill sent a special word of appreciation to the pressmen via Montague Browne who stopped his car on the morning of 20 January and thanked the press for the speed with which they had complied with the request. Lady Churchill was very touched he said. She had been feeling the strain.[20]

Three bulletins were issued on 19 January. The first in the morning stated that Churchill had spent a restless night and his condition had worsened. The second at midday stated: 'In the four hours since the last bulletin there has been no further deterioration.' The third bulletin was at 9.21 pm: 'Sir Winston has slept through the day, and there is no appreciable change in his condition since this morning. There will be another bulletin tomorrow morning.'[19]

Moran later wrote:

Day after day I was persuaded that he would be gone before the morning, but when the morning came he was still there. In bulletin, after bulletin, I felt I must prepare the public for his passing until I was at a loss what to say. From time to time the door of the bedroom was gently pushed open and one of the family would appear and stand by the bed and whisper: 'How long can it go on'. When I did not answer, I was left alone in the room, listening to the sound of his breathing. Randolph came in. I got up, and as I closed the door I saw him lift his father's hand to his lips. Lady Churchill drifted through the rooms. There was no expression on her beautiful face; she seemed to be in a trance.[11]

The first bulletin on 20 January was issued by Moran at 11.55 am. 'There is little to report. The restlessness has gone, and Sir Winston has slept through the night and morning.' The second bulletin was issued at 9.25 pm. It stated: 'The weakness of Sir Winston's circulation is more marked. There is nothing else to report. There will be another bulletin in the morning.'[20] When he left

Hyde Park Gate at 9.54 pm Moran was asked if Churchill was at a very low ebb. 'Yes,' he replied … 'his condition is very stationary.'[20]

On 21 January the first bulletin was issued at 12.16 pm, and this stated: 'There is no change in Sir Winston's condition. There will be a further bulletin this evening.' The second was issued at 9.35 pm: 'There was no change in Sir Winston's condition. There will be a further bulletin in the morning.'[21] The Prime Minister cancelled a visit to meet West German leaders in Bonn, and Sir Alec Douglas-Home (Prime Minister, 1963–4) cancelled a visit to his Scottish constituency.[21]

Brain recorded that Moran telephoned him on 22 January and said:

It was extraordinary that Churchill showed no evidence of dehydration and had passed several ounces of urine though he was not supposed to have had any food or drink for twelve days. 'Was that possible?' I said I thought it extremely unlikely. He said he thought someone might have been giving him fluids. I suggested getting his blood electrolytes done, but this fell through as he deteriorated.

Moran told Brain that Churchill had become pulseless and they prepared for the end, but he revived.[12] 'It was very embarrassing as official plans had been changed, etc. "They must think we are such ninnies!"' said Moran.[12] It was alleged that he (Churchill) had spoken to people.[12] Was that possible, Moran asked Brain?[12] Brain said he thought it very improbable.[12] Moran said that he had thought of publishing a statement about the illness in the *British Medical Journal* and *The Lancet* as Dawson had done in the case of King George V.[12] A statement had appeared in the *Evening Standard*'s 'Londoner's Diary' which had incensed Moran.[12] He thought that unofficial and inaccurate accounts might be published, but Brain said it was better to disregard the *Evening Standard* and do nothing.[12]

Moran issued the first bulletin on 22 January at midday which stated: 'Sir Winston had a quiet night and there is no change in his condition. There will be a further bulletin tonight.'[22] A second statement was issued at 9.47 pm which stated: 'Sir Winston had a quiet night and there is no change in his condition.'[22]

On 22 January Lady Churchill had a phone call from her grandson Winston to say that his wife, Minnie, had given birth to a son (Randolph) in the Westminster Hospital.[10] Howells commented that although they were overjoyed to hear the news, the joy was overshadowed by the fact that it was certain that Sir Winston would never see his great-grandson.[10]

The End

Howells recorded that the Churchill family retired to bed on the night of 24 January, giving instructions that the nurses should call them should there be any change.[10] Howells recorded that:

> Nurse Huddleston, and I took it, in turn, to sit at the bedside for the rest of the dark hours. It was about 5 o'clock when Mrs Soames returned as she had done every morning during the illness. There had been a change, and the three of us held a brief conference. It was decided that it would be better to let Lady Churchill get as much rest as possible, so she was not called. She came down a few minutes before seven and talked to Mrs Soames in the bedroom. They agreed to inform close members of the family. Mrs Soames telephoned from the morning room, also calling Lord Moran and Mr Montague Browne.[10]

Mary Soames wrote:

> I woke up at 5:30 on the morning of Sunday, 24 January and went downstairs. I met nurse Huddleston (who was on duty with Mr Howells) coming up to wake me – my father's condition had deteriorated, and she told me she did not think 'he could go on for very long'. We decided, however, not to wake my mother for a little while. About half-past six I was just going up to fetch her when she appeared. Lord Moran was sent for, and I started telephoning the other members of the family and Anthony Montague Browne. My mother and I sat on each side of my father. About a quarter-past seven Randolph and young Winston arrived and, soon after, Sarah and Celia. They all joined Clementine in Winston's room: Lord Moran and Anthony were also there.[6]

Lady Churchill sat by the bed holding her husband's right hand and was throughout on his right with young Winston on his left: other family members had gone into the drawing room for a while.[6] Mary Soames wrote:

Sitting exactly opposite my father, I suddenly noticed a change in him – his breathing seemed to alter. Through the open door, I signalled to one of the nurses, who observed the change and instantly ran along the passage to fetch the others. We gathered around him – Sarah, Celia and I kneeling at the foot of the bed, Randolph standing near the pillow by his son, Lord Moran on his right by my mother. I was dimly aware that at the back of the room the two nurses and Anthony had fallen to their knees. There was absolute silence – Winston gave two or three long, long sighs – nobody moved or spoke. Presently Clementine looked up at Lord Moran: 'Has he gone? she asked. He nodded. Presently, one by one we got up and silently left the room. I went back and remained with my mother some little time. Then we both kissed his hand and then his brow and left him.[6]

Montague Browne remembered that:

Early in the morning of 24 January one of the nurses telephoned to say that finality was very close. I went to Hyde Park Gate where the family was assembling. In his bedroom we stood, and as his breathing slowed, some of us knelt. Shortly after 8 o'clock, with a little sigh, his breathing stopped. It was the same hour on the same day of the month of January that his father had died.[9]

Moran later wrote:

For fourteen days he was not seen to move. His strength left him slowly, as if he was loath to give up life. On the night of 24 January it appeared that a crisis was at hand. His breathing became shallow and laboured, and at 8 o'clock in the morning it ceased. Mary, sitting by his side, looked up at me. I got up and bent over the bed, but he had gone.[11]

Young Winston later recalled:

The family assembled round his bed to take our leave of him. We knelt in the lamp-lit room in silent prayer, each with our own precious memories of this being we loved so deeply and who had meant so much to us all. Thus, quite peacefully, on the morning of 24 January 1965, he went out on the ebb tide.[1]

Howells recorded:

> It was now the final act. I went into the room where the family was gathered and said I think you had all better come in. My voice was a little hoarse, and I had to repeat myself. They came in one by one to join Lady Churchill and Mrs Soames, already kneeling at either side of Sir Winston's bed. Slowly the others sank to their knees around the room. He died a few minutes later, quite peacefully.[10]

Mary Soames recalled:

> During that day my mother and I spent a long period sitting there, in silent contemplation and recollection. Otherwise, Clementine remained most of the time in her room. She was perfectly calm, and addressed her mind to those matters which had to be discussed or decided. Anthony, who had through all these long days been a tower of strength, continued now to take an immense burden off Clementine, and dealt with the enquiries and messages which once again were at flood-tide.[6]

Murray wrote: 'On a grey Sunday morning that chill 24th of January 1965, at five minutes past eight o'clock … Sir Winston Churchill finally let go his hold on life. I saw him shortly afterwards, his features composed, and firm, and at peace'.[3] Soon afterwards, Lady Churchill discovered that there were no suitable candles to place in the room where her husband lay, and she asked Murray if he could find some. As it was Sunday no shops were open, but Murray was able to obtain the candles from the Savoy Hotel, and once they had been placed and lit, Lady Churchill asked him to 'sit with her for a while, there at the side of that humble bed in that small downstairs room at number 28 Hyde Park Gate'.[3]

Moran issued a statement at 8.36 am: 'Shortly after 8 am this morning, Sunday, January 24th, Sir Winston Churchill died at his London home.'[23] A spokesman at Hyde Park Gate (presumably Montague Browne) added: 'Sir Winston died in peace and without pain. Lady Churchill, his three surviving children and other members of his family were present.'[23]

Mary Soames recalls her mother asking her to telephone Violet Asquith and to invite her to come and take her leave if she so wished … 'Violet came to say a last goodbye. I took her to my father's room and left her.'[6] Violet Asquith wrote in her diary:

It is quite difficult to accept that this is <u>the</u> end … I could not face parting from his earthly presence – knowing that after today I sh[ou] ld never see his face again … I went to H.P. Gate at 2.30 – found Mary who was <u>most</u> sweet – quite calm & most understanding. Mary told me I c[ou]ld go in & see him & left me alone …[16]

Montague Browne recalled:

For some time before the coffin was closed, family and closest friends came to look on him for the last time. Violet Bonham Carter stood for ten minutes by him. She finally said: 'Goodbye Winston' and left silently. Jock, the yellow cat, of whom WSC was engagingly fond, came into the bedroom, jumped into the coffin, peered into the still face, and went away, never to re-enter the room again.[9]

Montague Brown went to Kensington Town Hall to register Churchill's death. The Registrar fired an unexpected question: 'What should I put down as Sir Winston's occupation?' Montague Brown considered that 'Retired' didn't seem right. So he said: 'Statesman'.[9]

On 25 January Violet Asquith delivered a eulogy on her departed friend in her maiden speech in the House of Lords:

I think it is hard to realise that that indomitable heart, to which we all owe our freedom and our very existence, has fought its long, last battle and is still. I count myself infinitely blessed in having known Winston Churchill as a close and dear and life-long friend. But, from the day of our first meeting in my early youth, I saw him always in a dual perspective. Through and beyond my friend, well known and dearly loved, I saw one of the greatest figures of all time upon the stage of history.[16]

Although Howells had not always found Churchill an easy patient to nurse, he wrote after the State Funeral Service:

As I stood there I felt a great emptiness, the legend had been so real to me … All of us felt a sense of loss, too personal to share even with each other. Memories flooded back as the world paid tribute … his courage … his humour … his pugnacity … his great love of people … his great love of life.[24]

Moran wrote:

> He was taken at night to Westminster, to the Hall of William Rufus, and there for three days he lay in state, while the people gathered in crowds that stretched over Lambeth Bridge to the far side of the river, to do honour to the man they loved for his valour. On the fourth day he was borne on a gun-carriage to St Paul's. There followed a long line of men in arms, marching to sorrowful music. With all the panoply of Church and State, and in the presence of his Queen, he was carried to an appointed place hard by the tombs of Nelson and Wellington, under the great Dome, while with solemn music and the beating of drums the nation saluted the man who had saved them and saved their honour.[11]

Medical Aspects

What can be added to this account of Winston Churchill's final illness? Perhaps first, that the accumulated recollections of so many of Churchill's family, friends and political colleagues present an extensive, comprehensive and most moving narrative of his last days, and the period leading up to them. It is true that no expense was spared, but deaths at home do not always occur with such timing, poignancy and peacefulness.

Churchill was clearly already fading at the time of his 90th birthday on 30 November 1964, and his decline following this was gradual but inexorable. Moran thought that Churchill had had a stroke on 10 January 1965, though Brain found no asymmetry of limb strength on 11 January. On 12 January, a definite left hemiparesis was recorded, but this apparently resolved over 24–48 hours. Clearly, there were fluctuating neurological signs, in a man known to have extensive cerebrovascular disease,[25-29] but in the context of Churchill's general condition at this time, with the attendant difficulties of detailed physical examination, and the limited significance of the findings in relation to the medical management of his terminal illness, these considerations are largely irrelevant. However, we may conclude that Churchill suffered at least a transient cerebral ischaemic attack (TIA) and in all probability another small completed stroke some twelve days before his death.

Churchill died with the greatest dignity. One might be forgiven for feeling that even Jock, the cat, understood how much Churchill meant to the nation and the world.

Chapter 33

Churchill's Doctors

I found that everything had been diagnosed and foreseen by Lord Moran[1]

In this chapter, we provide brief professional biographies of thirty-seven clinicians, including physicians, surgeons, anaesthetists, pathologists and general practitioners, who were involved in Churchill's care, from childhood up to the time of his death. Their involvement in looking after Churchill is described in the earlier chapters of this book.

In his childhood illnesses, Churchill's parents were able to engage doctors of reputation and skill. Later, following his distinguished military career and establishment as a major figure in British political life, with an international reputation, any doctor invited to see him did so without question. We are not aware of any doctor declining to see Churchill and most did not charge a fee.

From 1940 until his death in 1965, Churchill's personal physician was Sir Charles Wilson, later Lord Moran. Moran devoted himself to Churchill's care, travelling with him during the war and on most of his subsequent foreign travels, and was virtually always available at short notice for consultation when Churchill was in Britain. Moran, already a senior and distinguished physician in 1940, could call on any opinion he felt necessary, to Churchill's great advantage. The brief biographies presented here represent a catalogue of many of the most able specialists of their time.

Churchill lived a long life, during a period in which great advances were made in medical science and clinical practice, not least the availability of antibiotics (sulfonamides), which were almost certainly critically important in his recovery from pneumonia in 1943.

Some of the doctors involved in Churchill's care kept detailed records of their dealings with the great man, including comments about his reaction to the medical predicament in question as well as an objective clinical record. We have included these comments, because they help to provide a rich picture of the man – his fears, his frustration at being ill, his insights, his requests for detailed medical information, his supreme intelligence, and his enduring wit. But above all, his reaction to serious illness demonstrated his resilience, his sense of duty and his determination to continue to serve in high office. This is perhaps best manifested by his ability to continue during many stroke episodes due to cerebrovascular disease, as we have described. We believe this to be truly remarkable.

Dr Russell Brain, later Lord Brain, the pre-eminent neurologist of his generation, was closely involved in the assessment and management of Churchill's cerebrovascular disease, and with the permission of his son, Michael Brain DM FRCP, we have made many references to the case notes of his many encounters with Churchill. It is clear that while Moran had great respect for Brain's opinion and expertise, the two men did not always get along well at a personal level. We have provided evidence of a strained relationship at times, over many years, between the two men.

Churchill was invariably grateful to the doctors who cared for him, and he presented gifts to many, perhaps all of them after recovery from his various illnesses. Likewise, he was deeply appreciative of the care provided by the nurses who looked after him, particularly during his more prolonged later illnesses. We have already described some touching exchanges between Churchill and one or two of his nurses, and the later warm reflections of one of them.

The relationship between Churchill and his doctors was, for the most part purely professional, but we have identified two doctors, Sir Herbert Seddon and Sir Thomas Dunhill, with whom Churchill clearly formed closer personal friendships, to which we have alluded.

Dr Davis Evan Bedford CBE (1898–1978)

Bedford (Plate 22) entered the Middlesex Hospital, London, in 1916 but interrupted his studies in 1918 to serve as a surgeon sub-lieutenant on destroyers in the Royal Naval Volunteer Reserve. Bedford qualified in 1921[2] and specialised in cardiology first in France, then at the London Hospital (under Sir John Parkinson; see p. 444) and was appointed to the consultant staff at the Middlesex Hospital in 1926 at the age of 28.[2] Bedford's career was interrupted between 1939 and 1945, when he served with the Royal Army Medical Corps as a Brigadier in North Africa, when he was called upon to treat Churchill in Carthage (see p. 88)[3] and after Churchill had suffered a hip fracture (p. 333).[4] He was President of the British Cardiac Society and of the European Society of Cardiology. He was the first Editor of the *British Heart Journal*. In 1968, he was the Harveian Orator of the Royal College of Physicians; his Oration was entitled *Harvey's Third Circulation. De Circulo Sanguinis in Corde.*[5] He was appointed CBE in 1963.

Lord Brain Bt FRS (1895–1966)

Russell Brain (Plate 23) was a Consultant Physician at the London Hospital and Maida Vale Hospital for Nervous Diseases, London. Brain earned his living primarily from his private practice and as the author of *Diseases of the Nervous System, Clinical Neurology* and other medical and non-medical books.[6] He was President of the Royal College of Physicians from 1950–6, succeeding Lord Moran.[7,8] Brain assessed Churchill at Moran's request on 5 October 1949, 15 October 1949 and 8 December 1949 following Churchill's first stroke[9] and on multiple occasions in 1950–2 for further episodes of cerebrovascular disease,[10] in June 1953 after Churchill's second stroke,[11] in June 1955 after an ataxic stroke, again with an excellent recovery,[12] and a left hemisphere stroke in October 1956.[13]

Brain was knighted in 1952, made a baronet on 29 June 1954 and on 26 January 1962 was created Baron Brain, of Eynsham in the County of Oxford. In March 1964 he was elected a Fellow of the Royal Society.

Professor GAH Buttle OBE (1899–1983)

Buttle, affectionately known to many simply as 'B', enlisted in the regular Army at age 17 and in 1918 was commissioned as a lieutenant in the Royal Engineers.[14,15] After a year he decided to read medicine and entered St John's College, Cambridge. He qualified MRCS, LRCP from University College Hospital in 1924, received an honorary MD from Louvain in 1945, and was elected FRCP in 1970. Buttle joined the staff of the Wellcome Physiological Research Laboratories, where he remained for fourteen years, working first on digitalis and local anaesthesia then concentrating on antisera and drugs against streptococcal infections. He obtained Prontosil (sulfonamidochrysoïdine) from Professor Domagk. Domagk was Director of Bayer's Institute of Pathology and Bacteriology at Wuppertal and was awarded the Nobel Prize in Physiology or Medicine in 1939 for this discovery.

Buttle published papers on the *Pharmacology of the Sulphanilamide Group of Drugs* [16] and reported his findings on the action of sulfanilamide and its derivatives, with special reference to tropical diseases.[17]

At the outbreak of the Second World War Buttle transferred from the Royal Engineers reserve to the Royal Army Medical Corps, where he joined Brigadier Whitby (see p. 453) and became responsible for blood transfusion and resuscitation services first in the Middle East and then in Western Europe. Using his engineering skills, Buttle adapted gin and whisky bottles from messes in Cairo; and had needles, rubber tubing and bungs, and glass drip chambers made locally. Through his team of field transfusion officers Buttle transformed the surgery of the battlefield from El Alamein onwards.[18] It is of interest that to each bottle of blood products 1/1000 sulfanilamide was added as a preservative after Pulvertaft (see p. 445) had passed each bottle of blood as being bacteriologically sound.[19] More recently, it has become known that he treated Major (subsequently Major General) Orde Wingate in 1941 for cerebral malaria.[20] After the Second World War he was successively Wellcome Professor of Pharmacology at the School of Pharmacy, London (1945–66), with teaching duties at St Bartholomew's Hospital, London (1948–60), and then Professor of Pharmacology in Addis Ababa (1972–6) and in Riyadh (1974–8).

In 1942 he was appointed OBE for his contribution to war medicine.

Dr Derek HP Cope (1922–2015)

On leaving Epsom College in 1940, Cope was awarded the Freer Lucas entrance scholarship to the Middlesex Hospital, London, where he qualified in medicine in January 1945.[21] From September 1945 to April 1948 he worked as General Duty Orderly in the Royal Army Medical Corps, where he discovered his interest in, and aptitude for, anaesthetics. He was released from active military duty in May 1948 and began his training in earnest, obtaining a position as junior anaesthetist at the Middlesex Hospital. In 1951 he was appointed Senior Registrar and then in 1954 Consultant Anaesthetist at the Middlesex Hospital.

Mr Henry Couling (1837–1907)

Couling qualified from Guy's Hospital, London, in 1864 and received the Fellowship of the Royal College of Surgeons of Edinburgh in 1881. He was House Surgeon and Senior Obstetric Resident at Guy's Hospital before becoming in 1871 Assistant Surgeon at Sussex County Hospital, Brighton.[22] He acted in this role for twelve years. As a hospital surgeon he was considered to be sound in judgement, shrewd and conscientious in his work, kind beyond words to his patients and unsparing in the trouble he would take on their behalf; nor did he forget them when they left the hospital and had returned to their homes.[22] He soon became well known in private practice and made many friends before a severe illness compelled him for a time to give up work and seek health in a warmer climate.[22] On his return to Brighton he rapidly came to the front, enjoyed the full confidence of many leading members of the profession, and for years carried on one of the largest provincial private practices.[22]

Viscount Dawson GCVO KCB KCMG (1864–1945)

Bertrand Dawson (Plate 24) qualified in medicine at the London Hospital in 1890 and was elected to its honorary staff as assistant physician in 1896; he became full physician in 1906.[23] He became Physician-Extraordinary to King Edward VII in 1907 and attended the King on his deathbed. King George V confirmed him in his office and three years later made him a Physician-in-Ordinary. Henceforward, he was treated by the Royal Family not only as its medical adviser but as a trusted friend. He bore a heavy load of responsibility during the illness of King George V in 1928, when pleurisy was complicated by a lung abscess.[24] In January 1936, Dawson wrote the celebrated bulletin announcing that 'the King's life is drawing peacefully to its close', aided it is now known by Dawson late on the evening of 20 January 1936 administering morphine (grain 3/4) and cocaine (grain i) into the King's distended jugular vein.[24] He remained at the head of the medical households of Edward VIII, George VI and of Queen Mary.

On the outbreak of war in 1914, Dawson went to France as consulting physician to the British Armies, with the rank of Major General. Subsequently, he emerged as a leader of the profession. He was President of the Royal Society of Medicine (1928–30), a member of the Medical Research Council (1931–5), President of the BMA (1932 and again in 1943), and Senior Censor and then President of the Royal College of Physicians (1931–8).

Dawson understood his countrymen because he treated all men, whether dukes or dustmen, with the same sympathy and the same respect. His unselfishness and his humility are exemplified in a hundred stories of his dealings with patients of every social class. And with his qualities of humanity, he matched, in the words of *The Lancet*, 'a greatness of general ability rather than some particular excellence: in many ways, he was a shade better than the average first-class man'.[23]

He was created KCVO in 1911 and CB in 1916 for war services, GCVO in 1918, KCMG in 1919, he was raised to the peerage in 1920, was awarded KCB in 1926, made a Privy Councillor in 1929 and a Viscount in 1936.

Dr Peter Dinnick (1917–95)

Dinnick qualified from the Middlesex Hospital, London in 1939. During the Blitz he became the senior of only two resident anaesthetists. He later served as a specialist anaesthetist in the Royal Air Force in North Africa, and Italy.[25,26] At the end of the war he was a Squadron Leader, and returned to the Middlesex Hospital to be appointed to its consultant staff. Dinnick became Senior Anaesthetist at the early age of 42 in 1959, and for most of the next twenty-three years ran what was a very happy and successful anaesthetic department. He served as Vice President, Association of Anaesthetists, and was President of the Section of Anaesthesia of the Royal Society of Medicine.

Lieutenant-General Sir Robert Drew KCB CBE (1907–91)

Drew (Plate 25) graduated in medicine from the University of Sydney in 1930. He joined the Royal Army Medical Corps in 1931 and served in India from 1932–7 where he acquired great experience in tropical medicine. He was seconded to the (later Royal) Postgraduate Medical School, Hammersmith, in 1935.[27] He returned to the School during 1938–9 as a clinical tutor; his quality being recognized early in his career, since only doctors of the highest potential were selected for these posts. By 1938 he had gained the DTM&H of the University of London and Membership of the Royal College of Physicians (he was elected a Fellow in 1945) and was recognized as a specialist physician in tropical medicine.

After command of a field ambulance in the 4th British Division in the Second World War, he was given the task of training all the Army's medical officers in tropical diseases while he was Assistant Professor of Tropical Medicine at the Royal Army Medical College, London. He also acted as medical officer to the War Cabinet and gave vaccinations to Churchill, Eden and others. It is probably in this role that he assessed Churchill with Moran, Marshall and Whitby on at least two occasions (see pp. 73 and 127),[28] though his special expertise in treating infections would have made his opinion even more valuable and relevant.

Drew's ability, intelligence, social graces and phenomenal memory earned the respect and friendship of his younger colleagues who were later to become leaders of the civilian medical profession. This enabled him, as Director of Medicine of the Army Medical Services, to call for assistance from the most skilled and powerful doctors in the land. He rose to become Director General Army Medical Services and Vice-President of the Royal College of Physicians of London and was knighted in 1965.

Sir Thomas Dunhill GCVO CMG (1876–1957)

After matriculating at the University of Melbourne, Dunhill (Plate 26) studied pharmacy and was registered in June 1898, but he never practised.[29–31] Instead, in 1899 he began to study medicine. Dunhill's undergraduate career was impressive. He graduated in 1903 with three first-class honours and exhibitions in medicine and in obstetrics and gynaecology. In January 1906 Dunhill was commissioned as a captain in the Australian Army Medical Corps. On the outbreak of the First World War, he enlisted in the Australian Imperial Force as a major and was allotted to the 1st Australian General Hospital. In July 1918 he was appointed consulting surgeon to the Rouen area in France, and there he met and impressed many leading English surgeons, particularly George Gask, first Professor of Surgery in the University of London based at St Bartholomew's Hospital. Dunhill was mentioned in dispatches three times and was appointed CMG in 1919.

Dunhill returned to Australia in 1919. A brilliant and lucrative surgical career in Australia lay before him. In 1920, however, he accepted an invitation from Gask to join the professorial surgical unit at St Bartholomew's Hospital, London. Within a few years, he had established himself as the leading thyroid surgeon in England and the best general surgeon at St Bartholomew's. Dunhill was appointed surgeon to George V in 1928 and then successively to Edward VIII, George VI, becoming Sergeant Surgeon (senior surgeon in the Medical Household) in 1949, and finally Extra Surgeon to Elizabeth II. Dunhill looked after Churchill from at least 1941 until 1953. In particular, he repaired Churchill's inguinal hernia in 1947 (see p. 168).[32]

He was appointed KCVO in 1933 and GCVO in 1949.

Harold Edwards CBE (1899–1989)

Edwards (Plate 27) served in the Royal Engineers during the First World War (1917–19) before studying medicine. He qualified from King's College Hospital School of Medicine, London, in 1923. After graduating he spent the whole of his professional life at King's College Hospital, apart from further service in the army in the Second World War. He was appointed honorary surgeon at the age of 28 (five years after qualification) and retired in 1964. His surgery was 'punctilious, intense, and timeless; he cultivated in himself and among others a rigid discipline'.[32] His main interest was gastroenterology, particularly duodenal ulcer, Crohn's disease and diverticular disease. He was Dean of the Medical School from 1947–50.

Edwards was consultant surgeon to Southern Command, England (1942–4) with the rank of Brigadier, and then to Central Mediterranean Forces (1944–6). It was during this latter posting that he was called in to treat Churchill (see p. 150).[32] Edwards was President of the British Society of Gastroenterology (1961) and the Association of Surgeons of Great Britain and Ireland (1962) and Vice-President of the Royal College of Surgeons (1968–9).

He was appointed CBE in 1945.

Sir Crisp English KCMG (1878–1949)

English (Plate 28) qualified from St George's Hospital, London where he was William Brown scholar.[33–5] He won the Murchison scholarship of the Royal College of Physicians in 1900, the year that he qualified, and the Jacksonian prize of the Royal College of Surgeons in 1902 for his essay on *Fracture of the Skull, its Consequences Immediate and Remote, Including Pathology and Treatment*. He took the FRCS in 1903 and was a Hunterian Professor in 1904, giving three lectures on *The After Effects of Head Injuries*. English was elected an Assistant Surgeon in 1904 and Surgeon at St George's Hospital in 1912.

Initially, the First World War stalled his career intentions. He served with the Royal Army Medical Corps, as an operating surgeon in France and Italy and then in the Balkans as a consulting surgeon with the rank of colonel. His insistence on a regime of operating early and asepsis is credited with saving many lives.

English 'was an extremely dexterous, careful, and conscientious surgeon. There must be thousands who can testify to his skill and kindness and his unremitting care.'[35] 'He was a sound surgeon of wide interests, and being of handsome appearance and social and intellectual distinction he soon established himself in a very successful practice'[33] at 82 Brook Street, London. In 1933 he led the team operating on Princess Mary, the Princess Royal, only daughter of George V, sister of George VI and aunt of Queen Elizabeth II. He operated on two other princesses that year. English was never a prolific writer, but he made several useful contributions to surgical literature and published *Patients and Appendicitis* in 1946[36] *and Diseases of the Breast* in 1948.[37] He operated on Churchill for appendicitis in 1922 (see p. 20).

He was four times mentioned in despatches in the First World War was created CMG in 1917, and advanced to KCMG the next year for his distinguished services there.

Dr Herbert Robert Burnett Gibson (1885–1967)

Gibson joined the Indian Medical Service as a Lieutenant in 1909 aged 24 years.[38] His subsequent hospital ship experience gained him MD (Honours) from Edinburgh University for his thesis *Military Hospital Ships.*[38] He retired from military service with the rank of lieutenant colonel in 1926 and initially divided his time between the Winter Palace, Monaco (winter) and 18 Harley Street, London (summer), before devoting his whole time to his Winter Palace practice.[38] At the outbreak of the Second World War, he rejoined the military (age 55 years) as commanding officer of HMHS *Tairea.* Gibson received five medals for his service and retired to Monaco once more to resume his practice at the Winter Palace amongst a predominantly elderly population.[38] He submitted letters to the *British Medical Journal* until 1965.[38] Gibson treated Churchill in 1949 when he had suffered a stroke (see p. 182).

Dr Frederick Campbell Golding (1901–84)

Golding was born and educated in Australia, and his schooling was firstly in Sydney and then at Scots College in Melbourne.[39–42] He went to St Andrew's College of the University of Sydney to study medicine and qualified in 1926. A few years after qualification he came to England and obtained a post as registrar at the Royal Free Hospital. He then began to study diagnostic radiology after obtaining MRCP (Lond). After various appointments, including the directorship of the X-ray diagnostic department at the Royal Marsden Hospital, London, he came to the Middlesex Hospital, London in 1933 at the invitation of Sir Harold Graham-Hodgson to assist him in the development of the new X-ray diagnostic department. He was also Consultant Radiologist to the Royal National Orthopaedic Hospital, London.

His knowledge and teaching ability immediately made a great impression, and he was largely responsible for the important reputation developed by this department. In 1956 he succeeded to the post of Director of Diagnostic Radiology and held this until his retirement in 1967. He became Civilian Consultant in Radiology to both the Royal Navy and the Royal Air Force. He was also radiologist to the Medical Research Council Decompression Sickness Panel. He assessed Churchill in 1960 (see p. 309) and in 1962 (see p. 333).

Dr Thomas Hartigan (1871–1941)

Hartigan studied medicine in Dublin and Newcastle and graduated from Durham University in 1893, proceeding MD in 1907. He practised in London for many years, at Gloucester Terrace. His obituary in the *British Medical Journal* stated:

> With his quiet reserve, he was not an easy man to get to know, but behind this lay a fund of endearing qualities, not the least of which was his dry and never-failing sense of humour. He was the epitome of what a doctor ought to be: the kind physician with a power of imparting confidence and a sense of trust, given only to those possessed of real ability and a great human understanding. Neither rash nor too conservative in outlook in his dealings with patients, he held to the single objective of what was the very best which could be done for each one; added to this was a real kindness of heart, such as is rarely met.[43]
> He treated Churchill for appendicitis in 1922 (see p. 20).

Dr Christopher Langton Hewer (1896–1986)

Langton Hewer served in the Royal Army Medical Corps towards the end of the First World War and was appointed House Surgeon at St Bartholomew's Hospital in 1918, but thereafter concentrated on anaesthetics, being appointed to the Hospital staff in 1924 and retiring in 1961.[44,45] He worked with Boyle on the development of his eponymous continuous flow machine, and during the Second World War he was involved in the study of trichloroethylene as a battlefield alternative to ether and chloroform. His clinical skill was reflected in requests to anaesthetise members of the Royal Family, Winston Churchill and Bernard Shaw. The series *Recent Advances in Anaesthesia* first appeared in 1932 and continued under his editorship for fifty years. He was a founder member of the Association of Anaesthetists and also the first Editor of *Anaesthesia* in 1945, a position which he held for twenty years. He anaesthetized Churchill for his hip fracture in 1962 (see p. 333).

Dr Thomas Hunt CBE (1901–80)

Hunt (Plate 29) was educated at Magdalen College, Oxford and St Mary's Hospital Medical School, London.[46–8] He was appointed to the staff of St Mary's Hospital in 1930, ultimately becoming senior physician. In January 1940 Hunt joined the Royal Army Medical Corps. As a brigadier, he was consultant in Algeria and Iraq. With his headquarters in Baghdad, he visited most countries in the Middle East as well as India. He was appointed Senior Censor and Vice-President (1956), second Vice-President (1967), and Harveian Orator (1972) of the Royal College of Physicians. The subject of his Oration was *Digestive Disease: The Changing Scene.*[49] He wrote the Munk's Roll entry for Lord Moran.[50]

Until 1940 Churchill often consulted Hunt about his indigestion, and one day the future Prime Minister rang up asking for an appointment at 4.30 pm. Hunt was quite firm — he had another patient at that time. Churchill was nettled and chose an alternative physician.[48] Hunt was also involved in the decision, along with others, to decide whether or not Anthony Eden's health was robust enough for him to remain in office as the Prime Minister. The answer was a regretful but entirely firm 'No'.[48]

He treated Churchill again in 1958 (see p. 273). He was appointed CBE in 1964.

Professor Foster Kennedy FRSE (1884–1952)

Foster Kennedy trained in Belfast and qualified in 1906. His postgraduate training in neurology included a period at the National Hospital for Nervous Diseases, Queen Square, where he came under the influence of some of the founding fathers of British Neurology, including Henry Head, John Hughlings Jackson, William Gowers and Victor Horsley.[51,52] In 1910 he moved to New York, then during the First World War he served with distinction in France and was appointed a Chevalier de la Légion d'honneur. After the war, he returned to New York, later becoming Professor of Neurology at Cornell University. He is now best known for describing the Foster Kennedy syndrome and Kennedy's syndrome, and he was also among those who first described shell shock. Meticulous clinical observation was the hallmark of his career, and he became President of the American Neurological Association, and was elected a Fellow of the Royal Society of Edinburgh. However, his views on eugenics in relation to children with severe mental retardation were controversial and attracted opprobrium. He treated Churchill in 1931 following his road accident in New York (see p. 31).

Professor John Kinmonth (1916–82)

After Dulwich College, where Kinmonth passed the London First MB as an external student, he entered St Thomas's Hospital, London and qualified in 1938.[53–5] Appointed as house surgeon there he then became surgical registrar and resident assistant surgeon before entering the RAF medical service as a surgical specialist in 1943 and attaining the rank of wing commander. After war service spent mainly in West Africa, he returned in 1947 as a surgical research assistant at St Bartholomew's Hospital, London. There followed two years as a research fellow at the Harvard Medical School at Massachusetts General Hospital. On returning from the USA he became Assistant Director of the Surgical Professorial Unit at St Bartholomew's Hospital under Sir James Paterson Ross (see p. 449). In 1955 he was appointed surgeon to St Thomas's Hospital, London and Director of its Surgical Professorial Unit. He made outstanding contributions to surgery, especially in the peripheral vascular field. He was also responsible for setting up the cardiopulmonary by-pass work. Yet, it was his seminal research and publications on the lymphatic vascular system that earned him international renown.

In 1962, in collaboration with two colleagues in the United States (Charles Rob (see p. 446) of Rochester, New York, a former student contemporary, and Fiorindo Simeone of Boston) he published a combined work on vascular surgery. He was Arris and Gale Lecturer of the Royal College of Surgeons of England in 1953, Hunterian Professor of the College in 1954 and was elected to Council in 1977. Presidency of the European Society of Cardiovascular Surgery (1968), and of the Vascular Surgical Society of Great Britain (1973) followed. He was also Vice-President of the International Society of Cardiovascular Surgery. He was appointed Consultant in Vascular Surgery to the RAF in 1957. He treated Churchill in 1963 (see p. 351).

Dr Henry MacCormac CBE (1879–1950)

MacCormac was educated at the University of Edinburgh and graduated in 1903. After junior posts in London he was appointed to the Skin Department at the Middlesex Hospital, London, in 1912, a year after becoming assistant physician.[56–8] He was made full physician to the Department in 1920. During the First World War MacCormac served initially as a captain in the Royal Army Medical Corps but was later promoted to lieutenant colonel and was consulting dermatologist to the British Expeditionary Force in France. He was in medical charge of the 25th General Hospital, becoming Consulting Physician to Queen Alexandra's Military Hospital. In 1941 he was a Councillor at the Royal College of Physicians and in 1945 he delivered the Lumleian Lectures. He was President of the British Association of Dermatology in 1942. He treated Churchill from 1947–9 (see p. 359).

MacCormac was appointed CBE in 1919.

Dr Robert MacKenna (1903–84)

MacKenna entered Clare College, Cambridge, after attending classes at Liverpool University for one year; moving on to St Thomas's Hospital, London for clinical training.[59–61] After qualifying he worked as a clinical assistant in the dermatology departments of St Thomas's and of St John's Hospital for Diseases of the Skin. In 1927 he returned to Liverpool because both his parents were ill. He worked in his father's dermatological practice, and in the male venereal department of the Liverpool Stanley Hospital, where he later became honorary dermatologist. He resigned from his previous appointments in 1936 when he was appointed honorary dermatologist to the Royal Southern Hospital, Liverpool, where he also had teaching responsibilities.

At the outbreak of the Second World War, having previously volunteered for the Royal Army Medical Corps, he was mobilized as a lieutenant. In

1941 he was appointed adviser in dermatology to the War Office. When the invasion of Europe began it was considered that MacKenna had organized the best dermatological set-up of any army Britain had ever had. In 1943 he became War Office consultant in dermatology with the rank of acting colonel, local brigadier, an appointment he retained until 1964. In December 1945 he was released from military duty, being made an honorary colonel Royal Army Medical Corps in 1954. Soon after his release from the Army he was invited to be honorary dermatologist to St Bartholomew's Hospital, London. He treated Churchill from 1951 until 1960 (see p. 359).

MacKenna edited and revised the last three editions of his father's book *Diseases of the Skin*. His own book *Aids to Dermatology* ran into five editions. He edited *Modern Trends in Dermatology* for three series. He was a Councillor (1956–8) and Watson-Smith Lecturer (1957) of the Royal College of Physicians. He was President of the British Association of Dermatology in 1967.

Sir Geoffrey Marshall KCVO CBE (1887–1982)

Marshall (Plate 30) qualified at Guy's Hospital, London, in 1911. He became a Demonstrator in Physiology and Medical Registrar at Guy's Hospital. When war broke out in 1914 he served in the Royal Army Medical Corps as medical officer in France, and was in charge of the severely wounded transported by barge on the inland water transport unit. Thanks to his earlier specialization in physiology, he improvised means of administering gas and oxygen anaesthesia to these patients. For his services in France he was appointed OBE, and was twice mentioned in despatches. In 1919 Marshall was appointed Physician to Guy's Hospital, with a special interest in tuberculosis, and was recognized as one of the leading physicians in diseases of the chest.[62, 63] In 1934 he was invited to join the staff of Brompton Hospital, London. He was quick to adopt new and more active forms of treatment for tuberculosis and furthered the introduction and use of streptomycin; he was appointed Chairman of the Clinical Trials Committee of the Medical Research Council. During the Second World War Marshall was physician-in-charge at Brompton Hospital. 'He was magnificent in consultation, radiating confidence to the patient, who felt better at once. He had the ability to create within the doctor-patient relationship a feeling of warmth and friendship, which clearly existed between himself and the late

King George VI.'[62] He treated Churchill in 1943 (see p. 73) and in 1944 (see p. 127).

In 1951 his work as principal referee to the Civil Service Commission earned him his CBE and in 1951 he was knighted (KCVO) for his services to King George VI.

Lord Moran MC (1882–1977)

Charles Wilson (Plate 31) was appointed Dean of St Mary's Hospital Medical School, London, in 1920, a post he held until 1945. He became Churchill's doctor on 24 May 1940 and remained his personal physician until Churchill's death in 1965.[50] He treated Churchill for chest pain in December 1941 in Washington,[64] for pneumonia in London in February 1943,[28] for pneumonia and atrial fibrillation in Carthage in December 1943,[3] and for pneumonia in London in August 1944.[28] Moran also treated Churchill in 1949 when he suffered his first stroke[9] and was primarily responsible for managing the further episodes of cerebrovascular disease in 1950–2,[10] his second stroke in 1953[11] and Churchill's recovery from it,[65] the ataxic stroke in June 1955 again with an excellent recovery,[12] and a left hemisphere stroke in October 1956.[13] In 1958, he treated Churchill for pneumonia, atrial fibrillation and jaundice[66] and in 1962 cordinated treatment for Churchill's hip fracture.[4] He treated Churchill during his last illness (see p. 410).

Wilson was knighted in 1938, created Baron Moran of Manton in the County of Wiltshire in 1943 and was appointed Treasurer (1938–41), then President of the Royal College of Physicians (1941–50).[50]

Mr Philip Newman CBE DSO MC (1911–95)

Newman qualified at the Middlesex Hospital, London in 1934.[67] While still a registrar he joined the supplementary reserve of officers and, as a result, was posted to the 12th Casualty Clearing Station which was sent to France in 1940. In May 1940 the unit was at Béthune. Eventually the doctors were compelled to draw lots to determine who would be evacuated and who would stay with the prisoners. Newman drew the short straw and was taken prisoner. He was awarded the DSO for services at the evacuation of Dunkirk and after his escape to England he received the MC. After the war, Newman was appointed consultant orthopaedic surgeon at the Middlesex Hospital and the Royal National Orthopaedic Hospital, London. He was appointed a Hunterian Professor of the Royal College of Surgeons in 1954. In 1976 was elected President of the British Orthopaedic Association. He operated on Churchill's hip fracture in 1962 (see p. 333).

In 1976 he was appointed CBE.

Sir John Parkinson (1885–1976)

Parkinson (Plate 32) was appointed Assistant Physician to the London Hospital in 1920, Physician in 1927 and Physician to the Cardiac Department in 1933.[68] He was President of the Association of Physicians of Great Britain and Ireland and of the British Cardiac Society.[68] Parkinson and Evan Bedford were foremost in correlating the symptoms and electrocardiographic signs of myocardial infarction.[69,70] In 1930, Parkinson along with Louis Wolff and Paul White in the United States, described bundle-branch block associated with a short P-R period in healthy young people prone to paroxysmal tachycardia (the WPW syndrome).[71] Parkinson had first assessed Churchill in February 1942[64] and did so on multiple occasions subsequently and for the last time in 1953.[11]

He was knighted in 1948.[68]

Dr Otto Pickhardt (1887–1972)

Pickhardt attended Columbia University, New York and became a surgeon. He joined the Department of Surgery in Lenox Hill Hospital, New York in 1914 and remained affiliated with the Hospital until his death in 1972.[72]

Pickhardt served in the medical corps in both the First World War and Second World War. He was drafted into the First World War in January 1918 and served as a captain until October 1919. He served overseas and was stationed with the US Expeditionary Forces at the Russian Prisoners of War Camp at Sagan, Germany in 1919. In 1941, Pickhardt, who was then 55, again entered the Army as a lieutenant colonel. In March 1942 he established the 12th Evacuation Hospital, Lenox Hill Hospital Unit, which was made up of American doctors, nurses and enlisted men. The Unit was brought to the UK in January 1943 and was the first American military hospital based in tents in Britain.

After the war, Pickhardt returned to the Lenox Hill Hospital, serving as Director from 1945 to 1952. He is perhaps best known as the doctor who treated Churchill when he was hit by a car while visiting New York in 1931 (see p. 31). Pickhardt remained friendly with Churchill and when on duty in the UK during the Second World War he received a telegram inviting him to lunch with the Churchills at 10 Downing Street.

Professor Robert Pulvertaft OBE (1897–1990)

Known as 'Robin' to his family but 'Bulgy' to his friends (he was mildly exophthalmic), Pulvertaft (Plate 33) won a classics scholarship to Cambridge University but further studies were interrupted by the First World War.[73,74] He saw service as a lieutenant in Palestine, was later seconded to the Royal Flying Corps and became a bomber pilot in the Royal Air Force, in France. After demobilization he entered Trinity College, Cambridge, as a senior exhibitioner and took the Part II tripos in physiology. His medical studies were completed at St Thomas' Hospital, London, and after graduation he began a laboratory career at that same hospital. In 1931 he was appointed Director of Laboratories at Westminster Hospital, London and he acquired his Cambridge MD, with gold medal in 1933. He was subsequently appointed Professor at Westminster Hospital.

For the second time war interrupted his academic career and he joined the Royal Army Medical Corps as pathologist to the 64th General Hospital in Alexandria and he was soon appointed as Assistant Director of Pathology, with the rank of lieutenant colonel. This involved command of the Central Laboratory, housed in the 15th (Scottish) General Hospital in Cairo. Pulvertaft was interested in the bacteriology of war wounds and obtained a sample of Florey's penicillium. In his own laboratory Pulvertaft prepared extensive cultures of the mould in countless tanks of broth from which he extracted a crude filtrate which was then applied to infected wounds of battle casualties.[75] The Hospital's surgeons were impressed by the results. He treated Churchill in 1943 (see p. 88).

Pulvertaft was appointed OBE in 1944.

Lord Richardson Bt LVO (1910–2004)

John Richardson (Plate 34) undertook his clinical training at St Thomas' Hospital, London, where he won the Bristowe Medal and Hadden Prize, before qualifying in 1936 and being awarded a Perkins Fellowship.[76] His career was interrupted by being called up into the Royal Army Medical Corps in August 1939.[76] He saw service at Dunkirk and was later posted to North Africa as a medical specialist with the rank of lieutenant colonel. He looked after King George VI on a visit to the troops in 1942.[76] It was here that he met Harold Macmillan who was travelling with the royal party, which he described as 'the greatest good fortune of my life'; he was to act as Macmillan's personal physician for over forty years.

After the Second World War, Richardson returned to St Thomas' and, apart from an initial year off with pulmonary tuberculosis, spent twenty-eight years there as a Consultant Physician.[76] He was President of the Royal Society of Medicine (from 1969–71), President of the British Medical Association (from 1970–1) and recipient of its gold medal, and Master of the Society of Apothecaries (from 1971–2) and President of the General Medical Council from 1973–80.[76] He gave the Harveian Oration at the Royal College of Physicians in 1978 on *Harvey's Exhortation*, in which he emphasised William Harvey's exhortation to Fellows to keep their house in order. As his unpublished autobiography states, Richardson provided expert advice to Lord Moran on Churchill on several occasions.[77]

Richardson was made a Member (fourth class) of the Royal Victorian Order (MVO) in 1943, which was reclassified as Lieutenant (LVO) on 31 December 1984, for treating King George VI for sunburn. He was knighted in 1960, was made a baronet in Macmillan's resignation honours in 1963 and was created a life peer in 1979 taking the title Baron Richardson, of Lee in the County of Devon.[76]

Professor Charles Rob MC (1913–2001)

At Cambridge Rob joined the University Air Squadron, gained his wings and received a reserve commission in the RAF.[78] He went to St Thomas' Hospital, London, for his clinical training and graduated in 1937. At the outbreak of the Second World War, he returned from Montreal to London where he worked throughout the Blitz. When St Thomas' took over Hydestile Hospital, near Godalming, he was made resident assistant surgeon.

In April 1942 he joined the Royal Army Medical Corps and was posted to the 1st Parachute Brigade as a surgical specialist. In November of that year, the 1st Parachute Battalion was ordered to seize the airfield at Souk el Arba and the road junction at Beja, 90 miles east of Tunis. On 20 November

1942 Beja was bombed, causing many civilian casualties, and Rob performed more than 150 operations in a makeshift hospital in a former school. While he was treating his patients, a bomb fell outside the building, and Rob suffered fractures to his left tibia and kneecap. He continued to work and the next day performed twenty-two more operations. For this Rob was awarded the Military Cross. After the action in Tunisia, he went on to serve in command of a field surgical unit in Sicily and Italy, rising to the rank of lieutenant colonel.

After the war, he returned to the surgical staff of St Thomas'. In 1950 he was appointed Professor of Surgery at St Mary's Hospital, London. He became consultant vascular surgeon to the British Army. At a meeting of the British Medical Association in 1957, discussing the control of pain in a gangrenous limb, Rob told his audience: 'The best treatment for the condition is rest. The best way to rest is to sleep. The best way to get sleep is to relieve pain, and the best way to relieve pain is to give whisky - big and rapid doses up to the maximum tolerance of the individual.' His most famous patient would no doubt have approved! He treated Churchill in 1959 (see p. 303).

In 1960, he moved to the United States, to take up an appointment as Chairman of the Department of Surgery at the Strong Memorial Hospital in Rochester, New York. In 1978 he moved to East Carolina University in Greenville, North Carolina, as Professor of Surgery, and in 1983 joined the Uniformed Services University of the Health Sciences at Bethesda, near Washington DC.

Dr Dafydd Myrddin Roberts (1906–77)

Roberts qualified from Cardiff University in 1933 and was commissioned on 7 February 1941 as Flying Officer, Medical Branch RAF Volunteer Reserve with home postings. Roberts was promoted to Flight Lieutenant before he relinquished his commission on 5 January 1943 because of ill health.[38] Gilbert[79] stated that Roberts was invalided out of the Royal Air Force with a 90 per cent disability pension. After practising in Dublin in the early 1950s, he moved to the Alpes-Maritimes in 1953 living at Cap d'Ail, across the bay from Monte Carlo.[38] Roberts used David rather than Dafydd professionally. Gilbert[79] stated that he practised medicine in Monte Carlo, with the permission of the French authorities, on condition that he treated only British patients.

His first professional contact with Churchill was in 1956. Mary Soames quoted the letter of 3 March 1956 from her father to her mother: 'Nursing a sore throat with aid of Dr Roberts who I think is a good man (I had him last time you will remember).' The 'last time' refers to an earlier visit in January 1956, although there is no record of that attendance. Montague Browne described Roberts as 'conscientious and prompt'.[80] Mary Soames wrote: 'Both WSC and CSC liked him very much; Lord Moran was contemptuous of him – and, I suspect, jealous.'[81] Montague Browne wrote: 'I don't think Lord Moran much liked anyone but himself so much as laying a thermometer on his August Patient, but he did not come out unless summoned and this was infrequent.'[80] Moran's opinion of general practitioners, as his biographer has shown, is that they were not at the same 'level' as consultants.[82] Roberts continued to care for Churchill until 1962.

Roberts continued to practise in Monaco at Le Victoria, and as Physician at Princess Grace Hospital, until the 1970s when he returned to England.[38] He died on 28 July 1977 (six months after the death of Lord Moran) at the Cirencester Hospital, of bronchopneumonia, parkinsonism and cerebrovascular disease.[38]

Lady Churchill tried in vain to get Roberts some official recognition, not so much for his attentions to her husband as for those to the British community.[80] Early in their relationship, Churchill expressed gratitude to Roberts by presenting him with first editions of the *History of the English Speaking Peoples*: Volumes I and II at Christmas 1956; Volume III and Volume IV in March 1958.

Dr EC Robson Roose (1848–1905)

Roose (Plate 35) entered Guy's Hospital, London in 1867 and obtained his first medical qualification in 1870 (Licentiate of the Society of Apothecaries).[83] In 1872 he became a Member of the Royal College of Surgeons of England (MRCS). He was awarded the degree of Doctor of Medicine by a university in Bruxelles in 1877 after studying in Paris.[84] Roose became a Member of the Royal College of Physicians of Edinburgh (MRCPE) in 1875 and was elected to the Fellowship of the Royal College of Physicians of Edinburgh (FRCPE) in 1877.[83]

Roose was appointed Surgeon for District no. 6 of the Brighton and Hove Provident Dispensary in 1873.[85] In 1885 Roose closed his Brighton practice and thereafter practised only at 49 Hill Street, Mayfair, London.[86,87]

After Roose attended Mr Gladstone (Prime Minister four times) in one of his illnesses, his popularity steadily increased, and he built up a large and fashionable practice, although this apparently owed more to his social skills than any medical ones.[87, 88] Roose held no hospital appointment, but in 1895 was appointed Medical Attendant at the Turkish Embassy, London.[89] He was the Churchill family doctor and treated young Winston in 1886 when he had pneumonia and following a fall in 1896. Roose died on 12 February 1905 as a result of hepatic cirrhosis.[87]

Professor William Rose (1847–1910)

Rose entered the Medical School of King's College Hospital, London, aged 20. After qualifying in 1875 with first class honours in Surgery, he took the Fellowship of the Royal College of Surgeons of England (FRCS) in 1874.[90, 91] He acted for a time as House Physician at Brompton Hospital, London. Early in his career he attracted Sir William Fergusson's attention, and assisted Sir William in his private practice, instead of carrying on the family practice at High Wycombe as his father had hoped. Having been successively House Surgeon and Surgical Registrar to King's College Hospital, he was appointed Assistant Surgeon in 1876, became full Surgeon in 1885 and Professor of Surgery, and Consulting Surgeon in 1902. He practised privately from 17 Harley Street for many years. He was also Consulting Surgeon at the Royal Free Hospital. During the twenty-five years that Rose served on the staff of King's College Hospital he built up for himself a great reputation as a practical surgeon. He also acted as Surgeon to the London and Brighton and Great Eastern Railways and became a great expert in railway cases, and in the serious injuries that resulted. He treated Churchill following a fall in 1893.

Sir James Paterson Ross Bt KCVO (1895–1980)

Paterson Ross (Plate 36) entered St Bartholomew's Hospital Medical School, London, in 1912, with an entrance scholarship in science.[92] He was an outstanding student and was awarded the Treasurer's Prize and a junior scholarship in anatomy and physiology. His studies were interrupted during the First World War when he served as a sergeant dispenser to the 1st London General Hospital but was released and returned to St Bartholomew's

Hospital in 1915. He qualified with the Conjoint Diploma (MRCS LRCP) in 1917 and, after three months as a house surgeon, entered the Royal Navy as a Surgeon Lieutenant and was demobilised in 1919. After the war, Paterson Ross graduated in 1920 with distinctions in surgery and forensic medicine and was awarded the Gold Medal. At St Bartholomew's Hospital, he served as a Demonstrator in Physiology in 1920 and Pathology 1921–2. Shortly after, he went to Boston, Massachusetts, for neurosurgical training under Dr Harvey Cushing.

Returning to London in 1923, he joined Professor George Gask's newly established Surgical Professorial Unit at St Bartholomew's Hospital. Together with Gask, he developed a special interest in surgery of the sympathetic nervous system, and was awarded the Jacksonian Prize in 1931 for his essay on this subject. In the same year, he gave the first of three Hunterian Lectures; two others followed in 1933 and 1939. On Gask's retirement in 1935, Paterson Ross succeeded to the Professorial Chair at the age of 40.

He was appointed Civilian Consultant Surgeon to the Royal Navy and served as President of the Royal College of Surgeons of England, 1957–60. In 1949, when King George VI had developed signs of serious ischaemia in one leg, at the suggestion of the then Sergeant Surgeon, Sir Thomas Dunhill, Paterson Ross and James Learmonth were called into consultation and then undertook a lumbar sympathetic ganglionectomy operation. Paterson Ross was appointed Surgeon to HM Queen Elizabeth II in 1952. Paterson Ross assisted Dunhill (see p. 435) in operating on Churchill's inguinal hernia in 1947 (see p. 168).[32]

Paterson Ross was created KCVO in 1949 and made a Baronet in 1960.

Dr Joseph Rutter (1834–1913)

Rutter studied medicine at University College Hospital, London and qualified in 1860.[93] In 1860–1 he worked at University College Hospital, London as a physician assistant. He obtained MD (Lond) in 1862[94] and MRCP (Lond) in 1868.[95] Rutter's abilities at an early stage in his career prompted Sir James Clark (Physician-in-Ordinary to Queen Victoria) to offer him an appointment at Court.[93] Instead Rutter settled in Brighton in 1965 where he quickly gained an extensive practice. In 1870 he was appointed Physician in Ordinary to the Brighton and Hove Dispensary[96] and Consulting Physician at the Brighton and Hove Provident Dispensary.[97]

Rutter was appointed Assistant Physician at the Sussex County Hospital in 1873 and in 1884 he succeeded Dr EF Fussell as Physician at the Hospital.[98] He treated Churchill in 1886 for pneumonia.

Professor John Guyett Scadding (1907–99)

Scadding (Plate 37) trained at the Middlesex Hospital, qualifying in 1929. He was awarded the gold medal in the University of London MD examination in 1932.[99] He obtained an appointment at consultant level at age 27 (1934) in the new Academic Department of Medicine, with particular responsibility for respiratory disease, at Hammersmith Hospital, London (later to become the Royal Postgraduate Medical School), and in 1939 he was appointed Physician at Brompton Hospital, London.[99]

Scadding planned and conducted one of the first double-blind placebo-controlled trials (a study of sulfonamides in bacillary dysentery[100]) while working as Officer-in-Charge of the Medical Division of the 19th British General Hospital (some 3000 beds, under canvas), situated at Fayid, on the shore of the Great Bitter Lake.[99] He treated Churchill in Carthage in December 1943 (see p. 88).[3, 101]

After the Second World War Scadding was closely involved in the first MRC trial of streptomycin for the treatment of tuberculosis. As Dean of the Institute for Diseases of the Chest (now the National Heart and Lung Institute) at Brompton Hospital he played an important role in the establishment of academic respiratory medicine in the UK.[99] He was appointed the first Professor of Medicine at the Institute for Diseases of the Chest in 1963. He published on many aspects of respiratory disease, but was particularly well-known for his seminal work on pulmonary fibrosis and sarcoidosis, and he also published widely on medical semantics and the importance of clarity in definition in medical terminology and discourse.[99]

Professor Sir Herbert Seddon CMG (1903–77)

Seddon (Plate 38) graduated in 1928 from St Bartholomew's Hospital, London with honours and the University Gold Medal, passing his Final Fellowship Examination (FRCS) in the same year.[102] In 1930 he was appointed Instructor in Surgery to the University of Michigan at Ann Arbor. Seddon returned to the UK to take up appointment as Resident Surgeon at the Royal National Orthopaedic Hospital, Stanmore. There he spent eight pioneering years, but in 1939 he was appointed Nuffield Professor of Orthopaedic Surgery at Oxford.[102] There he undertook his work on peripheral nerve injuries which came to be accepted worldwide. The Institute of Orthopaedics in London had been created in 1946; two years later Seddon became Director of Studies and subsequently the first Professor of Orthopaedics in the University of London.[102] He became a member of the Medical Research Council for four years and was a member of the Advisory Medical Council of the Colonial Office and President of the British Orthopaedic Association.

Seddon treated Churchill after he had suffered a fracture of his fifth thoracic vertebra in November in 1960 (see p. 309). Seddon was also the leader of the surgical team responsible for treating Churchill's hip fracture in 1962 (see p. 333),[4] and he also treated Churchill again in 1963 for a disorder of his lower limbs (see p. 351).

Seddon's role with the Colonial Office led to extensive tours of Africa for which he was appointed CMG in 1951.[102] He received the accolade of Knight Bachelor in 1964. Churchill sent him a telegram: 'Warm congratulations on your most well deserved honour.'[103] Seddon replied: 'Your approbation means so much to me, and I am very grateful to you and to Lady Churchill for your kind message of congratulation.'[104]

Dr Kenneth Ward (1894–1981)

Ward was a general practitioner in Brasted, Kent, for many decades (1920s–1978)[105] and he acted as Churchill's general practitioner when he stayed at Chartwell. He was born in Brasted in 1894 and soon began accompanying his father on his medical rounds in a pony and trap.[105] Educated at Epsom College and Edinburgh University, Ward broke his studies in 1915 to serve as a medical officer in the Royal Navy.[105] After graduating he worked at the Edinburgh City Fever Hospital and then joined his father in general practice in the early 1920s. The Second World War found Ward on his own with a greatly increased workload. He developed the habit of rising at 5 am and working through until nearly midnight, continuing this practice until well after normal retiring age. He was possessed with extraordinary energy and enthusiasm; he truly enjoyed every minute of his work, so much so that he never took a holiday or indeed a night or weekend off work, Saturdays and Sundays being normal working days so far as he was concerned. Nothing was ever too much trouble. He finally retired in 1978 at the age of 84.

Professor Sir Lionel Whitby CVO MC (1895–1956)

At the outbreak of the First World War Whitby (Plate 39) enlisted in the Royal Fusiliers, was commissioned as machine-gun officer in the Royal West Kent Regiment, and served in Serbia, Gallipoli, Salonika and France. He rose to the rank of major, gained the MC for gallantry at Passchendaele in 1917 and was severely wounded in 1918, losing his right leg. He went up to Downing College, Cambridge, in 1918 to study medicine and then on to the Middlesex Hospital, London, in 1921. After qualification he was appointed Assistant Pathologist in the Bland-Sutton Institute at the Middlesex Hospital, and worked there until 1939.

Although his work was initially bacteriological, Whitby became increasingly interested in haematology – then a developing science – and, later, in experimental studies on the new sulfonamide compounds. These culminated in the introduction of sulfapyridine (M&B 693) for clinical use.[106,107] For this work Whitby was awarded the John Hunter triennial medal and prize by the Royal College of Surgeons, and in 1938 he delivered the Bradshaw lecture at the Royal College of Physicians on *The Chemotherapy of Bacterial Infections.*

After preliminary work begun in June 1939, Whitby took charge of the Army Blood Transfusion Service at the outbreak of the Second World War and so organised and developed it that blood or plasma was ultimately available to front-line units. For this major feat of organization which saved numberless lives, he rose to the rank of brigadier. He was awarded gold medals by the Royal Society of Medicine and Society of Apothecaries, and was appointed Commander of the American Legion of Merit and Chevalier de la Légion d'honneur. With the end of the war there commenced a chain reaction of honours and distinctions which lasted for the rest of his life.

His election as Honorary Fellow of Downing College, Cambridge in February 1945 and his appointment as Regius Professor of Physic (Medicine) at Cambridge later in the same year made him an obvious choice for the Mastership of Downing, to which he was elected in May 1947. This in turn brought him the post of Vice-Chancellor of the University (1951–3) and an Honorary Fellowship of Lincoln College, Oxford (1953). At the Royal College of Physicians he was a Councillor (1946–8). He treated Churchill in 1943 (see p. 73) and 1944 (see p. 119).[28]

In 1928 he was called in to attend King George V and was subsequently appointed CVO. He was knighted in January 1945.

Notes

Introduction
1. Lord Moran's Diaries. Letter from Lord Moran. *The Times*, 25 April 1966.
2. Lord Moran's Diaries. Letter from Lord Moran. *The Times*, 3 June 1966.
3. Moran. *Winston Churchill: The Struggle for Survival 1945–1965*. London: Constable & Company, 2006.
4. Lord Moran's Diaries. Letter from Sir Herbert Seddon. *The Times*, 17 May 1966.
5. Lord Moran's Diaries. Letter from Anthony Montague Browne. *The Times*, 6 June 1966.
6. Lovell, R. Choosing people: an aspect of the life of Lord Moran (1882–1977). *Med Hist* 1992; 36: 442–54.
7. Churchill Archives Centre, Churchill College, Cambridge. CHUR 2/530A-B/8-9. Letter from Lady Clementine Churchill to Lord Moran, 30 July 1964.
8. Soames, M. *Clementine Churchill*. London: Doubleday, 2003: pp. 546–73.
9. Lord Moran's Diaries. Letter from Randolph Churchill. *The Times*, 26 April 1966.
10. Lord Moran's Diaries. Letter from Randolph Churchill. *The Times*, 30 April 1966.
11. Lord Moran's Diaries and Sources. Letter from Lord Normonbrook. *The Times*, 24 May 1966.
12. Lord Moran's Diaries. Letter from John Colville. *The Times*, 27 April 1966.
13. Lord Moran's Diaries. Letter from Sir Reginald Watson-Jones. *The Times*, 13 May 1966.
14. Lord Moran's Diaries. Letter from Lord Brain. *The Times*, 10 May 1966.
15. Robitscher, JB. Doctors' privileged communications, public life, and history's rights. *Cleveland-Marshall Law Review* 1968; 17: 199–212.
16. Brain, WR. Encounters with Winston Churchill. *Med Hist* 2000; 44: 3–20.

Chapter 1. Pneumonia in March 1886 in Brighton
1. Churchill Archives Centre, Churchill College, Cambridge. CHAR 28/47/3. Letter to Lord Randolph Churchill from Dr Robson Roose, 15 March 1886 at 1 pm.
2. Churchill, WS. *My Early Life*. London: Macmillan & Co. Ltd, 1944: pp. 15–28.
3. Churchill, RS. *Winston S. Churchill. Volume I: Youth 1874–1900*. London: Heinemann, 1966: pp. 60–109.
4. Churchill, RS. *Winston S. Churchill. Companion Volume 1. Part 1 1874–1896*. London: Heinemann, 1967: pp. 97–160.
5. Lee, C, Lee, J. *The Churchills. A Family Portrait*. New York, NY: Palgrave Macmillan, 2010: pp. 29–46.
6. Churchill Archives Centre, Churchill College, Cambridge. CHAR 28/47/1. Letter to Lord Randolph Churchill from Dr Robson Roose, 14 March 1886 at 10.15 pm.
7. Churchill Archives Centre, Churchill College, Cambridge. CHAR 28/47/2. Letter to Lord Randolph Churchill from Dr Robson Roose, 15 March 1886 at 6 am.
8. Churchill Archives Centre, Churchill College, Cambridge. CHAR 28/7/93. Letter to Lady Randolph Churchill from Lord Randolph Churchill, 18 March 1886.

9. Churchill Archives Centre, Churchill College, Cambridge. CHAR 28/47/4. Letter to Lord Randolph Churchill from Dr Robson Roose, 15 March 1886 at 11 pm.
10. Churchill Archives Centre, Churchill College, Cambridge. CHAR 28/47/5. Letter to Lord Randolph Churchill from Dr Robson Roose, 16 March 1886.
11. Churchill Archives Centre, Churchill College, Cambridge. CHAR 28/47/6. Letter to Lord Randolph Churchill from Dr Robson Roose, 17 March 1886 at 7 am.
12. Churchill Archives Centre, Churchill College, Cambridge. CHAR 28/47/7. Letter to Lady Randolph Churchill from Dr Robson Roose, 17 March 1886.
13. Churchill Archives Centre, Churchill College, Cambridge. CHAR 28/7/91. Letter to Lady Randolph Churchill from Lord Randolph Churchill, 15 March 1886.
14. Vale, JA and Scadding, JW. Winston Churchill (1874–1965), Dr Robson Roose, MD Brux, FRCPE (1848–1905) and Dr Joseph Rutter, MD Lond, MRCP (1834–1913): treatment for pneumonia in March 1886. *J Med Biogr* 2018; online early: doi: 10.1177/0967772018754646.
15. Preston, SH, Haines MR. The social and medical context of child mortality in the late nineteenth century. In: Preston, SH, Haines, MR, eds. *Fatal Years: Child Mortality in Late Nineteenth-Century America*. Princeton, NJ: Princeton University Press, 1991: pp. 3–48.
16. Russell, J. The use of stimulants in pneumonia. *Br Med J* 1861; 1: 220–4.
17. Yeo, IB. An address on pneumonia. *Br Med J* 1884; 1: 1242–7.
18. Waters, ATH. Clinical lecture on pneumonia. *Br Med J* 1881; 2: 805–7.
19. Bristowe JS. Croonian lectures on disease and its medical treatment. *Br Med J* 1872; 1: 438–42.
20. Vale, JA and Scadding, JW. Sir Winston Churchill: treatment for pneumonia in 1943 and 1944. *J R Coll Physicians Edinb* 2017; 47: 388–94.
21. Vale, JA and Scadding, JW. In Carthage ruins: the illness of Sir Winston Churchill at Carthage, December 1943. *J R Coll Physicians Edinb* 2017; 47: 288–95.
22. Vale, JA and Scadding, JW. Sir Winston Churchill: pneumonia, pleurisy, jaundice and atrial fibrillation at Roquebrune-Cap-Martin and Chartwell, 1958. *J R Soc Med* 2019; 112: 11–21.

Chapter 2. Fall and Concussion in January 1893 in Branksome Dene

1. Court Circular. *The Times*, 11 January 1893.
2. Churchill, RS. *Winston S. Churchill. Volume I: Youth 1874–1900*. London: Heinemann, 1966: pp. 186–241.
3. Churchill, WS. *My Early Life*. London: Macmillan & Co. Ltd, 1944: pp. 39–56.
4. Vale, JA and Scadding, JW. Winston Churchill (1874–1965), Dr Robson Roose, MD Brux, FRCPE (1848–1905) and Dr Joseph Rutter, MD Lond, MRCP (1834–1913): treatment for pneumonia in March 1886. *J Med Biogr* 2018; online early: doi: 10.1177/0967772018754646.
5. Churchill, RS. *Winston S. Churchill. Companion Volume 1. Part 1 1874–1896*. London: Heinemann, 1967: pp. 350–405.
6. Seddon, H. Clinical records of Professor Harold Seddon relating to Sir Winston Churchill, 1960–1963, held by the Royal College of Surgeons of England (MS0279).
7. Moran. *Churchill: The Struggle for Survival 1945–60*. 2nd edn. London: Robinson, 2006: pp. 442–58.
8. Churchill Archives Centre, Churchill College, Cambridge. CHUR 28/152A/23/1-2. Letter from Winston Churchill to Jack Churchill, 3 February 1893.
9. Alizo G, Sciarretta, JD, Gibson, S, Muertos, K, Romano, A, Davis, J et al. Fall from heights: does height really matter?. *Eur J Trauma Emerg Surg* 2018; 44: 411–16.

10. Granhed, H, Altgärde, E, Akyürek, LM and David, P. Injuries sustained by falls – A review. *Trauma Acute Care* 2017; 2: 38.

11. Lallier, M, Bouchard, S, St-Vil, D, Dupont, J and Tucci, M. Falls from heights among children: a retrospective review. *J Pediatr Surg* 1999; 34: 1060–3.

12. VanWormer, JJ, Holsman, RH, Petchenik, JB, Dhuey, BJ and Keifer, MC. Epidemiologic trends in medically-attended tree stand fall injuries among Wisconsin deer hunters. *Injury* 2016; 47: 220–5.

Chapter 3. A Shoulder Injury in October 1896 in Bombay (Mumbai)

1. Churchill, WS. *My Early Life*. London: Macmillan, & Co. Ltd 1944: pp. 115–22.

2. Russell, DS. *Winston Churchill: Soldier*. London: Brassey's, 2005: pp. 135–85.

3. Manchester, W. *The Last Lion. Winston Spencer Churchill Visions of Glory 1874–1932*. New York: Little, Brown and Company, 1983: pp. 217–335.

4. Banta, JV. Churchill's shoulder: What if … ? *Finest Hour* 2007; 134: 40–3.

5. Churchill, RS. *Winston S. Churchill. Volume I Youth 1874–1900*. London: Heinemann, 1966: pp. 290–339.

6. Churchill, RS. *Winston S. Churchill. Companion Volume 1. Part 2 1896–1900*. London: Heinemann, 1967: pp. 852–5.

7. Churchill, RS. *Winston S. Churchill. Companion Volume 1. Part 2 1896–1900*. London: Heinemann, 1967: pp. 1006–9.

8. Churchill, WS. *My Early Life*. London: Macmillan & Co. Ltd, 1944: pp. 211–30.

9. Wallace, AL. Faithful but unfortunate: Churchill and his shoulder. *Shoulder & Elbow* 2019; 11: 4–8.

10. Churchill Archives Centre, Churchill College, Cambridge. CHAR 28/27/39. Letter from Winston Churchill to Lady Randolph Churchill, 6 April 1905.

11. Beasley, W. An approach to the natural: the Kenneth Russell Memorial Lecture. *ANZ J Surg* 2007; 77: 1045–52.

12. Brophy, RH and Marx, RG. The treatment of traumatic anterior instability of the shoulder: nonoperative and surgical treatment. *Arthroscopy* 2009; 25: 298–304.

Chapter 4. Donation of a Skin Graft in 1898 after the Battle of Omdurman

1. Moran. *Winston Churchill: The Struggle for Survival 1940–1965*. London: Constable & Company, 1966: pp. 521–33.

2. Churchill, WS. *My Early Life*. London: Macmillan & Co. Ltd, 1944: pp. 176–96.

3. Churchill, RS. *Winston S. Churchill. Volume I: Youth 1874–1900*. London: Heinemann, 1966: pp. 391–419.

4. Churchill, RS. *Winston S. Churchill. Companion Volume 1. Part 2 1896–1900*. London: Heinemann, 1967: pp. 973–4.

5. The Soudan Campaign. Back from Omdurman. *Morning Post*, 11 October 1898.

6. Churchill, WS. *My Early Life*. London: Macmillan & Co. Ltd, 1944: pp. 211–30.

7. Obituary: Sir Richard Molyneux. *The Times*, 21 January 1954.

8. Churchill Archives Centre, Churchill College, Cambridge. CHAR 20/198B/185. Letter from Sir Richard Molyneux to Winston Churchill, 22 January 1945.

9. Churchill Archives Centre, Churchill College, Cambridge. CHAR 20/198A-B/216. Letter from Winston Churchill to Sir Richard Molyneux, 28 January 1945.

10. Douglas, SR, Colebrook, L and Fleming, A. On skin-grafting: a plea for its more extensive application. *The Lancet* 1917; 190: 5–12.

Chapter 5. Appendicitis in October 1922 in London

1. Gilbert, M. *Winston S. Churchill Volume IV 1917–1922*. London: Heinemann, 1975: pp. 863–70.
2. Gilbert, M. *Churchill: A Life*. London: Heinemann, 1991: pp. 431–54.
3. Another speech by the Premier. Illness of Mr. Churchill. *The Times* 17 October 1922.
4. Beasley, AW. *Churchill The Supreme Survivor*. Frome: Mercer Books, 2013: pp. 48–59.
5. English, C. *Patients and Appendicitis*. London: J & A Churchill, 1946: pp. 43–60.
6. Churchill Archives Centre, Churchill College, Cambridge. WCHL 6/64. Clinical notes of Sir Crisp English regarding Winston Churchill and associated correspondence, 1922–42.
7. Mr. Churchill. Operation for appendicitis. *The Times*, 19 October 1922.
8. Roskill, S. *Hankey: Man of Secrets. Volume II 1919–1931*. London: Collins, 1972: pp. 279–303.
9. Gilbert, M. *The Churchill Documents Volume 10. Conciliation and Reconstruction, April 1921–November 1922*. Hillsdale MI: Hillsdale College Press, 2008: pp. 2061–99.
10. Gilbert, M. *Winston S. Churchill Volume IV 1917–1922*. London: Heinemann, 1975: pp. 871–92.
11. Gilbert, M. *The Churchill Documents, Volume 10. Conciliation and Reconstruction April 1921–November 1922*. Hillsdale MI: Hillsdale College Press, 2008: pp. 2100–29.
12. Jenkins, R. *Churchill*. London: Macmillan, 2001: pp. 370–92.
13. Mr. Churchill's message. 'I stand by Mr Lloyd George'. Fear of reaction. *The Times*, 28 October 1922.
14. Soames, M. *Speaking for Themselves*. London: Transworld, 1998: pp. 263–86.
15. Churchill, WS. *Thoughts and Adventures*. Wilmington, DE: ISI Books, 2009: pp. 213–29.
16. Mr. Churchill in tears. Labour triumph at Dundee. *The Times*, 17 November 1922.
17. Gilbert, M. *Winston S. Churchill Volume V: 1922–1939*. London: Heinemann, 1976: pp. 3–27.
18. Churchill Archives Centre, Churchill College, Cambridge. CHAR 2/442/18-19. Letter from Sir Crisp English to Winston Churchill, 18 October 1942.
19. Churchill Archives Centre, Churchill College, Cambridge. CHAR 2/531/8-9. Letter from Sir Crisp English to Winston Churchill, 19 May 1945.
20. Churchill Archives Centre, Churchill College, Cambridge. CHAR 2/531/7. Telegram from Winston Churchill to Sir Crisp English, 11 June 1945.

Chapter 6. A Serious Accident in December 1931 in New York

1. Churchill, WS. My New York Misadventure. *Finest Hour* 2007; 136: 24–8.
2. Packwood, A. *Churchill and the Great Republic*. Washington, DC: The Library of Congress, 2004: pp. 13–55.
3. Lough, D. *No More Champagne*. London: Head of Zeus, 2015: pp. 180–95.
4. Gilbert, M. *Winston S. Churchill. Volume V: 1922–1939*. London: Heinemann, 1976: pp. 420–7.
5. Thompson, WH. *Assignment: Churchill*. New York NY: Farrar, Straus and Young, 1955.
6. Churchill Archives Centre, Churchill College, Cambridge. CHAR 1/401A/51-52. Letter from Winston Churchill to Randolph Churchill, 20 January 1932.
7. Churchill Archives Centre, Churchill College, Cambridge. CHAR 1/399A/19/1. Account rendered by Dr Foster Kennedy to Winston Churchill.
8. Letter from Dr Otto Pickhardt to Phoenix Assurance Company, 15 January 1931. Available at: https://www.christies.com/lotfinder/books-manuscripts/churchill-winston-s-an-archive-of-correspondence-5382265-details.aspx (accessed 17 January 2019).

9. Churchill Archives Centre, Churchill College, Cambridge. RDCH 1/3/1. Telegram from Winston Churchill to Randolph Churchill, 15 December 1931.

10. Churchill Archives Centre, Churchill College, Cambridge. CHAR 8/290/38-39. Telegram from Winston Churchill to Hon. Esmond Harmsworth, 16 December 1931.

11. Churchill Archives Centre, Churchill College, Cambridge. CHAR 8/290/37. Letter from Literary Editor, *Daily Mail* to Winston Churchill, 29 November 1931.

12. Churchill Archives Centre, Churchill College, Cambridge. CHAR 28/145/93. Letter from Phoenix Assurance Company to WH Bernau, Lloyds Bank, 22 December 1931.

13. Churchill Archives Centre, Churchill College, Cambridge. CHAR 1/399B/151. Telegram from Winston Churchill to Professor Lindemann, 24 December 1931.

14. Churchill Archives Centre, Churchill College, Cambridge. CHAR 1/399A/85. Cable from Winston Churchill to Dr Hartigan, 28 December 1931.

15. Churchill Archives Centre, Churchill College, Cambridge. CHAR 8/290/43. Telegram from Winston Churchill to Hon. Esmond Harmsworth, 28 December 1931.

16. Churchill Archives Centre, Churchill College, Cambridge. CHAR 8/290/44. Telegram from Winston Churchill to Hon. Esmond Harmsworth, 30 December 1931.

17. Churchill Archives Centre, Churchill College, Cambridge. CHAR 1/222/36-37. Cable from Professor Lindemann to Winston Churchill, 31 December 1931.

18. Churchill Archives Centre, Churchill College, Cambridge. Telegram from Hon. Esmond Harmsworth to Winston Churchill, 1 January 1932.

19. Churchill Archives Centre, Churchill College, Cambridge. CHAR 1/401B/177-179. Letter from Winston Churchill to Randolph Churchill, 5 January 1932.

20. Churchill Archives Centre, Churchill College, Cambridge. CHAR 1/397A/79-80. Telegram from Winston Churchill to Louis Alber (President, Affiliated Lecture and Concert Association Incorporated), 2 January 1932.

21. Churchill Archives Centre, Churchill College, Cambridge. CHAR 1/401B/183. Account (2–22 January 1932) from Dr Graham, Nassau, Bahamas to Winston Churchill, 21 January 1932.

22. Churchill Archives Centre, Churchill College, Cambridge. CHAR 1/401B/160/1. Telegram from Winston Churchill to Dr Pickhardt, 3 January 1932.

23. Churchill Archives Centre, Churchill College, Cambridge. CHAR 1/397A/74/1. Telegram from Dr Pickhardt to Winston Churchill, 5 January 1932.

24. Churchill Archives Centre, Churchill College, Cambridge. CHAR 1/401B/177-179. Letter from Phoenix Assurance to Randolph Churchill, 5 January 1932.

25. Churchill Archives Centre, Churchill College, Cambridge. CHAR 1/397A/67-68. Telegram from Louis Alber (President, Affiliated Lecture and Concert Association Incorporated) to Winston Churchill, 7 January 1932.

26. Churchill Archives Centre, Churchill College, Cambridge. CHAR 1/401B/159/1. Telegram from Clementine Churchill to Dr Pickhardt, 7 January 1932.

27. Churchill Archives Centre, Churchill College, Cambridge. CHAR 1/397A/50/1. Telegram from Dr Pickhardt to Clementine Churchill, 8 January 1932.

28. Churchill Archives Centre, Churchill College, Cambridge. CHAR 1/401B/157/1. Telegram from Winston Churchill to Dr Pickhardt, 8 January 1932.

29. Churchill Archives Centre, Churchill College, Cambridge. CHAR 1/401B/155-156. Letter from Winston Churchill to Dr Otto Pickhardt, 8 January 1932.

30. Churchill Archives Centre, Churchill College, Cambridge. CHAR 1/397A/59-60. Letter from Winston Churchill to Louis Alber (President, Affiliated Lecture and Concert Association Incorporated), 11 January 1932.

31. Churchill Archives Centre, Churchill College, Cambridge. CHAR 1/401A/261. Account rendered by Mrs BM Maura, to Winston Churchill, 11 January 1932.

32. Churchill Archives Centre, Churchill College, Cambridge. CHAR 1/401A/289. Reference from Winston Churchill for Mrs Gertrude Sype, nurse and masseuse, 21 January 1932.
33. Churchill Archives Centre, Churchill College, Cambridge. RDCH 1/3/2. Letter from Clementine Churchill to Randolph Churchill, 12 January 1932.
34. Churchill Archives Centre, Churchill College, Cambridge. CHAR 28/145/105-106. Letter from WH Bernau, Lloyds Bank to Winston Churchill, 14 January 1932.
35. Churchill Archives Centre, Churchill College, Cambridge. CHAR 1/401A/12-13. Letter from Winston Churchill to Bernard Baruch, 18 January 1932.
36. Churchill Archives Centre, Churchill College, Cambridge. CHAR 1/400A/46. Letter from Dr Pickhardt for Winston Churchill to prove a medical need for alcohol, 26 January 1932.
37. Churchill Archives Centre, Churchill College, Cambridge. CHAR 1/401A/120. Letter from Winston Churchill to Duke of Marlborough, 26 January 1932.
38. Churchill Archives Centre, Churchill College, Cambridge. CHAR 1/400A/45 and 47-49. List of physicians provided by Dr Pickhardt for Winston Churchill.
39. Churchill Archives Centre, Churchill College, Cambridge. CHAR 1/400A/9/1. Letter from Winston Churchill to Dr Pickhardt, 14 February 1932.
40. Churchill Archives Centre, Churchill College, Cambridge. CHAR 1/399B/142/1-2. Letter from Winston Churchill to Louis Levy, 23 February 1932.
41. Churchill Archives Centre, Churchill College, Cambridge. CHAR 1/397A/27. Telegram from Louis Alber (President, Affiliated Lecture and Concert Association Incorporated) to Winston Churchill, 21 February 1932.
42. Churchill Archives Centre, Churchill College, Cambridge. CHAR 8/312/25. Letter from Winston Churchill to Thornton Butterworth, 1 April 1932.
43. Churchill Archives Centre, Churchill College, Cambridge. CHAR 1/400A/44/1. Letter from Dr Pickhardt to Winston Churchill, 25 April 1932.
44. Churchill Archives Centre, Churchill College, Cambridge. CHAR 1/400A/43/1. Letter from Winston Churchill to Dr Pickhardt, 4 May 1932.
45. Churchill Archives Centre, Churchill College, Cambridge. CHUR 2/339/198. Letter from Dr Pickhardt to Winston Churchill, 12 April 1957.
46. Churchill Archives Centre, Churchill College, Cambridge. CHUR 2/339/195. Letter from Winston Churchill to Dr Pickhardt, May 1957.
47. Seddon, H. Clinical records of Professor Sir Herbert Seddon relating to Sir Winston Churchill, 1960–3, held by the Royal College of Surgeons of England (MS0279).

Chapter 7. An Attack of Enteric Fever in September 1932 in Austria
1. HC Deb 21 March 1902; vol 105: cc740–811. Available at: https://api.parliament.uk/historic-hansard/commons/1902/mar/21/army-estimates-1902-3#S4V0105P0_19020321_HOC_287 (accessed 27 January 2019).
2. Ashley, M. *Churchill As Historian*. London: Secker and Warburg, 1968: pp. 1–11.
3. Gilbert, M. *Winston S. Churchill Volume V 1922–1939*. London: Heinemann, 1976: pp. 428–43.
4. Churchill Archives Centre, Churchill College, Cambridge. CHAR 8/311/7. Telegram to Winston Churchill from Lord Riddell, 4 August 1932.
5. Clarke, P. *Mr Churchill's Profession: Statesman, Orator, Writer*. London: Bloomsbury, 2012: pp. 116–51.
6. Churchill Archives Centre, Churchill College, Cambridge. CHAR 8/307/121-122. Letter to Lt Col Pakenham-Walsh from Winston Churchill, 23 August 1932.

7. Churchill Archives Centre, Churchill College, Cambridge. CHAR 8/307/123-125. Letter to Winston Churchill from Lt Col Pakenham-Walsh, 24 August 1932.

8. Churchill Archives Centre, Churchill College, Cambridge. CHAR 8/307/155. Letter to Professor Keith Feiling from Winston Churchill, 19 September 1932.

9. Gilbert, M. *The Churchill Documents Volume 12: The Wilderness Years 1929–1935.* 2nd edn. Hillsdale MI: Hillsdale College Press, 2009: pp. 471–9.

10. Churchill Archives Centre, Churchill College, Cambridge. CHAR 1/242/50. Account for professional services from Professor Dr Ludwig Petschacher, 21 September 1932.

11. Churchill Archives Centre, Churchill College, Cambridge. CHAR 1/242/41-49. Accounts for professional services from Sanatorium Dr Gebhard Hromada, 21 September 1932.

12. Kerschbaumer G. Margarethe Weissenstein. Available at: http://www.stolpersteine-salzburg.at/en/places_and_biographies?victim=Weissenstein,Margarethe (accessed 24 January 2019).

13. Mr. Churchill ill. Case not considered serious. *The Times*, 13 September 1932.

14. Mr. Churchill better. *The Times*, 14 September 1932.

15. Mr. Churchill. *The Times*, 15 September 1932.

16. Invalids. *The Times*, 16 September 1932.

17. Churchill Archives Centre, Churchill College, Cambridge. CHAR 8/311/32. Letter to Edward Marsh from Winston Churchill, 17 September 1932.

18. Mr. Churchill. *The Times*, 19 September 1932.

19. Invalids. *The Times*, 23 September 1932.

20. Mr. Churchill. *The Times*, 24 September 1932.

21. Gilbert, M. *Winston Churchill: The Wilderness Years.* London: Macmillan, 1981: pp. 48–68.

22. Churchill Archives Centre, Churchill College, Cambridge. CHAR 8/315/26-29. Letter to Duke of Marlborough from Winston Churchill, 25 September 1932.

23. Churchill Archives Centre, Churchill College, Cambridge. CHAR 8/311/45. Letter to Lord Riddell from Winston Churchill, 26 September 1932.

24. Churchill Archives Centre, Churchill College, Cambridge. CHAR 2/185/34. Letter to Winston Churchill from Sir Charles Mendl, 26 September 1932.

25. Stelzer, C. *Working With Winston: the Unsung Women Behind Britain's Greatest Statesman.* London: Head of Zeus Ltd, 2019: pp. 1–14.

26. Churchill Archives Centre, Churchill College, Cambridge. CHAR 1/242/61. Account for professional services from Beaumont House, 11 October 1932.

27. Mr. Churchill taken to nursing home. *The Times*, 23 September 1932.

28. Invalids. *The Times*, 1 October 1932.

29. Churchill Archives Centre, Churchill College, Cambridge. CHAR 8/311/46. Letter to CR Everitt from Violet Pearman, 1 October 1932.

30. Churchill, W. *Thoughts and Adventures.* Wilmington DE: ISI Books, 2009.

31. Mr. Winston Churchill better. *The Times*, 11 October 1932.

32. Churchill Archives Centre, Churchill College, Cambridge. CHAR 1/242/64, 68, 75, 81. Accounts for professional services from The Nurses Co-operation, October–November 1932.

33. Churchill Archives Centre, Churchill College, Cambridge. CHAR 8/315/46-47. Letter to George Harrap from Winston Churchill, 10 October 1932.

34. Churchill Archives Centre, Churchill College, Cambridge. CHAR 8/315/48. Letter to Winston Churchill from George Harrap, 11 October 1932.

35. Churchill Archives Centre, Churchill College, Cambridge. CHAR 8/315. Letter to Violet Pearman, personal secretary to Winston Churchill from James Harrap, 10 October 1932.
36. Churchill Archives Centre, Churchill College, Cambridge. CHAR 8/315/49. Letter to James Harrap from Winston Churchill, 12 October 1932.
37. Churchill Archives Centre, Churchill College, Cambridge. CHAR 8/309/47-48. Letter to Esmond Harmsworth from Winston Churchill, 18 October 1932.
38. Churchill Archives Centre, Churchill College, Cambridge. CHAR 8/313/113. Letter to Nancy Pearn, Curtis Brown from Violet Pearman, personal secretary to Winston Churchill, 20 October 1932.
39. Stelzer, C. *Working With Winston: the Unsung Women Behind Britain's Greatest Statesman.* London: Head of Zeus Ltd, 2019: pp. 15–45.
40. Hamblin, G. Frabjous days: Chartwell memories 1932–1965. *Finest Hour* 2002; 117: 19–25.
41. Gilbert, M. Winston S. *Churchill Volume V 1922–1939.* London: Heinemann, 1976: pp. 444–63.
42. Connor, BA and Schwartz, E. Typhoid and paratyphoid fever in travellers. *Lancet Infect Dis* 2005; 5: 623–8.
43. Harris, JB, Brooks, WA. Typhoid and paratyphoid (enteric) fever. In: Magill, AJ, Ryan, ET, Hill, DR, Solomon, T, eds. *Hunter's Tropical Medicine and Emerging Infectious Diseases.* 9th ed. London: Saunders/Elsevier, 2013: pp. 568–72.

Chapter 8. Chest Pain During Christmas 1941 at the White House

1. Moran. *Winston Churchill: The Struggle for Survival 1940–1965.* London: Constable & Company, 1966: pp. 5–23.
2. Gilbert, M. *Road to Victory.* London: Heinemann, 1986: pp. 1–22.
3. Churchill, WS. *The Grand Alliance: The Second World War Volume III.* London: Penguin Books, 1985: pp. 555–71.
4. Lavery, B. *Churchill Goes to War.* London: Conway, 2007: pp. 67–87.
5. Martin, J. *Downing Street the War Years.* London: Bloomsbury, 1991: pp. 66–9.
6. Churchill, WS. *The Grand Alliance: The Second World War Volume III.* London: Penguin Books, 1985: pp. 587–603.
7. Gilbert, M. *The Churchill Documents, Volume 16. The Ever-widening War 1941.* Hillsdale MI: Hillsdale College Press, 2011: pp. 1537–1718.
8. Kearns Goodwin, D. *No Ordinary Time.* New York: Touchstone, 1994: pp. 300–3.
9. Lovell, R. *Churchill's Doctor: A Biography of Lord Moran.* London: Royal Society of Medicine Services Ltd, 1992: pp. 157–75.
10. Lovell, R. Lord Moran's prescriptions for Churchill. *Br Med J* 1995; 310: 1537–8.
11. Meacham, J. *Franklin and Winston: a Portrait of a Friendship.* London: Granta Publications, 2003: pp. 139–65.
12. Churchill, WS. *The Grand Alliance: The Second World War Volume III.* London: Penguin Books, 1985: pp. 604–18.
13. Clinical records of Sir John Parkinson relating to Sir Winston Churchill 1942–54, held by the Royal College of Physicians.
14. Gilbert, M. *Road to Victory.* London: Heinemann, 1986: pp. 23–44.
15. Martin, J. *Downing Street the War Years.* London: Bloomsbury, 1991: pp. 70–4.
16. Lavery, B. *Churchill goes to war.* London: Conway, 2007: pp. 89–110.
17. Harvey, J, ed. *The War Diaries of Oliver Harvey 1941–1945.* London: William Collins Sons, 1978: pp. 85–206.

18. Gilbert, M. *Road to Victory*. London: Heinemann, 1986: pp. 44–59.
19. Gilbert, M. *Winston S. Churchill. Vol V.* London: Heinemann, 1976: pp. 781–93.
20. Baron, JH. Should we know about our leaders' health? *Standpoint* 2009; December.
21. Baron, JH. Churchill, Moran and the struggle for survival. *J R Coll Physicians Edinb* 2011; 41: 93–4.

Chapter 9. Pneumonia in February 1943 in London

1. Anon. Geoffrey Marshall obituary. *The Lancet* 1982; 320: 506.
2. Gilbert, M. *Road to Victory*. London: Heinemann, 1986: pp. 336–58.
3. Churchill, W. *The Hinge of Fate: The Second World War Volume IV*. London: Penguin, 2005: pp. 643–62.
4. Churchill, WS. War situation. Hansard 1943; 386: cc1453–531.
5. Pawle, G. *The War and Colonel Warden*. London: George G. Harrap, 1963: pp. 265–74.
6. Nicolson, N, ed. *Harold Nicolson: Diaries and Letters 1939–1945*. London: Collins, 1967: pp. 271–337.
7. Soames, M. *Clementine Churchill*. London: Doubleday, 2003: pp. 365–87.
8. Martin, J. *Downing Street the War Years*. London: Bloomsbury, 1991: pp. 94–100.
9. Danchev, A, Todman, D, eds. *War Diaries 1939–1945 Field Marshal Lord Alanbrooke*. London: Weidenfeld & Nicolson, 2001: pp. 376–86.
10. Moran. *Winston Churchill: The Struggle for Survival 1940–1965*. London: Constable & Company, 1966: pp. 84–9.
11. Gilbert, M, Arnn, LP. *The Churchill Documents, Volume 18: One Continent Redeemed, January–August 1943*. Hillsdale MI: Hillsdale College Press, 2015: pp. 536–871.
12. Rose, J. *Nursing Churchill*. Stroud: Amberley Publishing, 2018: pp. 141–66.
13. The Prime Minister's illness: Attack of acute catarrh. *The Times*, 20 February 1943.
14. Clinical records of Sir John Parkinson relating to Sir Winston Churchill 1942–54, held by the Royal College of Physicians.
15. Gilbert, M, Arnn, LP. *The Churchill Documents, Volume 18: One Continent Redeemed January–August 1943*. Hillsdale MI: Hillsdale College Press, 2015: pp. 304–535.
16. Dilks, D, ed. *The Diaries of Sir Alex Cadogan OM 1938–1945*. London: Cassell, 1971: pp. 481–560.
17. Harvey, J, ed. *The War Diaries of Oliver Harvey 1941–1945*. London: William Collins Sons, 1978: pp. 207–325.
18. Pugh, D. *Diary 1943*. Unpublished, 1943.
19. Anon. Plarr's Lives of the Fellows Online. Miles, Roger Paul Meredith (1915–1990). The Royal College of Surgeons of England. Available at: http://livesonline.rcseng.ac.uk/biogs/E007506b.htm (accessed 7 July 2017).
20. Vale, JA and Scadding, JW. Sir Winston Churchill: treatment for pneumonia in 1943 and 1944. *J R Coll Physicians Edinb* 2017; 47: 388–394.
21. Some clinical notes of Nurse Doris Miles and Nurse Dorothy Pugh relating to Churchill's illness in London in February 1943.
22. Nel, E. *Winston Churchill by His Personal Secretary*. Bloomington IN:: iUniverse, 2007: pp. 56–64.
23. Peck, J. *Dublin From Downing Street*. Dublin: Gill and Macmillan, 1978: pp. 67–83.
24. The Prime Minister better: No extension of lung inflammation. *The Times*, 22 February 1943.
25. Pawle, G. *The War and Colonel Warden*. London: George G. Harrap, 1963: pp. 232–41.
26. The Prime Minister: 'Pneumonia clearing'. *The Times*, 25 February 1943;4.
27. Avon. *The Eden Memoirs: The Reckoning*. London: Cassell, 1965: pp. 365–81.

28. The Prime Minister: Continuing to improve. *The Times*, 26 February 1943.
29. The Prime Minister: 'Further improvement'. *The Times*, 27 February 1943.
30. The Prime Minister: Condition continuing satisfactory. *The Times*, 1 March 1943.
31. The Prime Minister: Improving daily and getting up. *The Times*, 2 March 1943.
32. Rose, J. *Nursing Churchill*. Stroud: Amberley Publishing, 2018: pp. 167–208.
33. Gilbert, M. *Road to Victory*. London: Heinemann, 1986: pp. 359–86.
34. Flippin, HF, Schwartz, L and Domm, AH. Modern treatment of pneumococcic pneumonia. *JAMA* 1943; 121: 230–7.
35. Ministry of Health. *National War Formulary*. London: HMSO, 1943.
36. Lehr, D. Clinical toxicity of sulfonamides. *Ann N Y Acad Sci* 1957; 69: 417–47.

Chapter 10. Pneumonia and Atrial Fibrillation in December 1943 in Carthage

1. Packwood, A. *How Churchill Waged War: The Most Challenging Decisions of the Second World War*. Barnsley and Havertown PA: Frontline Books, 2018: pp. 183–204.
2. Churchill, W. *Closing the Ring: The Second World War Volume V.* London: Penguin Classics, 2005: pp. 372–87.
3. Gilbert, M. *Road to Victory*. London: Heinemann, 1986: pp. 550–69.
4. Churchill, W. *Closing the Ring: The Second World War Volume V.* London: Penguin Classics, 2005: pp. 287–301.
5. Hickman, T. *Churchill's Bodyguard*. London: Headline, 2005: pp. 157–75.
6. Moran. *Winston Churchill: The Struggle for Survival 1940–1965*. London: Constable & Company, 1966: pp. 125–32.
7. Martin, J. *Downing Street the War Years*. London: Bloomsbury, 1991: pp. 120–3.
8. Pawle, G. *The War and Colonel Warden*. London: George G Harrap, 1963: pp. 254–64.
9. Lavery, B. *Churchill Goes to War*. London: Conway, 2007: pp. 233–53.
10. Churchill, S. *Keep on Dancing*. New York: Coward, McCann & Geoghegan, 1981: pp. 98–139.
11. Macmillan, H. *War Diaries the Mediterranean 1943–1945*. London: PAPERMAC, 1985: pp. 273–310.
12. Ismay. *The Memoirs of Lord Ismay*. London: Heinemann, 1960: pp. 332–42.
13. Danchev, A, Todman, D, eds. *War Diaries 1939–1945 Field Marshal Lord Alanbrooke*. London: Weidenfeld & Nicolson, 2001: pp. 465–88.
14. Churchill Archives Centre, Churchill College, Cambridge. CHAR 20/130/1. Personal and Most Secret. Telegram to Foreign Secretary [Anthony Eden] from Prime Minister [Winston Churchill], 18 November 1943.
15. Avon. *The Eden Memoirs: The Reckoning*. London: Cassell, 1965: pp. 421–36.
16. Dilks, D., ed. *The Diaries of Sir Alexander Cadogan OM 1938–1945*. London: Cassell & Company, 1971: pp. 561–631.
17. Gilbert, M. *Road to Victory*. London: Heinemann, 1986: pp. 570–93.
18. Moran. *Winston Churchill: The Struggle for Survival 1940–1965*. London: Constable & Company, 1966: pp. 133–44.
19. Gilbert, M. *Road to Victory*. London: Heinemann, 1986: pp. 594–612.
20. Moran. *Winston Churchill: The Struggle for Survival 1940–1965*. London: Constable & Company, 1966: pp. 145–58.
21. Martin, J. *Downing Street the War Years*. London: Bloomsbury, 1991: pp. 124–33.
22. Danchev, A, Todman, D, eds. *War Diaries 1939–1945 Field Marshal Lord Alanbrooke*. London: Weidenfeld & Nicolson, 2001: pp. 489–505.
23. Lavery, B. *Churchill Goes to War*. London: Conway, 2007: pp. 255–66.

24. Mitchell, J, Feast, S. *Very Important Persons. Churchill's Navigator.* London: Grub Street, 2010: pp. 78–99.
25. Mitchell, J. Diary of a navigator pt 8. *Twenty Four* 2005; 16–21.
26. Churchill, S. *A Thread in the Tapestry.* London: Andre Deutsch, 1967.
27. Pawle, G. *The War and Colonel Warden,* London: George G. Harrap, 1963: pp. 265–74.
28. Grey-Turner, E. Pages from a diary. *Br Med J* 1980; 281: 1692–5.
29. Scadding, JG. A summons to Carthage, December 1943. *Br Med J* 1993; 307: 1595–6.
30. Soames, M. *Speaking for Themselves.* London: Transworld, 1998: pp. 471–95.
31. Hickman, T. *Churchill's Bodyguard.* London: Headline, 2005: pp. 177–200.
32. Lovell, R. *Churchill's Doctor: A Biography of Lord Moran.* London: Royal Society of Medicine Services Ltd, 1992: pp. 228–35.
33. Pulvertaft, RJV. *An Autobiography.* Unpublished, 2017.
34. Sakula, A. Churchill in Carthage, 1943: Dr Evan Bedford's war diary. *J Med Biogr* 2000; 8: 241–3.
35. Macmillan, H. *War Diaries the Mediterranean 1943–1945.* London: PAPERMAC, 1985: pp. 311–44.
36. Morgan, AD. Robert James Valentine Pulvertaft. *Munk's Roll* 1990; IX: 432–4.
37. Some medical notes of Brigadier D Evan Bedford relating to Sir Winston Churchill's illness in Carthage in 1943, held by the Royal College of Physicians.
38. Vale, JA and Scadding, JW. Sir Winston Churchill: treatment for pneumonia in 1943 and 1944. *J R Coll Physicians Edinb* 2017; 47: 388–94.
39. Self, ADH. Winston Churchill and M & B. *J Med Biogr* 2001; 9: 241.
40. Sakula, A. Winston Churchill and M & B: author's reply. *J Med Biogr* 2001; 9: 241.
41. Mr. Churchill: An attack of pneumonia. *The Times* 17 December 1943.
42. Gilbert, M, Arnn, LP. *The Churchill Documents, Volume 19: Fateful Questions, September 1943 to April 1944.* Hillsdale MI: Hillsdale College Press, 2017: pp. 1038–1291.
43. Clinical records of Sir John Parkinson relating to Sir Winston Churchill 1942–54, held by the Royal College of Physicians.
44. Colville, J. *The Fringes of Power.* London: Weidenfeld & Nicolson, 2004: pp. 436–49.
45. James, RR, ed. *Chips: The Diaries of Sir Henry Channon.* London: Weidenfeld, 1993: pp. 379–408.
46. Stelzer, C. *Working With Winston: the Unsung Women Behind Britain's Greatest Statesman.* London: Head of Zeus Ltd, 2019: pp. 15–45.
47. Soames, M. *Clementine Churchill,* London: Doubleday, 2003: pp. 365–87.
48. Wyatt, HV. Robert Pulvertaft's use of crude penicillin in Cairo. *Med Hist* 1990; 34: 320–6.
49. Pulvertaft, RJV. Local therapy of war wounds I. With penicillin. *The Lancet* 1943; 242: 339–48.
50. Grey-Turner, E. Pages from a diary. *Br Med J* 1980; 281: 1692–5.
51. Pawle, G. *The War and Colonel Warden.* London: Harrap, 1963: pp. 275–90.
52. Beasley, AW. *Churchill The Supreme Survivor.* Frome: Mercer Books, 2013: pp. 91–7.
53. Nel, E. *Winston Churchill by His Personal Secretary.* Bloomington IN: iUniverse, 2007: pp. 85–91.
54. Churchill, W. *Closing the Ring.* London: Penguin Classics, 2005: pp. 388–407.
55. Gilbert, M. *Road to Victory.* London: Heinemann, 1986: pp. 625–54.
56. Mr. Churchill to recuperate in sunshine. Control of affairs retained. *The Times,* 30 December 1943.
57. Flippin, HF, Schwartz, L and Domm, AH. Modern treatment of pneumococcic pneumonia. *JAMA* 1943; 121: 230–7.

58. Musher, DM, Rueda, AM, Kaka, AS and Mapara, SM. The association between pneumococcal pneumonia and acute cardiac events. *Clin Infect Dis* 2007; 45: 158–65.
59. Lip, GYH, Beevers, DG, Singh, SP and Watson, RDS. ABC of Atrial Fibrillation: aetiology, pathophysiology, and clinical features. *Br Med J* 1995; 311: 1425–8.
60. Long, PH. Sulfadiazine: the 2-sulfanilamidopyrimidine analogue of sulfanilamide. *JAMA* 1941; 116: 2399–401.
61. Long, PH. Sulphadiazine. *The Lancet* 1941; 237: 259.
62. Evans, W. The relative value of certain digitalis preparations in heart failure with auricular fibrillation. *Br Heart J* 1940; 2: 51–62.

Chapter 11. Recuperation in January 1944 in Marrakech
1. Churchill, W. *Closing the Ring: The Second World War Volume V*. London: Penguin Classics, 2005: pp. 388–407.
2. Grey-Turner, E. Pages from a diary. *Br Med J* 1980; 281: 1692–5.
3. Moran. *Winston Churchill: The Struggle for Survival 1940–1965*. London: Constable & Company, 1966: pp. 145–58.
4. Colville, J. *The Fringes of Power*. London: Weidenfeld & Nicolson, 2004: pp. 436–49.
5. Sakula, A. Churchill in Carthage, 1943: Dr Evan Bedford's war diary. *J Med Biogr* 2000; 8: 241–3.
6. Gilbert, M. *Road to Victory*. London: Heinemann, 1986: pp. 625–54.
7. Hickman, T. *Churchill's Bodyguard*. London: Headline, 2005: pp. 177–200.
8. Mitchell, J, Feast, S. *Very Important persons. Churchill's Navigator*. London: Grub Street, 2010: pp. 78–99.
9. Mitchell, J. Diary of a navigator pt 8. *Twenty Four* 2005; 16–21.
10. Pawle, G. *The War and Colonel Warden*. London: George G. Harrap, 1963: pp. 222–31.
11. Some medical notes of Brigadier D Evan Bedford relating to Sir Winston Churchill's illness in Carthage in 1943, held by the Royal College of Physicians.
12. Soames, M. *Clementine Churchill*. London: Doubleday, 2003: pp. 365–87.
13. Churchill Archives Centre, Churchill College, Cambridge. CHAR 20/154/8. Most Secret. Telegram to President Roosevelt from Colonel Warden [Winston Churchill], 1 January 1944.
14. Pawle, G. *The War and Colonel Warden*. London: Harrap, 1963: pp. 275–90.
15. Nicolson, N, ed. *Harold Nicolson: Diaries and Letters 1939–1945*. London: Collins, 1967: pp. 341–423.
16. Clinical records of Sir John Parkinson relating to Sir Winston Churchill 1942–54, held by the Royal College of Physicians.
17. Vale, JA and Scadding, JW. Sir Winston Churchill: treatment for pneumonia in 1943 and 1944. *J R Coll Physicians Edinb* 2017; 47: 388–94.

Chapter 12. Pneumonia in August–September 1944 in London
1. Gilbert, M. *Road to Victory*. London: Heinemann, 1986: pp. 887–922.
2. Churchill, WS. *Triumph and Tragedy: The Second World War Volume VI*. London: Penguin Classics, 2005: pp. 75–91.
3. Moran. *Winston Churchill: The Struggle for Survival 1940–1965*. London: Constable & Company, 1966: pp. 161–75.
4. Churchill Archives Centre, Churchill College, Cambridge. CHAR 20/169/43. Personal and Top Secret. Telegram from Prime Minister to General Alexander, 3 August 1944, 1944.

5. Churchill Archives Centre, Churchill College, Cambridge. CHAR 20/169/59. Top Secret and Personal. Telegram from General Alexander to Prime Minister, 4 August 1944, 1944.

6. Dixon, P. *Double Diploma*. London: Hutchinson, 1968: pp. 96–115.

7. Churchill Archives Centre, Churchill College, Cambridge. CHAR 20/169/115. Personal and Top Secret. Telegram from Prime Minister to Mr Duff Cooper, 9 August 1944.

8. Cooper, D. *The Duff Cooper Diaries*. London: Weidenfeld & Nicolson, 2005: pp. 279–487.

9. Pawle, G. *The War and Colonel Warden*. London: George G. Harrap, 1963: pp. 306–15.

10. Macmillan, H. *War Diaries the Mediterranean 1943–1945*. London: PAPERMAC, 1985: pp. 496–513.

11. Churchill, WS. *Triumph and Tragedy: The Second World War Volume VI*. London: Penguin Classics, 2005: pp. 92–103.

12. Churchill, WS. *Triumph and Tragedy: The Second World War Volume VI*. London: Penguin Classics, 2005: pp. 104–12.

13. Gilbert, M, Arnn, LP. *The Churchill Documents Volume 20: Normandy and Beyond, May–December 1944*. Hillsdale MI: Hillsdale College Press, 2018: pp. 1510–1837.

14. Mitchell, J, Feast, S. *Very Important persons. Churchill's Navigator*. London: Grub Street, 2010: pp. 100–14.

15. Soames, M. *Clementine Churchill*. London: Doubleday, 2003: pp. 388–416.

16. Colville, J. *The Fringes of Power*. London: Weidenfeld & Nicolson, 2004: pp. 478–95.

17. Avon. *The Eden Memoirs: The Reckoning*. London: Cassell, 1965: pp. 458–79.

18. Moran. *Winston Churchill: The Struggle for Survival 1940–1965*. London: Constable & Company, 1966: pp. 175–82.

19. Vale, JA and Scadding, JW. Sir Winston Churchill: treatment for pneumonia in 1943 and 1944. *J R Coll Physicians Edinb* 2017; 47: 388–94.

20. Vale, JA and Scadding, JW. In Carthage ruins: the illness of Sir Winston Churchill at Carthage, December 1943. *J R Coll Physicians Edinb* 2017; 47: 288–95.

21. Pugh, D. *Diary 1944*. Unpublished, 1944.

22. Clinical records of Sir John Parkinson relating to Sir Winston Churchill 1942–54, held by the Royal College of Physicians.

23. Danchev, A, Todman, D, eds. *War Diaries 1939–1945 Field Marshal Lord Alanbrooke*. London: Weidenfeld & Nicolson, 2001: pp. 586–98.

24. Gilbert, M. *Road to Victory*. London: Heinemann, 1986: pp. 930–53.

25. Harvey, J, ed. *The War Diaries of Oliver Harvey 1941–1945*. London: William Collins Sons, 1978: pp. 327–70.

26. Gilbert, M. *Road to Victory*. London: Heinemann, 1986: pp. 923–9.

27. Churchill, WS. *Triumph and Tragedy: The Second World War Volume VI*. London: Penguin Classics, 2005: pp. 129–42.

28. Pawle, G. *The War and Colonel Warden*. London: George G. Harrap, 1963: pp. 316–26.

29. Churchill Archives Centre, Churchill College, Cambridge. CHAR 20/147B/174. Letter from Winston Churchill to Brigadier Whitby, 16 October 1944.

30. Flippin, HF, Schwartz, L and Domm, AH. Modern treatment of pneumococcic pneumonia. *JAMA* 1943; 121: 230–7.

31. Ministry of Health. *National War Formulary*. London: HMSO, 1943.

32. Moran. *Winston Churchill: The Struggle for Survival 1940–1965*, London: Constable & Company, 1966: pp. 84–9.

33. Reid, J. Mepacrine and falciparum malaria. *QJM: An International Journal of Medicine* 1947; 16: 61–82.
34. Adams, ARD. Drug treatment of malaria. *Br Med J* 1959; 2: 183.

Chapter 13. A High Temperature in January 1945 on the Way to Yalta
1. Churchill, S. *A Thread in the Tapestry.* London: Andre Deutsch, 1967.
2. Colville, J. *The Fringes of Power.* London: Weidenfeld & Nicolson, 2004: pp. 520–8.
3. Pawle, G. *The War and Colonel Warden.* London: Harrap, 1963: pp. 346–56.
4. Moran. *Winston Churchill: The Struggle for Survival 1940–1965.* London: Constable & Company, 1966: pp. 216–41.
5. Martin, J. *Downing Street the War Years.* London: Bloomsbury, 1991: pp. 174–96.
6. Avon. *The Eden Memoirs: The Reckoning.* London: Cassell, 1965: pp. 504–27.
7. Churchill, S. *Keep on Dancing.* New York: Coward, McCann & Geoghegan, 1981: pp. 98–139.
8. Gilbert, M, Arnn, LP. *The Churchill Documents, Volume 21. The Shadows of Victory, January–July 1945.* Hillsdale MI: Hillsdale College Press, 2018: pp. 294–577.
9. Dilks, D, ed. *The Diaries of Sir Alexander Cadogan OM 1938–1945.* London: Cassell & Company, 1971: pp. 632–717.
10. Clay, C. Sulphonamide chemotherapy of intestinal infections. *Br Med J* 1943; 2: 35–6.
11. Scadding, JG. Comparative effects of sulphonamide drugs in mild bacillary dysentery. *The Lancet* 1944; 243: 784–6.
12. Scott, RB. On the effect of sulphaguanidine in acute bacillary dysentery. *J R Army Med Corps* 1945; 84: 159–62.
13. Scadding, JG. Sulphonamides in bacillary dysentery. Further observations on their effects. *The Lancet* 1945; 549–53.
14. Vale, JA and Scadding, JW. In Carthage ruins: the illness of Sir Winston Churchill at Carthage, December 1943. *J R Coll Physicians Edinb* 2017; 47: 288–95.
15. Bunting, JJ and Levan, NE. Toxic reactions of sulfaguanidine therapy. *JAMA* 1944; 125: 773–4.
16. Lynn, JM. Sulfonamide toxicity. *Calif Med* 1949; 70: 48–56.
17. Slatore, CG and Tilles, SA. Sulfonamide hypersensitivity. *Immunol Allergy Clin North Am* 2004; 24: 477–90.
18. Vale, JA and Scadding, JW. Sir Winston Churchill: treatment for pneumonia in 1943 and 1944. *J R Coll Physicians Edinb* 2017; 47: 388–94.

Chapter 14. Diagnosis of Inguinal Hernia in September 1945 at Lake Como
1. Soames, M. *Speaking for Themselves.* London: Transworld, 1998: pp. 532–61.
2. James, RR, ed. *Chips: The Diaries of Sir Henry Channon.* London: Weidenfeld, 1993: pp. 409–51.
3. Soames, M. *Winston Churchill: His Life As a Painter.* London: Collins, 1990: pp. 131–47.
4. Giangreco, PR. Leading Churchill myths #20; 'Churchill offered peace and security to Mussolini'. *Finest Hour* 2011; 149: 52–7.
5. Churchill Archives Centre, Churchill College, Cambridge. CHUR 2/140/22. Lt-Col WM Cunningham to Sarah Oliver, 18 August 1945.
6. Churchill Archives Centre, Churchill College, Cambridge. CHUR 2/140/21. Top Secret from Field Marshal Alexander to Brigadier Jacob, Cabinet Office, 24 August 1945.
7. Churchill Archives Centre, Churchill College, Cambridge. CHUR 2/140/20. Telegram from Winston Churchill to Field Marshal Alexander, 26 August 1945.

8. Churchill Archives Centre, Churchill College, Cambridge. CHUR 2/140/19. Telephone message from Field Marshal Alexander to Winston Churchill, 27 August 1945.
9. Churchill Archives Centre, Churchill College, Cambridge. CHUR 2/140/15-16. Letter from Field Marshal Alexander to Winston Churchill, 30 August 1945.
10. Gilbert, M. *Never Despair*. London: Heinemann, 1988: pp. 132–58.
11. Willett, P. *Makers of the Modern Thoroughbred*. London: Stanley Paul, 1984: pp. 243–64.
12. Churchill Archives Centre, Churchill College, Cambridge. WCHL 6/59. Papers relating to Brigadier Harold Edwards being called in to see WSC at Lake Como, September 1945, to treat a hernia.
13. Moran. *Winston Churchill: The Struggle for Survival 1940–1965*. London: Constable & Company, 1966: pp. 291–305.
14. Churchill, S. *Keep on Dancing*. New York: Coward, McCann & Geoghegan, 1981: pp. 98–139.
15. Scott, B. *Churchill at the Gallop*. Newbury, Berkshire: Racing Post Books, 2017: pp. 202–11.
16. Churchill Archives Centre, Churchill College, Cambridge. CHUR 1/134/182. Letter from Mr Harold Edwards FRCS to Mr Winston Churchill, 12 June 1947.
17. Churchill Archives Centre, Churchill College, Cambridge. CHUR 2/141A-B/16. Letter from Mr Harold Edwards FRCS to Mr Winston Churchill, 15 September 1945.
18. Churchill Archives Centre, Churchill College, Cambridge. CHUR 2/141A-B/14. Letter from Mr Winston Churchill to Mr Harold Edwards FRCS, 2 November 1945.
19. Barne, C. *Churchill's Colonel*. Barnsley: Pen & Sword Books, 2019: pp. x–xii.
20. Churchill Archives Centre, Churchill College, Cambridge. CHAR 2/365/39. Letter from Lt Colonel AM Barne 4th Queen's Own Hussars to Winston Churchill MP, 10 September 1945.
21. Churchill Archives Centre, Churchill College, Cambridge. CHAR 2/365/37-38. Letter from Winston Churchill MP to Lt Colonel AM Barne 4th Queen's Own Hussars, 17 September 1945.
22. Churchill, M. Painting at Lake Como. *Finest Hour* 2011; 152: 49–50.
23. Gilbert, M, Arnn, LP. *The Churchill Documents, Volume 22: Leader of the Opposition August 1945 to October 1951*. Hillsdale MI: Hillsdale College Press, 2019: pp. 52–89.
24. Gilbert, M, Arnn, LP. *The Churchill Documents, Volume 22: Leader of the Opposition August 1945 to October 1951*. Hillsdale MI: Hillsdale College Press, 2019: pp. 1–51.
25. Churchill Archives Centre, Churchill College, Cambridge. CHUR 2/141A-B/21. Telegram from Mr Winston Churchill to General Eisenhower, 1945.
26. Churchill Archives Centre, Churchill College, Cambridge. CHUR 2/141A-B/456. Letter from Lord Moran, President of the Royal College of Physicians, to Mr Winston Churchill, 24 September 1945.
27. Gilbert, M. *Never Despair*. London: Heinemann, 1988: pp. 159–79.
28. Gilbert, M. *Never Despair*. London: Heinemann, 1988: pp. 123–31.

Chapter 15. Repair of Inguinal Hernia in June 1947 in London
1. Gilbert, M. *Never Despair*. London: Heinemann, 1988: pp. 338–55.
2. Churchill, RS. *Winston S. Churchill. Volume I: Youth, 1874–1900*. London: Heinemann, 1966: pp. 110–85.
3. Soames, M. *Speaking for Themselves*. London: Transworld, 1998: pp. 532–61.
4. Connolly, JE. Churchill's inguinal hernia repair. *J Am Coll Surg* 2004; 198: 175–6.
5. Moran. *Winston Churchill: The Struggle for Survival 1940–1965*. London: Constable & Company, 1966: pp. 318–29.

6. Mather, J. Sir Winston Churchill: his hardiness and resilience. In: Langworth, R, ed. *Churchill Proceedings 1996–1997*. Washington, DC: The Churchill Center, 2000: pp. 83–97.

7. Keynes, G. *The Gates of Memory*. Oxford: Clarendon Press, 1981: pp. 185–95.

8. Beasley, AW. *Portraits of the Royal Australasian College of Surgeons*. Melbourne: Royal Australasian College of Surgeons, 1993.

9. Clinical records of Sir John Parkinson relating to Sir Winston Churchill 1942–54, held by the Royal College of Physicians.

10. Churchill Archives Centre, Churchill College, Cambridge. CHAR 2/417/223. Letter from Sir Thomas Dunhill to the Prime Minister, 21 May 1941.

11. Churchill Archives Centre, Churchill College, Cambridge. CHAR 2/441/103. Letter from K. Hill to the Prime Minister, 14 May 1942.

12. Churchill Archives Centre, Churchill College, Cambridge. CHAR 2/441/106. Invoice for Remington electric razor purchased from McReynolds Pharmacy 18th and G Streets NW, 4 June 1942.

13. Churchill Archives Centre, Churchill College, Cambridge. CHAR 2/441/111. Letter from Sir Thomas Dunhill to the Prime Minister, 14 July 1942.

14. Churchill Archives Centre, Churchill College, Cambridge. CHAR 2/441/114. Note for the Prime Minister concerning an appointment to see Sir Thomas Dunhill, 29 December 1942.

15. Churchill Archives Centre, Churchill College, Cambridge. CHAR 2/489/144. Winston Churchill's engagement diary for 29 September 1943.

16. Smith, JO. *Stones, Diamonds, Coronets, Kings and Their Surgical Custodians*. Melbourne: McLaren & Co., 1967.

17. Schein, M and Rogers, PN. Winston S Churchill's (1874–1965) inguinal hernia repair by Thomas P Dunhill (1876–1957). *J Am Coll Surg* 2003; 197: 313–21.

18. Vale, JA and Scadding, JW. Sir Winston Churchill: treatment for pneumonia in 1943 and 1944. *J R Coll Physicians Edinb* 2017; 47: 388–94.

19. Vale, JA and Scadding, JW. In Carthage ruins: the illness of Sir Winston Churchill at Carthage, December 1943. *J R Coll Physicians Edinb* 2017; 47: 288–95.

20. Churchill Archives Centre, Churchill College, Cambridge. CHUR 2/148/285-286. Letter from Sir Thomas Dunhill to Winston Churchill, 10 April 1946.

21. Churchill Archives Centre, Churchill College, Cambridge. CHUR 2/148/287. Telegram from Winston Churchill to Sir Thomas Dunhill, 11 April 1946.

22. Stelzer, C. *Working With Winston: the Unsung Women Behind Britain's Greatest Statesman*. London: Head of Zeus Ltd, 2019: pp. 95–131.

23. Churchill Archives Centre, Churchill College, Cambridge. CHUR 2/148/284. Message from Sir Thomas Dunhill to Winston Churchill, 15 May 1946.

24. Churchill Archives Centre, Churchill College, Cambridge. CHUR 2/148/279-280. Letter from Sir Thomas Dunhill to Winston Churchill, 24 August 1946.

25. Churchill Archives Centre, Churchill College, Cambridge. CHUR 2/148/277. Letter from Winston Churchill to Sir Thomas Dunhill, 30 September 1946.

26. Sir Thos. Dunhill: The gift of observation. *The Times*, 1 January 1958.

27. Smith, JO. *Sir Thomas Dunhill*. Melbourne: McLaren & Co., 1967.

28. Keynes, G. Sir Thomas Dunhill: the first Dunhill Memorial Lecture delivered at the International Goitre Conference in London on 6th July 1960. *Ann R Coll Surg Engl* 1961; 29: 160–9.

29. Moran. *Winston Churchill: The Struggle for Survival 1940–1965*. London: Constable & Company, 1966: pp. 503–18.

30. Churchill Archives Centre, Churchill College, Cambridge. CHUR 2/616/22-25. Engagement cards May–August 1947.
31. Gordon, R. *An Alarming History of Famous and Difficult Patients*. New York: St Martin's Press, 1997: pp. 20–5.
32. Mr. Churchill. *The Times*, 7 June 1947.
33. Churchill Archives Centre, Churchill College, Cambridge. CHUR 2/149A-B/74. Arrangements for the admission of Mr Winston Churchill to The Fife Nursing Home, 4 June 1947.
34. Anon. Plarr's Lives of the Fellows Online. Ross, Sir James Paterson (1895–1980). The Royal College of Surgeons of England. Available at: https://livesonline.rcseng.ac.uk/ biogs/ E000233b.htm (accessed 14 April 2020).
35. Obituary: KLS Ward. *Br Med J (Clin Res Ed)* 1981; 283: 1409.
36. Operation on Mr. Churchill 'Condition satisfactory'. *The Times*, 12 June 1947.
37. Churchill Archives Centre, Churchill College, Cambridge. CHUR 1/134/225. Letter from Mrs Christopher Langton Hewer to Mr Winston Churchill, 12 June 1947.
38. Churchill Archives Centre, Churchill College, Cambridge. CHUR 2/150A-B/505. Letter from Mrs Churchill to Commander Hunt, 16 June 1947.
39. Churchill Archives Centre, Churchill College, Cambridge. CHUR 2/150A-B/506. Letter from Lieutenant Commander Hunt to Mrs Churchill, 14 June 1947, 14 June 1947.
40. Churchill Archives Centre, Churchill College, Cambridge. CHUR 2/148/298. Message from Sir Thomas Dunhill to Winston Churchill, 1 July 1947.
41. Churchill Archives Centre, Churchill College, Cambridge. CHUR 2/148/299-300. Letter from Sir Thomas Dunhill to Winston Churchill, 12 July 1947.
42. Churchill Archives Centre, Churchill College, Cambridge. CHUR 2/148/302. Letter from Sir Thomas Dunhill to Winston Churchill, 1 August 1947.
43. Churchill Archives Centre, Churchill College, Cambridge. CHUR 2/148/301. Telegram from Winston Churchill to Sir Thomas Dunhill.
44. Churchill Archives Centre, Churchill College, Cambridge. CHUR 5/28A-B/7-11. Speech by the Rt Hon. Winston Churchill on the award of the *Sunday Times* Annual Literary Award for 1949 and Commemorative Gold Medal, 2 November 1949.
45. Golding, RE. Glimpses: 'Did you fly? Hmph!'. *Finest Hour* 1981; 34: 4–7.
46. Churchill Archives Centre, Churchill College, Cambridge. CHUR 4/49/100. List of personal friends to be given copies of *The Gathering Storm*, 1948.
47. Churchill Archives Centre, Churchill College, Cambridge. CHUR 2/185/147. Letter from Sir Thomas Dunhill to the Prime Minister, 26 April 1954.
48. Vale, JA and Scadding, JW. Sir Winston Churchill: pneumonia, pleurisy, jaundice and atrial fibrillation at Roquebrune-Cap-Martin and Chartwell, 1958. *J R Soc Med* 2019; 112: 11–21.

Chapter 16. First Stroke in August 1949 in Monaco

1. Moran. *Winston Churchill: The Struggle for Survival 1940–1965*. London: Constable & Company, 1966: pp. 333–8.
2. Clinical records of Sir John Parkinson relating to Sir Winston Churchill 1942–54, held by the Royal College of Physicians.
3. Vale, JA and Scadding, JW. In Carthage ruins: the illness of Sir Winston Churchill at Carthage, December 1943. *J R Coll Physicians Edinb* 2017; 47: 288–95.
4. Stelzer, C. *Working with Winston: the Unsung Women behind Britain's Greatest Statesman*. London: Head of Zeus Ltd, 2019: pp. 181–93.

5. Stelzer, C. *Working with Winston: the Unsung Women behind Britain's Greatest Statesman.* London: Head of Zeus Ltd, 2019: pp. 195–220.

6. Soames, M. *Clementine Churchill.* London: Doubleday, 2003: pp. 440–59.

7. Gilbert, M. *Never Despair.* London: Heinemann, 1988: pp. 479–99.

8. Macmillan, H. *Tides of Fortune 1945–1955.* London: Macmillan, 1969: pp. 151–84.

9. Wardell, M. Churchill's dagger. A memoir of La Capponcina. *Finest Hour* 1995; 87: 14–26.

10. Clinical records of Lord Brain relating to Sir Winston Churchill 1949–65 held by the Royal College of Physicians.

11. Griffiths, RW. Sir Winston Churchill's doctors on the Riviera 1949–1965: Herbert Robert Burnett Gibson (1885–1967) and Dafydd (David) Myrddin Roberts (1906–1977). *J Med Biogr* 2020; 28: 30–8.

12. Stelzer, C. *Working with Winston: the Unsung Women behind Britain's Greatest Statesman.* London: Head of Zeus Ltd, 2019: pp. 165–80.

13. Vale, JA and Scadding, JW. Did Winston Churchill suffer a myocardial infarction in the White House at Christmas 1941? *J R Soc Med* 2017; 110: 483–92.

14. Stelzer, C. *Working with Winston: the Unsung Women behind Britain's Greatest Statesman.* London: Head of Zeus Ltd, 2019: pp. 95–131.

15. Gilbert, M. *Never Despair.* London: Heinemann, 1988: pp. 500–14.

16. Vale, JA and Scadding, JW. Sir Winston Churchill: pneumonia, pleurisy, jaundice and atrial fibrillation at Roquebrune-Cap-Martin and Chartwell, 1958. *J R Soc Med* 2019; 112: 11–21.

17. Moran. *Winston Churchill: The Struggle for Survival 1940–1965.* London: Constable & Company, 1966: pp. 454–74.

18. Brain, WR. Encounters with Winston Churchill. *Med Hist* 2000; 44: 3–20.

19. Brain. Letters to the editor: Lord Moran's diaries in focus. *The Times*, 9 May 1966.

Chapter 17. Cerebrovascular Disease January 1950–March 1952 in London

1. Moran. *Winston Churchill: The Struggle for Survival 1940–1965.* London: Constable & Company, 1966: pp. 372–83.

2. Scadding, JW and Vale, JA. Winston Churchill: his first stroke in 1949. *J R Soc Med* 2018; 111: 316–23.

3. Gilbert, M. *Never Despair.* London: Heinemann, 1988: pp. 500–14.

4. Moran. *Winston Churchill: The Struggle for Survival 1940–1965.* London: Constable & Company, 1966: pp. 333–8.

5. Clinical records of Lord Brain relating to Sir Winston Churchill 1949–65 held by the Royal College of Physicians.

6. Beasley, AW. Churchill, Moran and the struggle for survival. *J R Coll Physicians Edinb* 2010; 40: 362–7.

7. Moran. *Winston Churchill: The Struggle for Survival 1940–1965,* London: Constable & Company, 1966: pp. 343–50.

8. Clinical records of Sir John Parkinson relating to Sir Winston Churchill 1942–54, held by the Royal College of Physicians.

9. Colville, J. *The Fringes of Power.* London: Weidenfeld & Nicolson, 2004: pp. 593–615.

10. Vale, JA and Scadding, JW. Did Winston Churchill suffer a myocardial infarction in the White House at Christmas 1941? *J R Soc Med* 2017; 110: 483–92.

11. Gilbert, M. *Never Despair.* London: Heinemann, 1988: pp. 696–724.

Chapter 18.   Churchill Unveils a Portrait of Lord Moran in July 1951
1. Davenport, G, McDonald, I, Moss-Gibbons, C, eds. *The Royal College of Physicians and its Collections.* London: James & James (Publishers) Ltd, 2001: pp. 126–35.
2. Brain, WR, Churchill, WS and Moran. Presentation of portrait to Lord Moran. *Journal of the Royal College of Physicians,* 1951.
3. Churchill, WS. Portrait of Lord Moran: a speech to the Royal College of Physicians, 10 July 1951. In: Churchill, RS, ed. *Stemming the Tide: Speeches 1951 and 1952.* Cambridge: The Riverside Press, 1954: pp. 90–2.
4. James, DG. Sir Winston Leonard Spencer Churchill (1874–1965). *J Med Biogr* 2010; 18: 215.
5. Prime Minister on healing. *The Times,* 1944.
6. Churchill, WS. *The Dawn of Liberation.* London: Cassell & Company Ltd, 1945: pp. 21–4.
7. Clinical records of Sir John Parkinson relating to Sir Winston Churchill 1942–54, held by the Royal College of Physicians.

Chapter 19.   Acute Stroke in June 1953 in London
1. Colville, J. *The Fringes of Power.* London: Weidenfeld & Nicolson, 2004: pp. 625–36.
2. Gilbert, M. *Never Despair.* London: Heinemann, 1988: pp. 827–45.
3. Stelzer, C. *Working With Winston: the Unsung Women Behind Britain's Greatest Statesman.* London: Head of Zeus Ltd, 2019: pp. 221–58.
4. Colville, J. *The Fringes of Power.* London: Weidenfeld & Nicolson, 2004: pp. 664–7.
5. Vale, JA and Scadding, JW. In Carthage ruins: the illness of Sir Winston Churchill at Carthage, December 1943. *J R Coll Physicians Edinb* 2017; 47: 288–95.
6. Moran. *Winston Churchill: The Struggle for Survival 1940–1965.* London: Constable & Company, 1966: pp. 399–407.
7. Clark, K. *The Other Half: a Self-Portrait.* New York: Harper & Row, 1977: pp. 124–47.
8. Soames, M. *Clementine Churchill.* London: Doubleday, 2003: pp. 460–89.
9. Moran. *Winston Churchill: The Struggle for Survival 1940–1965.* London: Constable & Company, 1966: pp. 408–18.
10. Scadding, JW and Vale, JA. Winston Churchill: his first stroke in 1949. *J R Soc Med* 2018; 111: 316–23.
11. Wheeler-Bennett J, ed. *Action This Day: Working with Churchill.* London: Macmillan & Co. Ltd, 1968: pp. 47–138.
12. Macmillan, H. *Tides of Fortune 1945–1955.* London: Macmillan, 1969: pp. 514–59.
13. Clinical records of Lord Brain relating to Sir Winston Churchill 1949–65 held by the Royal College of Physicians.
14. The National Archives – Prime Minister's Office. Postponement of the Bermuda Conference Owing to the Prime Minister's Illness. PREM11/517.98. 1953.
15. Moran. *Churchill the Struggle for Survival 1945–60.* London: Robinson, 2006.
16. Gilbert, M. *Never Despair.* London: Heinemann, 1988: pp. 847–57.
17. Butler. *The Art of the Possible: The Memoirs of Lord Butler.* London: Hamish Hamilton, 1971: pp. 154–82.
18. Wheeler-Bennett, J, ed. *Action This Day: Working with Churchill.* London: Macmillan & Co. Ltd, 1968: pp. 15–46.
19. Moran. *Winston Churchill: The Struggle for Survival 1940–1965.* London: Constable & Company, 1966: pp. 419–53.
20. Gilbert, M. *Never Despair.* London: Heinemann, 1988: pp. 858–92.

21. Moran. *Winston Churchill: The Struggle for Survival 1940–1965.* London: Constable & Company, 1966: pp. 454–74.

22. Vale, JA and Scadding, JW. Did Winston Churchill suffer a myocardial infarction in the White House at Christmas 1941? *J R Soc Med* 2017; 110: 483–92.

23. Clinical records of Sir John Parkinson relating to Sir Winston Churchill 1942–54, held by the Royal College of Physicians.

24. Scadding, JW and Vale, JA. Sir Winston Churchill: cerebrovascular disease January 1950–March 1952. *J R Soc Med* 2018; 111: 444–52.

Chapter 20. Churchill's Triumph at the Conservative Party Conference in October 1953 in Margate

1. Moran. *Winston Churchill: The Struggle for Survival 1940–1965.* London: Constable & Company, 1966: pp. 495–502.

2. Scadding, JW and Vale, JA. Sir Winston Churchill's acute stroke in June 1953. *J R Soc Med* 2018; 111: 347–58.

3. Scadding, JW and Vale, JA. Winston Churchill: his first stroke in 1949. *J R Soc Med* 2018; 111: 316–23.

4. Scadding, JW and Vale, JA. Sir Winston Churchill: cerebrovascular disease January 1950–March 1952. *J R Soc Med* 2018; 111: 444–52.

5. Moran. *Winston Churchill: The Struggle for Survival 1940–1965.* London: Constable & Company, 1966: pp. 454–74.

6. Macmillan, H. *Tides of Fortune 1945–1955.* London: Macmillan, 1969: pp. 514–59.

7. Soames, M. *Clementine Churchill.* London: Doubleday, 2003: pp. 460–89.

8. Stelzer, C. *Working with Winston: the Unsung Women Behind Britain's Greatest Statesman.* London: Head of Zeus Ltd, 2019: pp. 165–80.

9. Murray, E. *I was Churchill's Bodyguard.* London: WH Allen, 1987: pp. 169–79.

10. Colville, J. *The Fringes of Power.* London: Weidenfeld & Nicolson, 2004: pp. 625–36.

11. Stelzer, C. *Working with Winston: the Unsung Women Behind Britain's Greatest Statesman.* London: Head of Zeus Ltd, 2019: pp. 221–58.

12. Gilbert, M. *Never Despair.* London: Heinemann, 1988: pp. 858–92.

13. Butler. *The Art of the Possible: The Memoirs of Lord Butler.* London: Hamish Hamilton, 1971: pp. 154–82.

14. Gilbert, M. *Never Despair.* London: Heinemann, 1988: pp. 893–915.

15. The Rt Hon. Lord Owen, CH. The effect of Prime Minister Anthony Eden's illness on his decision-making during the Suez crisis. *QJM* 2005; 98: 387–402.

16. Braasch, JW. Anthony Eden's (Lord Avon) biliary tract saga. *Ann Surg* 2003; 238: 772–5.

17. Thorpe, DR. *The Life and Times of Anthony Eden First Earl of Avon, 1987–1977.* London: Pimlico, 2004: pp. 393–415.

18. Moran. *Winston Churchill: The Struggle for Survival 1940–1965.* London: Constable & Company, 1966: pp. 475–81.

19. Lovell, R. Lord Moran's prescriptions for Churchill. *Br Med J* 1995; 310: 1537–8.

20. Gilbert, M. *Never Despair.* London: Heinemann, 1988: pp. 1276–311.

21. Churchill, WS. The Conservative party conference: A speech at Margate 10 October 1953. In: Winston, RS, ed. *The Unwritten Alliance: Speeches 1953–59.* London: Cassell, 1961: pp. 57–67.

22. Moran. *Winston Churchill: The Struggle for Survival 1940–1965.* London: Constable & Company, 1966: pp. 482–7.

23. James, RR, ed. *Chips: The Diaries of Sir Henry Channon.* London: Weidenfeld, 1993: pp. 452–79.

24. Moran. *Winston Churchill: The Struggle for Survival 1940–1965*. London: Constable & Company, 1966: pp. 488–94.
25. Clinical records of Sir John Parkinson relating to Sir Winston Churchill 1942–54, held by the Royal College of Physicians.
26. Brain, WR. Encounters with Winston Churchill. *Med Hist* 2000; 44: 3–20.
27. Roberts, A. Winston wept: the extraordinary lachrymosity and romantic imagination of Winston Churchill. *Finest Hour* 2016; 174: 34–7.
28. Brooks, B. Pseudobulbar affect in stroke in statesmen: the peculiar case of Winston Spencer Churchill. *Neurology* 2012; 78: P04.003.
29. Viale, L, Catoira, NP, Di Girolamo, G and González, CD. Pharmacotherapy and motor recovery after stroke. *Expert Rev Neurother* 2018; 18: 65–82.
30. Yeo, S-H, Lim, Z-JI, Mao, J and Yau, W-P. Effects of central nervous system drugs on recovery after stroke: a systematic review and meta-analysis of randomized controlled trials. *Clin Drug Investig* 2017; 37: 901–28.
31. Wood, S, Sage, JR, Shuman, T and Anagnostaras, SG. Psychostimulants and cognition: A continuum of behavioral and cognitive activation. *Pharmacol Rev* 2014; 66: 193–221.
32. Ilieva, I, Boland, J and Farah, MJ. Objective and subjective cognitive enhancing effects of mixed amphetamine salts in healthy people. *Neuropharmacology* 2013; 64: 496–505.
33. Rothwell, PM, Algra, A, Chen, Z, Diener, HC, Norrving, B and Mehta, Z. Effects of aspirin on risk and severity of early recurrent stroke after transient ischaemic attack and ischaemic stroke: time-course analysis of randomised trials. *The Lancet* 2016; 388: 365–75.
34. Hankey, GJ. The benefits of aspirin in early secondary stroke prevention. *The Lancet* 2016; 388: 312–14.

Chapter 21. Acute Ataxic Stroke in June 1955 in London
1. Moran. *Winston Churchill: The Struggle for Survival 1940–1965*. London: Constable & Company, 1966: pp. 656–65.
2. Gilbert, M. *Never Despair*. London: Heinemann, 1988: pp. 1116–28.
3. Soames, M. *Clementine Churchill*. London: Doubleday, 2003: pp. 490–509.
4. Stelzer, C. *Working with Winston: the Unsung Women Behind Britain's Greatest Statesman*. London: Head of Zeus Ltd, 2019: pp. 165–80.
5. Moran. *Winston Churchill: The Struggle for Survival 1940–1965*. London: Constable & Company, 1966: pp. 666–85.
6. Moran. *Winston Churchill: The Struggle for Survival 1940–1965*. London: Constable & Company, 1966: pp. 686–92.
7. Clarke, P, ed. *Mr Churchill's Profession: Statesman, Orator, Writer*. London: Bloomsbury, 2012.
8. Churchill, WS. *A History of the English-Speaking Peoples. Volume 1: the Birth of Britain*. London: Cassell, 1956.
9. Murray, E. *I was Churchill's Bodyguard*. London: WH Allen, 1987: pp. 193–206.
10. Colville, J. *The Fringes of Power*. London: Weidenfeld & Nicolson, 2004: pp. 658–63.
11. Churchill Archives Centre, Churchill College, Cambridge. CHUR 2/220/21-22 Letter from Harold Macmillan to Winston Churchill, 15 June 1955.
12. Browne, AM. *Long Sunset*. High Halden, Ashford: Podkin Press, 2009: pp. 187–97.
13. Churchill, WS. The Guildhall Statue: A speech at the unveiling of a statue. In: Winston, RS, ed. *The Unwritten Alliance: Speeches 1953–59*. London: Cassell, 1961: pp. 266–8.
14. Clinical records of Lord Brain relating to Sir Winston Churchill 1949–65 held by the Royal College of Physicians.

15. Brain, WR. Encounters with Winston Churchill. *Med Hist* 2000; 44: 3–20.
16. Gilbert, M. *Never Despair*. London: Heinemann, 1988: pp. 1144–71.
17. Rowse, AL. *Memories of Men and Women*. London: Eyre Methuen Ltd, 1980: pp. 1–24.
18. Churchill Archives Centre, Churchill College, Cambridge. CHUR 1/66/6. Letter from John Colville to Winston Churchill, 17 July 1955.
19. Churchill Archives Centre, Churchill College, Cambridge. CHUR 2/217/79. Letter from President Eisenhower to Winston Churchill, 15 July 1955.
20. Churchill Archives Centre, Churchill College, Cambridge. CHUR 2/217/75-78. Letter from Winston Churchill to President Eisenhower, 18 July 1955.
21. Macmillan, H. *Tides of Fortune 1945–1955*. London: Macmillan, 1969: pp. 582–628.
22. Churchill, WS. The Cinque Ports: a speech in Hastings at the Court of Brotherhood and Guestling of the Cinque Ports on presentation of a portrait on 7 September 1955. In: Winston, RS, ed. *The Unwritten Alliance: Speeches 1953–59*. London: Cassell, 1961: p. 270.
23. Churchill Archives Centre, Churchill College, Cambridge. CHUR 1/54/38. Letter from Sir Winston Churchill to Lord Moran, 26 September 1955.
24. Scadding, JW and Vale, JA. Sir Winston Churchill's acute stroke in June 1953. *J R Soc Med* 2018; 111: 347–58.
25. Gorman, MJ, Dafer, R and Levine, SR. Ataxic hemiparesis: critical appraisal of a lacunar syndrome. *Stroke* 1998; 29: 2549—55.

Chapter 22. A Further Stroke in October 1956 in the South of France
1. Murray, E. *I was Churchill's Bodyguard*. London: WH Allen, 1987: pp. 219–33.
2. Moran. *Winston Churchill: The Struggle for Survival 1940–1965*. London: Constable & Company, 1966: pp. 699–711.
3. Churchill Archives Centre, Churchill College, Cambridge. CHUR 2/532A-B, image 279/285. Letter from Sir Winston Churchill to Wendy Reves, 4 September 1956.
4. Scadding, JW and Vale, JA. Winston Churchill: his first stroke in 1949. *J R Soc Med* 2018; 111: 316–23.
5. Scadding, JW and Vale, JA. Sir Winston Churchill: cerebrovascular disease January 1950–March 1952. *J R Soc Med* 2018; 111: 444–52.
6. Scadding, JW and Vale, JA. Sir Winston Churchill's acute stroke in June 1953. *J R Soc Med* 2018; 111: 347–58.
7. Scadding, JW and Vale, JA. Sir Winston Churchill: recovery from an acute stroke in June 1953 and triumph at the Conservative Party Conference in October 1953. *J R Soc Med* 2019; 112: 61–71.
8. Scadding, JW and Vale, JA. Sir Winston Churchill: a left hemisphere stroke or possible focal seizure on 20 October 1956. *J R Soc Med* 2018; 112: 185–91.
9. Soames, M. *Clementine Churchill*. London: Doubleday, 2003: pp. 490–509.
10. Murray, E. *I was Churchill's Bodyguard*, London: WH Allen, 1987: pp. 207–18.
11. Gilbert, M. *Never Despair*. London: Heinemann, 1988: pp. 1199–1241.
12. Soames, M. *Speaking for Themselves*. London: Transworld, 1998: pp. 593–614.
13. Churchill Archives Centre, Churchill College, Cambridge. CHUR 1/54, image 61/99. Letter from Dr David Roberts to Lord Moran, 25 October 1956.
14. Sir Winston Churchill 'Going on well'. *The Times*, 22 October 1956.
15. Lady Churchill on Riviera. *The Times*, 23 October 1956.
16. Browne, AM. *Long Sunset*. High Halden, Ashford: Podkin Press, 2009: pp. 208–15.
17. Sir W. Churchill Back from holiday. *The Times*, 29 October 1956.

18. Clinical records of Lord Brain relating to Sir Winston Churchill 1949–65 held by the Royal College of Physicians.
19. Churchill Archives Centre, Churchill College, Cambridge. CHUR 1/149, image 6. Letter from Lady Churchill to Dr David Roberts, 3 November 1956.
20. Anon. Cerebral vasodilators. *Br Med J* 1971; 2: 702–3.
21. Baltsavias, G, Yella, S, Al Shameri, RA, Luft, A and Valavanis, A. 'Intra-arterial administration of papaverine during mechanical thrombectomy for acute ischemic stroke'. *J Stroke Cerebrovasc Dis* 2015; 24: 41–7.
22. Gottstein, U and Paulson, OB. The effect of intracarotid aminophylline infusion on the cerebral circulation. *Stroke* 1972; 3: 560–5.
23. Bath, PMW. Theophylline, aminophylline, caffeine and analogues for acute ischaemic stroke. *Cochrane Database Syst Rev* 2004: 1–11.
24. Britton, M, de Faire, U, Helmers, C, Miah, K and Rane, A. Lack of effect of theophylline on the outcome of acute cerebral infarction. *Acta Neurol Scand* 1980; 62: 116–23.
25. Geismar, P, Marquardsen, J and Sylvest, J. Controlled trial of intravenous aminophylline in acute cerebral infarction. *Acta Neurol Scand* 1976; 54: 173–80.

Chapter 23. Pneumonia, Jaundice, Rigor and Atrial Fibrillation February–April 1958 on the Riviera and at Chartwell

1. Churchill Archives Centre, Churchill College, Cambridge. CHUR 2/530 A-B/49–50. Dr David Roberts to Sir Winston Churchill, 19 March 1958.
2. Soames, M. *Clementine Churchill*. London: Doubleday, 2003: pp. 490–509.
3. Murray, E. *I was Churchill's Bodyguard*. London: WH Allen, 1987: pp. 207–18.
4. Soames, M. *Speaking for Themselves*. London: Transworld, 1998: pp. 615–34.
5. Gilbert, M. *Never Despair*. London: Heinemann, 1988: pp. 1243–75.
6. Chancellor to meet Sir W. Churchill. *The Times*, 13 February 1958.
7. Browne, AM. *Long Sunset*. High Halden, Ashford: Podkin Press, 2009: pp. 216–32.
8. Moran. *Winston Churchill: The Struggle for Survival 1940–1965*. London: Constable & Company, 1966: pp. 732–47.
9. Murray, E. *I was Churchill's Bodyguard*. London: WH Allen, 1987: pp. 234–43.
10. Sir W. Churchill indisposed. Confined to bed. *The Times*, 19 February 1958.
11. Bulletin on Sir W. Churchill. 'Pneumonia at base of lung'. *The Times*, 20 February 1958.
12. Sir Winston Churchill 'bearing up'. Fever a little lower. *The Times*, 21 February 1958.
13. Sir W. Churchill's progress. 'Very definite improvement'. *The Times*, 22 February 1958.
14. Churchill Archives Centre, Churchill College, Cambridge. CHUR 1/60/49. Telegram from Sir Winston Churchill to HM The Queen, 21 February 1958.
15. Churchill Archives Centre, Churchill College, Cambridge. CHUR 1/60/83-84. Telegram from President Eisenhower to Sir Winston Churchill, 21 February 1958.
16. Churchill Archives Centre, Churchill College, Cambridge. CHUR 1/60/81. Telegram from Sir Winston Churchill to President Eisenhower, 22 February 1958.
17. Sir W. Churchill. Temperature back to normal. *The Times*, 24 February 1958.
18. Visitors for Sir W. Churchill. Further improvement. *The Times*, 25 February 1958.
19. Churchill Archives Centre, Churchill College, Cambridge. CHUR 1/60/223. Letter from Vice-President Richard Nixon to Sir Winston Churchill, 22 February 1958.
20. Churchill Archives Centre, Churchill College, Cambridge. CHUR 1/60/222. Letter from Sir Winston Churchill to Vice-President Richard Nixon, 4 March 1958.
21. Sir W. Churchill gains strength. Satisfactory progress. *The Times*, 26 February 1958.
22. Sir Winston churchill's progress. No more bulletins. *The Times*, 27 February 1958.

23. Churchill Archives Centre, Churchill College, Cambridge. CHUR 1/60/195. Telegram from Harold Macmillan MP and Hugh Gaitskell MP to Sir Winston Churchill, 27 February 1958.

24. Churchill Archives Centre, Churchill College, Cambridge. CHUR 1/60/207. Telegram from Sir Winston Churchill to Harold Macmillan MP and Hugh Gaitskell MP, 28 February 1958.

25. Sir Winston Churchill. *The Times*, 4 March 1958.

26. Churchill Archives Centre, Churchill College, Cambridge. CHUR 1/60/225. Letter from Brendan Bracken (Viscount Bracken) to Sir Winston Churchill, 27 February 1958.

27. Churchill Archives Centre, Churchill College, Cambridge. CHUR 1/60/268. Pol Roger & CIE to Doreen Pugh, La Pausa, 13 March 1958.

28. Churchill Archives Centre, Churchill College, Cambridge. CHUR 1/60/266. Sir Winston Churchill to Odette Pol Roger, 15 March 1958.

29. Lord Montgomery with Sir W. Churchill. *The Times*, 17 March 1958.

30. Final volume of Sir Winston Churchill's history. A crowded century surveyed. *The Times*, 17 March 1958.

31. Sir W. Churchill stays indoors. *The Times*, 20 March 1958.

32. Churchill Archives Centre, Churchill College, Cambridge. CHUR 2/530 A–B/49-50. David Roberts to Winston Churchill, 19 March 1958.

33. Sir Winston Churchill's health. *The Times*, 21 March 1958.

34. Sir W. Churchill progressing. Doctor's visit after relapse. *The Times*, 24 March 1958.

35. Lord Moran sees Sir W. Churchill. Progress maintained. *The Times*, 25 March 1958.

36. Sir W. Churchill's recovery. Returning home on Thursday. *The Times*, 1 April 1958.

37. Griffiths, RW. Sir Winston Churchill's doctors on the Riviera 1949–1965: Herbert Robert Burnett Gibson (1885–1967) and Dafydd (David) Myrddin Roberts (1906–1977). *J Med Biogr* 2020; 28: 30–8.

38. M. Coty dines with Sir W. Churchill. *The Times*, 3 April 1958.

39. Sir Winston Churchill back at Chartwell. *The Times*, 5 April 1958.

40. Churchill Archives Centre, Churchill College, Cambridge. CHUR 1/149/24. Lady Churchill to Dr Roberts, 3 April 1958.

41. Churchill Archives Centre, Churchill College, Cambridge. CHUR 1/149/31. Fee note from Dr DM Roberts to Sir Winston Churchill.

42. Sir W. Churchill not going to U.S. 'Inadvisable' at present. *The Times*, 10 April 1958.

43. Hunt, T. Clinical records of Dr Thomas Hunt CBE relating to Sir Winston Churchill held at the Library at the Wellcome Collection, London. GC/46/D.5.

44. Commons acclaim Sir W. Churchill. Return after four months. *The Times*, 24 April 1958.

45. Vale, JA and Scadding, JW. Sir Winston Churchill: treatment for pneumonia in 1943 and 1944. *J R Coll Physicians Edinb* 2017; 47: 388–94.

46. Vale, JA and Scadding, JW. In Carthage ruins: the illness of Sir Winston Churchill at Carthage, December 1943. *J R Coll Physicians Edinb* 2017; 47: 288–95.

47. Churchill Archives Centre, Churchill College, Cambridge. CHAR 1/285/149. Message from Dr Hunt, 22 August 1936.

48. Braun P. Hepatotoxicity of erythromycin. *J Infect Dis* 1969; 119: 300–6.

Chapter 24. Two Strokes: April 1959 at Chartwell and October 1959 in London

1. Moran. *Winston Churchill: The Struggle for Survival 1940–1965*. London: Constable & Company, 1966: pp. 748–70.

2. Vale, JA and Scadding, JW. Sir Winston Churchill: pneumonia, pleurisy, jaundice and atrial fibrillation at Roquebrune-Cap-Martin and Chartwell, 1958. *J R Soc Med 2019*; 112: 11–21.

3. Sandys, C. *Chasing Churchill.* London: HarperCollins, 2003: pp. 104–29.

4. Churchill Archives Centre, Churchill College, Cambridge. CHUR 1/91/290. Travel arrangements for Sir Winston Churchill's visit to Marrakech, 6 January 1961.

5. Churchill Archives Centre, Churchill College, Cambridge. CHUR 1/91/211. Alcohol imported for Sir Winston Churchill's visit to Marrakech, 18 January 1961.

6. Gilbert, M. *Never Despair.* London: Heinemann, 1988: pp. 1276–1311.

7. Murray, E. *I Was Churchill's Bodyguard.* London: WH Allen, 1987: pp. 244–89.

8. Churchill Archives Centre, Churchill College, Cambridge. CHUR 2/618/26-37. Engagement cards for Sir Winston Churchill January–December 1959.

9. Soames, M. *Clementine Churchill.* London: Doubleday, 2003: pp. 510–29.

10. Moran. *Churchill: The Struggle for Survival 1945–60.* 2nd edn. London: Robinson, 2006: pp. 442–58.

11. Clinical records of Lord Brain relating to Sir Winston Churchill 1949–65 held by the Royal College of Physicians.

12. Churchill, WS. Review at Woodford. A constituency speech at Hawkey Hall, Woodford. In: Winston, RS, ed. *The Unwritten Alliance: Speeches 1953–59.* London: Cassell, 1961.

13. Browne, AM. *Long Sunset.* High Halden, Ashford: Podkin Press, 2009: pp. 258–68.

14. Churchill Archives Centre, Churchill College, Cambridge. CHUR 1/54/76-77. Letter from Lord Moran to Sir Winston Churchill, 2 May 1959.

15. Lovell, R. Lord Moran's prescriptions for Churchill. *Br Med J* 1995; 310: 1537–8.

16. Scadding, JW and Vale, JA. Winston Churchill: his first stroke in 1949. *J R Soc Med* 2018; 111: 316–23.

17. Scadding, JW and Vale, JA. Sir Winston Churchill: cerebrovascular disease January 1950–March 1952. *J R Soc Med* 2018; 111: 444–52.

18. Scadding, JW and Vale, JA. Sir Winston Churchill's acute stroke in June 1953. *J R Soc Med* 2018; 111: 347–58.

19. Scadding, JW and Vale, JA. Sir Winston Churchill: acute ataxic stroke in June 1955 with excellent recovery. *J R Soc Med* 2018; 112: 226–35.

20. Scadding, JW and Vale, JA. Sir Winston Churchill: a left hemisphere stroke or possible focal seizure on 20 October 1956. *J R Soc Med* 2018; 112: 185–91.

21. Scadding, JW and Vale, JA. Sir Winston Churchill: recovery from an acute stroke in June 1953 and triumph at the Conservative Party Conference in October 1953. *J R Soc Med* 2019; 112: 61–71.

Chapter 25. Right Finger Gangrene in May 1959 in Washington

1. Browne, AM. *Long Sunset.* High Halden, Ashford: Podkin Press, 2009: pp. 258–68.

2. Scadding, JW and Vale, JA. Winston Churchill: two mild left hemisphere strokes, finger gangrene and syncope in 1959. *J R Soc Med* 2019; 112: 278–91.

3. Moran. *Winston Churchill: The Struggle for Survival 1940–1965.* London: Constable & Company, 1966: pp. 748–70.

4. Lord Moran (Charles McMoran Wilson) (1882–1977). Medical correspondence and notes held at the Library at the Wellcome Collection, London.PP/CMW/F.6/1-3.

5. Gilbert, M. *Never Despair.* London: Heinemann, 1988: pp. 1276–1311.

6. Murray, E. *I was Churchill's Bodyguard.* London: WH Allen, 1987: pp. 244–89.

7. Soames, M. *Clementine Churchill.* London: Doubleday, 2003: pp. 510–29.

8. Churchill Archives Centre, Churchill College, Cambridge. CHUR 2/618/26-37. Engagement cards for Sir Winston Churchill January–December 1959.

9. Churchill, WS. Adoption Meeting. A constituency speech at Hawkey Hall, Woodford 29 September 1959. In: Winston, RS, ed. *The Unwritten Alliance: Speeches 1953–59.* London: Cassell, 1961: pp. 318–22.

10. Churchill, WS. A General Election Speech. A constituency speech at Hawkey Hall, Woodford 29 September 1959. In: Winston, RS, ed. *The Unwritten Alliance: Speeches 1953–59.* London: Cassell, 1961: pp. 323–7.

11. Churchill Archives Centre, Churchill College, Cambridge. CHUR 5/62A-D/571-581. Sir Winston Churchill's speech when he planted a tree on 17 October 1959 at Churchill College, Cambridge.

Chapter 26. Fracture of Fifth Thoracic Vertebrae and Stroke in November 1960 in London

1. Moran. *Churchill: The Struggle for Survival 1945–60.* 2nd end. London: Robinson, 2006: pp. 442–58.

2. Howells, R. *Simply Churchill.* London: Robert Hale, 1965: pp. 52–62.

3. Scadding, JW and Vale, JA. Sir Winston Churchill's acute stroke in June 1953. *J R Soc Med* 2018; 111: 347–58.

4. Scadding, JW and Vale, JA. Sir Winston Churchill: recovery from an acute stroke in June 1953 and triumph at the Conservative Party Conference in October 1953. *J R Soc Med* 2019; 112: 61–71.

5. Churchill Archives Centre, Churchill College, Cambridge. CHUR 1/61/273. Letter from Sir Winston Churchill to Constable Clarke dated 12 December 1960.

6. Seddon, H. Clinical records of Professor Harold Seddon relating to Sir Winston Churchill, 1960–3, held by the Royal College of Surgeons of England (MS0279).

7. Churchill Archives Centre, Churchill College, Cambridge. WCHL 6/66 Notebook containing the nursing records on Sir Winston Churchill covering the period November–December 1960.

8. Churchill Archives Centre, Churchill College, Cambridge. CHUR 1/61/12. Professor Herbert Seddon's suggested statement for the Press, 16 November 1960.

9. Churchill Archives Centre, Churchill College, Cambridge. CHUR 1/61/125. Bulletin issued on 16 November 1960.

10. Sir Winston Churchill hurt in fall: Small bone in back broken. *The Times*, 17 November 1960.

11. Sir W. Churchill: 'Things going well'. *The Times*, 18 November 1960.

12. Churchill Archives Centre, Churchill College, Cambridge. CHUR 1/61/124. Bulletin issued on 17 November 1960.

13. Churchill Archives Centre, Churchill College, Cambridge. CHUR 1/61/49. Telegram from Her Majesty the Queen to Sir Winston Churchill, 16 November 1960.

14. Churchill Archives Centre, Churchill College, Cambridge. CHUR 1/61/48. Telegram from Sir Winston Churchill to Her Majesty the Queen, 21 February 1958.

15. Churchill Archives Centre, Churchill College, Cambridge. CHUR 1/61/54. Cable from President Eisenhower to Sir Winston Churchill, 17 November 1960.

16. Churchill Archives Centre, Churchill College, Cambridge. CHUR 1/61/52. Telegram to President Eisenhower from Sir Winston Churchill, 17 November 1960.

17. Richardson. Unpublished Autobiography of Lord Richardson. LVO FRCP.

18. Churchill Archives Centre, Churchill College, Cambridge. CHUR 1/61/123. Bulletin issued on 18 November 1960.

19. Sir W. Churchill: 'No anxiety'. *The Times*, 19 November 1960.

20. Churchill Archives Centre, Churchill College, Cambridge. CHUR 1/61/171. Letter from Dr DM Roberts to Sir Winston Churchill, 18 November 1960.

21. Churchill Archives Centre, Churchill College, Cambridge. CHUR 1/61/122. Bulletin issued on 19 November 1960.
22. Churchill Archives Centre, Churchill College, Cambridge. CHUR 1/61/121. Bulletin issued on 20 November 1960.
23. Sir Winston gets up for a while. *The Times*, 22 November 1960.
24. Gilbert, M. *Never Despair*. London: Heinemann, 1988: pp. 1312–39.
25. Sir W. Churchill: 'Going on all right'. *The Times*, 24 November 1960.
26. Churchill Archives Centre, Churchill College, Cambridge. CHUR 2/618/48. Engagement card for November 1960.
27. Sir Winston Churchill. *The Times*, 28 November 1960.
28. Sir Winston Churchill. *The Times*, 29 November 1960.
29. Sir Winston enjoys 86th birthday: Up for luncheon. *The Times*, 1 December 1960.
30. Sir W. Churchill X-Rayed. *The Times*, 6 December 1960.
31. Sir Winston Churchill. *The Times*, 7 December 1960.
32. Mr. Macmillan dines at Chartwell. *The Times*, 30 December 1960.
33. Churchill Archives Centre, Churchill College, Cambridge. CHUR 2/530A-B/40. Letter from Professor Herbert Seddon to Montague Browne, 31 January 1961.
34. Churchill Archives Centre, Churchill College, Cambridge. CHUR 2/530A-B/39. Letter from Montague Browne to Professor Herbert Seddon, 2 February 1961.
35. Churchill Archives Centre, Churchill College, Cambridge. CHUR 2/530A-B/41. Letter from Sir Winston Churchill to Professor Herbert Seddon, 2 February 1961.
36. Churchill Archives Centre, Churchill College, Cambridge. CHUR 2/530A-B/38. Letter from Professor Herbert Seddon to Anthony Montague Browne, 6 February 1961.
37. Vale, JA and Scadding, JW. Sir Winston Churchill KG: hip fracture in Monte Carlo ("Remember, I want to die in England") on 28 June 1962, femoral vein thrombosis and jaundice in London. *J R Soc Med* 2019; 112: 96–108.
38. Churchill Archives Centre, Churchill College, Cambridge. CHUR 2/530A-B/37. Letter from Professor Herbert Seddon to Sir Winston Churchill, 6 February 1961.
39. Churchill Archives Centre, Churchill College, Cambridge. CHUR 2/530A-B/36. Letter from Anthony Montague Browne to Professor Herbert Seddon, 8 February 1961.
40. Clinical records of Lord Brain relating to Sir Winston Churchill 1949–1965 held by the Royal College of Physicians.
41. Scadding, JW and Vale, JA. Winston Churchill: his first stroke in 1949. *J R Soc Med* 2018; 111: 316–23.
42. Scadding, JW and Vale, JA. Sir Winston Churchill: acute ataxic stroke in June 1955 with excellent recovery. *J R Soc Med* 2018; 112: 226–35.
43. Scadding, JW and Vale, JA. Sir Winston Churchill: a left hemisphere stroke or possible focal seizure on 20 October 1956. *J R Soc Med* 2018; 112: 185–91.
44. Scadding, JW and Vale, JA. Sir Winston Churchill: cerebrovascular disease January 1950–March 1952. *J R Soc Med* 2018; 111: 444–52.
45. Joint Formulary Committee. *British National Formulary: Alternative Edition*. London: The British Medical Association and The Pharmaceutical Society of Great Britain, 1957.
46. Lovell, R. Lord Moran's prescriptions for Churchill. *Br Med J* 1995; 310: 1537–8.
47. Macdonald, JB and MacDonald, ET. Nocturnal femoral fracture and continuing widespread use of barbiturate hypnotics. *Br Med J* 1977; 2: 483.
48. Browne, AM. *Long Sunset*. High Halden, Ashford: Podkin Press, 2009.

Chapter 27. Hip Fracture in June 1962 in Monte Carlo, Femoral Vein Thrombosis and Jaundice in London

1. Howells, R. *Simply Churchill*. London: Robert Hale, 1965: pp. 86–93.
2. Browne, AM. *Long Sunset*. High Halden, Ashford: Podkin Press, 2009: pp. 312–23.
3. Sandys, C. *Chasing Churchill*. London: HarperCollins, 2003: pp. 244–60.
4. Sir Winston Churchill to fly home. *The Times*, 29 June 1962.
5. Churchill Archives Centre, Churchill College, Cambridge. CHUR 1/62/69. Letter from Montague Browne to Dr David Roberts, 24 July 1962.
6. Churchill Archives Centre, Churchill College, Cambridge. CHUR 1/62/49. Letter from Sir Winston Churchill to Dr David Roberts, 24 August 1962.
7. Churchill Archives Centre, Churchill College, Cambridge. CHUR 1/62/55. Account from Dr David Roberts, 1962.
8. Churchill Archives Centre, Churchill College, Cambridge. CHUR 1/62/57. Account from Dr André Fissore, 1962.
9. Churchill Archives Centre, Churchill College, Cambridge. CHUR 1/62/58. Account from Dr M Gramaglia, 10 August 1962.
10. Churchill Archives Centre, Churchill College, Cambridge. CHUR 1/62/56. Account from Dr C-L Chatelin, 1962.
11. Churchill Archives Centre, Churchill College, Cambridge. CHUR 1/62/7. Letter from Sir Winston Churchill to the Speaker of the House of Commons, 28 June 1962.
12. Sir Winston Churchill satisfactory. *The Times*, 30 June 1962.
13. MacNeil, R. *The Right Place at the Right Time*. Boston: Little, Brown and Company, 1982: pp. 124–9.
14. Howells, R. *Simply Churchill*. London: Robert Hale, 1965: pp. 94–9.
15. Morton, G., Personal Communication.
16. Seddon, H. Clinical records of Professor Sir Herbert Seddon relating to Sir Winston Churchill, 1960–63, held by the Royal College of Surgeons of England (MS0279).
17. Sir W. Churchill gets out of bed. *The Times*, 2 July 1962.
18. Sir W. Churchill 'getting on well'. *The Times*, 3 July 1962.
19. Sir W. Churchill stronger. *The Times*, 4 July 1962.
20. Churchill Archives Centre, Churchill College, Cambridge. CHUR 1/62/21. Letter from journalists to Sir Winston Churchill, 3 July 1962.
21. Churchill Archives Centre, Churchill College, Cambridge. CHUR 1/62/20. Letter from Montague Browne to journalists, 3 July 1962.
22. Murray, E. *I Was Churchill's Bodyguard*. London: WH Allen, 1987: pp. 244–89.
23. Sir W. Churchill up for luncheon. *The Times*, 5 July 1962.
24. Sir W. Churchill has a quiet day. *The Times*, 6 July 1962.
25. Vale, JA and Scadding, JW. In Carthage ruins: the illness of Sir Winston Churchill at Carthage, December 1943. *J R Coll Physicians Edinb* 2017; 47: 288–95.
26. Sir W. Churchill is more rested. *The Times*, 7 July 1962.
27. Sir Winston Churchill sleeps well. *The Times*, 9 July 1962.
28. Sir Winston's leg 'more swollen'. *The Times*, 10 July 1962.
29. Sir W. Churchill – No extension of thrombosis. *The Times*, 11 July 1962.
30. Sir W. Churchill visited by son. *The Times*, 12 July 1962.
31. Gilbert, M. *Never Despair*. London: Heinemann, 1988: pp. 1312–39.
32. Sir Winston has a bronchial infection. *The Times*, 13 July 1962.
33. Sir W. Churchill: stitches removed. *The Times*, 14 July 1962.
34. Sir Winston in good spirits. *The Times*, 16 July 1962.
35. Sir W. Churchill walks unaided. *The Times*, 18 July 1962.

36. Sir Winston sees Mr. Macmillan. *The Times*. 21 July 1962.
37. Sir Winston: No more bulletins. *The Times*, 26 July 1962.
38. Sir W. Churchill 'Quite well'. *The Times*, 28 July 1962.
39. Sir Winston: No new attack of jaundice. *The Times*, 3 August 1962.
40. Vale, JA and Scadding, JW. Sir Winston Churchill: pneumonia, pleurisy, jaundice and atrial fibrillation at Roquebrune-Cap-Martin and Chartwell, 1958. *J R Soc Med 2019*; 112: 11–21.
41. Churchill Archives Centre, Churchill College, Cambridge. CHUR 1/62/33. Letter from Sir Winston Churchill to Professor Seddon, 1 August 1962.
42. Churchill Archives Centre, Churchill College, Cambridge. CHUR 1/62/34-35. Letter from Professor Seddon to Sir Winston Churchill, 2 August 1962.
43. Sir Winston is home again. *The Times*, 22 August 1962.
44. Howells, R. *Simply Churchill*. London: Robert Hale, 1965: pp. 100–6.
45. Soames, M. *Clementine Churchill*. London: Doubleday, 2003: pp. 510–29.
46. Churchill Archives Centre, Churchill College, Cambridge. CHUR 1/62/140. Letter from Sir Winston Churchill to Professor Herbert Seddon, 17 September 1962.
47. Churchill Archives Centre, Churchill College, Cambridge. CHUR 1/62/144-145. List of presents to medical advisors, 4 September 1962.
48. Churchill Archives Centre, Churchill College, Cambridge. CHUR 1/62/81. Letter from Professor Herbert Seddon to Sir Winston Churchill, 12 October 1962.
49. Scadding, JW and Vale, JA. Winston Churchill: his first stroke in 1949. *J R Soc Med* 2018; 111: 316–23.
50. Scadding, JW and Vale, JA. Sir Winston Churchill: cerebrovascular disease January 1950–March 1952. *J R Soc Med* 2018; 111: 444–52.
51. Scadding, JW and Vale, JA. Sir Winston Churchill's acute stroke in June 1953. *J R Soc Med* 2018; 111: 347–58.
52. Scadding, JW and Vale, JA. Sir Winston Churchill: acute ataxic stroke in June 1955 with excellent recovery. *J R Soc Med* 2018; 112: 226–35.
53. Scadding, JW and Vale, JA. Sir Winston Churchill: a left hemisphere stroke or possible focal seizure on 20 October 1956. *J R Soc Med* 2018; 112: 185–91.
54. Vale, JA and Scadding, JW. Sir Winston Churchill: treatment for pneumonia in 1943 and 1944. *J R Coll Physicians Edinb* 2017; 47: 388–94.
55. Portal, RW and Emanuel, RW. Phenindione hepatitis complicating anticoagulant therapy. *Br Med J* 1961; 2: 1318–19.
56. Perkins, J. Phenindione jaundice. *The Lancet* 1962; 279: 125–27.
57. Hargreaves, T and Howell, M. Phenindione jaundice. *Br Heart J* 1965; 27: 932–6.
58. Soames, M. *Speaking for Themselves*. London: Transworld, 1998: pp. 635–47.

Chapter 28. Vascular Episode in the Left Leg in August 1963 at Chartwell

1. Seddon, H. Clinical records of Professor Sir Herbert Seddon relating to Sir Winston Churchill, 1960–3, held by the Royal College of Surgeons of England (MS0279).
2. Churchill, WS. *Memories and Adventures*. New York: Weidenfeld & Nicolson, 1989: pp. 166–80.
3. Gilbert, M. *Never Despair*. London: Heinemann, 1988: pp. 1340–66.
4. Churchill Archives Centre, Churchill College, Cambridge. CHUR 2/618/79-85. Engagement cards for Sir Winston Churchill June–December 1963.
5. Churchill Archives Centre, Churchill College, Cambridge. CHUR 2/519A-C/216-217. Letter from Anthony Montague Browne to Lord Beaverbrook, 15 August 1963.

6. Churchill Archives Centre, Churchill College, Cambridge. CHUR 2/519A-C/214-215. Letter from Anthony Montague Browne to Lord Beaverbrook, 23 August 1963.
7. Churchill Archives Centre, Churchill College, Cambridge. CHUR 2/519A-C/213. Letter from Anthony Montague Browne to Lord Beaverbrook, 3 September 1963.
8. Soames, M. *Speaking for Themselves*. London: Transworld, 1998: pp. 635–47.
9. Churchill Archives Centre, Churchill College, Cambridge. CHUR 2/534/142. Letter from Doreen Pugh to Professor Seddon, 23 September 1963.
10. Churchill Archives Centre, Churchill College, Cambridge. CHUR 2/519A-C/212. Letter from Anthony Montague Browne to Lord Beaverbrook, 2 October 1963.
11. Macmillan, H. *The Macmillan Diaries, Vol II*. London: Macmillan, 1963.
12. Soames, M. *Clementine Churchill*. London: Doubleday, 2003: pp. 510–29.
13. Churchill Archives Centre, Churchill College, Cambridge. CHUR 1/135/226. Letter from Sir Winston Churchill to Lady Churchill, 30 September 1963.
14. Churchill Archives Centre, Churchill College, Cambridge. CHUR 1/135/227. Letter from Dr JW Barnett to Sir Winston Churchill, 10 October 1963.
15. Churchill Archives Centre, Churchill College, Cambridge. CHUR 1/136/184-5. Letter from Winston Churchill to Sir Winston Churchill, 24 September 1963.
16. Churchill Archives Centre, Churchill College, Cambridge. CHUR 1/136/186. Letter from Sir Winston Churchill to Winston Churchill, 30 September 1963.
17. Churchill Archives Centre, Churchill College, Cambridge. CHUR 1/136/187. Letter from Winston Churchill to Sir Winston Churchill, 14 October 1963.

Chapter 29. Churchill's Skin Diseases

1. Lord Moran (Charles McMoran Wilson) (1882–1977). Medical correspondence and notes held at the Library at the Wellcome Collection, London. PP/CMW/F. 6/1-3.
2. Vale, JA and Scadding, JW. Winston Churchill: inguinal hernia repair on 11 June 1947. *J R Soc Med* 2019; 112: 140–52.
3. Stelzer, C. *Working With Winston: the Unsung Women Behind Britain's Greatest Statesman*. London: Head of Zeus Ltd, 2019: pp. 95–131.
4. Churchill Archives Centre, Churchill College, Cambridge. CHUR 2/173/181. Letter from Miss Sturdee to Lord Moran, 13 February 1950.
5. Churchill Archives Centre, Churchill College, Cambridge. CHUR 2/173/284. Letter from Dr Henry MacCormac to Winston Churchill, 27 April 1949.
6. Churchill Archives Centre, Churchill College, Cambridge. CHUR 2/173/169. Letter from Winston Churchill to Lord Moran, 13 November 1950.
7. Churchill Archives Centre, Churchill College, Cambridge. CHUR 2/173/283. Letter from Miss Sturdee to Winston Churchill, 14 December 1950.
8. Churchill Archives Centre, Churchill College, Cambridge. CHUR 2/173/282. Letter from Winston Churchill to Mrs MacCormac, 29 January 1951.
9. Churchill Archives Centre, Churchill College, Cambridge. CHUR 2/173/280-281. Letter from Mrs MacCormac to Winston Churchill, 30 January 1951.
10. Gilbert, M. *Never Despair*. London: Heinemann, 1988: pp. 609–29.
11. Churchill, WS. Portrait of Lord Moran: a speech to the Royal College of Physicians, 10 July 1951. In: Churchill, RS, ed. *Stemming the Tide: Speeches 1951 and 1952*. Cambridge: The Riverside Press, 1954: pp. 90–2.
12. Churchill Archives Centre, Churchill College, Cambridge. CHUR 2/173/354-356. Letter from Dr Robert MacKenna to Winston Churchill, 25 July 1951.
13. Moran. *Winston Churchill: The Struggle for Survival 1940–1965*. London: Constable & Company, 1966: pp. 343–50.

14. Lovell, R. *Churchill's Doctor: A Biography of Lord Moran.* London: Royal Society of Medicine Services Ltd, 1992.

15. Moran. *Winston Churchill: The Struggle for Survival 1940–1965.* London: Constable & Company, 1966: pp. 639–45.

16. Safer, JD, Fraser, LM, Ray, S and Holick, MF. Topical triiodothyronine stimulates epidermal proliferation, dermal thickening, and hair growth in mice and rats. *Thyroid* 2001; 11: 717–24.

17. Gilbert, M. *Never Despair.* London: Heinemann, 1988: pp. 1276–1311.

18. Churchill Archives Centre, Churchill College, Cambridge. WCHL 6/66 Notebook containing the nursing records on Sir Winston Churchill covering the period November–December 1960.

19. Naldi, L and Rebora, A. Seborrheic dermatitis. *N Engl J Med* 2009; 360: 387–96.

20. Zander, N, Sommer, R, Schäfer, I, Reinert, R, Kirsten, N, Zyriax, BC, et al. Epidemiology and dermatological comorbidity of seborrhoeic dermatitis: population-based study in 161 269 employees. *Br J Dermatol* 2019; 181: 743–8.

21. Borda, LJ and Wikramanayake, TC. Seborrheic dermatitis and dandruff: a comprehensive review. *Journal of Clinical and Investigative Dermatology* 2015; 3: 1–22.

22. Naldi, L and Diphoorn, J. Seborrhoeic dermatitis of the scalp. *Br Med J (Clinical Evidence)* 2015; 2015: 1713.

23. Tulipan, L. Acne rosacea: a Vitamin B complex deficiency. *JAMA Dermatol* 1947; 56: 589–91.

Chapter 30. Did Churchill Suffer from the 'Black Dog'?

1. Moran. *Winston Churchill: The Struggle for Survival 1940–1965.* London: Constable & Company, 1966: pp. 161–75.

2. Simpson, S and Weiner, E. *The Oxford English Dictionary.* 2 edn. Oxford: Clarendon Press, 1989.

3. Storr, A. *Churchill: Four Faces and the Man.* London: Allen Lane The Penguin Press, 1969: pp. 203–46.

4. Storr, A. *Churchill's Black Dog and Other Phenomena of the Human Mind.* Glasgow: William Collins Sons & Co. Ltd, 1989: pp. 3–51.

5. Daniels, AM and Vale, JA. Did Sir Winston Churchill suffer from the 'black dog'? *J R Soc Med* 2018; 111: 394-406.

6. Ramsden, J. *Man of the Century. Winston Churchill and His Legend Since 1945.* London: HarperCollins Publishers, 2002: pp. 527–90.

7. Post, JM and Robins, RS. *When Illness Strikes the Leader.* New Haven and London: Yale Univeristy Press, 1993.

8. Moran. *Winston Churchill: The Struggle for Survival 1940–1965.* London: Constable & Company, 1966: pp. 454–74.

9. Owen, D. *In Sickness and in Power.* London: Methuen Publishing, 2008: pp. 1–105.

10. Ghaemi, N. *A First-Rate Madness.* London: Penguin Books, 2011: pp. 57–67.

11. Solomon, A. *The Noonday Demon: an Anatomy of Depression.* London: Chatto and Windus, 2001: pp. 361–400.

12. Norman, A. *Winston Churchill. Portrait of an Unquiet Mind.* Barnsley: Pen & Sword Military, 2012.

13. Norman, A. *Winston Churchill. Portrait of an Unquiet Mind.* Barnsley: Pen & Sword Military, 2012: pp. 197–201.

14. Best, G. *Churchill: A Study in Greatness.* London: Hambledon and London, 2001: pp. 141–57.

15. Attenborough, W. *Churchill and the 'Black Dog' of Depression*. Basingstoke: Palgrave Macmillan, 2014.

16. Attenborough, W. *Diagnosing Churchill: Bipolar or 'Prey to Nerves'?* Jefferson NC: McFarland & Company, Inc., 2019.

17. Gilbert, M. *In Search of Churchill*. London: HarperCollins, 1994: pp. 200–13.

18. American Psychiatric Association. Diagnostic and Statistical Manual of Mental Disorders. 5 edn. Arlington: American Psychiatric Association, 2013.

19. Soames, M. *Speaking for Themselves*. London: Transworld, 1998: pp. 39–57.

20. Gilbert, M. *Winston S. Churchill Volume III 1914–1916*. London: Heinemann, 1971: pp. 679–715.

21. Blunt, WS. *My Diaries: Being a Personal Narrative of Events, 1888–1914*. New York: A.A. Knopf, 1921.

22. CLAUSE 1.-(Suspension of death penalty for murder.). HC Deb 15 July 1948; 453: cc 1411–1545.

23. Soames, M. *Clementine Churchill*. London: Doubleday, 2003: pp. 68–87.

24. Riddell. *More Pages From My Diary: 1908–1914*. London: Country Life Ltd, 1934: pp. 24–9.

25. Churchill, WS. *Painting as a Pastime*. London: Odhams Press; Ernest Benn Ltd, 1948.

26. Soames, M. Life with my parents Winston and Clementine. *Finest Hour* 1996; 91: 14–17.

27. Churchill, S. *A Thread in the Tapestry*. London: Andre Deutsch, 1967.

28. Colville, J. *The Fringes of Power*. London: Weidenfeld & Nicolson, 2004.

29. Wheeler-Bennett, J, ed. *Action This Day: Working With Churchill*. London: Macmillan & Co. Ltd, 1968: pp. 47–138.

30. Moran. *The Anatomy of Courage*. London: Robinson, 2007.

31. Colville, JR. The personality of Sir Winston Churchill. In: Kemper, RC, ed. *Winston Churchill. Resolution, Defiance, Magnanimity, Good Will*. Columbia MO: University of Missouri Press, 1996: pp. 109–26.

32. Churchill Archives Centre, Churchill College, Cambridge. CHUR 2/220/21-22 Letter from Harold Macmillan MP to Sir Winston Churchill, 15 June 1955.

33. Browne, AM. *Long Sunset*. High Halden, Ashford: Podkin Press, 2009: pp. 187–97.

34. Soames, M. In: Browne, AM. *Long Sunset*. High Halden, Ashford: Podkin Press, 2009: pp. ix–xi.

35. Browne, AM. *Long Sunset*. High Halden, Ashford: Podkin Press, 2009: pp. 302–11.

36. Stelzer, C. *Working With Winston: the Unsung Women Behind Britain's Greatest Statesman*. London: Head of Zeus Ltd, 2019: pp. 195–220.

37. Churchill Archives Centre, Churchill College, Cambridge. CHOH 1 GMLL. Interview with Cecily Gemmell in 1986.

38. Gilbert, M. *Churchill*. London: BBC Enterprises, 1993.

39. Attenborough, W. *Diagnosing Churchill: Bipolar or 'Prey to Nerves'?* Jefferson NC: McFarland & Company, Inc., 2019: pp. 5–19.

40. Moran. *The Anatomy of Courage*, London: Robinson, 2007.

41. Moran. *Winston Churchill: The Struggle for Survival 1940–1965*. London: Constable & Company, 1966: pp. 133–44.

42. Moran. *Winston Churchill: The Struggle for Survival 1940–1965*. London: Constable & Company, 1966: pp. 175–82.

43. Moran. *Winston Churchill: The Struggle for Survival 1940–1965*. London: Constable & Company, 1966: pp. 286–90.

44. Moran. *Winston Churchill: The Struggle for Survival 1940–1965*. London: Constable & Company, 1966: pp. 306–17.
45. Moran. *Winston Churchill: The Struggle for Survival 1940–1965*. London: Constable & Company, 1966: pp. 639–45.
46. Moran. *Winston Churchill: The Struggle for Survival 1940–1965*. London: Constable & Company, 1966: pp. 732–47.
47. Moran. *Winston Churchill: The Struggle for Survival 1940–1965*. London: Constable & Company, 1966: pp. 748–70.
48. Moran. *Winston Churchill: The Struggle for Survival 1940–1965*. London: Constable & Company, 1966: pp. 133–44.
49. Moran. *Moran: Churchill at War 1940–45*. London: Robinson, 2002: pp. xxii–xxiv.
50. Grant, M. In: Moran. *Churchill: The Struggle for Survival 1945–60*. London: Robinson, 2006: pp. xv–xvii.
51. Attenborough, W. *Churchill and the 'Black Dog' of Depression*. Basingstoke: Palgrave Macmillan, 2014: pp. 187–97.
52. Colville, J. *The Fringes of Power*. London: Weidenfeld & Nicolson, 2004: pp. 478–95.
53. Attenborough, W. *Diagnosing Churchill: Bipolar or 'Prey to Nerves'?* Jefferson NC: McFarland & Company, Inc., 2019: pp. 202–22.
54. Moran. *Winston Churchill: The Struggle for Survival 1940–1965*. London: Constable & Company, 1966: pp. 777–90.
55. Attenborough, W. *Churchill and the 'Black Dog' of Depression*. Basingstoke: Palgrave Macmillan, 2014: pp. 214–17.
56. Attenborough, W. *Diagnosing Churchill: Bipolar or 'Prey to Nerves'?* Jefferson NC: McFarland & Company, Inc., 2019: pp. 233–5.
57. Pawle, G. *The War and Colonel Warden*. London: George G Harrap, 1963: pp. 2–8.
58. Gilbert, M. *Never Despair*. London: Heinemann, 1988: pp. 123–31.
59. Gilbert, M. *Never Despair*. London: Heinemann, 1988: pp. 180–206.
60. Gilbert, M. *Never Despair*. London: Heinemann, 1988: pp. 207–20.
61. Gilbert, M. *Never Despair*. London: Heinemann, 1988: pp. 221–54.
62. Gilbert, M. *Never Despair*. London: Heinemann, 1988: pp. 1243–75.
63. Scadding, JW and Vale, JA. Sir Winston Churchill's acute stroke in June 1953. *J R Soc Med* 2018; 111: 347–58.
64. Lovell, R. Lord Moran's prescriptions for Churchill. *Br Med J* 1995; 310: 1537–8.
65. Moran. *Winston Churchill: The Struggle for Survival 1940–1965*. London: Constable & Company, 1966: pp. 475–81.
66. Scadding, JW and Vale, JA. Sir Winston Churchill: recovery from an acute stroke in June 1953 and triumph at the Conservative Party Conference in October 1953. *J R Soc Med* 2019; 112: 61–71.
67. Brain, WR. Encounters with Winston Churchill. *Med Hist* 2000; 44: 3–20.
68. Bonham Carter, V. *Winston Churchill as I knew Him*. London: Eyre and Spottiswoode, 1965: pp. 261–76.
69. Bonham Carter, V. *Winston Churchill as I knew Him*. London: Eyre and Spottiswoode, 1965: pp. 15–23.
70. Bonham Carter, V. *Winston Churchill as I knew Him*. London: Eyre and Spottiswoode, 1965: pp. 377–407.
71. Bonham Carter, V. *Winston Churchill as I knew Him*. London: Eyre and Spottiswoode, 1965: pp. 408–32.
72. *National Collaborating Centre for Mental Health. Bipolar Disorder: the Assessment and Management of Bipolar Disorder in Adults, Children and Young People in Primary and*

Secondary Care. National Clinical Guideline Number 185. Updated edn. The British Psychological Society and The Royal College of Psychiatrists, 2018.

73. Vale, JA and Scadding, JW. Sir Winston Churchill: pneumonia, pleurisy, jaundice and atrial fibrillation at Roquebrune-Cap-Martin and Chartwell, 1958. *J R Soc Med* 2019; 112: 11–21.
74. Lord Moran (Charles McMoran Wilson) (1882–1977). Medical correspondence and notes held at the Library at the Wellcome Collection, London. PP/CMW/F.6/1-3.
75. Clinical records of Lord Brain relating to Sir Winston Churchill 1949–65 held by the Royal College of Physicians.
76. Clinical records of Sir John Parkinson relating to Sir Winston Churchill 1942–54, held by the Royal College of Physicians.
77. Some medical notes of Brigadier D Evan Bedford relating to Sir Winston Churchill's illness in Carthage in 1943, held by the Royal College of Physicians.
78. Breckenridge, C. The myth of the 'black dog'. *Finest Hour* 2012; 155: 28–31.

Chapter 31. Was Churchill an Alcoholic?

1. Langworth, RM. *Churchill in his own words.* London: Ebury Press, 2012: pp. 532–44.
2. Roberts, A. *Churchill: Walking with Destiny.* London: Allen Lane, 2018: pp. 32–54.
3. Robertson, I. Drunk in charge. *Br Med J* 1994; 309: 1237.
4. Churchill, WS. Unsubstantiated personal attack. *Br Med J* 1994; 309: 1517.
5. Hamblin, G. Never the worse for drink. *Br Med J* 1994; 309: 1517.
6. Robertson, I. Interpreting problems. *Br Med J* 1994; 309: 1519.
7. Rose, N. *Churchill: An Unruly Life.* London: Simon and Schuster, 1994: pp. 192–215.
8. Ponting, C. *Churchill.* London: Sinclair-Stevenson, 1994: pp. 276–92.
9. Charmley, J. *Churchill: The End of Glory.* London: Hodder and Stoughton, 1992: p. 549.
10. Wheeler-Bennett, J, ed. *Action this day: Working with Churchill.* London: Macmillan & Co. Ltd, 1968: pp. 158–217.
11. England Needs a Slap, and So Does China. *Wall Street Journal* 13 June 2019.
12. Langworth, R. Memo to Peggy Noonan and the WSJ: Churchill was NOT a drunk. Available at: https://richardlangworth.com/noonan-churchill-alcohol (accessed 21 June 2019).
13. Churchill, WS. *My Early Life.* London: Macmillan & Co. Ltd, 1944: pp. 136–48.
14. Churchill, W. *The Story of the Malakand Field Forc.*, London: Thomas Nelson, 1916: pp. 1–10.
15. Moran. *Winston Churchill: The Struggle for Survival 1940–1965.* London: Constable & Company, 1966: pp. 666–85.
16. Wheeler-Bennett, J, ed. *Action This Day: Working With Churchill.* London: Macmillan & Co. Ltd, 1968: pp. 47–138.
17. Brooks, C. Churchill the Conversationalist. In: Eade, C, ed. *Churchill by His Contemporaries.* London: Hutchison & Co. Ltd, 1955: pp. 240–8.
18. Langworth, RM. *Churchill in His Own Words.* London: Ebury Press, 2012: pp. 545–60.
19. James, RR. *Churchill: A Study in Failure 1900–1939.* London: Weidenfeld & Nicolson, 1970: pp. 285–350.
20. Roberts, A. *Churchill: Walking with Destiny.* London: Allen Lane, 2018: pp. 762–95.
21. Gilbert, M. *Churchill.* London: BBC Enterprises, 1993.
22. Gilbert, M. *In Search of Churchill.* London: HarperCollins, 1994: pp. 174–99.
23. Gilbert, M. *Finest Hour.* London: Heinemann, 1983: p. 336.
24. Langworth, RM. *Winston Churchill, Myth and Reality: What He Actually Did and Said.* Jefferson NC: McFarland & Company, Inc., 2017: pp. 85–90.

25. Hunt, D. *On the Spot*. London: Peter Davies, 1975: pp. 49–80.
26. Scadding, JW and Vale, JA. Sir Winston Churchill: acute ataxic stroke in June 1955 with excellent recovery. *J R Soc Med* 2018; 112: 226–35.
27. Rowse, AL. *Memories of Men and Women*. London: Eyre Methuen Ltd, 1980: pp. 1–24.
28. Campbell, TM, Herring, GC, eds. *The Diaries of Edward R Stettinius, Jr.* New York NY: New Viewpoints, 1975: p. 44.
29. King, M. Diary 23 August 1941. Available at: https://www.bac-lac.gc.ca/eng/discover/politics-government/prime-ministers/william-lyon-mackenzie-king/Pages/item.aspx?IdNumber=23171 (accessed 20 October 2019).
30. Gilbert, M. *The Churchill Documents, Volume 12: The Wilderness Years, 1929–1935*. 2nd edn. Hillsdale MI: Hillsdale College Press, 2009: pp. 1365–7.
31. American Psychiatric Association. *Desk Reference to the Diagnostic Criteria From DSM-5™*. Washington DC: American Psychiatric Publishing, 2013.
32. Kimball, W. 'Like Goldfish in a Bowl': The Alcohol Quotient. *Finest Hour* 2007; 134: 31–3.
33. Stelzer, C. *Working With Winston: the Unsung Women Behind Britain's Greatest Statesman*. London: Head of Zeus Ltd, 2019: pp. 15–45.
34. Gilbert, M. *In Search of Churchill*. London: HarperCollins, 1994: pp. 200–13.
35. Browne, AM. *Long Sunset*. High Halden, Ashford: Podkin Press, 2009: pp. 187–97.
36. Kidder, S. Present at the Creation: Danny Mander guarding the P.M. at Tehran, 1942–43. *Finest Hour* 2008; 138: 20–3.
37. Danchev, A, Todman, D, eds. *War Diaries 1939–1945 Field Marshal Lord Alanbrooke*. London: Weidenfeld & Nicolson, 2001: pp. 565–76.
38. Simpson, S, ed. *The Cunningham Papers*. Aldershot: Ashgate Publishing Ltd, 2006: p. 158.
39. Avon. *The Eden Memoirs: The Reckoning*. London: Cassell, 1965: pp. 458–79.
40. Roberts, A. *Churchill: Walking with Destiny*. London: Allen Lane, 2018: pp. 823–55.
41. Clinical records of Lord Brain relating to Sir Winston Churchill 1949–65 held by the Royal College of Physicians.
42. Moran. *Winston Churchill: The Struggle for Survival 1940–1965*. London: Constable & Company, 1966: pp. 384–95.
43. Vale, JA and Scadding, JW. Sir Winston Churchill: pneumonia, pleurisy, jaundice and atrial fibrillation at Roquebrune-Cap-Martin and Chartwell, 1958. *J R Soc Med* 2019; 112: 11–21.
44. Hunt, T. Clinical records of Dr Thomas Hunt CBE relating to Sir Winston Churchill held at the Library at the Wellcome Collection, London. GC/46/D.5.
45. Scadding, JW and Vale, JA. Winston Churchill: his first stroke in 1949. *J R Soc Med* 2018; 111: 316–23.
46. Scadding, JW and Vale, JA. Sir Winston Churchill: cerebrovascular disease January 1950–March 1952. *J R Soc Med* 2018; 111: 444–52.
47. Scadding, JW and Vale, JA. Sir Winston Churchill's acute stroke in June 1953. *J R Soc Med* 2018; 111: 347–58.
48. Scadding, JW and Vale, JA. Sir Winston Churchill: recovery from an acute stroke in June 1953 and triumph at the Conservative Party Conference in October 1953. *J R Soc Med* 2019; 112: 61–71.
49. Moran. *Winston Churchill: The Struggle for Survival 1940–1965*. London: Constable & Company, 1966: pp. 419–53.
50. Moran. *Winston Churchill: The Struggle for Survival 1940–1965*. London: Constable & Company, 1966: pp. 454–74.

51. Moran. *Winston Churchill: The Struggle for Survival 1940–1965.* London: Constable & Company, 1966: pp. 495–502.
52. Howells, R. *Simply Churchill.* London: Robert Hale, 1965: pp. 35–44.

Chapter 32.   Churchill's Terminal Illness in January 1965 in London
1. Churchill, WS. *Memories and Adventures.* New York: Weidenfeld & Nicolson, 1989: pp. 181–87.
2. Soames, M. *Speaking for Themselves.* London: Transworld, 1998: pp. 635–47.
3. Murray, E. *I was Churchill's Bodyguard.* London: WH Allen, 1987: pp. 244–89.
4. Gilbert, M. *Never Despair.* London: Heinemann, 1988: pp. 1340–66.
5. Churchill Archives Centre, Churchill College, Cambridge. CHUR 2/618/95-98. Engagement cards for October 1964–January 1965.
6. Soames, M. *Clementine Churchill.* London: Doubleday, 2003: pp. 530–45.
7. Howells, R. *Simply Churchill.* London: Robert Hale, 1965: pp. 164–76.
8. Coote, CR. *The Other Club.* London: Sidgwick & Jackson, 1971: pp. 102–13.
9. Browne, AM. *Long Sunset.* Ashford: Podkin Press, 2009: pp. 324–8.
10. Howells, R. *Simply Churchill.* London: Robert Hale, 1965: pp. 177–85.
11. Moran. *Winston Churchill: The Struggle for Survival 1940–1965.* London: Constable & Company, 1966: pp. 777–90.
12. Clinical records of Lord Brain relating to Sir Winston Churchill 1949–65 held by the Royal College of Physicians.
13. Churchill Archives Centre, Churchill College, Cambridge. CHUR 1/140/2. Letter to Lady Churchill from Anthony Montague Browne, 15 January 1965.
14. Sir Winston Churchill: Cerebral thrombosis. Night bulletin reports little change 'Slipping into deeper sleep'. *The Times,* 16 January 1965.
15. Bonham, Carter V. *Winston Churchill as I Knew Him.* London: Eyre and Spottiswoode, 1965.
16. Pottle, M, ed. *Daring to Hope: The Diaries and Letters of Violet Bonham Carter 1946–1969.* London: Weidenfeld & Nicolson, 2000.
17. Ground lost by Sir W. Churchill: "He is sleeping peacefully". Prayers in many Churches. *The Times,* 18 January 1965.
18. Lord Moran returns at 2 am. Visit to Sir W. Churchill 5 hours after bulletin. *The Times,* 19 January 1965.
19. No appreciable change, says night bulletin. Press, radio and TV leave after request. *The Times,* 20 January 1965.
20. Sir Winston 'at a very low ebb'. Circulation weaker, Lord Moran says in night bulletin. *The Times,* 21 January 1965.
21. Sir Winston 'No change'. *The Times,* 22 January 1965.
22. 'Restful day but some deterioration'. Night bulletin on Sir Winston. *The Times,* 23 January 1965.
23. The Nations Mourn Winston Churchill. Death 'in peace and without pain'. Service at St Paul's after Lying in State. *The Times,* 25 January 1965.
24. Howells, R. *Simply Churchill.* London: Robert Hale, 1965: p. 186.
25. Scadding, JW and Vale, JA. Winston Churchill: his first stroke in 1949. *J R Soc Med* 2018; 111: 316–23.
26. Scadding, JW and Vale, JA. Sir Winston Churchill: cerebrovascular disease January 1950–March 1952. *J R Soc Med* 2018; 111: 444–52.
27. Scadding, JW and Vale, JA. Sir Winston Churchill's acute stroke in June 1953. *J R Soc Med* 2018; 111: 347–58.

28. Scadding, JW and Vale, JA. Sir Winston Churchill: acute ataxic stroke in June 1955 with excellent recovery. *J R Soc Med* 2018; 112: 226–35.

29. Scadding, JW and Vale, JA. Sir Winston Churchill: a left hemisphere stroke or possible focal seizure on 20 October 1956. *J R Soc Med* 2018; 112: 185–91.

Chapter 33. Churchill's Doctors

1. Churchill, W. *Closing the Ring: The Second World War Vol V*. London: Penguin Classics, 2005: pp. 372–87.

2. Obituary: D Evan Bedford. *Br Med J* 1978; 1: 308–9.

3. Vale, JA and Scadding, JW. In Carthage ruins: the illness of Sir Winston Churchill at Carthage, December 1943. *J R Coll Physicians Edinb* 2017; 47: 288–95.

4. Vale, JA and Scadding, JW. Sir Winston Churchill KG: hip fracture in Monte Carlo ('Remember, I want to die in England') on 28 June 1962, femoral vein thrombosis and jaundice in London. *J R Soc Med* 2019; 112: 96–108.

5. Bedford, DE. Harvey's third circulation. De circulo sanguinis in corde. *Br Med J* 1968; 4: 273–7.

6. Brain, WR. Encounters with Winston Churchill. *Med Hist* 2000; 44: 3–20.

7. Pickering, GW. Walter Russell Brain, first Baron Brain of Eynsham, 1895–1966. *Biogr Mem Fellows R Soc* 1968; 14: 61–82.

8. Henson, RA. Walter Russell Brain, Baron Brain of Eynsham. *Munk's Roll* 1966; VI: 60–2.

9. Scadding, JW and Vale, JA. Winston Churchill: his first stroke in 1949. *J R Soc Med* 2018; 111: 316–23.

10. Scadding, JW and Vale, JA. Sir Winston Churchill: cerebrovascular disease January 1950–March 1952. *J R Soc Med* 2018; 111: 444–52.

11. Scadding, JW and Vale, JA. Sir Winston Churchill's acute stroke in June 1953. *J R Soc Med* 2018; 111: 347–58.

12. Scadding, JW and Vale, JA. Sir Winston Churchill: acute ataxic stroke in June 1955 with excellent recovery. *J R Soc Med* 2019; 112: 226–35.

13. Scadding, JW and Vale, JA. Sir Winston Churchill: a left hemisphere stroke or possible focal seizure on 20 October 1956. *J R Soc Med* 2019; 112: 185–91.

14. GAH Buttle. *Br J Pharmacol* 1983; 80: 223.

15. Wolstenholme, G. Gladwin Albert Hurst Buttle. *Munk's Roll* 1983; VII: 73–5.

16. Buttle, GAH. Pharmacology of the sulphanilamide group. *Br Med J* 1939; 2: 269–73.

17. Anon. Sulphanilamide in tropical disease. *Br Med J* 1939; 2: 84–5.

18. Anon. Obituary G A H Buttle. *Br Med J (Clin Res Ed)* 1983; 286: 1758–60.

19. Ellis, FP. Obituary G A H Buttle. *Br Med J (Clin Res Ed)* 1983; 287: 137–8.

20. Lock, S. A question of confidence. An editor's view. *Br Med J (Clin Res Ed)* 1984; 288: 123–5.

21. Cope, AP. Dr Derek Hubert Patrick Cope. Royal College of Anaesthetists. Available at: https://www.rcoa.ac.uk/obituaries/dr-derek-hubert-patrick-cope (accessed 21 September 2018).

22. Obituary: Henry Couling, M.R.C.S.,Eng., F.R.C.S.Edin. *Br Med J* 1907; 1: 1461–2.

23. Brown, GH. Dawson, Bertrand Edward, Viscount Dawson of Penn. *Munk's Roll* 1945; IV: 446–9.

24. Cook, GC. The practice of euthanasia at the highest level of society: the Lords Dawson (1864–1945) and Horder (1871–1955). *J Med Biogr* 2006; 14: 90–2.

25. Oswald Peter Dinnick. *Br Med J* 1995; 311: 1566.

26. Dr Oswald Peter Dinnick FRCA. An appreciation. *Hist Anaesth Soc Proc* 1995; 18.

27. Baird, J. William Robert MacFarlane (Sir) Drew. *Munk's Roll* 1991; IX: 133–6.
28. Vale, JA and Scadding, JW. Sir Winston Churchill: treatment for pneumonia in 1943 and 1944. *J R Coll Physicians Edinb* 2017; 47: 388–94.
29. Taylor, S. Surgical sketches: Sir Thomas Peel Dunhill (1876–1957). *World J Surg* 1997; 21: 660–2.
30. Anon. Plarr's Lives of the Fellows Online. Dunhill, Sir Thomas Peel (1876–1957). The Royal College of Surgeons of England. Available at: https://livesonline.rcseng.ac.uk/biogs/E005331b.htm (accessed 20 October 2019).
31. Vellar, ID. *Australian Dictionary of Biography*. Canberra: National Centre of Biography, Australian National University, 1981: Vol. 8.
32. Vale, JA and Scadding, JW. Winston Churchill: inguinal hernia repair on 11 June 1947. *J R Soc Med* 2019; 112: 140–52.
33. Anon. Plarr's Lives of the Fellows Online. English, Sir Thomas Crisp (1878–1949). The Royal College of Surgeons of England. Available at: https://livesonline.rcseng.ac.uk/biogs/E004022b.htm (accessed 20 October 2019).
34. Obituary: Thomas Crisp English K.C.M.G., M.B. Lond., F.R.C.S. *The Lancet* 1949; 254: 442–3.
35. I.B. Sir Crisp English, K.C.M.G., F.R.C.S. *Br Med J* 1949; 2: 548–9.
36. English, C. *Patients and Appendicitis*. London: J & A Churchill, 1946.
37. English, C. *Diseases of the Breast*. London: J. & A. Churchill Ltd, 1948.
38. Griffiths, RW. Sir Winston Churchill's doctors on the Riviera 1949–1965: Herbert Robert Burnett Gibson (1885–1967) and Dafydd (David) Myrddin Roberts (1906–1977). *J Med Biogr* 2020; 28: 30–8.
39. Windeyer, B. Frederick Campbell Golding. *Munk's Roll* 1984; VIII: 187–8.
40. Obituary: F C Golding FRCP, FFR, DMRE. *Br Med J (Clin Res Ed)* 1984; 289: 1464.
41. Harrison, J. Dr. F. Campbell Golding MB ChB FRCP DMRE FFR. *J R Nav Med Serv* 1985; 71: 63.
42. Windeyer, B. Obituaries: F. Campbell Golding, MB, ChM, FRCP, DMRE, FRCR. *Clin Radiol* 1985; 36: 2.
43. Obituary: Dr Thomas Hartigan. *Br Med J* 1941; 1: 612.
44. Boulton, TB. Editorial: C. Langton Hewer, MB, BS, FFARCS, MRCP, DA. *Anaesthesia* 1986; 41: 469–71.
45. Wildsmith, T. Dr Christopher Langton Hewer. Available at: https://www.rcoa.ac.uk/lives-of-the-fellows/dr-christopher-langton-hewer (accessed 20 October 2019).
46. Obituary: T C Hunt. *Br Med J* 1981; 282: 234.
47. Obituary: Thomas Cecil Hunt. *The Lancet* 1981; 317: 110.
48. Clarke, C and Jones, FA. Thomas Cecil Hunt. *Munk's Roll* 1980; VII: 286–8.
49. Hunt, T. Digestive disease: the changing scene. *Br Med J* 1972; 4: 689–94.
50. Hunt, TC. Charles McMoran Wilson, Baron Moran. *Munk's Roll* 1977; VII: 407–12.
51. Froggatt, P. Robert Foster Kennedy (1884–1952): Physician; Neurologist. Ulster History Circle. Available at: http://www.newulsterbiography.co.uk/index.php/home/printPerson/2115 (accessed 2 August 2019).
52. Royal Society of Edinburgh. Former Fellows of the Royal Society of Edinburgh. 1783–2002. Kennedy, Robert Foster 07/02/1884–07/01/1952. Royal Society of Edinburgh. Available at: https://www.rse.org.uk/publication/biographical-index-former-rse-fellows-1783-2002-part-2-k-z/ (accessed 2 August 2019).
53. John Bernard Kinmonth. *The Lancet* 1982; 320: 778.
54. JB Kinmonth. *Br Med J (Clin Res Ed)* 1982; 285: 1052.

55. Anon. Plarr's Lives of the Fellows Online. Kinmonth, John Bernard (1916–1982). The Royal College of Surgeons of England. Available at: https://livesonline.rcseng.ac.uk/biogs/E006660b.htm (accessed 20 October 2019).
56. Obituary: Henry MacCormac. *The Lancet* 1950; 256: 937–8.
57. Obituary: Henry MacCormac. *Br Med J* 1950; 2: 1449.
58. Brown, GH. Henry MacCormac. *Munk's Roll* 1950; IV: 552–3.
59. Obituary: R M B MacKenna. *Br Med J (Clin Res Ed)* 1984; 289: 1547.
60. Obituary: Robert Merttins Bird MacKenna. *The Lancet* 1985; 325: 61.
61. Vickers, HR. Robert Merttins Bird MacKenna. *Munk's Roll* 1984; VIII: 308–11.
62. Anon. Geoffrey Marshall obituary. *The Lancet* 1982; 320: 506.
63. Metcalfe, NH. Sir Geoffrey Marshall (1887–1982): respiratory physician, catalyst for anaesthesia development, doctor to both Prime Minister and King, and World War I Barge Commander. *J Med Biogr* 2011; 19: 10–14.
64. Vale, JA and Scadding, JW. Did Winston Churchill suffer a myocardial infarction in the White House at Christmas 1941? *J R Soc Med* 2017; 110: 483–92.
65. Scadding, JW and Vale, JA. Sir Winston Churchill: recovery from an acute stroke in June 1953 and triumph at the Conservative Party Conference in October 1953. *J R Soc Med* 2019; 112: 61–71.
66. Vale, JA and Scadding, JW. Sir Winston Churchill: pneumonia, pleurisy, jaundice and atrial fibrillation at Roquebrune-Cap-Martin and Chartwell, 1958. *J R Soc Med* 2019; 112: 11–21.
67. Anon. Plarr's Lives of the Fellows Online. Newman, Philip Harker (1911–1995). The Royal College of Surgeons of England. Available at: https://livesonline.rcseng.ac.uk/biogs/E008227b.htm (accessed 22 August 2018).
68. Evans, W. John (Sir) Parkinson. *Munk's Roll* 1976; VII: 443–6.
69. Parkinson, J and Bedford, DE. Successive changes in the electrocardiogram after cardiac infarction (coronary thrombosis). *Heart* 1928; 4: 195–239.
70. Parkinson, J and Bedford, DE. 'Cardiac infarction and coronary thrombosis'. *The Lancet* 1928; 211: 4–11.
71. Wolff, L, Parkinson, J and White, PD. 'Bundle-branch block with short P-R interval in healthy young people prone to paroxysmal tachycardia'. *Am Heart J* 1930; 5: 685–704.
72. 'Guide to the Dr. Otto C. Pickhardt papers 1919–circa 1970s (bulk 1942–1945) MS 488. New York. New-York Historical Society'. Available at: http://dlib.nyu.edu/findingaids/html/nyhs/pickhardt/bioghist.html (accessed 20 October 2019).
73. Morgan, AD. 'Robert James Valentine Pulvertaft'. *Munk's Roll* 1990; IX: 432–4.
74. Pulvertaft, DM. 'A newsletter on the Pulvertofts & Pulvertafts'. *Pulvertaft Papers* 1991; 2: 73–80.
75. Wyatt, HV. 'Robert Pulvertaft's use of crude penicillin in Cairo'. *Med Hist* 1990; 34: 320–6.
76. Paton, A. 'John Samuel Richardson'. *Munk's Roll* 2004; XII. Available at: https://history.rcplondon.ac.uk/inspiring-physicians/john-samuel-richardson (accessed 14 April 2020).
77. Richardson. Unpublished autobiography of Lord Richardson LVO FRCP.
78. Anon. Plarr's Lives of the Fellows Online. Rob, Charles Granville (1913–2001). The Royal College of Surgeons of England. Available at: https://livesonline.rcseng.ac.uk/biogs/ E008878b.htm (accessed 20 October 2019).
79. Gilbert, M. *Never Despair*. London: Heinemann, 1988: pp. 479–99.
80. Browne, AM. *Long Sunset*. High Halden, Ashford: Podkin Press, 2009: pp. 216–32.
81. Soames, M. *Speaking for Themselves*. London: Transworld, 1998: pp. 593–614.

82. Lovell, R. *Churchill's Doctor: A Biography of Lord Moran*. London: Royal Society of Medicine Services Ltd, 1992: pp. 228–35.

83. Vale, JA and Scadding, JW. Winston Churchill (1874–1965), Dr Robson Roose, MD Brux, FRCPE (1848–1905) and Dr Joseph Rutter, MD Lond, MRCP (1834–1913): treatment for pneumonia in March 1886. *J Med Biogr* 2018; online early: doi: 10.1177/0967772018754646.

84. Obituary: Robson Roose, M.D. Brux., F.R.C.P. Edin., M.R.C.S. Eng. *The Lancet* 1905; 165: 681.

85. Medical appointments. *The Lancet* 1873; 101: 721.

86. Obituary: Dr. Robson Roose. *Br Med J* 1905; 1: 391.

87. Power, D'A, Bevan, M. *Oxford Dictionary of National Biography*. Oxford: Oxford University Press, 2004.

88. Obituary: Death of Dr. Robson Roose. *The Standard (London)* 13 February 1905; Sect. Obituary: 3.

89. Appointments. *The Lancet* 1895; 146: 508–9.

90. Obituary: William Rose, M.B., B.S. Lond., F.R.C.S. Eng. *The Lancet* 1910; 175: 1654–7.

91. Obituary: William Rose, M.B., F.R.C.S. *Br Med J* 1910; 1: 1448–9.

92. Anon. Plarr's Lives of the Fellows Online. Ross, Sir James Paterson (1895–1980). The Royal College of Surgeons of England. Available at: https://livesonline.rcseng.ac.uk/biogs/ E000233b.htm (accessed 20 October 2019).

93. Obituary: Joseph Rutter, M.D. Lond., M.R.C.P. Lond., consulting physician to the Sussex County Hospital. *The Lancet* 1914; 183: 70–1.

94. Medical news. *The Lancet* 1862; 80: 634–6.

95. Medical news. *The Lancet* 1868; 92: 204–5.

96. Medical appointments. *The Lancet* 1870; 95: 178.

97. Churchill, RS. *Winston S. Churchill. Companion Volume 1. Part 1 1874–1896*. London: Heinemann, 1967: Vol 1. pp. 97–160.

98. Hospital and dispensary management: Sussex County Hospital. *Br Med J* 1884; 1: 491.

99. Scadding, JW. John Guyett Scadding's scepticism and pragmatism in addressing treatment uncertainties in clinical practice. *J R Soc Med* 2018; 111: 65–72.

100. Scadding, JG. Comparative effects of sulphonamide drugs in mild bacillary dysentery. *The Lancet* 1944; 243: 784–6.

101. Scadding, JG. A summons to Carthage, December 1943. *Br Med J* 1993; 307: 1595–6.

102. Anon. Plarr's Lives of the Fellows Online. Seddon, Sir Herbert John (1903–1977). The Royal College of Surgeons of England. Available at: https://livesonline.rcseng.ac.uk/biogs/E006924b.htm (accessed 22 August 2018).

103. Churchill Archives Centre, Churchill College, Cambridge. CHUR 2/534/141. Telegram from Sir Winston and Lady Churchill to Sir Herbert Seddon, 3 January 1964.

104. Churchill Archives Centre, Churchill College, Cambridge. CHUR 2/534/140. Letter from Sir Herbert Seddon to Sir Winston Churchill, 4 January 1964.

105. KLS Ward. *Br Med J (Clin Res Ed)* 1981; 283: 1409.

106. Whitby, LE. Chemotherapy of pneumococcal and other infections. *The Lancet* 1938; 231: 1210–12.

107. Whitby, LE. Chemotherapy of bacterial infections. *The Lancet* 1939; 232: 1095–1103.

Select Bibliography

For ease of reference the new edition of the Churchill Biography and Companion volumes produced by Hillsdale College are listed here, as the first edition books are not generally available. In the Notes the first edition is cited where available.

Official Biography of Winston S. Churchill
Churchill, RS. *Winston S. Churchill, Volume 1: Youth, 1874–1900*. Hillsdale MI: Hillsdale College Press, 2006.
Churchill, RS. *Winston S. Churchill, Volume 2: Young Statesman, 1901–1914*. Hillsdale MI: Hillsdale College Press, 2007.
Gilbert, M. *Winston S. Churchill, Volume 3: The Challenge of War, 1914–1916*. Hillsdale MI: Hillsdale College Press, 2008.
Gilbert, M. *Winston S. Churchill, Volume 4: World in Torment, 1916–1922*. Hillsdale MI: Hillsdale College Press, 2008.
Gilbert, M. *Winston S. Churchill, Volume 5: The Prophet of Truth, 1922–1939*. Hillsdale MI: Hillsdale College Press, 2009.
Gilbert, M. *Winston S. Churchill, Volume 6: The Finest Hour, 1939–1941*. Hillsdale MI: Hillsdale College Press, 2011.
Gilbert, M. *Winston S. Churchill, Volume 7: Road to Victory, 1941–1945*. Hillsdale MI: Hillsdale College Press, 2013.
Gilbert, M. *Winston S. Churchill, Volume 8: Never Despair, 1945–1965*. Hillsdale MI: Hillsdale College Press, 2013.
Gilbert, M. *Churchill: A Life*. London: Heinemann, 1991.
Gilbert, M. *In Search of Churchill*. London: HarperCollins, 1994.

The Churchill Documents
Churchill, RS. *The Churchill Documents, Volume 1: Youth, 1874–1896*. Hillsdale MI: Hillsdale College Press, 2006.
Churchill, RS. *The Churchill Documents, Volume 2: Young Soldier, 1896–1901*. Hillsdale MI: Hillsdale College Press, 2006.
Churchill, RS. *The Churchill Documents, Volume 3: Early Years in Politics, 1901–1907*. Hillsdale MI: Hillsdale College Press, 2007.
Churchill, RS. *The Churchill Documents, Volume 4: Minister of the Crown, 1907–1911*. Hillsdale MI: Hillsdale College Press, 2007.
Churchill, RS. *The Churchill Documents, Volume 5: At the Admiralty, 1911–1914.*. Hillsdale MI: Hillsdale College Press, 2007.
Gilbert, M. *The Churchill Documents, Volume 6: At the Admiralty, July 1914–April 1915*. Hillsdale MI: Hillsdale College Press, 2008.
Gilbert, M. *The Churchill Documents, Volume 7: 'The Escaped Scapegoat', May 1915–December 1916*. Hillsdale MI: Hillsdale College Press, 2008.

Gilbert, M. *The Churchill Documents, Volume 8: War and Aftermath, December 1916–June 1919*. Hillsdale MI: Hillsdale College Press, 2008.

Gilbert, M. *The Churchill Documents, Volume 9: Disruption and Chaos, July 1919–March 1921*. Hillsdale MI: Hillsdale College Press, 2008.

Gilbert, M. *The Churchill Documents, Volume 10: Conciliation and Reconstruction, April 1921–November 1922*. Hillsdale MI: Hillsdale College Press, 2008.

Gilbert, M. *The Churchill Documents, Volume 11: The Exchequer Years, 1922–1929*. Hillsdale MI: Hillsdale College Press, 2009.

Gilbert, M. *The Churchill Documents, Volume 12: The Wilderness Years, 1929–1935*. Hillsdale MI: Hillsdale College Press, 2009.

Gilbert, M. *The Churchill Documents, Volume 13: The Coming of War, 1936–1939*. Hillsdale MI: Hillsdale College Press, 2009.

Gilbert, M. *The Churchill Documents, Volume 14: At the Admiralty, September 1939–May 1940*. Hillsdale MI: Hillsdale College Press, 2011.

Gilbert, M. *The Churchill Documents, Volume 15: Never Surrender, May 1940–December 1940*. Hillsdale MI: Hillsdale College Press, 2011.

Gilbert, M. *The Churchill Documents, Volume 16: The Ever-widening War, 1941*. Hillsdale MI: Hillsdale College Press, 2011.

Gilbert, M. *The Churchill Documents, Volume 17: Testing Times, 1942*. Hillsdale MI: Hillsdale College Press, 2014.

Gilbert, M, Arnn, LP. *The Churchill Documents, Volume 18: One Continent Redeemed, January–August 1943*. Hillsdale MI: Hillsdale College Press, 2015.

Gilbert, M, Arnn, LP. *The Churchill Documents, Volume 19: Fateful Questions, September 1943 to April 1944*. Hillsdale MI: Hillsdale College Press, 2017.

Gilbert, M, Arnn, LP. *The Churchill Documents, Volume 20: Normandy and Beyond, May–December 1944*. Hillsdale MI: Hillsdale College Press, 2018.

Gilbert, M, Arnn, LP. *The Churchill Documents, Volume 21: The Shadows of Victory, January–July 1945*. Hillsdale MI: Hillsdale College Press, 2018.

Gilbert, M, Arnn, LP. *The Churchill Documents, Volume 22: Leader of the Opposition, August 1945 to October 1951*. Hillsdale MI: Hillsdale College Press, 2019.

Gilbert, M, Arnn, LP. *The Churchill Documents, Volume 23, Never Flinch, Never Weary, November 1951 to February 1965*. Hillsdale MI: Hillsdale College Press, 2019.

Books by Winston Churchill

Churchill, WS. *My Early Life*. London: Macmillan & Co. Ltd, 1944.

Churchill, WS. *A History of the English-Speaking Peoples. Volume 1: the Birth of Britain*. London: Cassell, 1956.

Churchill, W. *The Gathering Storm: The Second World War Volume I*. London: Penguin Classics, 2005.

Churchill, W. *Their Finest Hour: The Second World War Volume II*. London: Penguin Classics, 2005.

Churchill, W. *The Grand Alliance: The Second World War Volume III*. London: Penguin Books, 2005.

Churchill, W. *The Hinge of Fate: The Second World War Volume IV*. London: Penguin, 2005.

Churchill, W. *Closing the Ring: The Second World War Volume V*. London: Penguin Classics, 2005.

Churchill, W. *Triumph and Tragedy: The Second World War Volume VI*. London: Penguin Classics, 2005.

Churchill, WS. *Thoughts and Adventures*. Wilmington DE: ISI Books, 2009.

Books about Winston Churchill

Ashley, M. *Churchill as Historian*. London: Secker and Warburg, 1968.

Attenborough, W. *Churchill and the 'Black dog' of Depression*. Basingstoke: Palgrave Macmillan, 2014.

Attenborough, W. *Diagnosing Churchill: Bipolar or 'Prey to Nerves'?*. Jefferson NC: McFarland & Company, Inc., 2019.

Avon. *The Eden Memoirs: The Reckoning*. London: Cassell, 1965.

Barne, C. *Churchill's Colonel*. Barnsley: Pen & Sword Books, 2019.

Beasley, AW. *Churchill The Supreme Survivor*. Frome: Mercer Books, 2013.

Bonham Carter, V. *Winston Churchill as I knew him*. London: Eyre and Spottiswoode, 1965.

Browne, AM. *Long Sunset*. High Halden, Ashford: Podkin Press, 2009.

Butler. *The Art of the Possible: The Memoirs of Lord Butler*. London: Hamish Hamilton, 1971.

Churchill, S. *A Thread in the Tapestry*. London: Andre Deutsch, 1967.

Churchill, S. *Keep on Dancing*. New York NY: Coward, McCann & Geoghegan, 1981.

Clarke, P. *Mr Churchill's Profession: Statesman, Orator, Writer*. London: Bloomsbury, 2012.

Colville, J. *The Fringes of Power*. London: Weidenfeld & Nicolson, 2004.

Cooper, D. *The Duff Cooper Diaries*. London: Weidenfeld & Nicolson, 2005.

Coote, CR. *The Other Club*. London: Sidgwick & Jackson, 1971.

Danchev, A, Todman, D, eds. *War Diaries 1939–1945 Field Marshal Lord Alanbrooke*. London: Weidenfeld & Nicolson, 2001.

Dilks, D, ed. *The Diaries of Sir Alex Cadogan OM 1938–1945*. London: Cassell & Company, 1971.

Dixon, P. *Double Diploma*. London: Hutchinson, 1968.

Harvey, J, ed. *The War Diaries of Oliver Harvey 1941–1945*. London: William Collins Sons, 1978.

Hickman, T. *Churchill's Bodyguard*. London: Headline, 2005.

Howells, R. *Simply Churchill*. London: Robert Hale, 1965

Ismay. *The Memoirs of Lord Ismay*. London: Heinemann, 1960.

James, RR, ed. *Chips: The Diaries of Sir Henry Channon*. London: Weidenfeld, 1993.

Jenkins, R. *Churchill*. London: Macmillan, 2001.

Langworth, RM. *Winston Churchill, Myth and Reality: What he actually did and said*. Jefferson NC: McFarland & Company, Inc., 2017.

Lavery, B. *Churchill goes to war*. London: Conway, 2007.

Lee, C, Lee, J. *Winston and Jack: The Churchill brothers*. London: Celia Lee, 2007.

Lee, C, Lee, J. *The Churchills. A Family Portrait*. New York NY: Palgrave Macmillan, 2010.

Lough, D. *No more champagne*. London: Head of Zeus, 2015.

Lovell, R. *Churchill's Doctor: A Biography of Lord Moran*. London: Royal Society of Medicine Services Ltd, 1992.

Macmillan, H. *War Diaries the Mediterranean 1943–1945*. London: PAPERMAC, 1985.

Macmillan, H. *Tides of Fortune 1945–1955*. London: Macmillan, 1969.

Manchester, W. *The Last Lion. Winston Spencer Churchill Visions of Glory 1874–1932*. New York NY: Little, Brown and Company, 1983.

Martin, J. *Downing Street the War Years*. London: Bloomsbury, 1991.

Meacham, J. *Franklin and Winston: A Portrait of a Friendship*. London: Granta Publications, 2003.

Mitchell, J, Feast, S. *Very Important Persons. Churchill's Navigator*. London: Grub Street, 2010.

Moody, J. *From Churchill's War Rooms: Letters of a Secretary 1943–45*. Stroud: Tempus Publishing Limited, 2007.

Moran. *Winston Churchill: The Struggle for Survival 1940–1965.* London: Constable & Company, 1966.

Moran. *Churchill at War 1940–45.* London: Robinson, 2002.

Moran. *Churchill: The Struggle for Survival 1945–60.* London: Robinson, 2006.

Murray, E. *I was Churchill's Bodyguard.* London: WH Allen, 1987.

Nel, E. *Winston Churchill by His Personal Secretary.* Bloomington IN: iUniverse, 2007.

Nicolson, N, ed. *Harold Nicolson: Diaries and Letters 1939–1945.* London: Collins, 1967.

Packwood, A. *Churchill and the Great Republic.* Washington DC: The Library of Congress, 2004.

Packwood, A. *How Churchill Waged War: The Most Challenging Decisions of the Second World War.* Barnsley and Havertown PA: Frontline Books, 2018.

Pawle, G. *The War and Colonel Warden.* London: George G Harrap, 1963.

Peck, J. *Dublin From Downing Street.* Dublin: Gill and Macmillan, 1978.

Pottle, M, ed. *Daring to Hope: The Diaries and Letters of Violet Bonham Carter 1946–1969.* London: Weidenfeld & Nicolson, 2000.

Roberts, A. *Churchill: Walking with Destiny.* London: Allen Lane, 2018.

Rose, J. *Nursing Churchill.* Stroud: Amberley Publishing, 2018.

Roskill, S. *Hankey: Man of Secrets. Volume II 1919–1931.* London: Collins, 1972.

Russell, DS. *Winston Churchill: Soldier.* London: Brassey's, 2005.

Sandys, C. *Chasing Churchill.* London: HarperCollins, 2003.

Scott, B. *Churchill at the Gallop.* Newbury, Berkshire: Racing Post Books, 2017.

Soames, M. *Speaking for Themselves.* London: Transworld, 1998.

Soames, M. *Clementine Churchill.* London: Doubleday, 2003.

Soames, M. *Winston Churchill: His Life as a Painter.* London: Collins, 1990.

Stelzer, C. *Working with Winston: The Unsung Women Behind Britain's Greatest Statesman.* London: Head of Zeus Ltd, 2019.

Thompson, WH. *Assignment: Churchill.* New York NY: Farrar, Straus and Young, 1955.

Wheeler-Bennett, J, ed. *Action this day: Working with Churchill.* London: Macmillan & Co. Ltd, 1968.

Index

WSC – Sir Winston Churchill

4th Hussars (cavalry regiment), 10, 11,
92, 152, 159–60
21st Lancers (cavalry regiment), 16–17

Abraham, Frieda, 288
accidents: falling from bridge at
Branksome Dene (1893), 6–10, 45–6,
326, 329; disembarking in Bombay
(1896), 11–15; falls down stairs in
Jodhpore (1899), 12–13; knocked
down by car in New York (1931), 32–3,
43–6; fall at London home fracturing
thoracic vertebra (1960), 8, 309–32; fall
at Monte Carlo fracturing hip (1962),
328, 333–50
Acheson, Dean, 296
Adenauer, Konrad, 214, 258; visits WSC
on French Riviera, 273–4; visits WSC
in London, 298–9, 300, 301
Aitken, Sir Max, 184
Ajaccio (Corsica), 132–3
Alamein, Battle of (1942), 82, 345, 432;
veterans' reunion, 190
Alanbrooke, Alan Brooke, 1st Viscount *see*
Brooke, Sir Alan
Alber, Louis, 31, 37, 38, 39, 45
alcohol: Alcohol Use Disorder, 398, 404,
408–9; Alcohol Withdrawal Syndrome,
5, 398, 408, 409; and depression, 397;
inebriation, 397, 398–400, 404–6;
use in treatment of pneumonia, 4–5;
WSC's drinking, 41, 81, 111, 163, 188,
397, 398–409
Alexander, Harold (*later* 1st Earl
Alexander of Tunis): Commander-
in-Chief of Middle East Command,

92, 110, 117, 147, 356; planning for
Operation SHINGLE, 113, 124; WSC
tours operations in Italy, 127, 128–9,
133, 134; Supreme Allied Commander
of Mediterranean Forces, 151; offers
WSC use of villa on Lake Como,
151–2, 167; visits WSC at Como, 161;
Minister of Defence, 201
Alexandria (Egypt), 90
Alexandria (Virginia), 63
Algiers, 73, 89, 96, 130
Allen, George Roland Gordon, 132
Allison, James, 21
amfetamines, 237, 240, 244–5, 294, 375,
392, 396–7
aminophylline, use in treatment of
strokes, 271–2
amnesia *see* memory loss
Anderson, Sir John (*later* 1st Viscount
Waverley), 105
Anderson, Sir Kenneth, 87
anhedonia, 396
Annigoni, Pietro, portrait of Lord Moran,
206, 207–8
Antibes, 165–6; Villa Sous le Vent, 162,
165, 166
Anzio, Battle of (1944), 124
Aouina, El (Tunisia), 92–3
appendicitis, 20–1, 29; appendicectomy and
post-operative care, 22–3, 29–30, 176
ARCADIA Conference (Washington;
1941–2), 57
ARGONAUT Conference *see* Yalta
Conference (1945)
Arthur of Connaught, Princess, 2nd
Duchess of Fife, 175
Ascalon (aircraft), 91, 92–3, 119–21, 130,
134

Ascot, St George's School, 1
Ashley, Maurice, 47, 51
aspirin, 80, 87, 195, 237, 245
Asquith, Herbert Henry (*later* 1st Earl of
  Oxford and Asquith), 257, 393
Asquith of Yarnbury, Violet Bonham
  Carter, Baroness, 257, 322, 411, 418,
  426–7; on WSC's 'black dog', 393–4
asthma, 1, 272
Atbara Fort (Sudan), 16
Athens, 351
atomic weapons *see* nuclear weapons
atrial fibrillation, 101–2, 104–6, 109, 116,
  126, 192, 261, 283, 286, 343, 349, 358
Attenborough, Wilfred, 375–6, 382, 384,
  386, 388
Attlee, Clement (*later* 1st Earl Attlee), 99,
  103, 104, 105, 191, 196, 201, 250, 388
Avon, Anthony Eden, 1st Earl of *see*
  Eden, Anthony

Bad Nauheim (Germany), 106, 173
Bahamas, 37–41; Polly Leach Hotel, 37
balanitis, 368
Baldwin, Stanley (*later* 1st Earl Baldwin
  of Bewdley), 20, 52
Balmoral Castle, 233, 234, 235, 243
Balsan, Consuelo (*earlier* Duchess of
  Marlborough), 64
Bangalore, 16
Bankart, (Arthur Sidney) Blundell, 14–15
Banta, J.V., 'Churchill's shoulder: What
  If ...?' 12
Barlow-Wheeler, William Hubert
  ('Hugh'), 307
Barne, Anthony, 152, 159–60, 167
Barnett, J.W., 357
Baron, J.H., 71
Barrington-Ward, Robert ('Robin'), 86
Baruch, Bernard, 32, 263, 295, 296, 303
Bath (Somerset), 296–7
BBC: *Churchill* (1993), 382, 401; *Ninety
  Years On* (1965), 411, 415
Beasley, A.W., 14–15, 21, 114, 170, 195
Beaverbrook, Max Aitken, 1st Baron:
  friendship with WSC, 77, 249, 414;

Minister of Supply, 57; with WSC in
  Washington for 1941–2 ARCADIA
  Conference, 57, 59, 64; with WSC
  during recuperation at Marrakech
  (1943–4), 122; WSC stays with at villa
  at Cap d'Ail (1949), 183–4; and news
  blackout on WSC's second stroke, 215;
  WSC takes recuperative holiday at
  Cap d'Ail villa (1953), 233–6; WSC's
  further holidays at Cap d'Ail villa (1955;
  1958; 1959), 251, 259, 265, 306, 368,
  405; meets WSC following episode of
  pneumonia and jaundice at Roquebrune
  (1958), 282; WSC attends annual dinner
  (1959), 305; and WSC's sixth stroke,
  298–9; visits WSC following 1960 fall,
  320; and WSC's acute leg ischaemia
  (1963), 352, 354, 355
Bedford, 248
Bedford, (Davis) Evan, 393, 397,
  430–1; treats WSC during episode of
  pneumonia and atrial fibrillation at
  Carthage (1943), 95, 97, 99, 100–17;
  examination of WSC following 1962
  hip operation, 342, 343–4
Beethoven, Ludwig van, deafness, xvii
Bergamo, 182
Bermuda, 64; Bermuda Conference
  (1953), 210, 216, 217, 218–19, 240, 242
Bernau, William, 36, 40
Berwick, RMA, 64
Best, Geoffrey, *Churchill: A Study in
  Greatness*, 375
Bevan, Aneurin, 198, 201, 285, 388
Bevin, Ernest, 158
Bevir, Sir Anthony, 81, 103
Bidault, Georges, 223
Biggam, Sir Alexander, 99
Biggin Hill airfield (Kent), 187, 307
bipolar disorders, xvii, 372, 374, 375, 376,
  384, 394–5
Birkenhead, F.E. Smith, 1st Earl of, 22,
  251, 276
Birstingl, Martin, 175, 176
'black dog' (depression and melancholia),
  viii, 39, 44, 372–97

Blackpool, 50, 52
Blake, Helen, 178
Blindheim (Germany), 48
Boer War, 59, 396, 411
boils (furuncles), 364–7, 371
Bombay (Mumbai), 11–12
Bonham Carter, Lady Violet *see* Asquith
    of Yarnbury, Violet Bonham Carter,
    Baroness
Bournemouth, Branksome Dene, 6–7,
    45, 326
Boyle, Henry Edmund Gaskin, 439
Bracken, Brendan (*later* 1st Viscount
    Bracken), 42, 81–2, 140, 215, 278, 388,
    390–2
Bradfield College (Berkshire), 77
Brain, Michael, 430
Brain, (Walter) Russell Brain, 1st
    Baron: professional biography, 431;
    assessments of WSC following first
    stroke in 1949, 184, 187–9, 190, 191–3,
    393; further assessments of WSC
    for cerebrovascular disease (1950–2),
    195, 203, 204, 430; awards WSC
    Honorary Fellowship of Royal College
    of Physicians, 206; and attempts to
    persuade WSC to reduce workload,
    201, 202, 217; and WSC's second
    stroke in 1953, 213–14, 216–17, 219,
    221, 223–6, 227–8; assessment of
    WSC following third stroke in 1955,
    253–5, 260, 261; assessment of WSC
    following fourth stroke in 1956, 267–8,
    270; assessment of WSC following
    fifth stroke in April 1959, 292–3, 301;
    and WSC's ischaemia in right little
    finger, 301; and WSC's episode of loss
    of consciousness and sixth stroke in
    October–November 1959, 296–302;
    examination of WSC following 1960
    fall fracturing thoracic vertebra, 329;
    and WSC's final illness and last days,
    415–19, 423, 428
    Views and opinions on: Lord Moran,
    430; Moran's publication of *The
    Struggle for Survival*, 193, 254–5;

publication of case notes, xviii;
    WSC's drinking, 400, 406; WSC's
    resumption of work after second
    stroke, 226; WSC's vitality, 374
Branksome Dene (Dorset), 6–7, 45, 326
Bratton, Allen, 79
Bridges, Sir Edward (*later* 1st Baron
    Bridges), 144
Brighton and Hove: Bedford Hotel, 2;
    Brunswick Road School, 1; Brunswick
    Terrace, 9; Orleans Club, 2; Sussex
    County Hospital, 3
Bristol University, 190
Bristowe, J.S., 'Croonian lectures on
    disease and its medical treatment', 4–5
Britannia, SS, 11
bronchitis, 312, 345
bronchopneumonia, 275–80, 286
Brook, Sir Norman (*later* 1st Baron
    Normanbrook), 220, 225, 226
Brooke, Sir Alan (*later* 1st Viscount
    Alanbrooke): Chief of Imperial
    General Staff, 73; and WSC's bout
    of pneumonia following return from
    1943 Casablanca Conference, 73–4,
    80; with WSC in Middle East for 1943
    Cairo and Tehran conferences, 89; and
    WSC's episode of pneumonia and atrial
    fibrillation in Carthage, 93, 94–5, 96,
    108–9, 110–11, 113, 117; and WSC's
    bout of pneumonia on return from
    Italy (1944), 136; travels to Canada with
    WSC for 1944 Quebec Conference,
    137, 140; with WSC on journey to
    Crimea for 1945 Yalta Conference, 147;
    WSC reads autobiography, 298; on
    WSC's drinking, 406
Broughton-Alcock, William, 22–3
Brown, Francis, 98
Browne, Sir Anthony Montague *see*
    Montague Browne, Sir Anthony
Bruxelles, 48
Buckley, G.K., 346
Bullock, Walter, 35
Bunting, J.J., 'Toxic reactions of
    sulfaguanidine therapy', 149

Butler, Richard Austen ('Rab'; *later* Baron Butler of Saffron Walden): Chancellor of the Exchequer, 213, 231, 236; and WSC's second stroke, 213, 215, 217, 218–19, 220–1, 222, 224, 226; on WSC's speech to 1953 Party Conference, 238–9; Leader of the House, 278, 300; and WSC's episode of pneumonia and jaundice during 1958 holiday on French Riviera, 278; on WSC's 85th birthday, 300

Buttle, Gladwin Albert Hurst, 97, 106–7, 116, 431–2

by-election, Newport (1922), 20, 22

Byrne, Thomas, 16–17

Cadogan, Sir Alexander, 76, 91, 147

Cairo, 17–18, 65, 92, 95, 96, 112; Cairo Conference (1943), 89, 91

Cambridge, 307–8; Churchill College, 248, 290, 307–8; King's College, 307

Camrose, William Berry, 1st Viscount, 85, 136, 215, 223, 232, 233, 388

Canary Islands, 288, 289

Canford (Dorset), 6

Cannes, Villa Rêve d'Or, 27

Cantasano, Edward F., 33, 41

Cap d'Ail (French Riviera), 333, 447; La Capponcina, 183–7, 233–6, 251, 259, 265, 306, 368, 405

Cap Martin (French Riviera) *see* Roquebrune-Cap-Martin

Capri, 131, 132, 306

carbuncles, 366–7, 371

Carlton Club, 7

Carthage, 93–115, 408

Casablanca Conference (1943), 73, 114, 121

cerebrovascular disease, 194–205, 227–9, 261, 270, 302, 331, 349, 430; *see also* strokes; transient ischaemic attacks (TIA)

cervical vertebrae *see* spinal injuries

Chaldecott, J.H., 22

Chamberlain, Sir Austen, 20

Chandos, Oliver Lyttelton, 1st Viscount, 413

Chanel, Coco, 263

Channon, Sir Henry ('Chips'), 105, 150, 240, 241

Charles, Sir Noel, 133

Charmley, John, *Churchill: The End of Glory*, 398

Chartwell (Kent), 161, 178, 214–23, 247, 249, 255, 257, 282, 291, 327; rebuilding and refurbishment, 27, 150, 248, 269

Chatelin, Charles-Louis, 334, 336

Chequers (Buckinghamshire), 67, 84, 223, 230–1, 403, 412

Cherwell, Frederick Lindemann, 1st Viscount ('the Prof'): and WSC's motor accident in New York, 36, 43, 44; with WSC on research trip to battlefields in Belgium, Holland and Germany, 48; travels to Canada with WSC for 1944 Quebec Conference, 138, 139; and WSC's second stroke, 215; accompanies WSC on Sicilian holiday following retirement as Prime Minister, 248; with WSC during holidays at La Pausa, Roquebrune, 263, 264; and WSC's drinking, 400

Chiang Kai-shek, 65, 91

Chicago, 42

Chicago Tribune, 47

Christian Scientists, 278

Christina (yacht), 274, 289, 306, 351

Chubb, Percy, 59

Churchill (television series; 1993), 382, 401

Churchill, Arabella (WSC's granddaughter), 412

Churchill, Clementine (*later* Baroness Spencer-Churchill; WSC's wife): early married life, 376; campaigning with WSC during 1922 election, 25; with WSC for convalescent holiday in south of France (1922–3), 27; in United States for WSC's lecture tour (1931–2), 31; and WSC's motor accident in New York, 38, 40, 45; with WSC during research trip to battlefields in Belgium, Holland and Germany (1933), 48; and WSC's attack of enteric fever in

Austria, 49, 50; and WSC's bout of pneumonia following return from 1943 Casablanca Conference, 75, 77, 79, 81, 84; suffers burn to hand, 83; and WSC episode of pneumonia and atrial fibrillation in Carthage (1943), 95, 99, 100, 104, 105–6, 107, 108–9, 110, 112–13; Christmas in Carthage, 113; with WSC during recuperation in Marrakech, 119, 122–3, 124; and WSC's bout of pneumonia on return from Italy (1944), 134–5; travels to Canada with WSC for 1944 Quebec Conference, 138–40, 385, 386; refurbishment of houses during WSC's 1945 holiday at Lake Como, 150, 166; and WSC's inguinal hernia, 157–8, 177; 1949 summer holiday in Italy with WSC, 182–3; with WSC in Strasbourg for Inaugural Session of Council of Europe, 183; and WSC's first stroke, 185; and WSC's cerebrovascular disease, 197, 202; at 1953 Coronation celebrations, 210; and WSC's second stroke, 213, 214–15, 218, 231–2; and WSC's recuperative holiday at Cap d'Ail (September 1953), 234–5; at 1953 Party Conference, 237; represents WSC at Nobel Prize ceremony, 240; and WSC's retirement as Prime Minister, 246–7; holiday in Sicily with WSC (April 1955), 247–8; and WSC's third stroke, 249; WSC paints portrait, 257; holiday with WSC at Cap d'Ail (September 1955), 259; 48th wedding anniversary, 262; and WSC's working holiday at La Pausa, Roquebrune (September 1956), 263–4; and WSC's fourth stroke, 267, 268; joins WSC during further holiday at La Pausa (February–April 1958), 273, 274, 279, 281–2; and WSC's episode of pneumonia and jaundice, 276, 281–2; returns to England for WSC's convalescence at Chartwell, 282, 283; with WSC on holiday in Morocco and

Canary Islands (January–February 1959), 288–9, 292; and WSC's fifth stroke, 291, 292; and WSC's gangrene in right little finger, 304, 305; sailing holiday with WSC to Greece and Turkey (July–August 1959), 306; undergoes operation on eyelid, 306; in Cambridge with WSC for foundation ceremony for Churchill College, 307; and WSC's episode of loss of consciousness and sixth stroke, 297, 298–300; and WSC's fall at London home fracturing thoracic vertebra (November 1960), 309–10, 312, 327; and WSC's fractured hip following 1962 fall at Monte Carlo, 335, 336, 337, 339, 341–2, 343, 344, 345, 346; and WSC's acute leg ischaemia, 353, 356–7; 55th wedding anniversary, 355; suffers stress-related illness, 356–7, 358; and WSC's 90th birthday, 411–12; and WSC final illness and last days, 413, 414, 415, 416, 417, 418, 421–2; birth of great-grandson, 423–4; and WSC's death, 424–6
  Views and opinions on: Dafydd Roberts, 448; doctors' attempts to persuade WSC to reduce workload, 202; mepacrine medication, 140, 142; Moran's *The Struggle for Survival*, xviii; possibility of WSC dying at war's end, 124; WSC's 1959 trip to Washington, 292, 304; WSC's drinking, 111; WSC's episode of pneumonia at Carthage, 108–9, 111, 112, 122; WSC's resumption of activities after second stroke, 231–2, 239, 240; WSC's smoking, 108, 111
Churchill, Diana (*later* Sandys; WSC's daughter), 31, 79, 81, 190–1, 239, 281, 304, 318, 322, 323, 341, 377, 379
Churchill, Mary (WSC's daughter) *see* Soames, Mary
Churchill, Mary ('Minnie'; née d'Erlanger; WSC's granddaughter-in-law), 412, 423

Churchill, Lord Randolph (WSC's father): Private Secretary to Viceroy of Ireland, 1; and WSC's episode of childhood pneumonia, 2–3; and WSC's accident falling from bridge, 7–8, 9; Anthony Storr's account of, 373; death, 425

Churchill, Lady Randolph (WSC's mother): family background, 60, 61; and WSC's episode of childhood pneumonia, 2–3; and WSC's accident falling from bridge, 7–8; and WSC's dislocated shoulder in India, 12, 14; Anthony Storr's account of, 372–3

Churchill, Randolph (WSC's son): biography of WSC, 5, 9; and WSC's accident in New York, 34, 37, 40, 45; Lord Rothermere's concerns for 'health', 404; with entourage to Middle East for 1943 Cairo and Tehran conferences, 88; at Carthage with WSC, 93, 107, 108–9, 110, 112, 114; in Algiers following injury in aircraft crash, 130; disagreements with father, 166, 173; stands in 1950 General Election, 194; lunches with parents at Savoy (October 1959), 297; visits WSC on 86th birthday, 323; and WSC's fractured hip following 1962 fall at Monte Carlo, 337, 344; with WSC during last holiday on Onassis's yacht, 351; at WSC's 90th birthday, 412; and WSC's final illness and last days, 414, 417, 422; and WSC's death, 424, 425

Churchill, Randolph (WSC's great-grandson), 423–4

Churchill, Sarah (*later* Oliver; *afterwards* Baroness Audley; WSC's daughter): childhood and early life, 25, 48; with entourage to Middle East for 1943 Cairo and Tehran conferences, 88–9; at Carthage with WSC, 93, 98, 114; and WSC's episode of pneumonia and atrial fibrillation, 94, 96, 107, 108; with WSC during recuperation in Marrakech, 119, 120; with WSC

on journey to Crimea for 1945 Yalta Conference, 144–7; with WSC during holiday on Lake Como following 1945 election defeat, 151, 153–5, 160, 161; learns of WSC's first stroke, 185; with WSC during holiday at Roquebrune (1958), 274; visits WSC on 86th birthday, 323; at WSC's 90th birthday party, 412; and WSC's final illness and last days, 414; and WSC's death, 424, 425

Churchill, Sir Winston: early childhood and schooling, 1; develops pneumonia aged 11, 2–5; at Harrow, 5, 6, 157; develops hernia, 168; entrance examination for Sandhurst, 6, 9–10; suffers accident falling from bridge, 6–10, 45–6, 326, 329; convalescence in London and Brighton, 9; joins 4th Hussars, 10; posting to India, 11–16, 407; suffers shoulder injury disembarking in Bombay, 11–15; at Battle of Omdurman, 15, 16–17, 396; donates skin graft, 17–19; falls down stairs in Jodhpore, 12–13; writing and publication of *The River War*, 16, 356; President of Board of Trade, 395; Home Secretary, 377, 378, 385–7, 395, 396; First Lord of the Admiralty, 356, 377, 378, 393; during First World War, 356, 377, 390, 391, 393–4; Secretary of State in Coalition government, 20, 30, 55; develops acute appendicitis, 20–1, 29; appendicectomy and post-operative course, 21, 22–5, 29–30, 176; awarded Companion of Honour, 23; campaigning for 1922 election, 20, 23, 25–6; loses seat, 26; convalescence in south of France, 26–7; writing of memoirs, 26, 27; travels to United States for 1931–32 lecture tour, 31–2; knocked down by car in New York, 32–3; treatment in Lenox Hill Hospital, 33–5, 42–3; recuperation in New York and Bahamas, 35–41; writes articles on accident for *Daily Mail*, 32,

35, 36–7, 40, 42, 43; completion of
lecture tour and return to England,
41–2; writing and publication of
Marlborough: his life and times, 47, 48,
51, 53, 54; research trip to battlefields
in Belgium, Holland and Germany, 47,
48, 55–6; attack of enteric fever in
Austria, 48–50, 54–6; returns to
England, 50–1; relapse and recovery,
51–4, 56; holiday at Marrakech
(December 1935), 403–4; Mackenzie
King visits at Chequers (August 1941),
403; travels to Washington for 1941–2
ARCADIA Conference, 57–8; stays at
White House, 58–61, 65–6; speech to
Congress, 60–1; suffers chest pain,
61–2, 65–6, 69–72, 187–8; travels to
Ottawa, 62–3, 73; speech to Canadian
Parliament, 63; returns to Washington,
63; signs *Declaration by the United
Nations* on war aims, 63; short stay at
villa in Florida, 63–4, 66; returns to
England via Bermuda, 64–5; cardiac
assessments by John Parkinson, 61–2,
65–9, 70–1, 188; at January 1943
Casablanca Conference, 73, 114, 121;
develops pneumonia on return to
London, 73–84, 86–7, 429;
recuperation at Chequers, 84–6; travels
to Middle East for Cairo and Tehran
conferences (November–December
1943), 88–92, 383–4, 405–6; flies on to
Tunisia, 92–4; develops pneumonia
and atrial fibrillation at Carthage,
94–118, 192, 408; planning for
Operation OVERLORD, 103, 118;
appointment of 'Jumbo' Wilson as
Supreme Commander Mediterranean,
99–100, 110; planning for Operation
SHINGLE, 113, 124; Christmas in
Carthage, 113–14; leaves Carthage for
Morocco, 114–15, 119–21;
recuperation at Marrakech, 101, 110,
121–4; meetings with generals during
convalescence, 122, 123–4; returns to
England via Gibraltar, 124–5; further

cardiac assessment by Parkinson,
125–6; tours operations in Italy and
South of France (August 1944),
127–34; prescribed mepacrine as
antimalarial, 128–9, 138, 140, 141–2;
meets Marshal Tito, 127, 131; audience
with Pope Pius XII and meetings with
Italian Crown Prince and government
in Rome, 133–4; develops pneumonia
on return to London, 134–42; travels
to Canada on *Queen Mary* for Quebec
Conference (September 1944), 136,
137–41, 385–7; illness on journey to
Crimea for Yalta Conference (January
1945), 143–9; 1945 General Election
defeat, 150, 383, 387–9; holiday at Lake
Como, 150–62, 166–7; diagnosis of
inguinal hernia, 154–8, 167; fitting of
truss, 157–8, 168, 359; writing of war
memoirs, 150, 167, 177, 178, 179–80,
183, 191, 390; returns to England via
Genoa and French Riviera, 161–6, 167;
first referral to dermatologist, 359, 369;
referral to Sir Thomas Dunhill,
169–73; operation to repair hernia, 156,
173–7, 181, 359, 360; post-operative
recovery and recuperation, 177–81;
Commons' capital punishment debate
(July 1948), 377; recurring skin
conditions, 360–71; publication of *The
Second World War* book series, 180, 223,
226, 236; re-examined by cardiologist
(May 1949), 182; summer holiday in
Italy, 182–3; speech to Inaugural
Session of Council of Europe in
Strasbourg (August 1949), 183; flies on
to Monte Carlo for stay at
Beaverbrook's villa at Cap d'Ail, 183–7;
suffers first stroke, 184–93; returns to
England, 187, 190; assessments by
Russell Brain, 187–9, 190, 191–3;
working holiday in Madeira (December
1949–January 1950), 190–1, 194;
further assessments for cerebrovascular
disease (1950–2), 194–205; 1950
General Election, 191, 194–5;

acceptance speech for Honorary Fellowship and unveiling of portrait of Moran at Royal College of Physicians (July 1951), 203, 206–9, 364; regains premiership following 1951 election victory, 196–203; 77th birthday, 402; death and funeral of George VI, 196; 1952 Budget, 196, 198; encouraged to reduce workload, 199–203, 217; suffers acute stroke following 1953 Coronation celebrations, 210–28, 243–4, 309, 407; recovery at Chartwell, 214–23, 244–5, 407; resumes prime ministerial duties, 224–6, 228, 229–33, 239–42, 245; joins Queen at races and for weekend at Balmoral, 231–3, 234, 235, 243; recuperative holiday at Beaverbrook's villa at Cap d'Ail (September 1953), 233–6; writing of *A History of the English-Speaking Peoples*, 235, 236, 247, 249, 250, 255–6, 263–4; addresses Party Conference at Margate (October 1953), 220, 235, 236–9, 243, 244–5, 392; awarded Nobel Prize for Literature, 239–40, 399; attendance at Bermuda Conference (December 1953), 210, 216, 217, 218–19, 240, 242; retires as Prime Minister, 246–7; holiday in Sicily (April 1955), 247–8; retains seat at 1955 General Election, 248–9; suffers third stroke, 249–51, 253–6, 259–61, 402–3; resumes seat in Parliament as backbencher, 250–1; Guildhall speech at unveiling of statue by Lord Mayor, 251–3, 254, 260, 261; speech at Hastings at presentation of portrait as Lord Warden of the Cinque Ports, 258; holiday at Beaverbrook's villa at Cap d'Ail (September 1955), 251, 259, 265; 81st birthday and 48th wedding anniversary, 259, 262; working holiday at La Pausa, Roquebrune (September–October 1956), 262–7; suffers fourth stroke, 264–72; recovery and return to London, 266–9, 271–2; returns to political activity during Suez crisis, 262, 267, 268; develops pneumonia and jaundice during recuperative holiday at La Pausa (February–April 1958), 273–82, 286–7, 407; returns to England for convalescence at Chartwell, 282–6; further episode of atrial fibrillation, 283, 286; returns to House of Commons, 284, 285; stays again at Beaverbrook's villa at Cap d'Ail (September 1958), 368–9; holiday in Morocco and Canary Islands (January–February 1959), 288–9, 292; returns to London, 290; further holiday at La Pausa (March–April 1959), 290; suffers fifth stroke on return to England, 290–5, 301; speech at Woodford constituency (April 1959), 290, 292, 293; visits United States (May 1959), 293–6, 302, 303, 303–4; stays at White House and British Embassy in Washington, 295–6, 303–4; ischaemia and gangrene in right little finger, 291, 301, 303–4, 306, 308; sailing holiday in Greece and Turkey (July–August 1959), 306; travels on to stay at Cap d'Ail and Roquebrune, 306–7; retains seat in 1959 General Election, 307; in Cambridge for foundation ceremony for Churchill College, 307–8; episode of loss of consciousness (October 1959), 296–8, 301–2; suffers sixth stroke, 298–301; 85th birthday, 300; fall at London home fracturing thoracic vertebra, 8, 309–32; suffers further mild stroke, 319–21, 330–1; 86th birthday, 322; fall at Monte Carlo fracturing hip, 333–7, 349–50; returns to England, 335–8; at Middlesex Hospital, 338–47; hip operation, 328, 339–41; post-operative course and recuperation, 341–7, 350; develops jaundice and femoral vein thrombosis during convalescence, 344, 346, 347, 349–50; returns home from hospital, 347–9, 350; 88th birthday, 349; last

holiday on Onassis's yacht at Monte
Carlo (June–July 1963), 351; develops
acute leg ischaemia on return to
England, 352–8; 55th wedding
anniversary, 355; retirement from
Parliament, 410; 90th birthday, 411–12,
415; final social engagements, 412–14;
suffers further probable stroke, 414–18,
428; last days, 414–24; birth of
great-grandson, 423–4; death, 424–7,
428; State funeral, 416, 428
  Character and characteristics:
American ancestry, 60; bathing, 85,
184, 231, 353, 367; bravery, 19, 67,
215, 246; card-playing, 138, 148,
183–4, 235, 262, 274, 299; clubs,
7, 251, 412–13; codenames and
pseudonyms, 122, 130, 161, 176,
233; as commanding officer, 394;
conversation skills, 158, 220, 225,
378; cross-examination skills, 156,
175–6, 192–3; determination, 28,
85, 124, 189, 200, 220, 226, 228,
430; diet and eating, 85, 237, 266,
289, 316, 402, 411, 413; drinking,
41, 81, 111, 163, 188, 397, 398–409;
emotionality, 159, 224, 227–8, 245;
film-watching, 85, 348; finances,
26, 31, 35, 36, 37, 42, 43, 47, 163,
187, 240, 388; gambling, 164–5,
274, 403–4; generosity, 187; golf-
playing, 14, 378; as great European,
158; handwriting, 185, 191, 249,
250, 253, 292, 413; honours and
awards, 23, 179, 203, 206–7, 239–40,
258; humour, 246, 261, 378, 430;
kindness, 86, 245, 378; loyalty, 378;
magnanimity, 413; mental health,
372–97; military strategist, 19, 406;
monarchist, 158; musical tastes, 411,
412; nightwear, 76, 94, 113, 188,
189; 'nine lives', 8, 326; obesity, 181;
obstinacy, 78, 91, 309; optimism,
252, 396; oratory, 4, 203, 211–12,
238–9, 240, 241; painting, 27, 70,
101, 123, 154–5, 156, 163, 165, 167,

183, 234, 248, 257, 259, 269, 289,
290, 292, 296, 348, 378; pets, 314,
416, 427, 428; polo-playing, 12–13,
14, 27; portraits and statues, 219,
252, 258, 298, 391; rabbit-shooting,
180; racehorses, 155, 187, 264;
reading, 75, 133, 138, 139, 176,
298, 299, 300, 346; reputation, xvii,
xviii, 43, 181, 246, 411, 413, 427–8;
resilience, 44, 271, 373, 376, 396,
430; selflessness, 19; sense of duty,
245, 430; speaking voice, 211, 212,
213, 214, 216, 223, 227, 253, 292–3,
299, 301, 407; stamina and vitality,
124, 302, 374, 393, 416; swimming,
131, 132, 159, 163, 183; tearfulness,
91, 125, 159, 196, 224, 245; temper,
86, 111, 305, 316–17, 325, 331–2,
335, 406; tobacco smoking, 4, 108,
111, 163, 174, 188, 344, 348, 370;
uniforms and dress, 91, 119, 155,
347, 411; V-sign, 256, 337, 338, 347,
412; walking stick, 309, 329; work
output, 73, 75, 85, 87, 117–18, 141,
199–203, 239; writing processes,
179, 188, 247, 249, 255–6
Churchill, Winston (WSC's grandson),
323, 357, 358, 398, 412, 414, 420, 423,
424, 425
Churchill College, Cambridge, 248, 290,
307–8
cigars *see* smoking
Clark, Sir James, 450
Clark, Jane, Lady, 211
Clark, Sir Kenneth (*later* Baron Clark),
211
Clark, Mark, 133
Clark, Miss (nurse in Cairo), 96, 115
Clarke (police constable), 309
Clifford, Sir Bede Edmund Hugh, 37
Coldstream Guards, 2nd Battalion, 93
Colebrook, L., 'On skin-grafting', 19
Collier's (magazine), 35, 54
Collins, Henry ('John'), 92, 112, 114,
114–15, 134
'Colonist II' (racehorse), 187

Columbine (aircraft), 296
Colville, Sir John ('Jock'): Assistant
   Private Secretary to WSC, 104; and
   WSC's episode of pneumonia and
   atrial fibrillation at Carthage (1943),
   104, 106, 108, 112, 113, 114; and
   WSC's recuperation at Marrakech,
   119, 122; and WSC's cardiac
   assessment following return from
   Marrakech, 125; and WSC's bout
   of pneumonia on return from Italy
   (1944), 135, 136; travels to Canada with
   WSC for 1944 Quebec Conference,
   138–40, 385–7; and WSC's journey
   to 1945 Yalta Conference, 143; and
   death of George VI, 196; and WSC's
   possible resignation as Prime Minister,
   198–9, 202; and WSC's second stroke,
   211–12, 214–15, 218, 220, 222, 224;
   with WSC during recuperative holiday
   at Cap d'Ail, 233, 235; at 1953 Party
   Conference, 237–8, 239; accompanies
   WSC on Sicilian holiday following
   retirement as Prime Minister, 248;
   receives commemorative silver
   V-sign, 256; drafts speeches for WSC,
   259; joins WSC on 1959 holiday in
   Morocco, 288, 289; at the opera in
   London with WSC, 290; with WSC
   during last holiday on Onassis's yacht,
   351; at WSC's 90th birthday party, 412;
   on WSC's 'black dog', 376, 379–80,
   385–7; on WSC's drinking, 400, 402
Colville, Lady Margaret ('Meg'), 211,
   233, 288, 289, 290, 351, 412
Commonwealth Prime Ministers'
   Conference (London; 1953), 210
Como, Lake, 150–1, 153–67; Villa d'Este,
   152; Villa Le Rose, 151, 152–3, 154,
   160
concussion, 8, 10, 33, 43
confusion, mental, 34, 283, 300, 302;
   following 1960 fall, 315–23, 326,
   331–2; following 1962 hip operation,
   342, 343, 349–50
Connelly, John, 176–7

Conservative Party Annual Conference:
   (1949), 190; (1953), 220, 235, 236–9,
   243, 244–5, 392
Conservative Trades Union Congress,
   WSC's speech (1949), 190
Cooper, Lady Diana (née Manners; *later*
   Viscountess Norwich), 86, 123, 124, 130
Cooper, Duff (*later* 1st Viscount
   Norwich), 86, 123, 130
Cope, Derek H.P., 340, 341, 432
Coronation (1953), 198, 199, 210
Corsica, 132–3
Coty, René, 277, 282
Couling, Henry, 8, 9, 432–3
Council of Europe, 183
Coward, Sir Noël, 411
Cowell, Sir Ernest, 110
Cranborne, Elizabeth, Viscountess *see*
   Salisbury, Elizabeth, Marchioness of
Cranborne, Robert Gascoyne-Cecil,
   Viscount *see* Salisbury, Robert
   Gascoyne-Cecil, 5th Marquess of
Crathie Church (Deeside), 233
Cripps, Sir Stafford, 187
Cunningham, Sir Andrew (*later* 1st
   Viscount Cunningham of Hyndhope),
   88, 135, 137, 406
Cunningham, Delia (née Holland-
   Hibbert), 152
Cunningham, Jeremy, 153
Cunningham, Sir John, 89, 90, 113, 124,
   132
Cunningham, William M., 151, 152,
   152–3
Curtis Brown (literary agents), 51, 53
Cushing, Harvey, 450
Cyclothemic Disorder, 374, 393, 394–5

Daily Mail, WSC's articles for, 32, 35,
   36–7, 40, 42, 43, 54
Daniels, Anthony, 372–97
Dardanelles, 306; Dardanelles campaign
   (1915–16), 219, 390, 391, 393
Davies, Cyril, 153, 161, 163
Dawson of Penn, Bertrand Dawson, 1st
   Viscount, 21, 23–4, 30, 172, 423, 433–4

de Gasperi, Alcide, 211–12
de Gaulle, Charles, 258
de Valera, Eamon, 233
deafness, 202, 225, 240, 289, 305, 348;
    hearing aid, 240, 263
Deakin, Sir William ('Bill'), 190–1, 390
Defoe, Daniel, *Moll Flanders*, 75
depression and melancholia *see* 'black dog'
Derby (horse race; 1953), 210
dermatitis, 359–61, 369–70, 371
DeSalvo, Christine, 98
Desert Victory (film; 1943), 82
Detroit, 42
Devers, Jacob, 124
diabetes mellitus, 353, 358
Digby, Pamela (*later* Churchill; *then*
    Harriman), 81
Dill, Sir John, 57
Dinnick, Peter, 340, 341, 434
Disraeli, Benjamin (*later* 1st Earl of
    Beaconsfield), 252, 264
Ditchley Park (Oxfordshire), 85
Dixon, Piers, 319, 411, 412
Dixon, Sir Pierson, 130–1, 210
Domagk, Gerhard, 431–2
Doncaster Race Course, 231, 232–3
Douglas, S.R., 'On skin-grafting', 19
Douglas-Home, Sir Alec (*later* Baron
    Home of the Hirsel), 410, 423
D'Oyly Carte Opera Company, 290
DRAGOON, Operation (Allied invasion
    of Southern France; 1944), 127, 131,
    132–3
Drew, Sir Robert, 136, 141, 434–5
drunkenness *see* inebriation
Duke, Sir Charles, 289
Duke of York, HMS, 57, 58, 64
Dulles, John Foster, 269
Dundas, Sir Ambrose Dundas Flux, 265
Dundee, 21, 25–6; parliamentary
    constituency, 23, 26
Dunhill, Sir Thomas, 169–81, 430, 435,
    450
dysentry, 148–9, 451
dyspepsia *see* indigestion
dysphasia, 204–5, 269–70, 292, 301

ear: labyrinthine lesion, 187; skin disease,
    369; *see* also deafness
East Grinstead (Sussex), Queen Victoria
    Hospital, 306
eczema, 360, 361–2, 371
Eddy, Mary Baker, 278
Eden, Anthony (*later* 1st Earl of Avon):
    Foreign Secretary, 65, 67, 76, 78,
    82, 90, 229, 383; at 1943 Cairo and
    Tehran conferences, 91, 405–6; and
    WSC's episode of pneumonia and
    atrial fibrillation at Carthage, 104,
    105; and WSC's 1944 tour of Italian
    operations, 129–30; and WSC's bout
    of pneumonia on return to London,
    135, 136, 137; with WSC on journey
    to 1945 Yalta Conference, 144, 147;
    ill-health and recuperation following
    gallstones operation, 210, 219, 223,
    439; as potential successor to WSC as
    Prime Minister, 198, 218, 219, 223,
    236, 240; dines with WSC before 1953
    Party Conference, 236–7; valediction
    at WSC's last Cabinet meeting, 246;
    Prime Minister, 256, 264, 439; visits
    WSC during recuperation from 1962
    hip operation, 346; visits WSC shortly
    before 90th birthday, 411; views on
    WSC's health and character, 65, 82–3,
    91, 406
Edinburgh, 218
Edinburgh, Prince Philip, Duke of *see*
    Philip, Prince, Duke of Edinburgh
Edward VII, King, 433
Edward VIII, King (*later* Duke of
    Windsor), 433, 435
Edwards, Anthony William Fairbank, 157
Edwards, Harold, 152, 155–9, 167, 168,
    436
Eisenhower, Dwight D. ('Ike'): Supreme
    Allied Commander in North Africa,
    93, 110, 115; WSC stays at villa in
    Carthage, 93–4; planning for Operation
    SHINGLE, 113; meetings with WSC
    at Marrakech, 122; Supreme Allied
    Commander of Allied Expeditionary

Force, 136; offers WSC use of villa at Antibes, 162, 165, 166; President, 210, 222; 1953 Bermuda Conference, 210, 216, 218, 242; WSC's correspondence with following third stroke, 256–7, 258, 261; suffers myocardial infarction, 259; invites WSC to visit White House, 273, 276, 278, 282, 295; WSC stays with at White House (May 1959), 295, 296, 303; WSC's correspondence with following 1960 fall, 313; visits WSC during recuperation from 1962 hip operation, 346

Eisenhower, Mamie, 313

elections *see* by-elections; General Elections

Elizabeth, Queen consort, 58

Elizabeth II, Queen: Coronation, 198, 199, 210; WSC's correspondence with following second stroke, 218, 234; WSC's first audience with following stroke, 224; WSC joins at races and for weekend at Balmoral, 231–3, 234, 235, 243; WSC's correspondence with during episode of pneumonia on French Riviera (1958), 276; WSC's correspondence with following 1960 fall, 313, 323; WSC's audience with following 1962 fall at Monte Carlo, 336; sends greetings on WSC's 90th birthday, 411; and WSC's final illness, 416; at WSC's funeral, 428; physicians, 435, 450

English, Sir (Thomas) Crisp, 20–1, 22, 23–4, 27–30, 436–7

enteric fever, 48–56

epilepsy, 270, 297, 302

Epsom Downs Racecourse (Surrey), 187, 210

Eton College, 5

Europa, SS, 31

Evans, Horace Evans, 1st Baron, 276, 278

Everest, Elizabeth (WSC's nanny), 3, 380, 452

Everitt, C.R., 51

extrasystoles (extra heart beats), 66, 67, 68, 126, 173, 180–1, 182, 189, 192, 224, 242–3, 284, 343

eye conditions, 322

falls *see* accidents

Feiling, Sir Keith, 47, 48, 50

femoral vein thrombosis, 344, 347, 349, 350

Fergusson, Sir William, 449

Fields, Dame Gracie, 306

Fifth Army (Allied formation in Italy), 127

First World War, 304, 356, 377, 393–4; Dardanelles campaign, 219, 390, 391, 393

Fisher, Herbert Albert Laurens, 24

Fissore, André, 334, 336

Fitzroy, Edward, 86

Fleming, A., 'On skin-grafting', 19

Florence, 127

Forbes, Donald, 268, 293, 307

Forester, Cecil Louis, 346

Fraser, Ernest ('Bill'), 112

Frederick William, German Crown Prince, 99

Freyberg, Bernard Freyberg, 1st Baron, 280

furuncles *see* boils

Fussell, Edward Francis, 451

Gage, Harold Courtney, 287

Gaitskell, Hugh, 278, 300, 336

Gale, Sir Richard, 113, 124

gall stones, 287, 346

Gallipoli campaign (1915–16) *see* Dardanelles campaign

Galvin, George Wild ('Dan Leno'), 178

Gammell, Sir James, 124

gangrene, 303–4; *see also* ischaemia

Garda, Lake, 182–3

Gardone Val Trompia (Italy), 182–3

Gask, George, 435, 450

Geismar, Peter, 271

Gemmell, Cecily ('Chips'), 183, 381–2

General Elections: (1922), 20, 23, 25–6;
(1945), 150, 383, 387–9; (1950), 191,
194–5; (1951), 196; (1955), 248–9;
(1959), 292, 293, 307; (1964), 410
Geneva Summit (1955), 256
Genoa, 162–4, 167; Villa Pirelli, 162–3
George V, King, 18, 23, 27, 433, 435, 453;
death, 423, 433
George VI, King, 58, 75, 80, 85, 124, 125,
128, 136, 169, 433, 435, 446, 450; death
and funeral, 196
Gettysburg (Pennsylvania), 48, 296
Ghaemi, Nassir, *A First-Rate Madness*,
374–5
Gibraltar, 88, 106, 124
Gibson, Herbert Robert Burnett, 184,
188, 437
Gilbert, Sir Martin, 21, 50, 63, 85, 98,
117, 120, 163, 184, 200, 293, 364, 382,
401, 447; on WSC's 'black dog', 375–6,
383; and WSC's drinking, 401, 402,
405
Gilbert and Sullivan, *The Gondoliers*, 290
Gilliatt, Elizabeth, 185, 191, 233, 247
Gilliatt, Sir William, 233
Gladstone, William Ewart, 264, 402, 449
Golding, (Frederick) Campbell, 8, 45,
310–11, 325, 326, 341, 437–8
Gordon, Richard, 175
Gort, John Vereker, 6th Viscount, 90
Gourock (Renfrewshire), 57
Gowers, Sir William, 440
Graham, Dr (Nassau physician), 37, 39
Graham-Hodgson, Sir Harold, 438
Gramaglia, M. (anaesthetist at Monte
Carlo), 336
Grant, Matthew, 384
Greenock (Renfrewshire), 138
Gregorio, Nicholas John, 98
Grenz rays, 365, 370–1
Grey-Turner, Elston, 93, 96, 100, 110,
111
Grimond, Joseph ('Jo'; *later* Baron
Grimond), 336, 410
Guest, Alice (née Grosvenor; *later*
Viscountess Wimborne), 376

Guest, Cornelia, Lady (née Spencer-
Churchill; *later* Baroness Wimborne), 6
Guest, Sir Ivor (*later* 1st Baron
Wimborne), 6
Guest, Ivor (*later* 1st Viscount
Wimborne), 376
Gustaf VI Adolf, King of Sweden, 240

Hailstone, Bernard, portrait of WSC as
Warden of the Cinque Ports, 258
Haley, Sir William, 392
Halifax (Nova Scotia), 140
Hamblin, Grace, 53–4, 106, 398, 404–5
Hampton Roads (Virginia), 58
Hamsell Manor (Kent), 356
Hankey, Sir Maurice (*later* 1st Baron
Hankey), 22
Hardy-Roberts, Sir Geoffrey, 341
Harmsworth, Esmond *see* Rothermere,
Esmond Harmsworth, 2nd Viscount
Harrap, George, 53
Harriman, Averell, 147–8, 388–9
Harrow School, 5, 6, 27, 157, 259, 412
Hartgill, William Clavering, 99
Hartigan, Thomas, 21, 22, 24, 25, 29, 36,
438
Harvey, John, 307
Harvey, Oliver (*later* 1st Baron Harvey of
Tasburgh), 65, 67, 76, 80, 137
Haselden, Mrs (nurse in Cairo), 96, 115
Hastings, 258
Hatfield House (Hertfordshire), 252
Hawkey, Sir James, 52
Head, Sir Henry, 440
Heath, Sir Edward, 322
Henley, Sylvia, 412, 418
Henry VII, King, 256
Henry VIII, King, 256
hernia, inguinal, 154–8, 167, 171;
operation to repair, 156, 173–7, 181,
359, 360
Herriot, Édouard, 159
Hewer, Christopher Langton, 176–7, 181,
438–9
'High Hat' (racehorse), 155
Hill, Kathleen, 170, 388

hip fracture, 333–50; operation, 328, 339–41; post-operative course and recuperation, 341–50
Hodge, Alan, 236, 247, 249, 250, 255, 263
Holland-Hibbert, Delia (*later* Cunningham), 152
Hollis, Sir Leslie, 57, 64, 88, 119, 386
HOPE NOT, Operation (WSC's State funeral arrangements; 1965), 416
Hopkins, Harry, 58, 62, 76, 81, 87, 103, 147
horse racing, 155, 187, 210, 232–3, 264
Horsley, Sir Victor, 440
Hove *see* Brighton and Hove
Howells, Roy: nurse to WSC, 309, 427; and WSC's 1960 fall at London home, 309–10, 316–17, 321, 324, 325, 332; and WSC's 1962 fall at Monte Carlo, 333–5, 337, 338; and WSC's recuperation from fractured hip, 338, 341, 342, 343, 345, 349; and WSC's acute leg ischaemia, 353, 354; and WSC's 90th birthday, 412; and WSC's final illness and last days, 413–14, 415–18, 420, 423–4; and WSC's death, 424, 426, 427; on WSC's drinking, 408
Huddleston, Ann, 417, 424
Hunt, Sir David, 402
Hunt, Frank de Vine, 177
Hunt, Thomas, 283–7, 397, 407, 439
HUSKY, Operation (Allied invasion of Sicily; 1943), 87
Hutton (St Mary's Hospital nurse), 311
Hylton-Foster, Sir Harry, 336

incontinence, 320, 331, 332
India, 11–16, 407; independence, 64; Indian Nationalism, 31, 42, 50
indigestion, 20, 27, 70, 125, 388, 439
inebriation (drunkenness), 397, 398–400, 404–6
inguinal hernia, 154–8, 167, 171; operation to repair, 156, 173–7, 181, 359, 360
Inönü, Ismet, 92
insomnia *see* sleeping problems and medication

intertrigo, 368–9, 371
intestinal haemorrhage, 51, 52, 55, 56
Ireland, 1, 7
ischaemia: of finger, 291, 301, 303–4, 306, 308; of leg, 352–8
ischaemia, cerebral *see* strokes; transient ischaemic attacks
Ischia, 131
Ismay, Sir Hastings ('Pug'; *later* 1st Baron Ismay), 78–9, 85, 88, 90, 118, 138, 144, 390, 403
itching *see* pruritus

Jackson, John Hughlings, 440
Jacob, Sir Ian, 57, 130, 151, 398, 401–2
James, Walter, 6
jaundice, 280–7, 346, 349–50, 397, 407
'Jock' (cat), 416, 427, 428
Jodhpore, 12–13
Johnson, Boris, 394
Johnson, Samuel, 372, 374

Keefe, Gillian ('Sunny'), 338–9, 343–7
Kelly, Denis, 176, 178, 179, 184, 187, 247, 249, 250, 390
Kelly, Thomas James, 114, 119, 120–1
Kennedy, Foster, 34, 45, 439–40
Kennedy, John Fitzgerald, Addison's disease, xvii
keratosis, 365–6, 371
Kerr, Archibald Clark (*later* 1st Baron Inverchapel), 383
Keyes, Sir Roger (*later* 1st Baron Keyes), 12
Keynes, Sir Geoffrey, 169, 172–3
kidney injuries and damage, 8, 10, 86, 116, 149
Kimball, Warren, 404
Kimberley, HMS, 133
King, Ernest, 147
King, (William Lyon) Mackenzie, 403
King George V, HMS, 124
Kinmonth, John, 355, 356, 357, 440–1
Kinna, Patrick, 91, 98, 112, 117

Kirkwood, Jock, 248
Kitchener, Sir Herbert (*later* 1st Earl
　Kitchener), 16
Knox, Adrienne, 417

Langworth, Richard, 399
Lascelles, Sir Alan ('Tommy'), 124, 199,
　204–5, 218
Lavery, Brian, *Churchill Goes to War*, 57,
　92
Law, (Andrew) Bonar, 20, 27
Lawrence, Thomas Edward ('Lawrence of
　Arabia'), 26
Layton, Elizabeth, 77, 85, 115, 153, 161
Learmonth, Sir James, 450
Leathers, Frederick Leathers, 1st
　Viscount, 138, 139
Lee, Celia, 1
Leeds, 194, 201
Leeming, Felicity, 417
Leghorn (Livorno), 133
Lend-Lease programme, 139, 144, 147
Leno, Dan (George Wild Galvin), 178
Levan, N.E., 'Toxic reactions of
　sulfaguanidine therapy', 149
Life (magazine), 248, 388
Lincoln, Abraham, 375
Lindemann, Frederick *see* Cherwell,
　Frederick Lindemann, 1st Viscount
　('the Prof')
Lloyd, Selwyn (*later* Baron Selwyn-
　Lloyd), 285, 410
Lloyd George, David (*later* 1st Earl
　Lloyd-George of Dwyfor), 20, 23, 30,
　257
London: Addison Road Station, 138;
　Army Medical College, Millbank, 128;
　Beaumont House Nursing Home, 51,
　52; Bryanston Square, 69; Cabinet
　War Rooms, 73, 128; Carlton Club,
　7; Claridge's Hotel, 166, 387–8;
　Devonshire Place, 76, 125; Dorchester
　Hotel, 166; Dorset Square, 21, 22;
　Drapers Hall, 259; Fife Nursing
　Home, 174–5, 176; Grosvenor Square,
　9; Guildhall, 252; Hyde Park Gate,
150, 178, 196–7, 248, 297, 309, 347,
　418; Hyde Park Hotel, 248; Kensington
　Public Library, 414; Kensington
　Town Hall, 427; Lancaster House,
　210; Mansion House, 259; Middlesex
　Hospital, 338–47; Morpeth Mansions,
　52; Palace of Westminster, 428; Royal
　Academy, 286, 290; Royal College of
　Physicians, 166; Savoy Hotel, 297, 412–
　13, 426; St Bartholomew's Hospital,
　169, 175, 435; St Mary's Hospital,
　76–7, 311; St Paul's Cathedral, 428;
　St Thomas' Hospital, 168; Storey's
　Gate, 135; Sussex Square, 21, 24;
　Westminster Hospital, 356, 357, 423
Longfellow, Henry Wadsworth, *King
　Robert of Sicily*, 221, 285
Louise, Queen consort of Sweden, 240
Lovell, Richard, 59, 114, 237, 329, 365
Luce, Clare Boothe, 248
Luce, Henry, 248, 255
Lugano, Lake, 154, 156, 160
Lyneham, RAF (Wiltshire), 106, 335
Lyttelton, Oliver *see* Chandos, Oliver
　Lyttelton, 1st Viscount

Macaulay, Thomas Babington, 1st Baron,
　176, 241
MacCormac, Henry, 359–63, 370, 441
MacCormac, Sir William, 168
MacKenna, Robert M.B., 202, 290, 318,
　363–9, 441–2
Mackenzie, Sir Morell, 99
Macmillan, Lady Dorothy, 131
Macmillan, Harold (*later* 1st Earl of
　Stockton): wartime Minister Resident
　in the Mediterranean, 89; and WSC's
　episode of pneumonia and atrial
　fibrillation in Carthage (1943), 98–9,
　99–100, 107, 112–13, 117; planning for
　Operation SHINGLE, 113; Christmas
　in Carthage, 113–14; and WSC's 1944
　tour of Italian operations, 131, 133–4;
　at Strasbourg for Inaugural Session
　of Council of Europe (1949), 183,
　185–6; learns of WSC's first stroke,

185–6; and WSC's second stroke, 213, 217, 220, 229–30; on WSC's speeches following resumption of work after stroke, 238, 241; Foreign Secretary, 251; and secondment of Montague Browne as Private Secretary to WSC, 251, 255, 257–8, 381; Prime Minister, 278, 290, 292, 305; and WSC's episode of pneumonia and jaundice during 1958 holiday on French Riviera, 278; visits WSC after 1960 fall at London home, 326–7; and WSC's fractured hip following 1962 fall at Monte Carlo, 335, 336, 346; visits WSC at Chartwell (September 1963), 356, 358; resignation as Prime Minister, 356; visits WSC shortly before 90th birthday, 411; speaks at Other Club dinner following WSC's death, 413; Lord Richardson as personal physician, 446

MacNeil, Robert, 338
Macready, Sir Gordon, 57
Madeira, 190–1, 194; Reid's Hotel, 191
Majestic, RMS, 42
malaria, 128–9, 141–2, 432
Malenkov, Georgy, 214
Malta, 89–90, 143, 145–6; Luqa Airfield, 145; San Anton Palace, 147
Manchester, 194
Manchester, William, *The Last Lion*, 11
Mander, Danny, 405–6
manic depression *see* bipolar disorders
Margate (Kent), Conservative Party Annual Conference (1953), 220, 235, 236–9, 243, 244–5, 392
Marie Antoinette, Queen of France, 299–300
Marlborough, John Churchill, 1st Duke of, WSC's biography of, 47, 48, 51, 53, 54, 328
Marlborough, John Spencer-Churchill, 7th Duke of, 1
Marlborough, Charles Spencer-Churchill, 9th Duke of ('Sunny'), 41, 50, 55, 328

Marlborough, Lily, Dowager Duchess of, 7, 8, 9
Marrakech, 101, 110, 114, 121–4, 289–90, 292, 348; Hotel Mamounia, 289, 290, 403; Villa Taylor, 121, 123
Marriott, Marjorie, 339
Marsh, Sir Edward: Private Secretary to WSC, 20; drafting of articles for WSC, 49, 51–2, 54
Marshall, Sir Geoffrey: professional biography, 442–3; relations with WSC, 74; provides second opinion on WSC's pneumonia following return from Casablanca Conference (February 1943), 74–87; and WSC's pneumonia and atrial fibrillation at Carthage (December 1943), 99, 104–5; and WSC's pneumonia on return from Italy (1944), 135, 136–7
Marshall, George, 63, 147
Marston, Lettice, 183, 390
Martin, Sir John: Principal Private Secretary to WSC, 57; with WSC in United States for 1941–2 ARCADIA Conference, 57, 60, 63–4; and WSC's bout of pneumonia following return from 1943 Casablanca Conference, 73–4; with WSC in Middle East for 1943 Cairo and Tehran conferences, 88, 91; and WSC's episode of pneumonia and atrial fibrillation at Carthage, 93, 98, 99, 100, 104, 107, 108, 112, 114; travels to Canada with WSC for 1944 Quebec Conference, 138, 386, 387; with WSC on journey to 1945 Yalta Conference, 143, 144, 146, 147
Martin-Jones, Miss (physiotherapist), 314
Mary, Princess Royal, 437
Mary, Queen consort, 18, 169, 433
Masterton Smith, Sir James, 22
Maugham, Somerset, 234
Mauritius, HMS, 124
May & Baker (chemical company), manufacture of sulfonamides, 74
McIntire, Ross T., 122
Meerut, 12

memory loss, 68, 231, 254, 257, 259, 261, 270, 285, 289, 301, 302, 345

Mendl, Sir Charles, 50–1

mepacrine (medication), 128–9, 138, 140, 141–2

methyl salicylate (oil of wintergreen), 87

Mickleburgh, Miss (secretary to Sir John Parkinson), 125

Milan, 153, 157

Miles, Doris (née Clayton Greene), 76–87

Miles, Roger, 77, 86

Miller Fisher syndrome, 260

Mitchell, John Lewis, 92–3, 114, 119–20

Moatti, Pierre-Jean, 277

Mohammed V, King of Morocco, 289

Molyneux, Edward, 234

Molyneux, Sir Richard, 16–19

Monaco, 164, 265, 274, 336, 437; *see also* Monte Carlo

Monckton, Bridget ('Biddy'), Viscountess, 288, 289

Monckton, Sir Walter (*later* 1st Viscount Monckton of Brenchley), 289

Montag, Charles, 160, 161, 162

Montague Browne, Sir Anthony: Private Secretary to WSC, 246, 251, 255, 257–8; with WSC during holidays on French Riviera, 251, 262, 273–5, 405, 448; and WSC's fourth stroke, 267; and WSC's episode of pneumonia and jaundice (1958), 276, 277–8, 280–1; with WSC during 1959 holiday in Morocco, 289; prepares constituency speeches for WSC, 293, 307; with WSC during 1959 trip to Washington, 294, 295–6, 303–4; and gangrene in WSC's right little finger, 303–4, 308; with WSC during 1959 sailing holiday to Greece and Turkey, 306; in Cambridge with WSC for foundation ceremony for Churchill College, 307–8; and WSC's episode of loss of consciousness and sixth stroke (October–November 1959), 296–7, 298; and WSC's 1960 fall fracturing thoracic vertebra, 311, 327–8;

with WSC during 1962 holiday at Monte Carlo, 333–6; and WSC's fall fracturing hip, 333–6, 337; and WSC's hip operation and recuperation, 339, 341, 342, 343, 349; with WSC during last holiday on Onassis's yacht (1963), 351; and WSC's acute leg ischaemia, 352, 354, 355, 356, 357, 358; and WSC's 90th birthday, 411, 412; and WSC's final illness and last days, 413, 416, 417–18, 420, 421–2; and WSC's death, 424, 425, 426, 427; on WSC's 'black dog', 381; on WSC's drinking, 397, 405; on Lord Moran, 448; *Long Sunset* (memoirs; 1995), 332

Montague Browne, Noel ('Nonie'), 288, 306, 351, 412

Monte Carlo, 162, 164–5, 167, 183, 186–7, 281, 295–6, 306, 333–7, 351, 447–8; Casino, 235, 274; Hôtel de Paris, 164, 166, 187, 275, 333–4, 335–6, 405; Princess Grace Clinic, 334–6, 337, 448; Sporting Club, 234

Monte Cassino, 133, 151

Montgomery, Bernard (*later* 1st Viscount Montgomery of Alamein): New Year 1944 with WSC in Marrakech, 122; created Field Marshal, 136; WSC's correspondence with following first stroke, 186; visits WSC on French Riviera, 279; at the opera in London with WSC, 290; unveiling of statue of WSC in Woodford, 298; visits WSC on 86th birthday, 323; weekends at Chartwell, 351, 355, 358; misses WSC's 90th birthday party, 412

Moran, Charles Wilson, 1st Baron: personal physician to WSC, 58, 290, 429; professional biography, 443; WSC's views on and relations with, 58, 62, 78, 112, 294; with WSC in North America for 1941–2 ARCADIA Conference, 57–8, 59–65; diagnosis of WSC's episode of chest pain, 61–2, 65–6, 69–72, 187–8; treatment of WSC's pneumonia following return from 1943

Casablanca Conference, 74–9, 82–7; with WSC in Middle East for 1943 Cairo and Tehran conferences, 88–9, 90, 91, 92, 383–4; treatment of WSC's pneumonia and atrial fibrillation at Carthage, 93–118; and WSC's recuperation at Marrakech, 114, 119, 120–1, 122–3, 124; and WSC's cardiac assessment on return from Marrakech, 125; and WSC's 1944 tour of Italian operations, 128–9, 130; prescription of mepacrine, 128–9, 138, 140, 141–2; and WSC's bout of pneumonia on return to London, 134–42; travels to Canada with WSC for 1944 Quebec Conference, 138–41, 385–7; with WSC on journey to Crimea for 1945 Yalta Conference, 143–9; with WSC during holiday on Lake Como following 1945 election defeat, 153, 160, 161; and WSC's inguinal hernia, 154–5, 168–9; invites WSC to speak at dinner for Royal College of Physicians, 166; first refers WSC to dermatologist, 359, 360; and WSC's referral to Sir Thomas Dunhill, 169, 170–2; and WSC's hernia operation, 173–6, 177, 181; and WSC's recurring skin conditions, 360, 362–3, 365, 366–7; and WSC's re-examination by cardiologist (May 1949), 182; and WSC's first stroke, 184–9, 192–3; further assessments of WSC for cerebrovascular disease (1950–52), 194–205; unveiling of portrait at Royal College of Physicians, 206–9, 364; encourages WSC to reduce workload, 199–203, 217; and WSC's second stroke, 211, 212–28, 229; further assessments of WSC during recovery from second stroke, 230–2, 233, 237, 240–5; prescription of amfetamine, 237, 239, 240, 244–5, 294, 375, 392, 396–7; offers to accompany WSC on Sicilian holiday following retirement as Prime Minister, 247–8; and WSC's third stroke, 249–61; visits WSC and

wife after their forty-eighth wedding anniversary, 262; and WSC's fourth stroke, 265–7, 268–71; and WSC's episode of pneumonia and jaundice during 1958 holiday on French Riviera, 274–9, 280–2, 286–7; further assessments of WSC for jaundice and atrial fibrillation on return to England, 282–7; and WSC's fifth stroke, 290–5, 301; and WSC's 1959 trip to Washington, 293–5, 303; and WSC's ischaemia and gangrene in right little finger, 291, 303–5, 306, 308; with WSC during 1959 sailing holiday to Greece and Turkey, 306; and WSC's episode of loss of consciousness and sixth stroke, 296–301; and WSC's 1960 fall at London home fracturing thoracic vertebra, 309–32; and WSC's further mild stroke following fall, 319–21, 330–1; and WSC's fractured hip following 1962 fall at Monte Carlo, 335, 336, 337, 341, 342, 346; and WSC's acute leg ischaemia (1963), 352–5, 357–8; and WSC's 90th birthday, 412; and WSC's final illness and last days, 415–24; and WSC's death, 424–6, 428; writing and publication of *The Struggle for Survival*, xviii, 193, 254–5, 383, 384–5 *Views and opinions on*: Dafydd Roberts, 448; general practitioners, 448; Lord Brain, 254–5, 430; Sir Herbert Seddon, 312; Sir Thomas Dunhill, 171–2; WSC's behaviour as patient, 111, 148, 222, 229, 317, 412; WSC's 'black dog', 374, 375, 379–80, 382–92, 393, 396; WSC's death and funeral, 421, 425, 428; WSC's donation of skin graft, 19; WSC's drinking, 188, 397, 400, 406–8; WSC's 'nine lives', 326; WSC's potential longevity, 140, 303; WSC's resumption of work after second stroke, 226, 229, 231–2, 241–2; WSC's smoking, 108, 188; WSC's work output, 87
Moran, Dorothy, Lady, 187, 208

Moran, (Richard) John Wilson, 2nd
  Baron, 384
Morning Post, WSC as special
  correspondent, 16–17
Morrison, Herbert (*later* Baron Morrison
  of Lambeth), 183, 196, 200
Morse, Sir John, 131
Morton, Sir Desmond, 88, 96, 98, 400
Mount Vernon (Virginia), 63
Mountbatten, Lord Louis (*later* 1st Earl
  Mountbatten of Burma), 170
Murray, Edmund: WSC's bodyguard,
  233; with WSC during recuperative
  holiday at Cap d'Ail (September 1953),
  233–4; with WSC during holiday
  in Sicily (April 1955), 248; with
  WSC during holidays at La Pausa,
  Roquebrune (1956–8), 263, 264–5, 266,
  273, 282; and WSC's fourth stroke,
  264–5, 266, 269, 270, 271; and WSC
  episode of pneumonia and jaundice
  (1958), 274–5, 276, 279; with WSC
  during 1959 holiday in Morocco and
  Canary Islands, 288, 289; with WSC
  during 1959 trip to Washington, 295;
  with WSC during 1959 sailing holiday
  to Greece and Turkey, 306; with WSC
  during 1962 holiday at Monte Carlo,
  333; and WSC's recuperation from
  fractured hip, 339, 342–3, 345; and
  WSC's final illness and last days, 418,
  419–20; and WSC's death, 426
Mussolini, Benito, 150, 154

Nairn, Margaret, 123
Naples, 130–2, 133, 134; Villa Rivalta,
  131, 134
Nares, Eric, 151
Nassau (Bahamas), 37–41; Polly Leach
  Hotel, 37
National Union of Conservative and
  Unionist Associations, annual
  conference (1932), 50, 52
Nauheim baths, 106, 173
Nazi Party, 54, 374
Nemon, Oscar, statue of WSC, 252

New York, 31–7, 41, 296, 303; Brooklyn
  Academy of Music, 41; Fifth Avenue,
  32–3; Lenox Hill Hospital, 33–5, 42–3,
  444–5; Waldorf Astoria Hotel, 32, 33,
  35, 41
Newman, Philip, 339–41, 342, 344, 346,
  349, 443–4
Newport by-election (1922), 20, 22
News of the World, 378; WSC's articles
  for, 47, 49, 54
Nice, 276, 279; Airport, 184, 233, 267,
  279, 281, 282, 337; Hotel Continental,
  36
Nicolson, Sir Harold, 73, 124–5
nikethamide (stimulant), 271
Ninety Years On (television programme;
  1965), 411, 415
Nixon, Richard, 277
Nobel Prize: Literature, 239–40, 399;
  Physiology or Medicine, 431
Noonan, Peggy, 398–9
Norfolk (Virginia), 64
Norfolk, Bernard Fitzalan-Howard, 16th
  Duke of, 416
Norman, Andrew, *Winston Churchill:
  Portrait of an unquiet mind*, 375
Normandy, Battle of (1944) *see*
  OVERLORD, Operation
Northolt, RAF (Middlesex), 89, 130, 134,
  143–4
Nova Levante (Italy), 183
nuclear weapons, 87, 158, 307

Oberon, Merle, 183
OCTAGON Conference *see* Quebec
  Conference (1944)
Ogier, John L.E., 152, 153, 155, 160, 161,
  163, 164, 167
Oldham, 194
Oliver, Sarah *see* Churchill, Sarah
Omdurman, Battle of (1898), 15, 16–17,
  396
Onassis, Aristotle, 274, 282, 288, 289,
  306, 320, 351, 414
Onassis, Christina, 289
Orion, HMS, 146–7

Orpen, Sir William, portrait of WSC, 219, 391
Osler, Sir William, 100
Other Club, The, 251, 276, 286, 290, 292, 293, 412–13
Ottawa, 62–3, 73
Oudenaarde (Flanders), 48
OVERLORD, Operation (Battle of Normandy; 1944), 131; planning for, 103, 118
Owen, David Owen, Baron, *In Sickness and in Power*, 374

Pakenham-Walsh, Ridley, 47, 48
papaverine (drug), 271
paratyphoid fever, 48–56
Paré, Ambroise, 349
Paris, Galerie Druet, 161
Parkinson, Sir John: cardiologist to WSC, 65, 169, 209, 393, 430; professional biography, 444; assessments of WSC following chest pain suffered in Washington (1942), 61–2, 65–9, 70–1, 188; and WSC's bout of pneumonia following return from 1943 Casablanca Conference, 75–6; and WSC's pneumonia and atrial fibrallation in Carthage (December 1943), 99, 103–6; assessment of WSC following return from convalescence in Marrakech (January 1944), 125–6; and WSC's bout of pneumonia on return from Italy (August 1944), 136; assessments of WSC before and after hernia operation (1947), 173–4, 180–1; re-examines WSC (1949), 182; advises Moran on WSC's 'muzzy feeling' (1951), 196; assessments of WSC after second stroke (1953), 225, 227, 242–3
Pavia, 162
Pearl Harbor, Japanese attack (1941), 57
Pearman, Violet, 51, 52, 53
Pearn, Nancy, 53
Peck, Sir John, 78, 130, 401–2, 405
penicillin, development and trialling, 106–7, 117

Petschacher, Ludwig, 49–50, 54–5
Philip, Prince, Duke of Edinburgh, 231, 233, 336
Phoenix Assurance Company, 36, 38, 40
physiotherapy, 314, 316, 345
Pickhardt, Otto, 34–5, 37, 38, 40, 41, 42–3, 45, 444–5
Pim, Sir Richard, 88
Pirelli, Giovanni Battista, 162
Pitblado, Sir David, 211
Pius XII, Pope, 133
pleurisy, 99, 275, 277, 278, 280
Plymouth, 65, 88, 124; parliamentary constituency, 194
pneumonia: childhood incidence, 4; mortality rates, 4, 86, 116, 141; prescription of alcohol, 4–5; treatment, 4–5, 86–7, 116–17, 141, 429
pneumonia, WSC's episodes: (1886), 1–5; (February 1943), 73–87, 429; (December 1943), 94–118, 192, 408; (1944), 134–42; (1958), 274–80, 286; (1962), 341, 350
Poe, Edgar Allan, 299
polo, 12–13, 14, 27
Pol-Roger, Odette, 279, 399
Pompano (Florida), 63–4
Ponting, Clive, *Churchill*, 403–4
Port Said, 11
Portal, Sir Charles (*later* 1st Viscount Portal of Hungerford), 57, 64
Portal, Jane (*later* Lady Williams), 210, 233, 235, 239, 241, 383, 390
Portsmouth Football Club, 290
Post, Jerrold M., *When Illness Strikes the Leader*, 373–4
Potsdam Conference (1945), 389
Pound, Sir Dudley, 57, 64
Powell, Robin, 333, 335
Pownall, Sir Henry, 381–2
'Premonition' (racehorse), 234
'Pretendant, Le' (racehorse), 264
Prince of Wales, HMS, 57
pruritus (itching), 359, 360, 362–3, 365–71
psoriasis, 369, 370, 371

Pugh, Doreen, 288, 289, 300
Pugh, Dorothy, 76–87, 135–41
Pugh, Robert, 135, 138
Pugh, Roger, 76
Pulvertaft, Robert, 96–108, 116, 432, 445

Quebec Conference (OCTAGON; 1944), 136, 137, 140–1
Queen Mary, RMS, 138–40, 385–7

Rabat (Morocco), 134, 289
Rainier, Prince of Monaco, 265, 336
Ramillies (Belgium), 48
Ramsden, John, 373
Ranke, Leopold von, 176
Rattigan, Sir Terence, 411
Renown, HMS, 87–8, 89–90
Reves, Emery, 262, 263, 267, 273, 274, 290, 306
Reves, Wendy Russell, 262, 263, 267, 273, 290
Rhodes James, Sir Robert, 400–1
Richardson, John Richardson, Baron, 300, 302, 314–15, 445–6
Riddell, George Riddell, 1st Baron, 47, 50, 378
rigor, 275
Rob, Charles, 304–5, 308, 440, 446–7
Roberts, Andrew, 400, 401, 406
Roberts, Dafydd (David) Myrddin: professional biography, 447–8; WSC's doctor in South of France, 184, 263, 315, 368–9, 448; and WSC's fourth stroke, 265–6, 268, 270–1; and WSC's episode of pneumonia and jaundice (1958), 274–82; and WSC's fifth stroke, 293; and WSC's 1962 fall fracturing hip, 333–5, 336
Robertson, Ian, 398, 404
Robins, Robert S., *When Illness Strikes the Leader*, 373–4
Robitscher, Jonas B., xviii
Rogers, A.D.D. ('Tim'), 152, 155, 160, 161, 163–5, 167
Rogers, Kelly, 64
Rome, 127, 133–4

Roose, Bertrand ('Bertie'), 1
Roose, (Edward Charles) Robson, 1–4, 8, 9, 448–9
Roosevelt, Eleanor, 58
Roosevelt, Franklin Delano: disability, xvii; WSC stays with during 1941–2 ARCADIA Conference, 57–60, 62, 63, 64; at 1943 Casablanca Conference, 114, 121; WSC's correspondence with while recuperating from pneumonia following conference, 82, 83, 84; at 1943 Cairo and Tehran conferences, 91, 92, 405; WSC correspondence with during bout of pneumonia and recuperation in North Africa (December 1943), 103, 110, 117, 122; WSC's correspondence with during tour of Italian operations (August 1944), 134; at Quebec Conference (September 1944), 136, 140; at Yalta Conference (January 1945), 143
Roquebrune-Cap-Martin (French Riviera), 165; La Pausa, 262–7, 273–82, 290, 306–7
Rose, Jill, 77
Rose, William, 8, 9, 449
Ross, Sir James Paterson, 168, 173, 175, 176–7, 178, 440, 449–50
Rothermere, Harold Harmsworth, 1st Viscount, 35, 403–4
Rothermere, Esmond Harmsworth, 2nd Viscount, 35, 36–7, 44, 53, 165
Rowan, Sir Leslie, 104–5, 130
Rowse, Alfred Leslie, 247, 255–6, 402–3
Royal College of Physicians: Harveian Oration, 166, 446; presidency, 166, 203, 206, 208; WSC proposes Toast of the College at luncheon (1944), 209; WSC's acceptance speech for Honorary Fellowship and unveiling of portrait of Moran (1951), 203, 206–9, 364
'Run, Rabbit, Run' (song), 411
Russell, J., 'The use of stimulants in pneumonia', 4
Rutter, Joseph, 3, 4, 450–1
Rycroft, Sir Benjamin, 306

Safi (Morocco), 289
Salisbury, Elizabeth, Marchioness of (*earlier* Viscountess Cranborne), 309, 403
Salisbury, Robert Gascoyne-Cecil, 5th Marquess of (*earlier* Viscount Cranborne), 198–9, 215, 217, 219, 220, 224, 236, 309, 403; WSC visits at Hatfield (June 1955), 252
Salmonella paratyphi, 54–6
Salzburg, 48–50
San Remo (Italy), 235
Sandhurst (Royal Military College), 399; entrance examination, 6, 9–10
Sandys, Celia, 333, 334, 335, 337–8, 412, 424, 425
Sandys, Diana *see* Churchill, Diana
Sandys, Duncan (*later* Baron Duncan-Sandys), 80, 186, 239
Sandys, Edwina, 319, 411, 412
Sandys, Julian, 412
Sawyers, Frank, 91, 119, 130, 134, 144, 146, 148, 153, 161, 163, 402
Scadding, John Guyett, 95, 103–4, 111–12, 116–17, 148, 451
Scharnhorst (German battleship), sinking of, 119
Schumann, Robert, mental health, xvii
seasickness, 58, 89
seborrhoeic dermatitis, 359–61, 369–70, 371
seborrhoeic keratosis, 365–6, 371
secobarbital, use and side effects, 331–2
Seddon, Sir Herbert: professional biography, 451–2; friendship with WSC, 181, 327–8, 348–9, 430, 452; assessments and treatment of WSC following 1960 fall at London home, 8, 45–6, 310–32; operation on WSC's hip following 1962 fall at Monte Carlo, 328, 339–41; post-operative course, 341, 344, 346–7, 348–9; and WSC's acute leg ischaemia (1963), 352–5, 357–8; on Moran's *The Struggle for Survival*, xviii
Sefton, William Molyneux, 4th Earl of, 18

Shaw, George Bernard, 439
Shawcross, Sir Hartley (*later* Baron Shawcross), 293
Shepherd, Ivan, 288, 291, 295
SHINGLE, Operation (Allied amphibious landing in Italy; 1944), 113, 124
shingles, 306
Shock, Sir Maurice, 263, 264
shoulder injuries: (1893), 8; (1896), 11–15; (1899), 12–13; (1931), 44, 45; (1960), 309, 313–14, 316, 318–19, 330
Sicily: wartime, 87, 129; WSC visits (1955), 247–8
Sidney Street siege (1911), 396
Siena, 134, 151
Simeone, Fiorindo, 440
Sink the Bismarck! (film; 1960), 348
skin diseases, 202, 317–18, 359–71
skin grafts, 18–19
sleeping problems and medication, 39, 44, 59, 95, 184, 201, 225, 315–16, 318, 324, 331–2, 389, 413
Smith, Frederick Edwin *see* Birkenhead, F.E. Smith, 1st Earl of
Smith, Julian Ormond, 170, 172
Smith, Walter Bedell, 89, 124
smoking, 4, 108, 111, 163, 174, 188, 344, 348, 370
Sneyd-Kynnersley, Herbert William, 1
Soames, Christopher (*later* Baron Soames), 180, 240, 247, 248, 259, 317; and WSC's second stroke, 211, 212, 213, 214–15, 216, 219; with WSC during recuperative holiday at Cap d'Ail (September 1953), 233–5; and WSC's third stroke, 249–50; at WSC's 90th birthday party, 412; and WSC's final illness and last days, 416
Soames, Mary (née Spencer-Churchill; WSC's daughter): early childhood, 25; wartime life, 73, 79, 108, 403; and WSC's second stroke, 211, 212, 213, 214, 219; with WSC during recuperative holidays at Cap d'Ail (1953; 1955), 233–5, 259; represents

WSC at Nobel Prize ceremony, 240;
joins WSC during 1958 holiday at
Roquebrune, 281; and WSC's 1960 fall
fracturing thoracic vertebra, 315; visits
WSC on 86th birthday, 323; mother
stays with at Hamsell Manor, 356; and
WSC's retirement from Parliament,
410; at WSC's 90th birthday party, 412;
and WSC's final illness and last days,
414, 416, 417, 421; and WSC's death,
424, 426, 427
    Views and opinions on: 1959 General
    Election result, 307; Dafydd
    Roberts, 448; Montague Browne,
    381; parents' campaigning in
    Dundee, 25; WSC's 90th birthday
    party, 412; WSC's 1960 fall, 315;
    WSC's 'black dog', 376, 379; WSC's
    condition after fourth stroke, 269,
    270–1; WSC's death, 424–5, 426;
    WSC's drinking, 402; WSC's
    holiday at Lake Como following
    1945 election defeat, 150, 167;
    WSC's holiday in Sicily following
    retirement as Prime Minister, 248;
    WSC's Hyde Park Gate home,
    347; WSC's ill-health on return
    from Casablanca Conference, 73,
    79; WSC's recovery from 1962
    hip operation, 344, 350; WSC's
    retirement as Prime Minister,
    247; WSC's second stroke and
    subsequent resumption of work,
    212, 214, 219, 239
Solomon, Andrew, *The Noonday Demon*,
375
Spaatz, Carl, 113
Spencer-Churchill, John ('Jack'; WSC's
brother), 1, 7, 9, 12, 79
Spencer-Churchill, (Henry Winston)
Peregrine (WSC's nephew), 1
Spencer-Cox, William Leigh, 110
spinal injuries: (1893), 8, 10, 45–6; (1931),
44, 45–6; (1960), 8, 309–32
St Albans, Hill End asylum, 175
St George's School, Ascot, 1

St Leger (horse race; 1953), 231, 232–3,
234
Stalin, Joseph, 67, 87, 92, 143, 158, 405
Stamfordham, Arthur Bigge, 1st Baron,
23, 27
Statendam, SS, 41
Stettinius, Edward, 63, 147, 403
Stockholm, 240
Storr, Anthony, on WSC's 'black dog',
372–4, 375, 379, 384
Straight, Whitney, 145
Strang, Sir William (*later* 1st Baron
Strang), 224
Strasbourg, 183, 186
strokes: (1949), 184–93; (1953), 210–28,
243–4, 309, 407; (1955), 249–50,
253–6, 259–61, 402–3; (1956), 264–72;
(April 1959), 290–5, 301; (November
1959), 298–301; (1960), 319–21,
330–1; (1965), 414–18, 428; *see also*
cerebrovascular disease; transient
ischaemic attacks (TIA)
Sturdee, Nina Edith ('Jo'; *later* Lady
Onslow), 171, 191, 194, 360
Sudan, 16–17
Suez crisis (1956), 262, 267, 268
sulfonamides (antibacterial medications),
use and side effects, 86–7, 116–17, 141,
148–9, 429, 431–2, 453
Sunday Chronicle, 54
Sunday Dispatch, 54
Sunday Times, literary awards, 179
Swinton, Philip Cunliffe-Lister, 1st Earl
of, 226

Taylor, Edith, 121
Taylor, Maxwell D., 296
Taza Pass (Morocco), 120
Tedder, Sir Arthur (*later* 1st Baron
Tedder), 90, 93, 98, 108, 110, 113,
114–15, 117
Tehran Conference (1943), 67, 91–2,
383–4, 405–6
Thompson, Charles ('Tommy'): WSC's
aide-de-camp, 57, 73, 403; with
WSC in United States for 1941–42

ARCADIA Conference, 57, 63–4; and WSC's bout of pneumonia following return from 1943 Casablanca Conference, 80, 87; with WSC in Middle East for 1943 Cairo and Tehran conferences, 88, 91; and WSC's episode of pneumonia and atrial fibrillation in Carthage, 93, 95, 98, 100, 108, 113; and WSC's recuperation in Marrakech, 121, 122–3; with WSC during 1944 tour of Italian and South of France operations, 130, 132, 134; travels to Canada with WSC for 1944 Quebec Conference, 138, 140, 386; with WSC on journey to Crimea for 1945 Yalta Conference, 143–5

Thompson, Walter: WSC's bodyguard, 31; with WSC during 1931–32 lecture tour, 31, 40–1, 42; with WSC in Middle East for 1943 Cairo and Tehran conferences, 88, 91; and WSC's episode of pneumonia and atrial fibrillation in Carthage, 95–6; and WSC's recuperation at Marrakech, 119–20

Thomson (nurse attending WSC after 1960 fall), 311

Thomson, Charlotte, 1

Thomson, Kate, 1

thoracic vertebrae *see* spinal injuries

Thorneycroft, Peter (*later* Baron Thorneycroft), 202

Thornton Butterworth (publishers), 42, 51

Thrale, Hester Lynch (*later* Piozzi), 372

TIA *see* transient ischaemic attacks

Time (magazine), 248, 388

Tito, Josip Broz, 127, 131

'Toby' (budgerigar), 314

Todd, Robert Bentley, 4

Todd's paresis, 270

Tolstoy, Leo, 298

transient ischaemic attacks (TIA), 203–4, 301, 428

Trevelyan, George Macaulay, xviii; *England Under Queen Anne*, 255

Trieste, 152

Trinity House (charity), 250

Trollope, Anthony, *Phineas Finn*, 138, 139

Truman, Harry S, 296

Tube Alloys (nuclear weapons development programme), 87

Tunis, 92–3, 96, 106, 108; American General Hospital, 97–8; RAMC General Hospital, 95

typhoid fever, 54, 55; vaccination, 55, 89

Umberto, Prince of Piedmont (*later* King Umberto II of Italy), 131, 133

Valetta, 89, 146

Valiant Years, The (documentary film; 1960–1), 327

Venice, 48

vertebrae *see* spinal injuries

vertigo, 187

V-sign, 337, 338, 347, 412; commemorative silver, 256

Wall Street crash (1929), 31, 40

Wallace, A.L., 'Faithful but unfortunate: Churchill and his shoulder', 13

Walthamstow East (parliamentary constituency), 307

Ward, Kenneth L.S., 177, 353–5, 357, 358, 360, 452

Wardell, Michael, 183–4

warts, 365–6, 371

Washington, DC, 58–62, 63, 295–6; British Embassy, 296; Capitol Building, 60; Foundry Methodist Church, 60; Mayflower Hotel, 59; White House, 58–60, 296

Washington, George, 60; tomb, 63

Waters, A.T.H., 'Clinical lecture on pneumonia', 4

Wathen, Guy, 163

Weissenstein (Salzburg family), 49

Welldon, James Edward Cowell, 6, 27

Westminster, Anne ('Nancy'), Duchess of, 189

Westminster, Hugh Grosvenor, 2nd Duke of, 189

Whitby, Sir Lionel, 79, 82, 83, 86, 95, 137, 138, 140, 141, 145, 146, 386, 432, 435, 453
White, Ian, 359–71
White, Paul Dudley, 444
Whiteley, Sir John, 89–90
Wilson, Sir Charles *see* Moran, Charles Wilson, 1st Baron
Wilson, Charles Paul, 237–8
Wilson, Harold (*later* Baron Wi 423
Wilson, Sir Henry Maitland ('Jumbo'; *later* 1st Baron Wilson), 99–100, 110, 113, 117, 124, 131, 132, 356
Wilson, John (*later* 2nd Baron Moran), 123
Wimborne, Alice, Viscountess (née Grosvenor), 376
Wimborne, Cornelia, Baroness (née Spencer-Churchill), 6
Wimborne, Ivor Guest, 1st Baron, 6
Wimborne, Ivor Guest, 1st Viscount, 376
Winant, John Gilbert ('Gil'), 88

Windsor Castle, 280; St George's Chapel, 196
Wodehouse, John ('Jack'), Lord (*later* 3rd Earl of Kimberley), 25
Wolff, Louis, 444
Wood (St Mary's Hospital nurse), 311
Woodford (Essex), 293, 298, 307; parliamentary constituency, 150, 195, 248–9, 259, 293, 307
Woolton, Frederick Marquis, 1st Earl of, 241, 261
Worcester (Massachusetts), 32
World Day of Prayer for Peace (1942), 63

Yalta Conference (ARGONAUT; 1945), 143, 148
Yeo, I.B., 'An address on pneumonia', 4
Yeoman, Philip, 312, 313, 316, 318, 332, 337, 353
Yetman, F.B., 337
Young Conservatives' Association, WSC speech (December 1955), 259

Zweig, Stefan, *Marie Antoinette*, 300